Donated by
Jack Hartnell 6/14/90

Sam Crocker's Boats

A Design Catalog

Sam Crocker's Boats

S. Sturgis Crocker

INTERNATIONAL MARINE PUBLISHING COMPANY
Camden, Maine

© 1985 by International Marine Publishing Company

Typeset by Journal Publications, Inc., Camden, Maine
Printed and bound by The Alpine Press, Stoughton, Massachusetts

All rights reserved. Except for use in a review, no part of this book may be reproduced or utilized in any form or by any means, electronic or mechanical, including photocopying, recording, or by any information storage and retrieval system, without written permission from the publisher.

Published by International Marine Publishing Company
21 Elm Street, Camden, Maine 04843
(207) 236-4342

Library of Congress Cataloging-in-Publication Data

Crocker, Sam.
    Sam Crocker's Boats.

  1. Sailboats. 2. Crocker, Sam. I. Crocker, Sturgis. II. Title. III. Title: Boats.
VM351.C67   1985   623.8'223   84-48687
ISBN 0-87742-195-1

*For Sam Crocker, a builder's designer, an owner's designer,
and my father*

Contents

Foreword xi
By Bud McIntosh

Preface xv

Introduction 1
By Joel White

Design No.

6	*Samari*	6
23		9
24		10
28		10
39	*Idlewilde*	12
40	*Urchin*	14
41		16
42	*Grey Gull*	18
43	*Skookum*	20
47	*Fearless*	22
54		23
63		25
68		26
68B	*Nawanna*	30
75	*Wakaya*	31
76	*Fremari*	34
77	*Kittiwake*	38
78		42
80	*Tern*	43
82	*Black Arrow*	46
85	*Eleanor III*	48

86	*Aunt Abby*	51
88	*Grey Gull II*	57
90	*Barbette*	61
95	*Valiant*	64
97	*W. W. Lufkin*	67
98	*Jacinta*	69
100	*Sea Dawn*	74
103	*Sea Fan*	79
104		81
106	*Joloma II*	84
110	*Amos Judd*	88
113	*Fearless*	92
115	*Retriever*	94
122	*Vagrant*	98
125	*Sea Crest*	101
128	*Charity*	104
131	*Mahdee*	107
142	*Skookum III*	110
143	*Little Bear*	113
147		114
153		120
154	*Roaring Bessie*	121
155	*Ida S.*	125
157	*Pole Star*	127
159		131
160		136
162		138
163	*Brunette*	140
166	*Ranger*	142
168	*Land's End*	145
171		149
175		150
176	*Sirius*	153
178	*Blue Peter*	157
180		163
188	*Milky Way*	166
190	*Ben Gunn*	169
191	*Mercury*	172
195	*Fomalhaut*	175

198		178
202	*Tyrone*	182
203	*Blue Peter*	186
207		189
212	*Eastwind*	189
216	*Devil*	193
218		195
227	*Free and Easy*	199
234	*Emily Marshall*	203
236	*Dog Watch*	206
238	*Dolphin*	208
243	*Masconomo*	211
245	*Limulus*	215
248	*Marion 26*	217
253	*Sparhawk*	219
263	*Akbar*	224
266	*Crocker 20*	226
268	*Dolphin*	228
269	*Metacomet*	229
270	*Aunt Emma*	232
273	*Last Call*	239
277A	*Calista III*	243
280	*Sallee Rover*	246
283		248
284	*Chief Gramatan*	250
291	*Dorothy*	252
292	*Stromboli*	255
297	*Torino*	257
301	*Golden Eagle*	261
302	*Macaw*	263
304	*Gull*	266
305		269
310	*Cousin Elizabeth*	272
311	*Jingo*	275
313	*Green Heron*	279
325	*Five Ply*	281
327	*Scaup*	284
337	*Dione*	288
338		290
344	*Mary Harding*	294

Foreword
By Bud McIntosh

SAM CROCKER WOULD HAVE THOUGHT IT entirely fitting and proper to have a couple of boatbuilders introduce this collection of his work to the public. (And I know other designers who would tremble at such a thought — as well leave their pet canary in the tender charge of a couple of cats.) Sam was, among other rare things, the perfect boatbuilder's designer. He was also, of course, a lot more than that: brilliant and innovative designer-engineer, superb draftsman, creator of a vast and varied fleet of handsome and useful boats. Perhaps these are the important things to have in mind when you look through this book. It provides a fascinating education for you who love boats, and offers (I think) the pure pleasure you can get from true art.

I'll leave any detailed practical assessment of these designs to Joel White, who is better fitted, by training and detachment, to handle it. What I want to tell you is something of what Sam Crocker meant to us boatbuilders, especially when we were young and cocky and somewhat ignorant, and just a bit afraid at times, that we'd undertaken more than we could handle. Sam was good for us. We were his friends, who loved what he loved.

Our first boat for Sam set the pattern for what was to come. We wondered about a clause in the contract: Could we live up to the standard implied in the term "yacht finish"; and what did it mean, anyway? Sam said something like this: "It's not necessarily the same for every builder; but I expect work equal to the best I've seen you do in the past; and it's tied in with the price you're getting for the job; and the owner's a damn fool if he thinks he ought to get more than he's paying for."

And we built the boat (a big cutter) with Sam serene, helpful, impartial in minor disputes. We launched her on a midnight tide after spreading an inch of lime on the whiffy and thinking silent prayers for the integrity of the railway. Champagne corks popped high into the dark sky, and Sam's knuckles were white when she floated — *just right,* where he wanted her, and looking as pretty as a picture with the spotlight on her.

She went away to the west'ard next day, and we at the shop were wracked with doubts and fears. The last payment on the contract was still to come, and all kinds of things could go wrong with the boat. (We'd been through this before, and seen that last payment gnawed to a fraction to pay for a better paint job, or adjustment to the rigging, or a change in the gear shift, and naught for us to do but grin and bear it.) Then we got a letter from Sam, describing the trip home, and a few jobs he'd done on the boat, and his instructions to the owner to pay up as per contract for a job well done. The last paragraph was the best, though — something like, "We tried her out yesterday against that big sloop you saw and *Christmas!* we went by her like . . . ." I forget the rest, but it had to be pretty good to match Sam's glee over what he and we had done together.

* * *

We went on, through some hard years, to build a couple of schooners, a big keel catboat (that one was sheer joy from start to finish), a chubby little cutter that was the prototype for the Green Bay class, and then Sam's biggest raised-deck ketch, which strained the shop's pelvis somewhat in the gestation process. Last, I think, was a 40-foot centerboard cutter with fiddlehead and trailboards, lovely to look at even when she was only half-finished. Some slight argument arose at the end of that job because of extras and changes beyond the original contract; and Sam, beholden to the owner and certainly not to us builders, stepped in and arbitrated the dispute with absolute fairness.

Somewhere in there we built Cliff's powerboat, design number 216, if you're curious. Cliff was a young man of some talent and great ambition, who worked with us at the shop between excursions to build airfields in Africa or yachts on Grand Cayman Island. He owned a very small barge, which he had used to carry coal to the offshore Coast Guard stations — five tons a trip, towed, as I remember, behind a Friendship sloop with a 1907 Hupmobile engine. He yearned for something better: If only the towboat could carry another five tons, and travel twice as fast . . . . So he took his dream to Sam, who, as we well knew, would not rest until he'd figured out the perfect boat for the purpose. (The man liked boats, in case you wonder.)

A week later, the lines, offsets, and construction plan arrived. We went to Woody's sawmill in the snow and sawed out keel, stem, and frame stock; picked over 10,000 feet of box boards to get what we thought would plank and deck her; laid down the body plan and built a set of molds and a transom as big as a barn door. And three weeks later, she was planked, decked, and ready for the two engines. (These were six-cylinder Chevies, not new, that cost, as I remember, $25. So far as I know, they were identical, each complete with transmission, coil, and carburetor.)

I'd like to tell you about the steering gear, and the power hoist on that boom, and a few other things that we invented, or fabricated, or stole from wrecks; but this is supposed to be an appreciation of Sam Crocker, master designer and good friend. So I stop and think: Was there ever another who would do a design like this for free, watch it take shape in crudeness incredible, and pray as earnestly as we did that we could get both those Chevies running at the same time and see what she'd do, b'God? Talk about kids — he was worse than we were.

But then, when the Coast Guard decided to do its own coaling, Cliff appeared to be stuck with a white elephant. Luckily, the fort guarding Portsmouth Harbor needed a vessel to tow a target for young gunners to practice on. With hardly time for an oil change, our boat got the job. Johnny Marshall went as crew, his main duty to try to get the other engine going again. When both engines quit at once, boat and target tended to drift together. This seemed to stimulate the young marksmen.

But this duty ended, also. Maybe they wanted a more reliable towboat; maybe, for all I know, the Humane Society stepped in before it was too late. Whatever — Cliff sold her, reluctantly, to a fisherman down to Rhode Island, who replaced those magnificent gas engines with a pair of opposite-turning pudgy little diesels. And he put in real boughten fuel tanks and numerous other weighty things, and she never cracked 12 knots again. But Sam and Cliff and the rest of us at the boat shop were happy about it. That boat had done better than anyone had a right to expect, and we'd sure had a lot of fun.

* * *

Once in a while, Bill Simms or Myron Cowden stops in at the shop, and we get to talking about creaking joints and the deplorable sameness of modern sailboats. Now if we could shed 50 years apiece and get Sam back on the job, we'd build you some boats worth looking at. And tough, and able, and comfortable, and fast. If you have any doubts, look through this book and see what our good friend and teacher could do. He was quite a man.

Preface

IT HAS BEEN SEVERAL YEARS SINCE I suggested to International Marine President Roger Taylor that I would like to record my father's plans in a book. He thought it a good idea, and suggested I pick out some of the best designs and write a little about them. It seemed a simple, straightforward job when I started, but the further I went, the more complicated it became. Dad was working on design number 344 when he died in 1964, and the first thing I had to do was sort out all the designs and make sure that I had a complete set for each design selected for the book.

Some designs never got beyond the sketching stage for various reasons, expense probably being the strongest. The designs selected are all boats that were built and turned out to satisfy the owners' requirements. In most cases, there are photos; Dad was never far from his camera. I have tried to make a representative selection to show his versatility and his ability to listen to a client's wants and desires and respond to them with a good looking, able boat.

My father was not only an exacting engineer, but he was also an able free-hand artist; in fact, a lot of his designs started out on the backs of envelopes during the commute home from Boston on the B&M Railroad. Later, Dad would develop the designs, usually on a ¾-inch scale. This scale was used as much as possible, because when the design was turned over to a builder, he could get by with his regular rule (every ¹⁄₁₆-inch equaling 1 inch on the drawing).

Having built several boats himself, Dad's designs and specifications were complete. He could picture the finished product from either the builder's or the owner's point of view and make enough drawings so that everything was understood to start with and nothing left to chance. Anything not covered in the drawings was covered in the specifications. If a particular section needed a separate drawing or full-size detail, it was always there, in many cases even to the placement of fastenings. Spar hardware, in most cases custom made, was always proportioned so that you didn't get a tang good for 2,000 pounds and a turnbuckle for the same stay good for 5,000 pounds. Block lists were made and were exact. The builder seldom found a front shackle where a side shackle would have been better. Every builder I ever met made it clear that they would rather build from my father's plans and specifications than from any other's.

Of course, not all of the plans selected for this book appeal to me or will appeal to individual readers. In fact, the plans were often not what my father would have drawn for himself. The point is, they were what the client wanted, and I have many appreciative letters that bear this out. I have tried to give a little history of each design as far as I can determine from memory, magazine and newspaper clippings, and material on file, but I have hesitated to editorialize much, because, as I say, these boats weren't designed for me. More than once I heard Dad say that the most challenging part of yacht design was anticipating the client's questions and apprehensions and being ready with an answer. I remember in particular the owner of one fairly large boat. He had been rather fussy all through the designing and building, and when it came time for launching, Dad expected him to be upset if she didn't float exactly right. Having supervised construction and knowing the builder was right on the lines, Dad stayed late at the office the night before and went over all his figures. The next day, before the boat was launched, he placed a postage stamp on the stem where she should float at that stage of completion. It was only a two-cent stamp, but it was in the right place.

The only help Dad ever had in designing was when he would employ his brother John or myself to do some tracing when he got overloaded. This accounts for those drawings initialed J.A.C. or S.S.C. The originals were all his own work.

My father studied naval architecture at the Massachusetts Institute of Technology from 1909 to 1911. For the next four years he worked for George Owen of Newton, Mass. He designed and built some boats in a small shop in Marion, Mass., until World War I came along, at which point he went to work in the Lawley Yard, in charge of planking the 110-foot submarine chasers. After the war he was associated with Murray & Tregurtha in the design and building of F-5-L flying boats, through which he developed his own method of building the hulls of planes — a method subsequently approved and adopted by the supervisors of the Philadelphia Navy Yard. One of the designs he assisted with was the NC-4, which in 1919 became the first seaplane to cross the Atlantic. In May 1924, after five years with John Alden, Dad opened an office at 333 Washington Street in Boston. During World War II and the Korean conflict, he helped out at Simms Brothers Yard in Dorchester, Mass., building sub chasers and aircraft-rescue boats, meanwhile keeping the office going by stopping in at night on his way home. In 1956 I fixed up a corner of the loft on the second floor of my shop at the Boat Yard, and Dad moved his office there with the idea of taking it a little easier. But all this did was eliminate the commute on the B&M, because he kept right on drawing until his death.

I think he carried as much enthusiasm into every design as did the prospective owner. Quite often he couldn't wait to see the boat that a set of lines would produce, so a model was made, usually on a ⅜-inch scale. Some of these models were made by professional model makers, but he liked to work in wood himself, and when he had time, he made them himself, teaching me in the process. A model is supposed to be an exact reproduction of the full-size vessel, so his were made to his own accurate methods by making a sheet-metal template of each section of the body plan and the block, worked down until each section fit exactly (as opposed to the lift method, in which accuracy depends on getting the lifts exactly the right thickness and glued up without slipping out of line of the wet glue when clamped; then cutting exactly to the waterline created by the glue lines of the lifts). There is no way to see if enough or too much wood has been taken off unless templates are used. After all, $\frac{1}{16}$ inch equals 2 inches on a $\frac{3}{8}$-inch scale. Another trick he had was to put a piece of mahogany through the planer on a clapboard and glue this in a block for a model with the thick edge on the centerline. This created the effect of a swept boot top with the thin edge at the low point of the sheer and widening at the stern and stem on the finished model.

I wish Dad could have lived to take advantage of today's calculators and computers. All of his calculations were done with planimeter, adding machine, and slide rule, and he used to grumble about the time it took. Nonetheless, he went through the process with every design. He simply had to be sure that the finished product would perform as expected. On the other hand, perhaps it's just as well he didn't have access to a computer, because we might not have had such pleasing profiles. That isn't to say that modern technology hasn't produced some handsome boats. It has, and some of them sail better than the older wooden boats. One just has to get used to the modern straight sheer and high freeboard as opposed to the older low freeboard and sweeping sheer. My father, however, loved more traditional, wood boats. Once he was approached to design a boat to be built in fiberglass, and I can remember him trying to apply himself to the drawing. Finally, he threw down his pencil and said, "I just can't get interested!"

I hope there will be much to interest readers in this record of my father's work. My writing and comments probably leave a lot to be desired, but after all, this is primarily a picturebook. If it pleases a sailor's eye with a lot of pretty pictures, it will have served its purpose.

All the photographs that appear in this book have come from the files that were kept with each boat Dad designed. In most cases, as I've mentioned, these photographs were taken by Dad. In some cases, however, they were provided to him by the boat owners. In all cases where the photographs were taken by someone else we have provided a credit line for the photographer.

Sam Crocker's Boats

Introduction
By Joel White

MY FAVORITE PICTURE OF SAM CROCKER* shows him sitting in the bow of a partially planked boat in full business suit and necktie, felt hat, shiny shoes, and an unlit pipe. He is also wearing glasses, a small mustache, and an attentive, friendly look — but no smile. One assumes that he was inspecting the construction of one of his designs, and that the builder, perhaps, took the photograph.

I have a feeling that the men who built to his designs liked Sam Crocker as a person, respected him as a naval architect, and enjoyed his visits of inspection. The quality of boats that resulted from this collaboration between architect and builder speaks well for Sam's designs and the men who built them. D.C. (Bud) McIntosh, George Chaisson, F.F. Pendleton, Reid & Pendergast, Reuben Bigelow, Simms Brothers, Carl Beetle, Harvey Gamage, Goudy & Stevens and of course, Sturgis Crocker — all of these and many more built Crocker boats along the New England coast from the 1920s through the present day. Crocker designs are still being built and will probably continue to be built in the next century. Anyone with an interest in practical cruising yachts, boats with good looks and sailing qualities, will have to consider a Crocker boat when choosing a design.

The collection of designs drawn by Crocker during his lifetime, many of which are presented in this book, can only be described as remarkable. Perhaps more than any other naval architect, he concentrated on a specific category of small boat — the sailing cruiser. While he did turn out other types, this was his particular interest and talent. Some of his designs — the Amantha cutter, for example — produced dozens of fine little cruising boats that are seen frequently in the harbors of New England and less often in other areas of the United States.

It is hard to tell if this single-minded concentration on cruising-boat design was Crocker's choice or was due to the commissions he received. In fact, it was probably a little of each. Certainly, when a designer produces a string of successful boats of a certain type, potential clients for boats of that type will think

---

* In *More Good Boats,* by Roger C. Taylor, page 84.

of his name when choosing an architect. In the movie industry, this is called type casting, and to a certain extent, Sam Crocker was type cast. A scanning of his complete design list will show that indeed, on occasion, he turned out widely varied projects: hydroplanes, a 60-foot Customs Service patrol boat, a rum-runner or two with three Liberty gasoline engines (standard equipment for rum-runners), sailing dories, a tugboat for his son Sturgis's boatyard. But the bulk of the collection consists of cruising boats from 20 to 60 feet overall.

Some of his cruisers were entered in local races and did well on occasion. But except for *Malabar IV,* a boat he designed with Charles MacGregor in 1922 that won the 1923 New London to Bermuda race, Sam's reputation was not built on the racing circuit. As far as I know, none of his designs ever won a Bermuda Race or a Fastnet, but they did win recognition as fast and able cruisers. Many of them made long passages and traveled to far parts of the globe. Take *Lands End,* number 168, a 39-foot ketch. She was built in 1935 by Britt Brothers. In the same year she sailed to Bermuda, then Newfoundland, weathering a hurricane along the way. In 1936 she was in the Bermuda Race. In 1939 she voyaged to Labrador, circumnavigating Newfoundland. She was then shipped to Seattle and sailed to Icy Bay, Alaska, and back. In 1946 she sailed from Seattle to San Francisco and the next year was shipped back to the East Coast. For the next 25 years, *Lands End* cruised between Massachusetts and Cape Breton. This winter she has rested in a Center Harbor, Me., storage shed, awaiting next summer's adventures. To date she has afforded 50 years of cruising pleasure to the same family.

Despite the preponderance of sailing craft in his collection, Crocker turned out several powerboat designs, both pleasure and commercial. Several nice fishing vessels came from his board, particularly *Metacomet,* a 62-footer for Russell Ginnell, and a big one, *Nova Julia,* a 90-footer built by A.D. Story in 1930. Crocker's power designs reflect his attention to detail and feeling for line and proportion, but I believe sailing craft were his first love.

As an example of his versatility, a family who summered near my home for many years owned three boats: a 38-foot motorsailer, an 18-foot daysailer used by the children, and a 28-foot power craft used as a ferry to the family's island. All of these were designed by Crocker, and all served their purpose admirably. The motorsailer was *Blue Peter,* design number 203, built in 1930, and a most interesting boat. Her accommodations were particularly nice and roomy for a boat of her size. One of my early cruising memories is the evening I was invited aboard *Blue Peter* in Northeast Harbor, Me. Going below, I found the charcoal stove working away at supper and the cabin filled with comfort, serenity, and good cheer. As the owner mixed cocktails, I realized for the first time that cruising didn't have to be like a camping trip.

Blue Peter had an unusual companionway hatch that was built like a small, sliding deckhouse. It allowed the helmsman to steer the boat by remote autopilot while remaining under cover in inclement weather. A recent trend in sailing-yacht design is the use of large deckhouses to give the helmsman shelter while under sail. Much has been written in the yachting press about this "new" idea. Well, Sam Crocker was using the same idea on quite small yachts as far back as 1929, on the 49-foot ketch *Amos Judd,* and again in 1935 on the 39-foot ketch *Brunette,* to mention only a couple. On the *Judd,* the wheelhouse covered most of a large cockpit with a steering station inside the wheelhouse as well as one right aft. On *Brunette,* the structure is more of a sunken deckhouse, part of the whole cabin structure, with an inside wheel and hinged seats over the two quarter berths. She has a conventional cockpit and outside wheel aft, with the mizzen stepped in the forward end. Both of these boats show unusual approaches to cruising-boat layout. It would be interesting to know whether Crocker proposed the wheelhouses or the owners demanded them. In any case, the concept shows a flexible design approach. The most remarkable thing is that both vessels are good looking, something that is hard to achieve with a large deck structure on a small boat.

Crocker's flexibility notwithstanding, there is such a thing as a typical Crocker design. The typical Crocker boat has short ends; good sheer with considerable height at the bow; hollow waterlines forward, flaring out to more than average width on deck; a long, low cabinhouse with oval ports down each side; a somewhat old-fashioned looking (nowadays) rig with long upper spreaders; a big, comfortable cockpit — all blended to give a staunch, workmanlike feeling to the vessel and a general sense of looking "right." She may have a rather plumb stem with pronounced knuckle just above the waterline, as in *Lands End,* or better yet, a clipper bow balanced by a short counter stern, as in *Free and Easy,* number 227. Many Crocker boats were ketch rigged. Most of the boats above 34 feet overall had double spreaders, and the upper speaders were very long, giving the boats a special high-shouldered look.

Crocker also designed a considerable number of raised-deck craft, with the topsides carried up to a sufficient height to allow headroom. These are my least favorite of his designs, and I suspect not his favorites, either. This style of boat gives the greatest amount of useful space below, but it is difficult to make such a boat aesthetically pleasing. As Sturgis Crocker points out in the preface to this book, Sam tried hard to give his clients what they asked for in a design, even if it was not what he would have chosen for himself. As proof of his success at pleasing clients, his listings show a remarkable number of repeat customers. Topping the list of whose who commissioned more than one boat is S.K. Dimock, who came back at least nine times that I can document. Others had three, four, or even six boats designed and built. A naval architect can receive no higher praise.

The thing that immediately strikes a builder about a set of Crocker plans is his understanding of wooden yacht construction. You may think that all designers of wooden yachts would have this understanding, but not so. Crocker's construction plans are outstanding in their clarity, completeness, and — happily — simplicity. That he had done considerable boatbuilding himself is obvious in, for example, the layout of backbone timbers. Wherever possible, the heavy backbone members are straight edged, which saves time during lofting, cutting out, and assembly. The stopwaters are shown in the right place, the bolts are clearly shown, and the assembly sequence is considered. Detail and clarity are balanced.

Moreover, few Crocker designs hold any unusual or "trick" ideas. Crocker was neither an innovator nor a gadget man. He stuck to proven, well-thought-out construction techniques. His specifications were detailed and correct. Builders often find contradictions and ambiguities in other designers' spec sheets, but not in his. Crocker usually drew spar and rigging details in more than average detail, leaving the builder with no doubts as to what the architect had intended. Few people realize what a timesaver a good set of drawings can be, freeing the builder from the need to spend hours trying to interpret the designer's thoughts and thus allowing him to proceed quickly from one building operation to the next. Crocker's lines plans were always carefully drawn and included abundant dimensional information, all of which helped the builder in laying down.

A perfect example of the simplicity of Crocker's construction plans is number

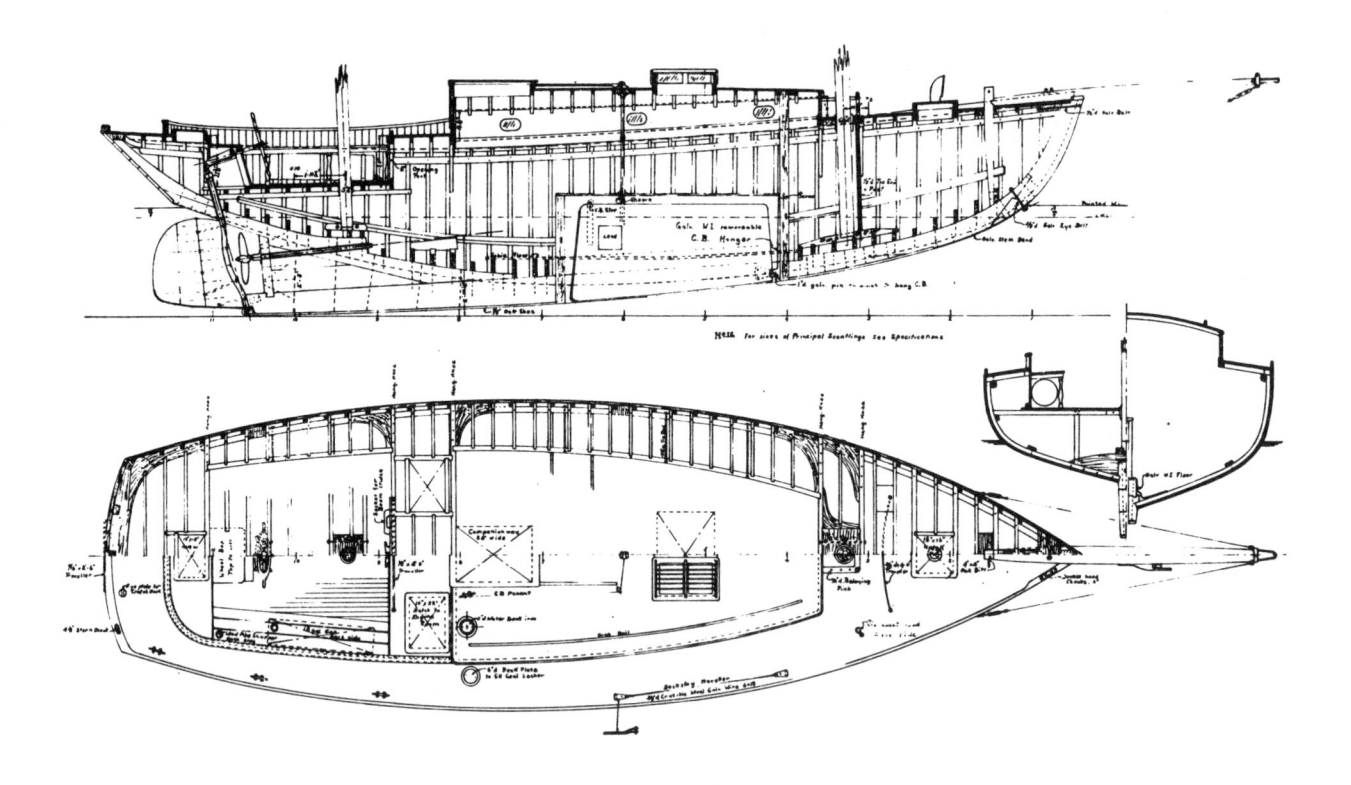

The construction plans and the lines for design number 100, Sea Dawn.

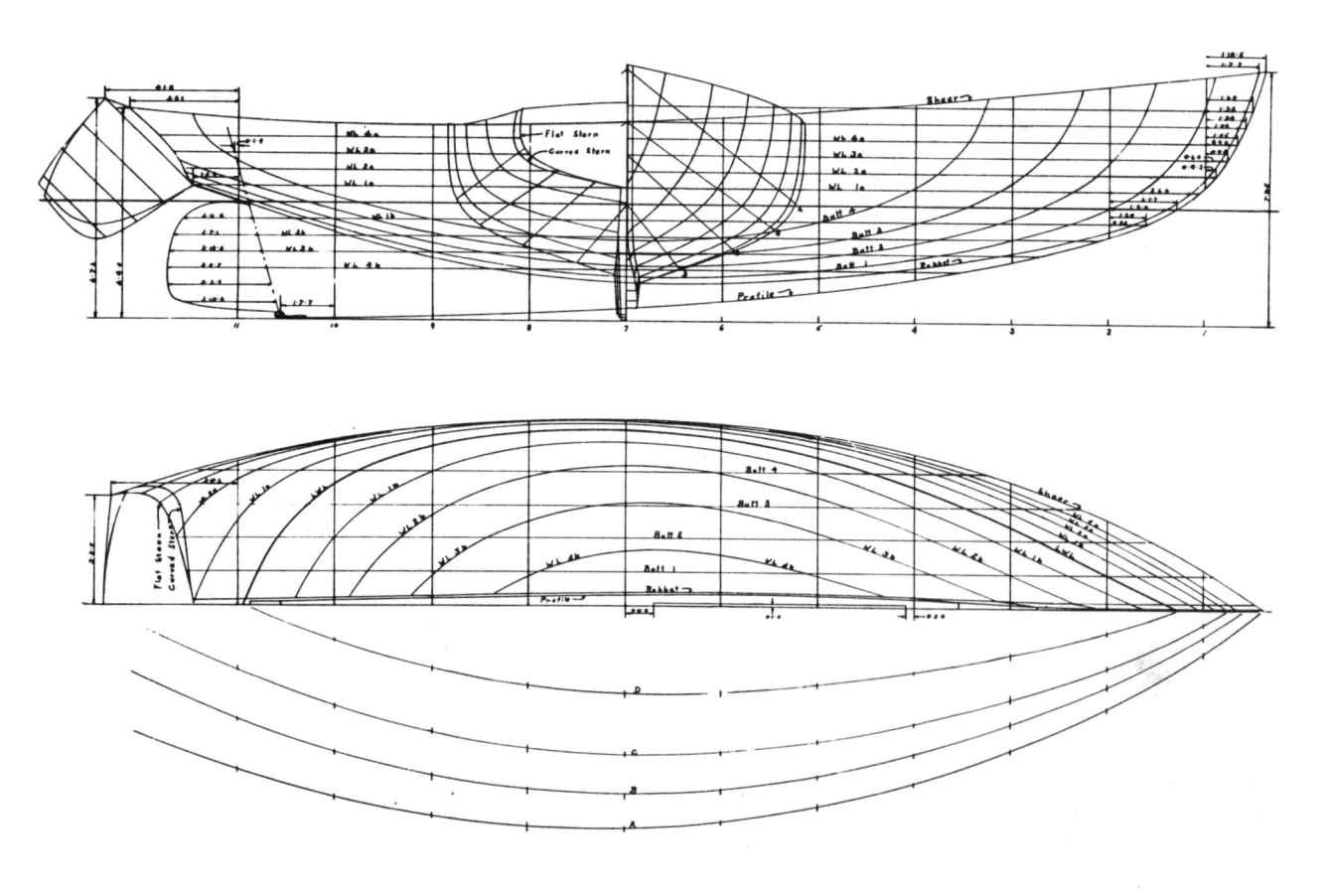

100, a "How-To-Build" design for *Rudder* magazine. *Sea Dawn,* as she is named, is a 36-foot centerboard cruising hull, and you can see Crocker's efforts to keep her straightforward and easy for amateurs to build. There are no reverse curves in her sections; her rabbet rises from its deepest point amidships in a fair curve to the counter stern aft. The backbone structure consists of a few heavy pieces, many with straight edges. There is no ballast casting as she is designed to use all-inside ballast. And yet, in spite of these concessions to easy building, she is a handsome, seaworthy, and eminently practical boat. Apparently, there was over time demand for a number of different rigs for the boat. The original design was dated 1927, but there are sailplan drawings and revisions dating all the way to 1959. From this it would seem that a considerable number of the boats must have been built. In addition to *Sea Dawn,* Crocker designed *Trade Winds* in 1949, a 26-foot sloop, again for *Rudder*'s "How-To-Build" series. This is still another simple yet attractive boat of sensible size for amateur building: large enough to cruise two, yet small enough that the project doesn't become overwhelming.

I have before me, thanks to the librarian of *WoodenBoat* magazine, a list of Crocker designs that were published in the yachting press, together with copies of those printed designs. The designs are visual testimony to one man's thinking about his work over 45 years, from 1915 to 1960. Most striking is the similarity of the early work to the late. Not that the man was in a rut; rather, I think, he developed early the design concepts that seemed right to him and found little that he wanted to change four decades later. The middle and later designs are better than the very early ones as his eye improved with practice. But his basic ideas of a proper cruising boat varied little throughout his working years. Almost all Crocker boats were wooden, and while rigs became simpler and more efficient, the hull shapes did not change greatly.

Indeed, Sam Crocker's boats have a timeless quality. Looking at the lines drawing for the 52-foot cutter *Mercury,* published in *Rudder,* October 1938, I see a handsome set of lines with great power and grace. Even now, decades later, I would challenge anyone to improve on them for offshore racing. Sam Crocker was fortunate enough to have spent his working years during the heyday of American wooden-yacht building, his career coming to an end before the near-demise of the craft in the 1960s and 1970s. I am sure he would be heartened to learn that in the 1980s able craftsmen are again building to his designs in wood.

6 SAMARI

Design Number 6
Length Overall: 25 feet
Length on Waterline: 22 feet
Beam: 8 feet 6 inches
Draft: Centerboard up:
    2 feet 8 inches
Sail Area: 435 square feet
Displacement: 6,200 pounds

DAD DESIGNED *SAMARI* FOR PERSONAL USE while working as a draftsman for George Owen of Newton, Mass. She was named after my grandfather and grandmother (Sam and Mary), who financed the building of the boat by Guy Gardiner of Swampscott, Mass. I remember my father telling me what a job it was to talk my grandfather into spending $660 for a 25-foot yawl complete!

She was kept in Barnstable, Mass., until the family moved to Manchester, Mass., in 1920. We used her there until 1922 or 1923, when she was sold to Asler Abbot. He or a subsequent owner brought her through a hurricane in June 1924 while 100 miles offshore. Another owner eventually sailed her to Italy.

Another boat practically identical to this one was number 22, *Mariana*. The difference was that *Mariana* was sloop rigged and only drew 2 feet 8 inches with her centerboard up. She was designed and built by my father in 1916, when he had a little shop in Marion, Mass. F.S. Blanchard, who bought her from him, says,

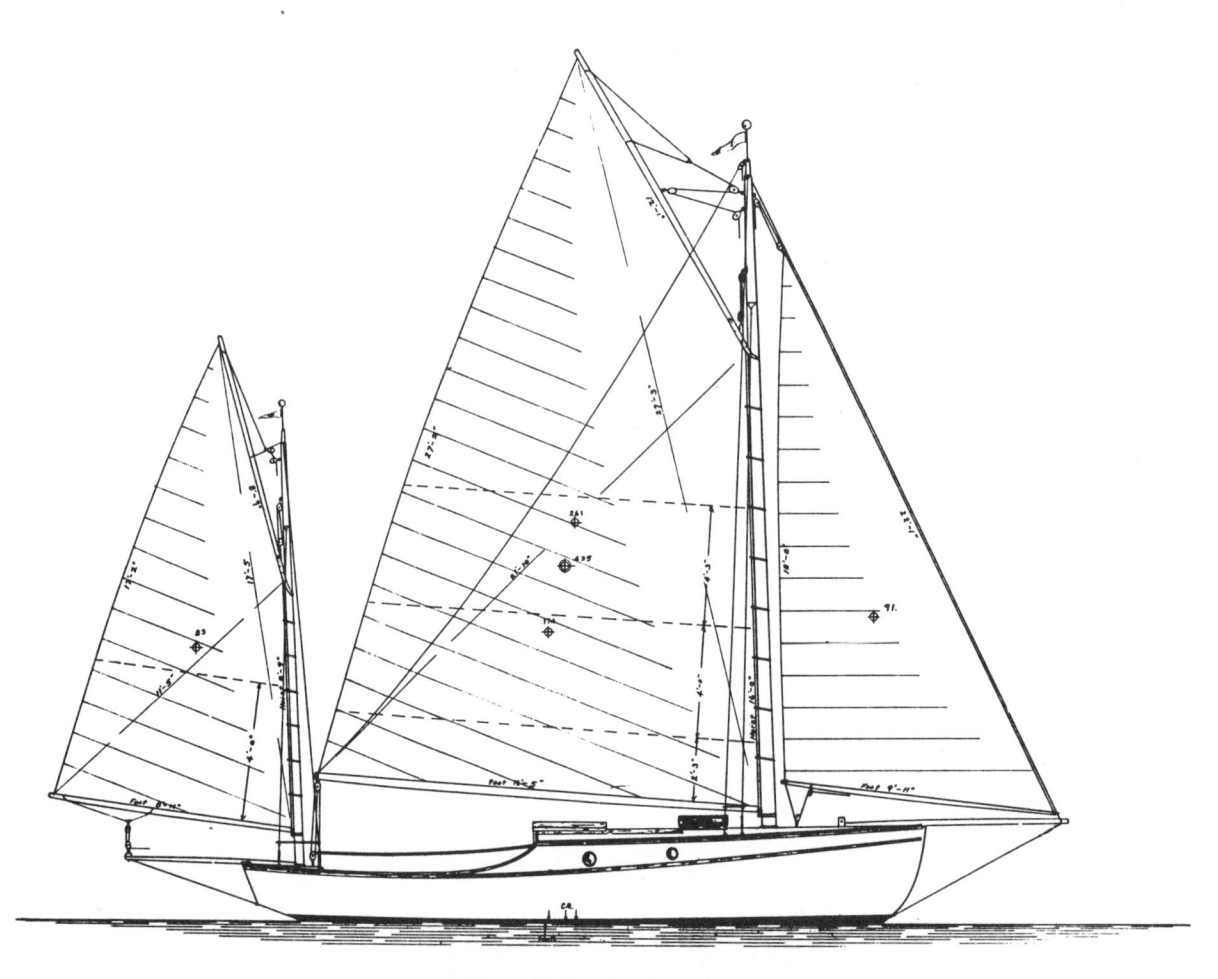

The sailplan for Samari.

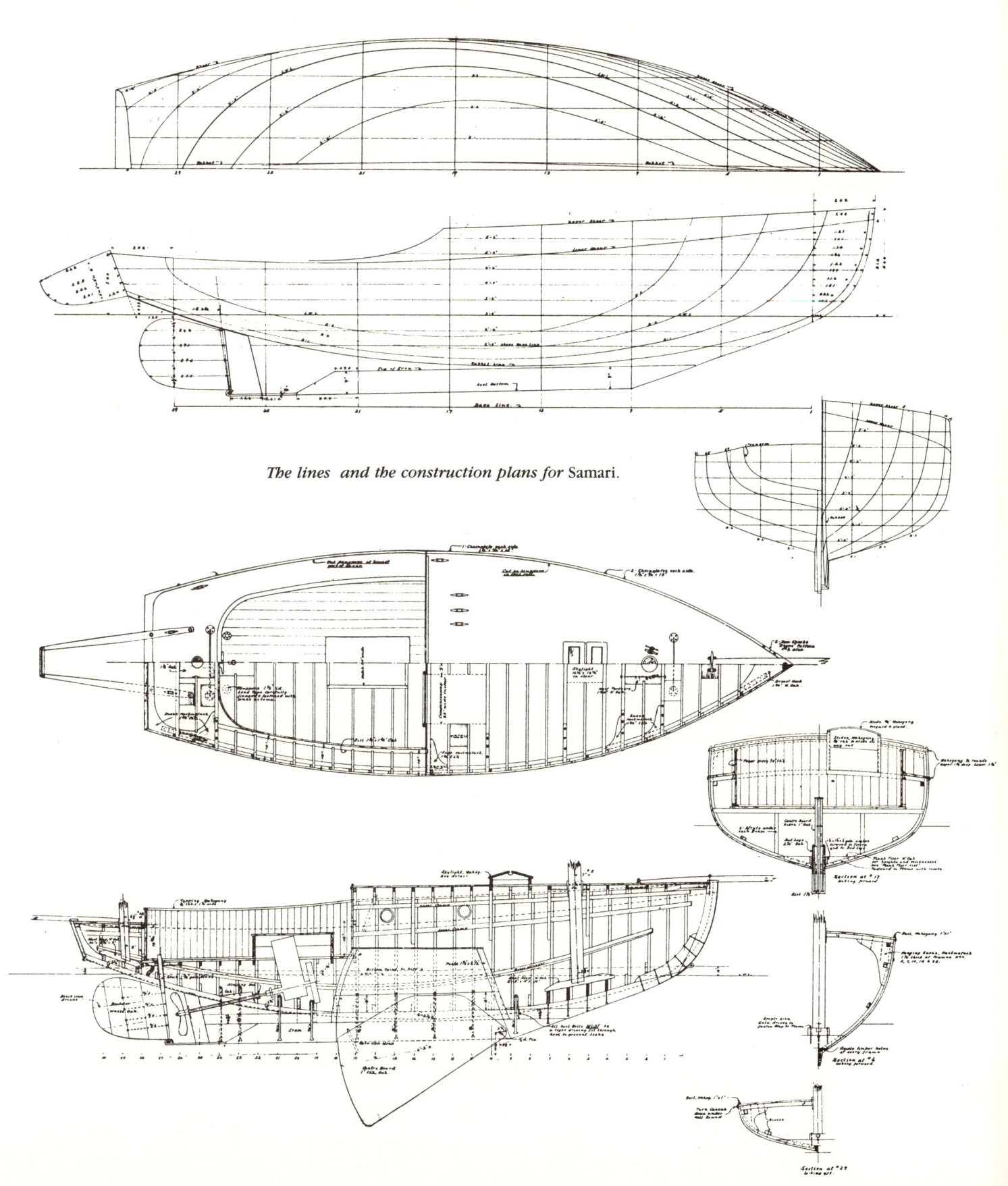

The lines and the construction plans for Samari.

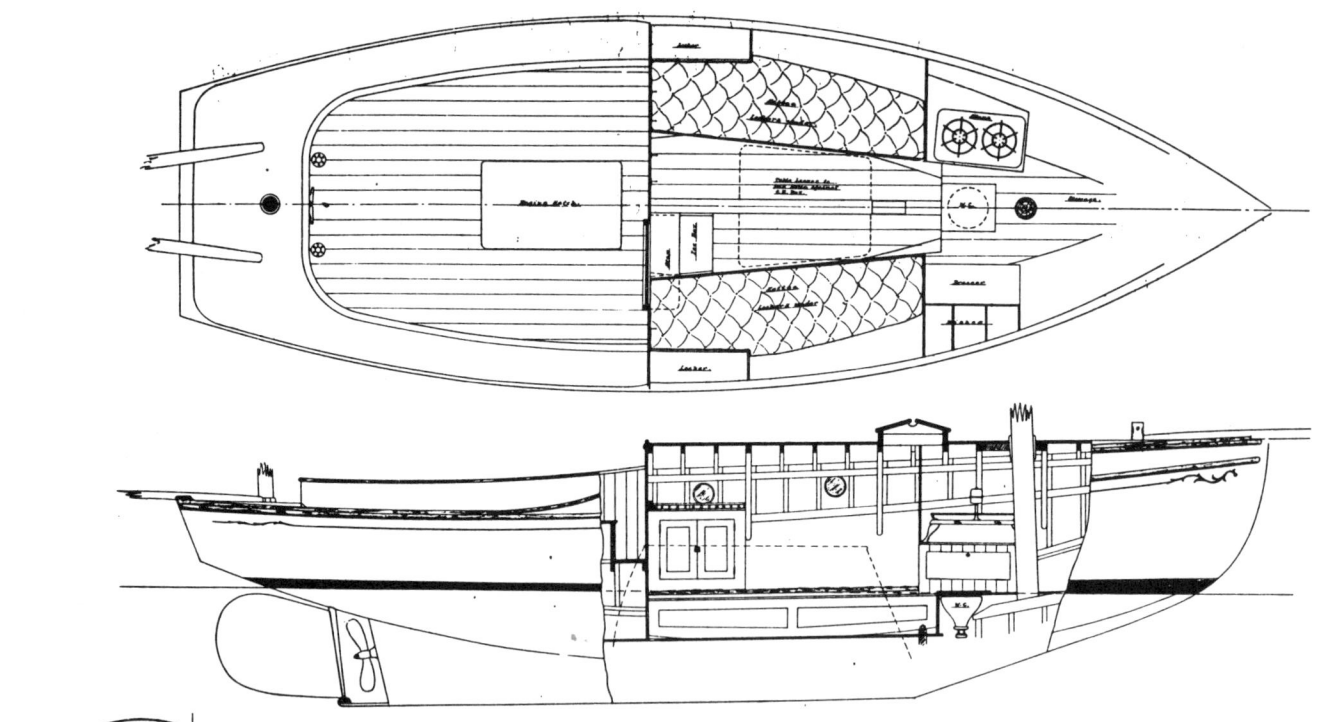

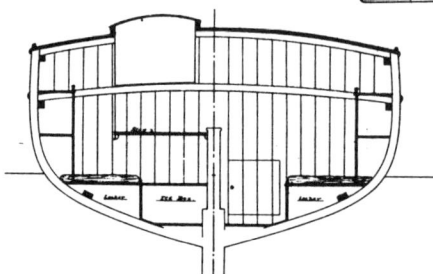

The interior accommodations for Samari.

Samari cruising along under full sail.

8

Two people can sleep comfortably in the cabin, which, owing to the raised deck, extends the full width of the boat. Two or three can sleep in the cockpit, fully protected by the awning, on kapok mattresses as the seats and engine-box top are all on the same level, and the space between is filled in by specially designed boards so that a level space of about 7 feet by 6½ feet is provided.

This boat combined shoal draft with some very seaworthy qualities, as indicated by Blanchard's cruise from Plymouth, Mass., around Nova Scotia and Cape Breton, to Gaspe in the Gulf of St. Lawrence, and later back to Boston from Montreal (as told in the January 1921 *Yachting*, "Cruising on the Installment Plan").

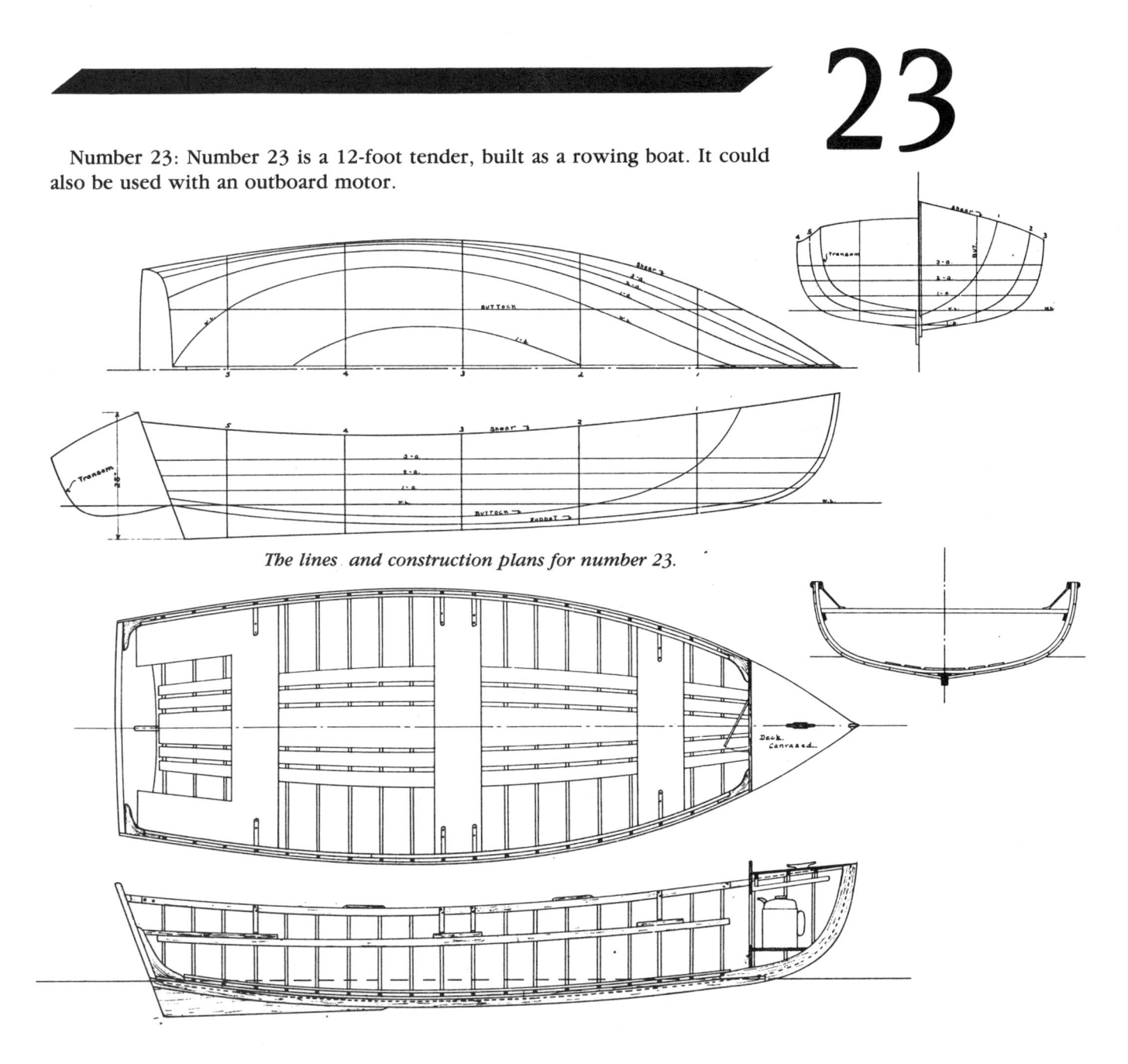

23

Number 23: Number 23 is a 12-foot tender, built as a rowing boat. It could also be used with an outboard motor.

The lines and construction plans for number 23.

24

Number 24: This design is similar to number 23 except that it is more heavily constructed amidships so as to accommodate the six-horsepower Gray Marine engine shown in the drawing. Also note the outboard rudder. There are no photos available for either of these boats, and I'm not certain they were ever built.

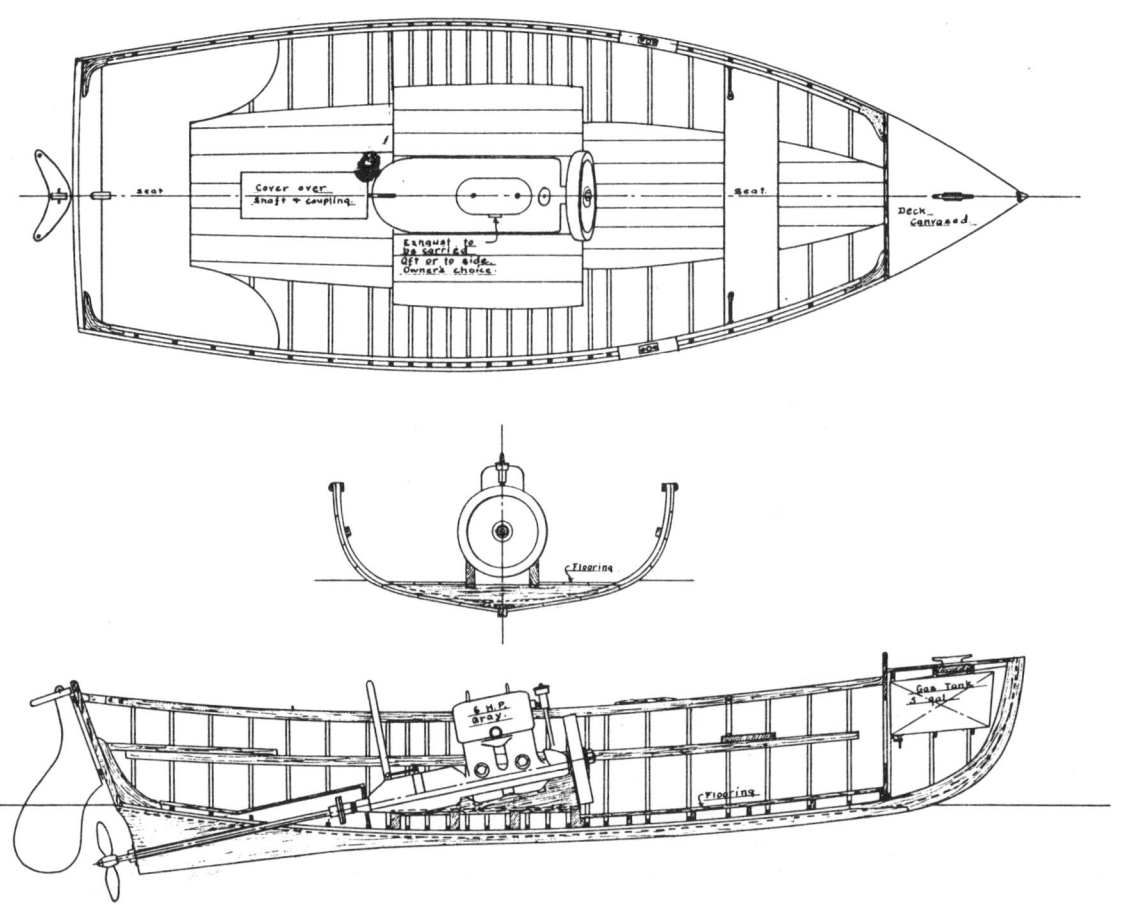

The construction plans for number 24.

28

Number 28: This is a light, easy-rowing, 11-foot sailing skiff. With the triangular lateen rig, she made a handy sailing tender. Also shown is 28B, probably a more efficient conventional marconi rig. This rig requires a halyard and cannot be stowed in the boat without the mast overhanging.

Left and below: *The lateen and marconi sailplans for number 28.*

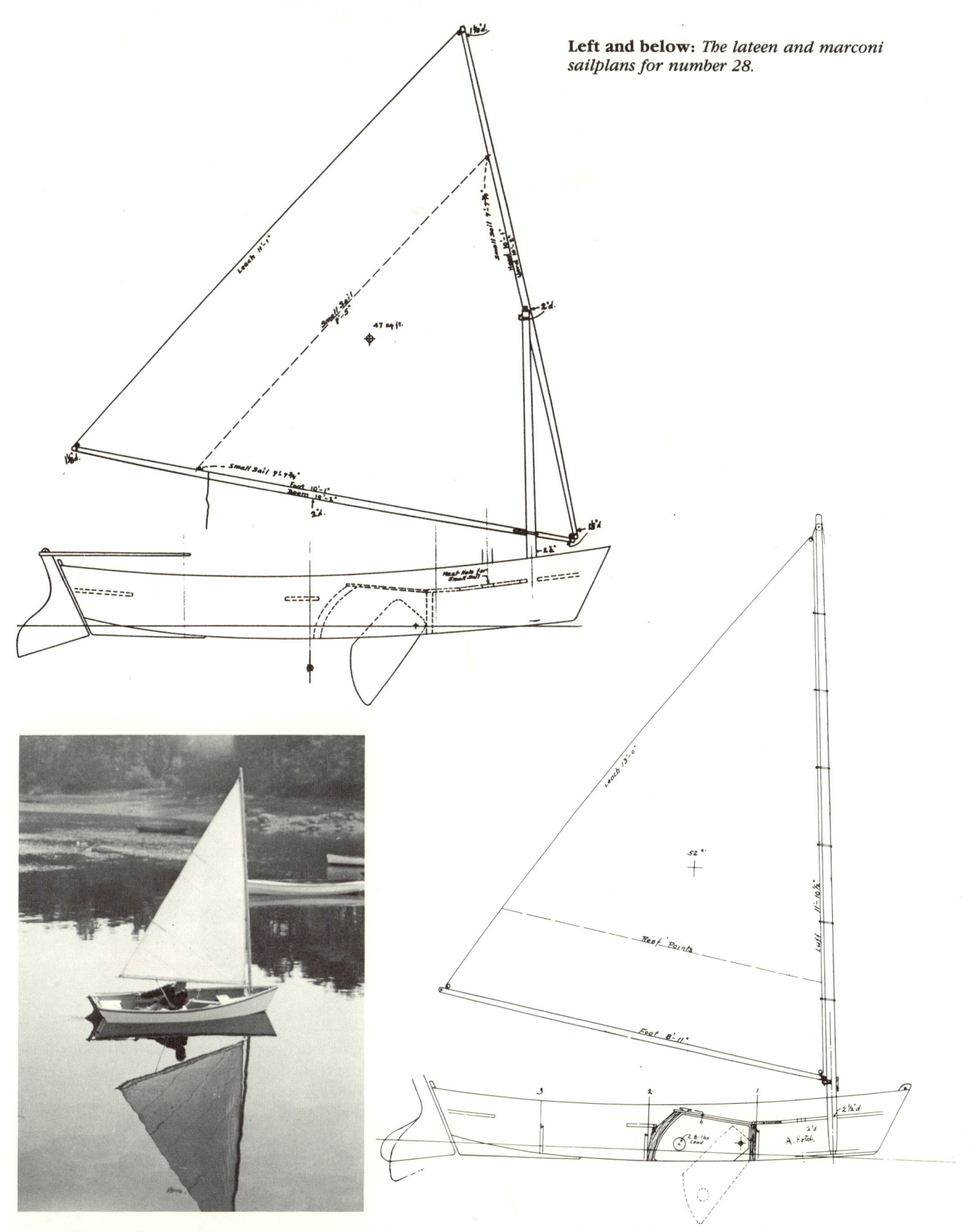

Above: *Number 28 under sail.*

11

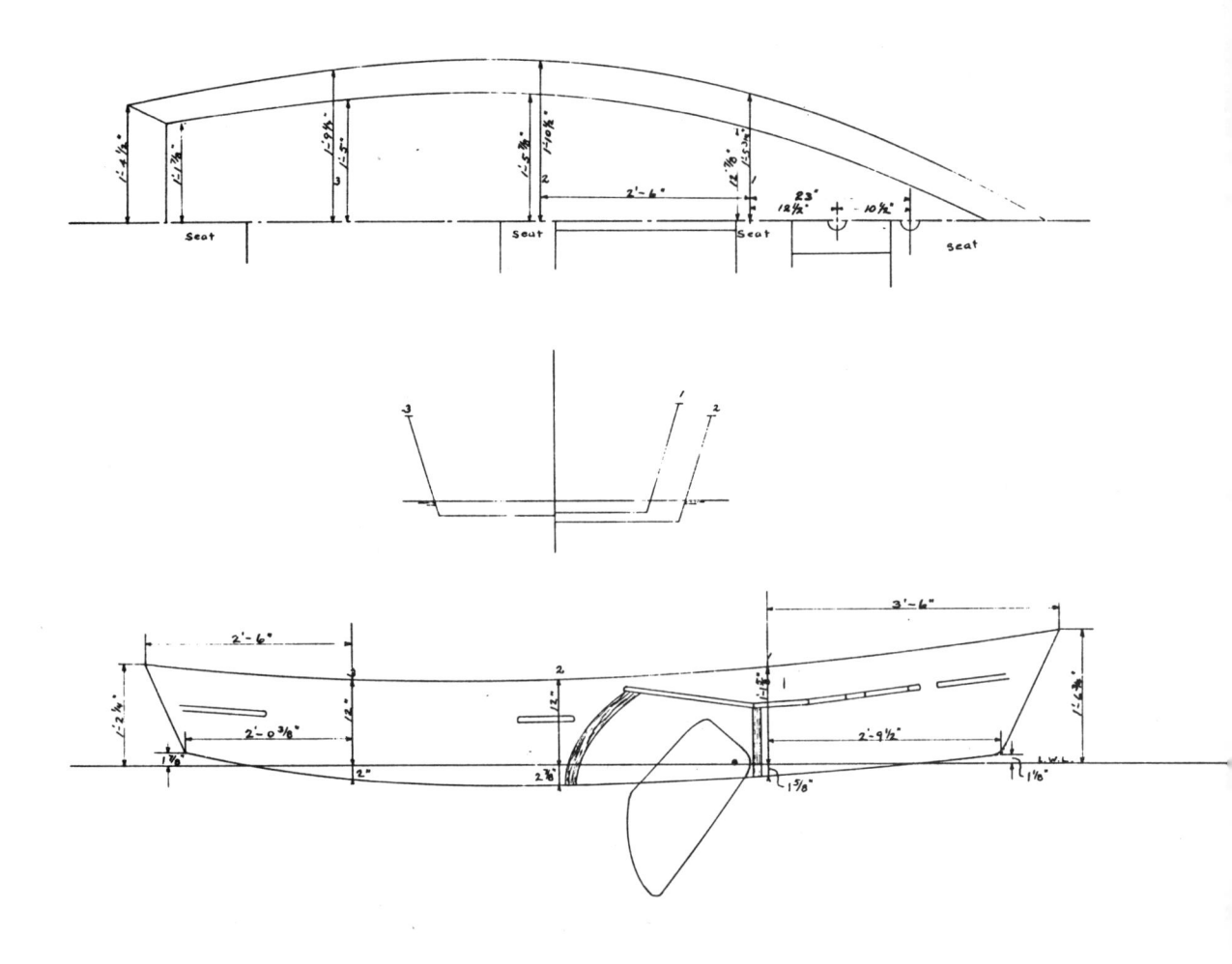

The construction plans for design number 28.

39 IDLEWILDE

Design Number 39
Length Overall: 36 feet
Length on Waterline: 34 feet 6 inches
Beam: 12 feet 6 inches
Draft: 4 feet
Sail Area: 456 square feet
Displacement: 24,750 pounds

Idlewilde was designed in Manchester before Dad opened his office in Boston. She was quite heavy and was used in all kinds of fishing around Nantucket and Martha's Vineyard. She even had a steering wheel at the masthead for swordfishing. Charles A. Morse & Son of Thomaston, Me., built her for Capt. Isaac Morton of Edgartown, Mass. With her 6-foot-square fishwell, generous sailplan, and living quarters for four in the forecastle, she might be a good boat for today's offshore lobstering. She could certainly save on fuel. Her 24-to-27-horsepower, three-cylinder standard motor pusher her along at 10 miles an hour.

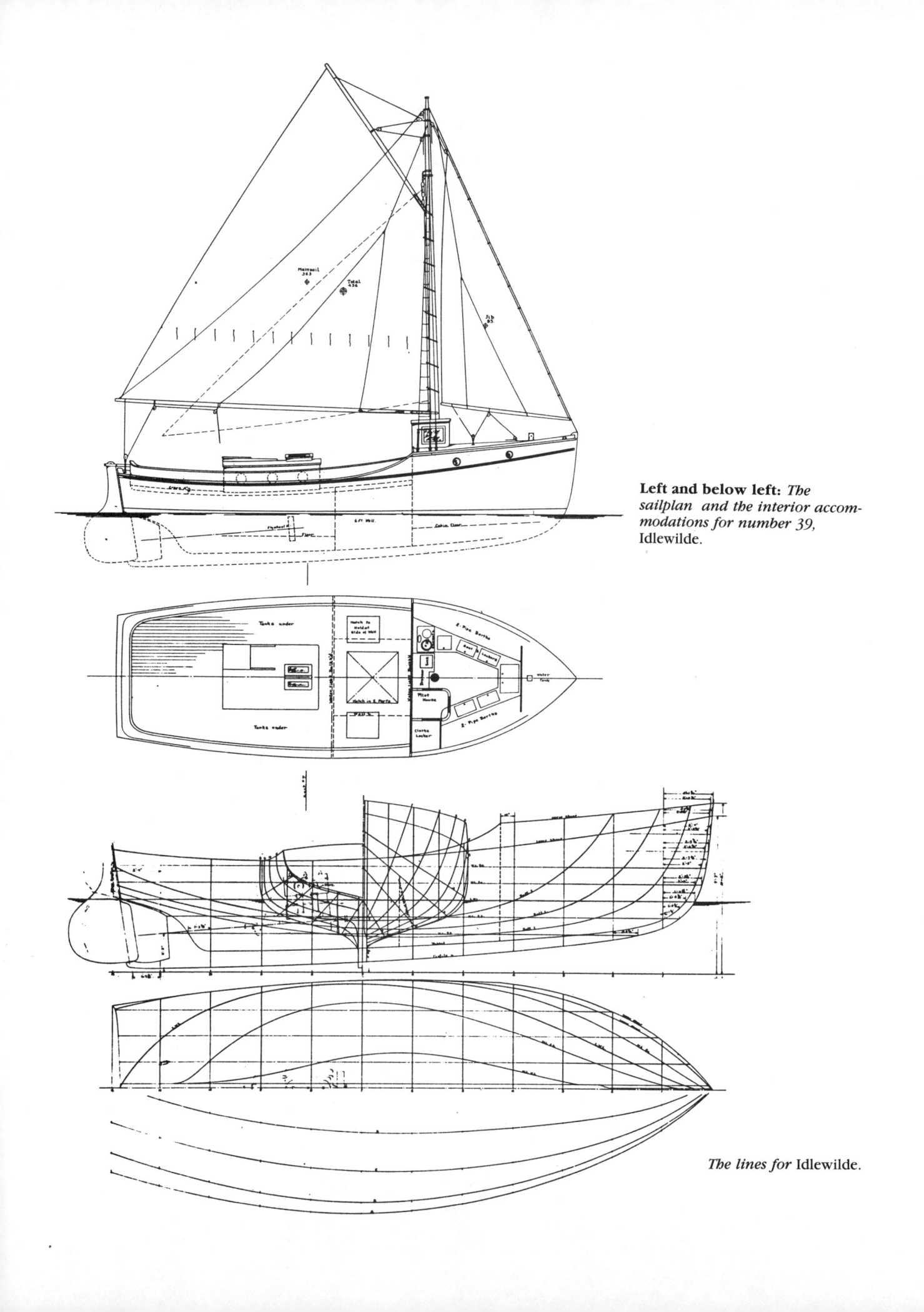

Left and below left: *The sailplan and the interior accommodations for number 39, Idlewilde.*

The lines for Idlewilde.

40 URCHIN

Design Number 40
Length Overall: 31 feet 11 inches
Length on Waterline: 23 feet 6 inches
Beam: 8 feet 6 inches
Draft: 5 feet 6 inches
Sail Area: 575 square feet
Displacement: 11,000 pounds

Design numbers 40, 43, and 76 are very similar. All were designed at home while Dad was working in John Alden's office. Number 40, of course, was the first, and she was designed to be rigged as a yawl or a sloop, with the mainmast in the same location for either boat. She was built by F.F. Pendleton in Wiscasset, Me., and called *Wiscasset.* Rigged as a yawl, she was subsequently sold to Bradford Smith who called her *Brant* and won the Gloucester to Cape Elizabeth race in 1925.

The next number 40 was the sloop *Urchin,* sold to Alger Sheldon. In an early Detroit-Mackinac race, she won second place, even though she was smallest in a field of 15.

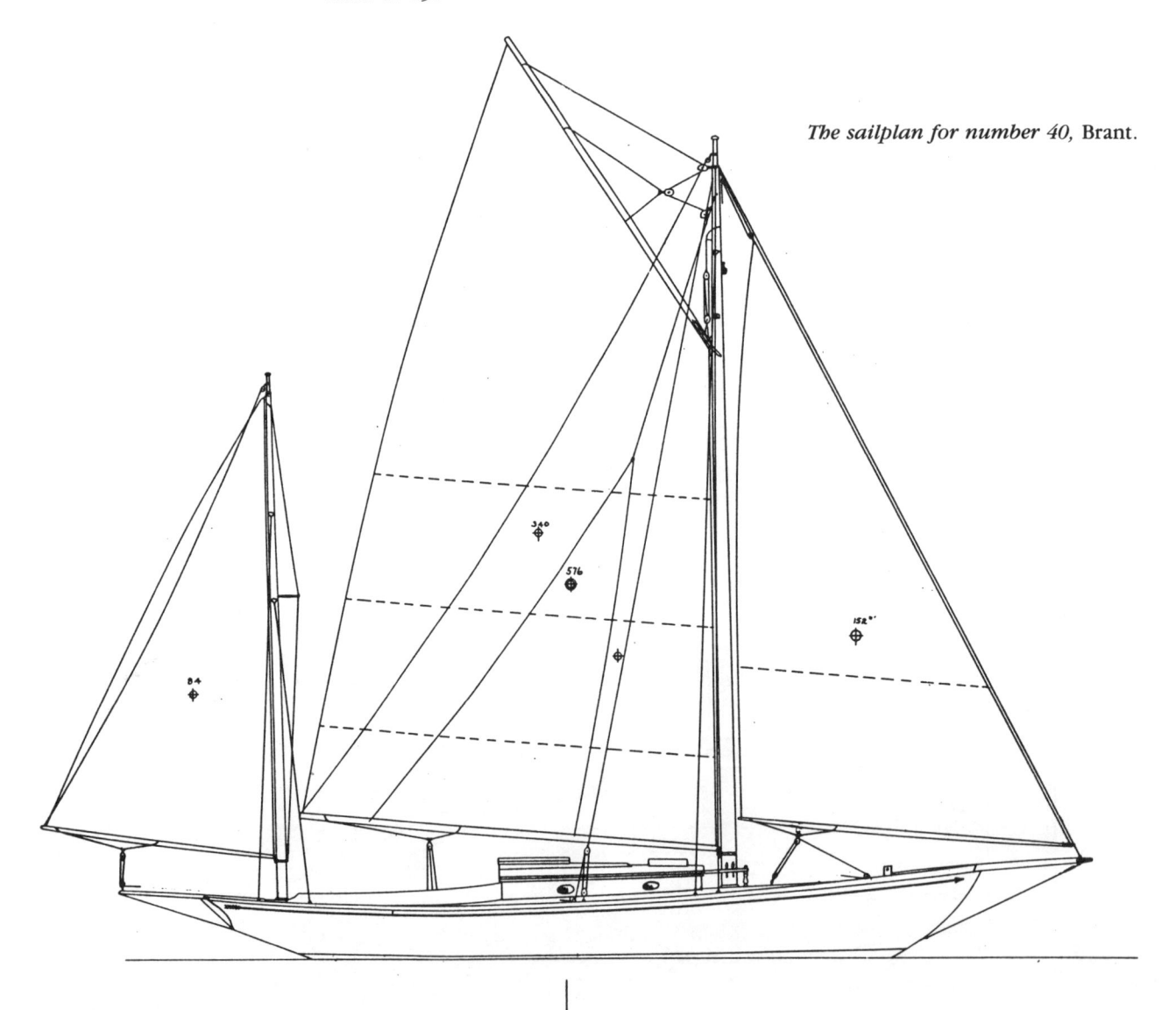

The sailplan for number 40, Brant.

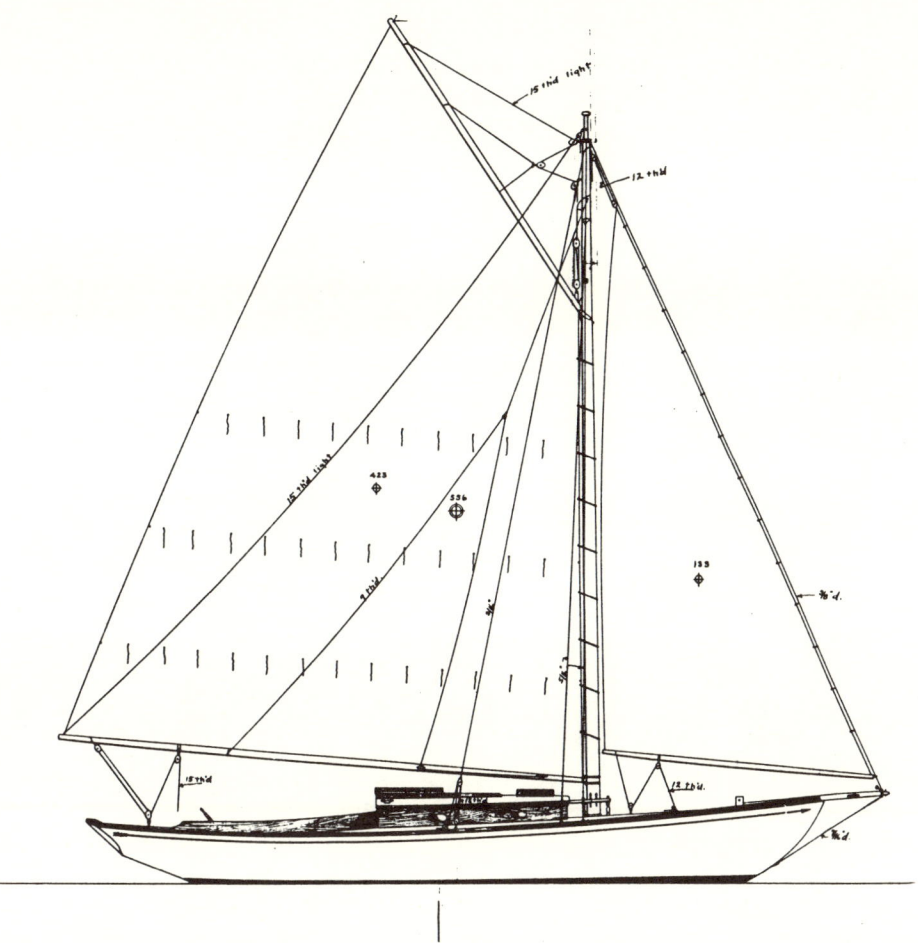

Above and below: *Design number 40's sailplan as a gaff-rigged sloop. The lines for number 40.*

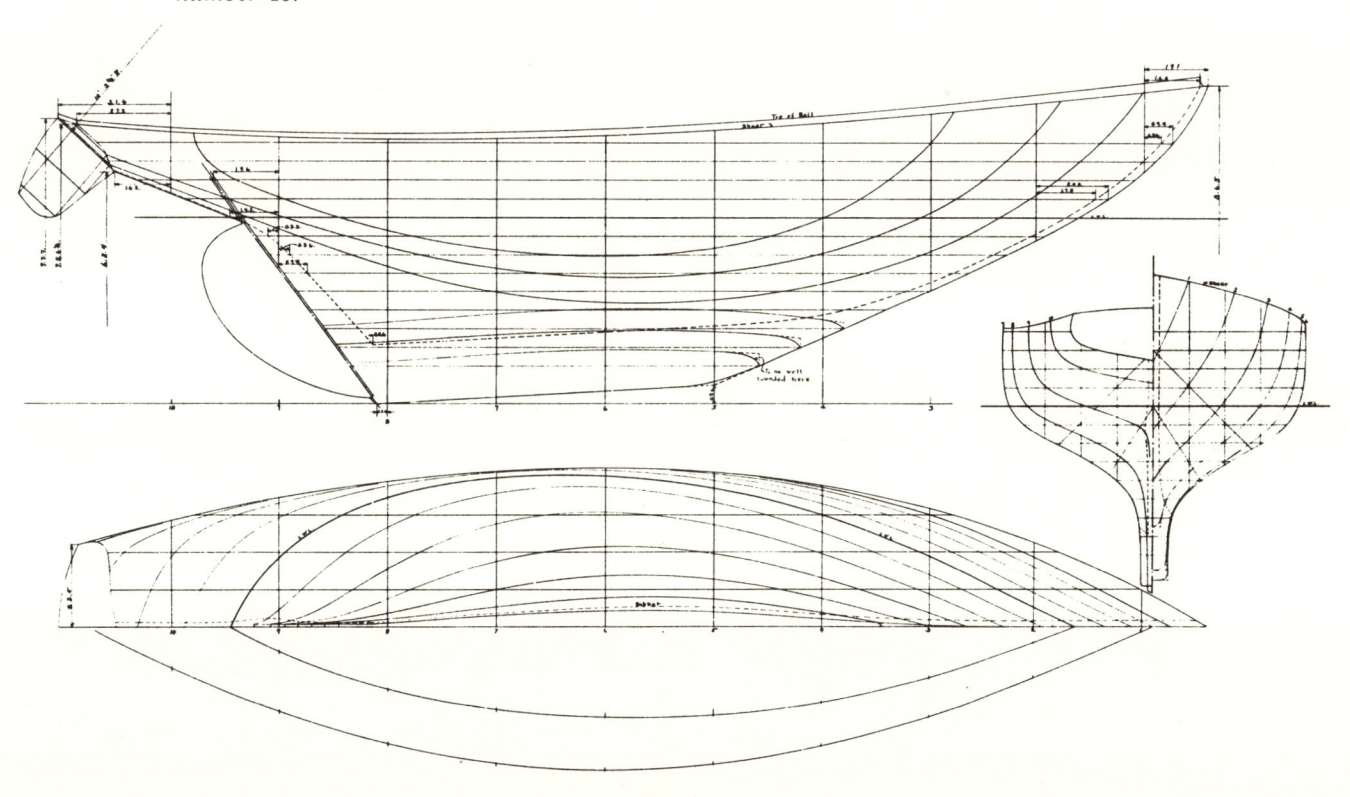

The start of the 1926 Detroit-Mackinac race showing Urchin *(2),* Kittiwake *(9), and* Nawana *barely visible under number 12's main. Photograph courtesy of The Detroit News.*

41

Number 41: This was a light, easy-to-row tender with good carrying capacity. Guy Gardiner in Swampscott, Mass., built a lot of these and shipped them all over the country. Often he built them in different lengths simply by spacing the molds differently. We had one 11 feet long with a centerboard and a lateen rig, similar to number 28A, which was kept in the inner harbor behind the railroad

16

Left: *The sailplan for number 41.*

Below: *The lines for number 41.*

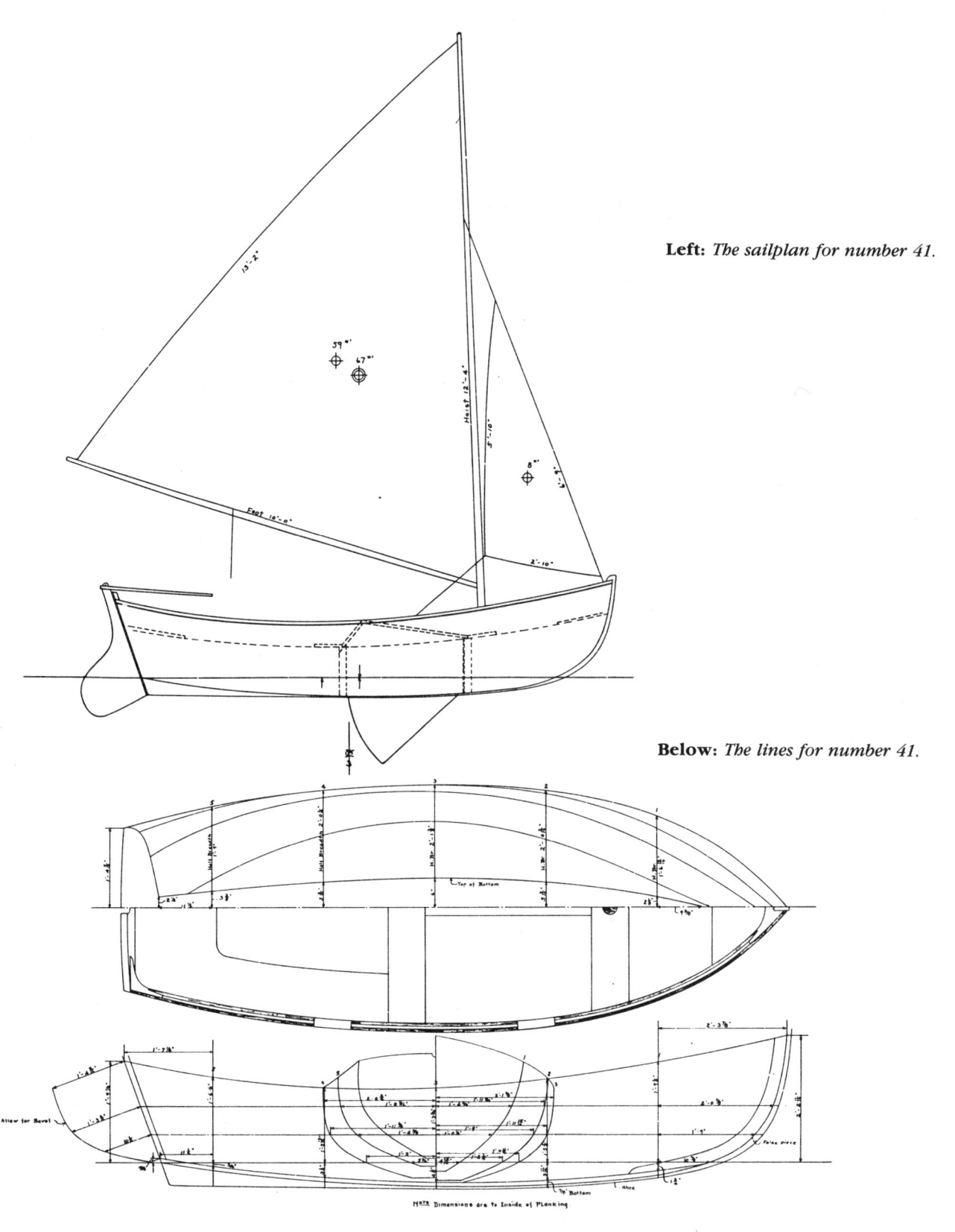

drawbridge. I could put the sail on the stub mast, sail up to the drawbridge, pull the lower spar aft to disengage it from the mast, then push it forward to lay the upper spar horizontal, sail under the bridge, and reverse the process on the other side — all while sitting in the bottom of the boat. I put a lot of miles under her keel as a kid.

42 GREY GULL

Design Number 42
Length Overall: 32 feet
Length on Waterline: 30 feet 9 inches
Beam: 9 feet
Draft: 2 feet 6 inches
Sail Area: 252 square feet
Displacement: 11,450 pounds

This was the first *Grey Gull,* designed for Prof. "Pop" Turner, headmaster of the Hill School in Pottstown, Penn. She was built in Swampscott, Mass., in 1924 by Guy Gardiner. As a teacher, Pop had a lot of vacation time in the summer and used to take fishing parties out from Scituate, Mass., to Minot's Light. With her big cockpit, she was ideal for this, and nobody could get fouled up in the engine with the house over it. Also, this house made working on the engine much more pleasant in bad weather (which is when they most often act up — or don't act at all). However, with that sailplan, she wouldn't be entirely helpless without an engine. The Lathrop two-cylinder pushed her at 8½ m.p.h. Number 61 was the same boat, but with a raised deck aft and bigger house over the engine, she offered a lot more cabin space. Both boats could be steered either from under cover or out in the cockpit.

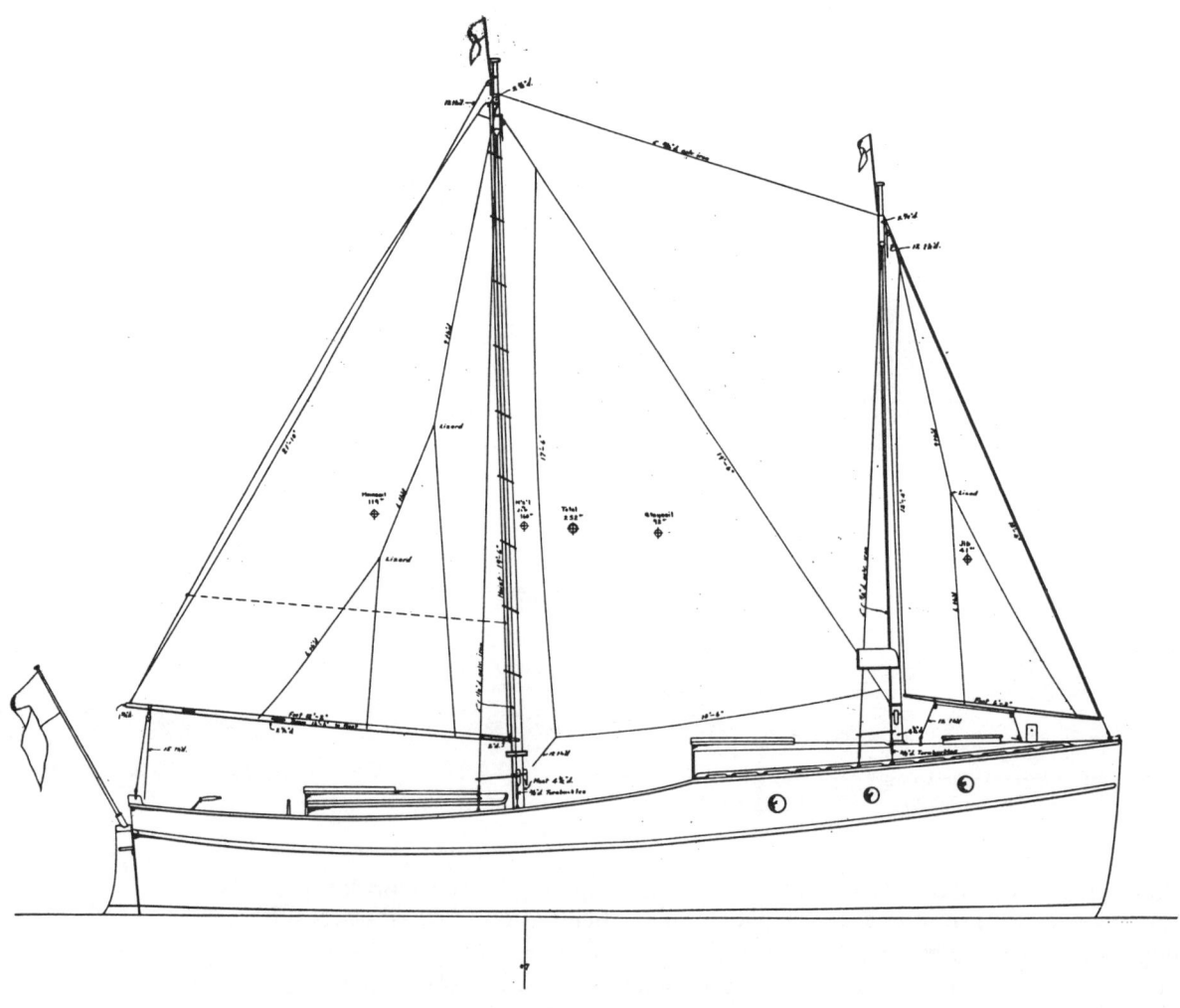

The sailplan for number 42, Grey Gull.

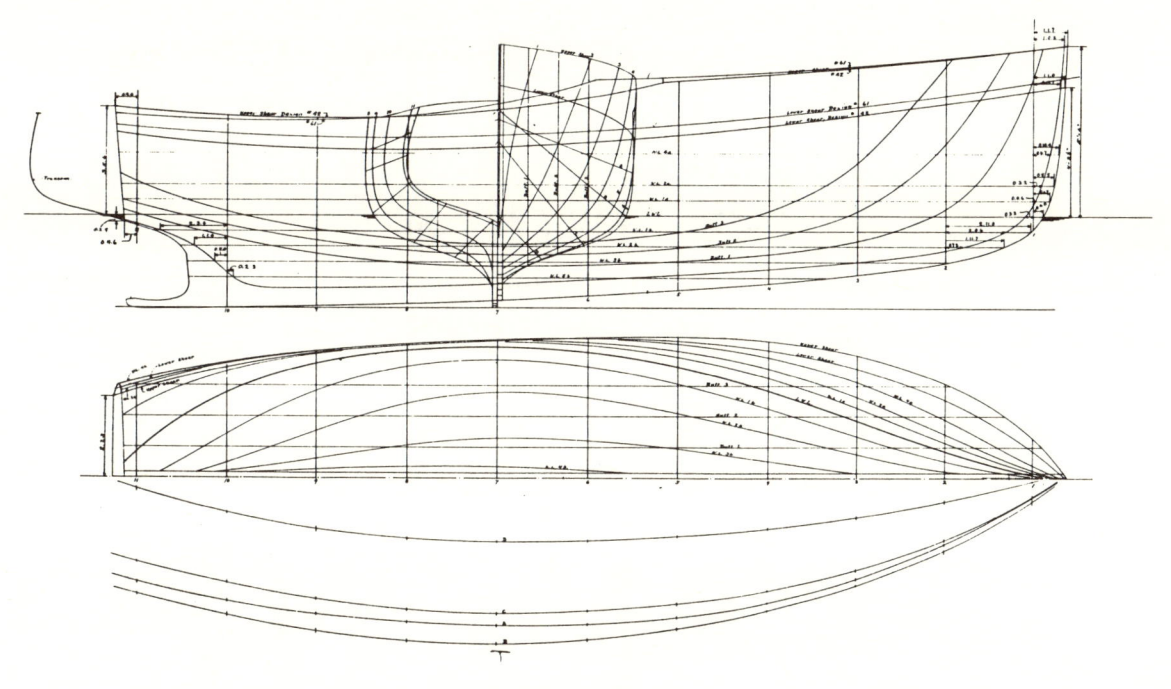

The lines for number 42.

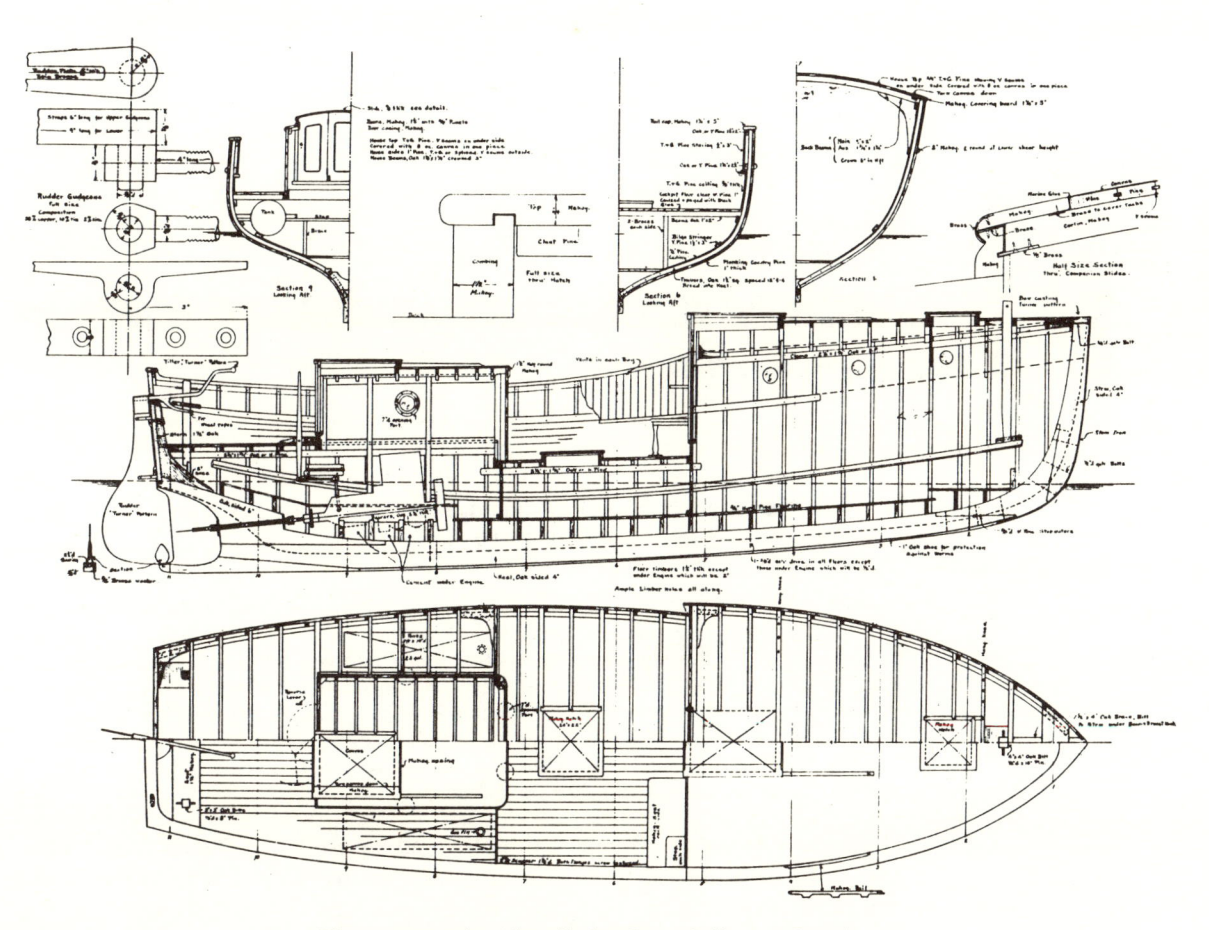

The construction details for Grey Gull, number 42.

19

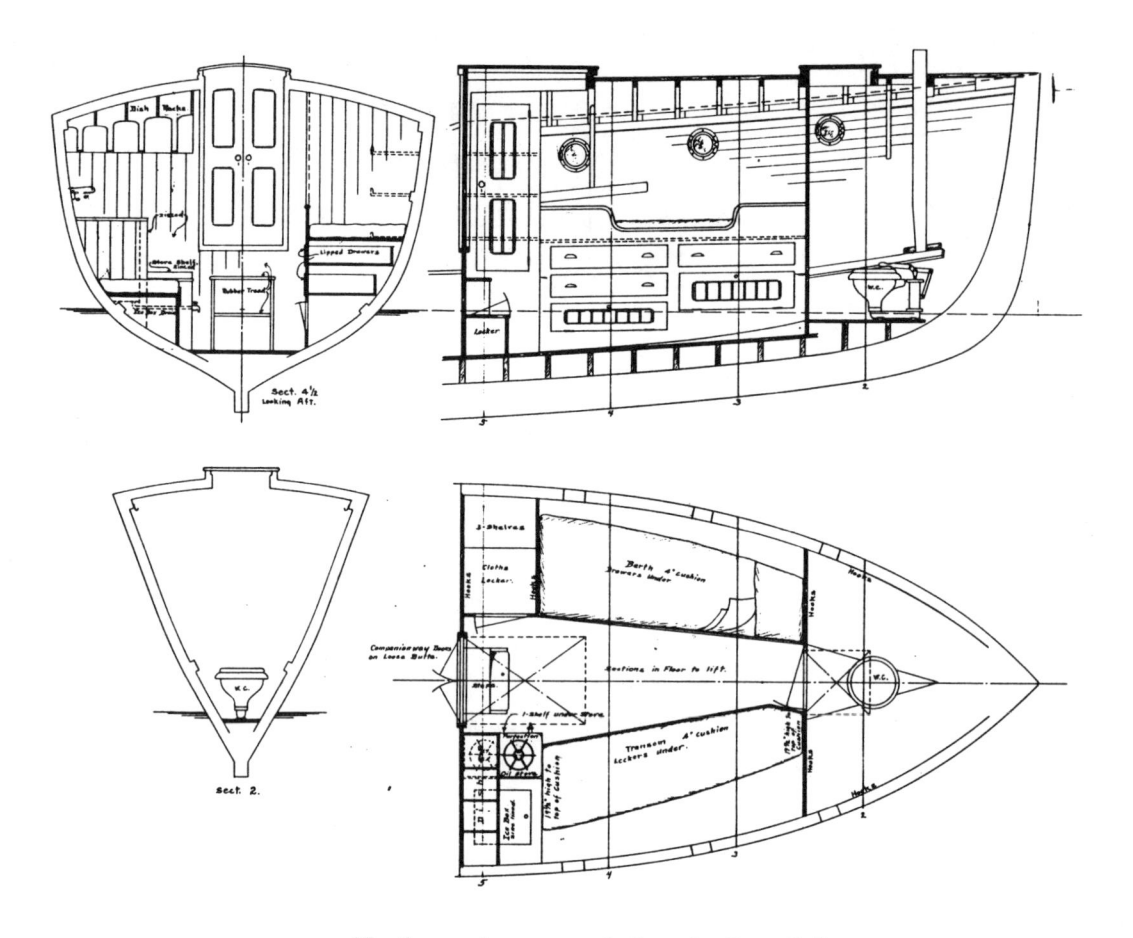

The forward accommodations for Grey Gull.

43 SKOOKUM

Design number 43 — as mentioned, she came from the same lines as number 40 — was the single-head-sloop-rigged *Skookum*, built for James Dean. Dean reported in a letter of November 1, 1924:

I am glad to inform you that my boat *Skookum*, which you built for me in the winter of 1923-1924, has been entirely satisfactory.

She is a good sailer, and in one race at Cohasset, which was not fluky, she came in second, beating two 21-footers, *Fly* and *Fancy*, Herreshoff boats. For a cruising boat I consider her speedy. She is well balanced and is the driest and best small boat in a seaway that I have ever sailed on. Although she will not point as close under jib alone, she will handle and go to windward under this sail, a rather unusual and satisfactory feature, considering her bowsprit.

The second number 43 was a double-head sloop called *Aquilla* by John C. Scully. Then came a yawl called *Samari*, used by my father until she was sold to Evans Dick, who renamed her *Youth*. She was later *Phalarope* and *Sparrowhawk*.

20

The sailplan for Aquilla.

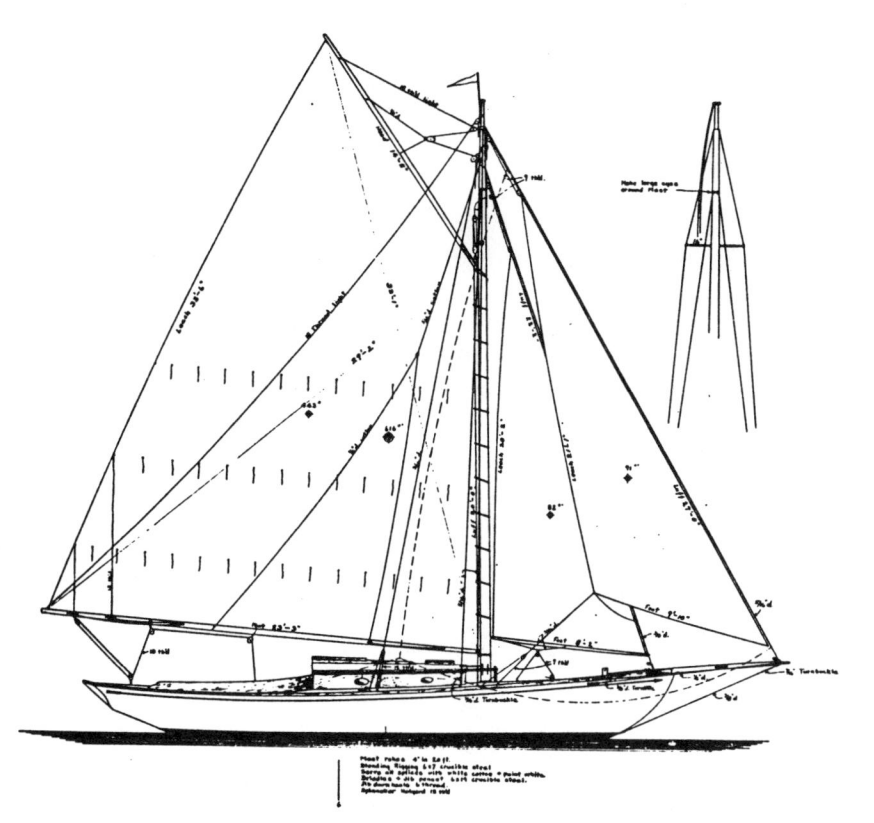

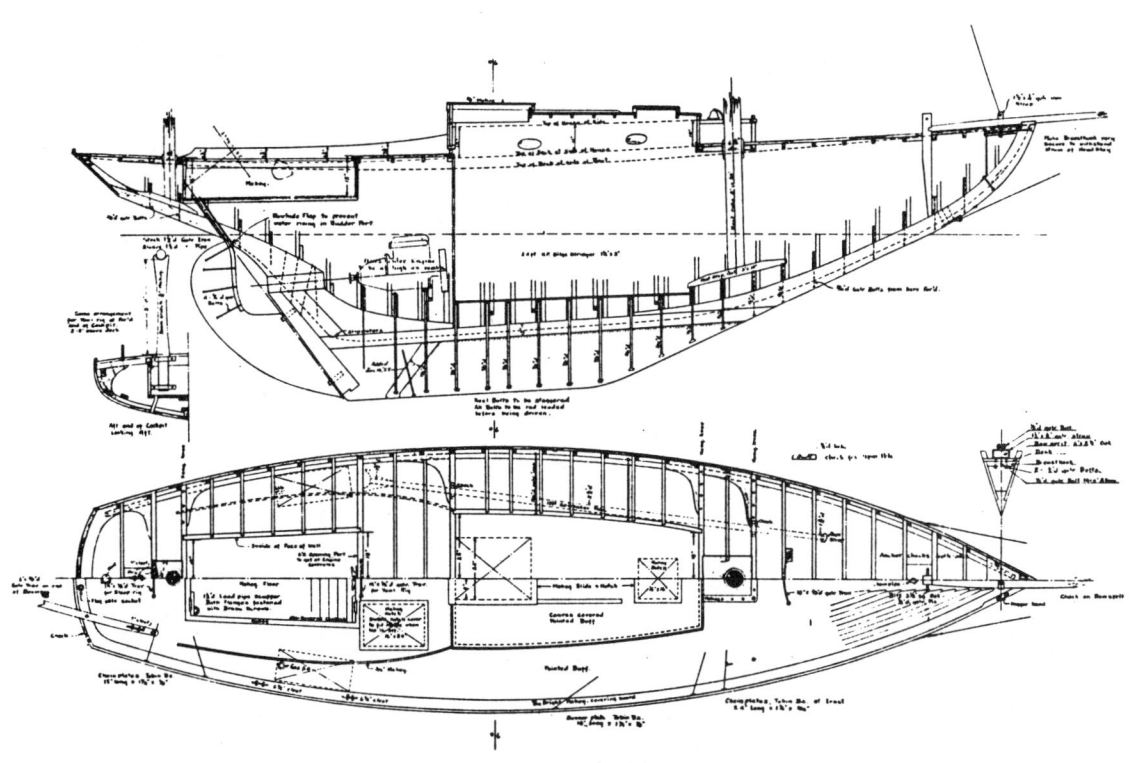

Youth, *design number 43.*

The construction plans for number 43.

21

47 FEARLESS

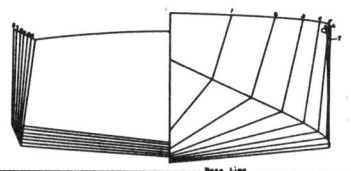

Design number 47: This 21-foot hydroplane called *Fearless,* was designed for E.B. Phillips of Georges Mills, N.H. She is rather interesting, being chine construction and lightly built, with a step in the bottom and rudder forward. I don't know what powered the V drive, but a note says she was capable of making 35 m.p.h. Somehow that rudder forward looks awfully vulnerable. She was used on Lake Sunapee in New Hampshire.

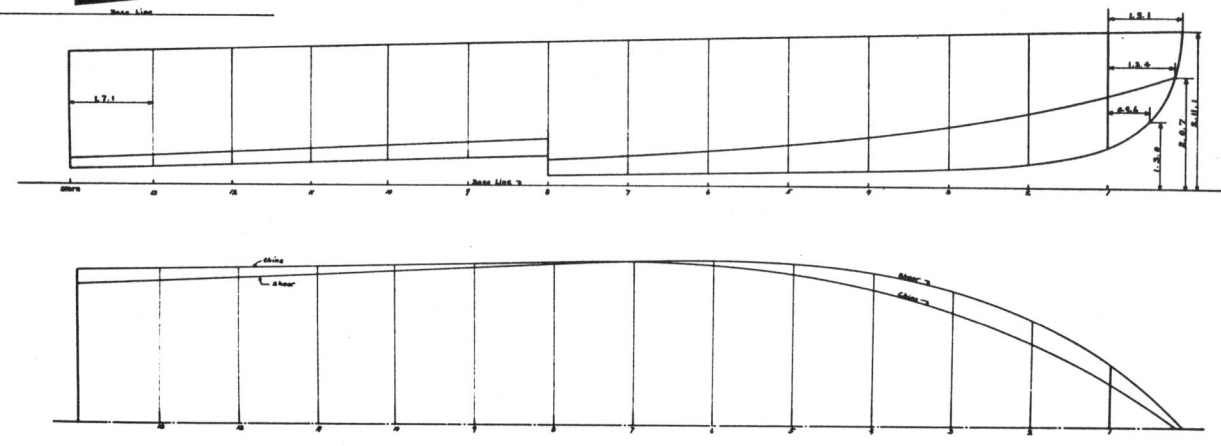

The lines for number 47, Fearless.

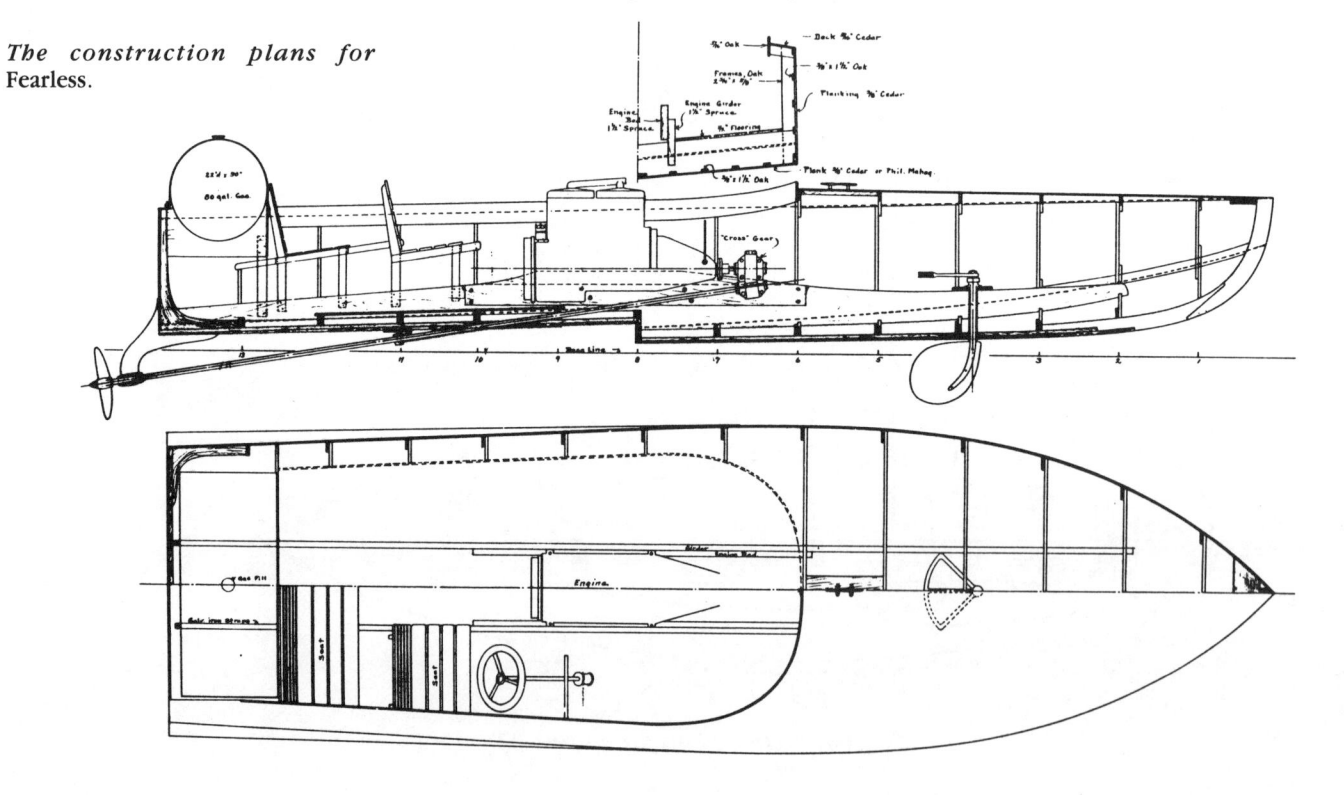

The construction plans for Fearless.

54

This design shows a profile similar to the old *Samari* (number 6) except she is marconi rigged and has a trunk cabin. Underwater she was flat bottomed and had a centerboard.

Right and below: *The sailplan for number 54 and the lines for the same vessel.*

Design Number 54
Length Overall: 26 feet 4 inches
Length on Waterline: 24 feet 6 inches
Beam: 8 feet
Draft: 1 foot 6 inches
Sail Area: 295 square feet
Displacement: 4,800 pounds

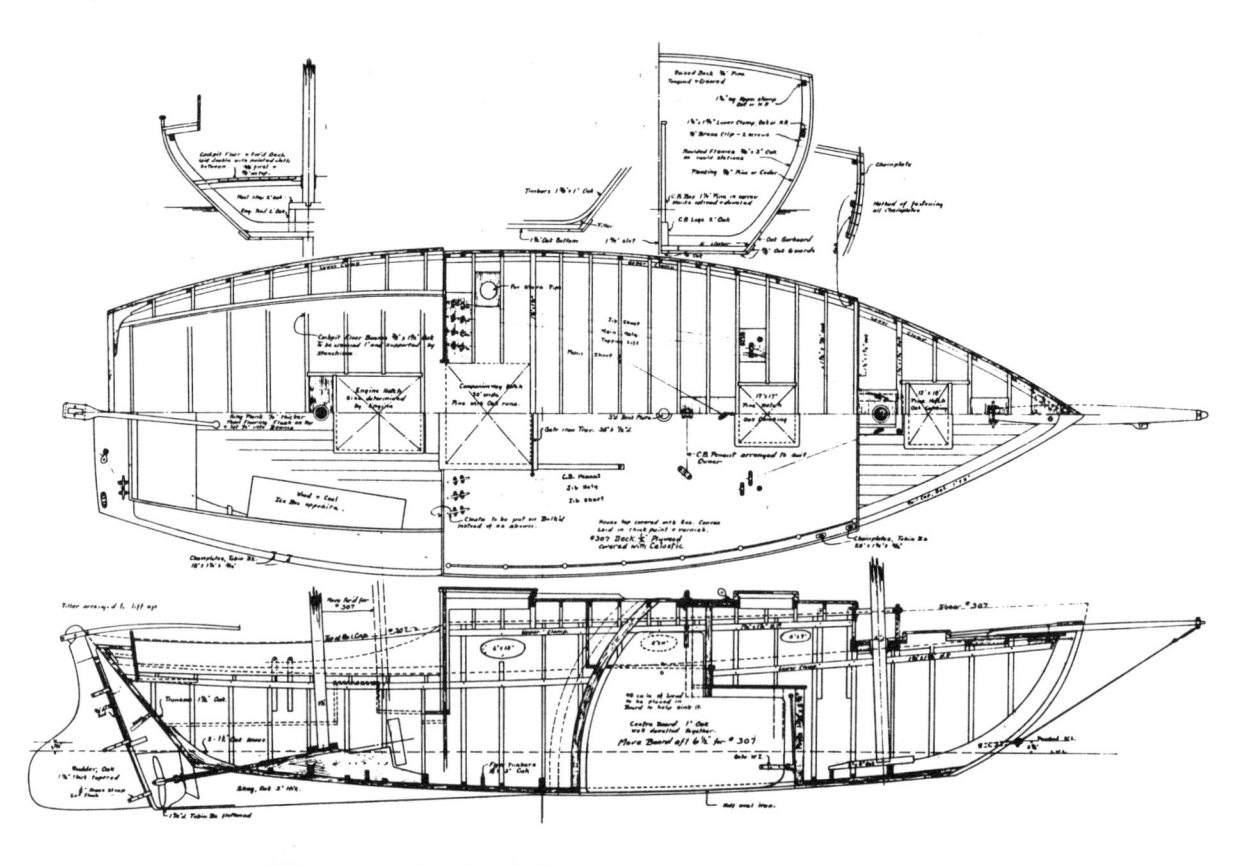

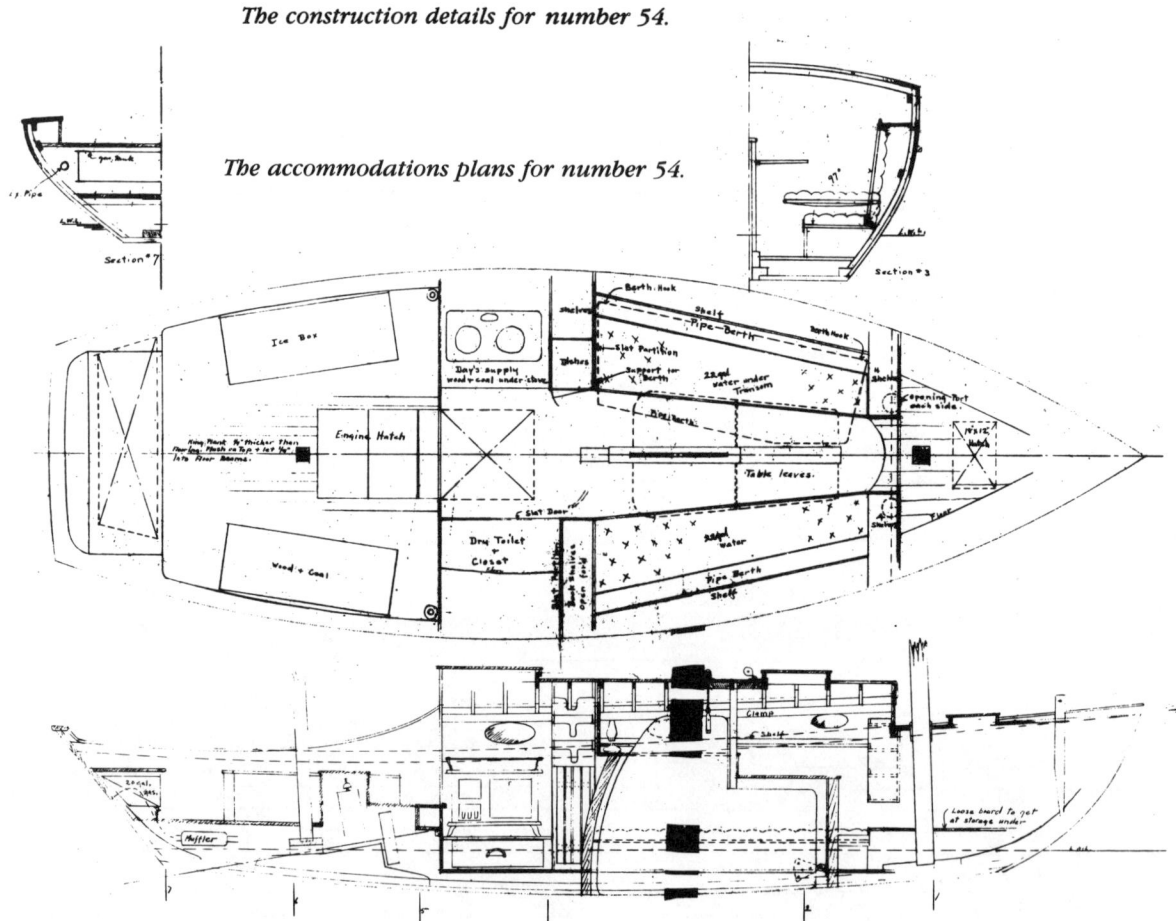

The construction details for number 54.

The accommodations plans for number 54.

63

Number 63: This V-bottom cat would certainly be an easy boat to build out of plywood. As can be seen by the faint lines on the drawing, she apparently had a bowsprit added and a sliding hatch over the foredeck.

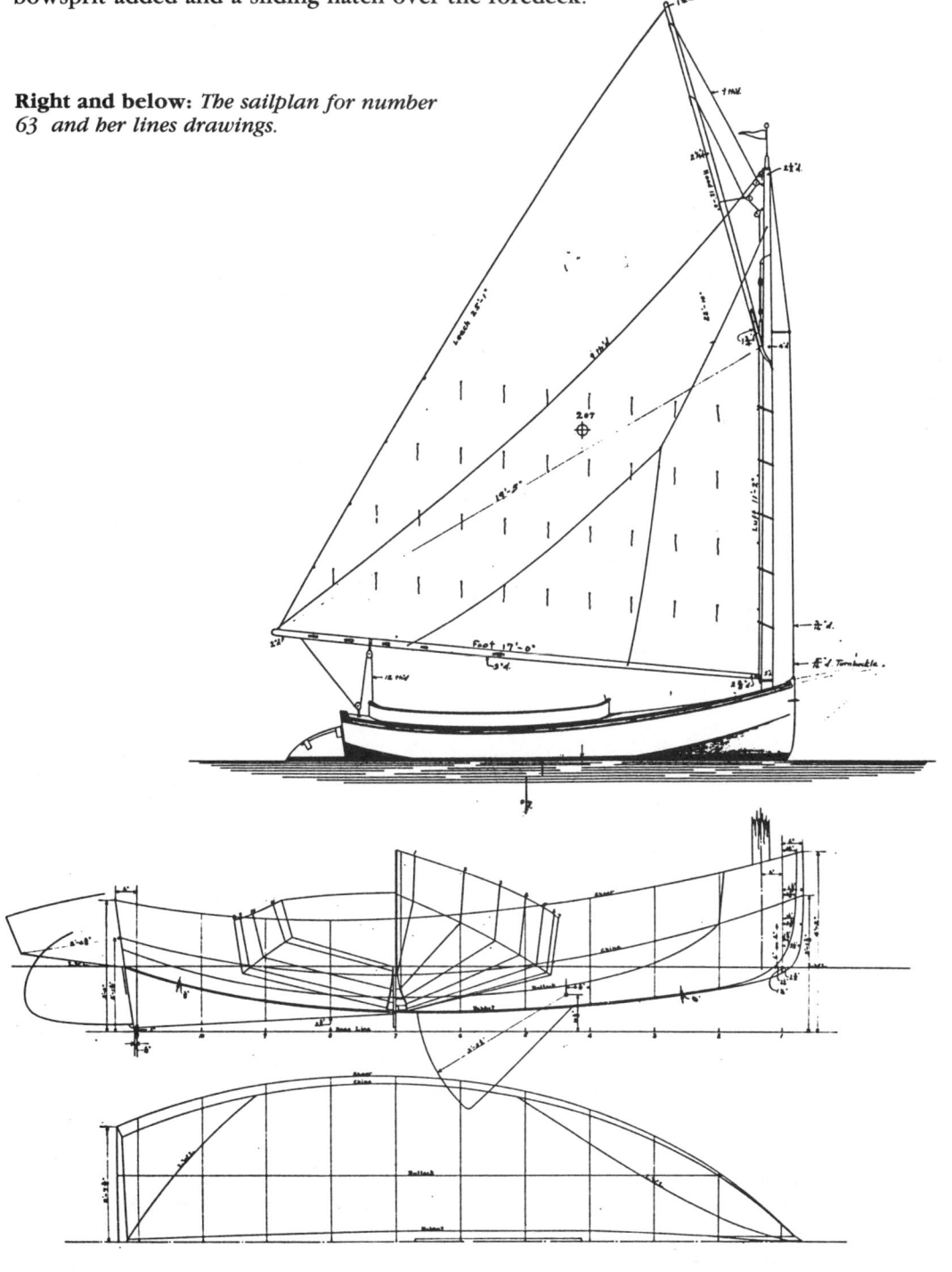

Right and below: *The sailplan for number 63 and her lines drawings.*

25

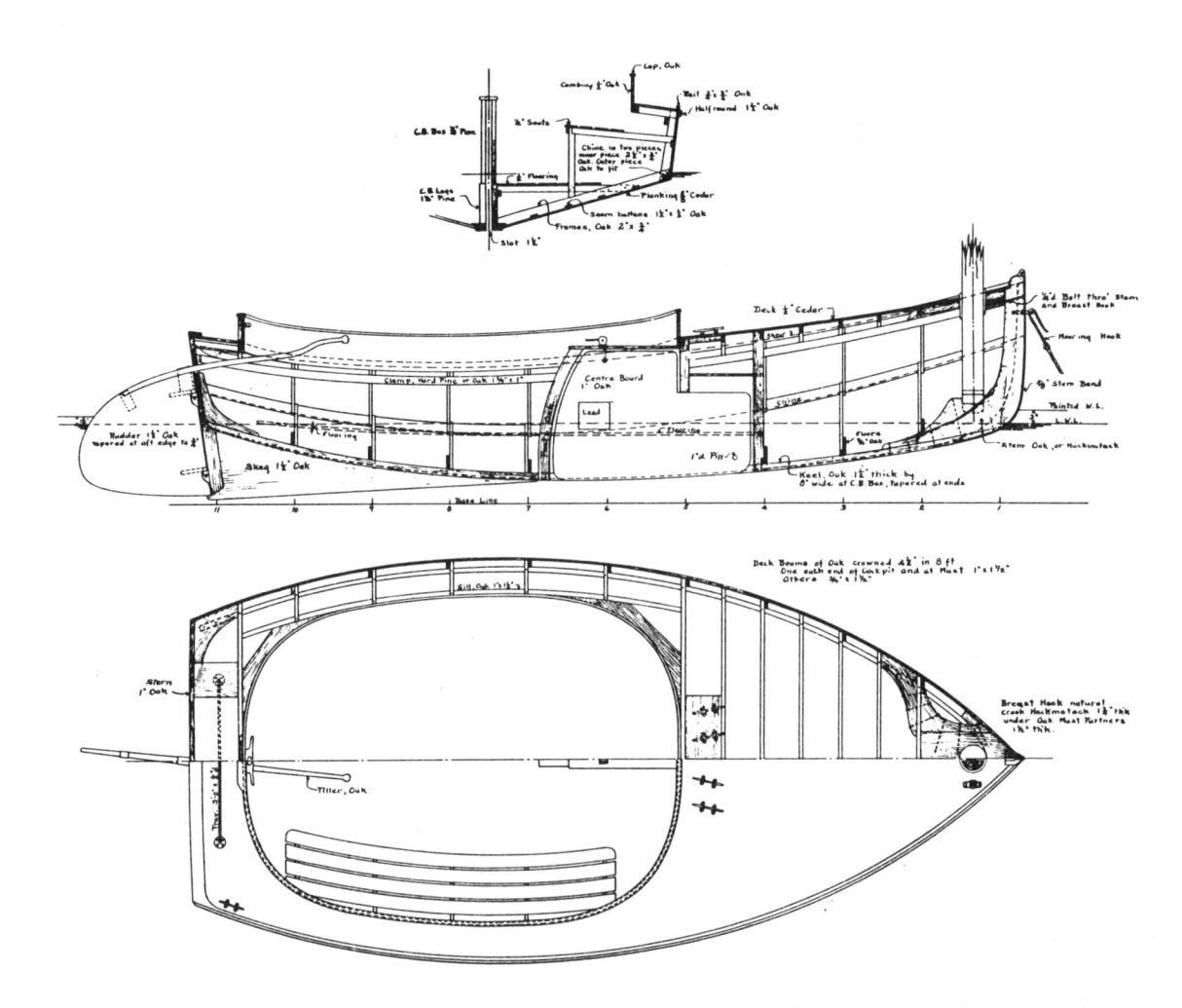

The construction details for number 63.

68

Design Numbers 68 and 68A
Length Overall: 41 feet 6 inches
Length on Waterline: 30 feet 9 inches
Beam: 12 feet
Draft: 6 feet 2 inches
Sail Area: 1041 square feet
Displacement: 26,600 pounds

Number 68 was the first of several medium-length yawls. She was built for Dr. C.A. Thomas and called *Saros*. She was subsequently called *Sequoia, Champernowne,* and *Riptide;* the last I know of her was as *Boro Gove III,* owned by Don Gardiner of Marblehead, Mass.

Number 68A was built for my father from the same lines on speculation. We used her out of Manchester and called her *Pontiac*. She was the winner of the Tilden Thurber ocean race in 1928 and 1929. She was eventually sold and moved to Chicago, where she was called *Vagabond*.

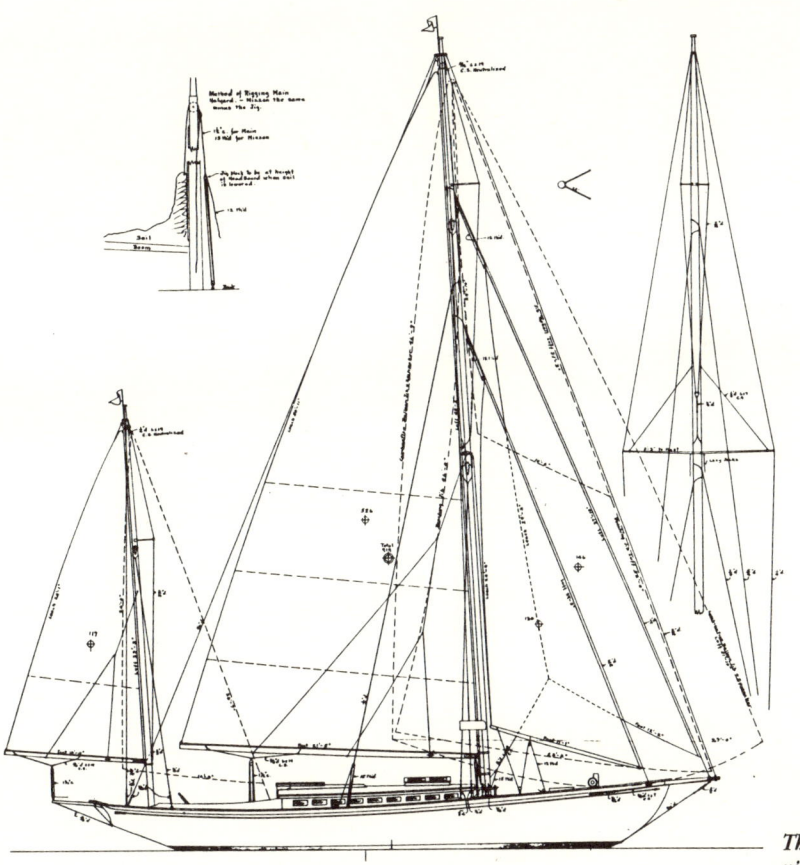

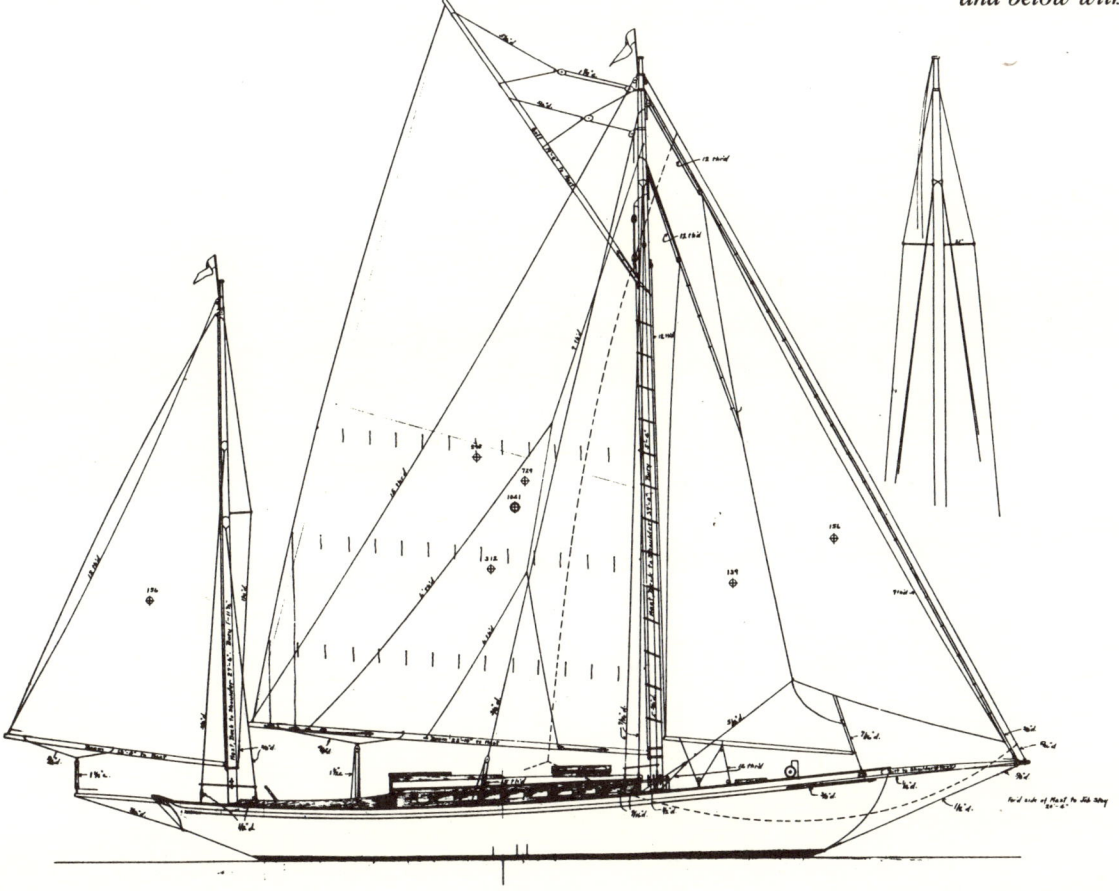

The sailplans for number 68 rigged first with a marconi main, and below with a gaff main.

27

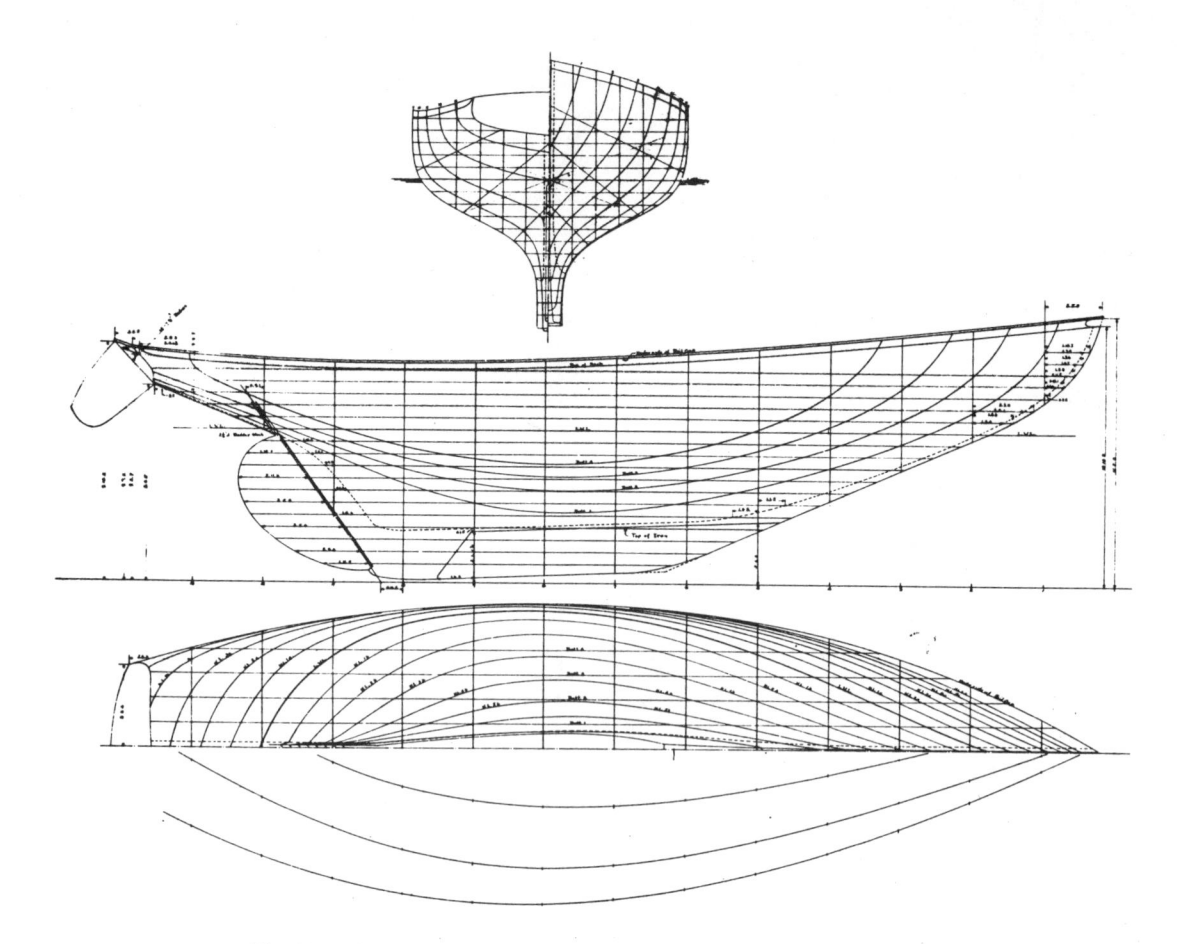

The lines for number 68 and her construction details.

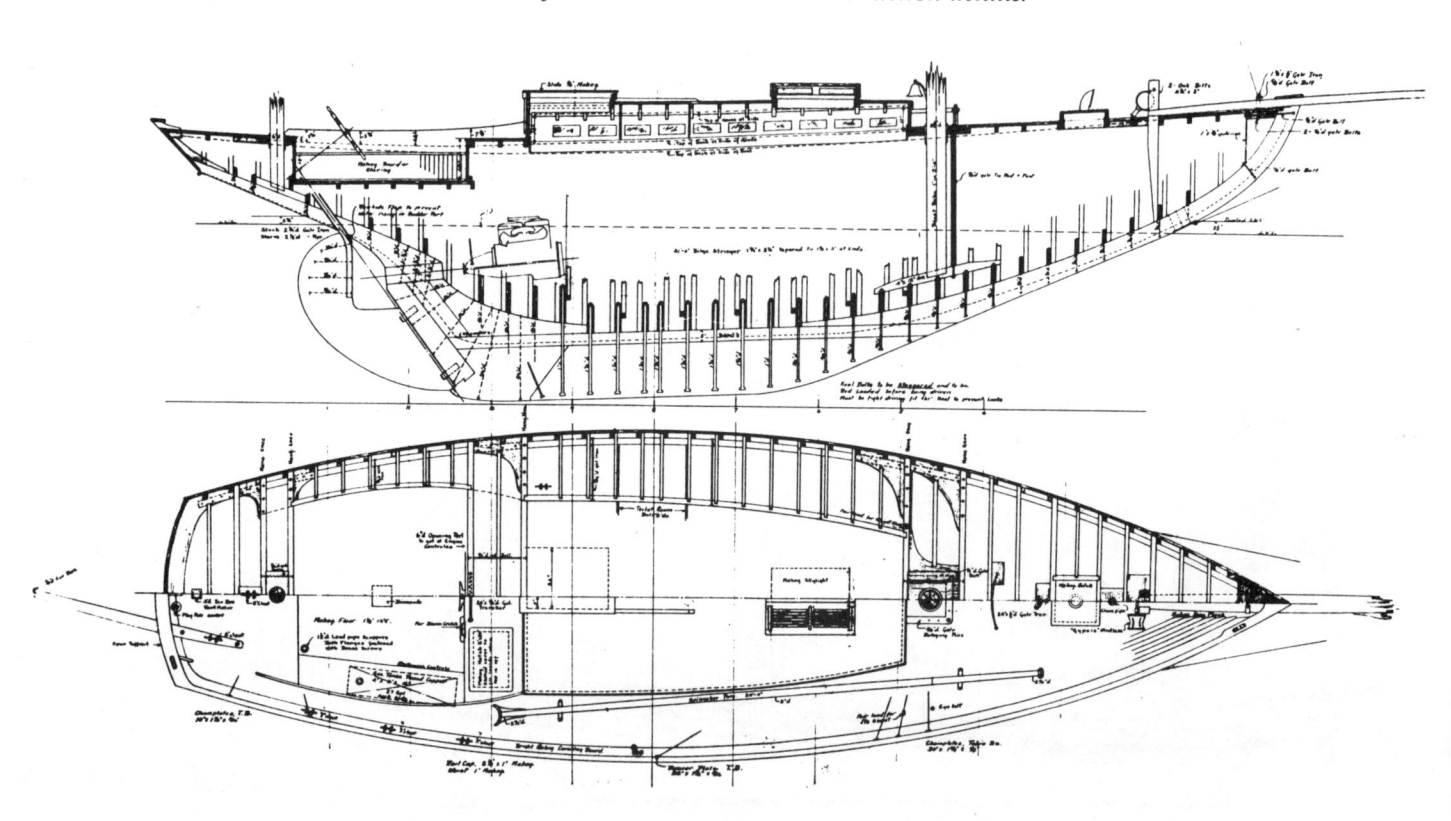

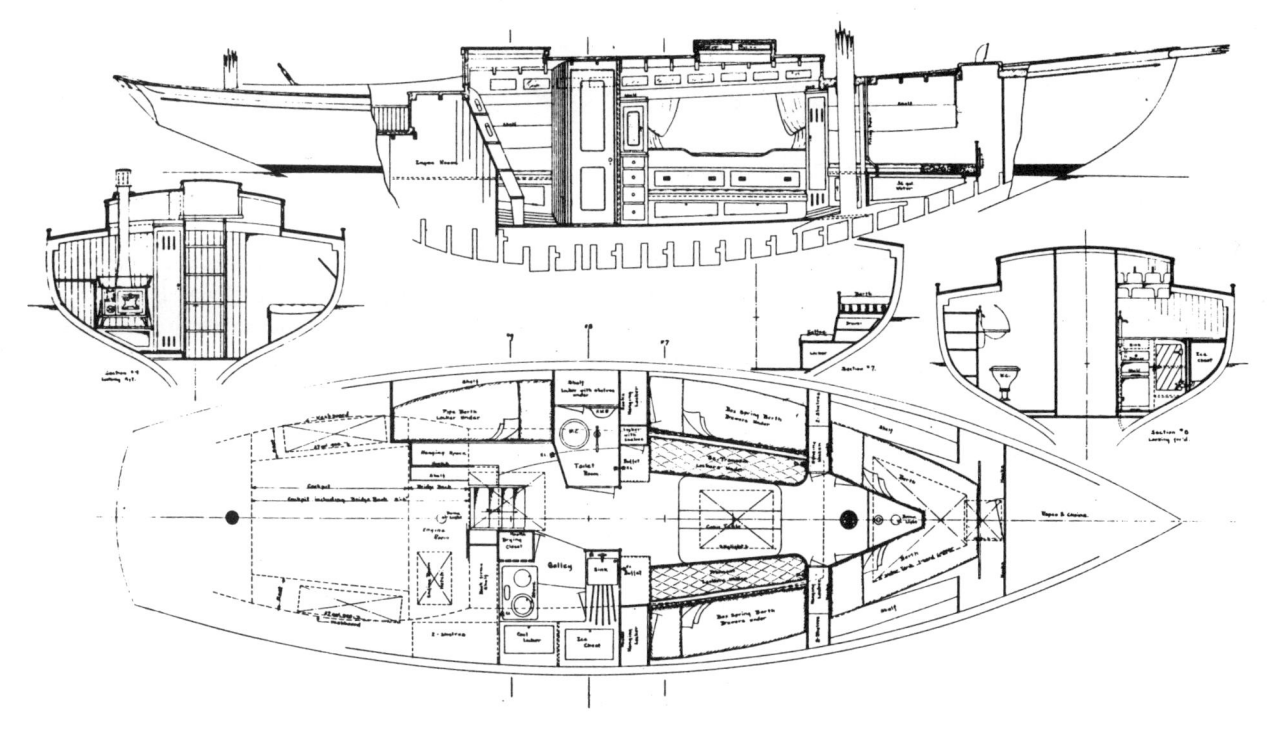

The interior plans for number 68.

Number 68 courtesy of Edwin Levick.

68B NAWANNA

Number 68B was built from the same lines as numbers 68 and 68A but was rigged as a schooner and called *Nawanna*. She sailed on the Great Lakes. She had a different layout, with two staterooms. I'll bet a good many heads were bumped going from one stateroom to the other.

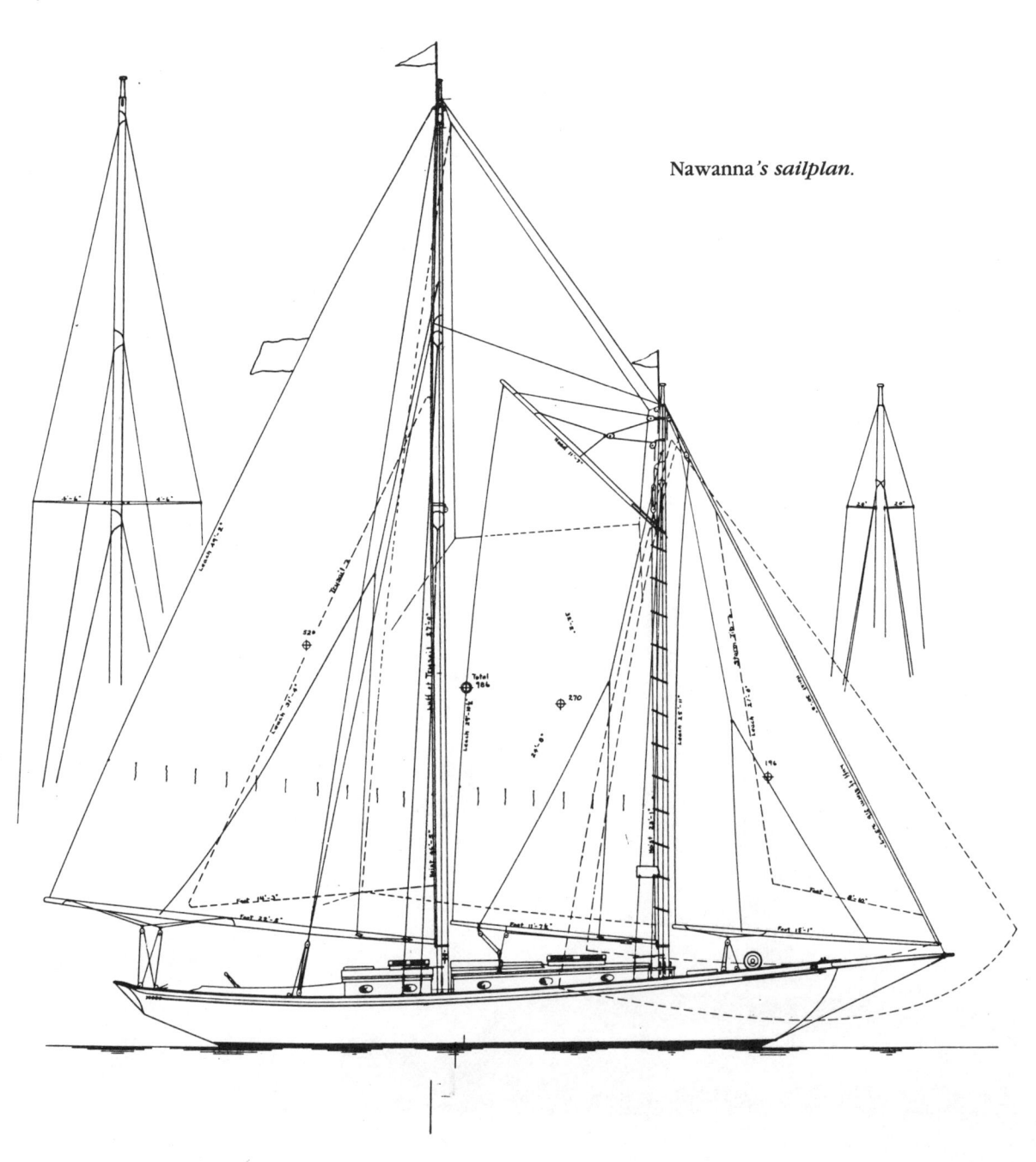

Nawanna's sailplan.

A pen and ink drawing by Sam Crocker, showing Nawanna's *main cabin and her sea berths.*

WAKAYA 75

Wakaya was a raised-deck motor cruiser with a trunk cabin for extra headroom. There was also a small house over the engine that contained the head — not too handy an arrangement at times, I imagine. She had a small rig, but I can't imagine her going to weather very well. At least one other boat was built from these lines with a more conventional powerboat profile. The raised deck was carried farther aft and not carried to the bow, leaving a well deck forward, where she had an anchor davit, which, of course, made anchoring easier. She also had a standing top over part of the cockpit. A 30-horsepower, three-cylinder Lathrop powered her.

Design Number 75
Length Overall: 32 feet
Length on Waterline: 31 feet 6 inches
Beam: 9 feet
Draft: 3 feet
Displacement: 9,660 pounds

The profile of Wakaya and her lines.

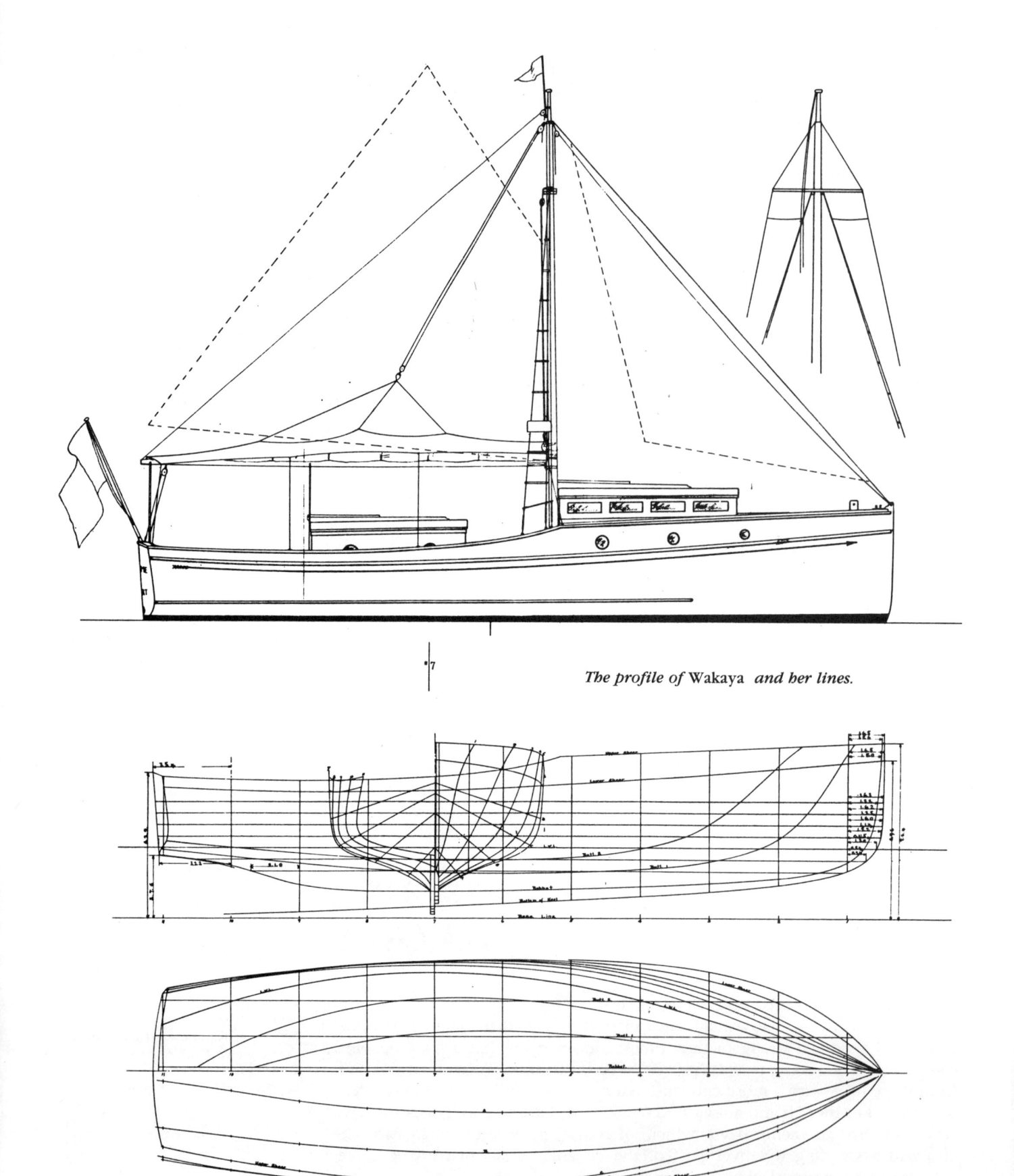

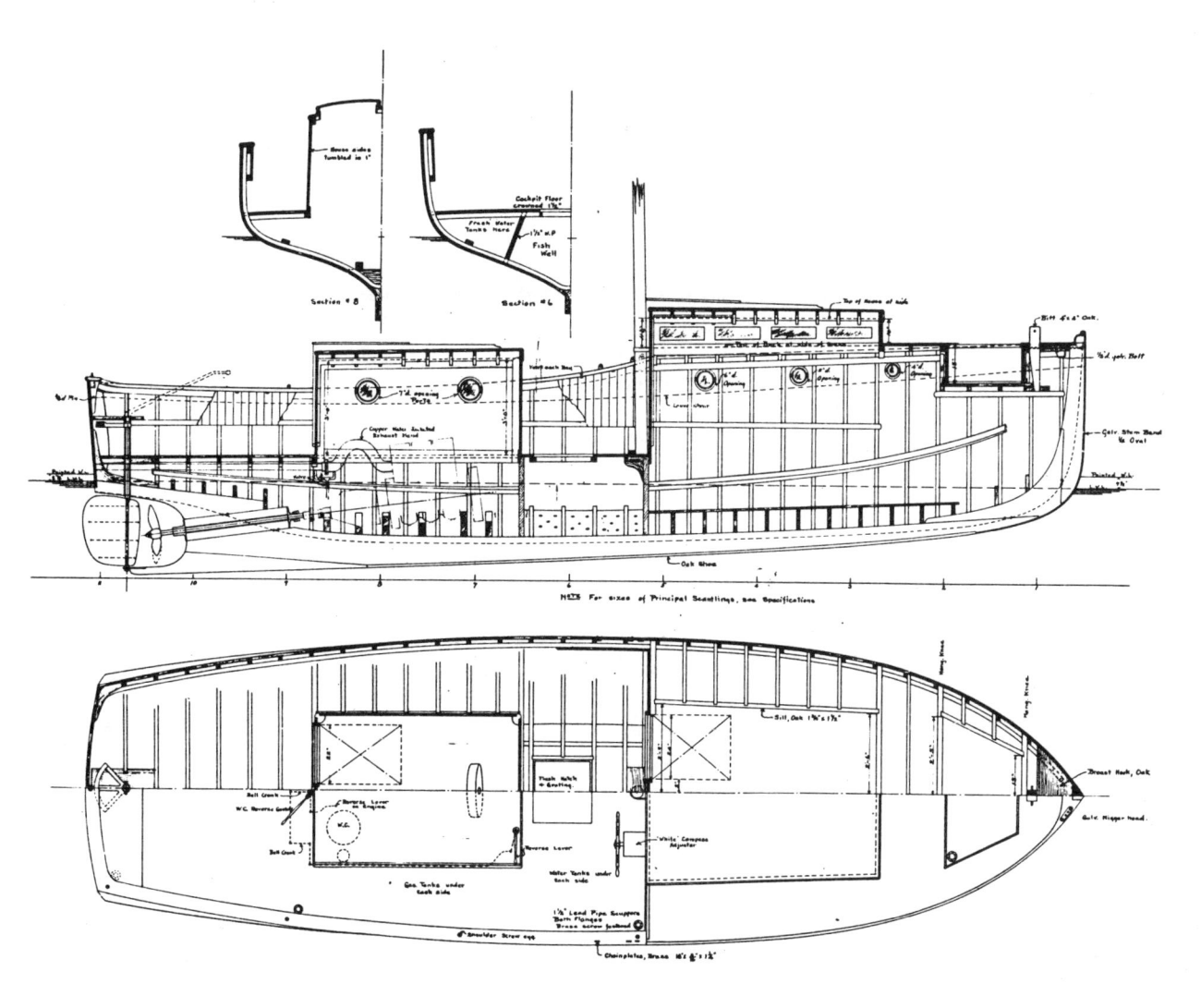

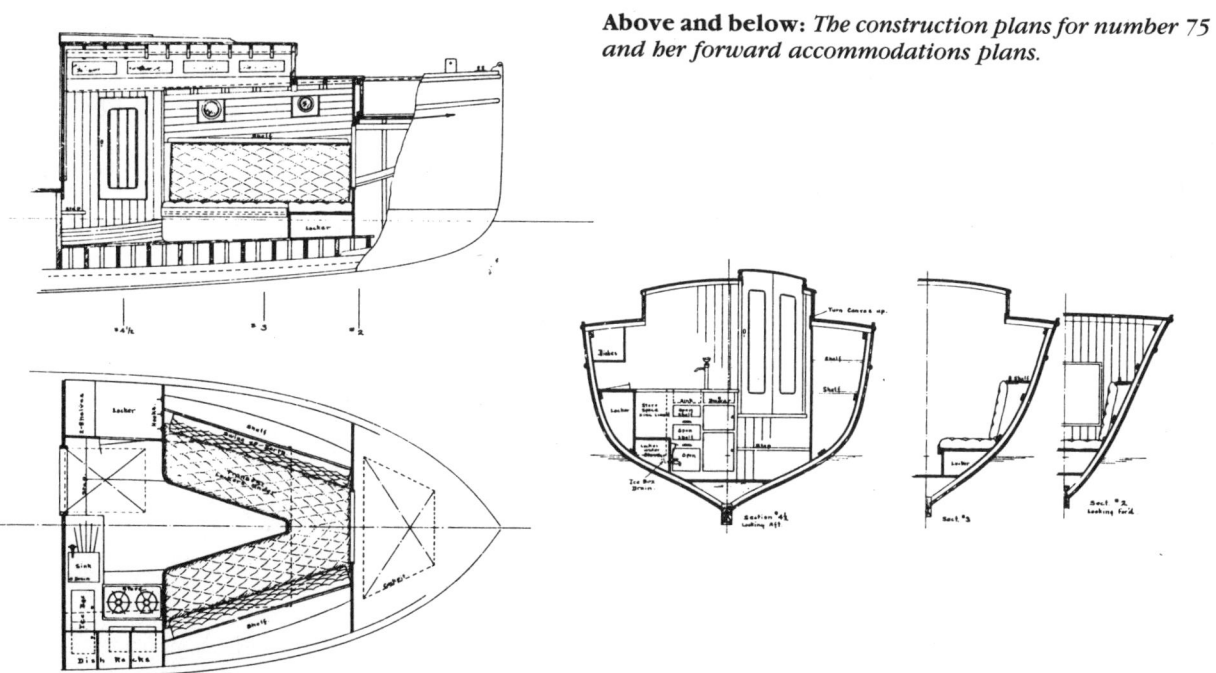

Above and below: *The construction plans for number 75 and her forward accommodations plans.*

76 FREMARI

Design Number 76
Length Overall: 31 feet 11 inches
Length on Waterline: 23 feet 6 inches
Beam: 8 feet 6 inches
Draft: 5 feet 6 inches
Sail Area: 569 square feet
Displacement: 11,000 pounds

The first number 76, drawn to the same lines and dimensions as number 40, was *Fremari,* built for F.L. Woods. Later she was *Crocodile,* for U.H. Crocker and *Chiquite,* for Murray G. Peterson and then passed to several other owners, most of whom changed her name.

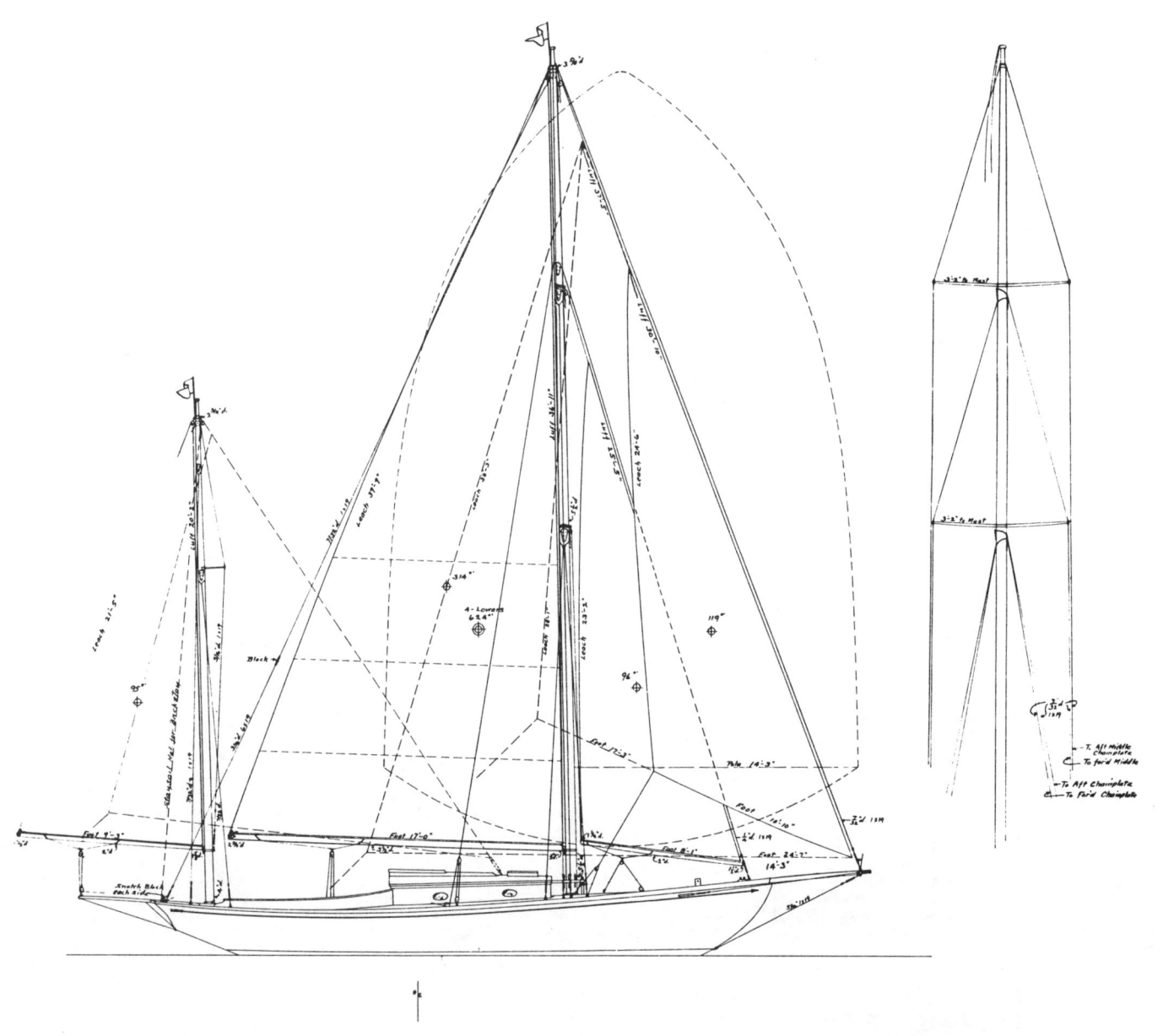

The sailplan for Fremari.

34

Number 76B, built for Gardiner Akin, was called *Minerva,* later owned by A.P. Loring, Jr., and still later, by Frank Vining Smith.

Number 76C, *Caronia,* built for A.F. Spare in 1925, was later *Amantha,* owned by Gardiner Akin, Jr. G.B. Hollister changed the name to *Chantey;* then B.T. Woodle changed it to *Brownie.* Capt. Conant Taylor acquired her in 1932. It was this boat that was so glowingly written about by Roger Taylor in *Good Boats.*

Practically all of these boats were built in Maine and brought to Manchester by my father for a trial trip.

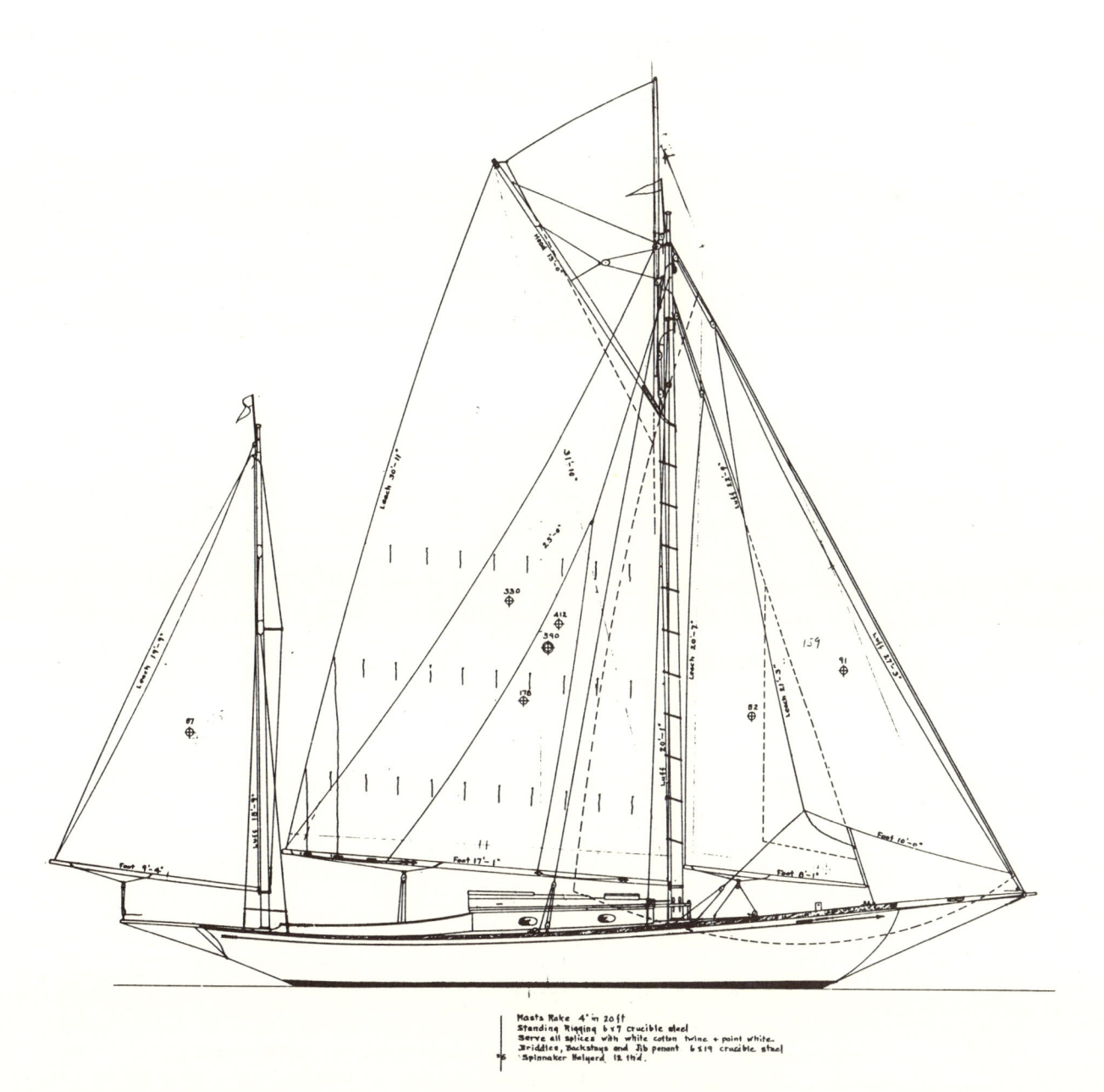

Number 76's sailplan with a gaff main.

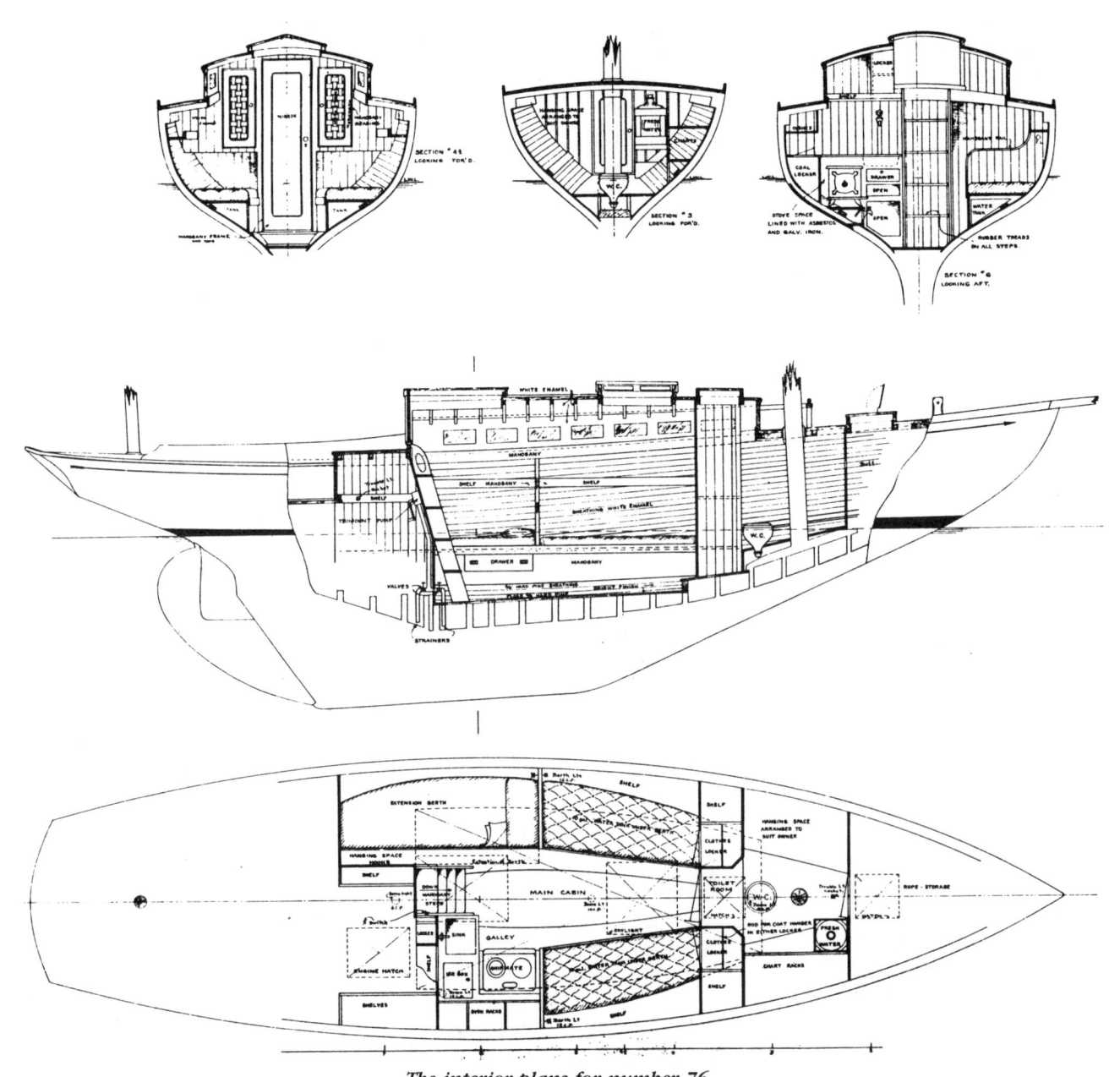

The interior plans for number 76.

A. Spare, owner of *Caronia,* wrote on October 18, 1930,

We had a peach of a cruise last week. We sailed to Hadley's Harbor Saturday night, through Woods Hole and the Sound to Menemsha on Sunday, and Monday from Menemsha to Vineyard Sound Lightship, Hen & Chickens Lightship, and back to Padanaram. The Monday sail was about 26 miles and she sailed herself the whole distance except when we changed courses and into the harbor at Padanaram. These courses included close hauled, started sheets, sheets broad off and dead before the wind wing and wing, the wind moderate S.W. and quite steady. I have read and heard about perfect self-steerers, but I never saw one before. Her balance is absolutely perfect, and when sailing herself the rudder is always amidships. No one ever designed a better cruising boat, and I do not see how she could possibly be improved upon.

Fremari *off Marblehead. Photograph courtesy of W.B. Jackson.*

77 KITTIWAKE

Design Number 77
Length Overall: 37 feet
Length on Waterline: 27 feet 3 inches
Beam: 10 feet 10 inches
Draft: 4 feet 9 inches
Sail Area: 811 square feet
Displacement: 18,700 pounds

Kittiwake was designed and built in 1925 for Neil D. McMath of Detroit, who later became affiliated with Bill Lee of Harwichport, Mass., in the building of the Stone Horses. The contract was signed in October 1925 by Israel Snow, Jr., of Newcastle, Me. I have snapshots showing the boat loaded on a flatcar, presumably for delivery to the Great Lakes, after her trials in Maine. A letter from her third owner in 1944 tells of her fine performance in the long-distance races on the lake and the fact that she had taken the Mackinawa Schooner Trophy for the third consecutive year. She won two third places and one fourth place in three Mackinac races and one third place and one fifth place in two 60-mile-long distance races.

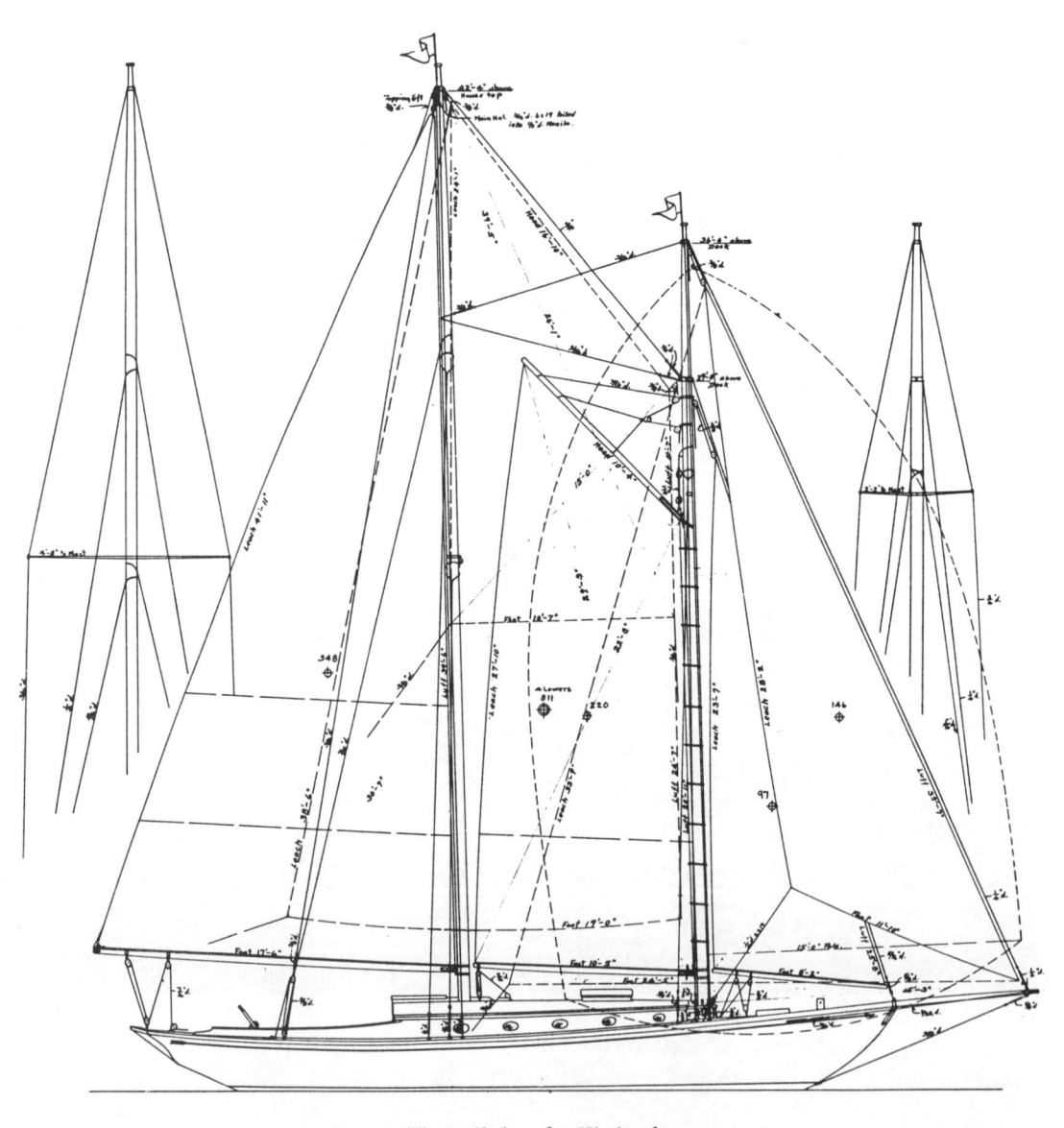

The sailplan for Kittiwake.

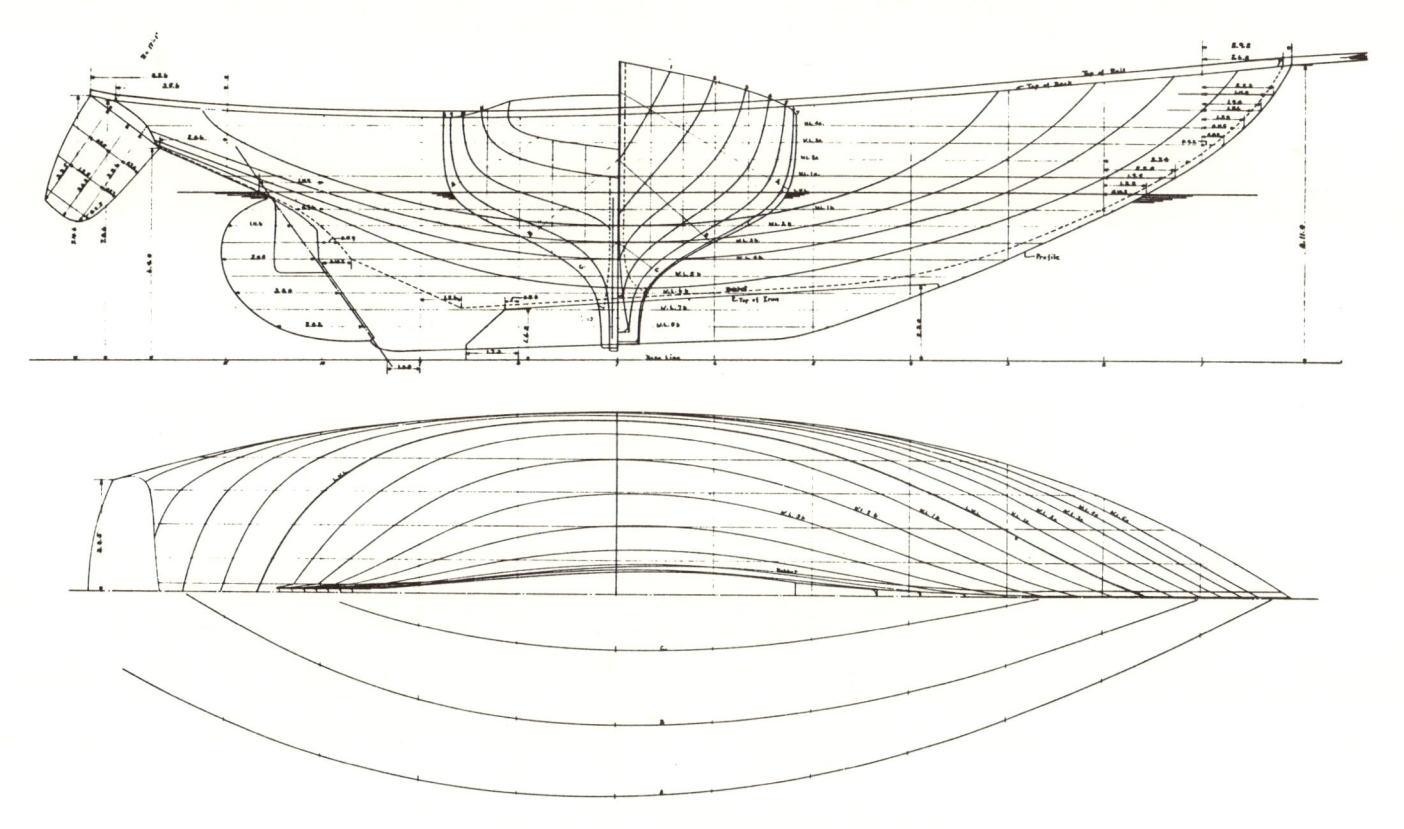

Kittiwake's *lines* and her construction plans.

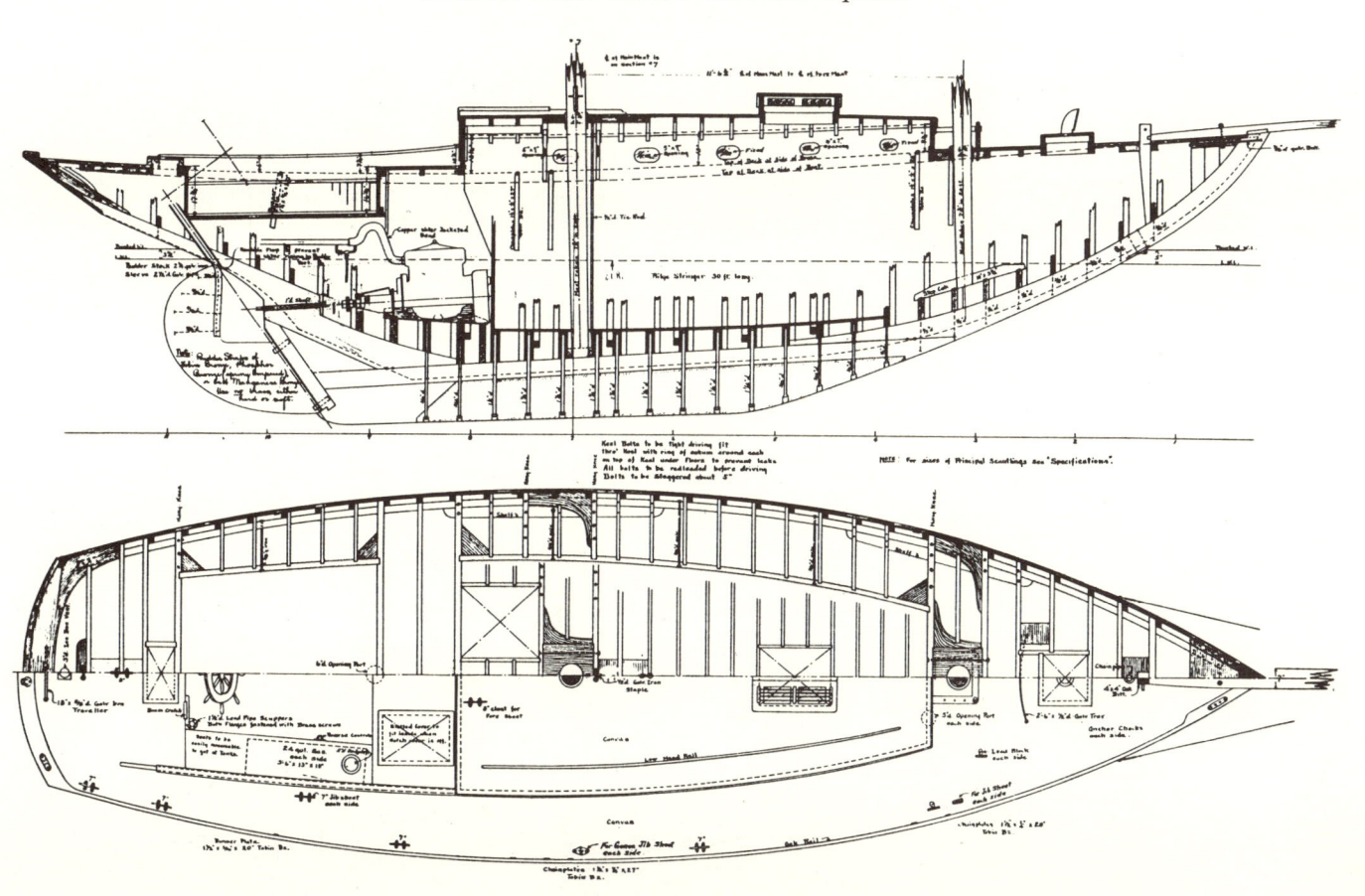

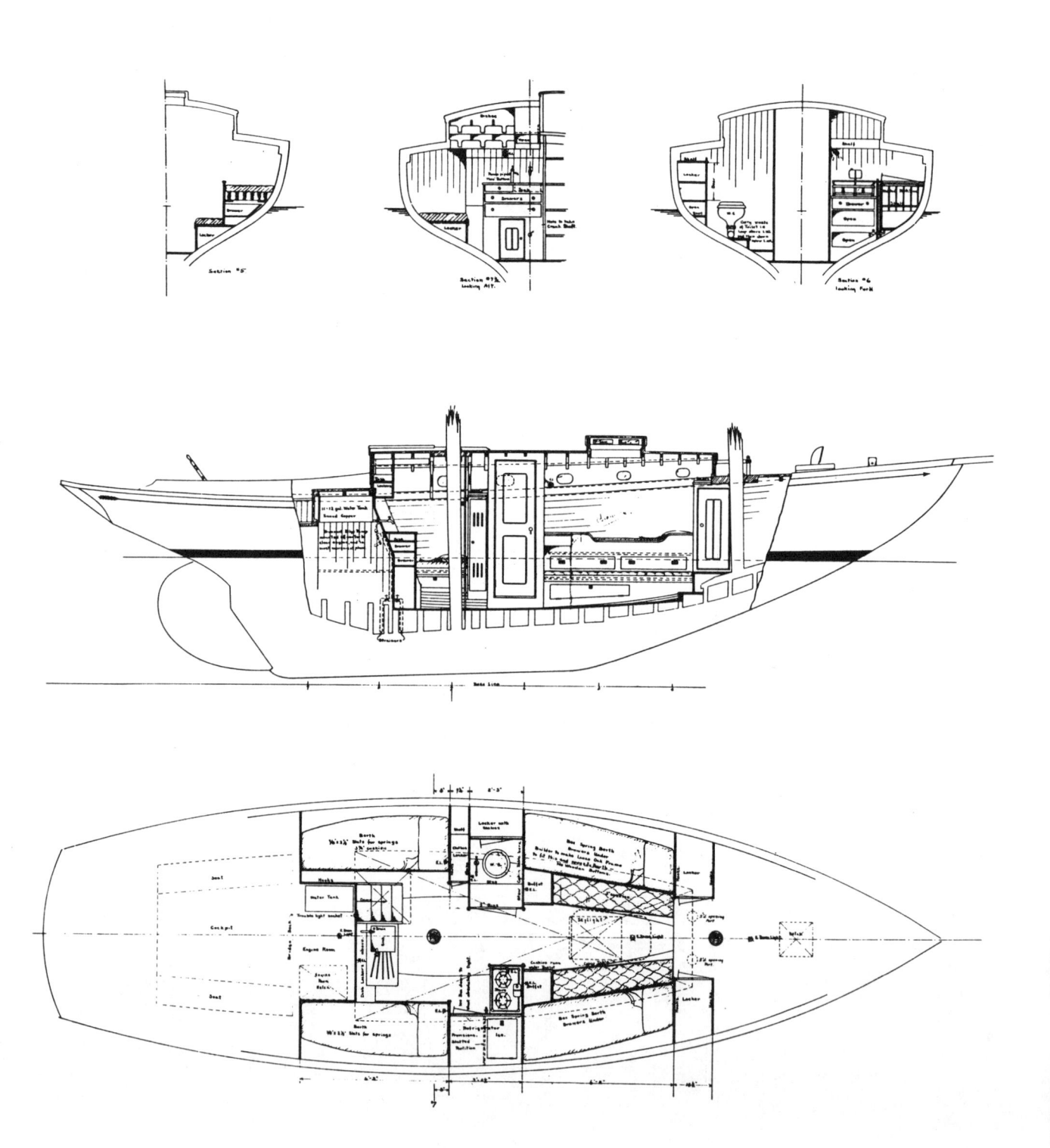

The accommodations for Kittiwake.

Number 77, Kittiwake.

78

Design Number 78
Length Overall: 26 feet
Length on Waterline: 24 feet 10 inches
Beam: 7 feet 6 inches
Draft: 2 feet 6 inches
Displacement: 5,220 pounds

I enclose this design even though all we have is the lines. It was a very popular hull, and many were built for lobsterboats. Number 194 was the *Alamo,* designed for our neighbor G.L. (Lock) Allen and built by George Chaisson in Swampscott from these lines with more freeboard in 1938. She was a comfortable little motorsailer, and we did a lot of fishing from her until Lock sold her in 1949. Another boat built from these lines was *Schoodic,* built in 1927 by Guy Gardiner in Swampscott. He put on a raised deck forward and an auxiliary yawl rig. She had a two-cylinder Palmer engine with reverse gear but no self-starter. Her cruising speed was 8 m.p.h.

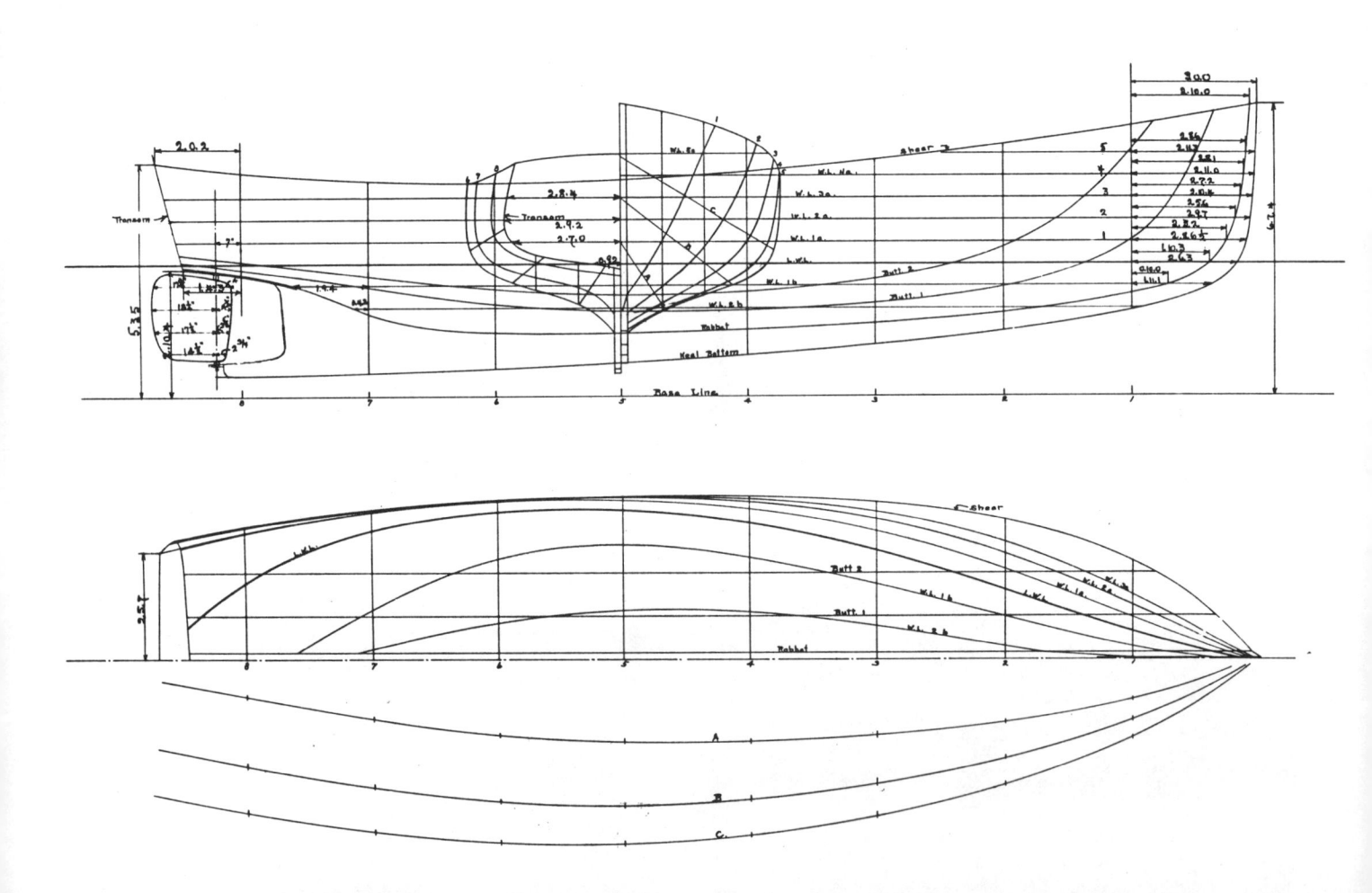

The lines for number 78.

TERN 80

The schooner *Tern* was built through the winter of 1925-1926 by Israel Snow for A.L. Pope of West Hartford, Conn. The photograph shows Pope at the wheel, with my father enjoying the sail on the cruise from Maine to Manchester in spring 1926. Sunny but cold! In Dad's files I found a clipping from the *Hartford Daily Times* (October 15, 1929), a copy of the log for a cruise from Hartford to Bar Harbor, Me., which is quite interesting. I guess she was in use most of the time, because in that year alone she logged 2,500 miles. A Kermath four-cylinder engine gave a speed of six knots when she was under power.

Design Number 80
Length Overall: 49 feet
Length on Waterline: 36 feet 3 inches
Beam: 14 feet 5 inches
Draft: 5 feet
Sail Area: 1247 square feet
Displacement: 38,000 pounds

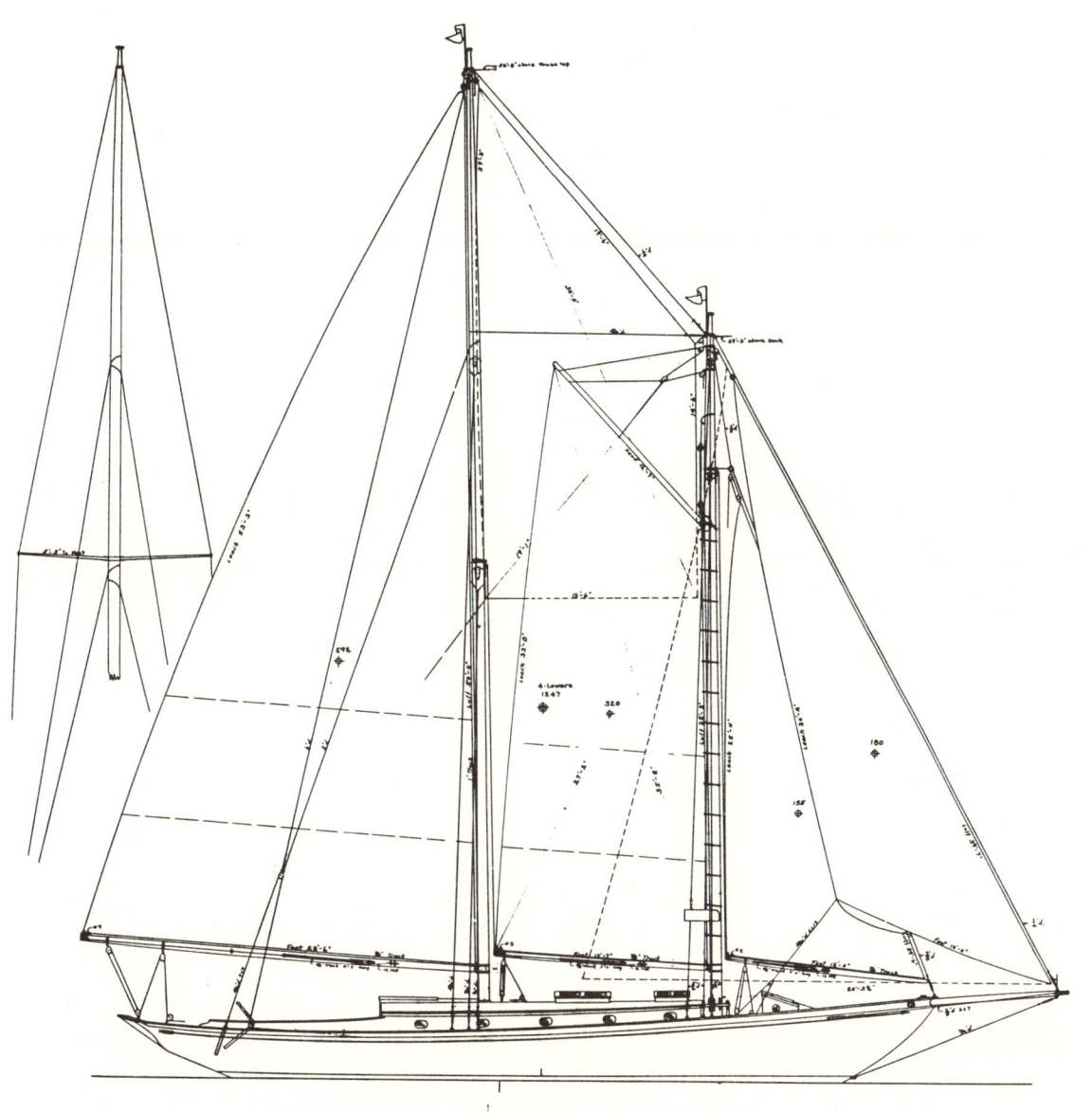

The sailplan for the schooner Tern, *number 80.*

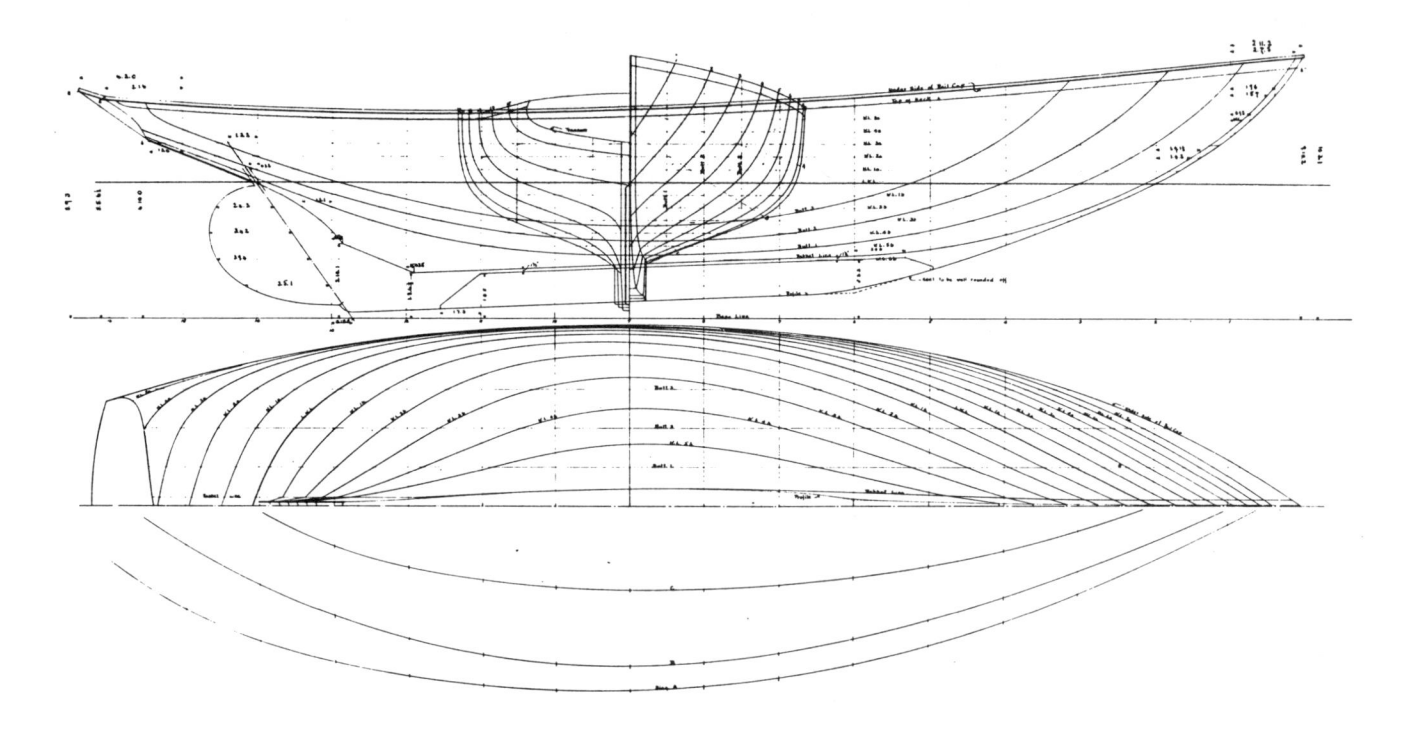

The lines for Tern *and her construction plans.*

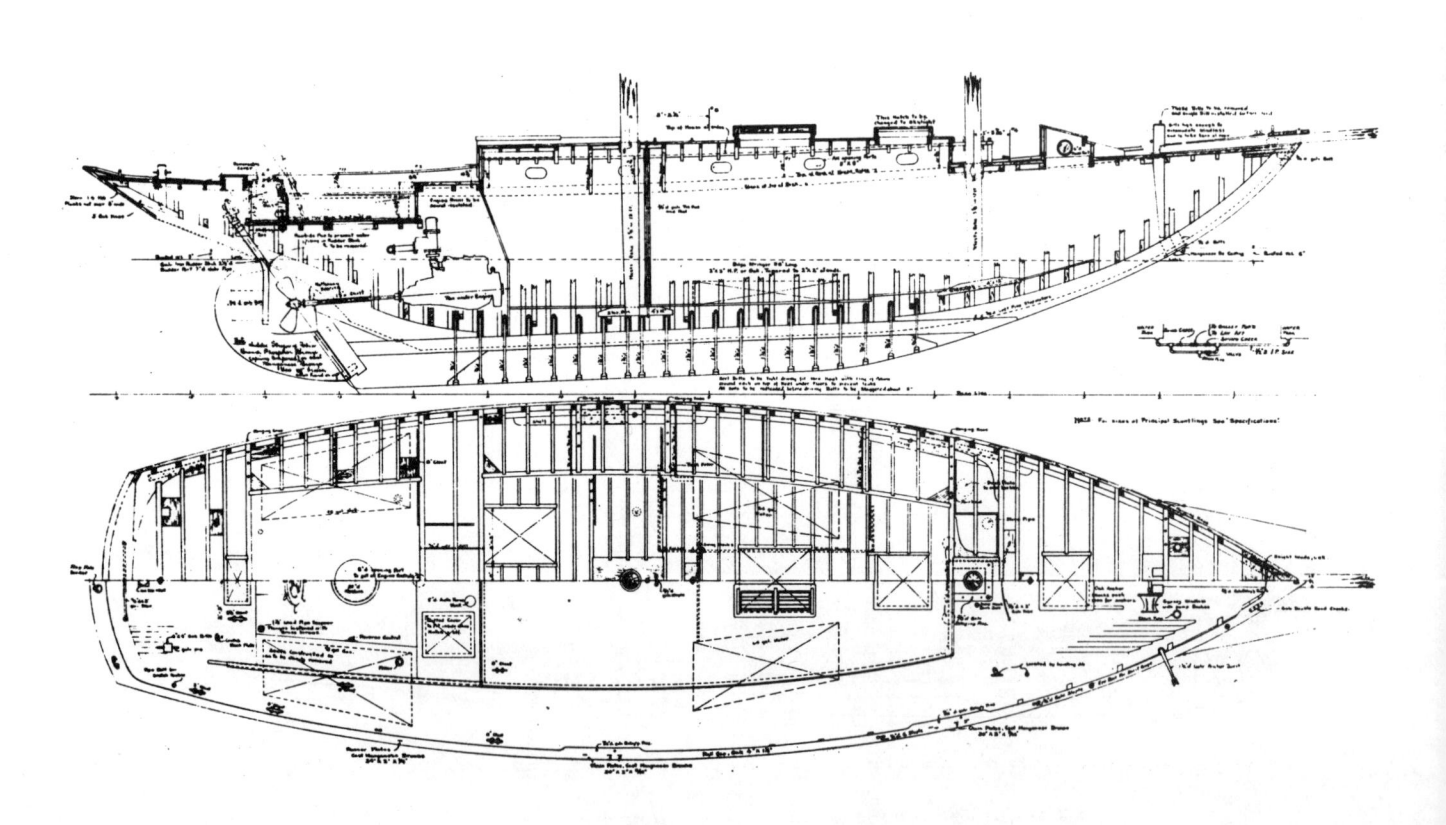

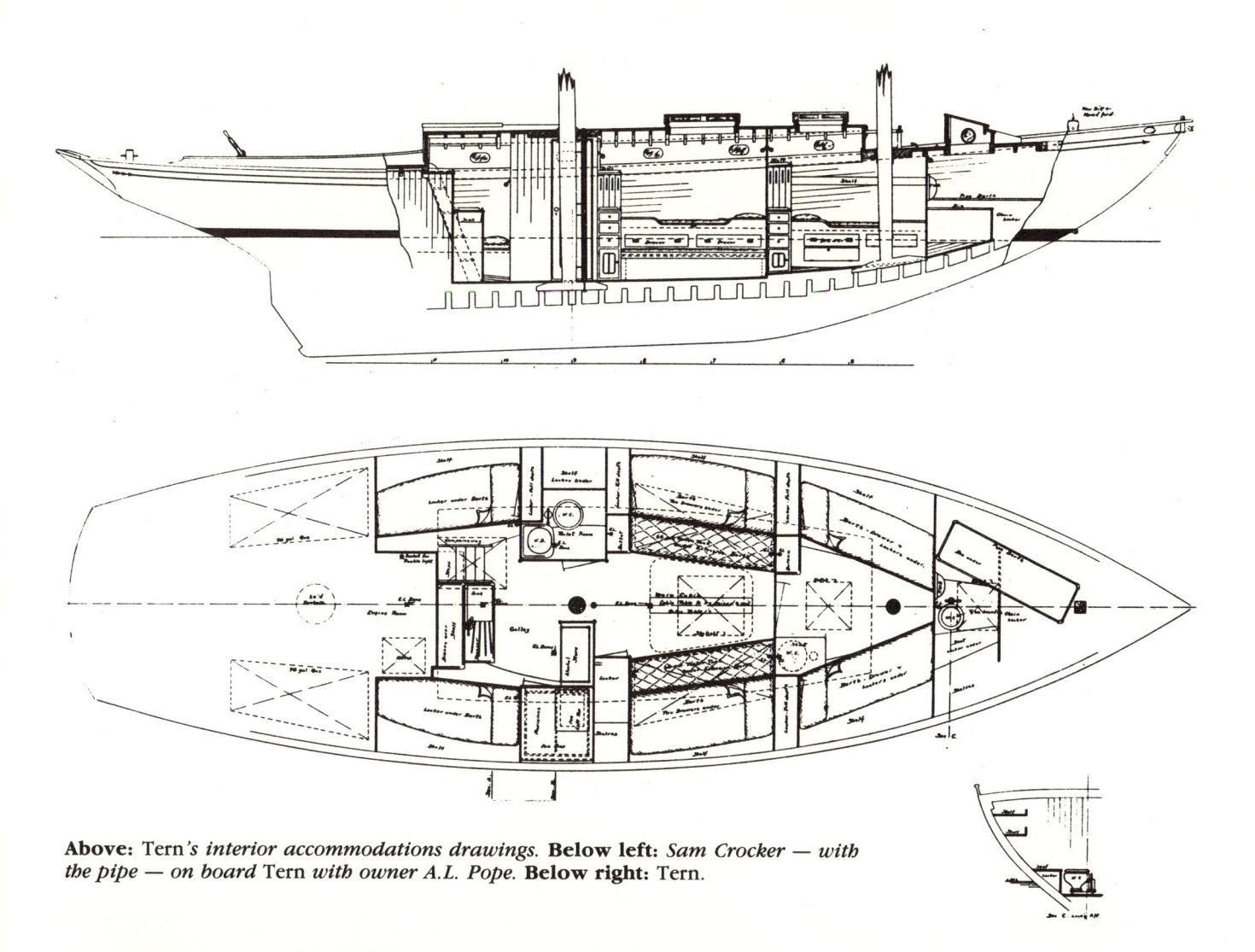

Above: Tern's *interior accommodations drawings.* **Below left:** *Sam Crocker — with the pipe — on board* Tern *with owner A.L. Pope.* **Below right:** *Tern.*

82 BLACK ARROW

Design Number 82
Length Overall: 49 feet
Length on Waterline: 39 feet 6 inches
Beam: 14 feet
Draft: 5 feet
Sail Area: 1196 square feet
Displacement: 41,500 pounds

Black Arrow was another boat built by Israel Snow. The drawings are dated 1926 so I suppose she came along after *Tern*. Not the prettiest of profiles, with all that deckhouse, but such comfort in bad weather! The six-cylinder Kermath gas engine pushed her along at better than nine knots. I enclose part of a letter dated August 29, 1944, from Dad to G.W. Ford Yacht Agency, which sold her to Lt. Alton D. Miller in 1944:

> . . . I have yours of the 28th re the *Black Arrow II*. All I can say about her is that she is what her original owner, Mr. Somonds, wanted, and he was very well satisfied with her. She is a nice model boat from her lower sheer down; and if anyone likes her profile from the lower sheer up, then I would say that she was O.K., but personally I don't care much for it. She is planked with Native Maine cedar and fastened with galvanized hatch nails. You may keep the enclosed picture . . . .

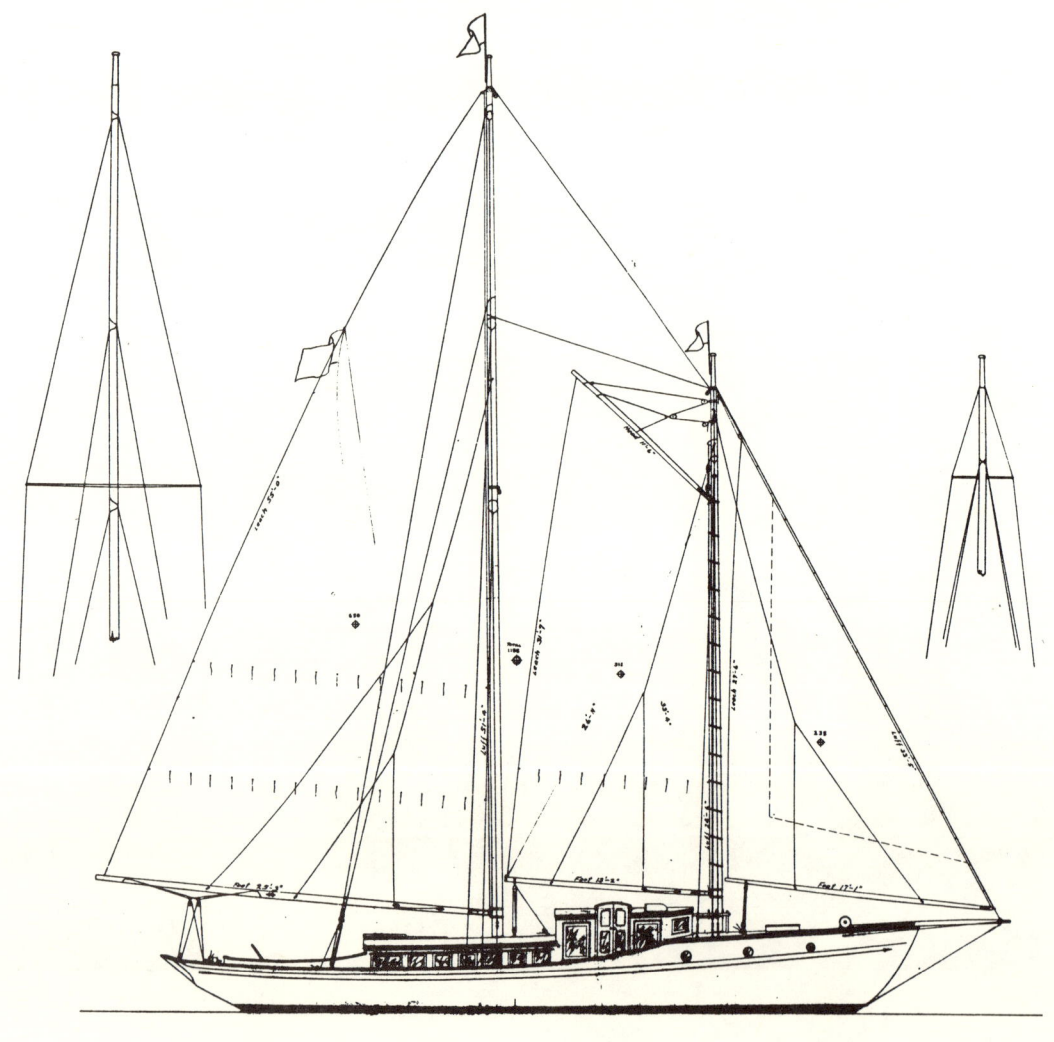

Black Arrow's sailplan.

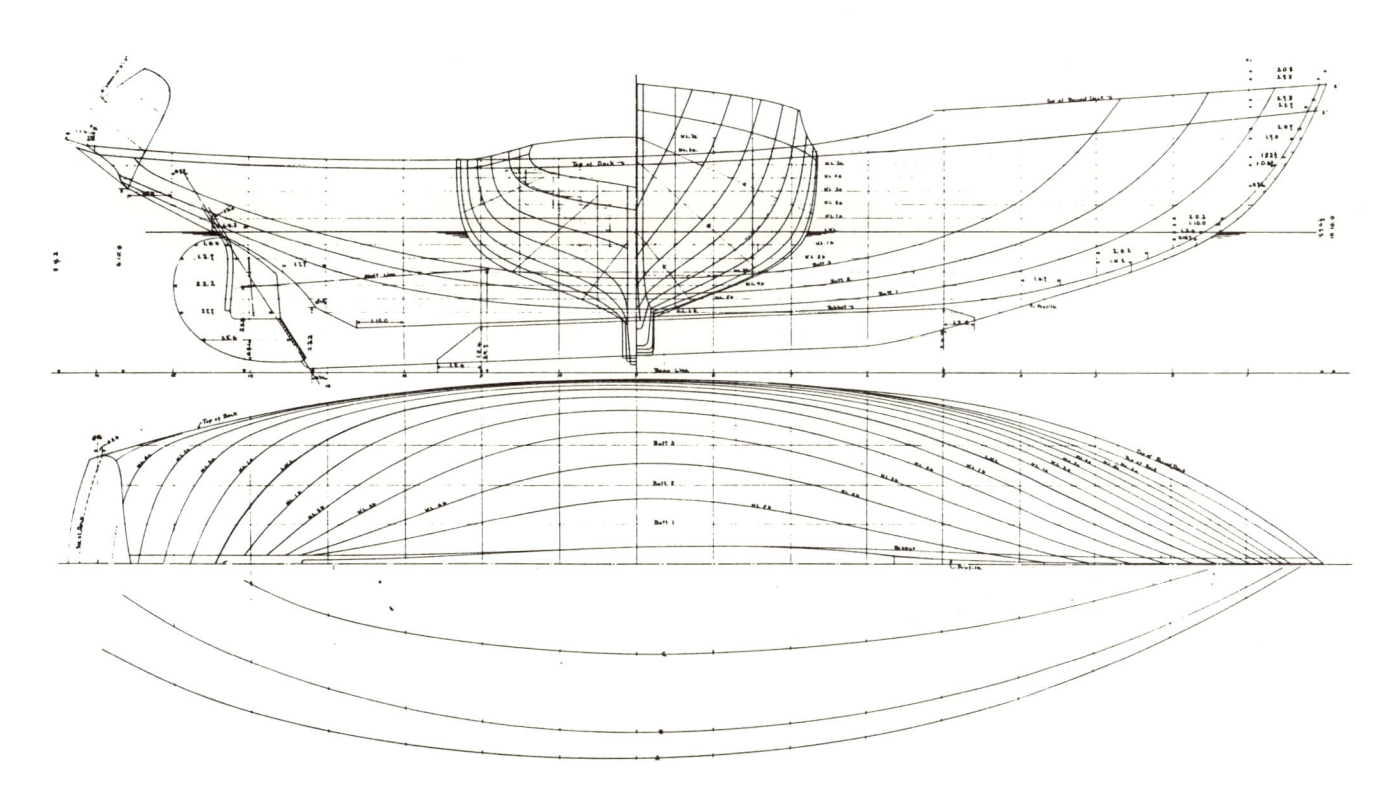

The lines and construction plans for number 82, Black Arrow.

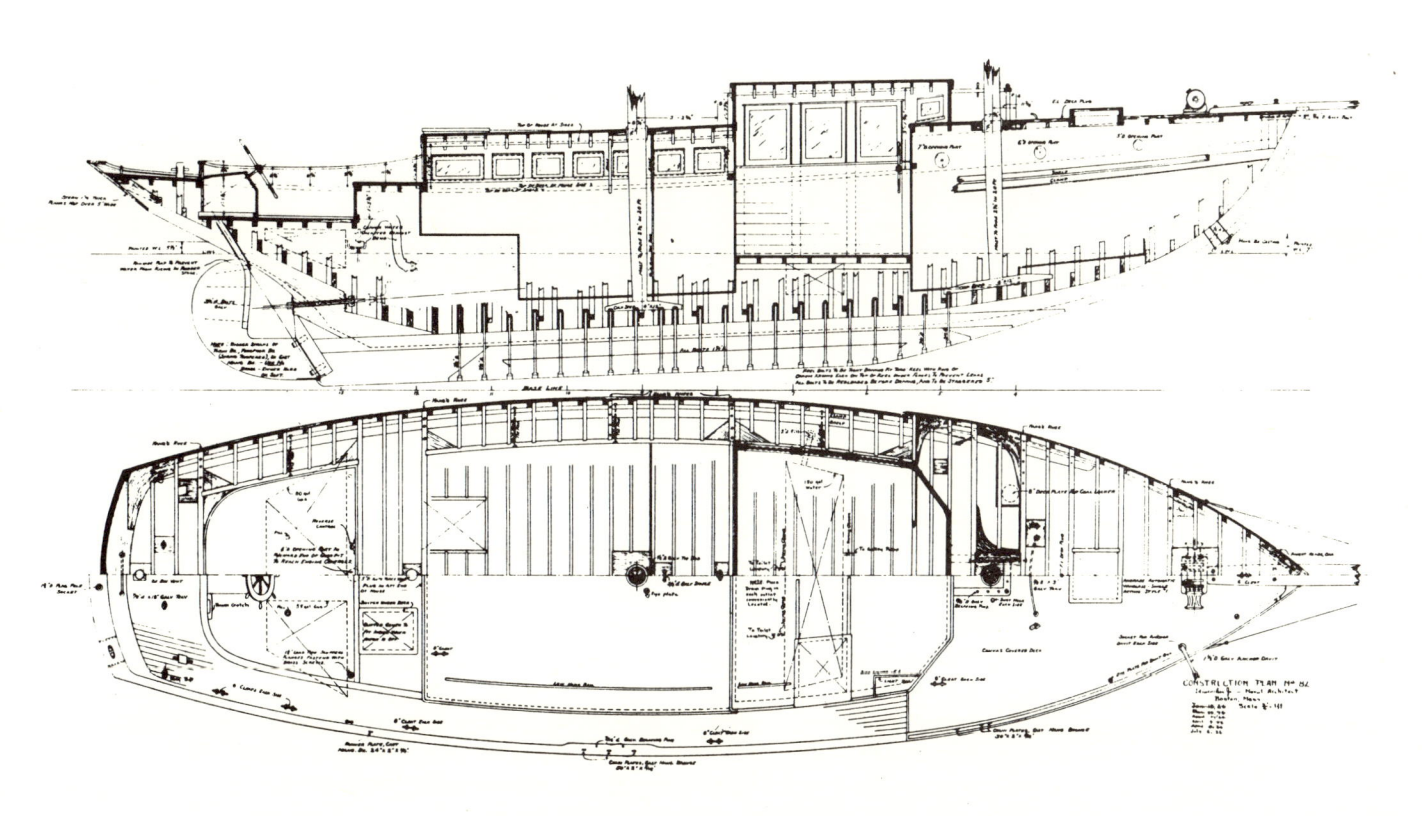

47

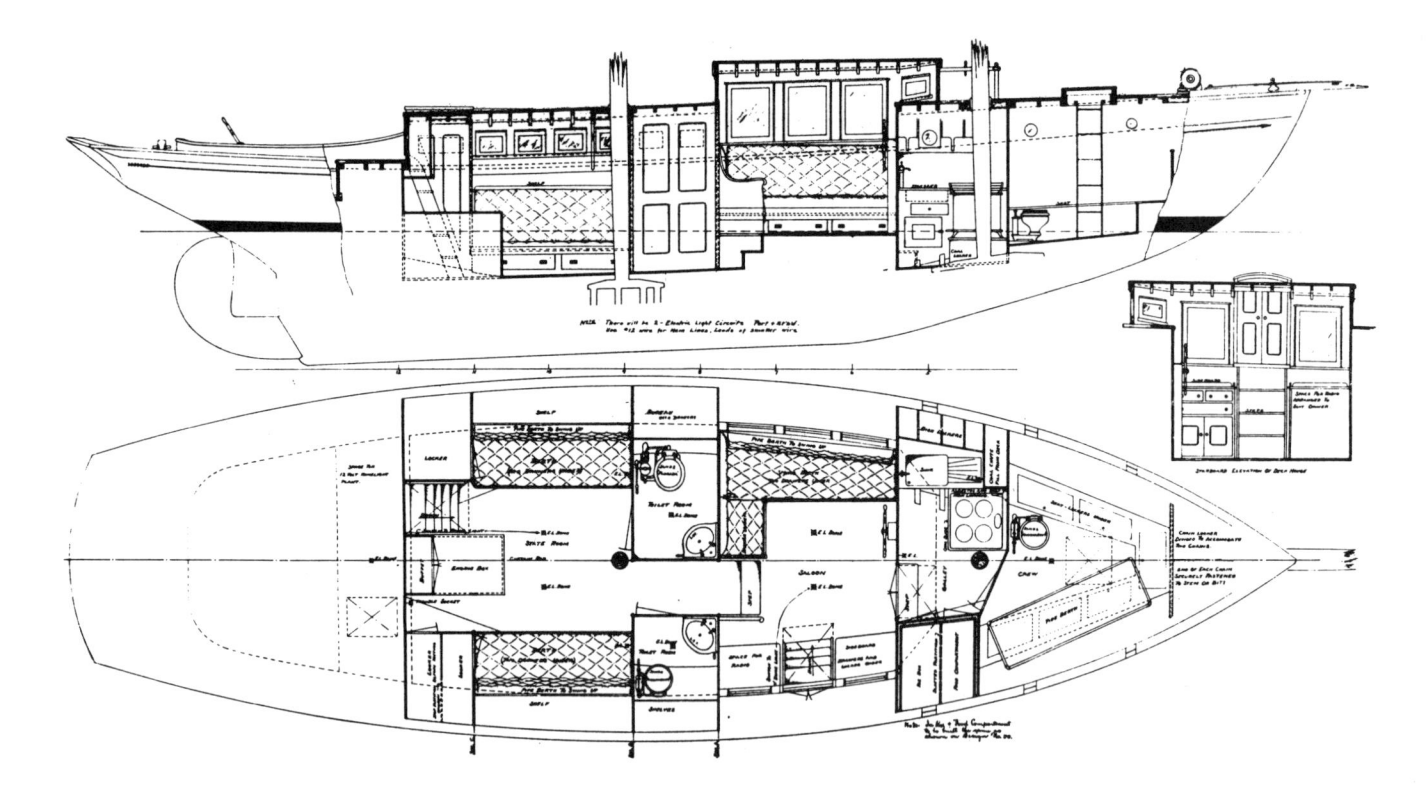

The accommodations plans for Black Arrow.

85

ELEANOR III

Design Number 85
Length Overall: 51 feet
Length on Waterline: 49 feet 9 inches
Beam: 31 feet
Draft: 3 feet 6 inches
Displacement: 32,000 pounds

The contract for this twin-screw powerboat, *Eleanor III,* was signed in March 1926 by the Falmouth Foreside Yacht Yard in Falmouth Foreside, Me., for William A. Sanborn. Specifications called for two six-cylinder, 65-horsepower Kermath gas engines, which gave her a speed of better than 12 m.p.h. One nice feature was that one could go from one end of the boat to the other without going on deck. I imagine the tub in the toilet room between the two staterooms was as good as a whirlpool bath when running in the trough of the sea. Dad is second from the left in the back row of the photo on page 50.

48

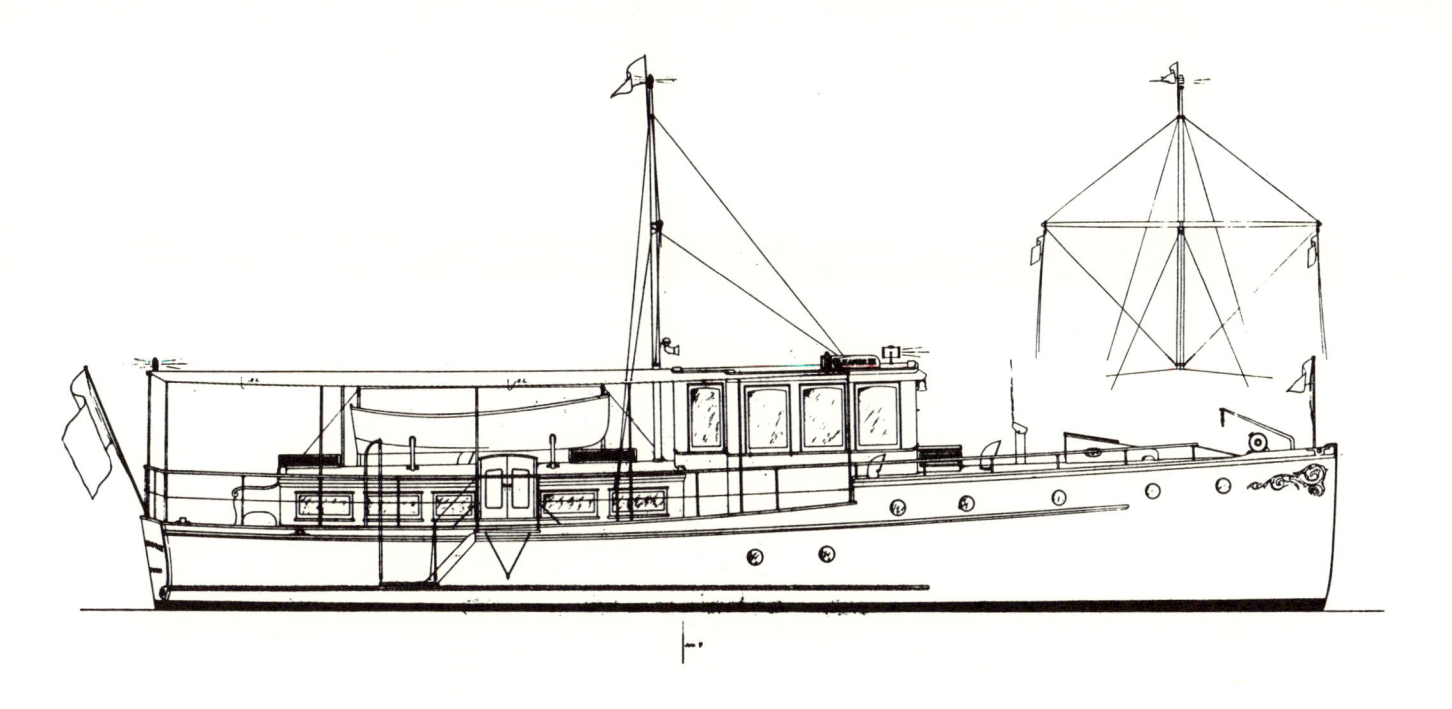

The profile for number 85 and her lines drawings.

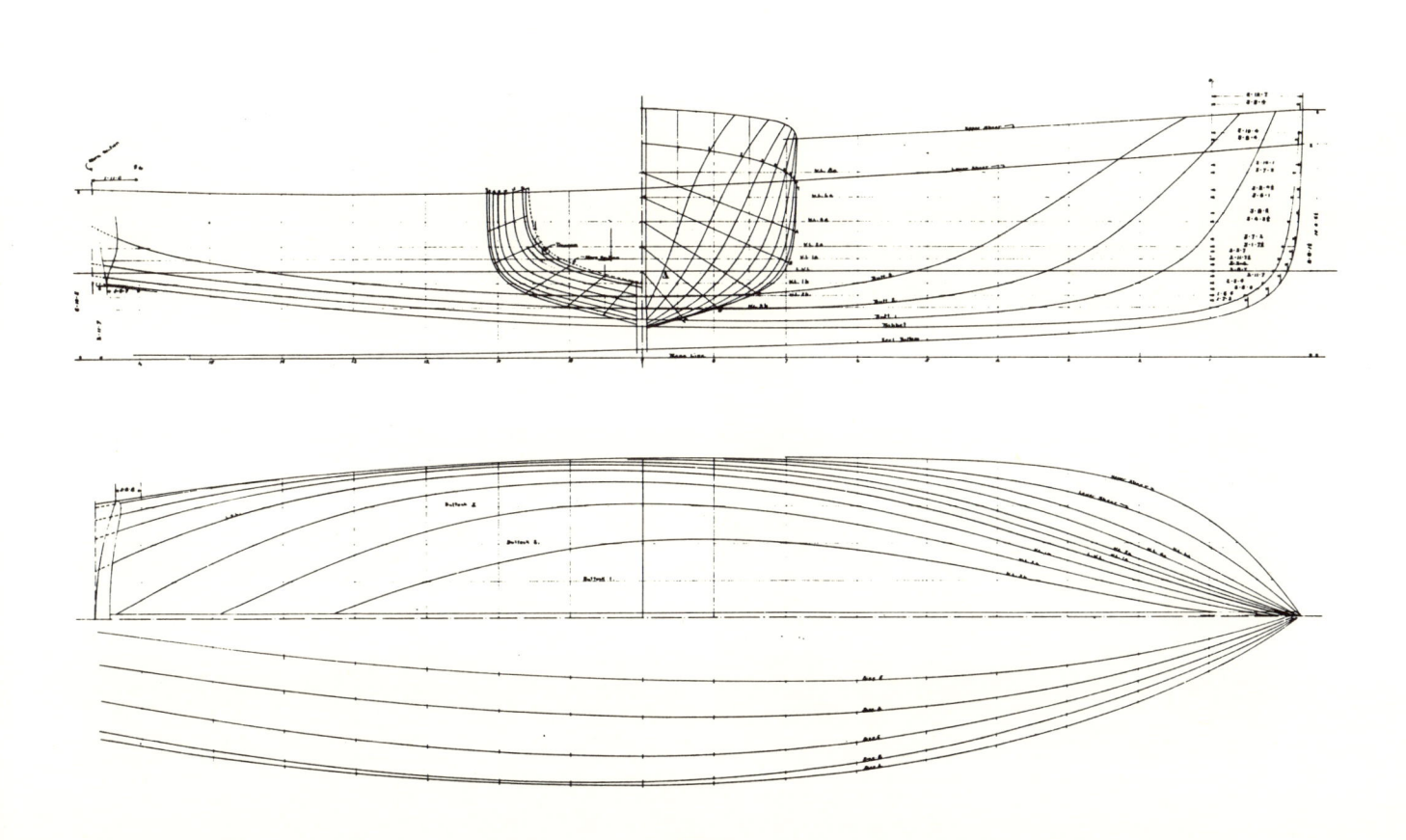

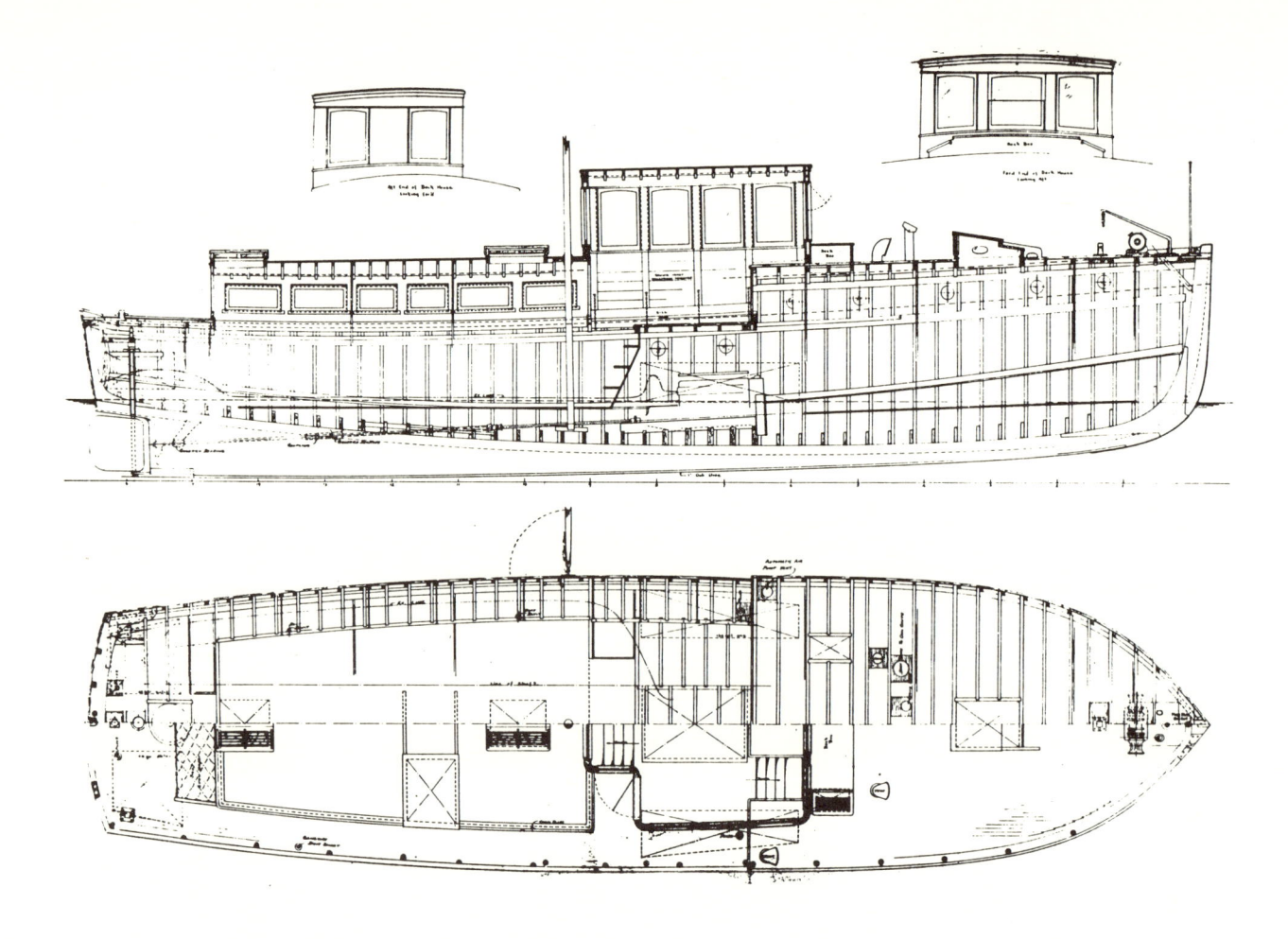

Above: *The construction details for number 85.* **Below left:** *The* Eleanor III's *construction gang.* **Below right:** *Number 85 at anchor.*

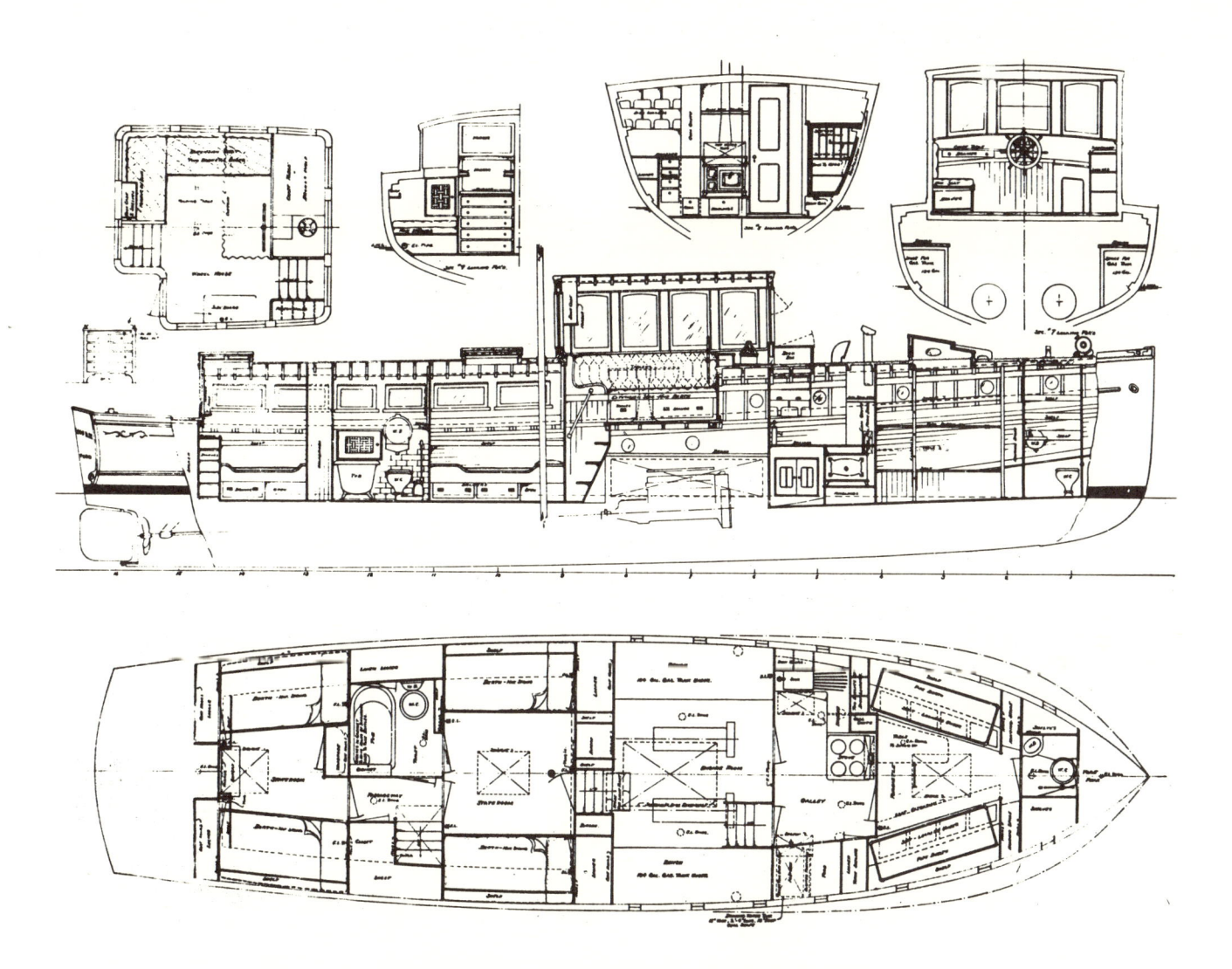

The interior accommodations for number 85.

AUNT ABBY 86

Aunt Abby, another boat for S.K. Dimock, was designed in 1926. Dimock wanted a limited-draft boat for Florida waters, and he was happy with her. Her pleasing profile and comfortable cabin appealed to a lot of people, and there were several more built, although the draft increased to 4 feet. Also, a client in California built one, stretched her out to 40 feet, and used her for swordfishing as shown in the photo. *Aunt Abby* was changed to a marconi sloop in 1936 (see photo).

Design Number 86
Length Overall: 35 feet
Length on Waterline: 28 feet 7 inches
Beam: 10 feet 10 inches
Draft: 3 feet 9 inches
Sail Area: 668 square feet
Displacement: 17,700 pounds

Here is a copy of a letter from Dimock's captain:

I think I wrote you from Southport about the first two runs. The day we came to Southport three boats were nearly lost. I saw the men on the boats and they told me about their trip. One 52' houseboat rolled down on her side going into Winyah Bay and they didn't think she would come back, but they finally got her head to the wind and she came out of it. A Matthews 38 and another 40' cruiser found they would have to make shelter or be swamped, so they tried for an inlet. The sea of course was breaking all feather white on the bar, so they couldn't tell where the best water was, but took a chance. They both struck and were pounded over by the seas into the inlet. They all said it was a lucky thing they ever got in. I did not mention much about that trip in my last letter as I considered it a common occurrence of going to sea and thought nothing of it, but as there has been so much talk about it, I thought I would write a few lines about it. The *Aunt Abby* did not complain in any way. I kept the whole mainsail on her, staysail and jib, and she lugged it fine. We shipped some water, of course, but nothing to be alarmed at. If we could have steered her as we liked and favored her a little, a lot of that could have been avoided. The *Aunt Abby* can handle herself all right and would stand a lot of that.

Above left and left: *Number 86 rigged for swordfishing, and* Aunt Abby *under sail.*

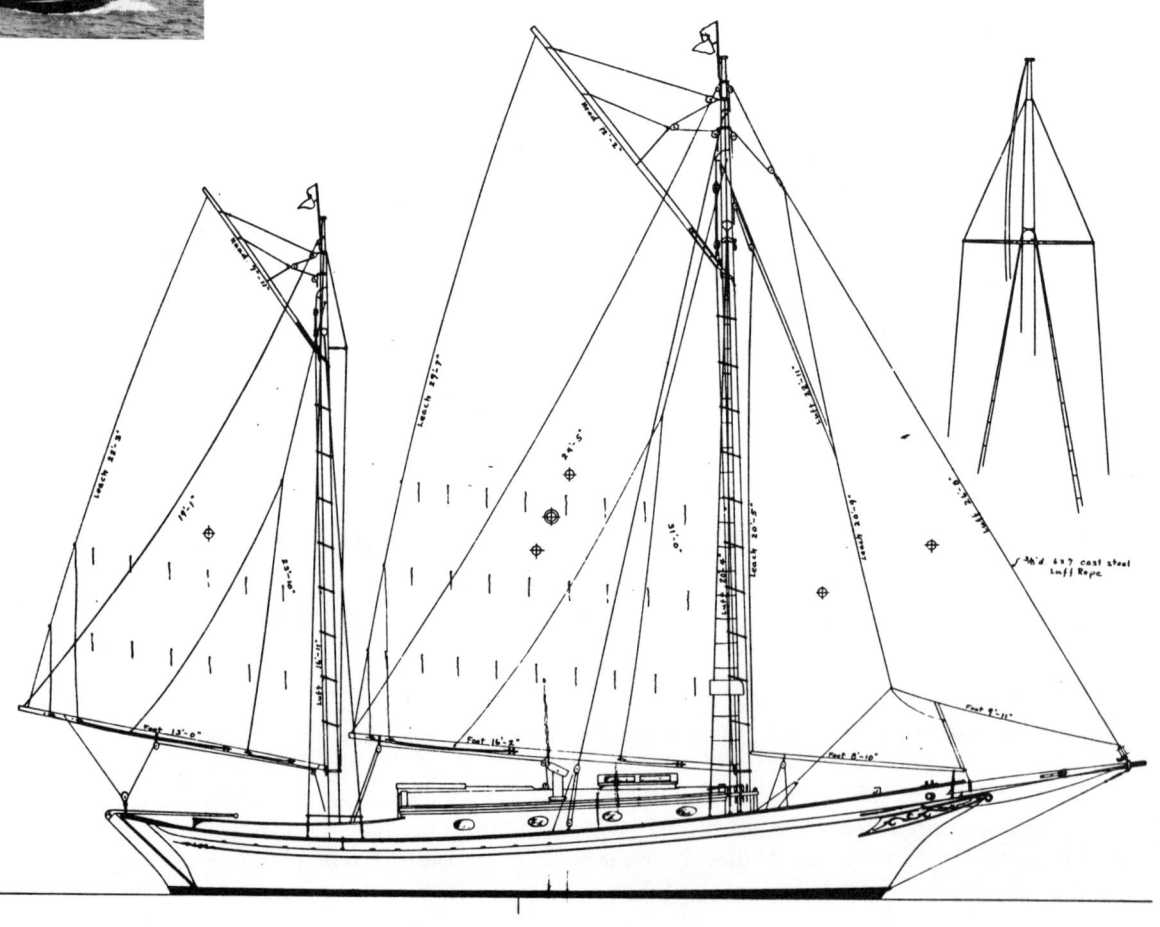

The sailplan for Aunt Abby.

Left: *Number 86 with a marconi rig.*

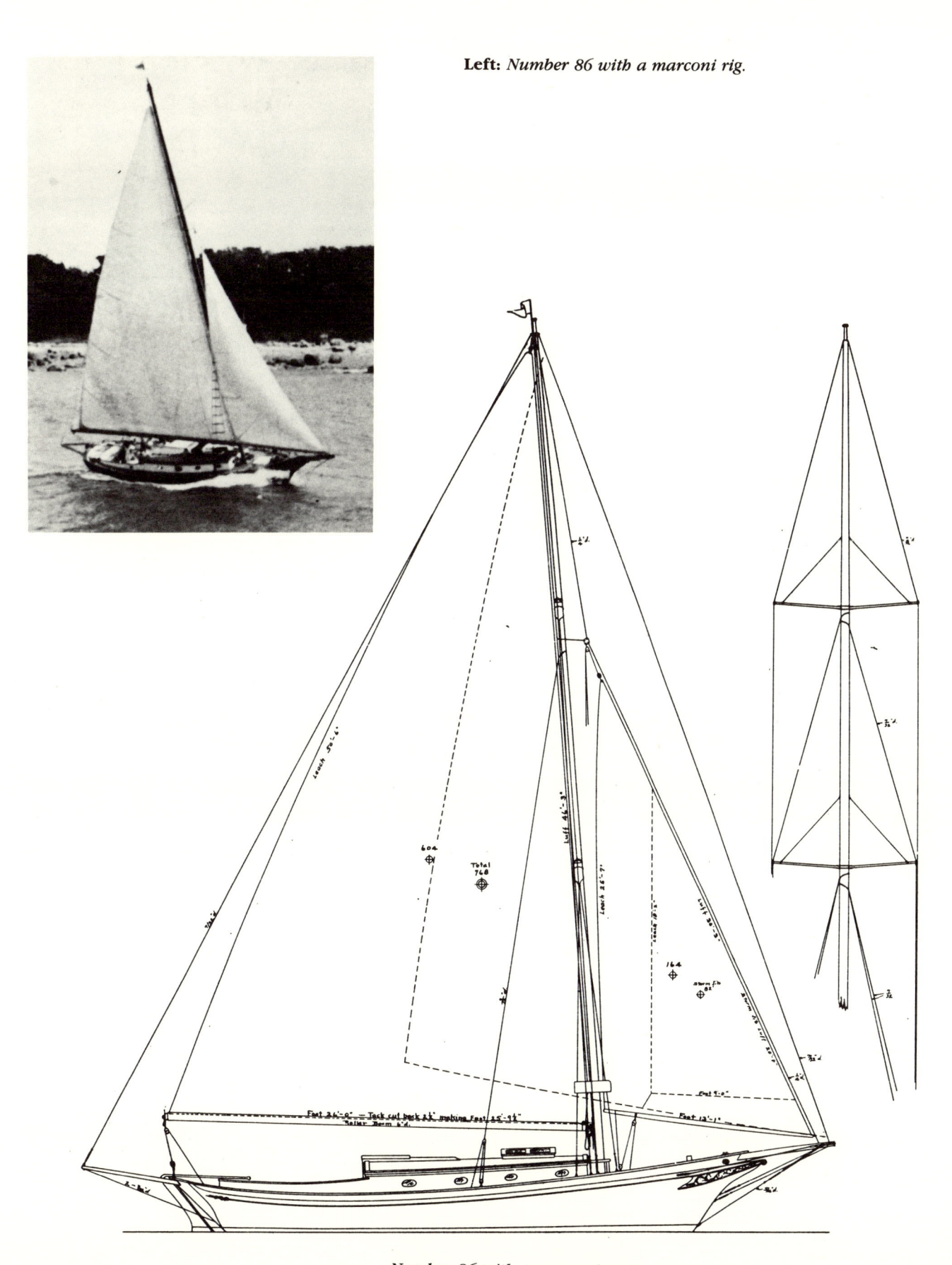

Number 86 with a marconi main.

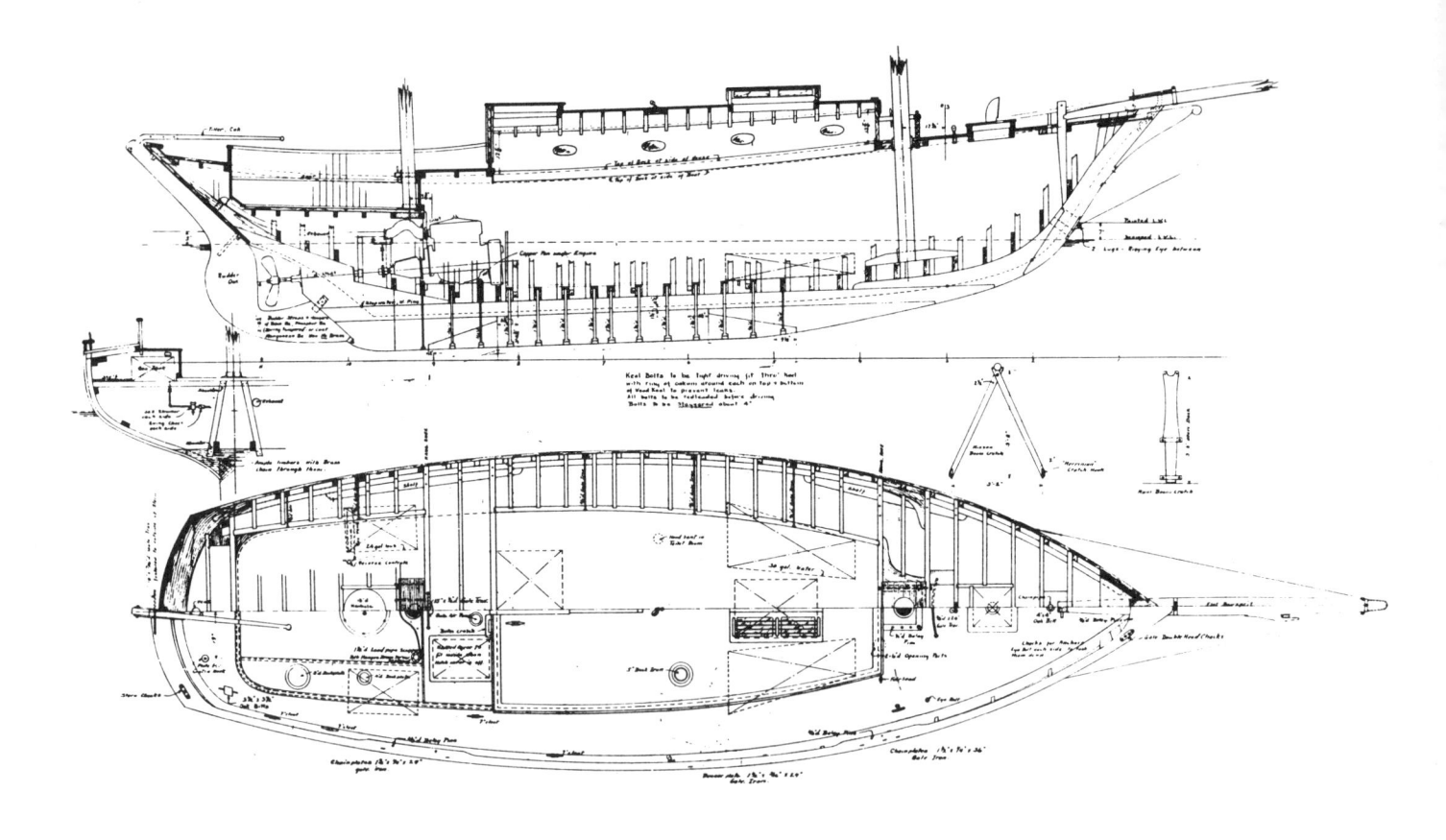

The construction drawings for number 86 also her interior plans.

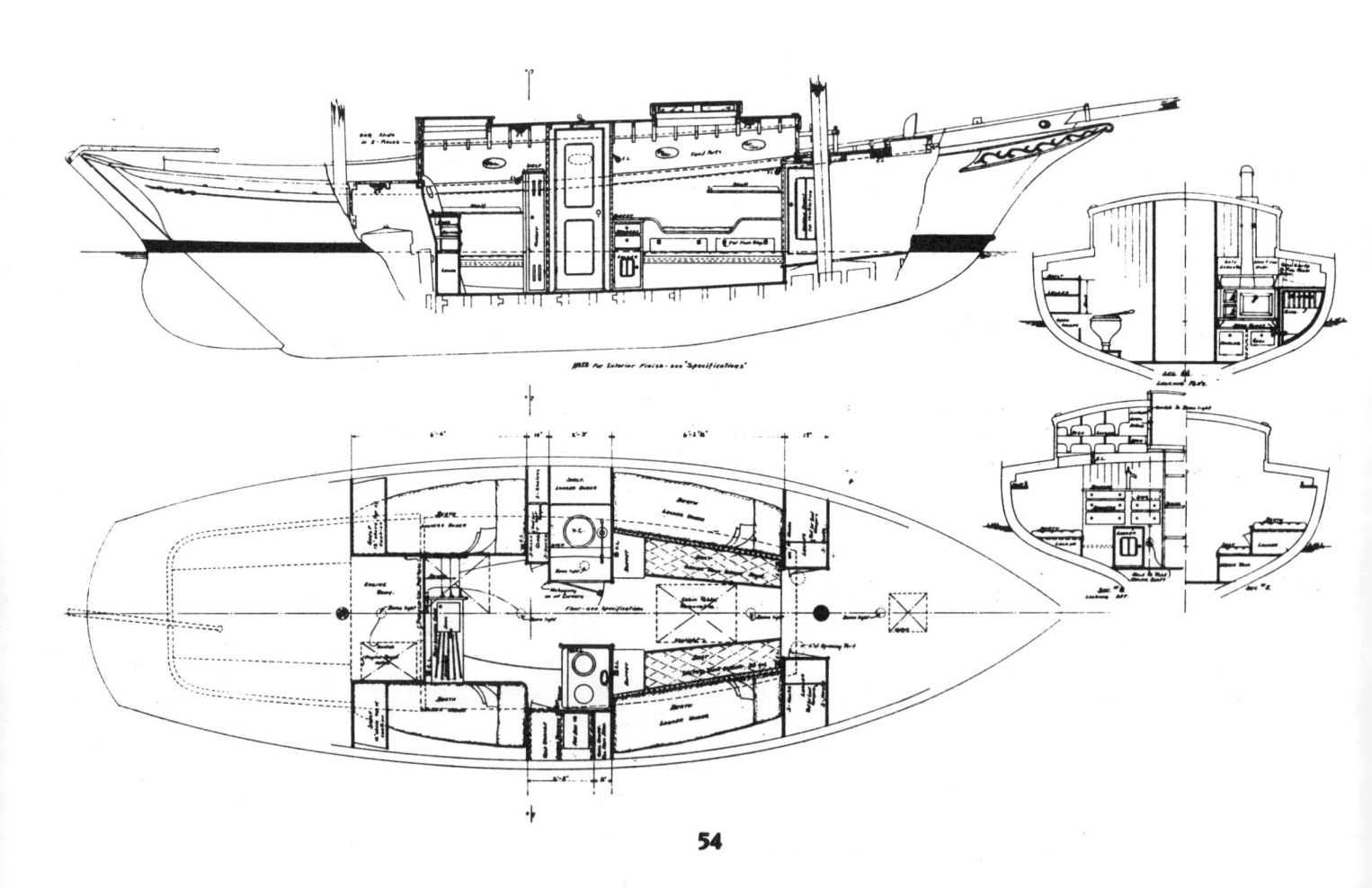

54

The two designs numbered 136, *Aunt Sara* and *Corolla,* should be mentioned here, because they are so like *Aunt Abby*. Still another similar boat was *Falcon,* built for a Dr. Hussey with gaff-headed ketch rig. Although over 80 years old, the doctor took her on an extensive cruise in the West Indies, and on his return sailed direct from the West Indies to New York via Bermuda. He was back only a short time when the boat caught fire in the Hudson and was demolished.

Number 86 under a schooner rig.

55

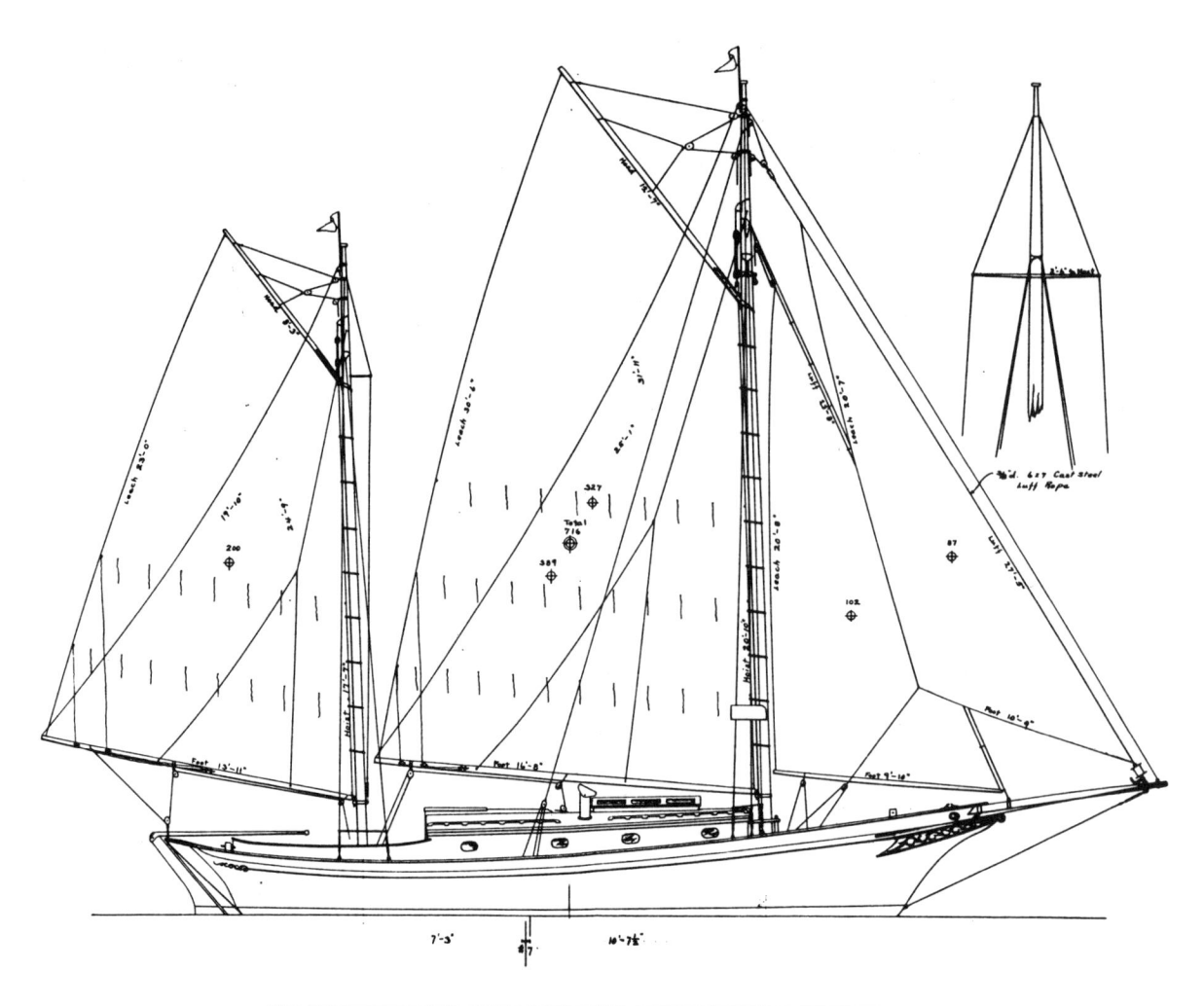

Above: *Number 136,* Aunt Sara.

Right: Aunt Sara *under sail.*

GREY GULL II 88

Grey Gull II was the first boat built from this design. She was designed for Pop Turner, who had number 42. She was built in Cohasset, Mass., in 1927 by H.H. Ellsworth. She was planned for cruising comfort and was also a smart sailer, winning the Huntington-Cornfield light race and the Bayside Block Island race twice. *Tortuga,* the next boat to be built from these plans, was built by F.D. Rolphein Quincy for Schuyler Dillon of Boston in 1930. She was the same as *Grey Gull* except for the double-head rig and a little smaller main. In 1950 trailboards and billet head were drawn for *Grey Gull,* making her clipper bowed.

Boris L. Leonardi, editor of *Rudder* magazine, praised the *Grey Gull* design in this letter to my father, dated November 12, 1945:

Design Number 88
Length Overall: 36 feet 2 inches
Length on Waterline: 32 feet 2 inches
Beam: 11 feet 1 inch
Draft: 4 feet 6 inches
Sail Area: 830 square feet
Displacement: 22,100 pounds

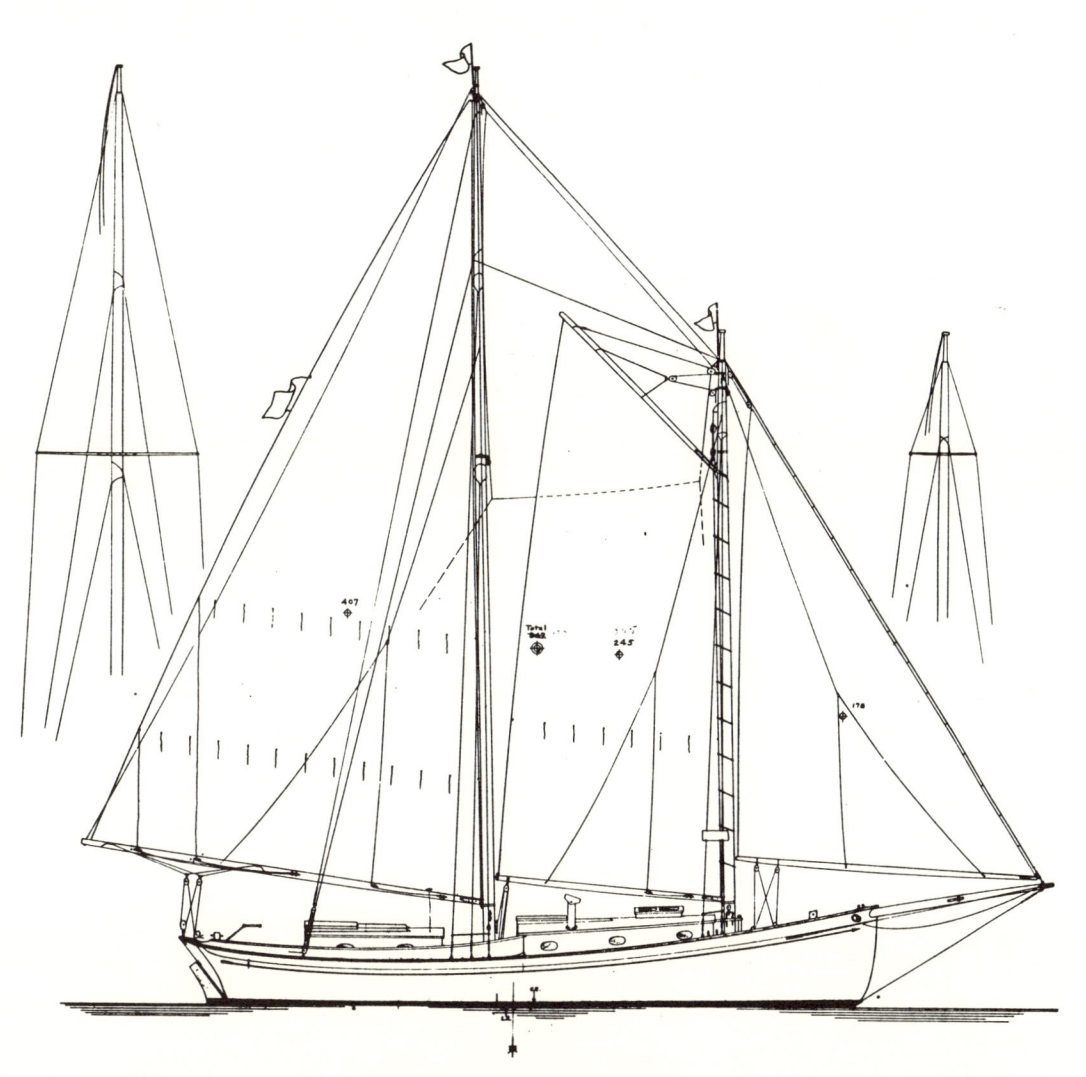

The sailplan for number 88.

57

For some time I have wanted to write to you and tell you that I have made two passages on the *Grey Gull II* designed by you.

I sailed her from the Chesapeake to New York, and recently back again. We had a variety of weather and sea conditions, and she behaved like a perfect lady under all circumstances.

On the last trip we encountered a brisk southerly immediately upon leaving Sandy Hook, and a good sea built up. I decided to stand out all night, and then stand in next day. She sailed herself with her helm lashed for 36 hours, sailing as close to the wind as she would were a man at the helm, and this in spite of a heavy sea. It was a superb performance.

I have always admired your work, and take this opportunity to tell you so.

In 1945 *MacCaboy* was developed from these lines for Dave Strater of New Hampshire. Bud McIntosh built the hull, and Strater had his own cabinetmaker do the interior. When I saw her several years ago, I thought it an awfully nice job. She had two inches more freeboard, and the after cabin was arranged a little differently. She also carried a little more sail and had a permanent backstay.

The sailplan for Toruga.

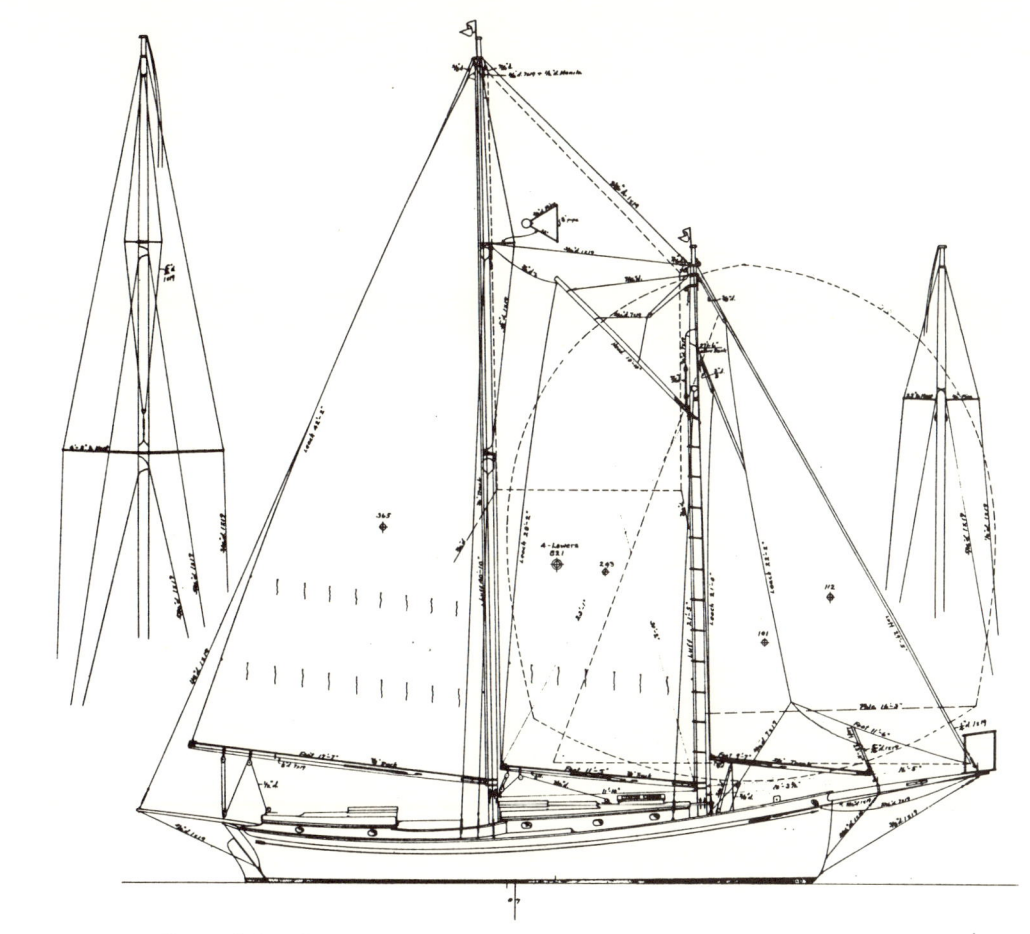

The sailplan for MacCaboy *also note her aft cabin, the lines for number 88.*

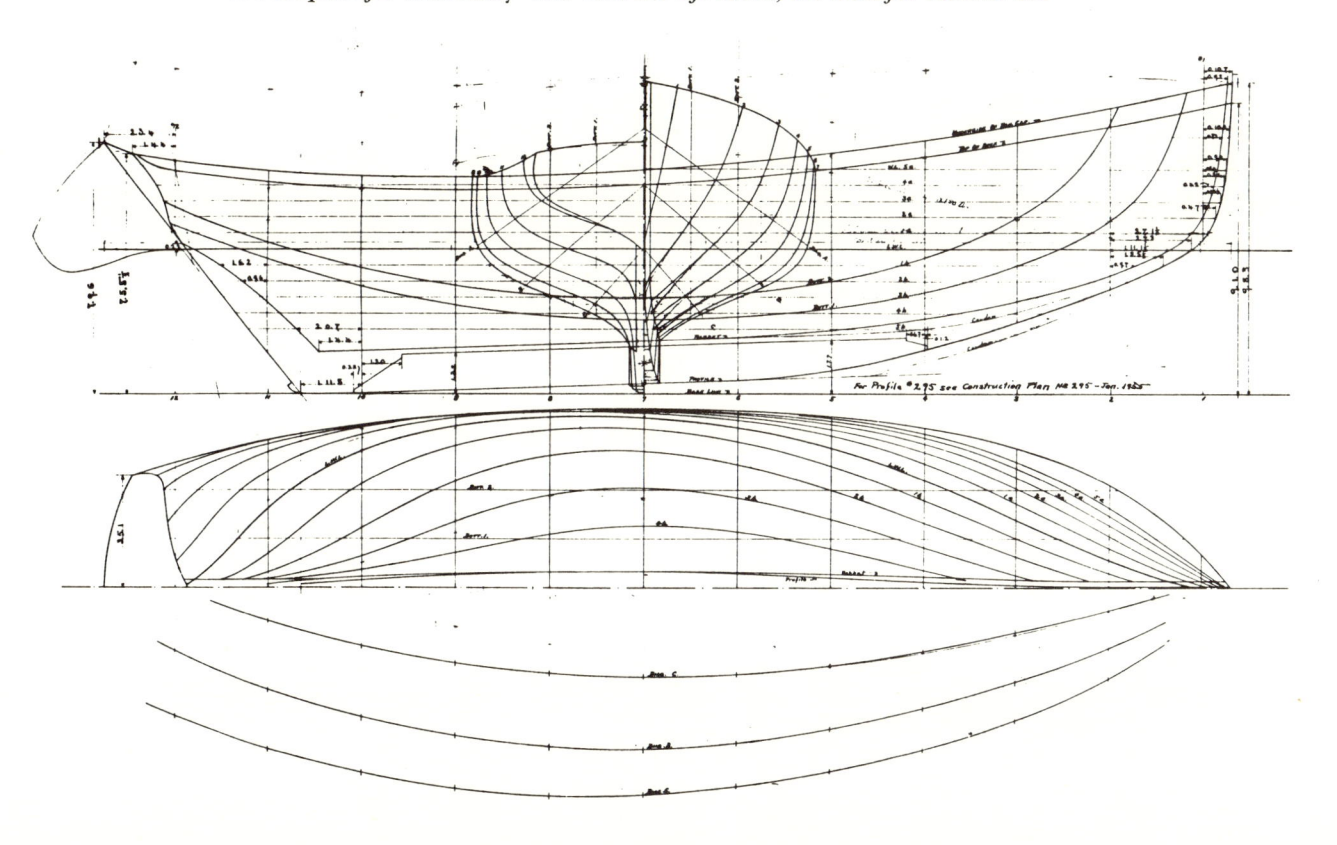

59

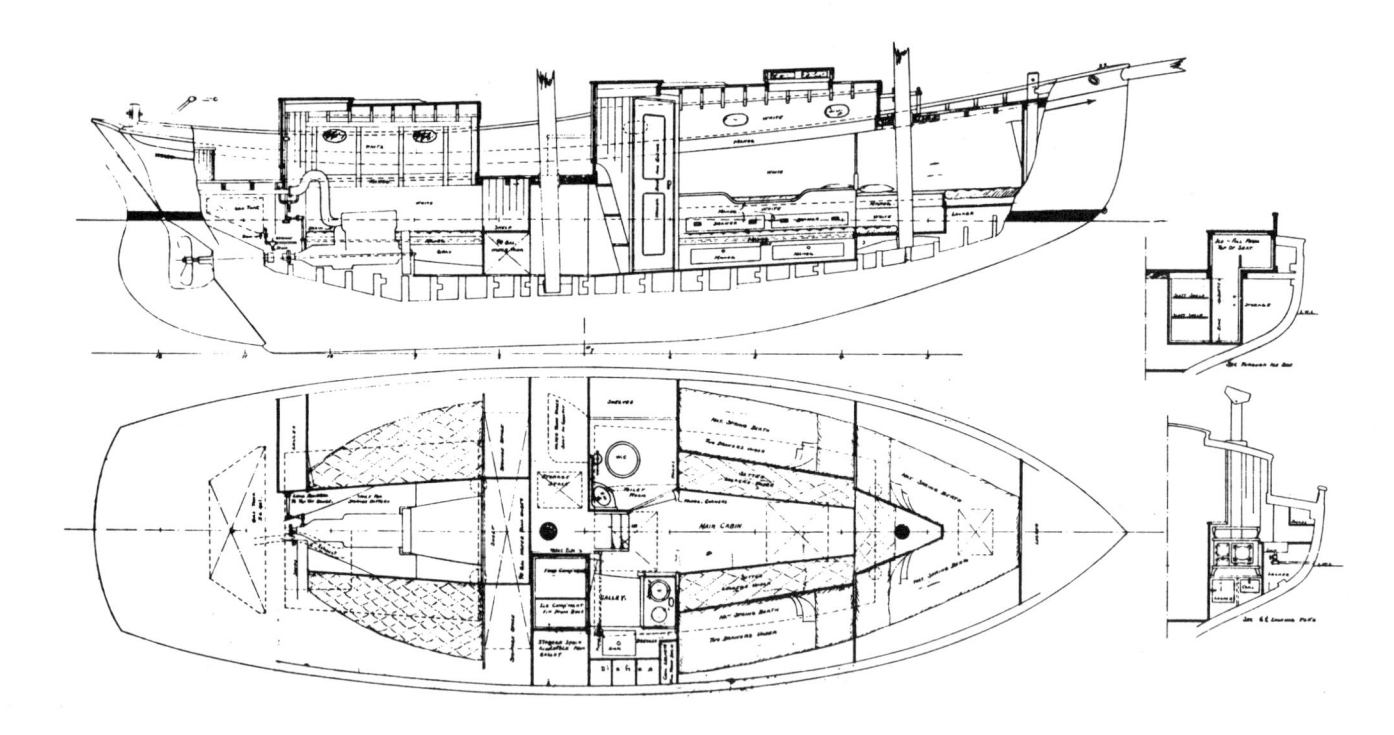

The interior plans and the construction plans for number 88.

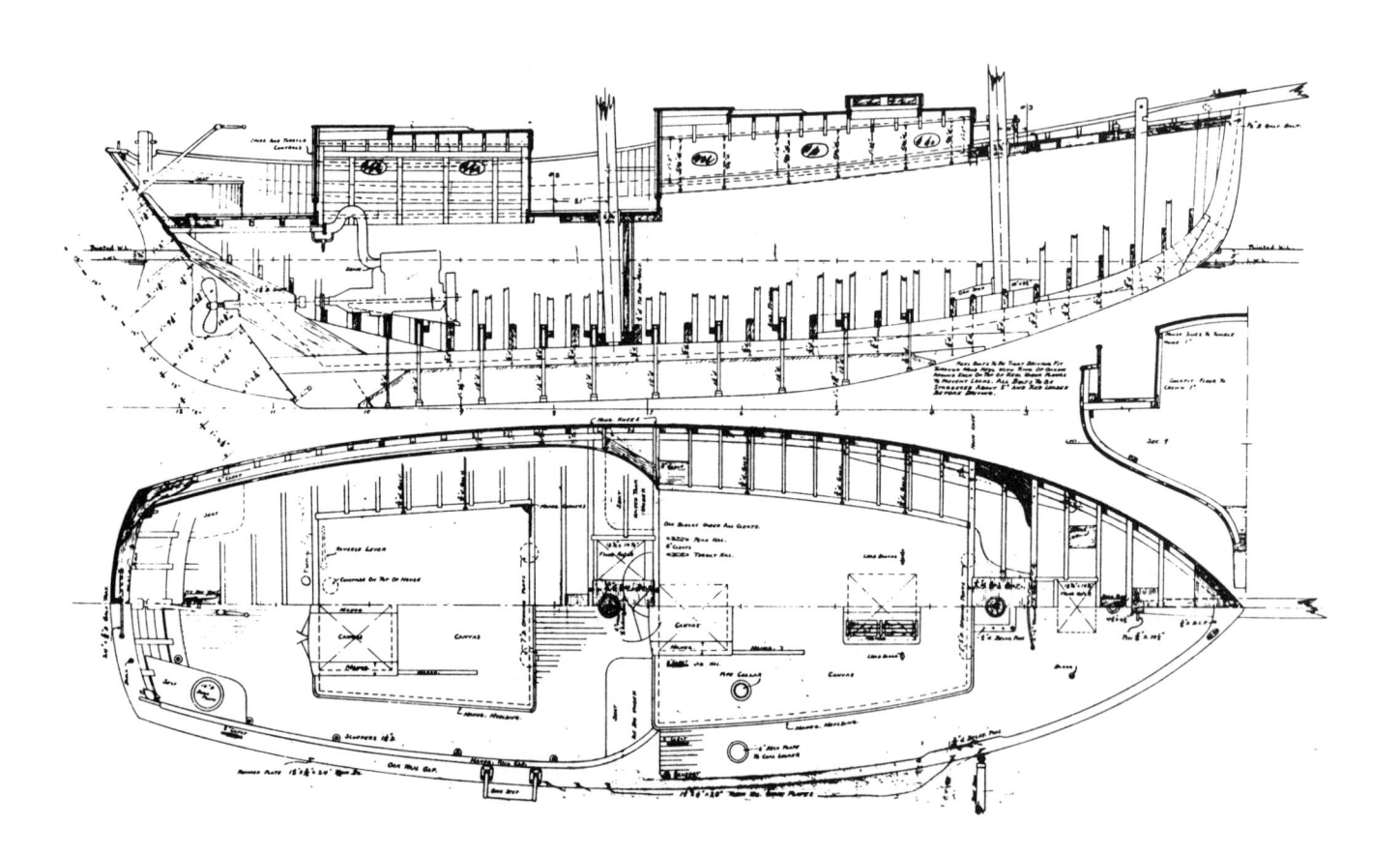

BARBETTE 90

Barbette was built in the winter of 1926 and 1927 by George Lawley Corporation for T.P. Archer of Detroit. Not only was she a comfortable cruiser, especially with that 4-foot-by-6-foot storeroom on the port side, but she had a fine racing record as well. She won the Detroit-to-Mackinac race in 1927 and 1929. The following excerpt describes one of *Barbette*'s victories:

Encountering the strongest winds that sailors have been called upon to weather in years in local waters, Tom Archer's large yawl *Barbette* achieved top honors and a leg on the Historical Free Press Cup in the Bayview Yacht Club's annual All Night race that started Saturday night.

Design Number 90
Length Overall: 50 feet 9 inches
Length on Waterline: 37 feet 9 inches
Beam: 14 feet
Draft: 5 feet
Sail Area: 1502 square feet
Displacement: 41,000 pounds

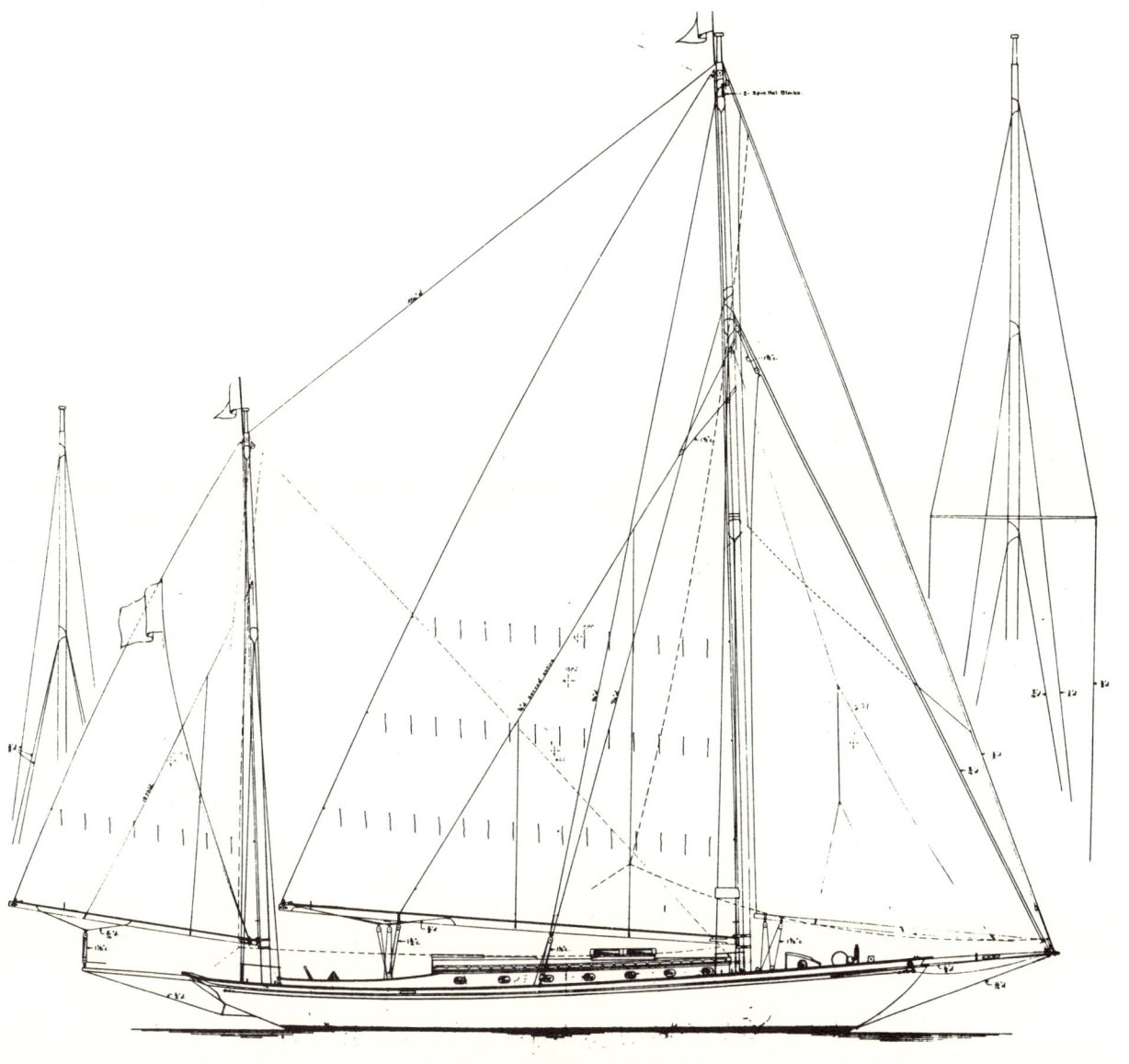

Barbette's *sailplan.*

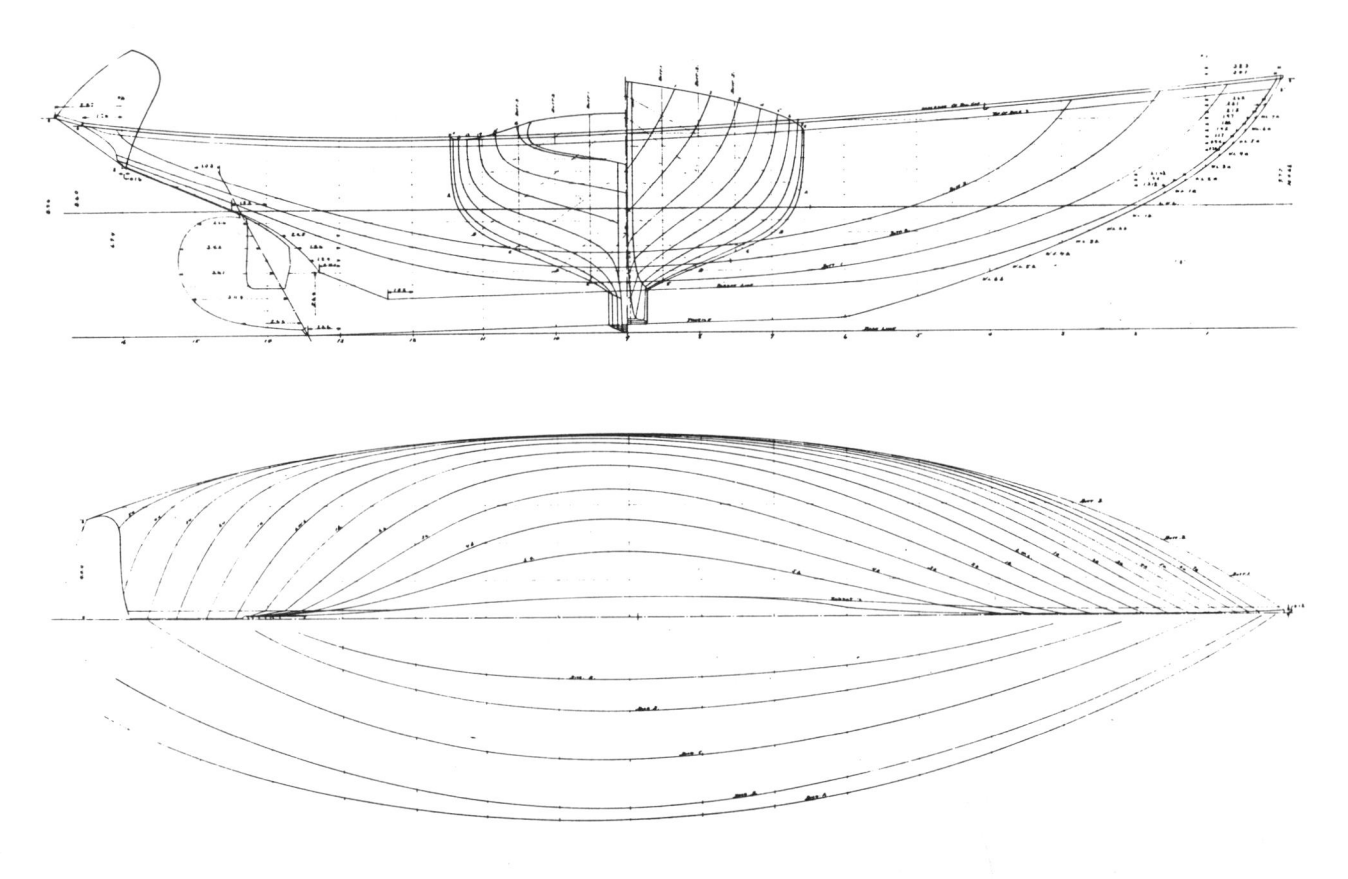

The lines for number 90, Barbette.

Like a phantom ghost, Archer's fleet craft traversed the course which approximated more than 60 miles at a speed which veteran tars say never again will be equaled, in the same race.

The *Barbette* was the only boat in the 22 craft entered whose owner dared to carry full canvas in the heavy wind. In heavy gales, which included three squalls, rain and hail, Archer's stately craft never faltered, though at times half of the cabin was underwater as green seas poured over the entire ship.

All Records Fall

All records for the course were shattered by many hours, the *Barbette* rounding the large triangle in 6 hours and 52 minutes, which breaks the old record held by Milt Gross's *Ardette* by more than 12 hours. Trailing *Barbette* by just 14 minutes was Al Tobin's *Arethusa* of the Corinthian Yacht Club.*

**Editorial Note: International Marine has made several attempts to substantiate the times cited in the previous press clipping. However, the records of the Bayview Yacht Club are no longer available for this particular race. There is, however, reason to feel that* Barbette's *winning time is somewhat suspect.*

The course for this event is a large dog-legged triangle about 68 statute miles in length. Using Barbette's *designed waterline length of 37 feet 9 inches as a starting point, then her hull speed would be on the order of 8.6 knots. Given the description of the race it is safe to assume that her waterline length was extended somewhat. But, to have averaged a speed in excess of 10 knots is somewhat suspicious. That* Barbette *won this race, and in a record shattering fashion is, however, without question.*

We understand that this question has sparked a lively debate within the public rooms at the Bayview Yacht Club. We particularly appreciate the efforts of past Commodore William J.A. Nagle, and club member Bob Roadstrum for their valuable assistance on this matter.

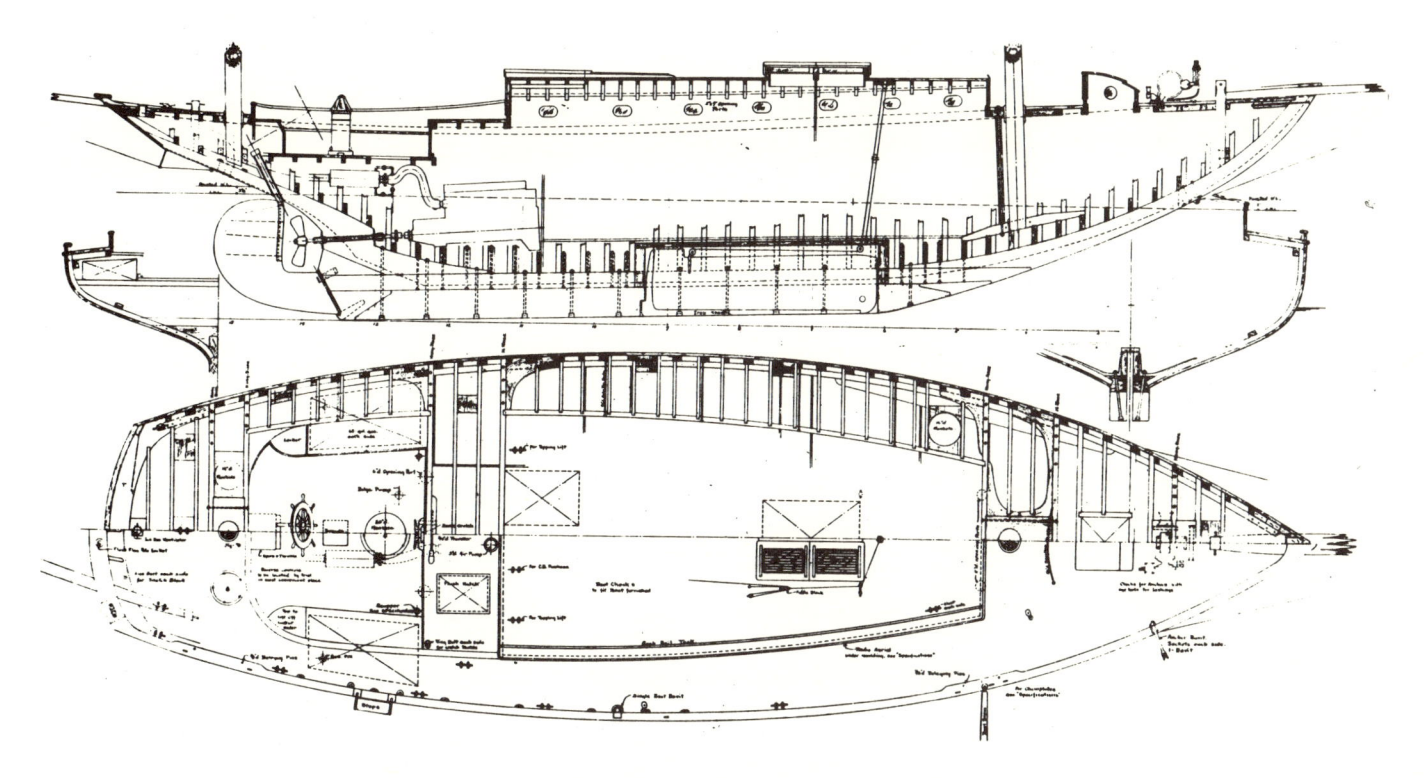

Barbette's *construction plans and her interior plans.*

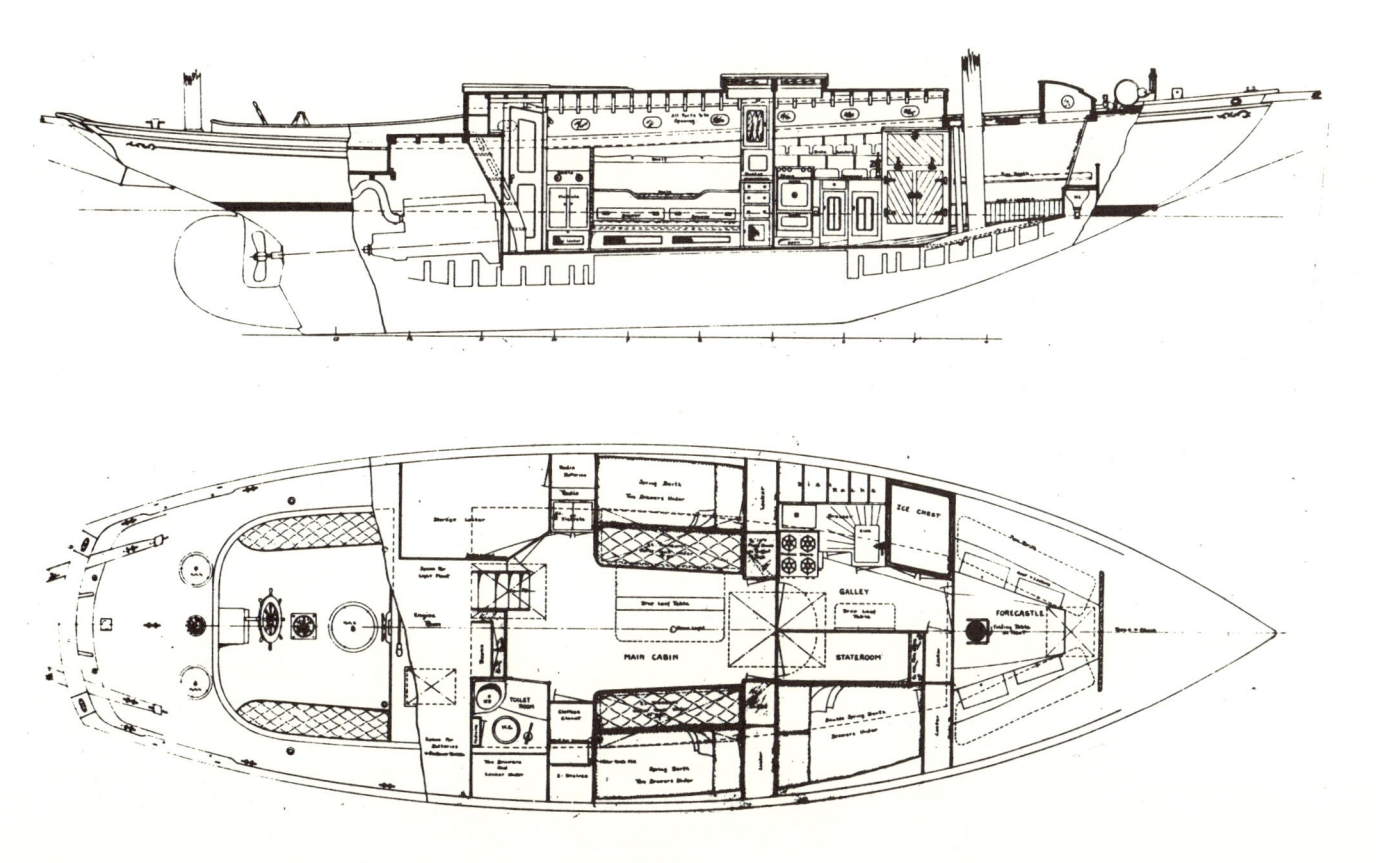

Number 90, Barbette, *under sail.*

95

VALIANT

Length Overall: 40 feet
Length on Waterline: 25 feet
Beam: 9 feet
Draft: 5 feet 5 inches
Sail Area: 740 square feet
Displacement: 10,350 pounds

Valiant was designed and built for E.B. Phillips of Georges Mills, N.H. He also had the 21-foot hydroplane, number 47, in 1924; number 113, a 65-foot diesel powerboat; two launches, number 117 and number 120; number 129, a 28-foot centerboard sloop; and number 135, a 28-foot launch with aft cabin for Lake Sunapee. Built at Lawley's in 1927 of double-plank construction, she lasted well; in fact, I had a request from her present owner only a few years back for a set of her plans. It seems a lot of boat for an inland lake, but she went to Sunapee in New Hampshire when completed. Later she was owned by Robert Coulson of Marblehead, Mass. She was changed to marconi rig in 1937.

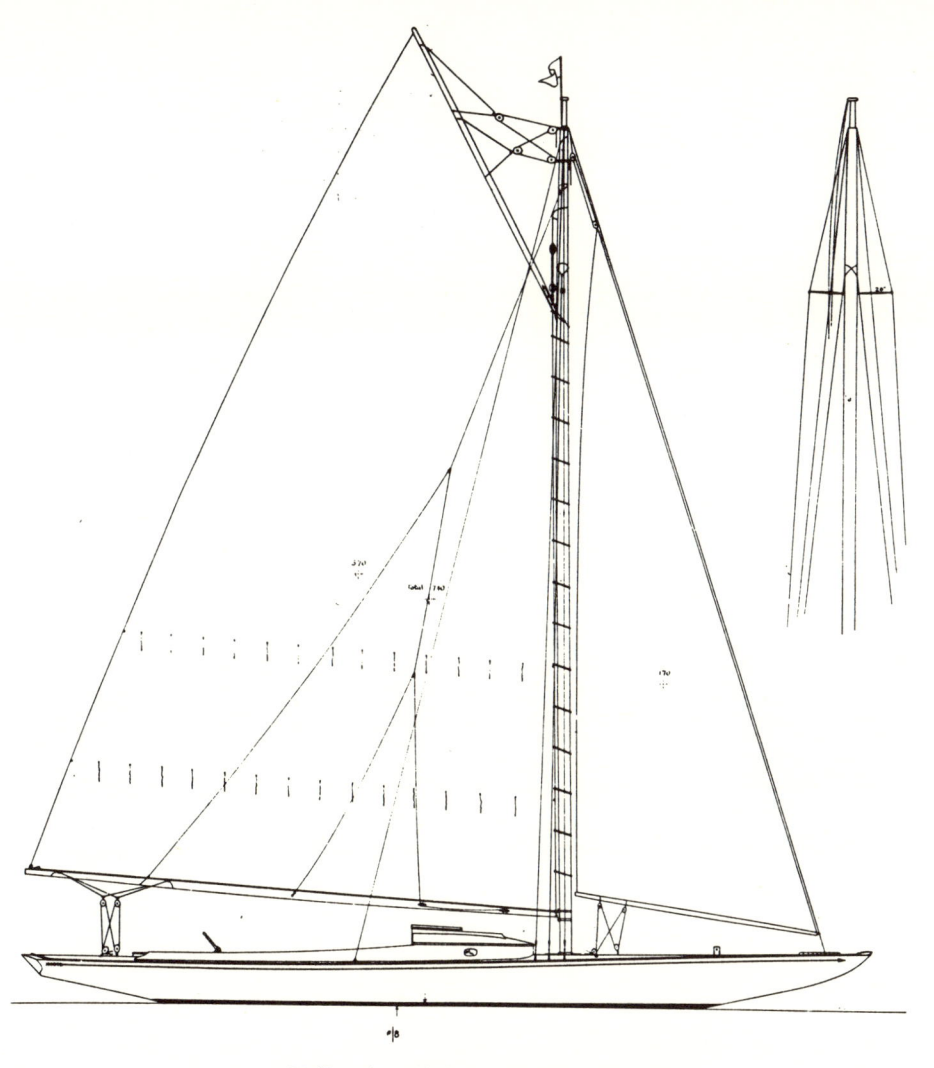

Valiant's *sailplan and lines drawings*.

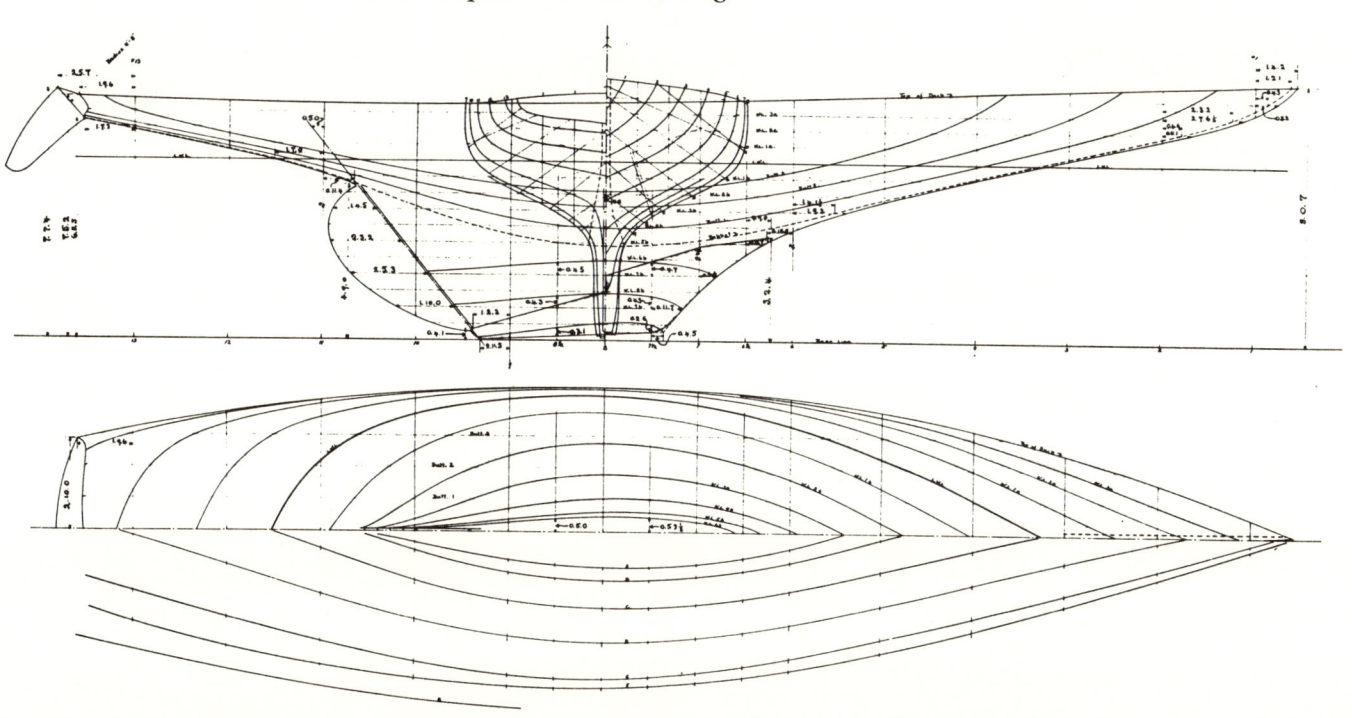

Valiant's *construction details.*

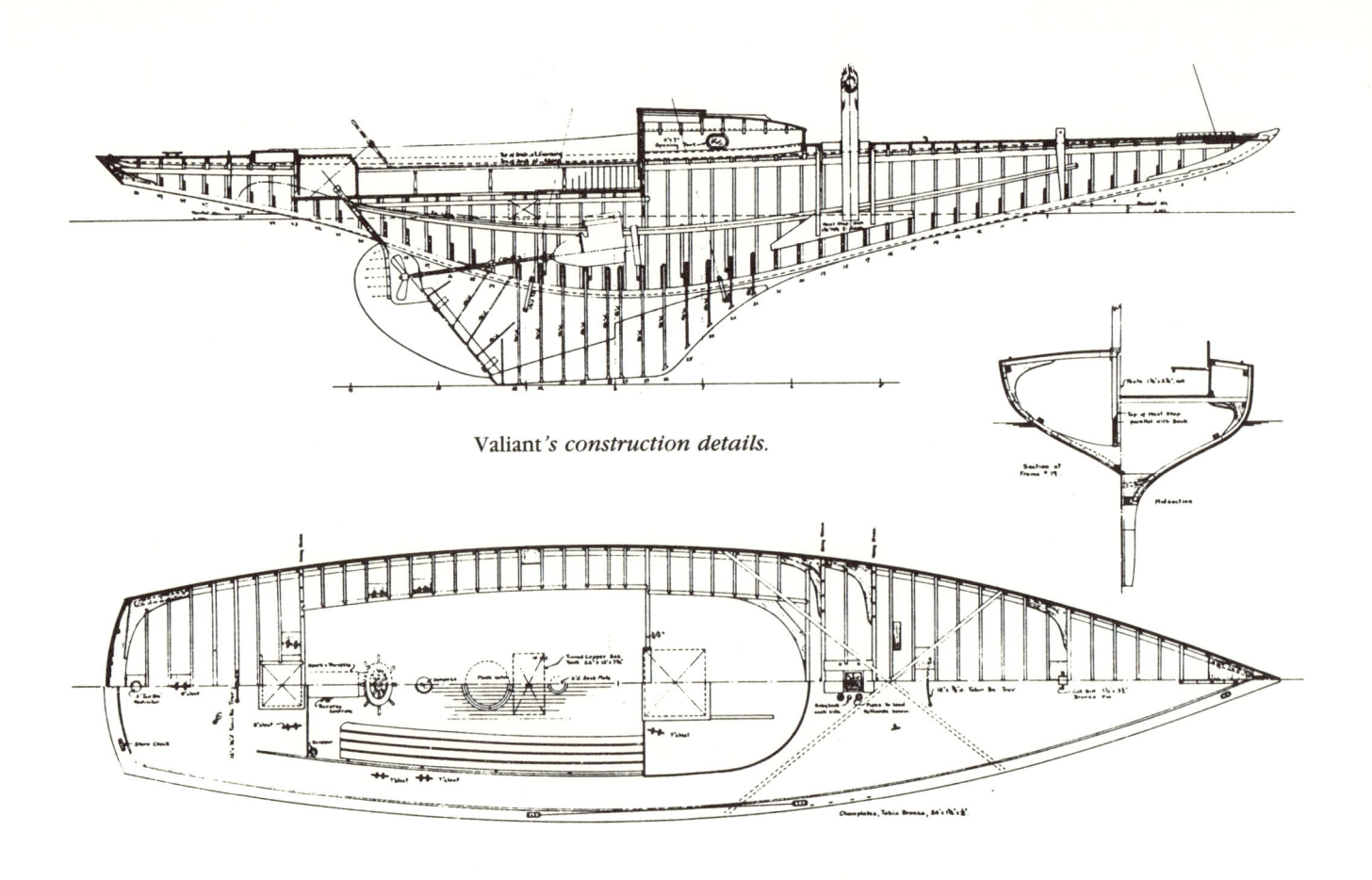

Valiant *just prior to launching.*

66

W.W. LUFKIN 97

The *W.W. Lufkin,* a 60-foot patrol boat for the Customs Service, was built in Gloucester, Mass., by Jake Storey in 1927. Power was supplied by a pair of 200-horsepower Murray & Tregurtha gas engines, which gave her a top speed of 25 m.p.h. She cruised at 18 m.p.h. with two-thirds throttle. She was used summer and winter in the apprehension of rum-runners, so there was a hot water heating plant provided. I believe at one point she was badly damaged by fire and then turned over to the Sea Scouts of Revere, who called her *Olympia II.*

Design Number 97
Length Overall: 60 feet
Length on Waterline: 58 feet 6 inches
Beam: 13 feet
Draft: 3 feet 11 inches
Displacement: 54,800 pounds

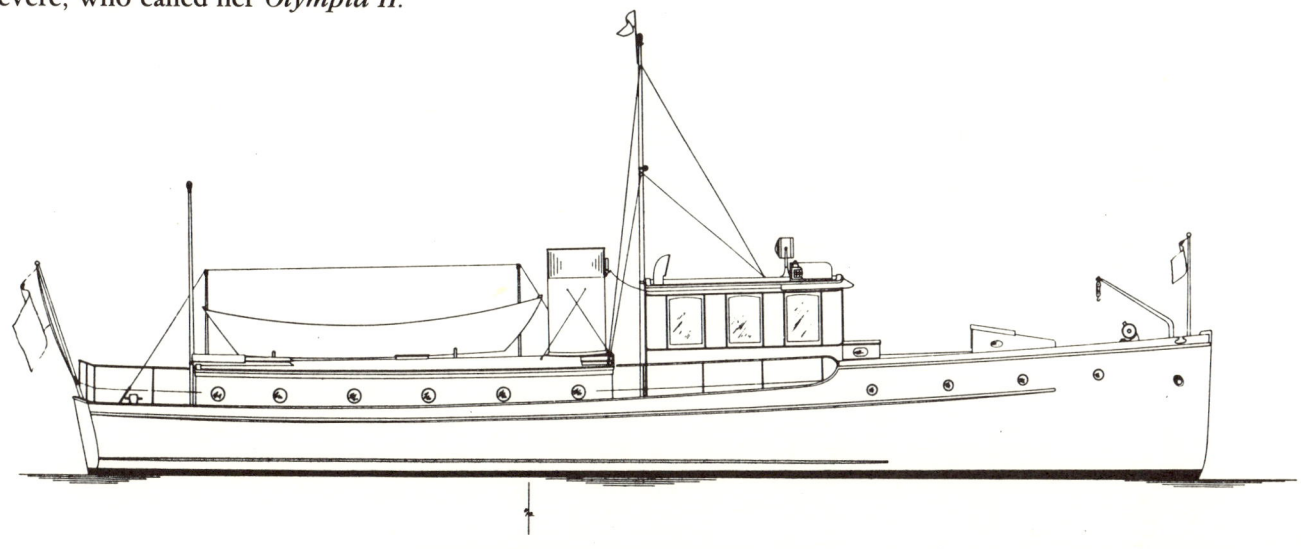

W.W. Lufkin's *profile and her lines.*

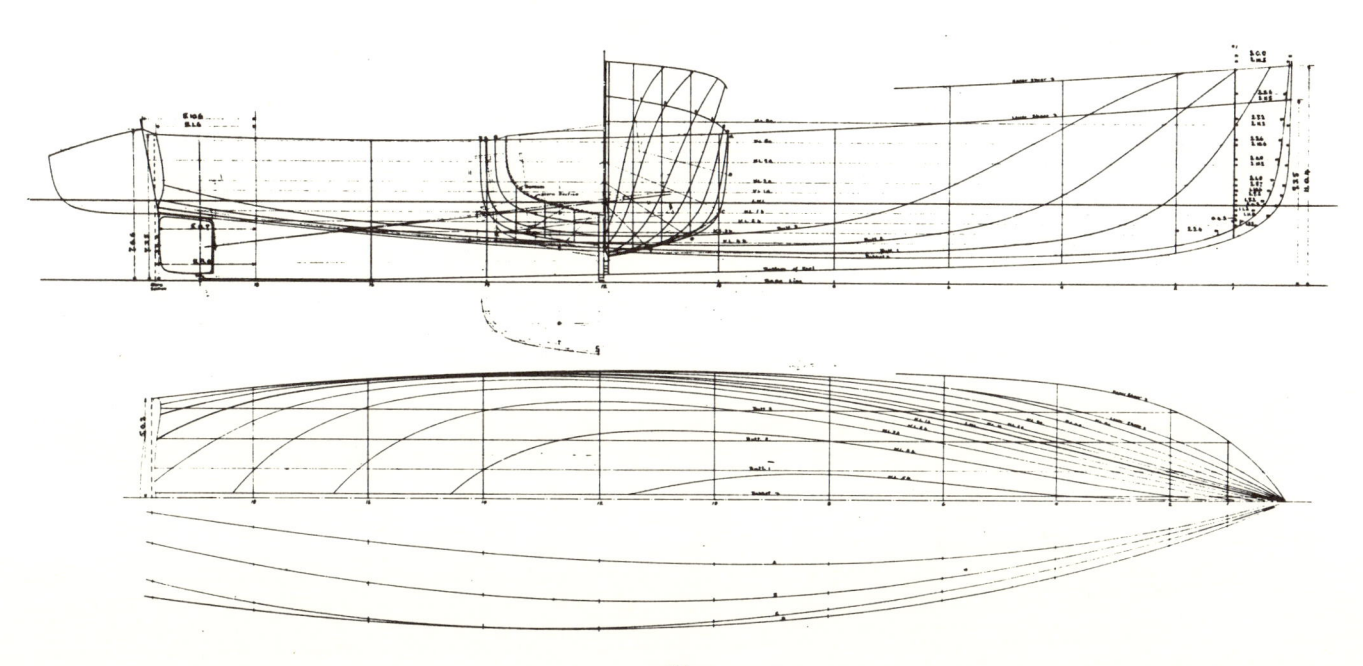

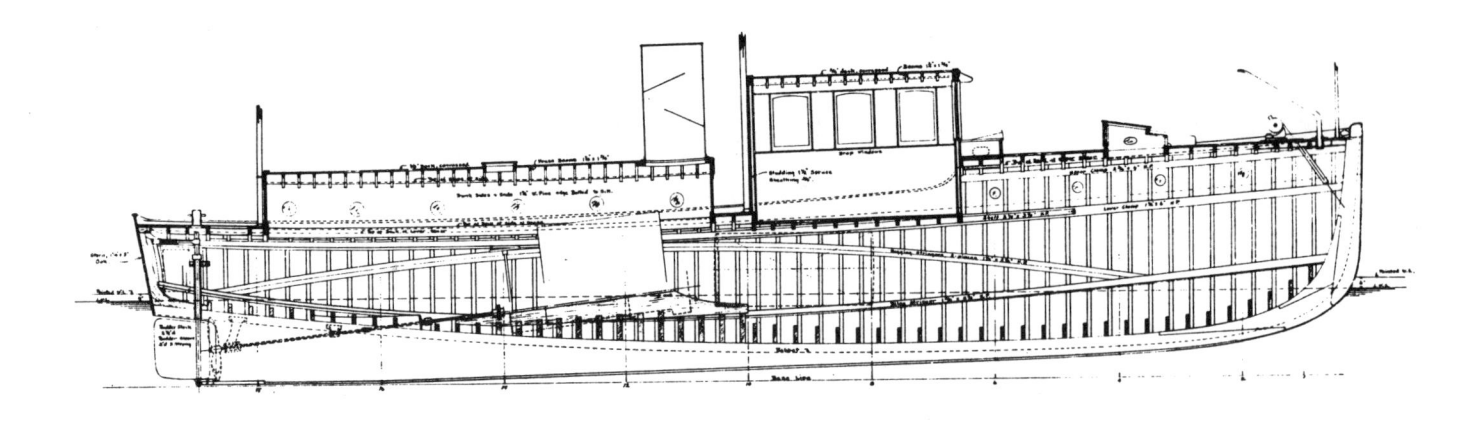

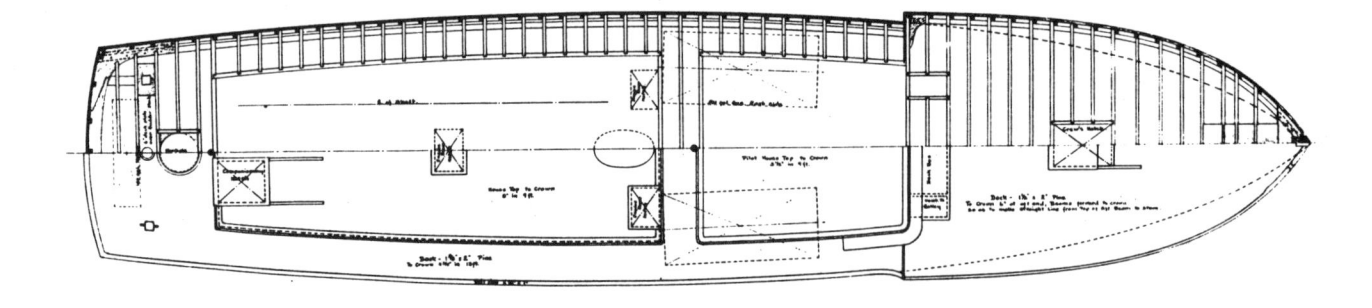

The construction plans for number 97 and her interior accommodations.

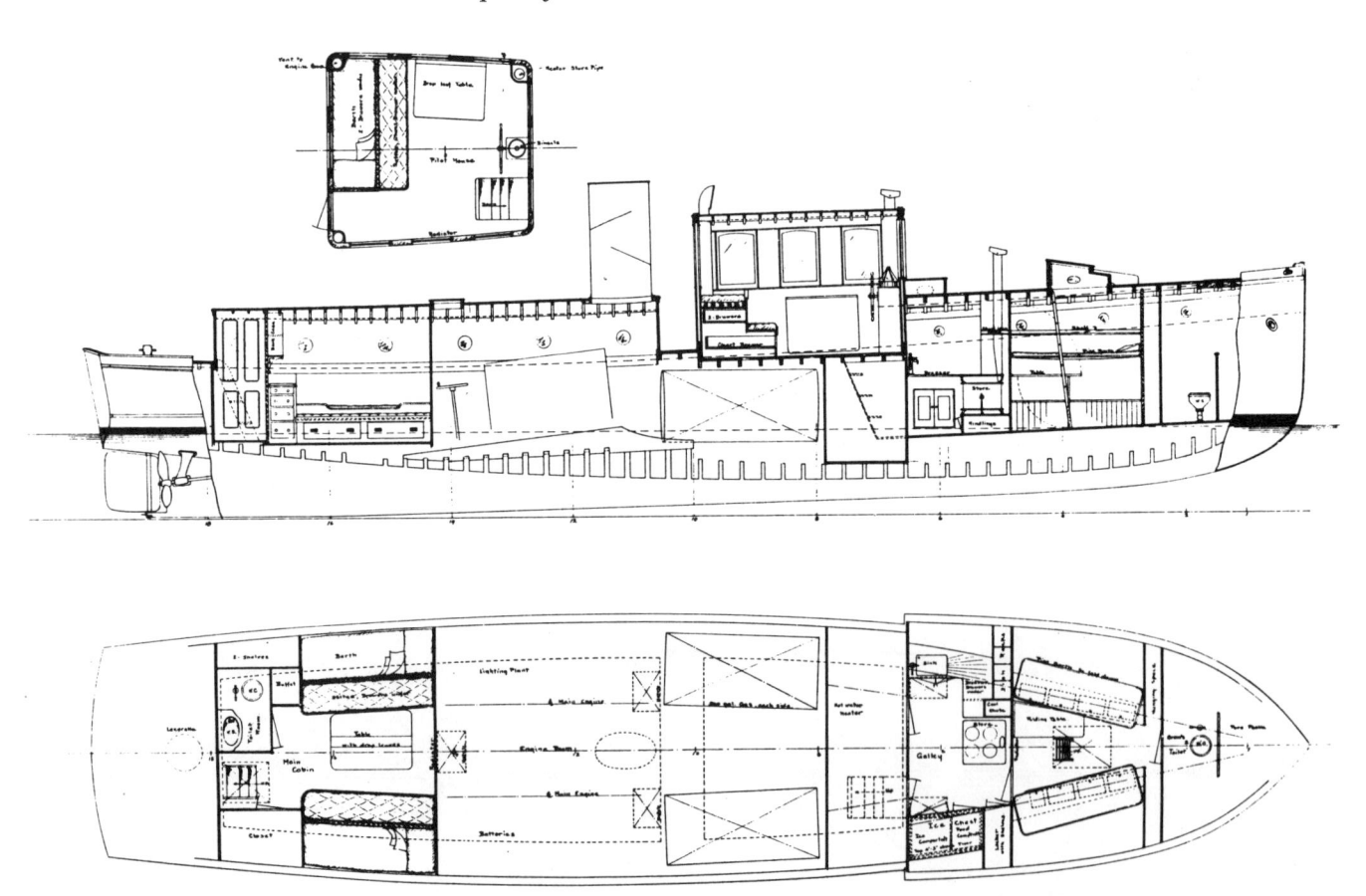

68

W.W. Lufkin. *Photograph courtesy of L.R. Jones, Boston Herald.*

JACINTA 98

Jacinta was built in 1931 by W.J. Reid at Winthrop, Mass., for J.E. Gerich of Milwaukee. Her frame was double sawn oak on 18-foot centers and used natural crooks as far as possible. Planking was Philippine mahogany to finish 1⅞ inches thick and fastened with ⅜-inch-diameter-by-4-inch galvanized hatch or ring nails. After the deck was strapped with 3/26-inch-by-3½-inch galvanized iron, the 2-inch white pine deck was laid

Design Number 98
Length Overall: 76 feet 3 inches
Length on Waterline: 56 feet 3 inches
Beam: 17 feet 6 inches
Draft: 9 feet 6 inches
Sail Area: 2693 square feet
Displacement: 121,000 pounds

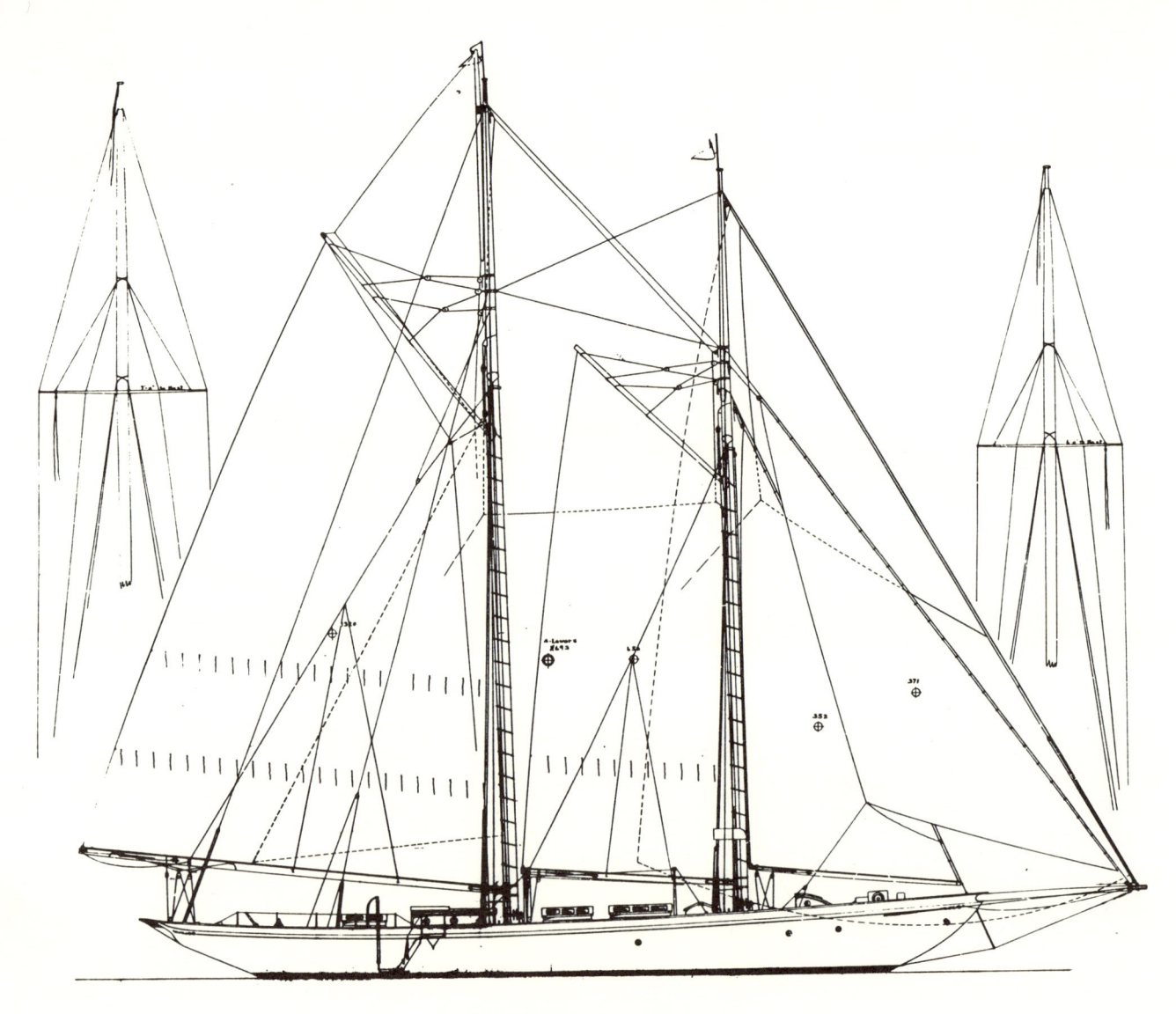

The sailplan for Jacinta.

and left unfinished. She carried a 14-foot inboard launch on the port side and a 12-foot tender to starboard. She spent her first summer cruising to her home port of Milwaukee on Lake Michigan. She was quite luxuriously furnished, with a bathroom complete with bathtub set in green tile, hot and cold running water, a double and single stateroom aft, captain's stateroom forward, and berths for four in the forecastle. A smart sailer, she won the Wind Point Race her first year in 1931 — a race in which she started five minutes late and finished 30 minutes in the lead. Her 180-horsepower Sterling Petrel could push her up to 11 knots, and she cruised comfortably at seven-plus knots with the engine turning 1,200 r.p.m.

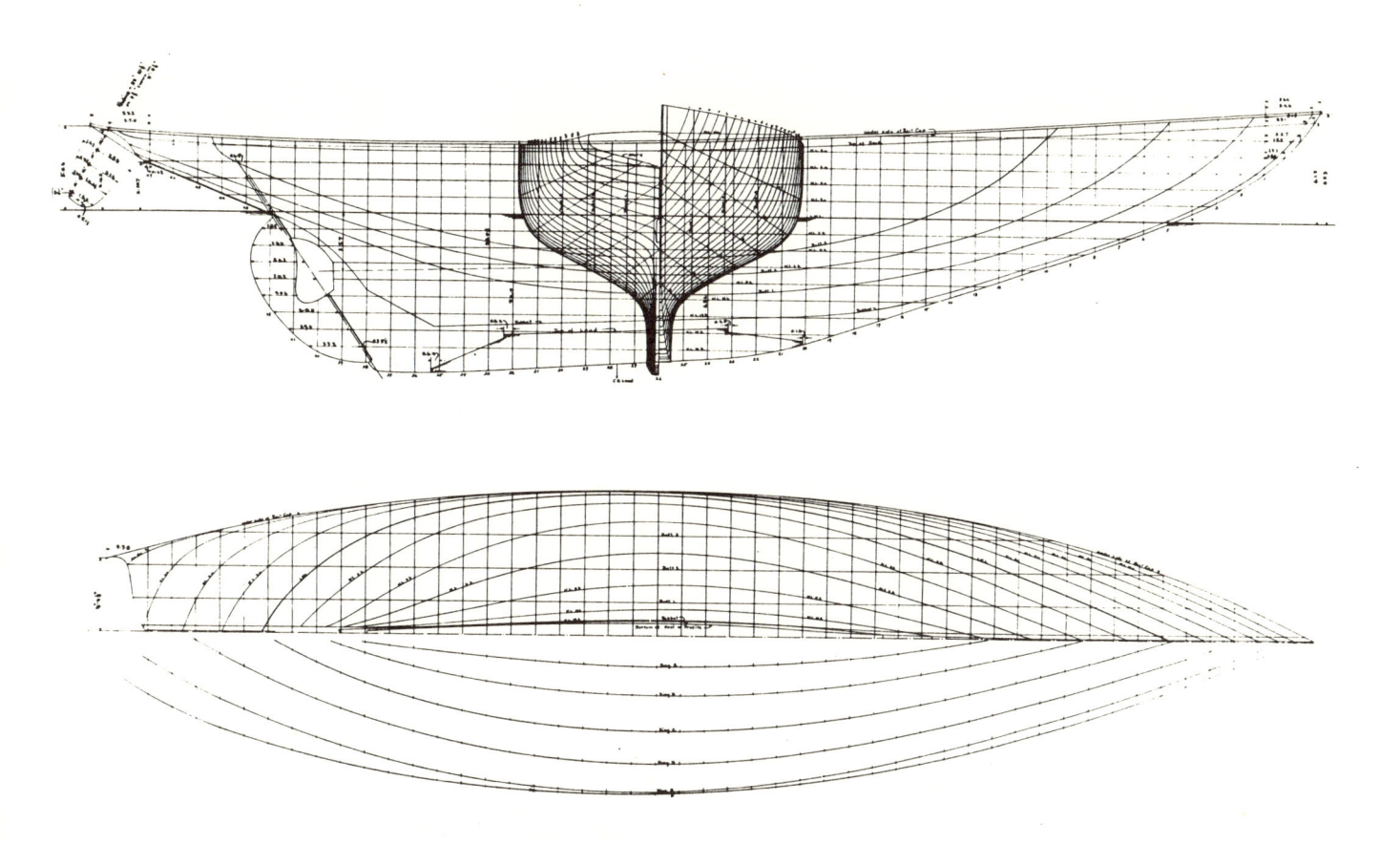

The lines and construction plans for Jacinta.

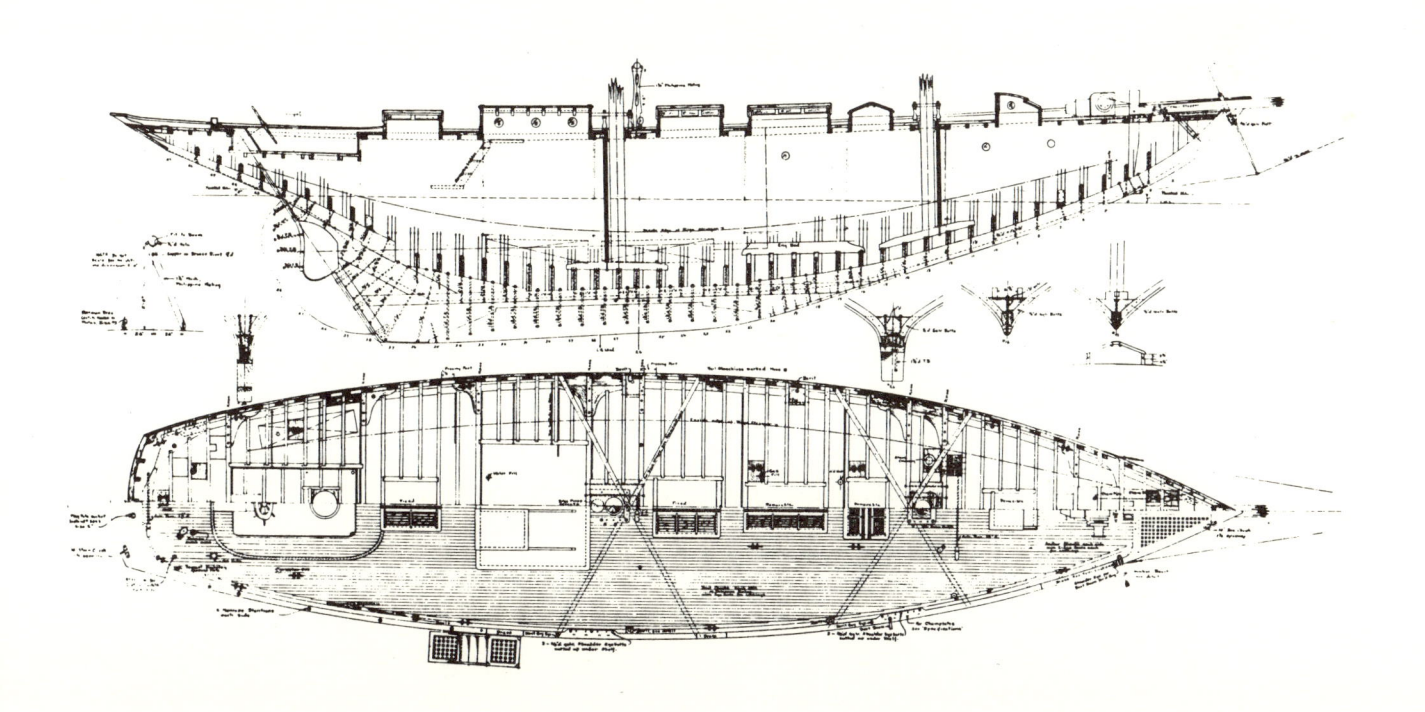

71

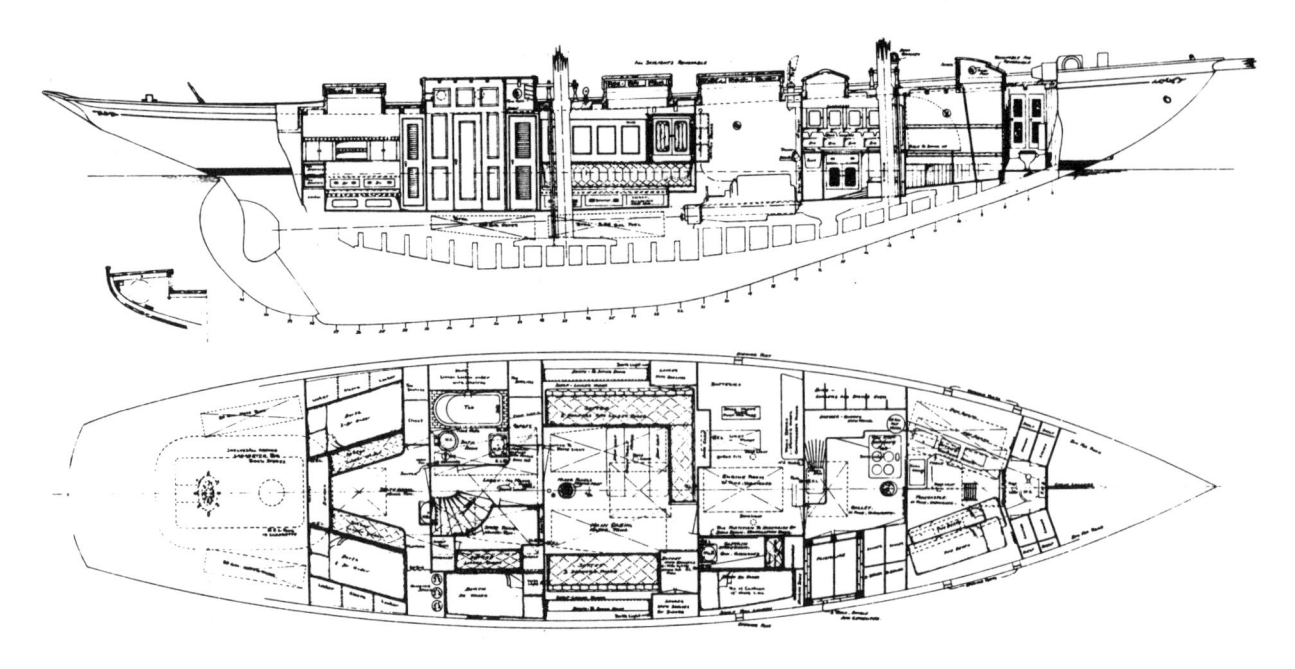

Above: *The accommodations plans for* Jacinta.

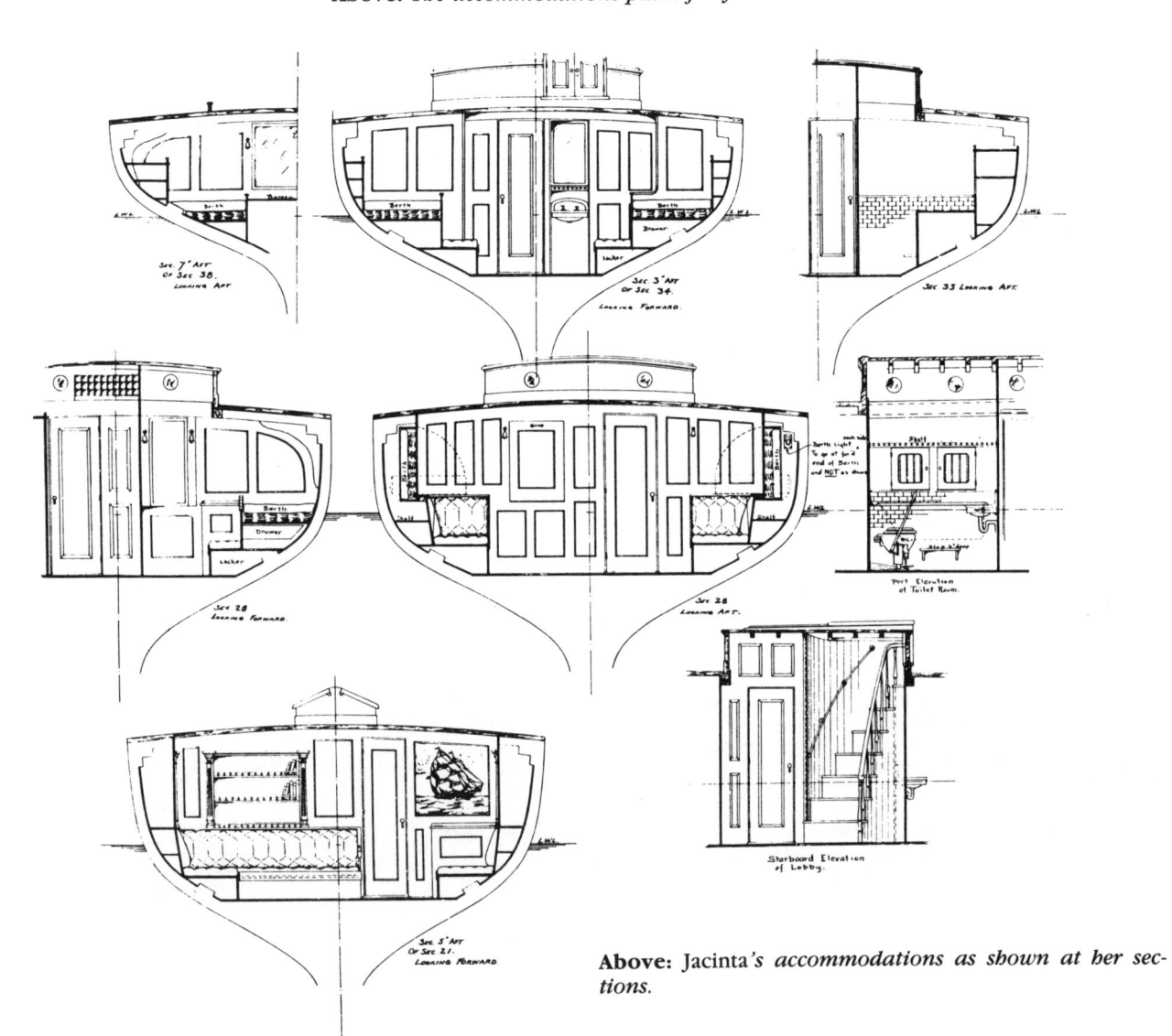

Above: Jacinta's *accommodations as shown at her sections.*

Jacinta *under sail*.

100 SEA DAWN

Design Number 100
Length Overall: 36 feet
Length on Waterline: 29 feet
Beam: 11 feet
Draft: 3 feet 6 inches
 with centerboard up
Sail Area: 672 square feet
Displacement: 17,200 pounds

These plans were traced from a set of blueprints that were made from the original drawings. They are the only originals that I find missing, and I can only assume they were given to *Rudder* magazine as she was designed for their "How-To-Build" series. I don't know how many boats were built from these lines, but there must have been quite a few. I have 12 or 13 different rigs that were drawn up for the design.

With inside ballast, this was a good boat for the amateur, as he wouldn't have to build a keel pattern or pay for a casting. If you could cope with the installation of the centerboard and have it tight, you would come up with a satisfactory cruising boat. Naturally, it wasn't long before someone wanted to put a keel on one, and my father's comment shows how impractical it is to take a boat designed for one purpose and try to make something else out of it.

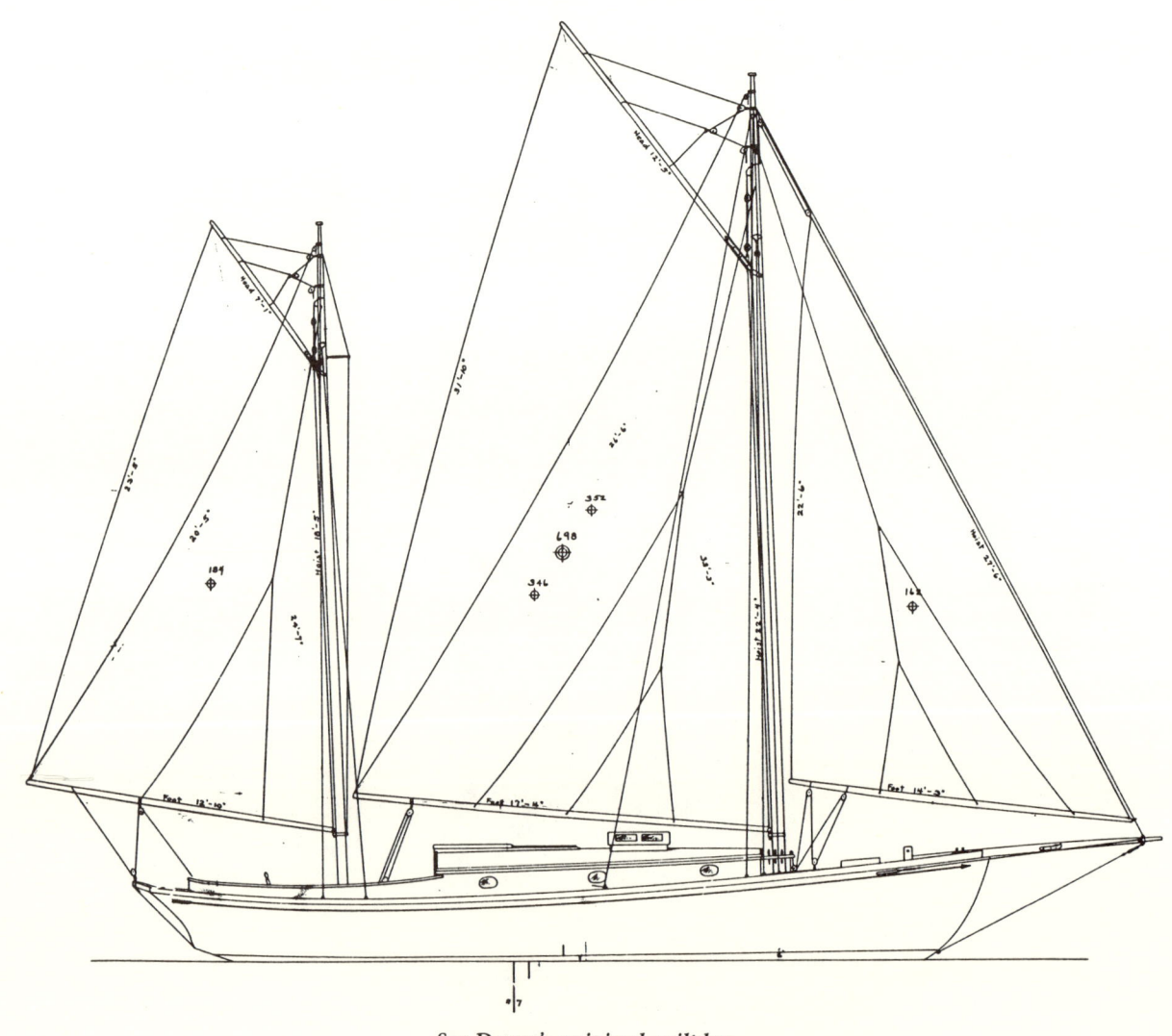

Sea Dawn's original sailplan.

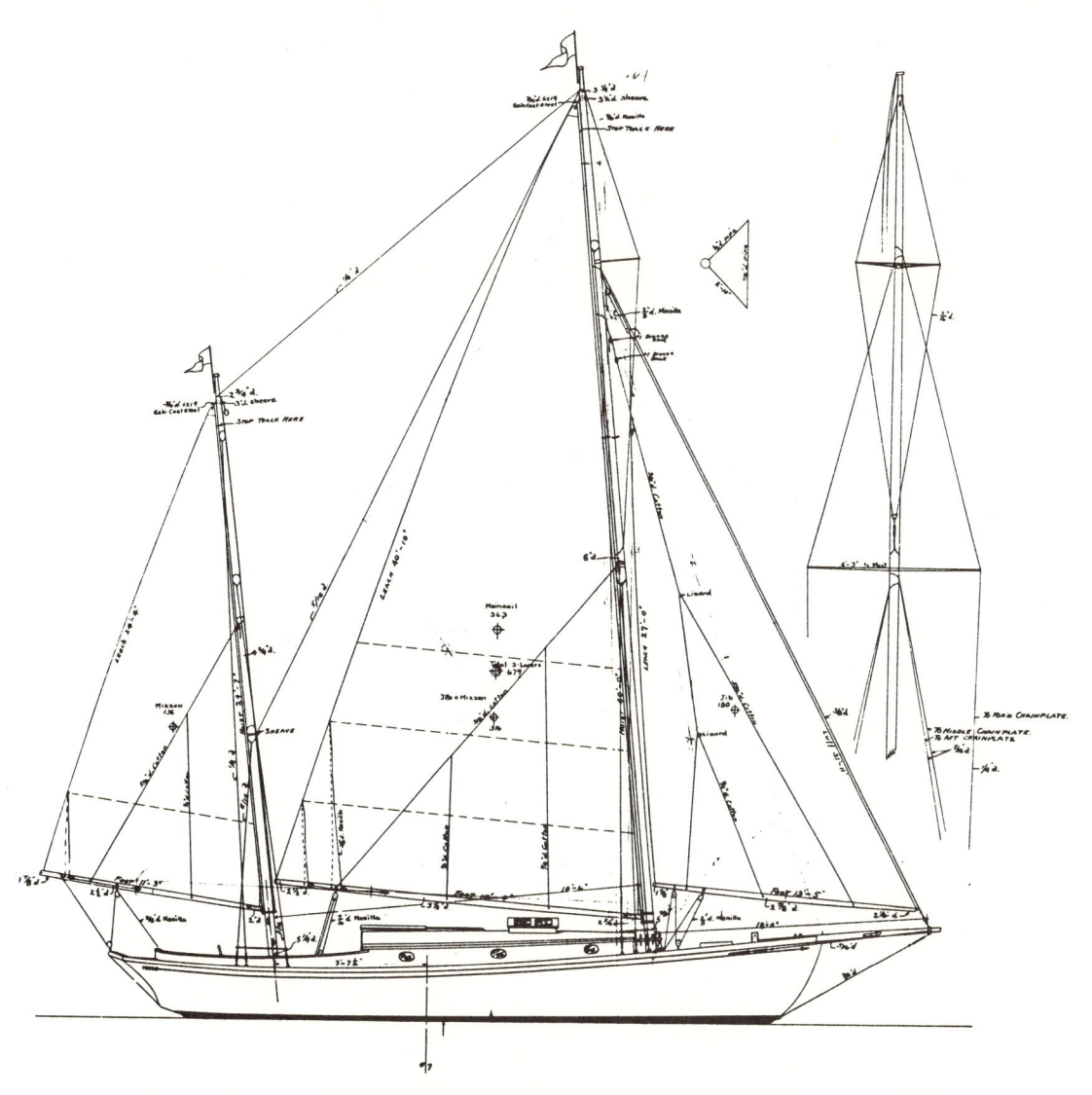

Number 100 as a ketch, with a marconi main.

Dad said: I have never designed or made drawings of a ballasted keel for this boat and do not recommend it, with the hull lines she has. Owners of a few of these boats have put on keels in accordance with their own ideas, with the consequence that the boats have fallen short of expectations. They have been poor steerers, have had too much initial stability, etc. You can't simply put a keel on this boat and expect her to perform. To make a keel boat of *Sea Dawn* would mean an entirely new design as her hull lines do not go with a deep-ballasted boat.

In writing the specifications for *Sea Dawn,* Dad finally decided not to specify any amount of ballast, because if amateurs built the boat it would be easy for them to lose displacement in setting her up and in bending frames, and they would be apt to increase the scantling sizes perhaps an eighth of an inch here and there, little realizing that this would increase the hull weights anywhere from 10 percent to 15 percent. However, if the boat were fairly accurately built, she would need about 4,500 pounds of ballast, and of course, this amount could be varied to get the feeling of stiffness the owner desired.

As a gaff cutter.

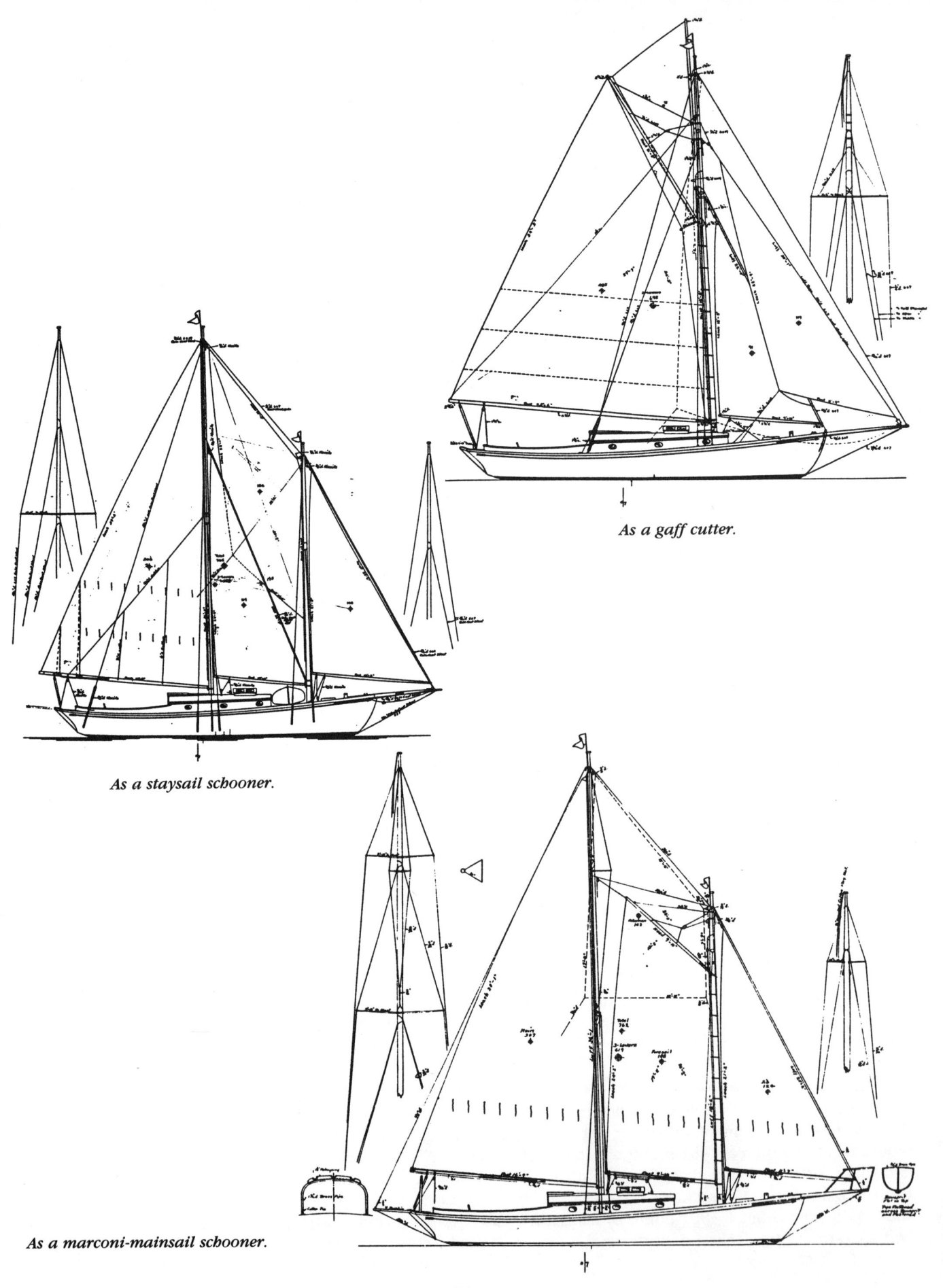

As a staysail schooner.

As a marconi-mainsail schooner.

76

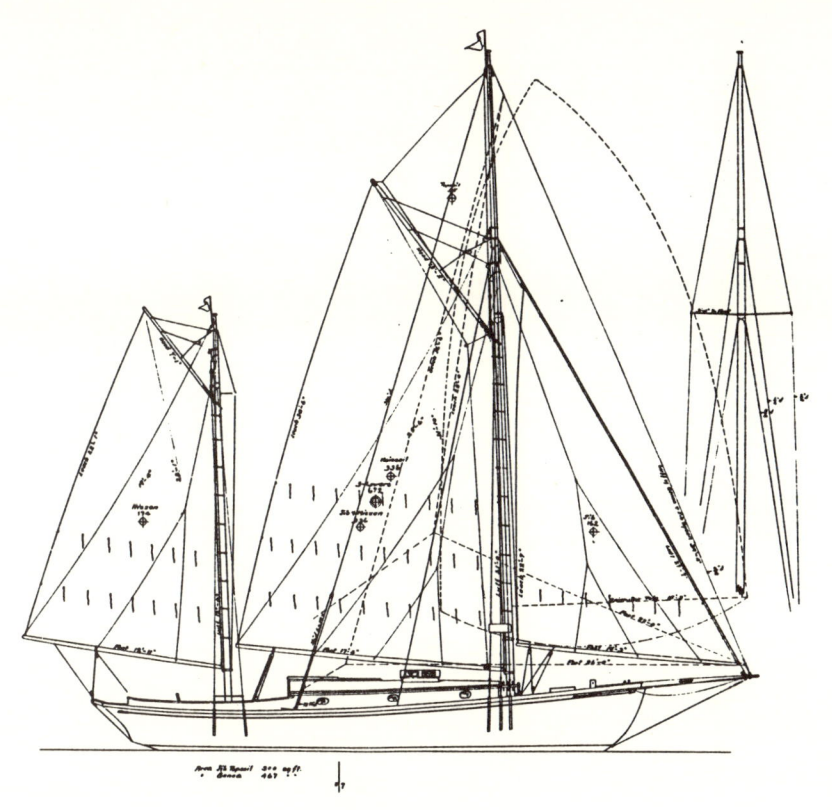

Gaff-rigged ketch.

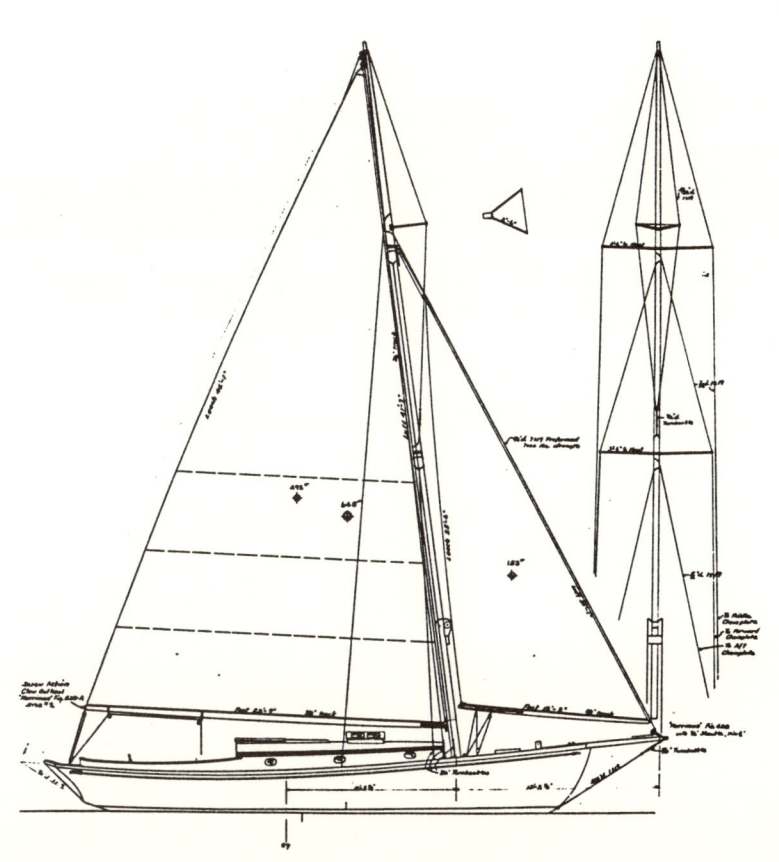

As a marconi sloop with double spreaders.

77

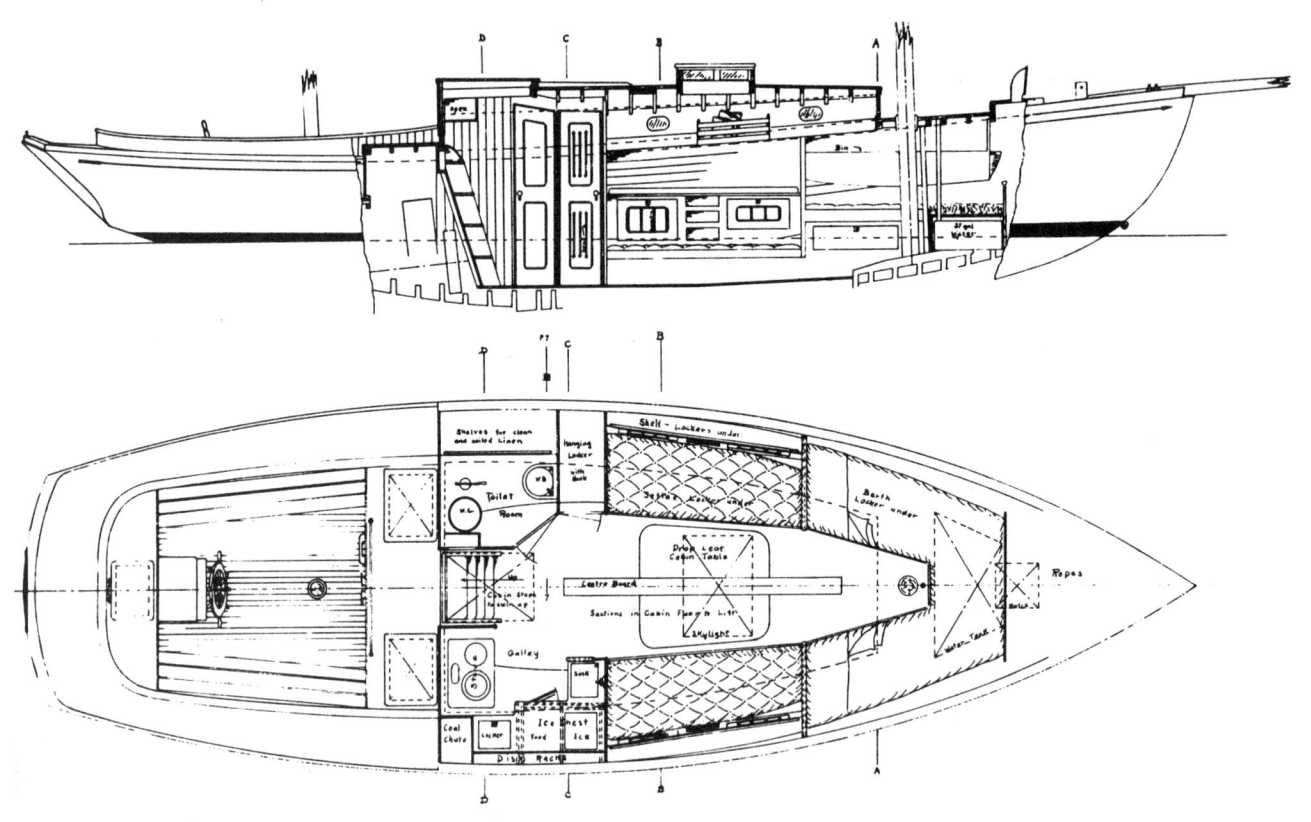

The accommodations drawings for number 100.

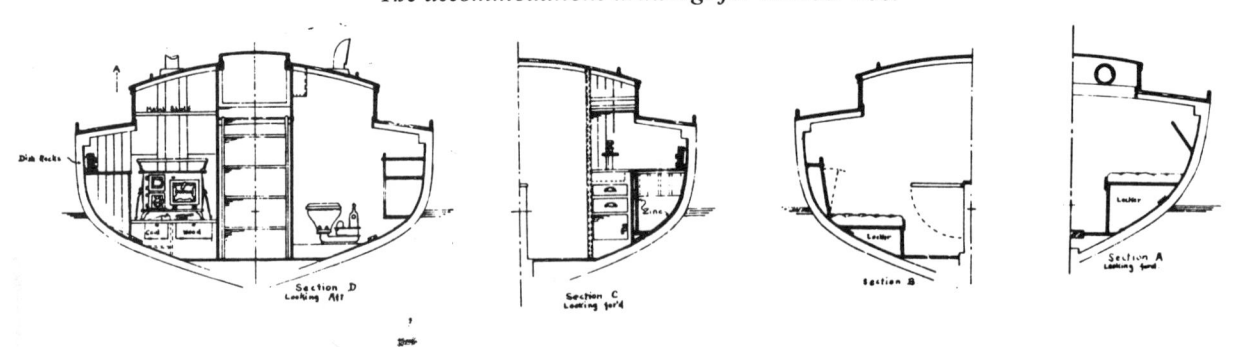

Number 100 under sail with a contemporary ketch rig.

As a gaff rigged ketch with her original sailplan.

SEA FAN 103

Sea Fan, the cat yawl for S.K. Dimock, was built by C.A. Anderson of Wareham, Mass., in 1928. With the mizzen on a sprit and the sail furling around the mast, she could certainly be moored in close quarters. After her trials, she was freighted to Florida for use in shoal inlets and rivers. A Universal flexi-four turning an 18-inch-by-16-inch, three-blade propeller powers her.

Design Number 103
Length Overall: 21 feet
Length on Waterline: 20 feet 10 inches
Beam: 9 feet
Draft: 2 feet 2 inches
Sail Area: 257 square feet
Displacement: 5,500 pounds

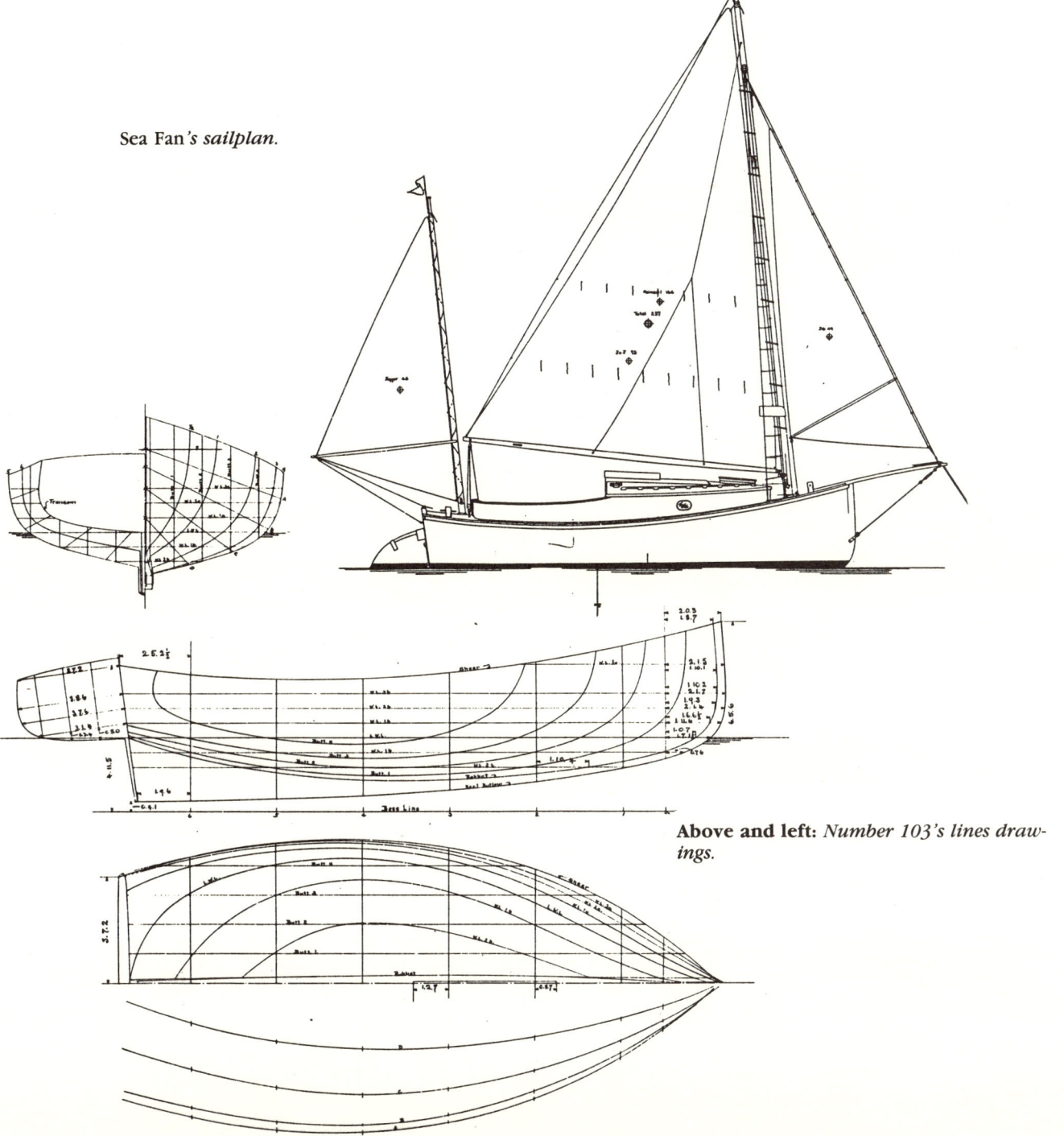

Sea Fan's *sailplan.*

Above and left: *Number 103's lines drawings.*

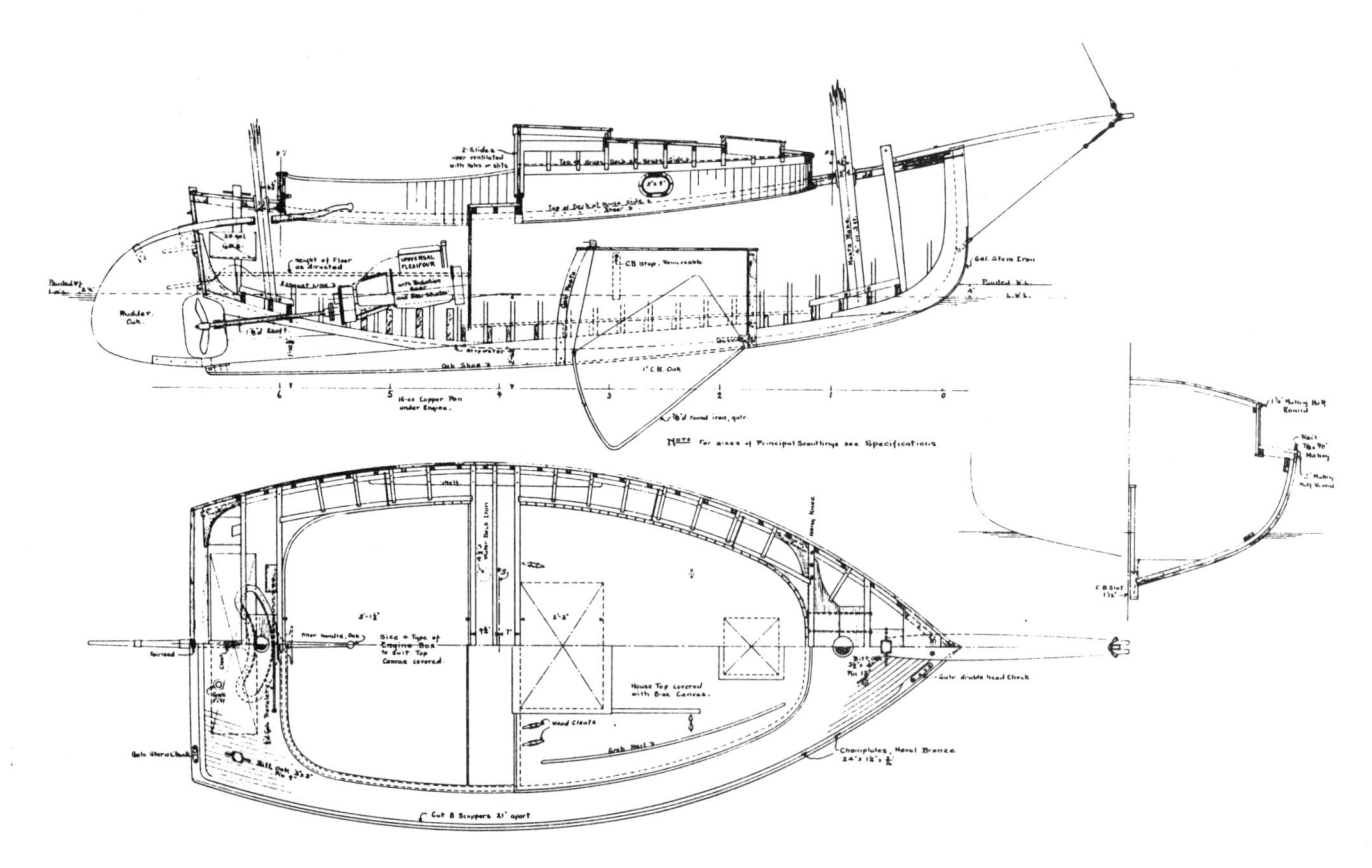

The construction plans and Sea Fan's *accommodations plans.*

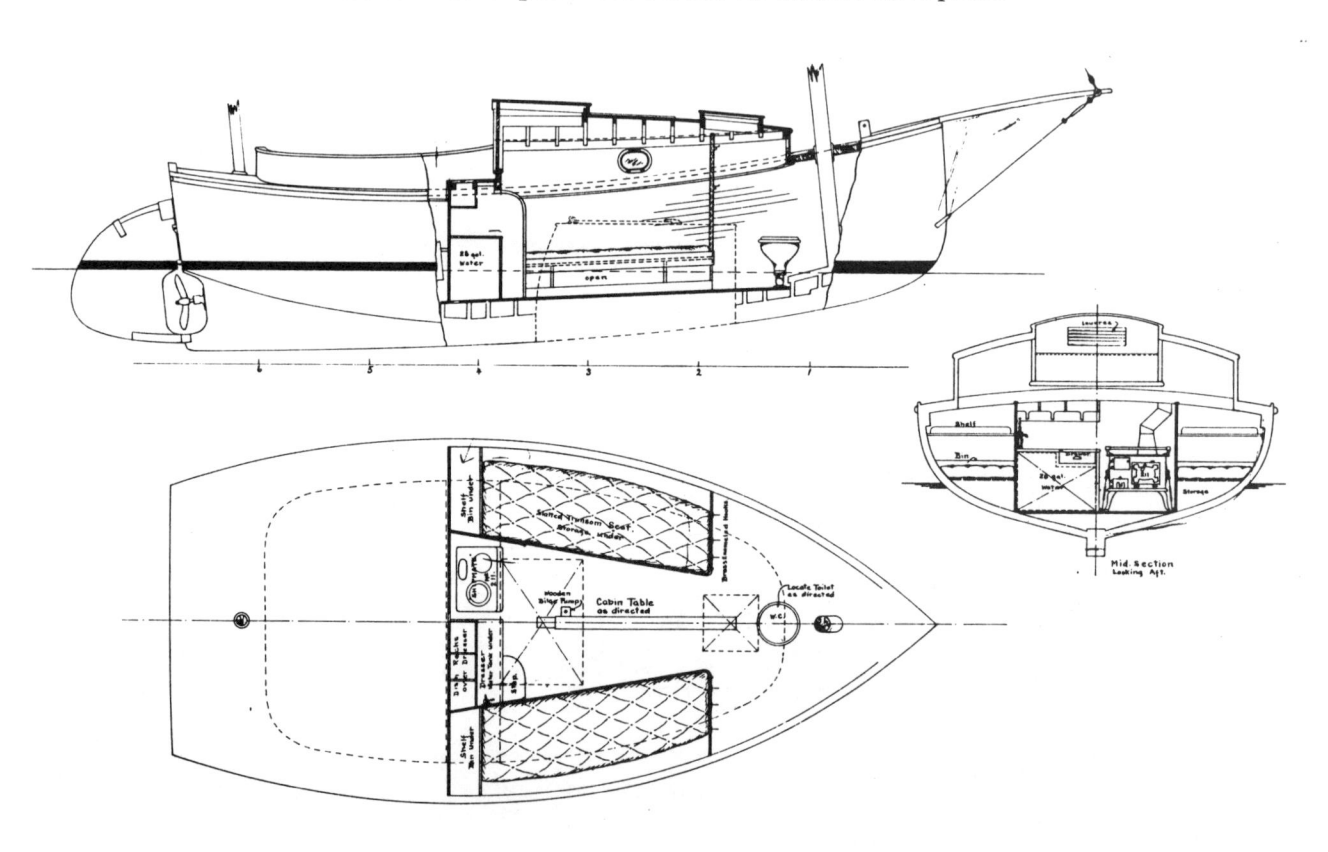

104

These three designs are all similar. In fact, the lines for numbers 104 and 229 are the same, but the rigs are a little different. The *Wanderer,* number 104, was designed in 1928 and built by Guy Gardiner at Swampscott. I built number 229, *Extra Dry,* for Jane P. Guild in 1945 while working at Calderwood Boat Yard.

Number 119 was a 13-foot, one-design class designed for a Chicago yacht club for youngsters to learn to sail in.

The side decks on all three boats were wide enough so that they could be laid flat in the water without any water getting into the cockpit. They also had watertight bulkheads fore and aft.

Design Numbers 104, 119, and 229
Length Overall: 18 feet
Length on Waterline: 14 feet 5 inches
Beam: 6 feet 5 inches
Draft: 1 foot 4 inches
Sail Area: 104 and 229; 179 square feet, 119; 85 square feet
Displacement: 1,660 pounds

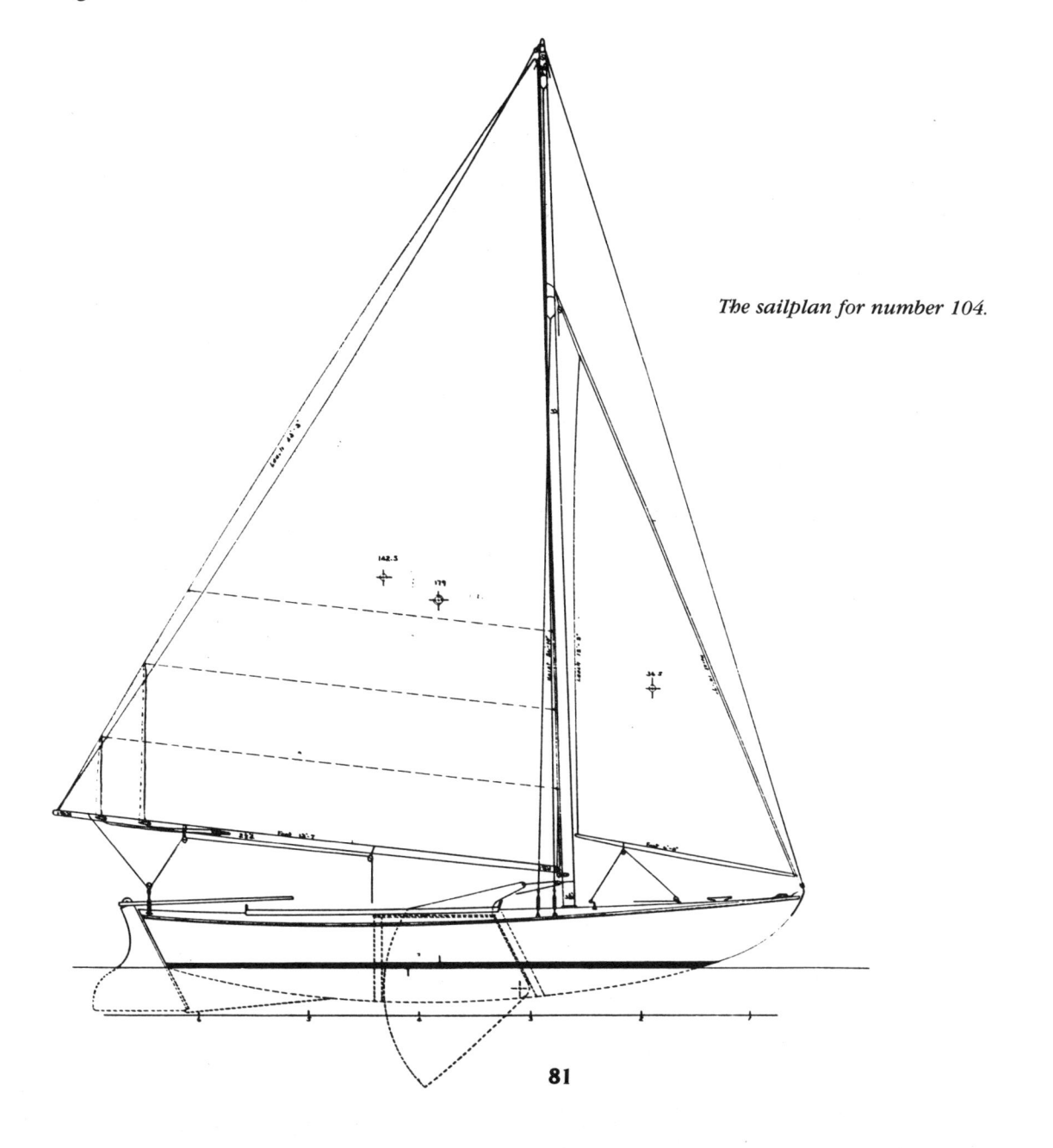

The sailplan for number 104.

Number 119 under sail.

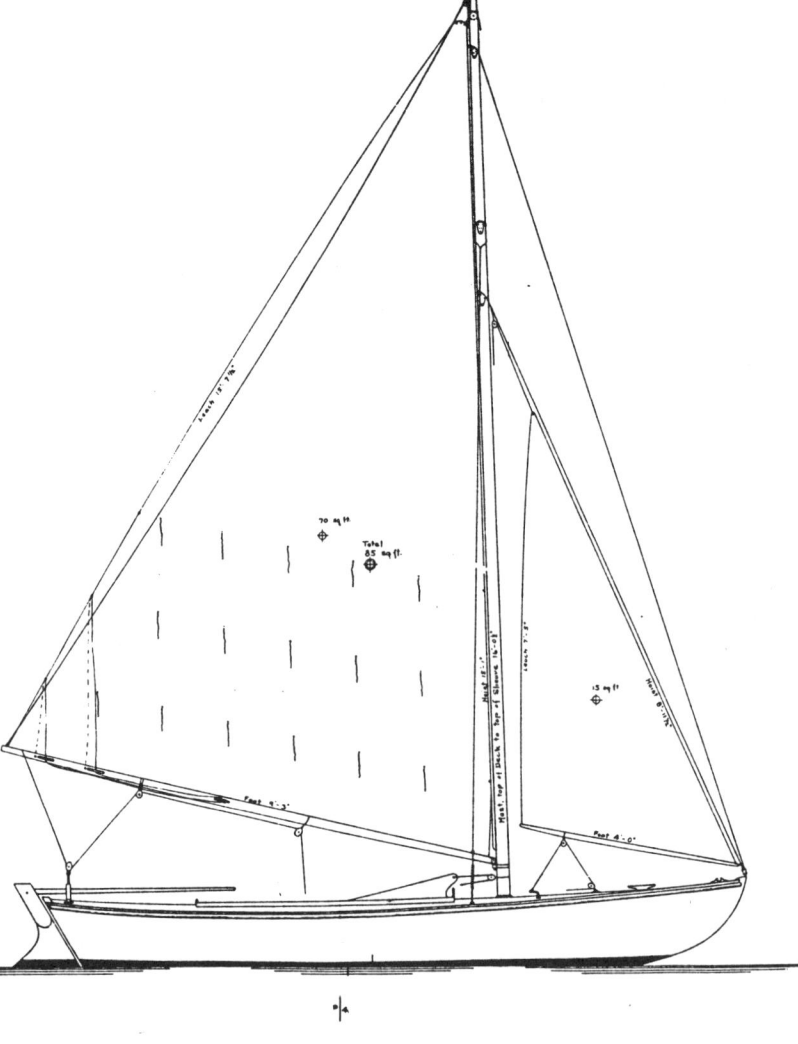

The sailplan and lines drawings for number 119.

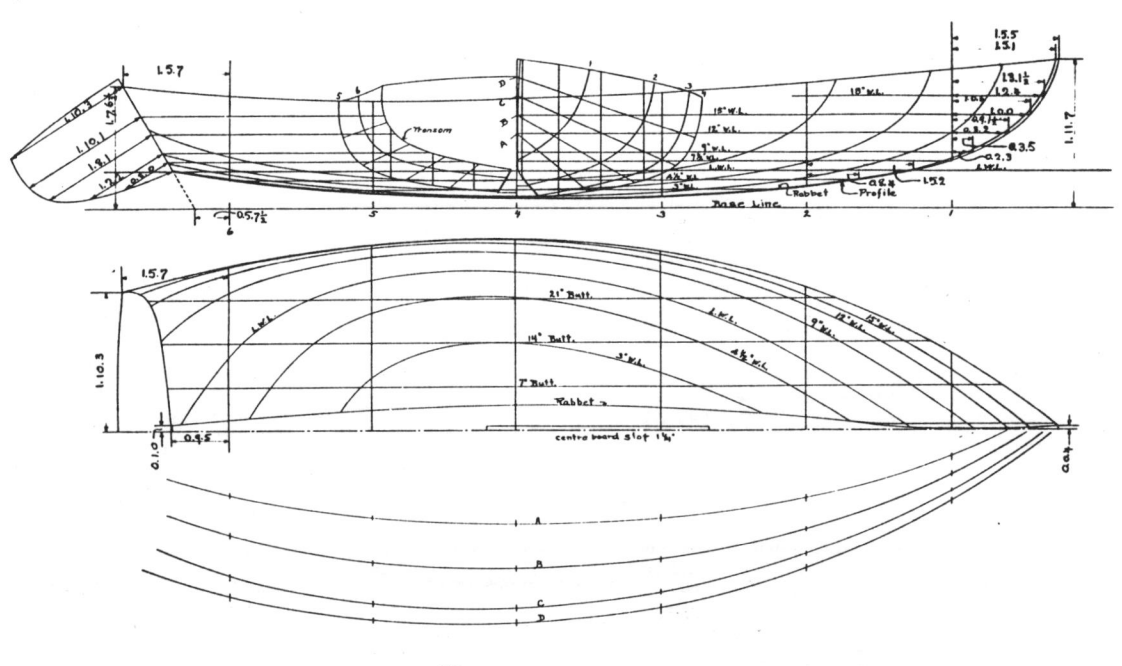

The construction plans for 119.

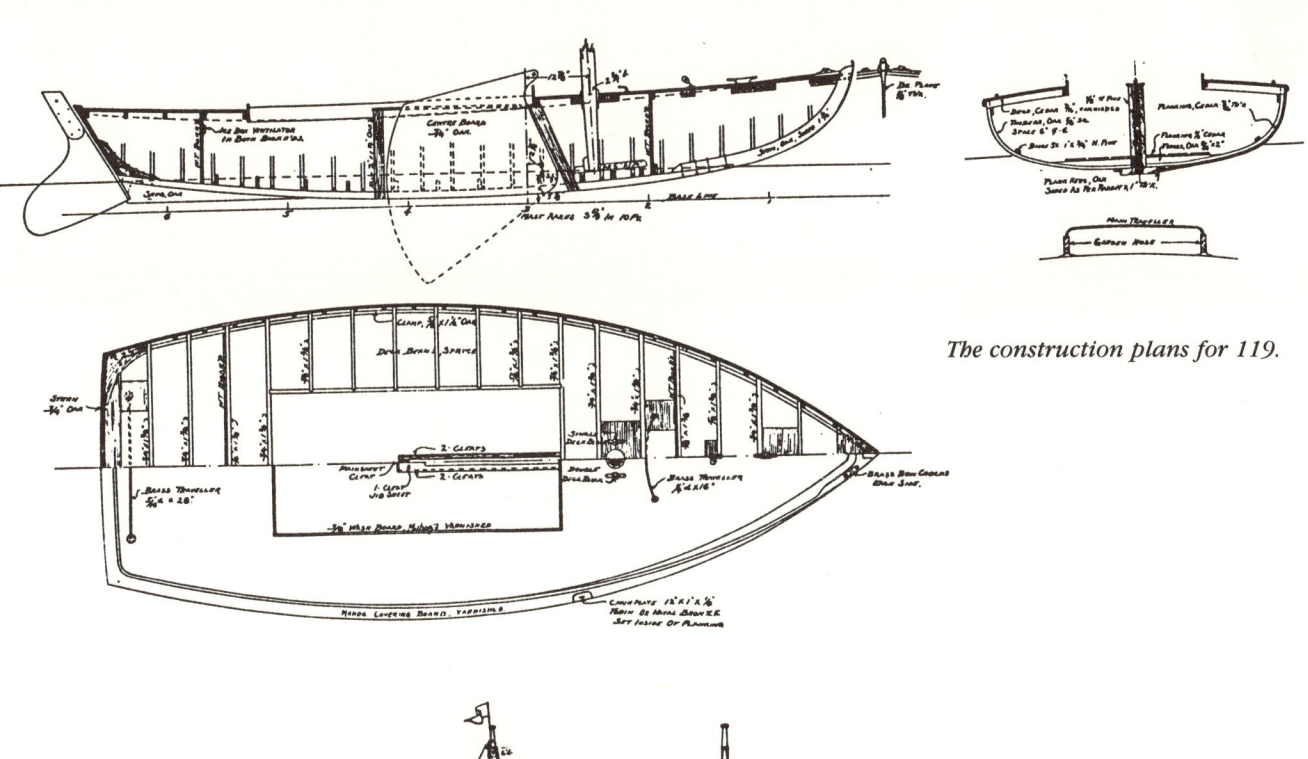

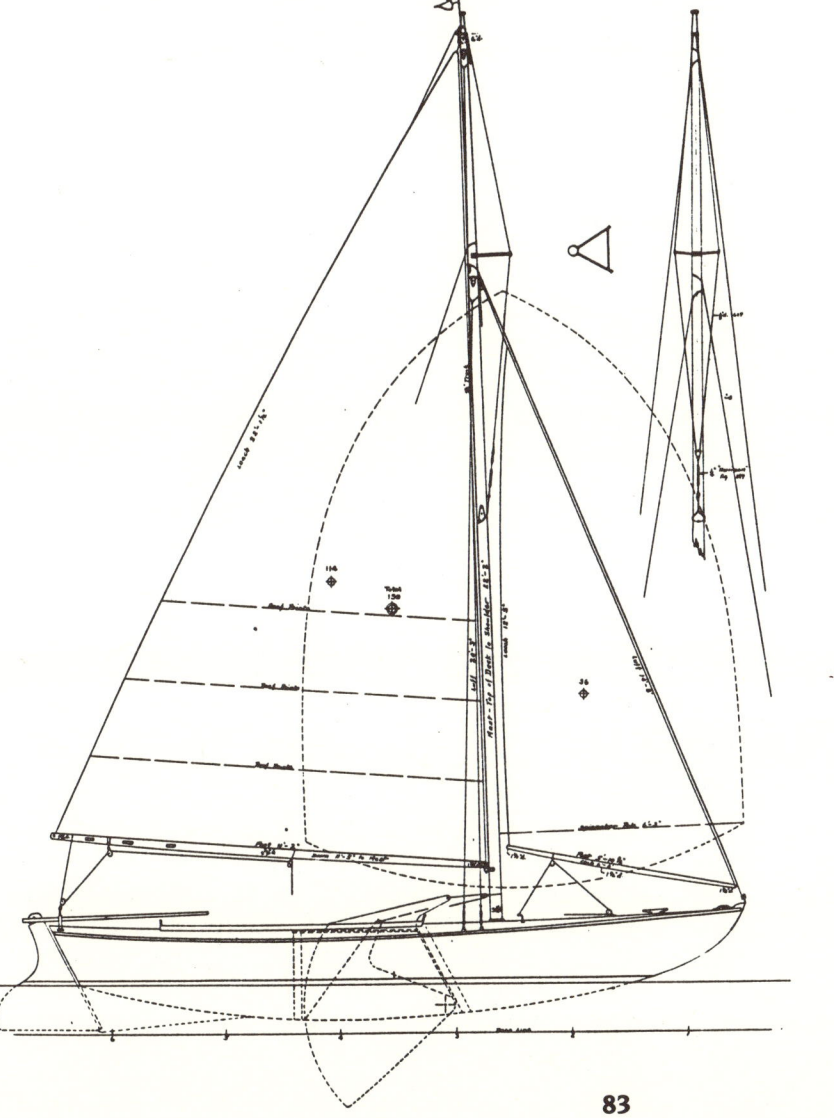

The sailplan for 129.

83

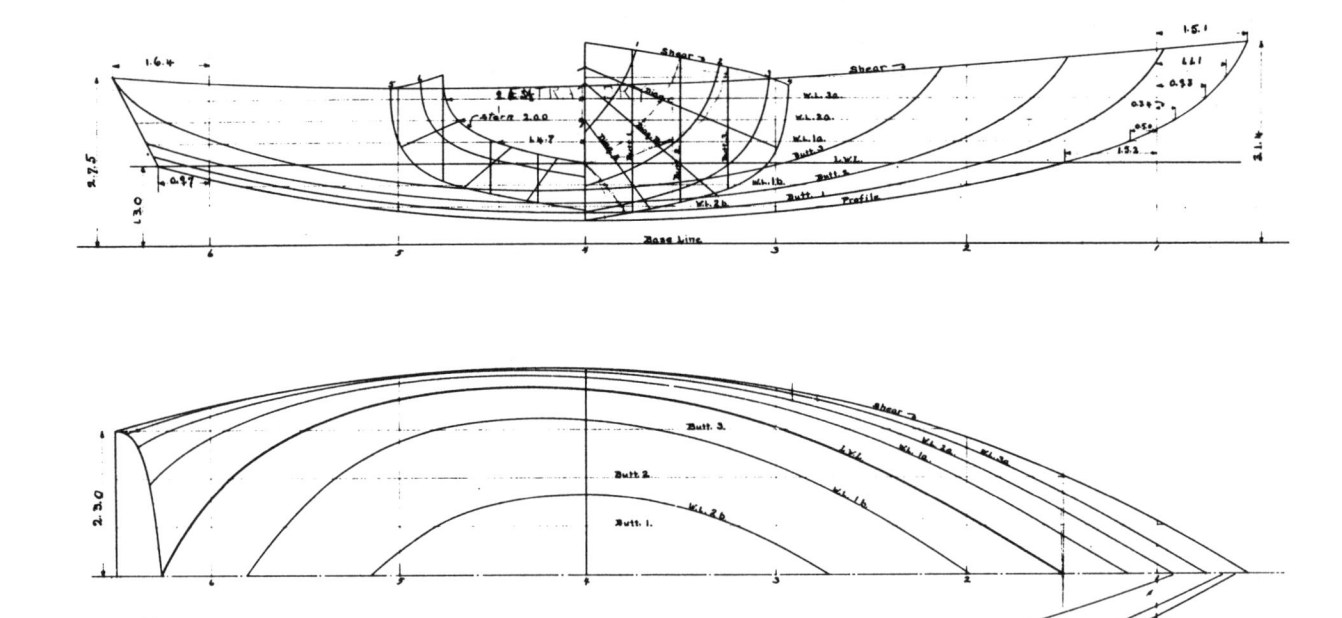

The lines for number 129.

106 JOLOMA II

Design Number 106
Length Overall: 37 feet
Length on Waterline: 28 feet
Beam: 10 feet 10 inches
Draft: 4 feet 11 inches
Sail Area: 755 square feet
Displacement: 20,700 pounds

Joloma II was built in 1928 by W.J. Reid of Winthrop, Mass., for A.W. Olds of Windsor, Conn., and is a good example of the comfort to be gained by not cramming a small boat full of berths. With four comfortable berths, there is ample room for locker, shower, and cabinet space. My father always said that there is no use in putting in a berth without a locker to go with it. The engine, set in its own compartment, was a Scripps F-4, which cruised her at better than 8¼ m.p.h. She was changed to sloop rig in 1951, as shown in design number 106B.

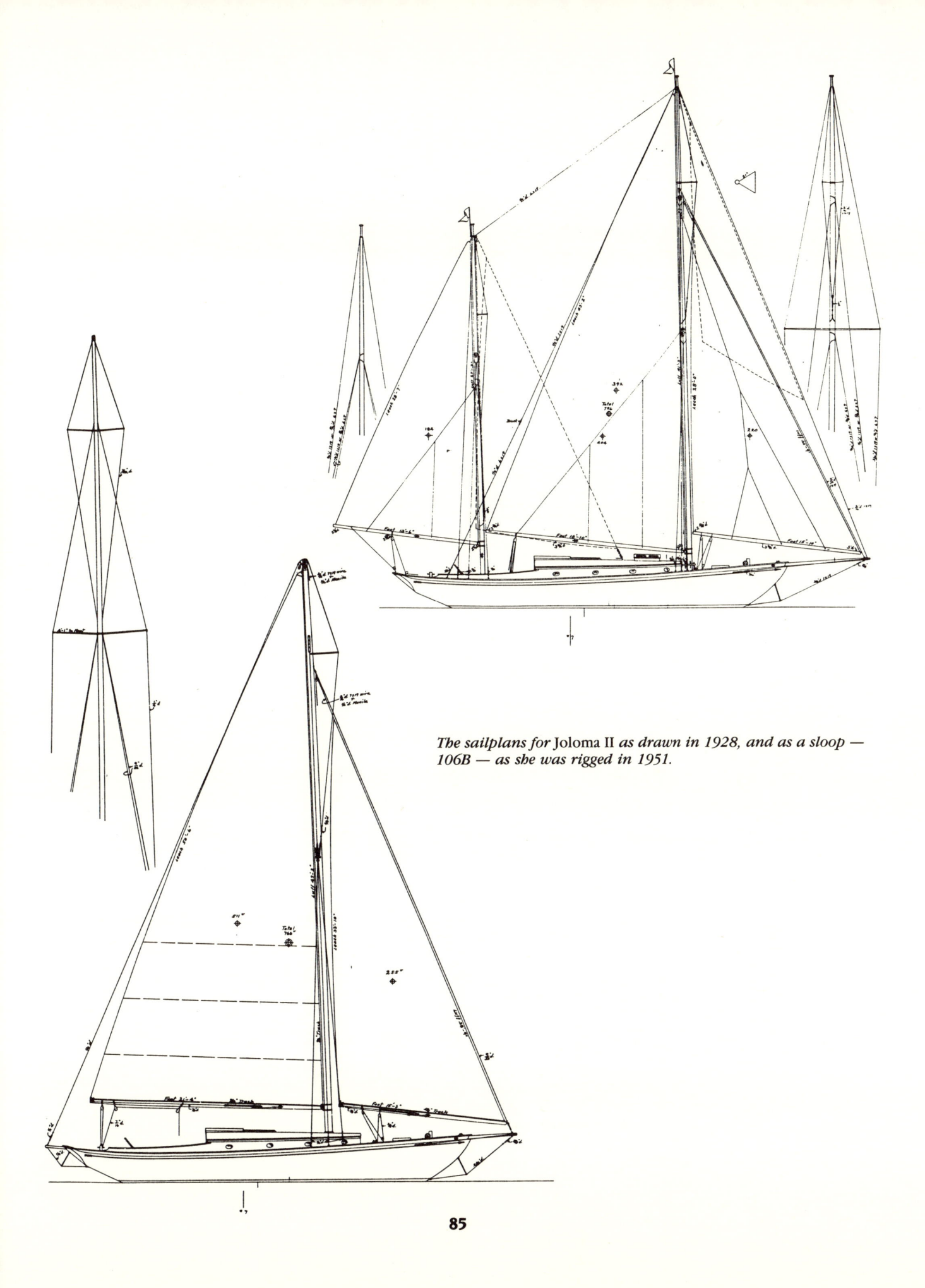

The sailplans for Joloma II *as drawn in 1928, and as a sloop — 106B — as she was rigged in 1951.*

85

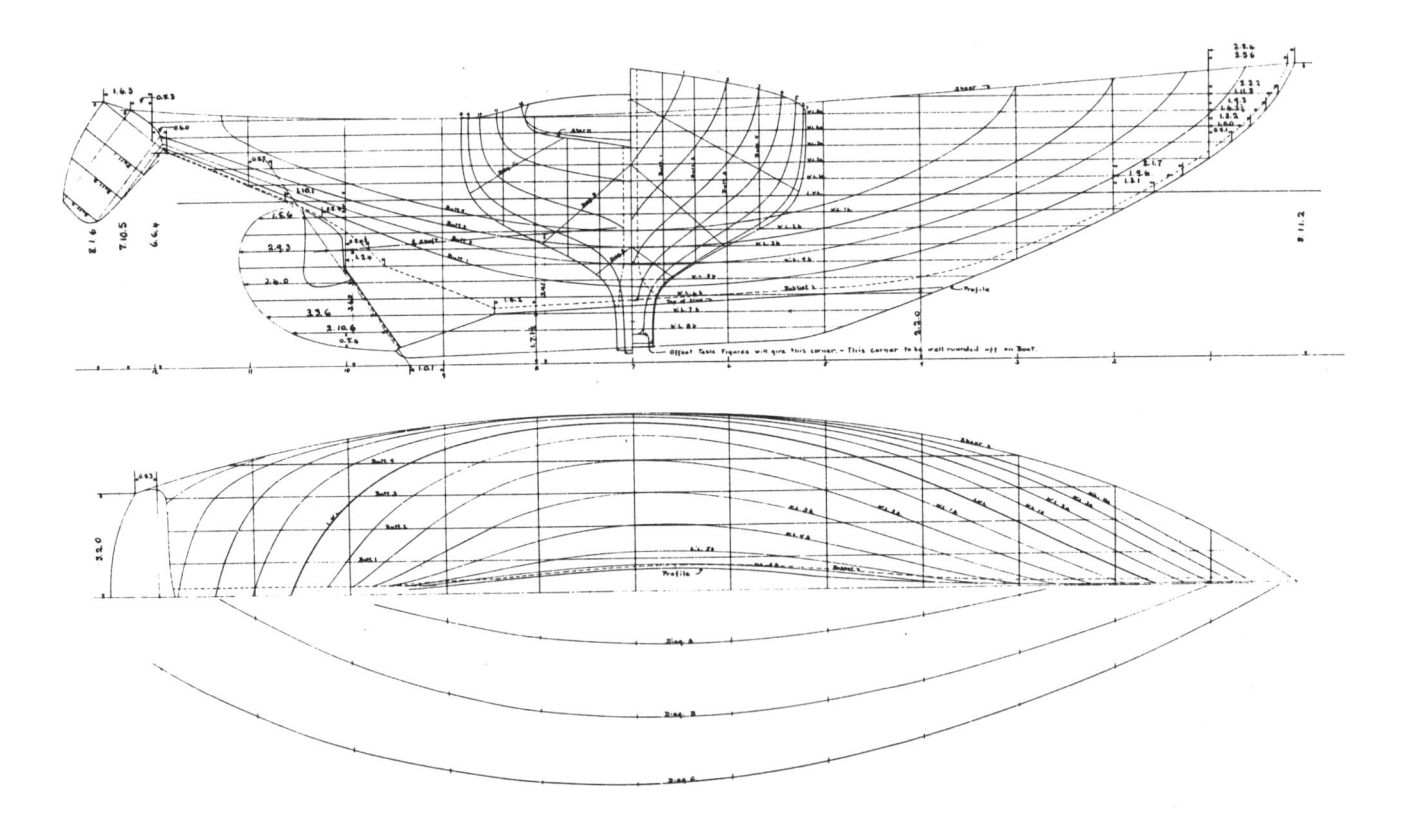

The lines for 106 and her construction plans.

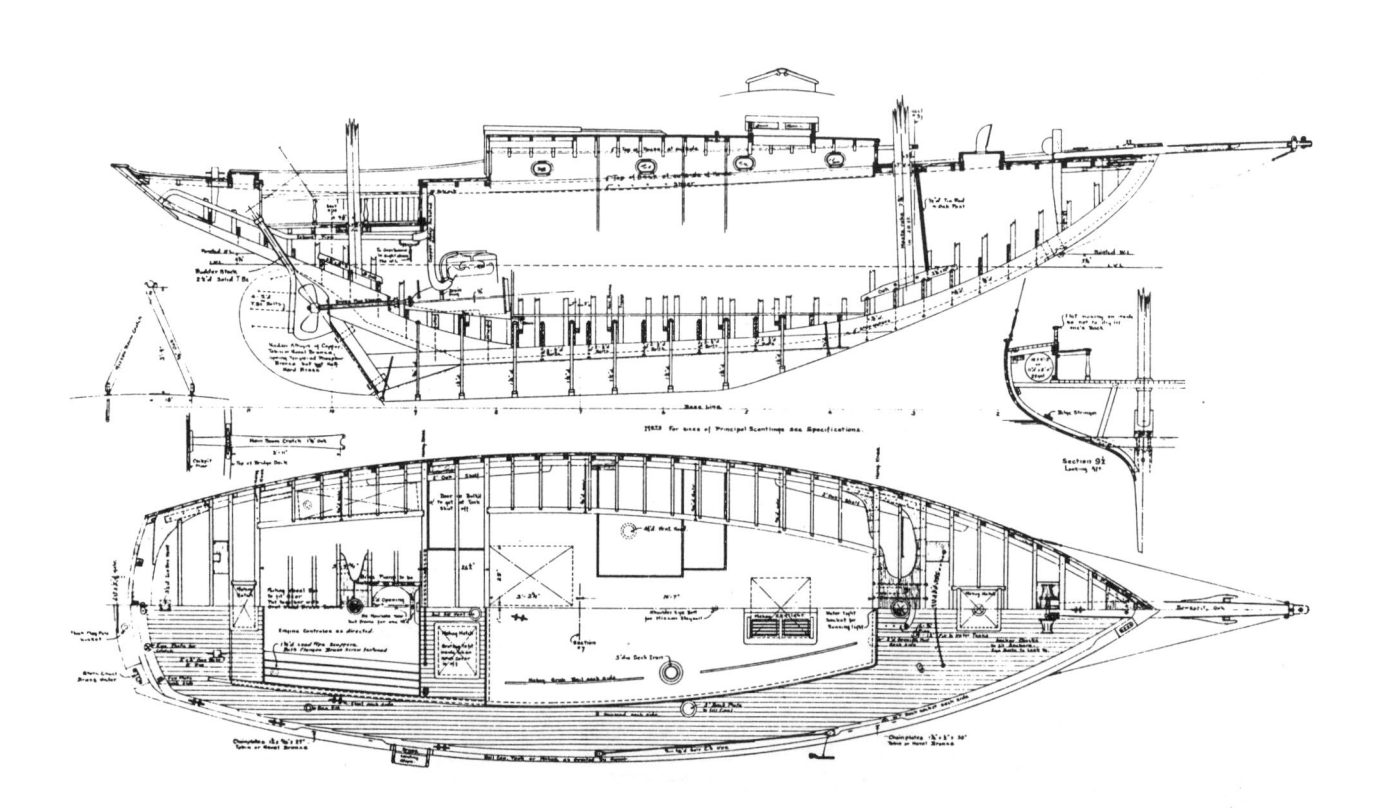

86

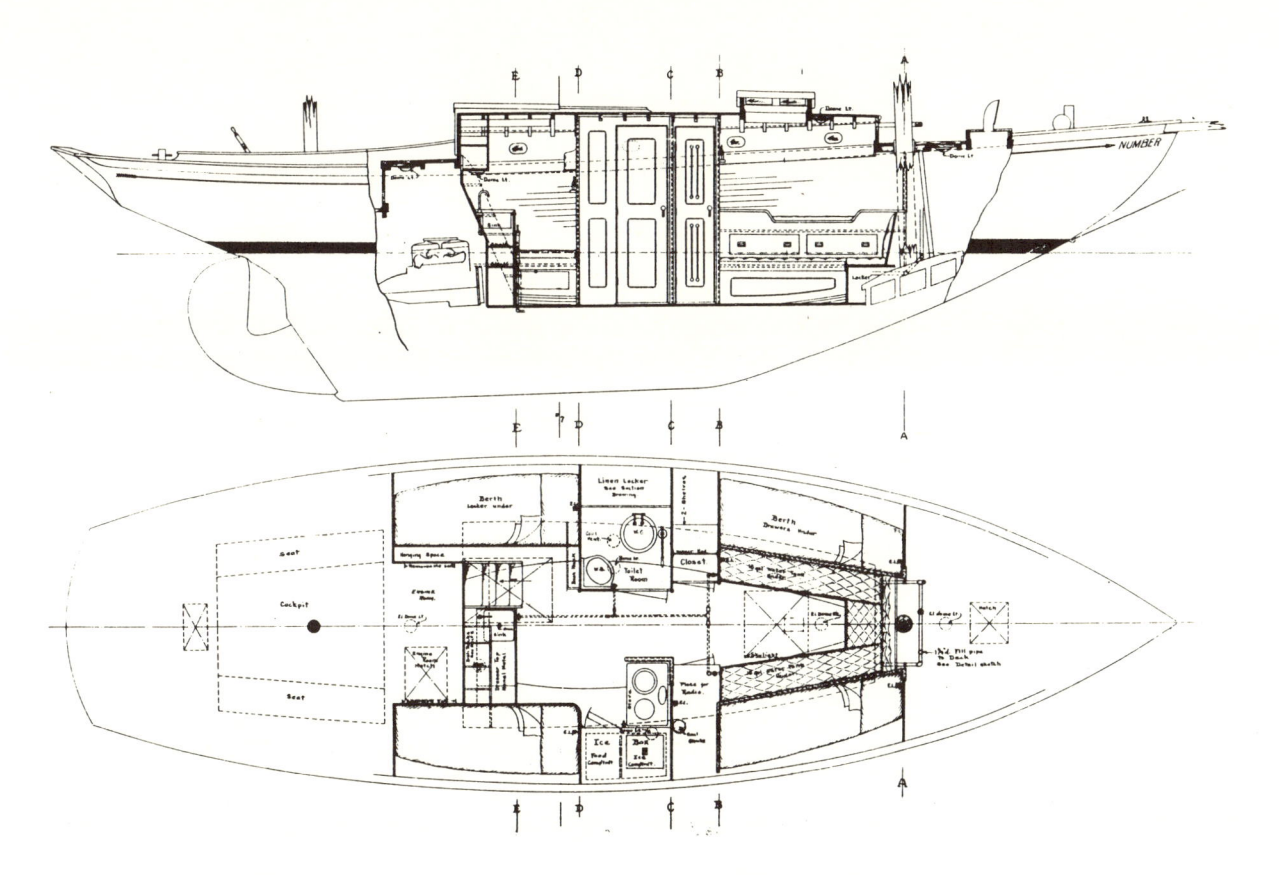

Above: Joloma II's *accommodations, and* **left**, *under sail.*

87

110 AMOS JUDD

Design Number 110
Length Overall: 49 feet
Length on Waterline: 42 feet
Beam: 14 feet
Draft: 4 feet 8 inches
Sail Area: 1250 square feet
Displacement: 41,800 pounds

Amos Judd was built in the winter of 1928 and 1929 by W.J. Reid of Winthrop, Mass., for S.K. Dimock of Hartford, Conn. She had ample accommodations, and with a spacious forecastle for a crew of two with their own trunk cabin, she must have been very comfortable, especially with that deckhouse. The centerboard was entirely below the cabin floor. A four-cylinder Cummins diesel engine gave her a speed of eight knots and, through a hatch in the deckhouse floor, was readily accessible. She was owned at one time by Pop Turner, shown at the wheel.

Here is an excerpt from a letter my father wrote to Dimock, telling him about the delivery trip from New London, Conn., and how the boat performed:

We got down and grub aboard Friday night, and Saturday got underway. It was rather moderate until we got out into Fisher's Island Sound with the wind about westerly, increasing, and it looked as if we were going to have a windy day, and believe me, we did. By about 2 o'clock in the afternoon we were off Newport and Sakonnet, and by that time the sea had had a chnace to make up so that it was really quite heavy. Capt. Bill and Reid estimated it about a 30 mile breeze, and I think it was, judging from other breezes that I have been in when I knew from weather observatories the actual velocity. As I say, the middle of the afternoon it had had a chance to make up quite a sea. Of course, we were running dead before it, which with a great many boats is a difficult point of sailing, hard to keep the boat on course unless you have a spinnaker to set. With this boat we had only the three lowers, and we had everything on her, and do you know she was the most perfect thing in these conditions that I was ever on. Bill Reid said a 100 ft. heavy fishing schooner could not have been better. On most boats you would have torn your arms out trying to keep them on course, but on this boat the only thing you had to guard against was to keep from falling asleep at the wheel, she was so easy, and did not require any helming at all. Once in a while, with an especially heavy surge under her quarter, you might give her half a spoke, but for the majority of the run you just held the wheel steady and the sea would pick her up, she would take a little lurch to windward, slowly, and then when the sea passed under her, and her stern began to drop down, her bow would swing right off onto the course again without any helming. Really, it was wonderful. And how she was going!

We went into Padanaram about 6 o'clock, just dark. We laid there Saturday night, went ashore and got some fresh scallops, and Sunday morning I turned out at 6 o'clock, slept like a log all night. I told the two Bills if they would get the anchor (it was moderate then) and start the motor, I would get breakfast while they were running out up the bay. We got out into the bay and it breezed up pretty well, about so'west, but we were so near to the Canal that we did not bother to put any sail on her. So we let her go under power thro the Canal, and right here let me say that your engine is a wonder. She goes like a train of cars, and really makes a very strong 8 knots, about 8¼ — real knots, not miles. We left Padanaram at just half past six, and we were thru the Canal at half past nine. Now, if that isn't good going, I would like to know. We had the whole day ahead of us so we shut the engine off and put the sail on. We loated along until we got up to Plymouth, when I thought we were going to be becalmed, but while we were down to dinner it breezed up so'west and we had a wonderful sail to Winthrop. We got into Winthrop at 5 o'clock in the afternoon. How she would reach along. A so'wester along that shore is apt to be puffy, but when the puffs would strike her she would just settle down and start to go. Gosh, she feels great, stiff as a church, and how she would foot along. I know you are going to be crazy about her, and she will make a wonderful boat for your purpose because she sails right side up, and she can't possibly scare anybody. We

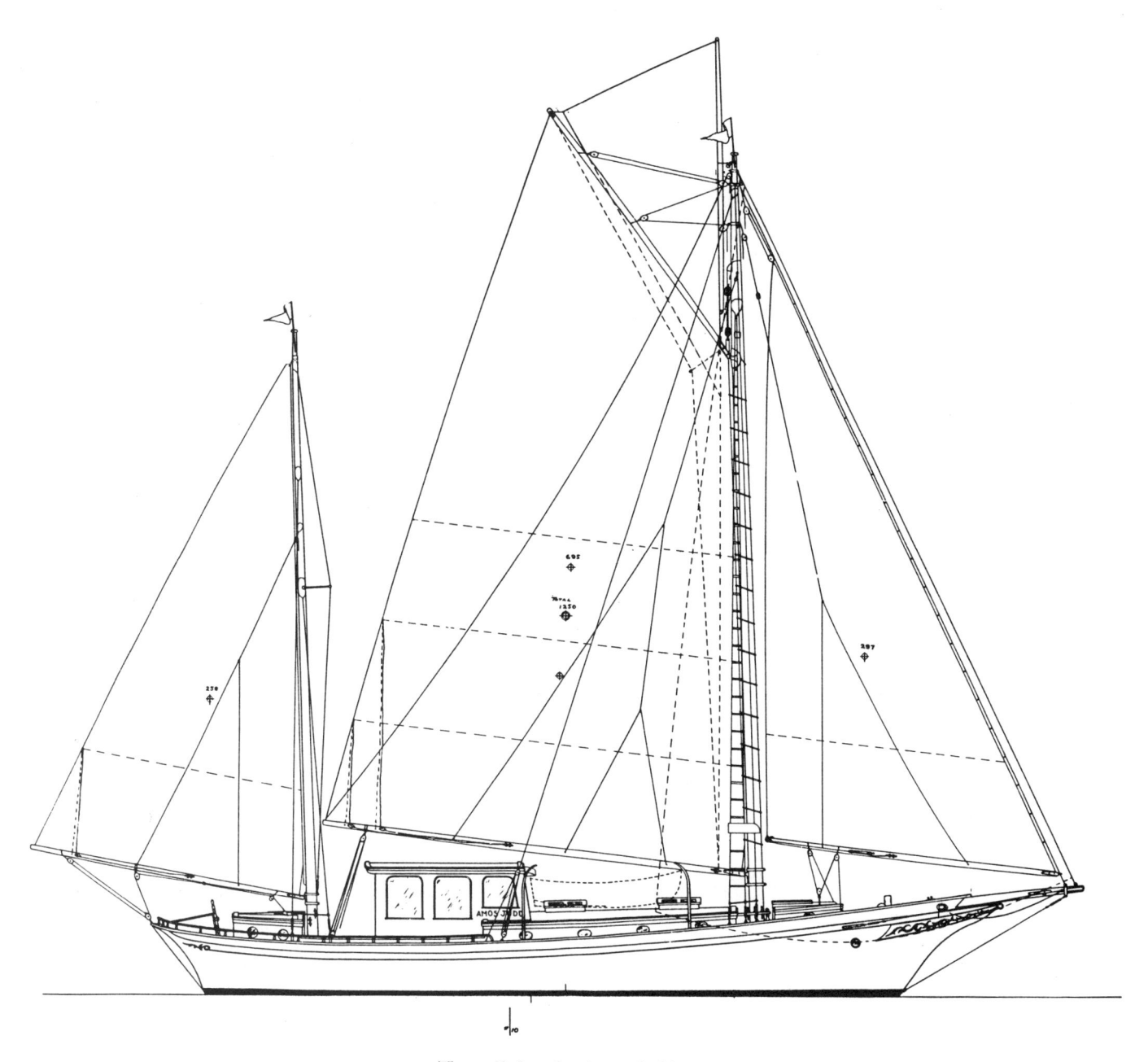

The sailplan for Amos Judd.

passed an Alden marconi ketch between Minot and Nantasket that would roll way out of water when a puff hit her, and she did not seem to be going any, and there we were steamboating, a puff would hit us and we would just simply start ahead. Bill said he never saw any boat of her size that would feel a little puff the way she would and turn it into forward energy instead of just laying over.

Another thing I want to tell you is that in all that heavy going Saturday, the twisting motion that a boat gets under those conditions was absolutely absent. You couldn't hear a sound anywhere in the boat. She is solid as a rock. Capt. Bill says he has pumped her since he had her about every two weeks, getting perhaps 3 or 4 buckets out. Saturday morning, before we started, I pumped her myself (she had not been pumped for a week) and I got about 4 strokes before she sucked air, so I would call her absolutely tight.

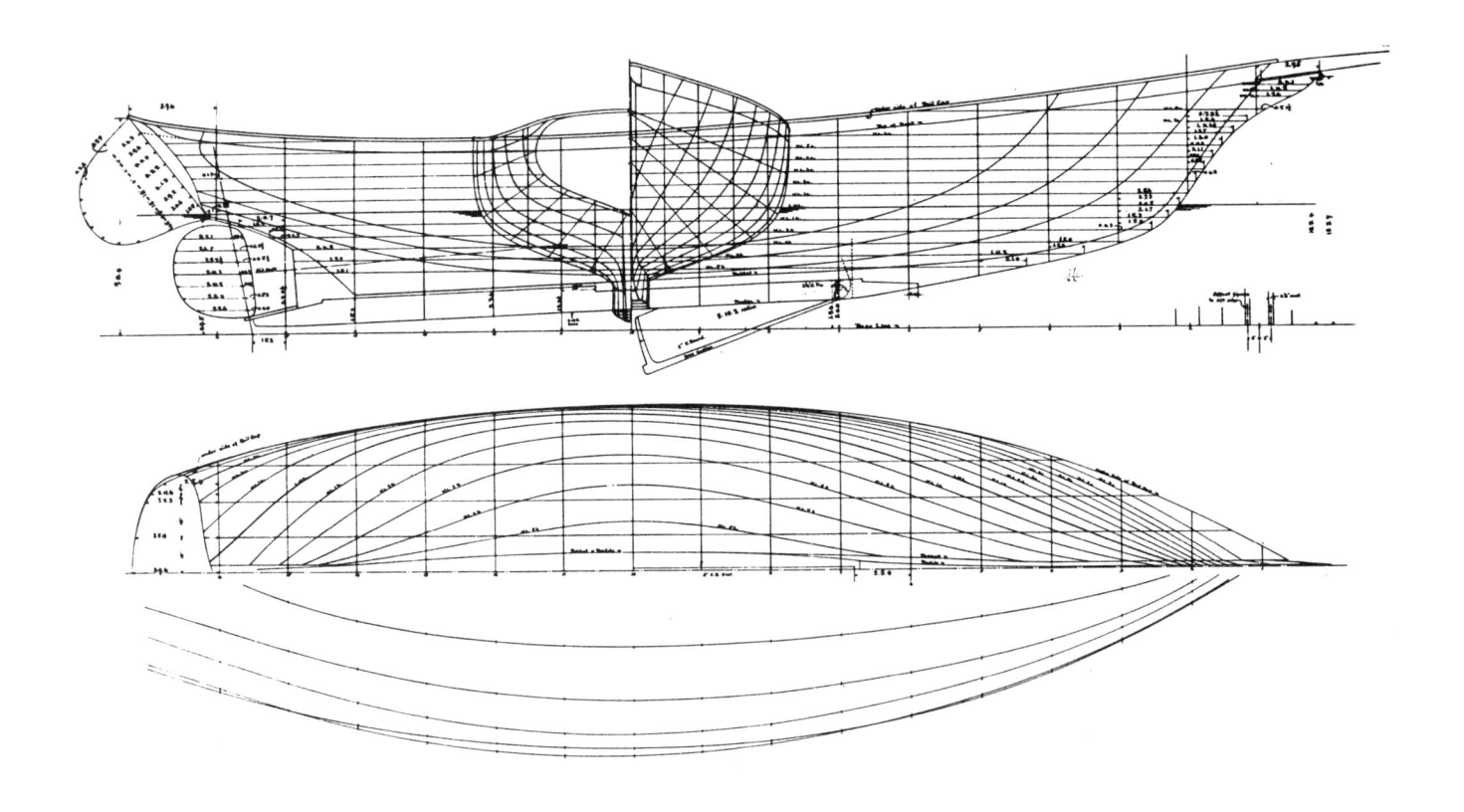

The lines for Amos Judd *and her construction drawings.*

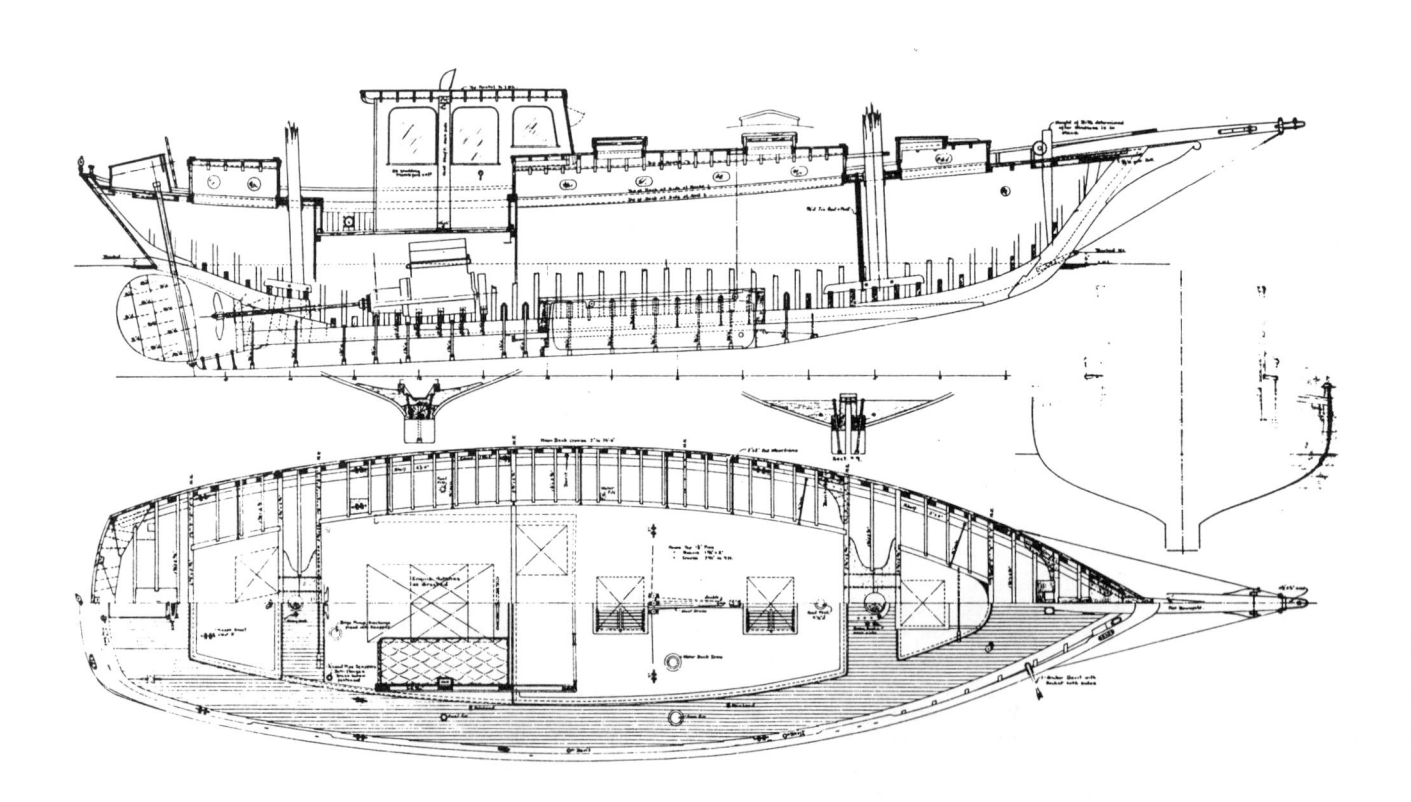

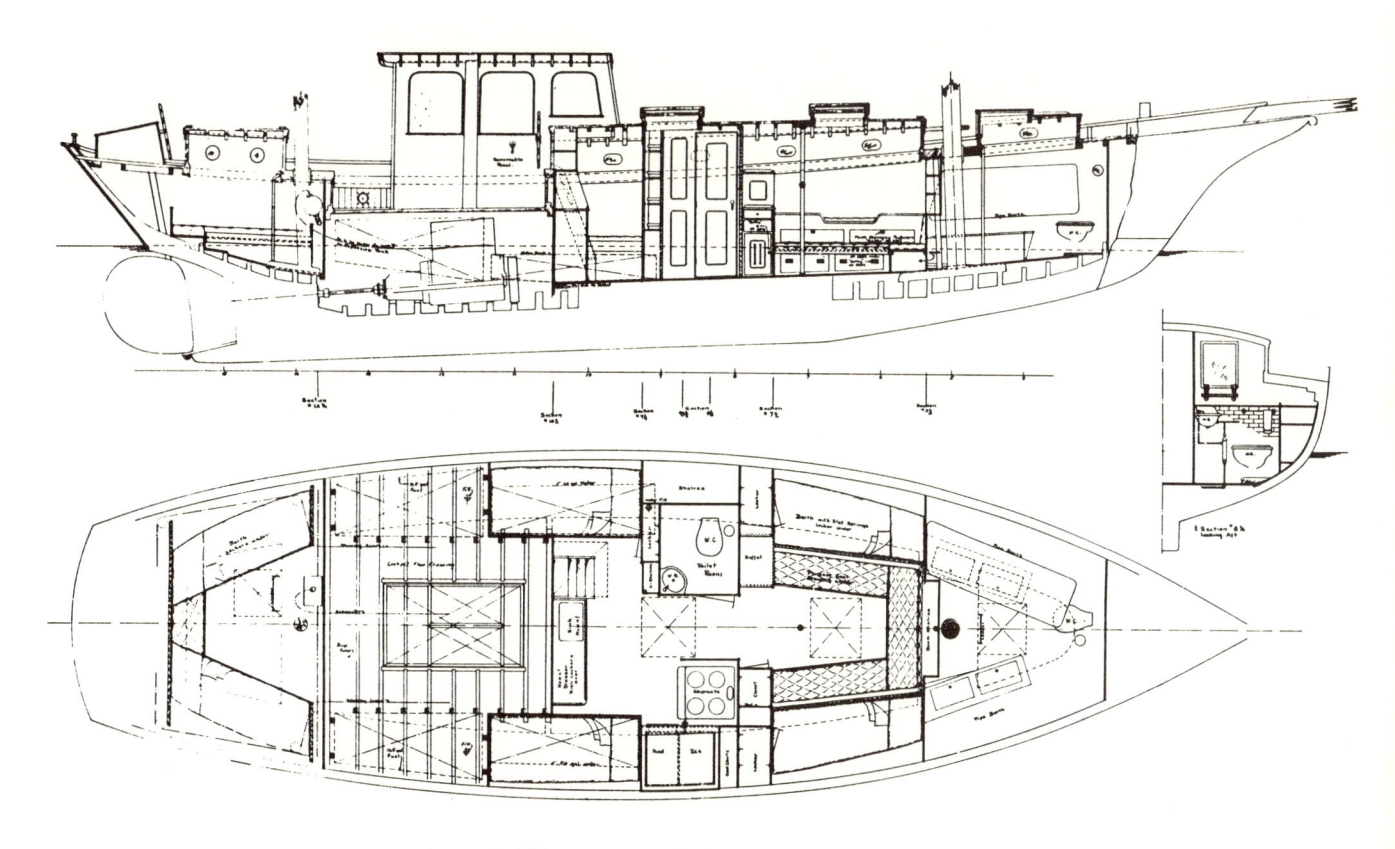

Amos Judd's *accommodations plans and under sail.*

113 FEARLESS

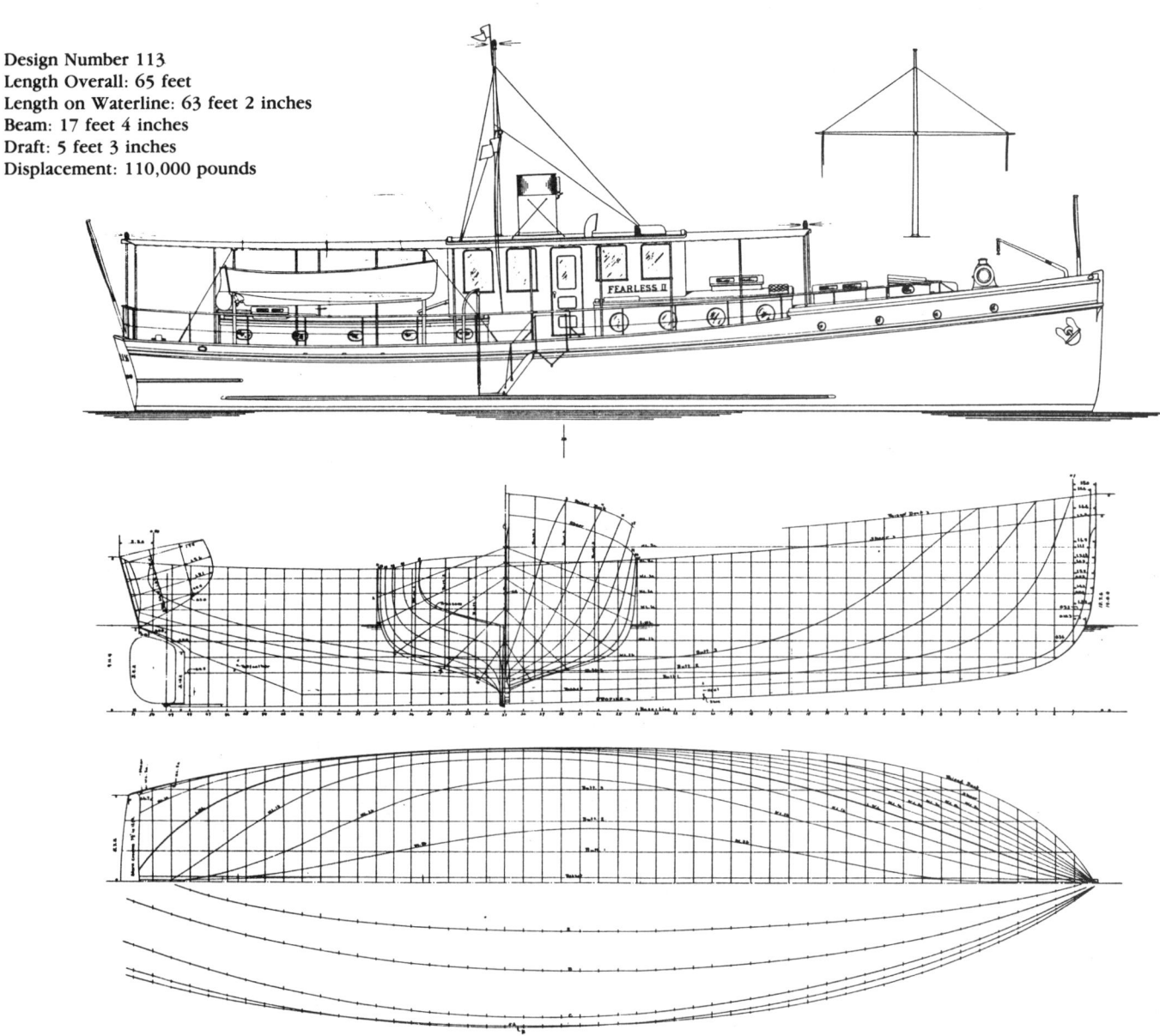

Design Number 113
Length Overall: 65 feet
Length on Waterline: 63 feet 2 inches
Beam: 17 feet 4 inches
Draft: 5 feet 3 inches
Displacement: 110,000 pounds

Number 113's profile and her lines drawings.

Fearless II was a twin-screw diesel cruiser built at W.J. Reid's at the same time as *Amos Judd*. She was another boat for E.B. Phillips of Georges Mills, N.H. Similar in type and construction to the larger Boston beam trawlers of the times, planked with hard pine on double-sawn oak timbers on 15-inch centers, she had probably three times the displacement of the average cruiser of the same length. She had hot and cold running water under pressure, hot water heat in all compartments, and with 1,000 gallons of fuel was capable of extended cruises. She carried a motor launch on one side and sailing tender on the other. Cruising speed was 12 m.p.h. She was eventually sold to a party on the West Coast.

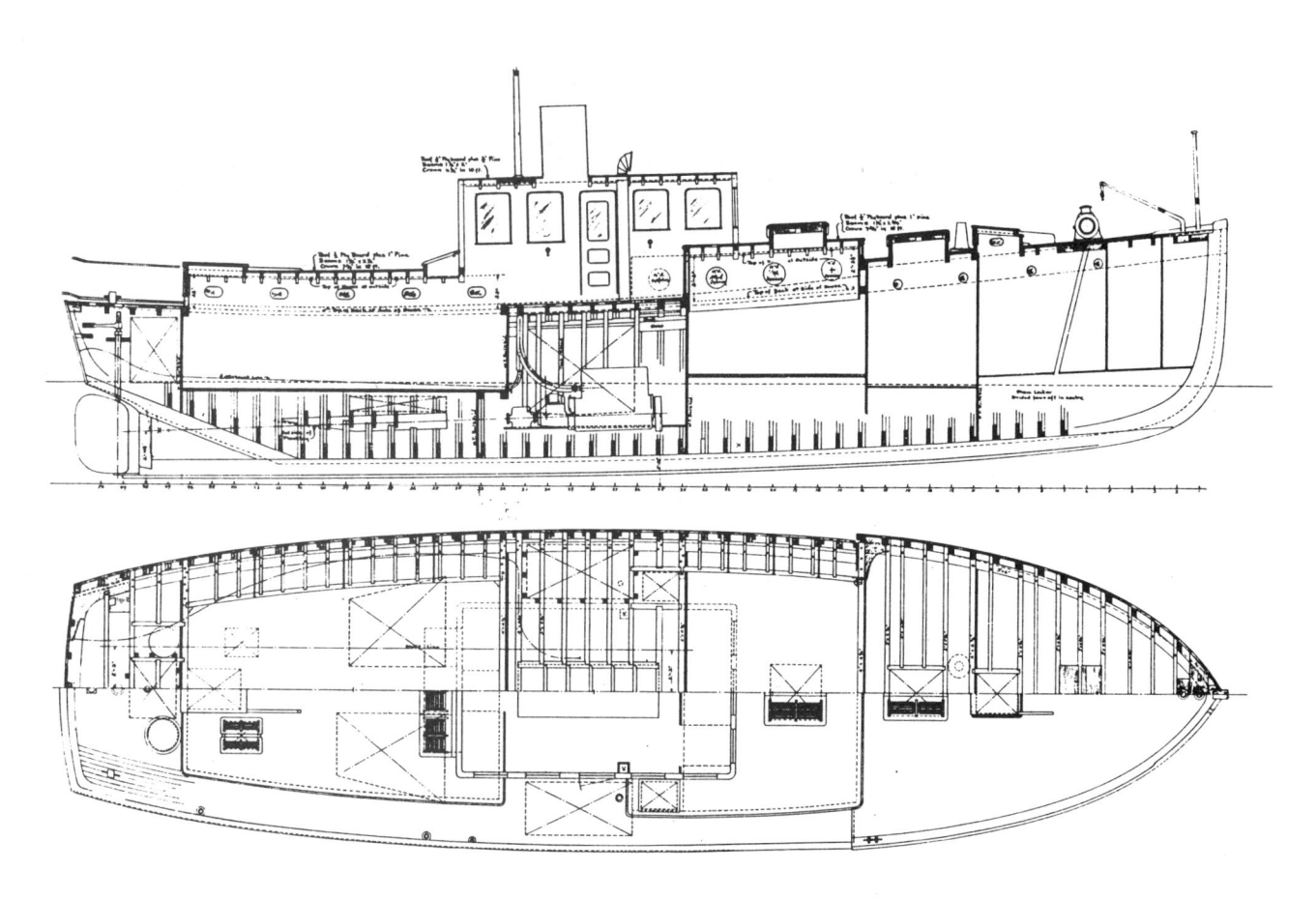

The construction plans for number 113 and her accommodations plans.

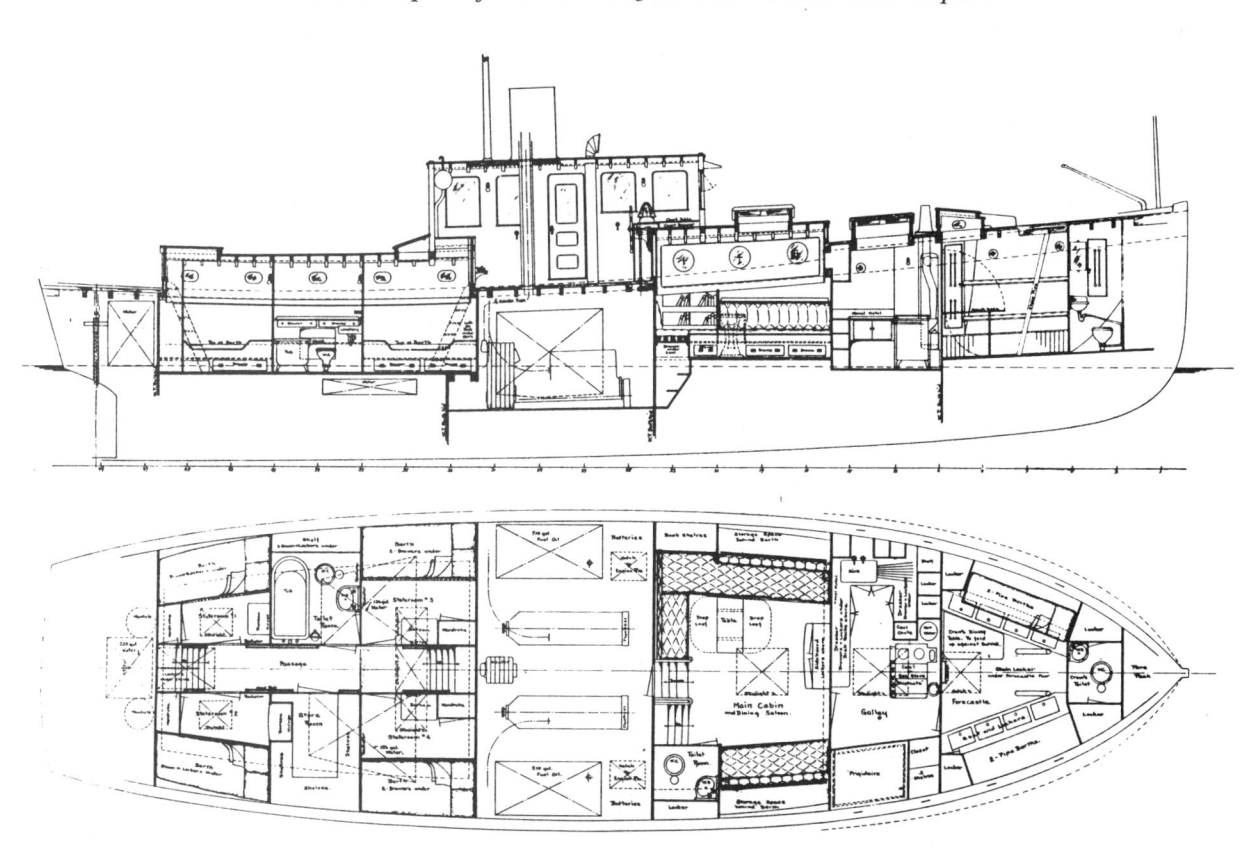

115 RETRIEVER

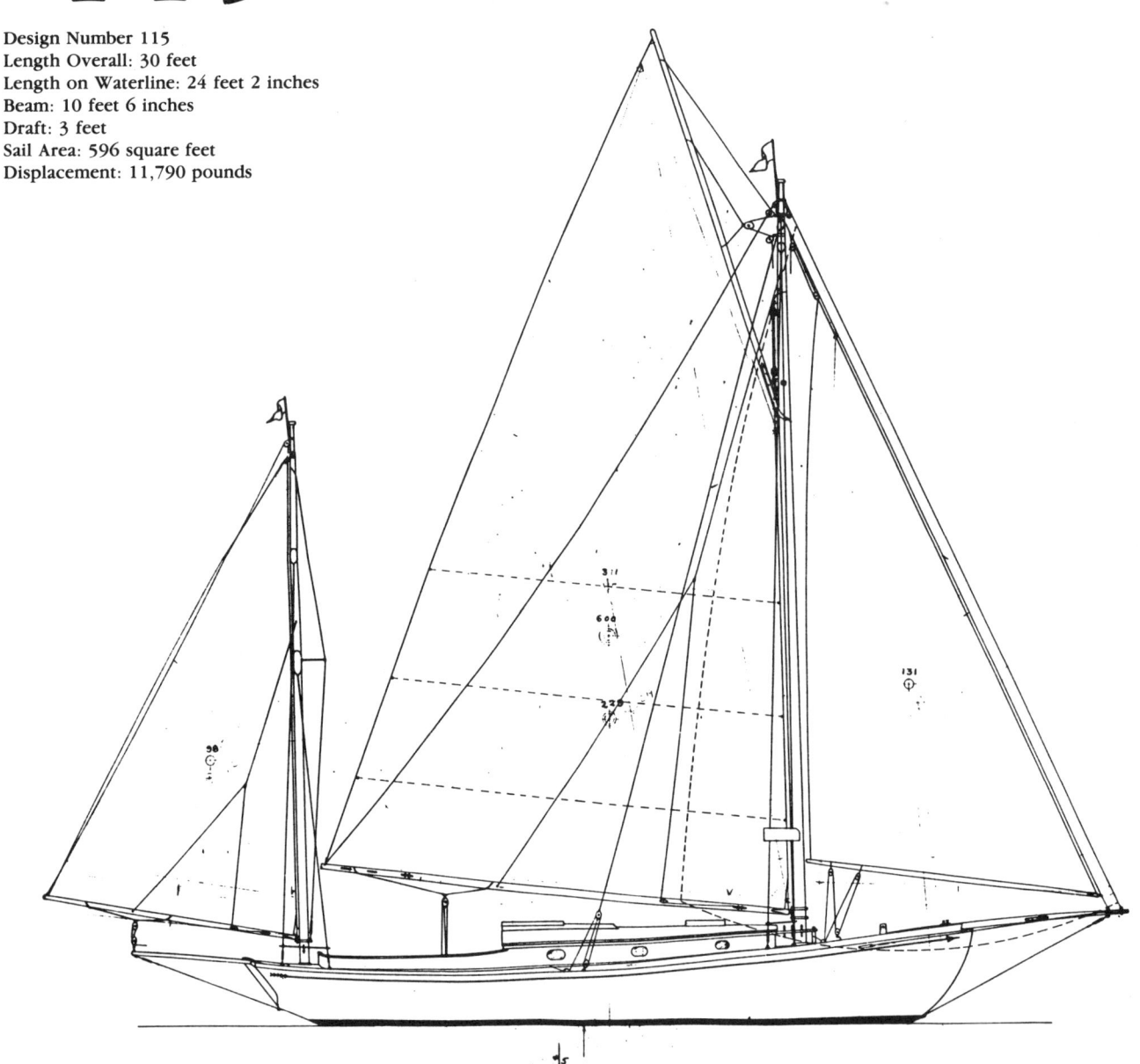

Design Number 115
Length Overall: 30 feet
Length on Waterline: 24 feet 2 inches
Beam: 10 feet 6 inches
Draft: 3 feet
Sail Area: 596 square feet
Displacement: 11,790 pounds

Retriever's sailplan.

Retriever was a well-known shoal-draft yawl built for Arthur Rotch of Marblehead, Mass., by S.F. McFarland of South Bristol, Me., in 1929. She was a smart and comfortable sailer with a winning race record, including Class B in the Jeffrey's Ledge Race of 1932. Auxiliary power was provided by a Gray 4-40.

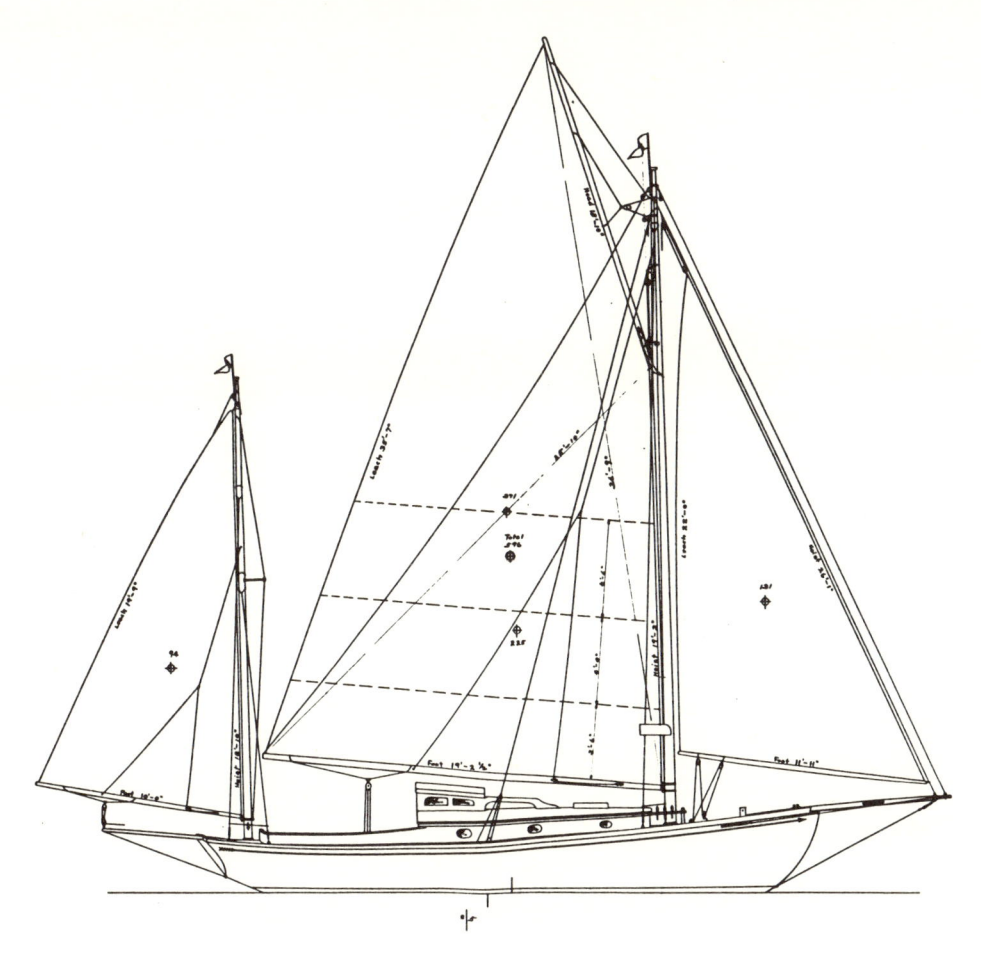

Number 115's sailplan — Note the addition of the doghouse in this profile, and her lines drawings.

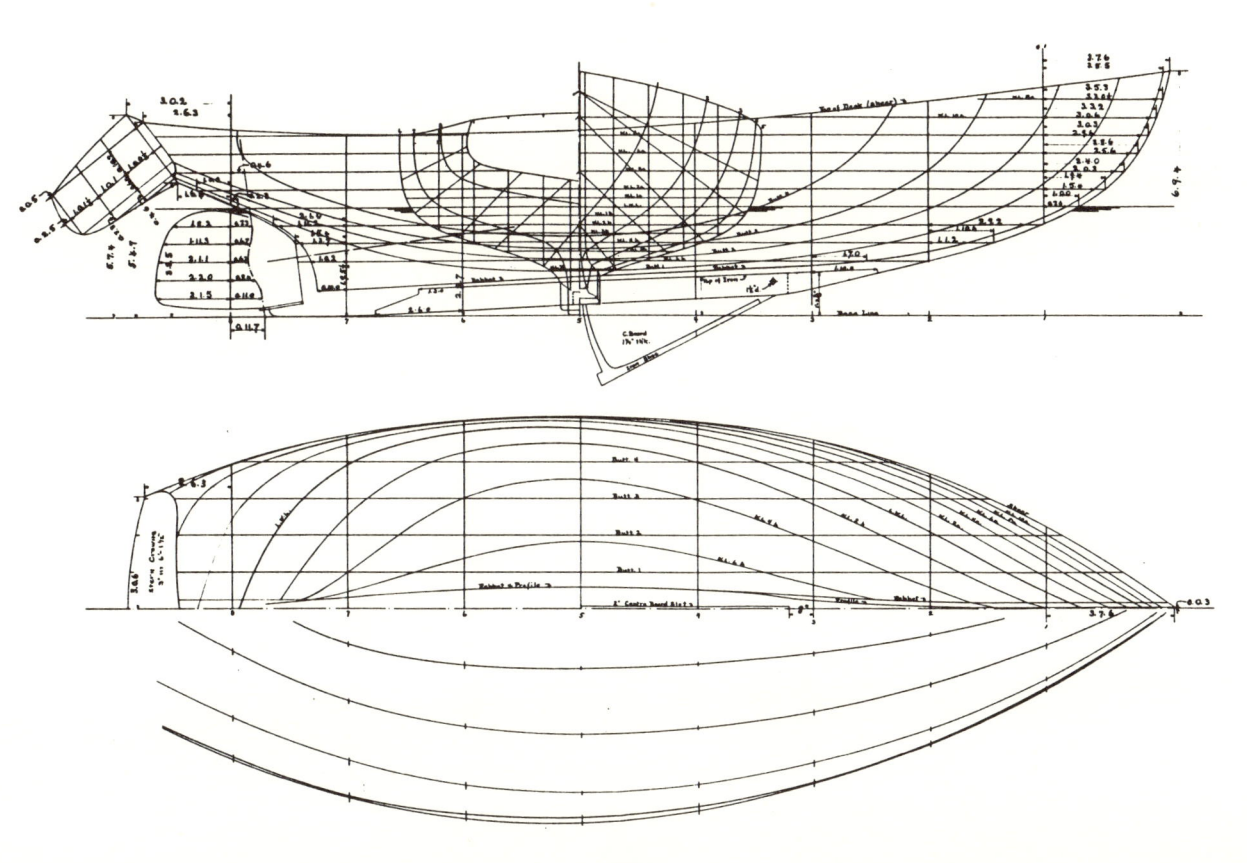

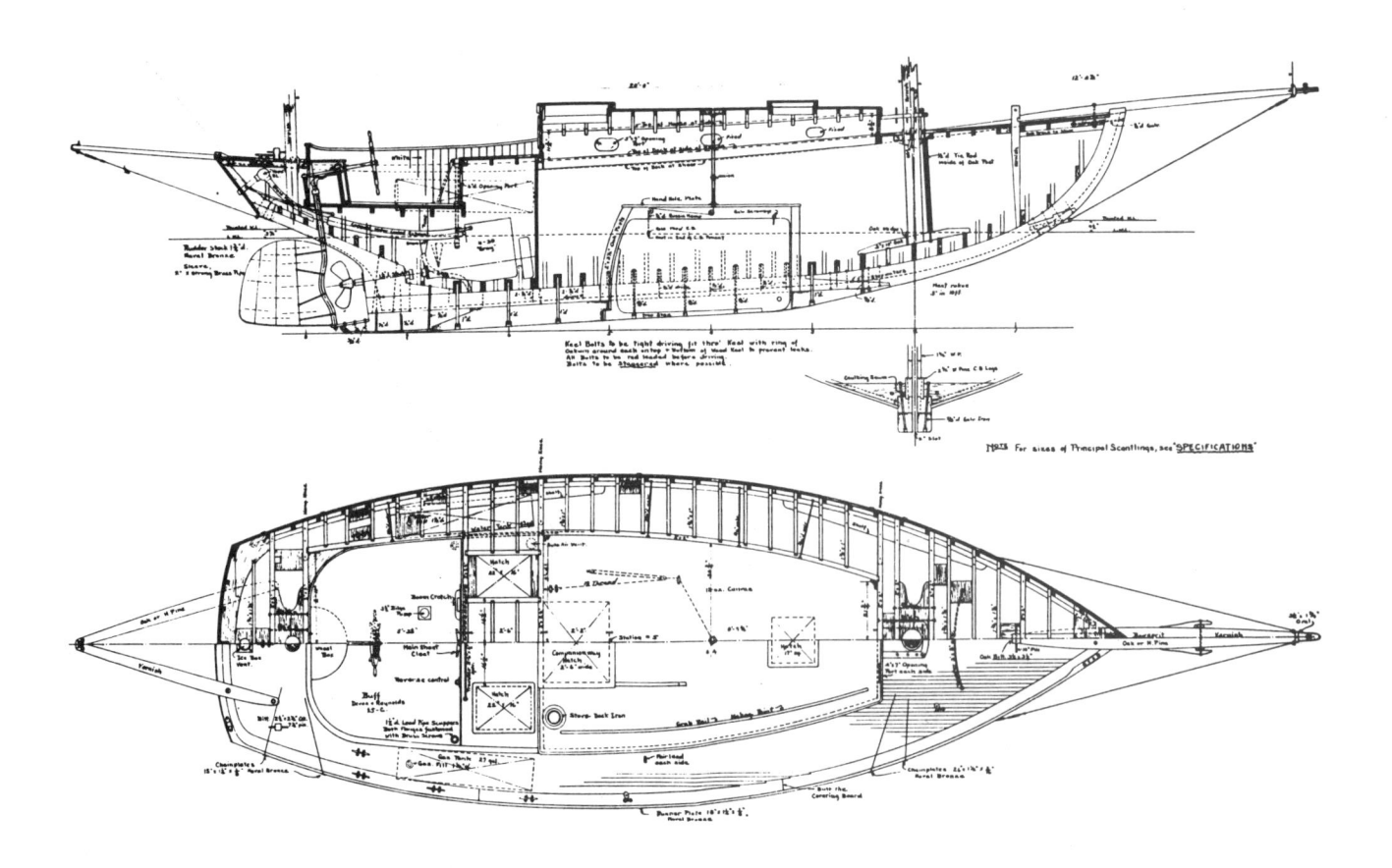

Number 115's construction drawings and her accommodations plans.

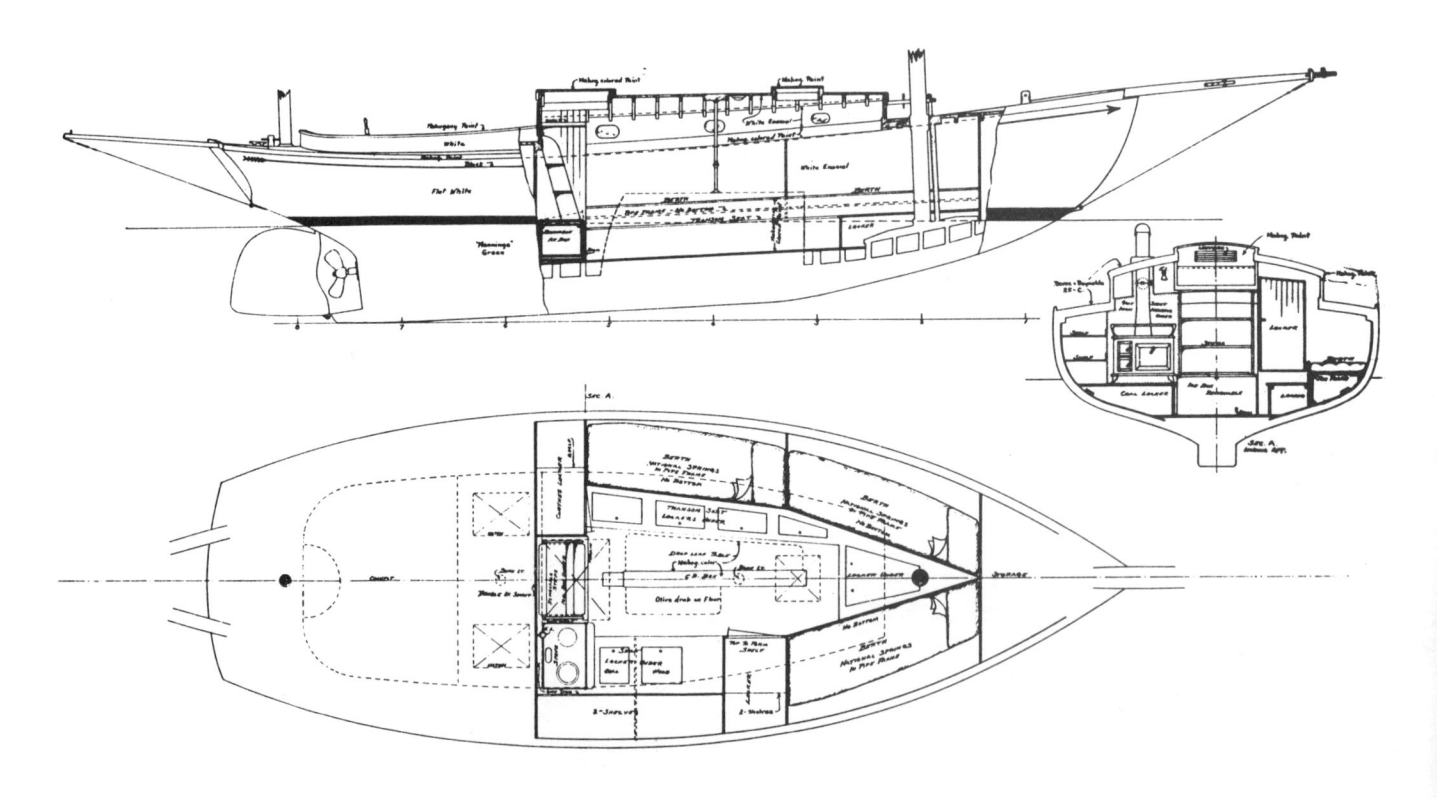

Retriever *enjoying a pleasant sail*.

122 VAGRANT

Design Number 122
Length Overall: 47 feet
Length on Waterline: 32 feet
Beam: 12 feet
Draft: 6 feet
Sail Area: 1066 square feet
Displacement: 32,000 pounds

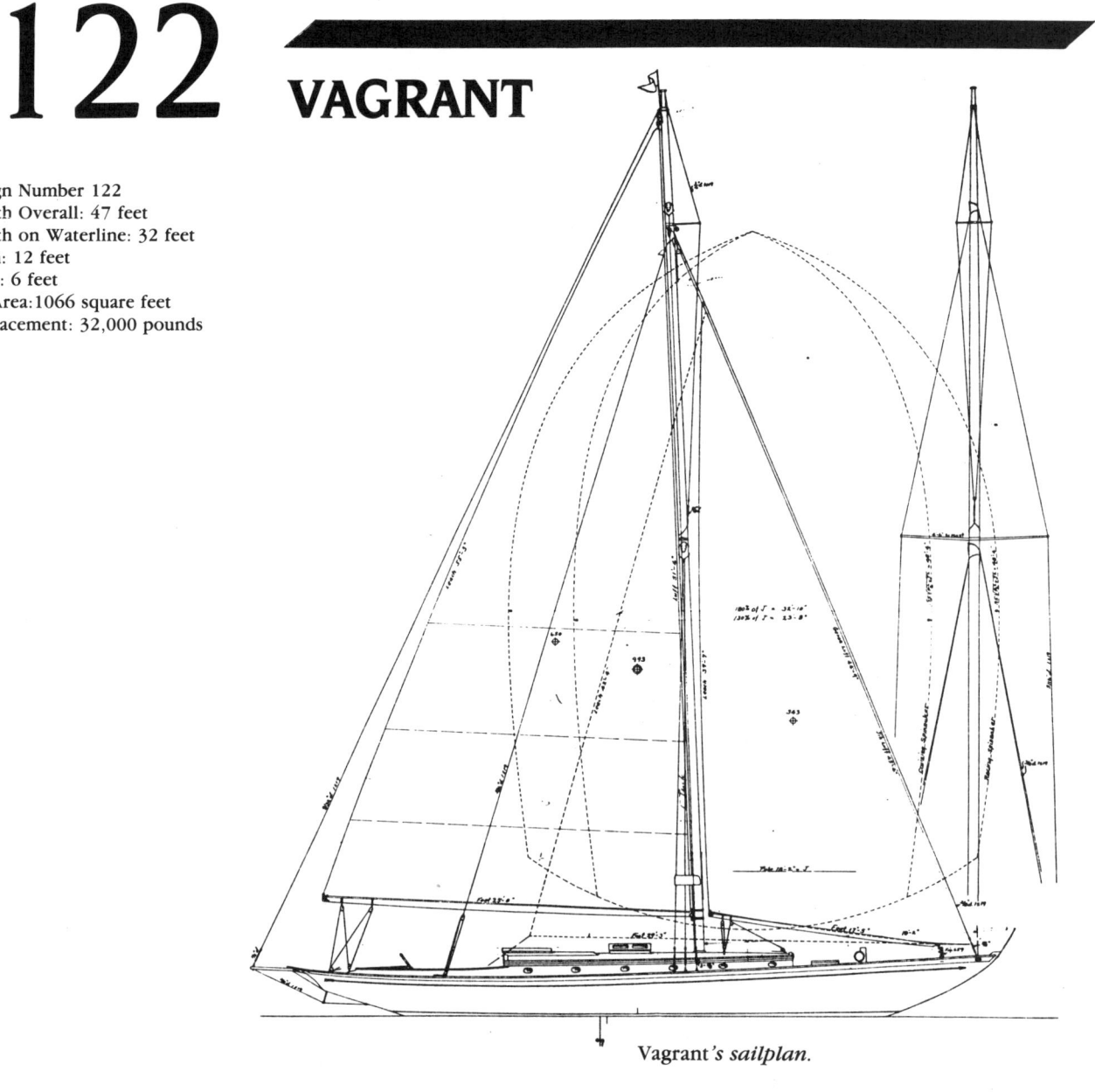

Vagrant's sailplan.

    Vagrant was launched in 1930 for then Commodore of the Cruising Club of America William H. Coolidge of Manchester, Mass. She was built in W.H. Reid's yard in Winthrop, Mass. She is still in existence and can be seen as you drive north on I-95: Just as you cross the bridge from Portsmouth, N.H., into Kittery, Me., she is the boat under covers on the right.
    Vagrant had several owners and won a lot of races including the Chicago-Mackinac in 1934. In 1942 she was sold to a man in Washington, D.C., who, on his first cruise, had a collision with a tramp steamer and was sunk in 60 feet of water. After she was raised and repaired, L. Mortimer Pratt owned her and used her in Manchester and Maine. Her present owner is restoring her and has decks and superstructure all recovered with glass. I hope he has the perseverence to complete the job, because she certainly was a nice boat.

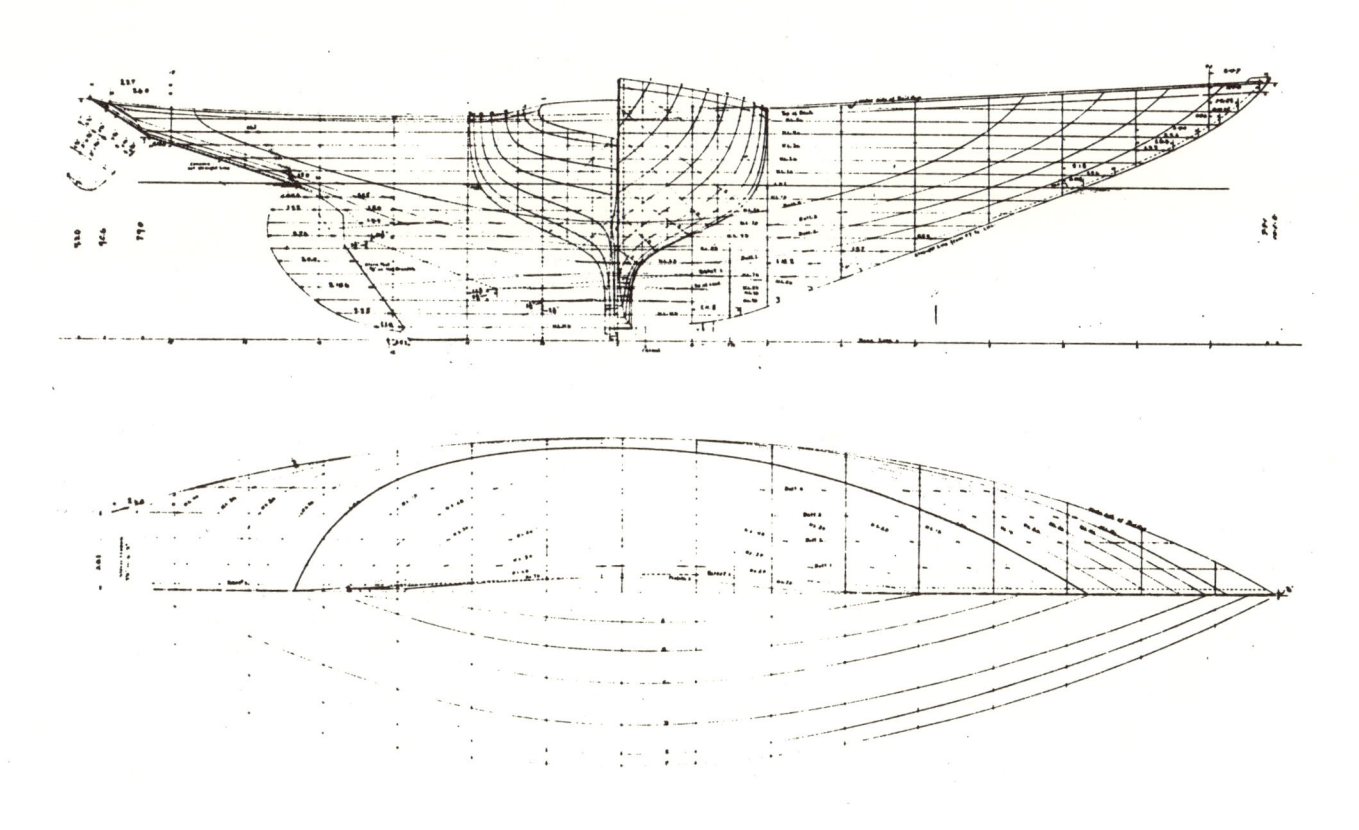

Vagrant's *lines* and her construction drawings.

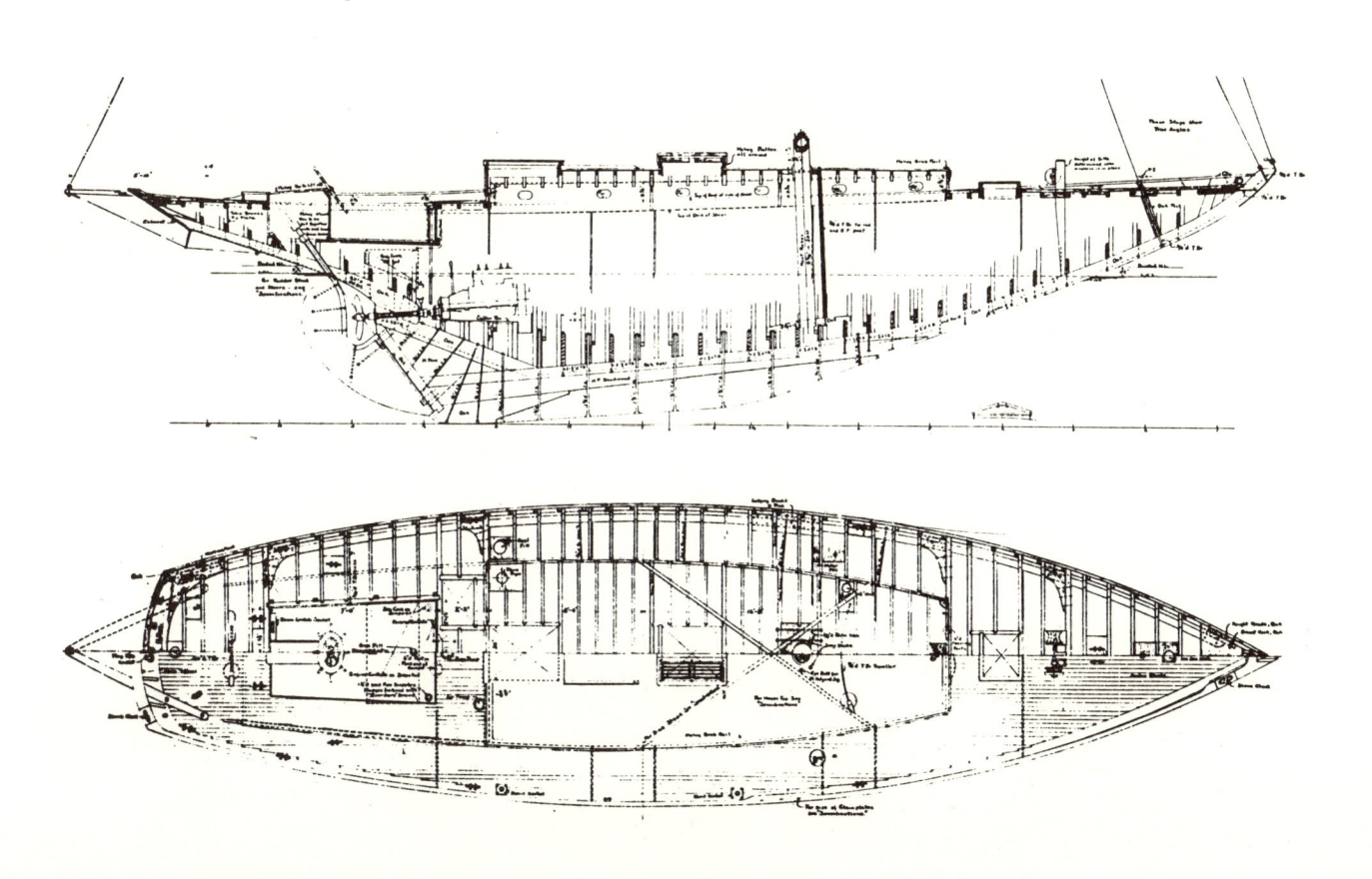

99

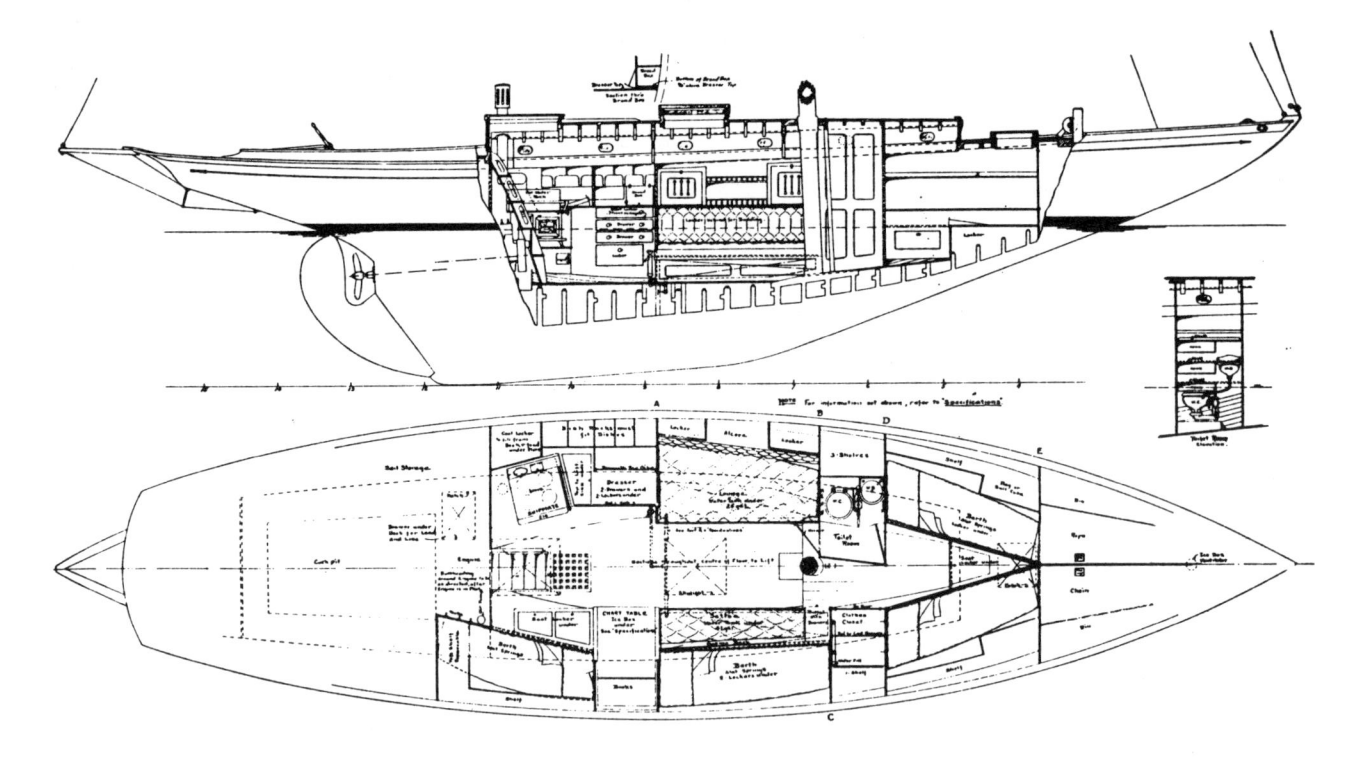

Above and right: Vagrant's *accommodations plans* and Vagrant *under sail.*

SEA CREST 125

Design Number 125
Length Overall: 37 feet
Length on Waterline: 29 feet 4 inches
Beam: 11 feet 9 inches
Draft: 4 feet
Sail Area: 806 square feet
Displacement: 20,000 pounds

Sea Crest's *sailplan*.

    This design was done in the winter of 1929-1930. At least four of them were built through 1937.

    Sea Crest, built in 1936 by V. Cole in Portland, Me., for C.C. Emerson, is probably the best known boat of this design. She was owned by Dr. Paul B. Sheldon in 1937, who made many cruises north along the Labrador coast. On one of these cruises, she ran up on an uncharted rock and was left high and dry as the tide went out. Luckily, the rock was fairly flat and level on top, and *Sea Crest* was able to balance on the flat of her keel until the tide returned. I guess the doctor was pretty happy with her, because in a letter to another man contemplating building a boat in 1961 he stated, "After having owned no other boat in 25 years or nearly that, if I lost her I'd hope to duplicate her. Sam Crocker's boat has been just right. Three times to Bermuda, once from Maine to Florida and the rest you know about."

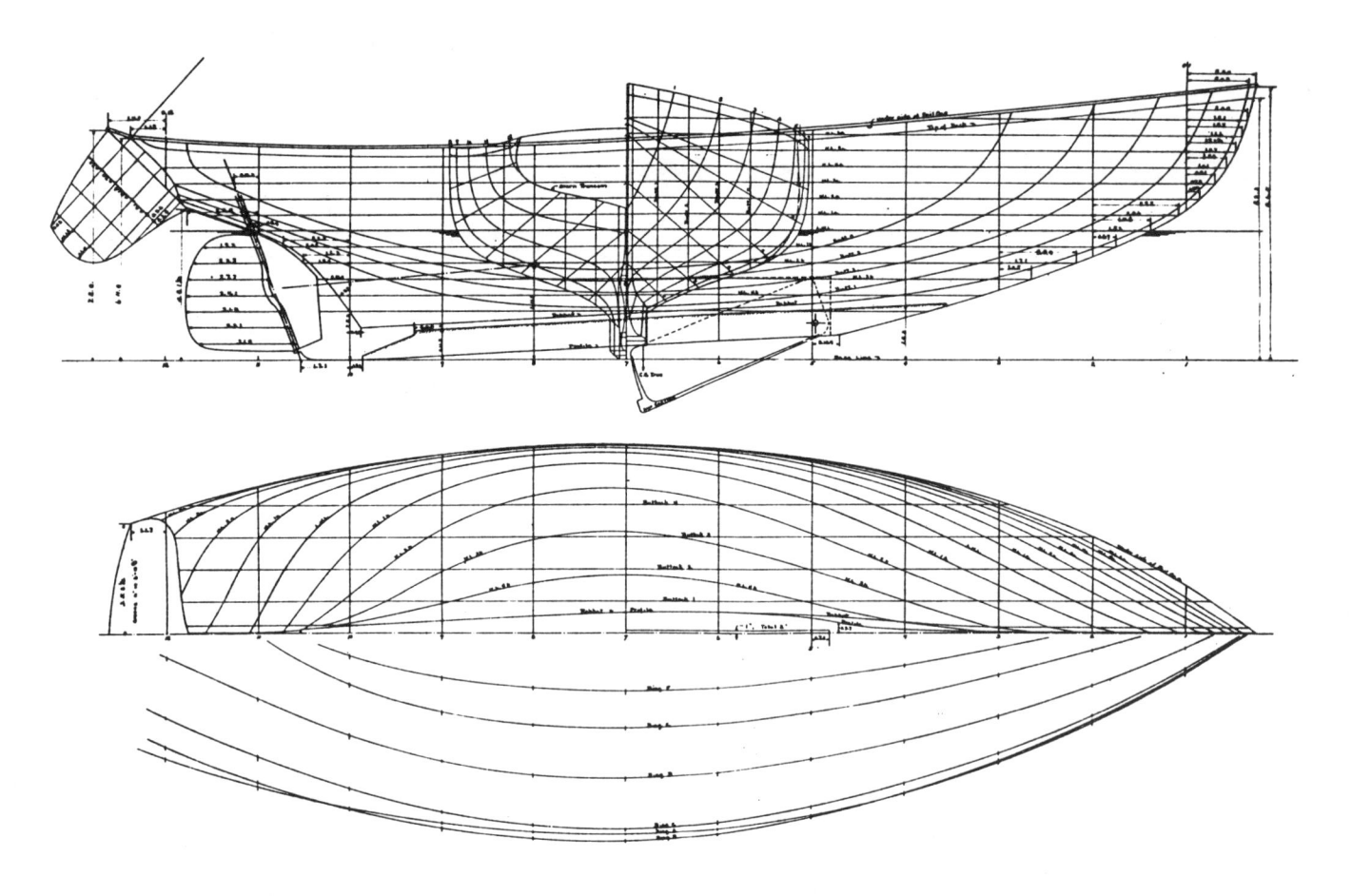

Sea Crest's *lines drawings* and her construction plans.

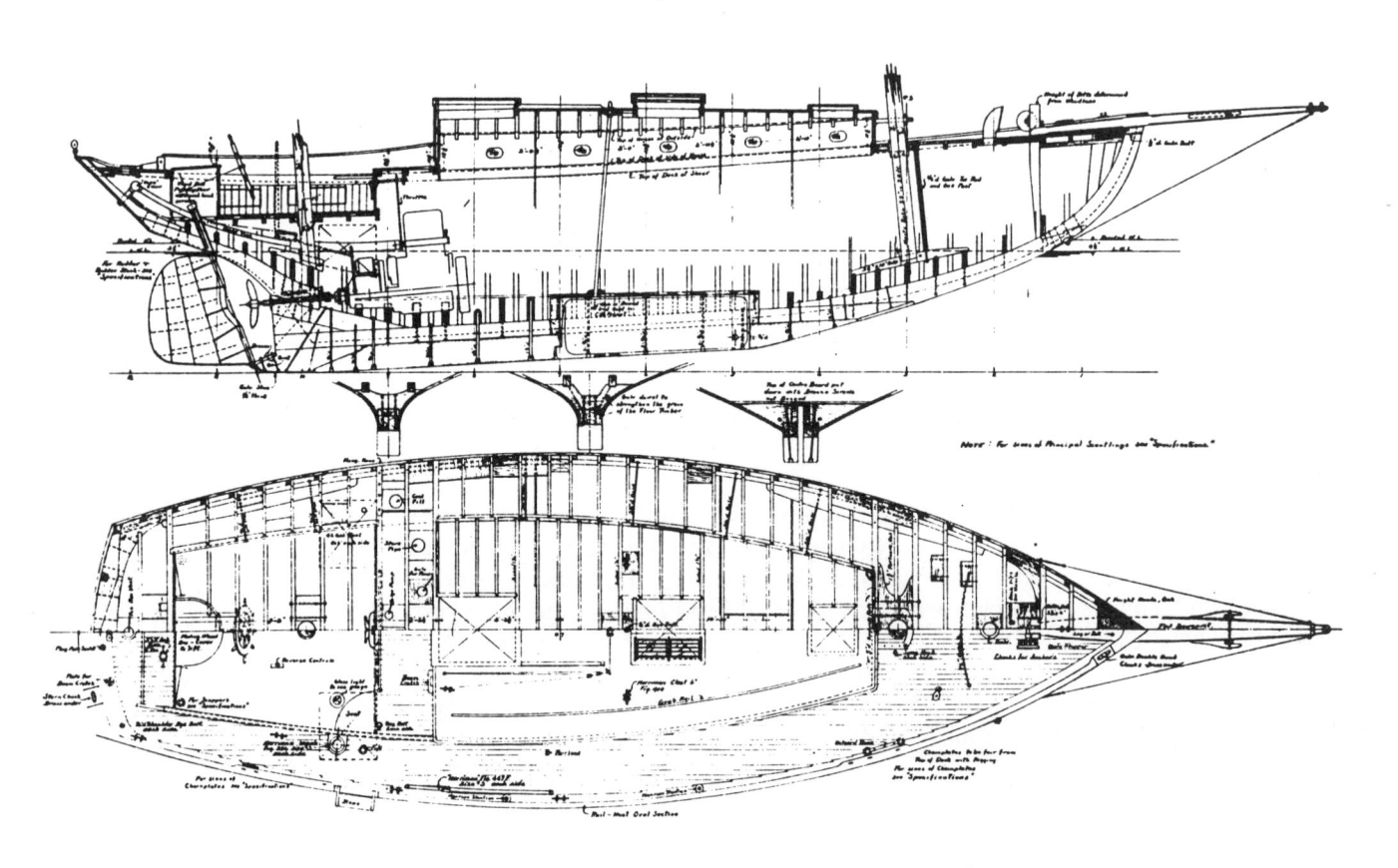

Sea Crest's accommodations drawings.

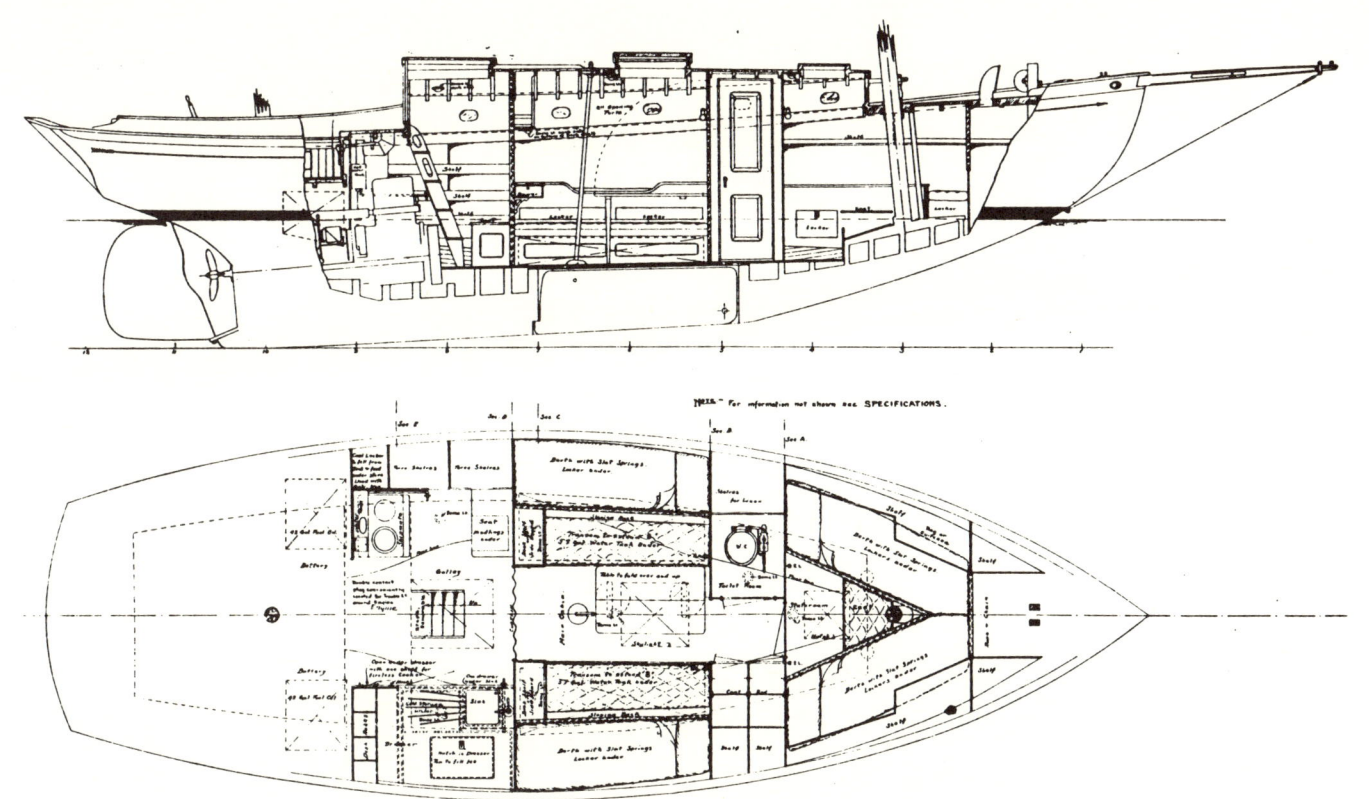

Sea Crest high and dry somewhere in Labrador! Photograph courtesy of Dr. Paul B. Sheldon.

The Cruising Club of America awarded a Blue Water Medal to *Sea Crest* and Sheldon. Part of the citation reads:

Dr. Paul B. Sheldon of the Cruising Club of America has cruised for sixteen years, 1947-1962, on the coasts of Labrador and Newfoundland and adjacent waters. He has made 24 crossings of Cabot Strait, ten passages through the Straits of Belle Isle, and circumnavigated Newfoundland twice. He has made four cruises to Labrador. One included Lake Hamilton as far as Goose Bay, one as far as Port Manvers, and on two Saglek Bay was reached. The longer cruises averaged about two thousand miles.

128 CHARITY

Design Number 128
Length Overall: 46 feet
Length on Waterline: 34 feet 1 inch
Beam: 12 feet
Draft: 6 feet 3 inches
Sail Area: 1226 square feet
Displacement: 32,300 pounds

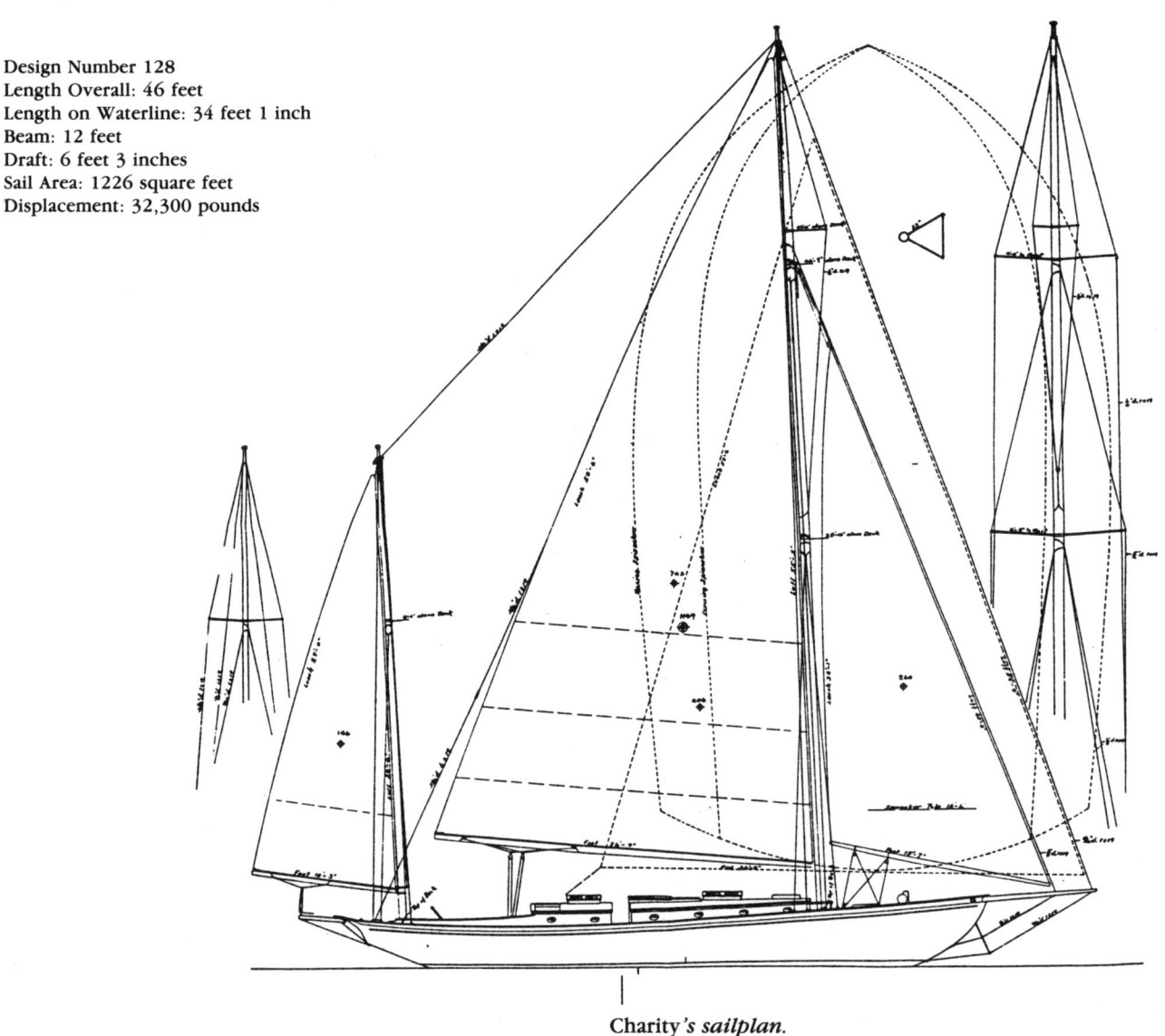

Charity's *sailplan*.

Charity was launched at W.J. Reid's in 1930 for G.B. Hollister and proved a comfortable cruising boat and able sailer. She won the New Bedford Race Week in 1930, 1931, and 1932 as well as the Whaler's Race out of Padanaram in 1933. I know about that one, because I was aboard. Soon after daybreak on the way back from rounding Block Island, we were assured that a win was inevitable. An old timer we had aboard as a guest pulled off his boot to show he had accidentally put one of his socks on inside out. Said it was a sure sign. The photo, taken in the Crocker Memorial Race of 1984, shows her looking not too different than she did more than 50 years earlier.

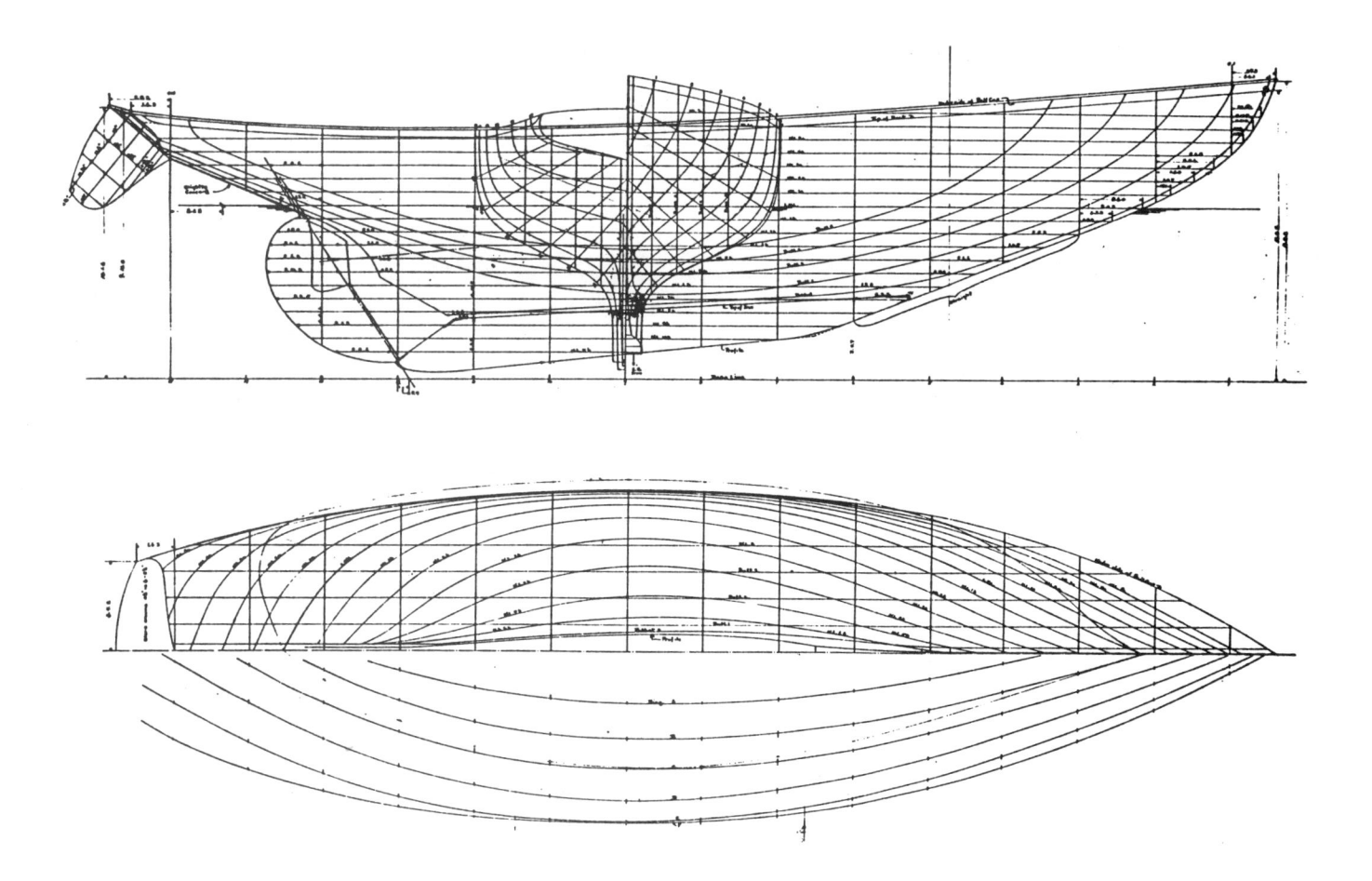

The lines for number 128 and her construction drawings.

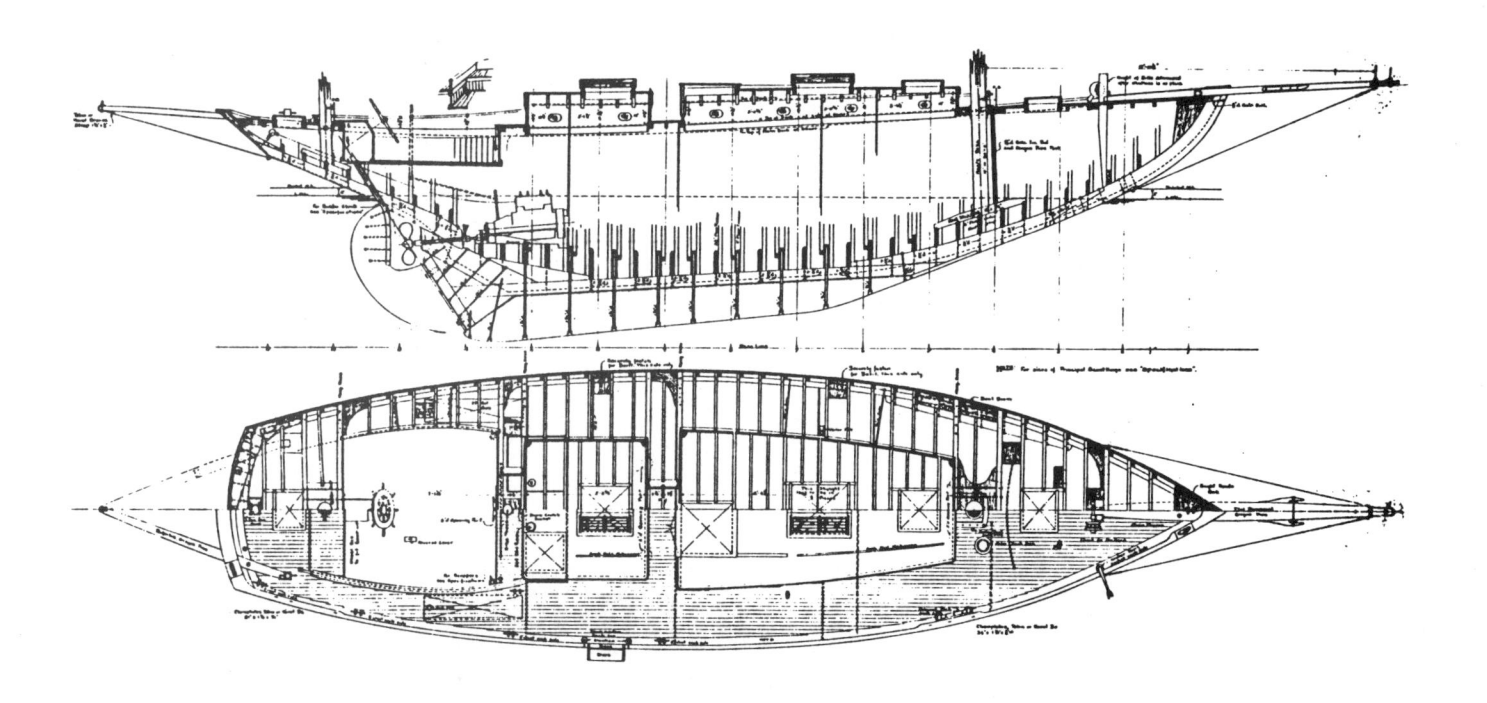

105

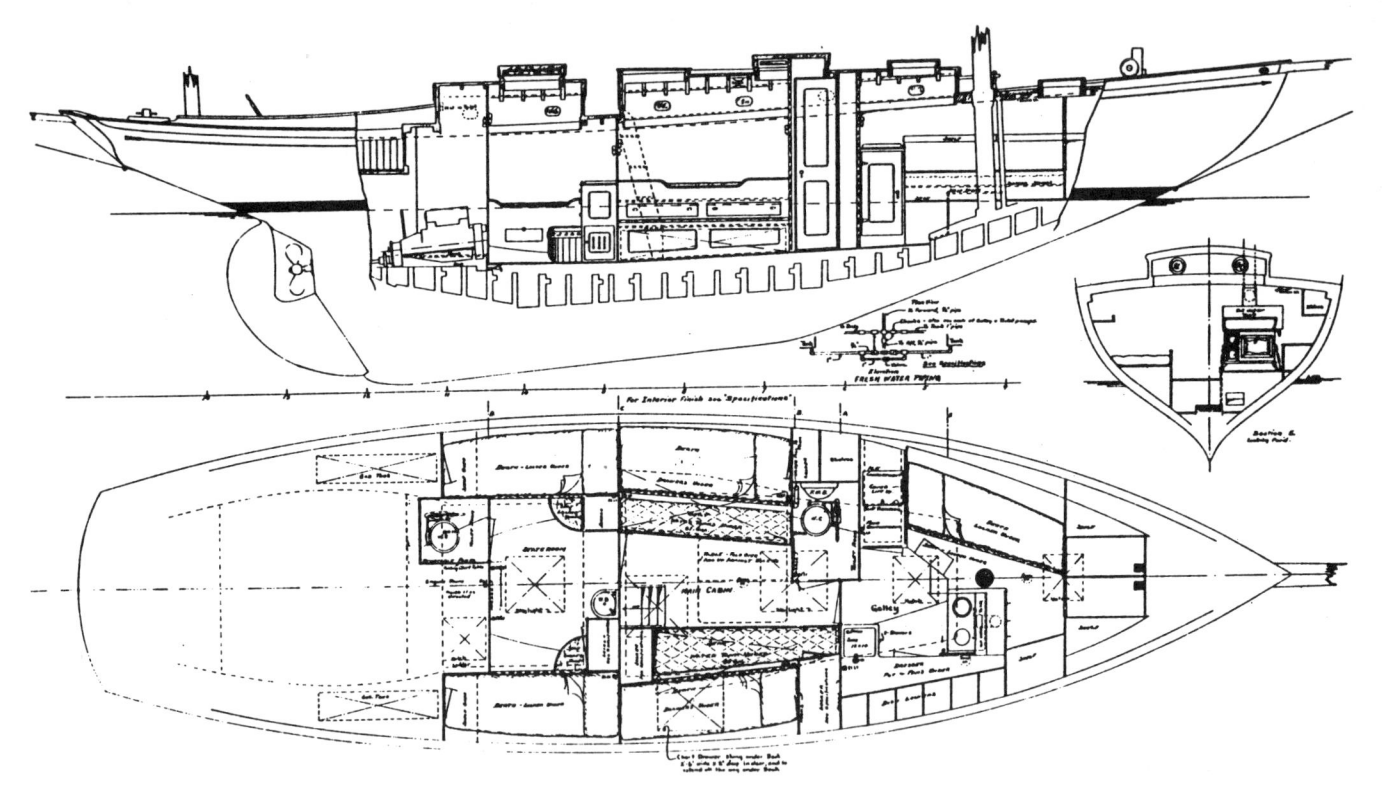

Above and right: *The interior plans for* Charity *and as she appeared in the 1984 Crocker Memorial Race.*

MAHDEE 131

Design Number 131
Length Overall: 53 feet 3 inches
Length on Waterline: 45 feet 11 inches
Beam: 14 feet 11 inches
Draft: 6 feet
Sail Area: 1604 square feet
Displacement: 58,300 pounds

Number 131's sailplan.

Mahdee, an electric-drive schooner, was designed for A.W. (Sandy) Moffat and launched from G.F. Lawson & Son's yard in Dorchester, Mass., in 1931. Sandy was one of Dad's earliest clients when the office was opened at 333 Washington Street, having owned the first 32-footer design, number 40, called *Brant* ex. *Wiscasset.* Later he had me build *Cousin Elizabeth. Mahdee* was powered by a 25-horsepower electric motor, which was directly connected to the propeller shaft with a controller located alongside the wheel, and had the same speed of rotation either ahead or reverse. Two 10-kilowatt Winton generator plants, mounted forward alongside the foremast, gave her 7.6 knots of cruising speed. On one generator she would do 5.7 knots. She could run for awhile on the 56-cell oxide batteries, but normally, they floated on the line. Exhaust from the gasoline generators was carried up the foremast and out the top. In an article in the February 1921 *Yachting,* Sandy wrote, "*Mahdee* has proved herself a grand sea boat, although she has, so far, only had the opportunity to make little jaunts between Long Island Sound and the Maine coast. As a power

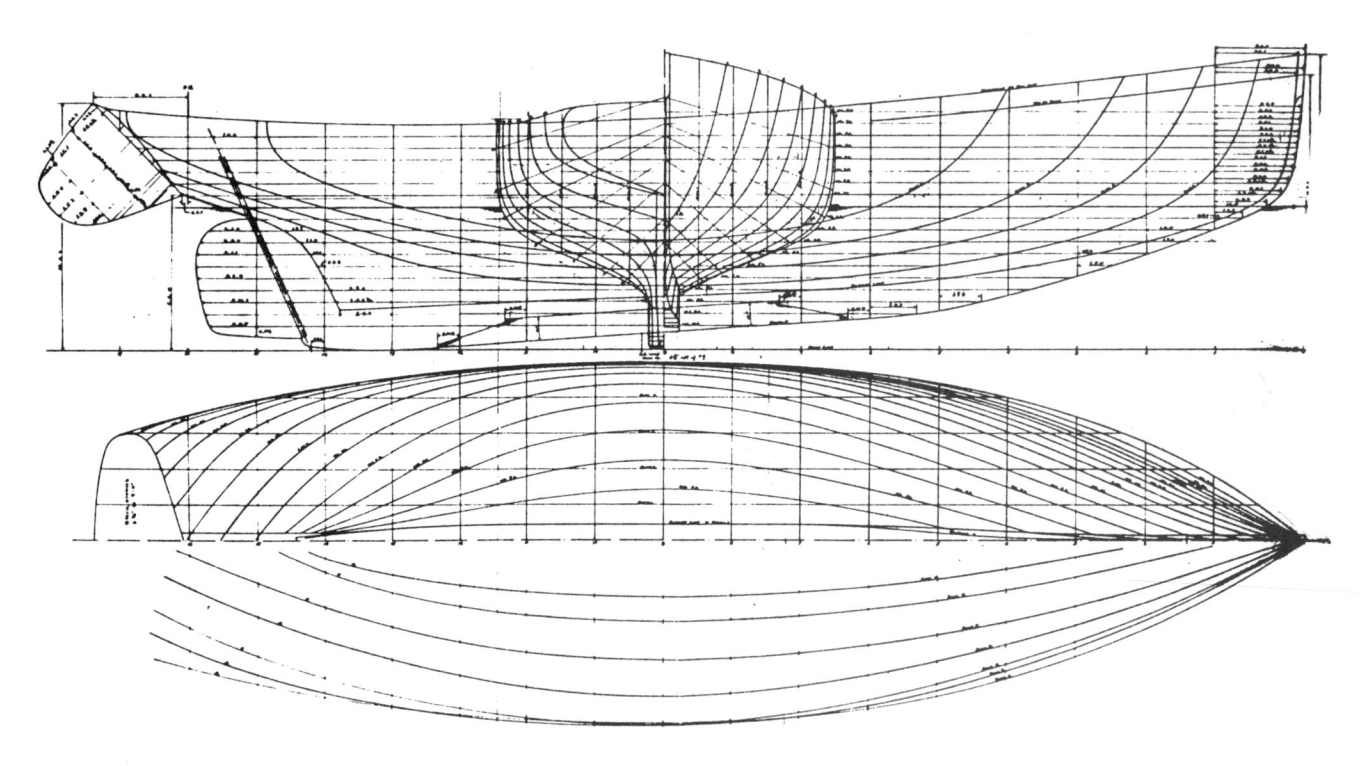

The lines for 131 and her construction drawings.

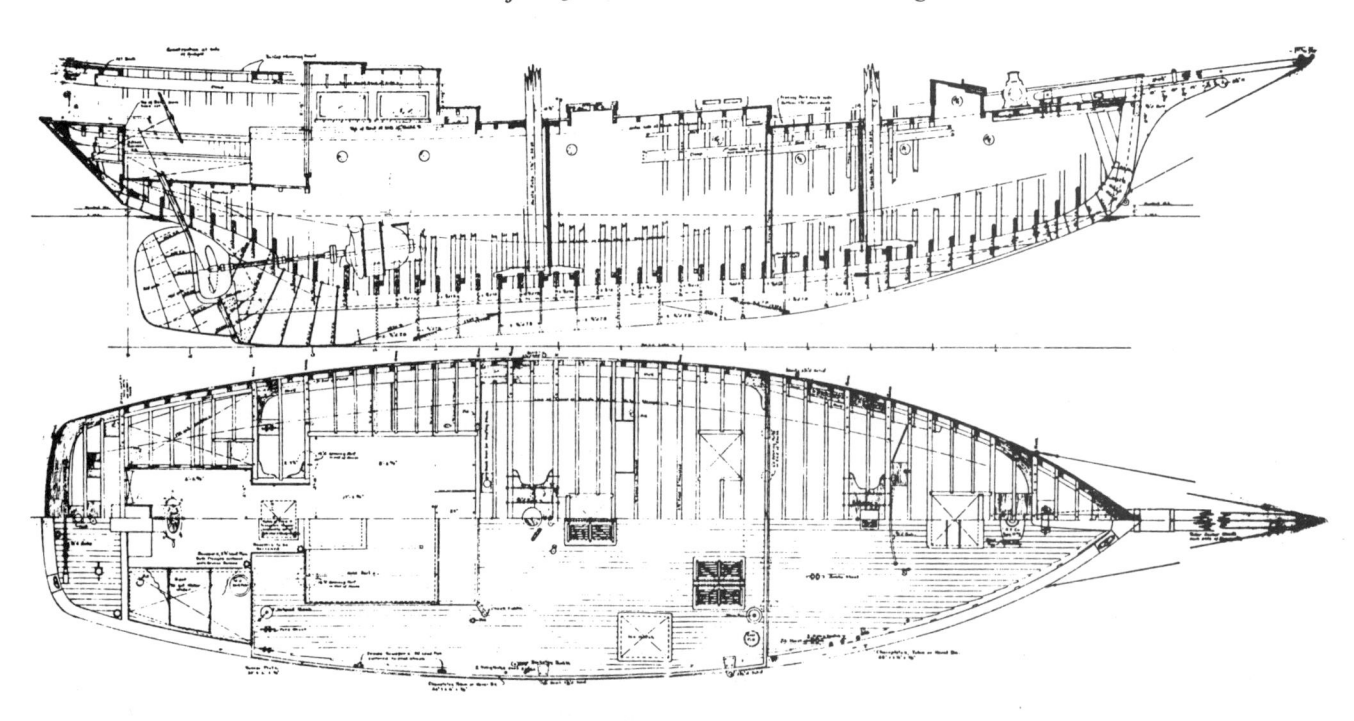

boat she handles with the ease of a steam towboat, but as a racer she would have to have weather that few of the competition would be found to start in."

After Sandy owned her, a billet head was added to her stem, making her clipper bowed. The diesel electric drive was changed to a Chrysler Majestic with 2½-to-1 reduction gear, and the sliding Gunter rig was done away with. Finally, she also went to the West Coast.

108

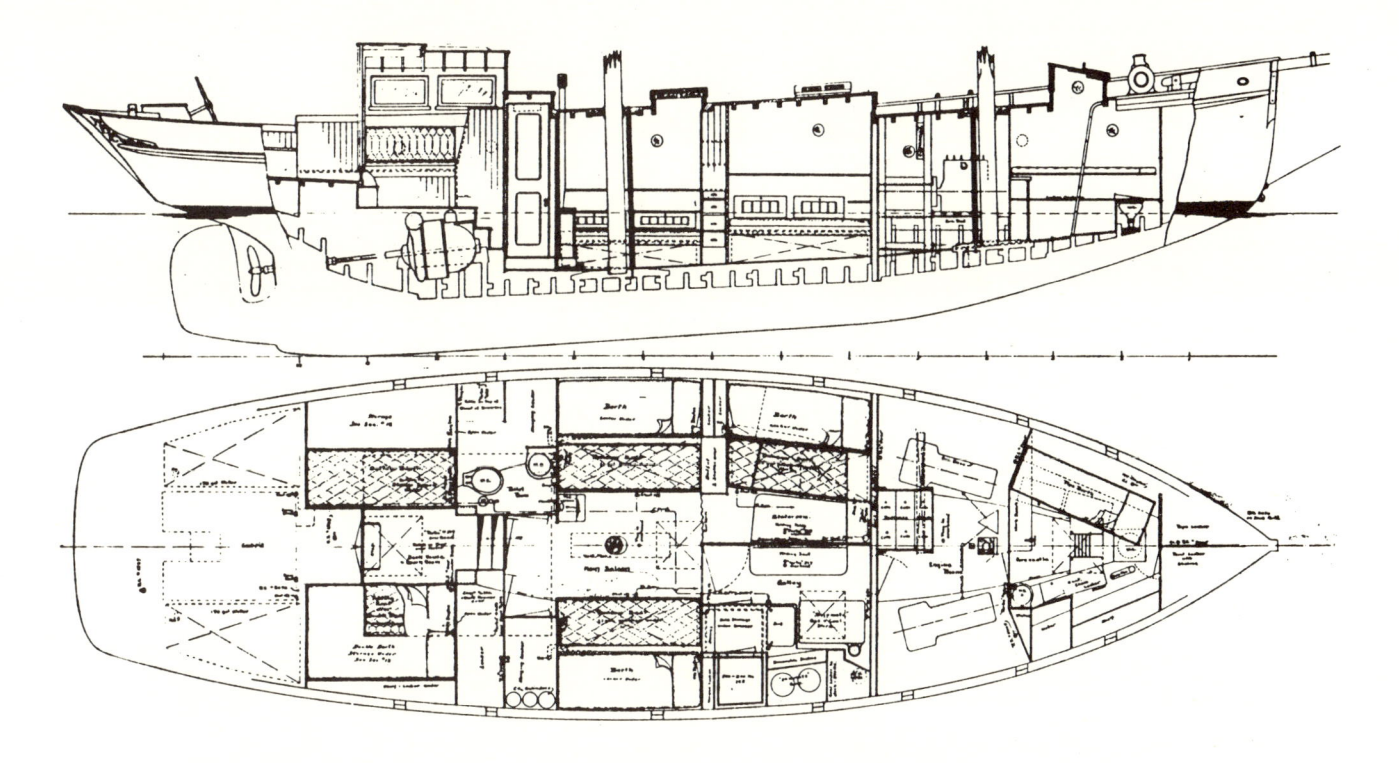

Mahdee's *accommodations plans, and moving along smartly off Marblehead, Mass. Photograph courtesy of W.B. Jackson.*

142 SKOOKUM III

Design Number 142
Length Overall: 63 feet
Length on Waterline: 46 feet
Beam: 14 feet 5 inches
Draft: 6 feet 6 inches
Sail Area: 1743 square feet
Displacement: 61,800 pounds

Skookum III was the third boat of this name that James Dean of Cohasset, Mass., had from my father's design. The first was one of the 32-foot sloops (number 43), and the second was number 91, a 43-foot sloop. *Skookum III* was built by Britt Brothers in 1935, one of the last boats to be built in their West Lynn shop before it was destroyed by fire. She was one of the first boats I worked on. As a teenager, I went to Britt Brothers after school, drove a lot of bungs, cut off a lot of bolts, and did some painting and anything else a kid could do. Of course, there was no smoking in the shop, so all the men chewed tobacco. I remember being awfully careful where I sat on the staging while driving bungs in the topsides, but every once in a while, my hand would land in a puddle of tobacco juice as I shifted positions.

Skookum III had a six-cylinder, 60-horsepower Lathrop Mystic gas engine and a four-horsepower, two-kilowatt, 32-volt generating set for electricity.

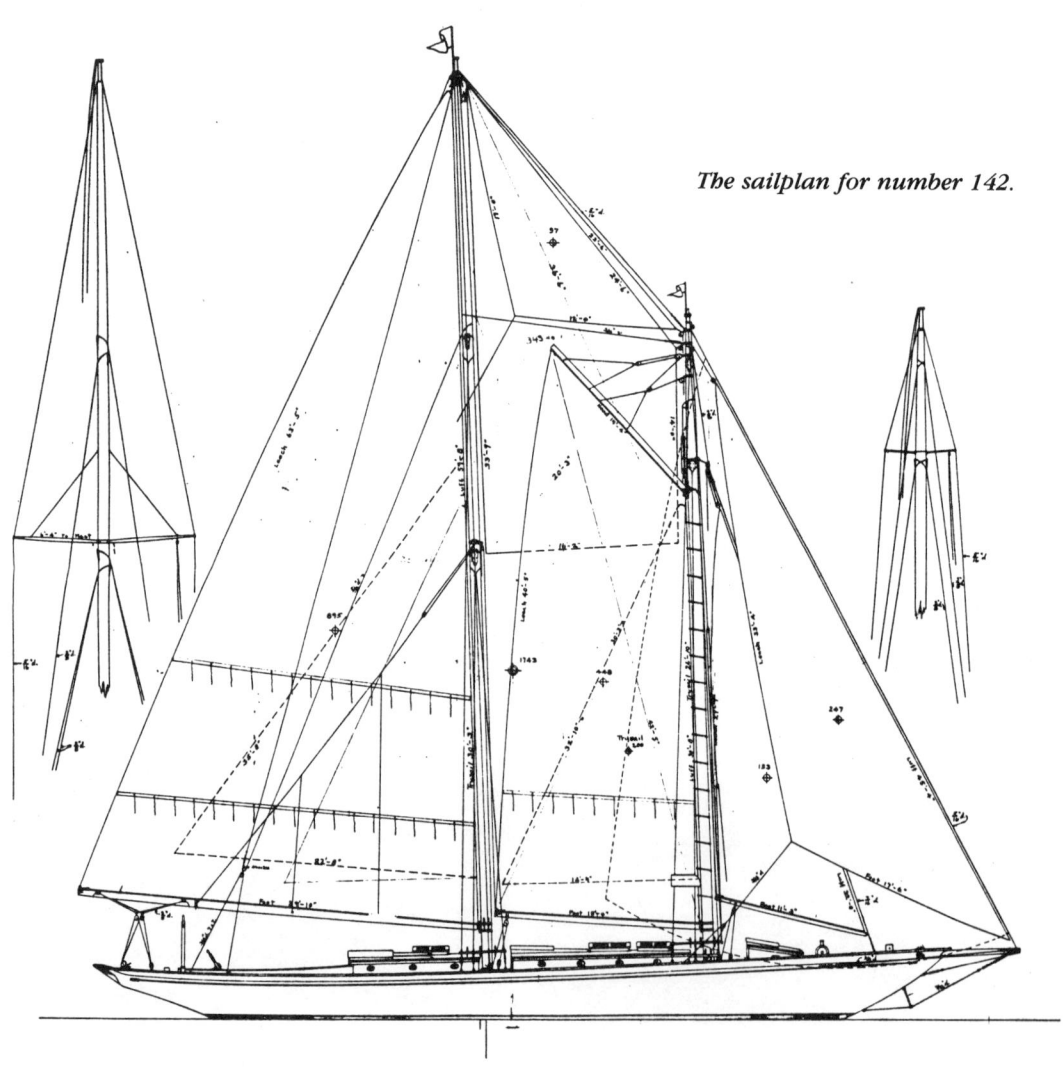

The sailplan for number 142.

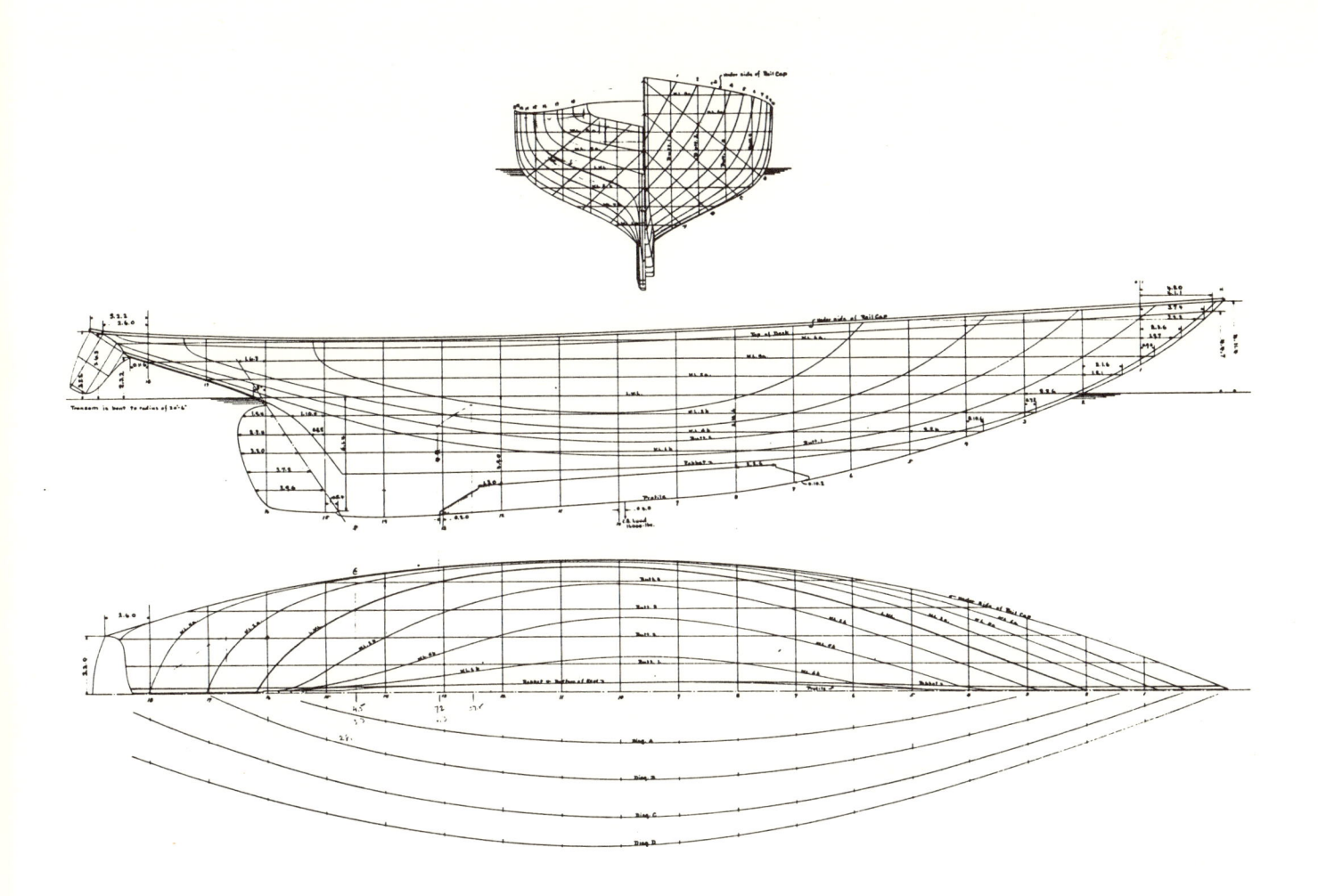

Skookum III's *lines drawings* and her *construction plans*.

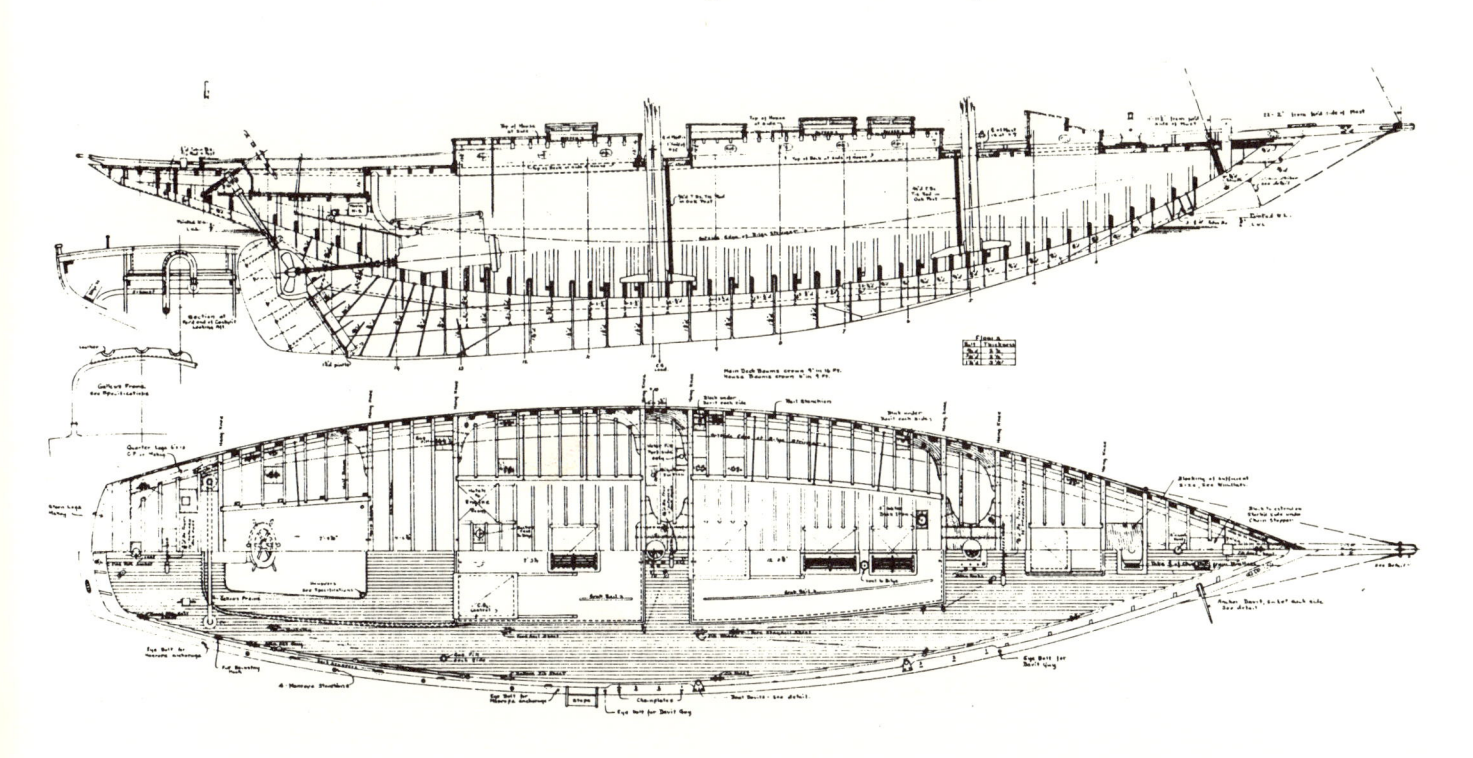

111

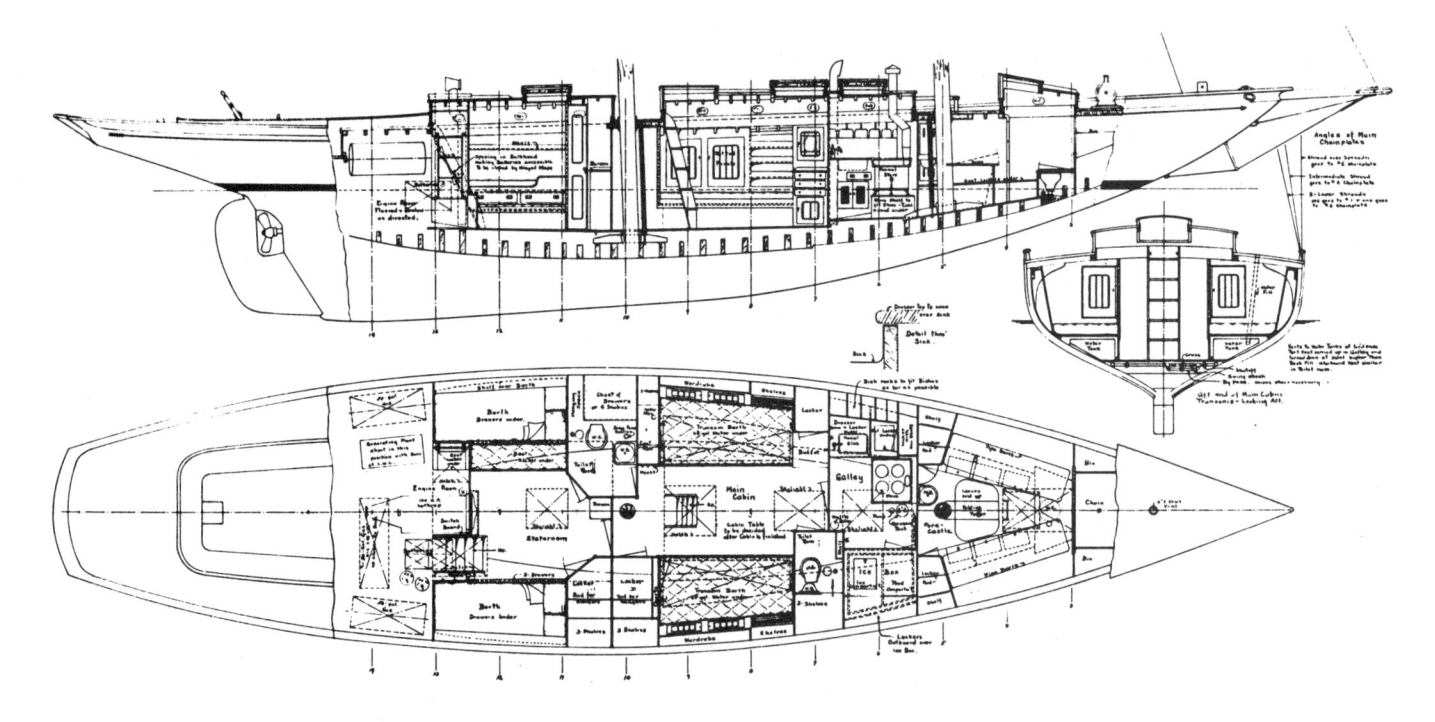

The accommodations plans for number 142.

Skookum III *under sail.*

LITTLE BEAR 143

Little Bear was designed in 1931 for Fred Lyman of Marblehead, Mass. George Chaisson built the bare hull, and Fred finished the boat in his yard. Dad only drew the lines and profiles, and unfortunately, the lines drawing is unavailable. Still, I include her in this book, because she was the forerunner of *Roaring Bessie,* number 154, as is evidenced by the similarity of profiles.

Design number 144 is the same boat lengthened to 28 feet and given a schooner rig. There is no record of this boat ever having been built. It would certainly be a good boat to have as she has a pretty good profile.

Design Number 143
Length Overall: 23 feet
Length on Waterline: 21 feet
Beam: 8 feet 2 inches
Draft: 4 feet 2 inches
Sail Area: 333 square feet
Displacement: 5,600 pounds

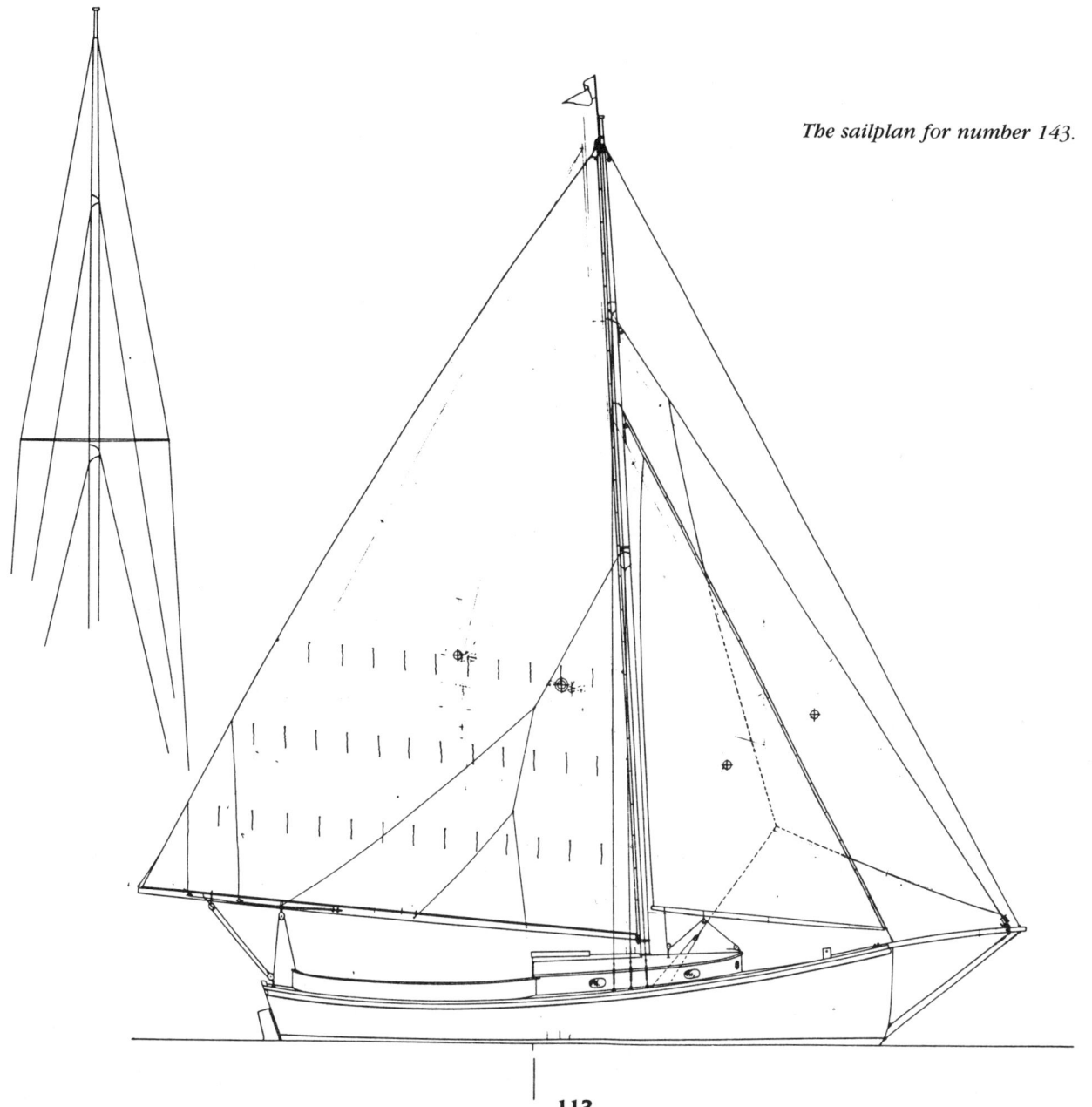

The sailplan for number 143.

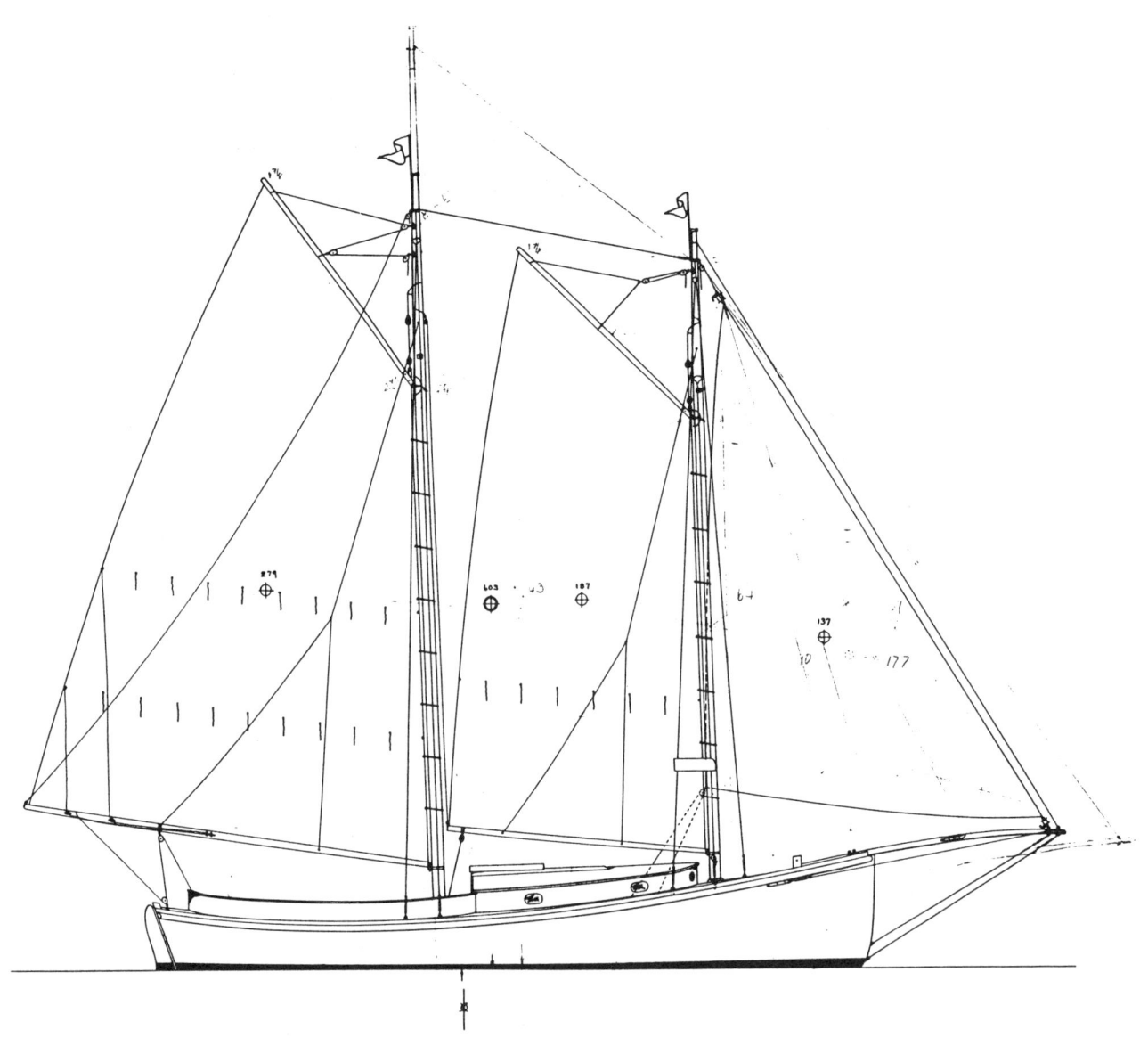

The sailplan for number 144.

147

Design Numbers 147 and 152
Length Overall: 22 feet 2 inches
Length on Waterline: 20 feet
Beam: 7 feet 6 inches
Draft: 4 feet 7 inches
Sail Area: 344 square feet
Displacement: 6,100 pounds

In 1932 a committee of five Boston Yacht Club members considered several architects' designs for a small, able cruising boat that could be raced as a one-design and yet have sufficient accommodations for two persons. Number 147 was the unanimous choice. "Something to shoot at" was the slogan on their brochure. The cost was to be under $1,000 for the hull, ironwork, and full suit of sails. The cabin was quite sparse, and engine and head were extras.

Left and above: *The original sailplan for number 147, and her accommodations plans.*

Right: *Number 147 with a gaff cutter rig.*

Left: *Number 147 as a yawl.*

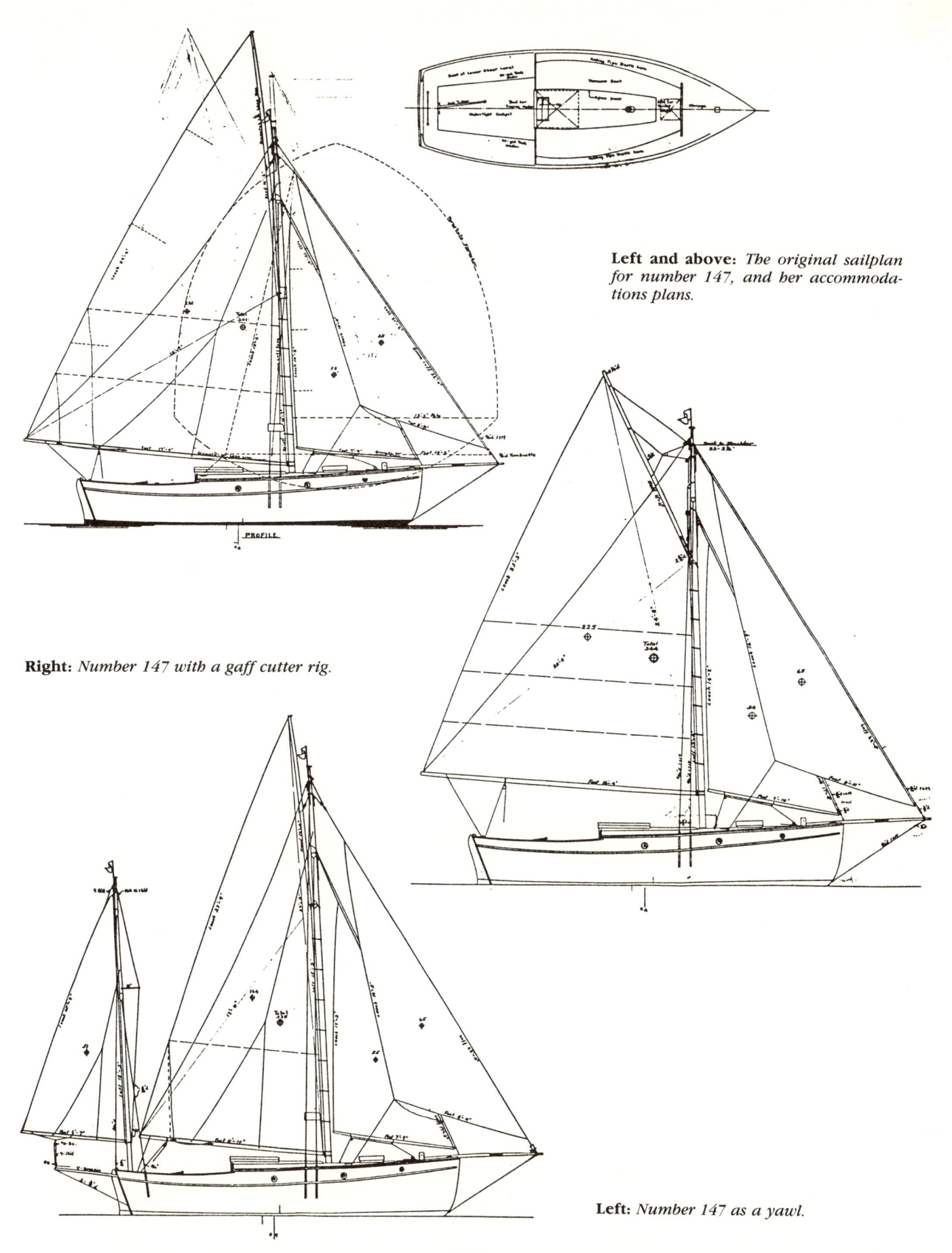

115

Right: *The lines drawings for number 147.*

Right and below: *The construction plans for number 147, and her interior details.*

116

Target *class boat under sail in Boston Harbor.*

Number 152: *Spaniel,* built in 1932 by W.J. Reid for J.J. Storrow, was a variation of the *Target,* having an inboard rudder and overhanging stern. She had several different owners and rig changes from sliding Gunter double head, to marconi double head, to marconi single head.

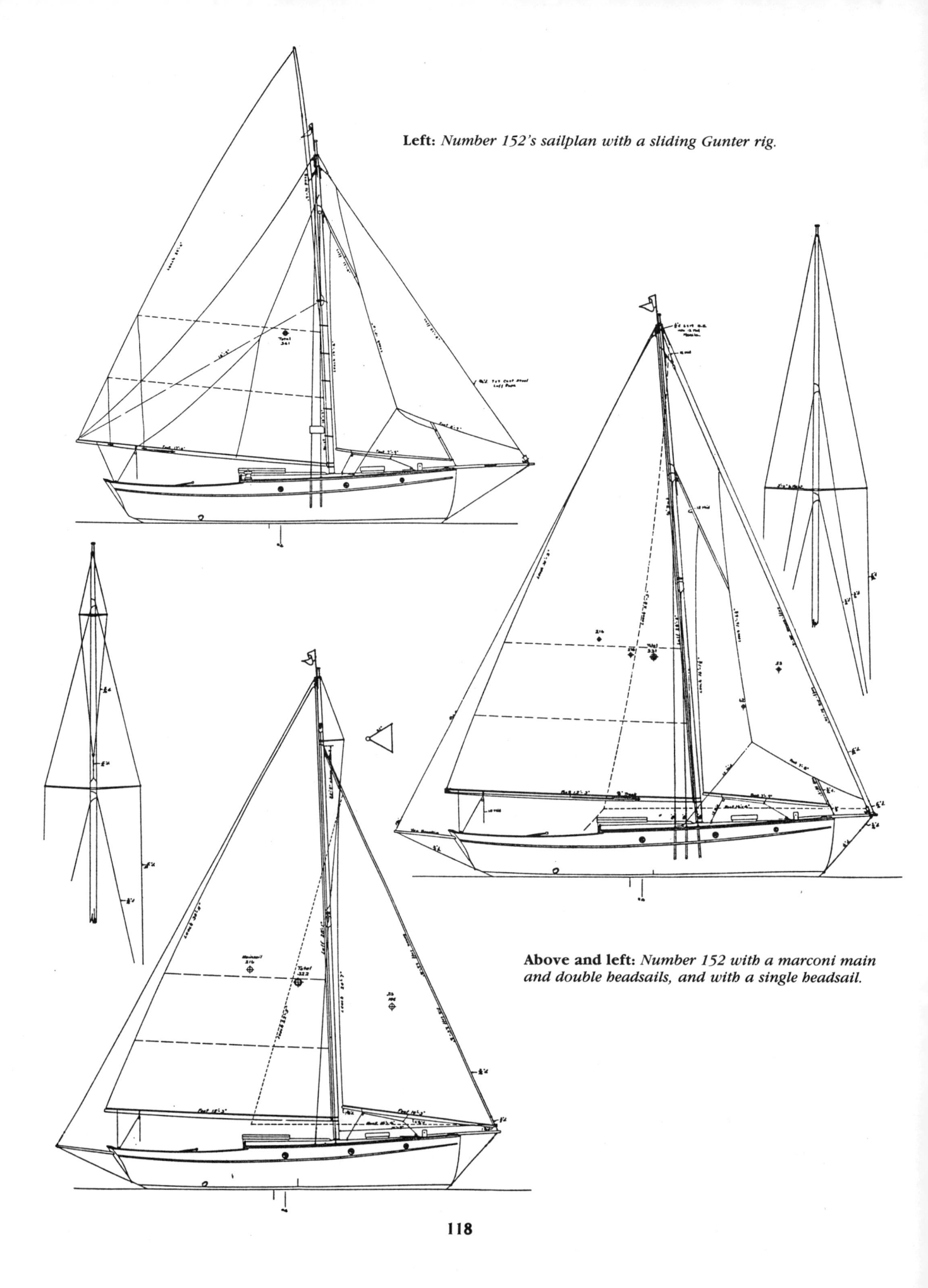

Left: *Number 152's sailplan with a sliding Gunter rig.*

Above and left: *Number 152 with a marconi main and double headsails, and with a single headsail.*

The lines for number 152.

Above and below: *The construction plans for number 152, and her accommodations plans.*

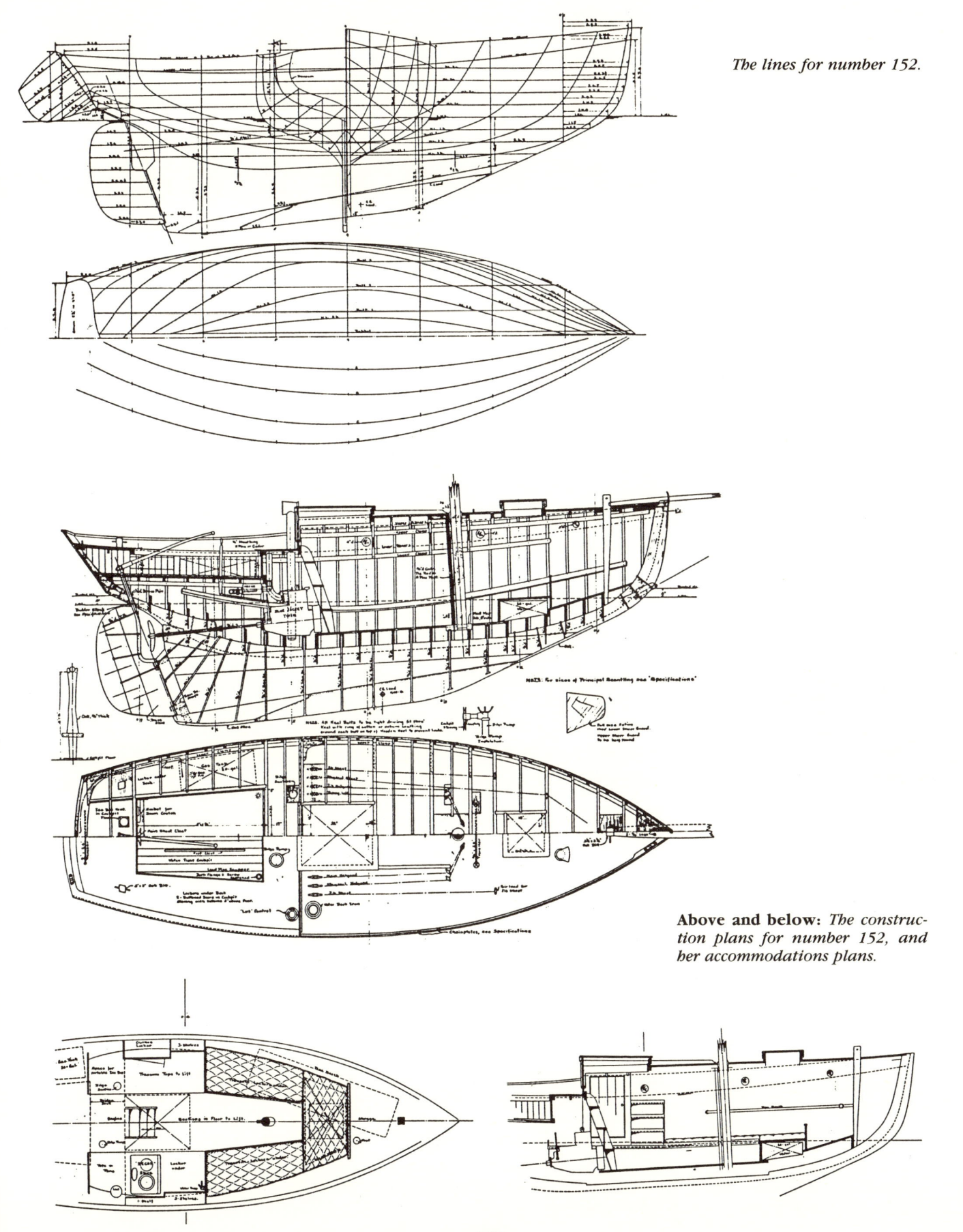

153

Right and below right: *The sailplan and construction details for number 153.*

Number 153 under sail.

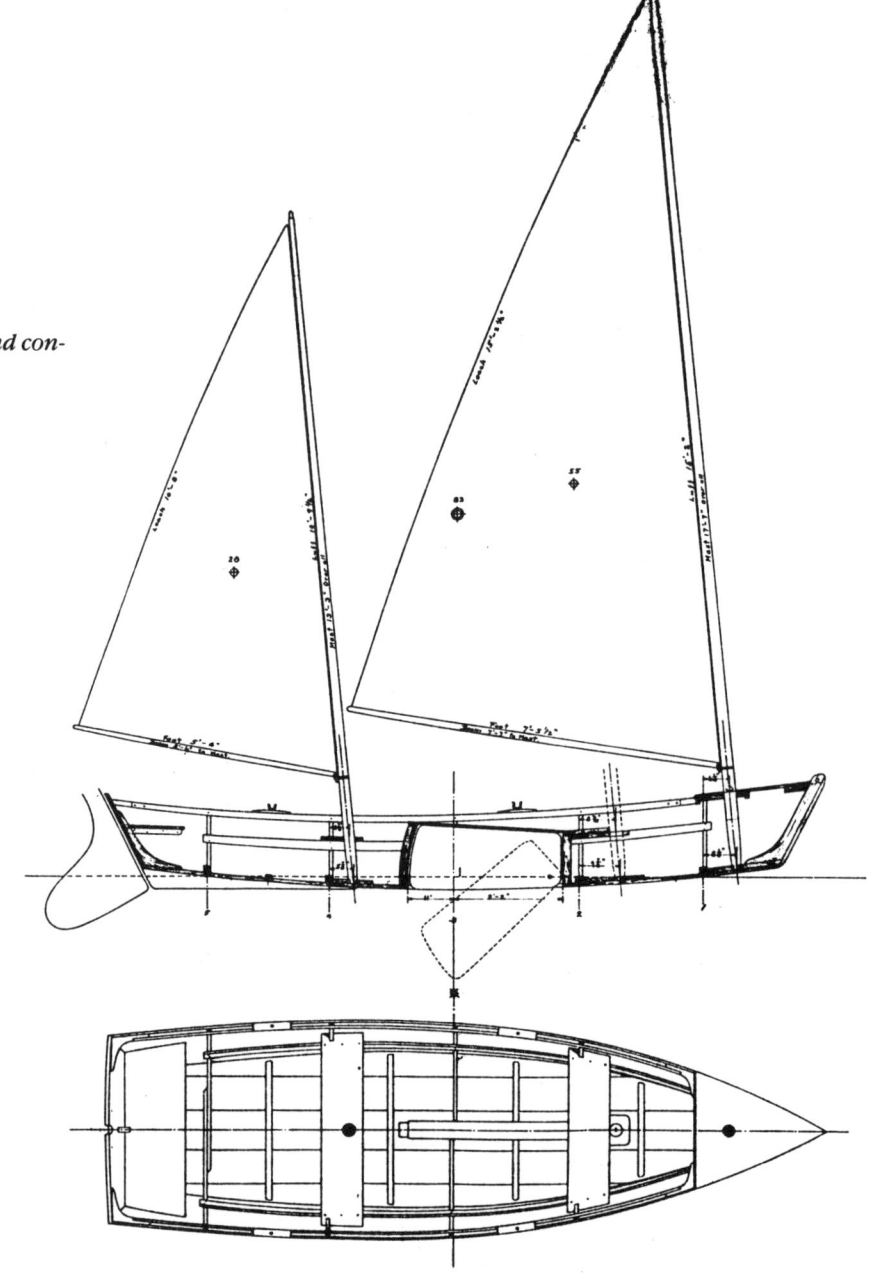

Number 153: This 14½-foot Essex sharpie was built on our front porch in 1933, the first of several boats built there. We had quite a workshop in the cellar, where all the parts were gotten out for assembly on the piazza. After ripping something over 100 feet of planking in one day, we decided to get a bandsaw. This was the first of our power tools. With the ketch rig, we could take down the mizzen and step the main farther aft or take down the main and step the mizzen in its place, depending on how much sail we wanted for various conditions.

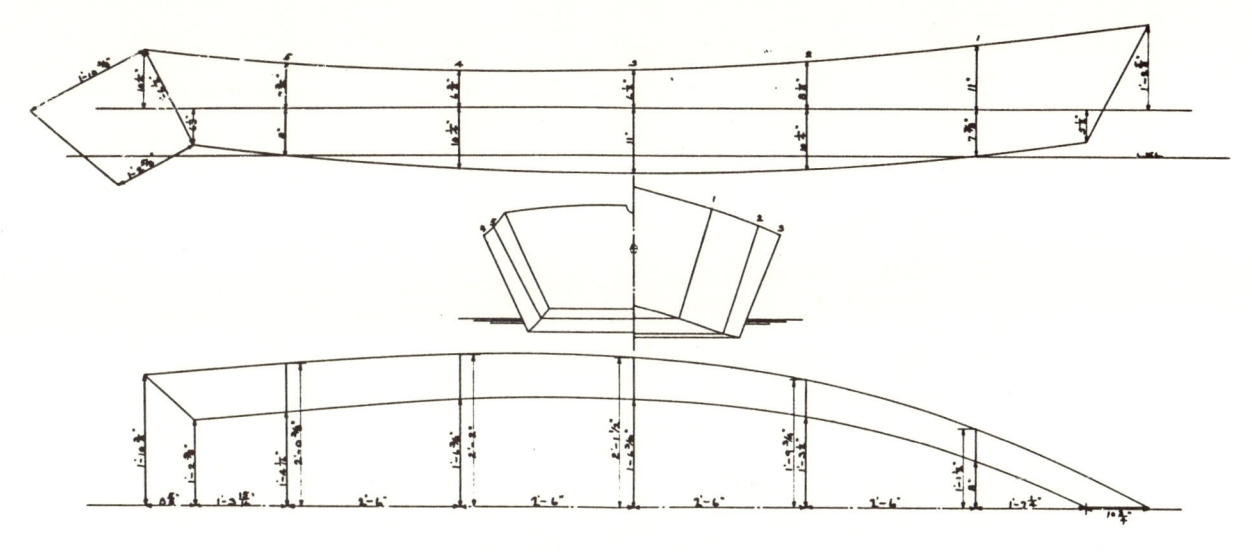

The lines for number 153.

I think it was on this boat that, wanting to impress my visiting Uncle John, I came out on the porch smoking a cigarette. He said, "What are you doing with a cigarette in your mouth? Don't you know all boatbuilders chew tobacco?" He cut off a piece and offered it to me, and of course, I took it. The boat was upside down, all planked, and I was underneath, securing the centerboard box, when I couldn't control my stomach any longer. I can still see the expression on my father's face and hear his voice as he bent down to see what was going on. My uncle was holding onto his sides laughing, while my mother was furious. I never chewed again.

ROARING BESSIE 154

Here is *Roaring Bessie,* referred to earlier in connection with design number 143. Quite a few boats were built to these lines with several different rigs and cabin layouts. There were 3,900 pounds of outside ballast. Some boats had lead; some iron. *Roaring Bessie* was the first of these boats, built for Dick Lyman and Burnham Porter in 1932. They were impressed with Fred Lyman's *Little Bear* (number 143) but wanted something a little bigger, so the *Bessie* was created. Originally gaff rigged, she was converted to marconi with running backstays in 1936 and permanent backstay with boomkin still later. All of these so-called *Amantha*-class boats were comfortable and able sailers and won their share of races. I don't know how many have been built, but the plans have been sold all over the world; Ken Meyers in Hampton, N.H., has one under construction in his backyard right now. My father wasn't much of a drinker, but from the grin on his face at the launching of *Fulmar* in 1937, he must have gotten hold of something (or something got hold of him). That's George Chaisson beside him.

Design Number 154
Length Overall: 30 feet 3 inches
Length on Waterline: 28 feet 8 inches
Beam: 10 feet 9 inches
Draft: 4 feet 9 inches
Sail Area: 654 square feet
Displacement: 14,000 pounds

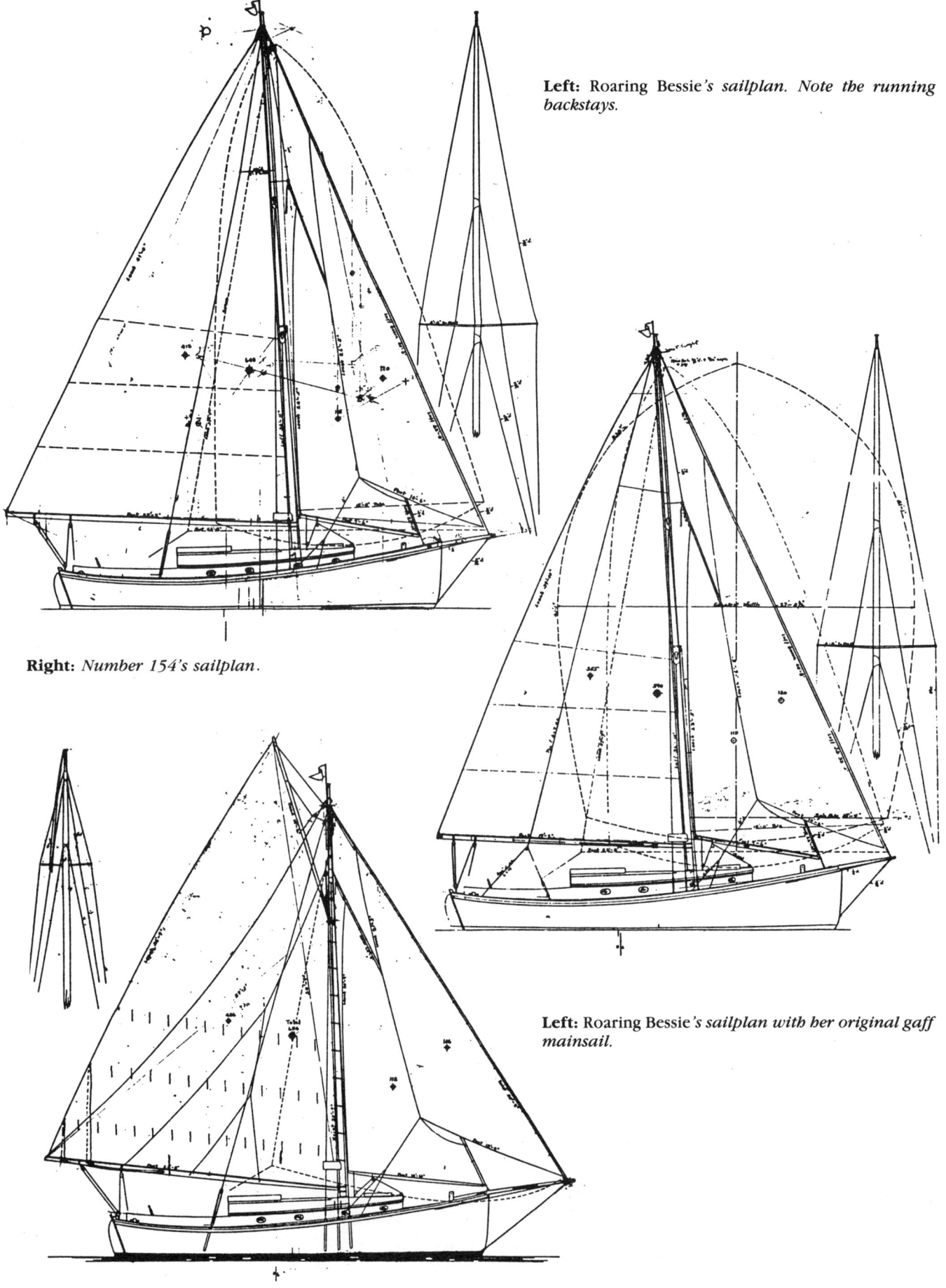

Left: Roaring Bessie's *sailplan. Note the running backstays.*

Right: *Number 154's sailplan.*

Left: Roaring Bessie's *sailplan with her original gaff mainsail.*

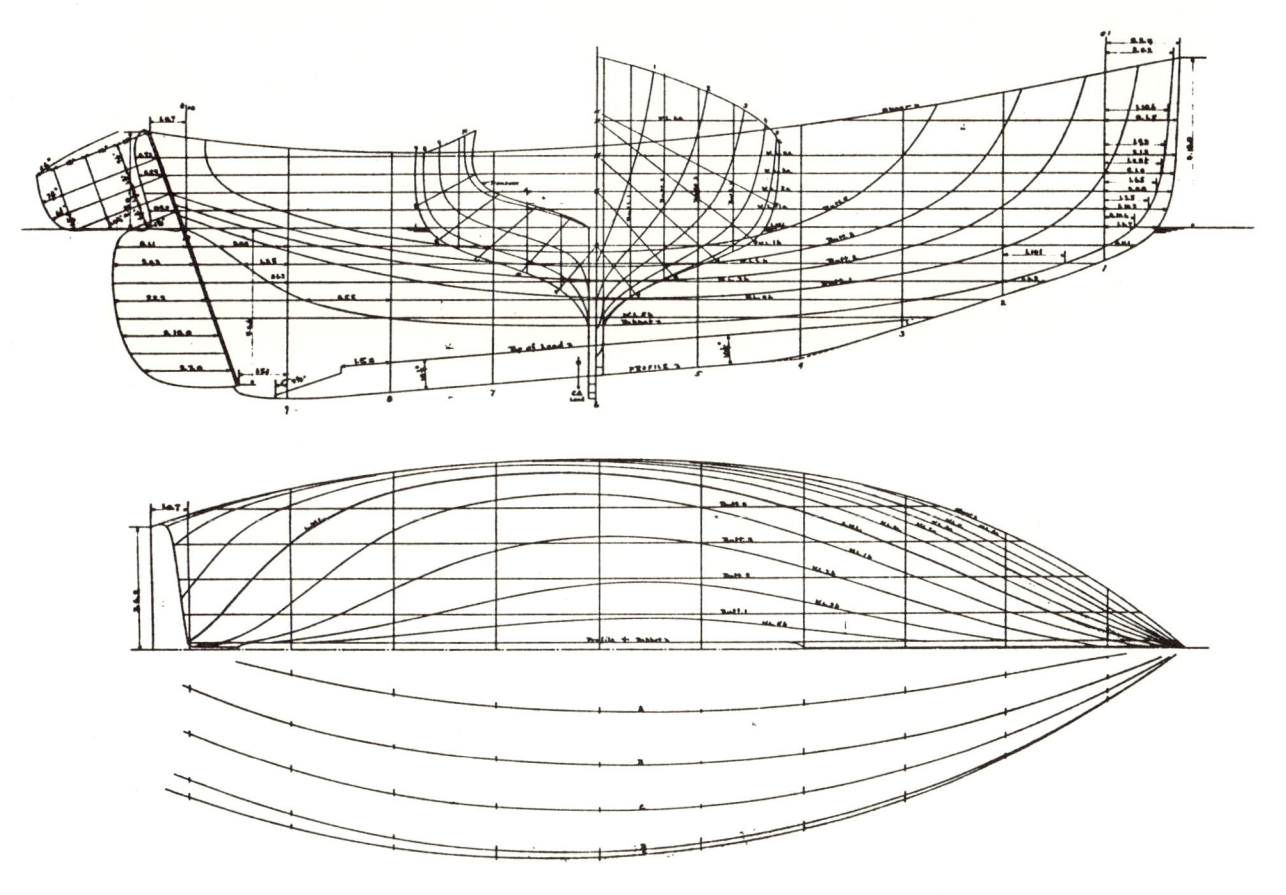

Roaring Bessie's *lines drawings, and her construction plans.*

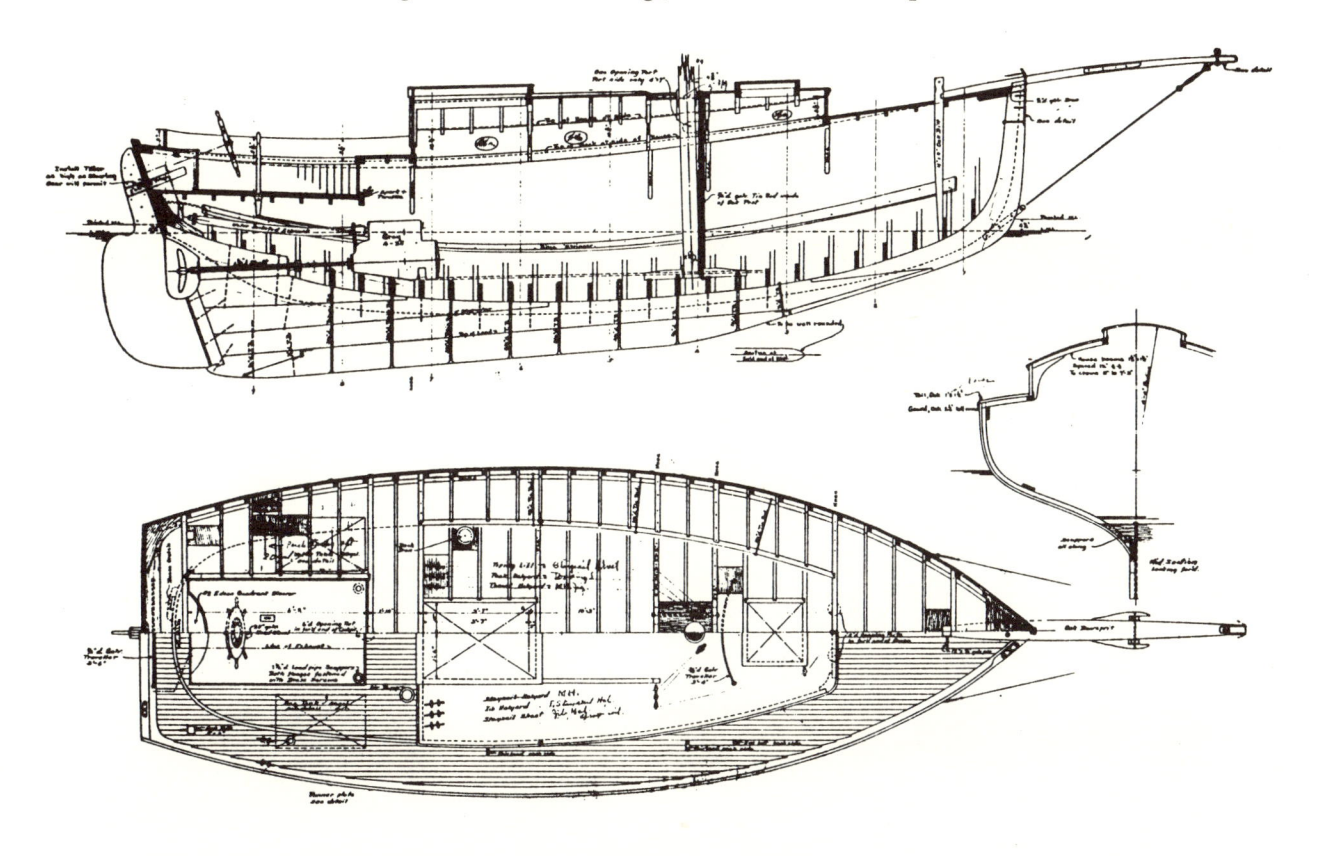

123

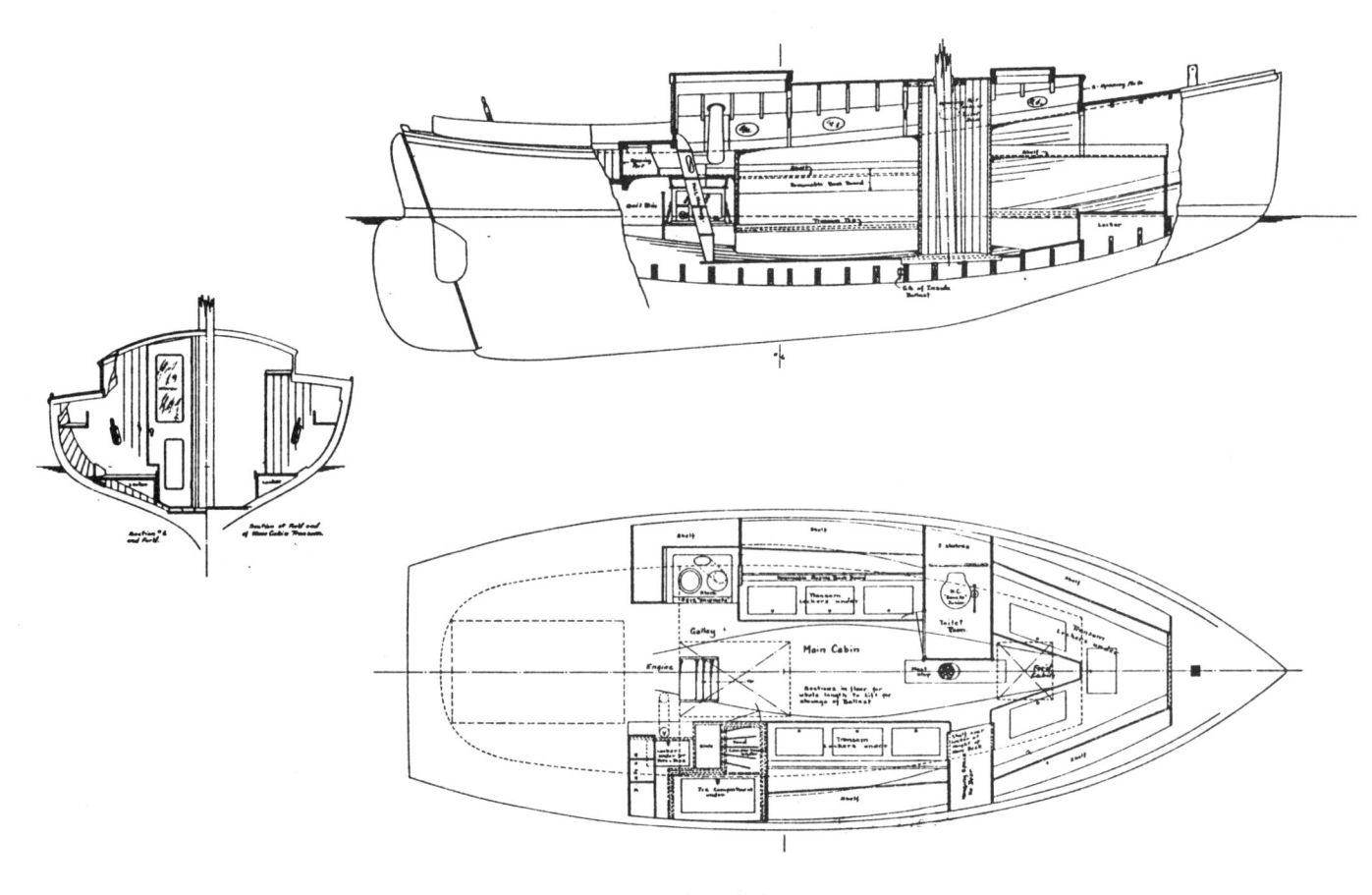

Above: Roaring Bessie's *accommodations plans.* **Below left:** *Sam Crocker and George Chaisson at a launching.* **Below right:** Roaring Bessie *under sail.*

124

IDA S 155

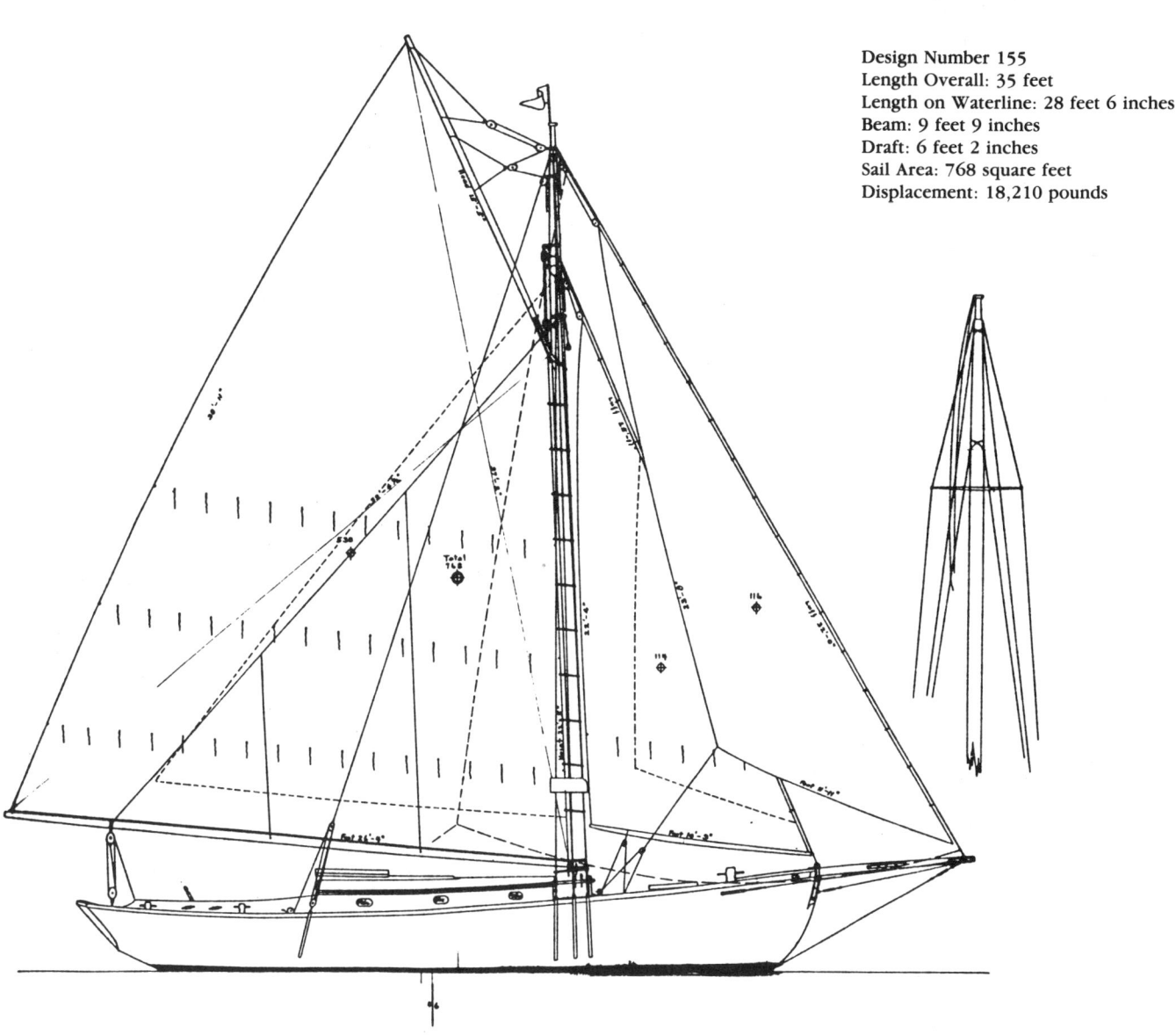

Design Number 155
Length Overall: 35 feet
Length on Waterline: 28 feet 6 inches
Beam: 9 feet 9 inches
Draft: 6 feet 2 inches
Sail Area: 768 square feet
Displacement: 18,210 pounds

The sailplan for Ida S.

Ida S. was launched in 1933 from Bill Reid's yard in Winthrop, Mass., for Channing Williams of Jamaica Plain, Mass., her home port being Marblehead. She was planked with dark Philippine mahogany and finished bright. I bet Reid was some pleased with the simplicity of the cabin layout. It seems to take forever to complete a cabin interior with all the lockers, cabinets, and drawers, but this one was done practically as soon as the hull was. And what a simple toilet. A 4-44 Gray provided power.

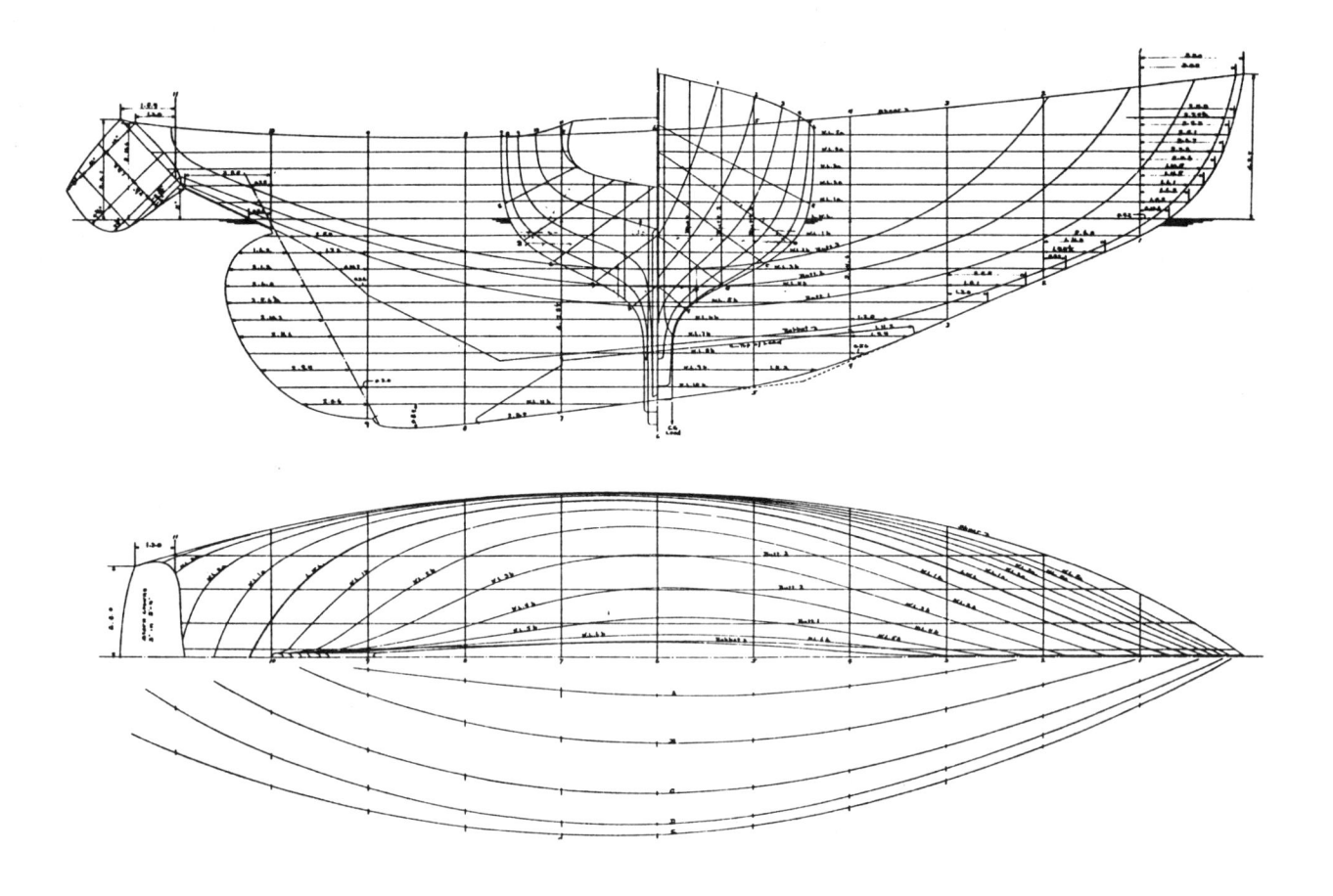

The lines for number 155 and her construction details.

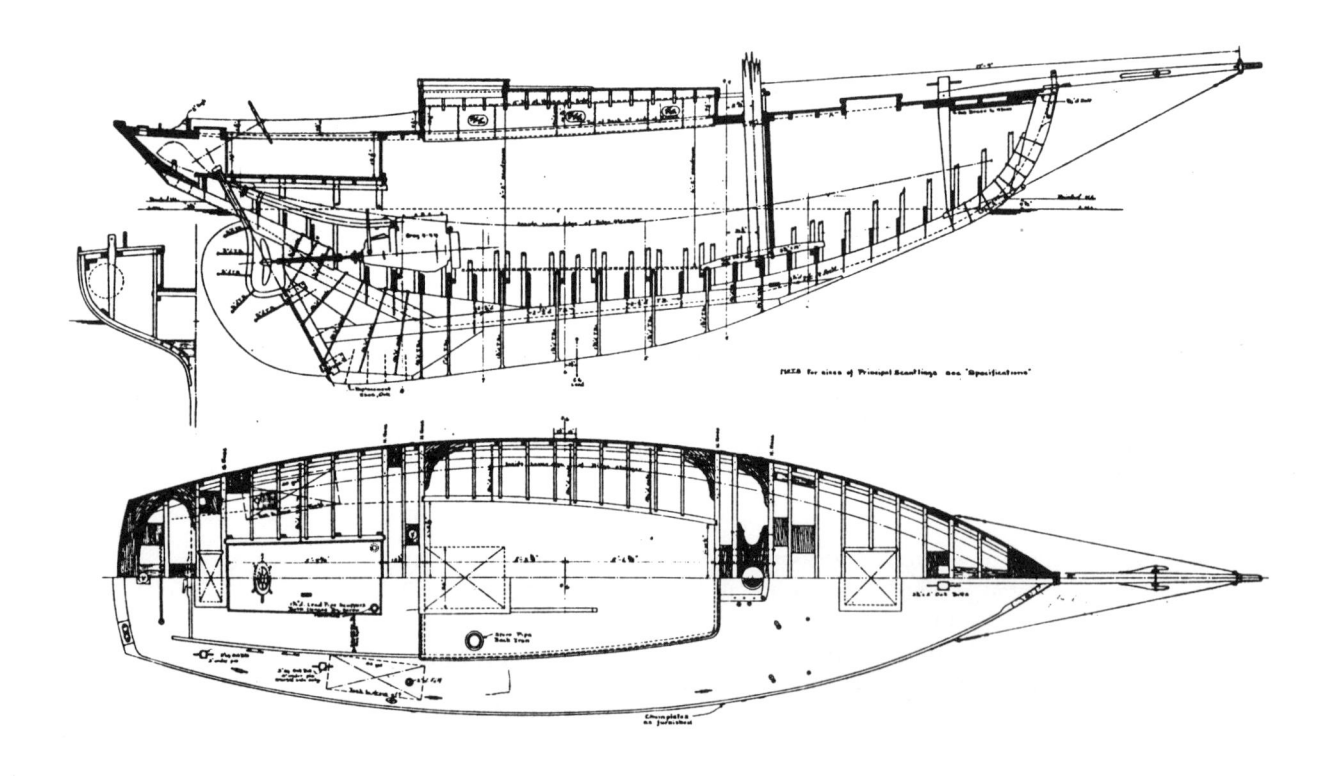

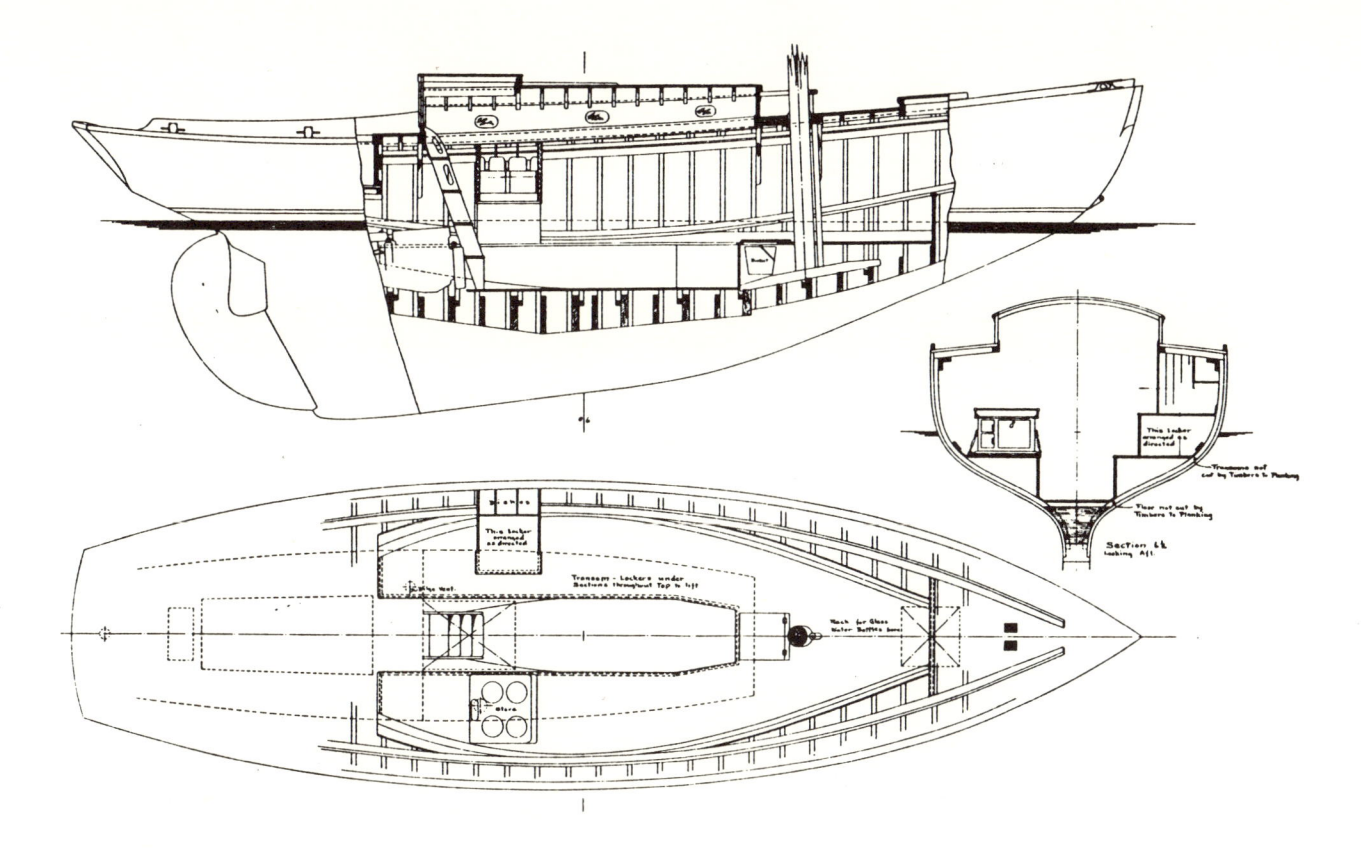

The accommodations plans for Ida S.

POLE STAR 157

Pole Star was launched in 1933 from the yard of R. Bigelow of Monument Beach, Mass., for Lincoln and Richard Dow of Cambridge, Mass. She is another example of Dad's ability to design a lot of boat into a small space and still come up with an able performer. While primarily a cruising boat, she was more than ordinarily successful in races along the New England coast. She won the following races in her class: 1933 Jeffrey's Ledge; 1934 Whaler's Race; 1935 New London to Marblehead and Jeffrey's Ledge; 1936 Jeffrey's Ledge; 1937 Whaler's Race and Edgartown Regatta; 1938 New London to Marblehead and Jeffrey's Ledge; 1939 Jeffrey's Ledge.

In 1984 she was being rebuilt by M. Christian Nye in the Virgin Islands.

Design Number 157
Length Overall: 34 feet
Length on Waterline: 30 feet 4 inches
Beam: 10 feet 11 inches
Draft: 5 feet 3 inches
Sail Area: 752 square feet
Displacement: 18,000 pounds

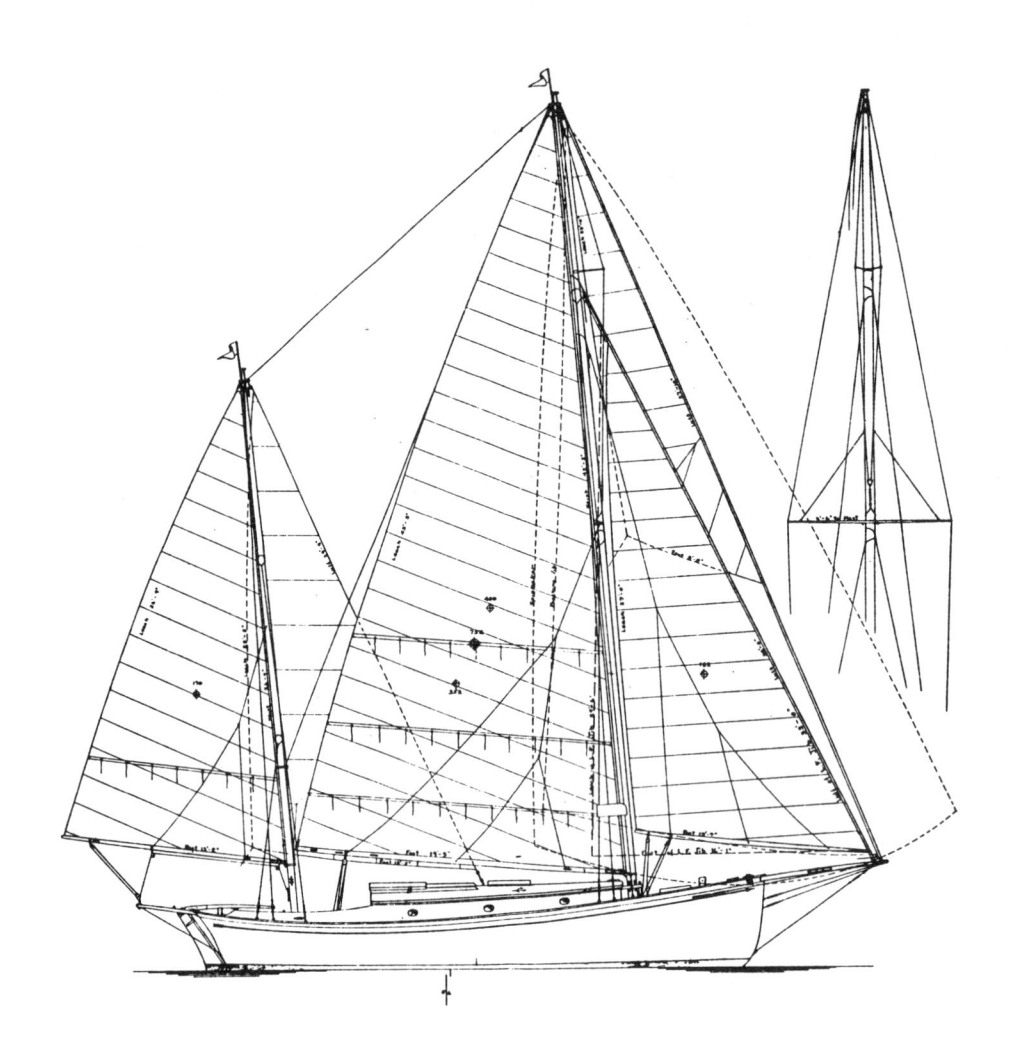

The sailplan for Pole Star *and her lines drawings.*

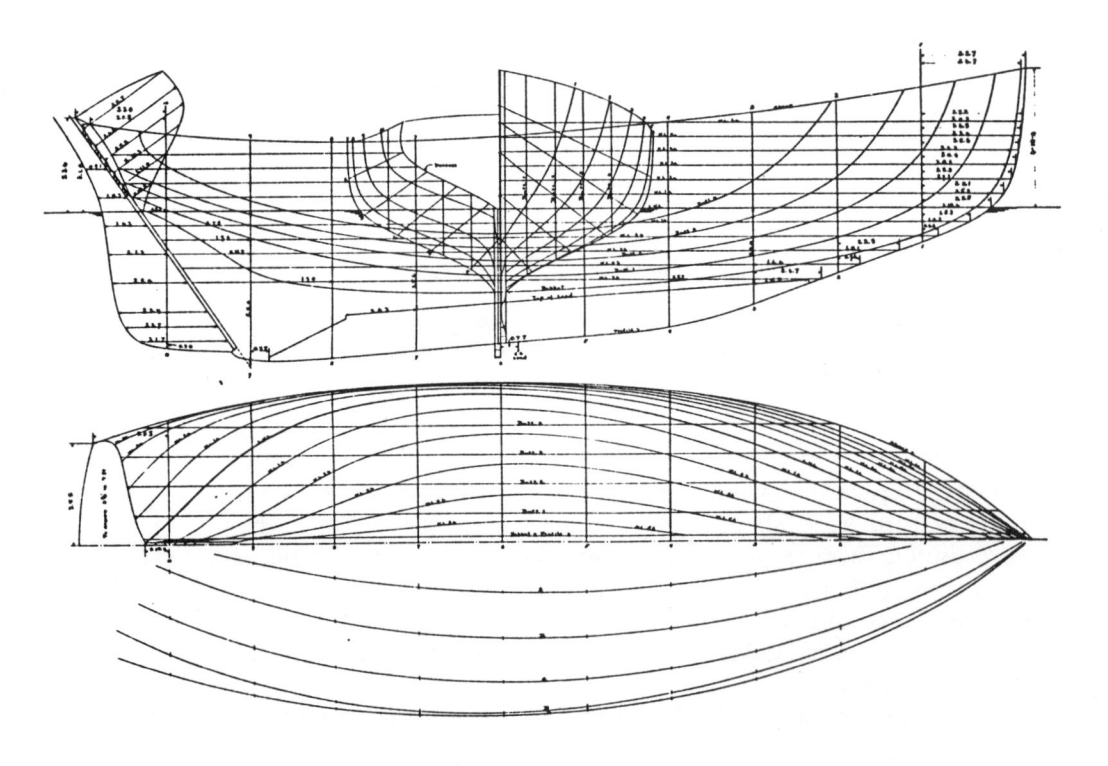

128

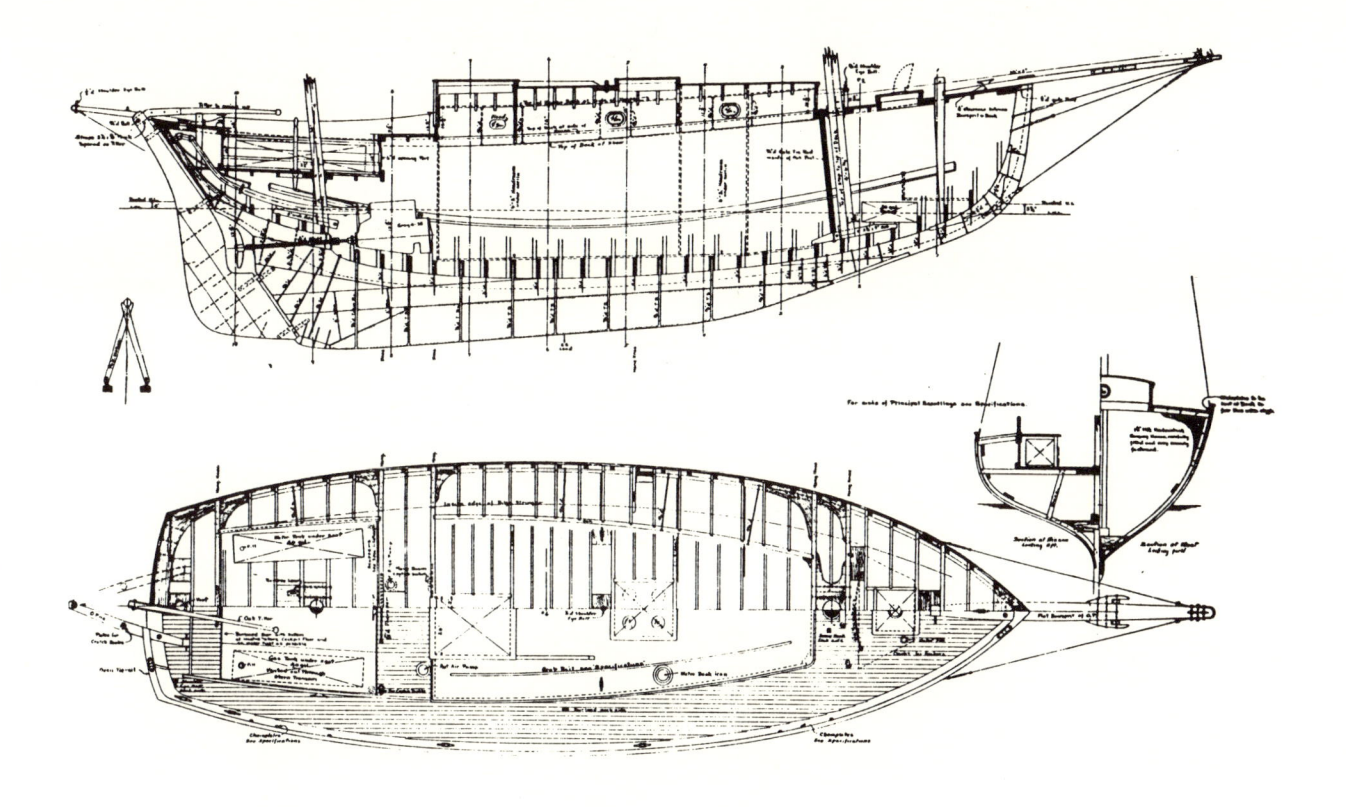

The construction details for Pole Star *and her accommodations drawings.*

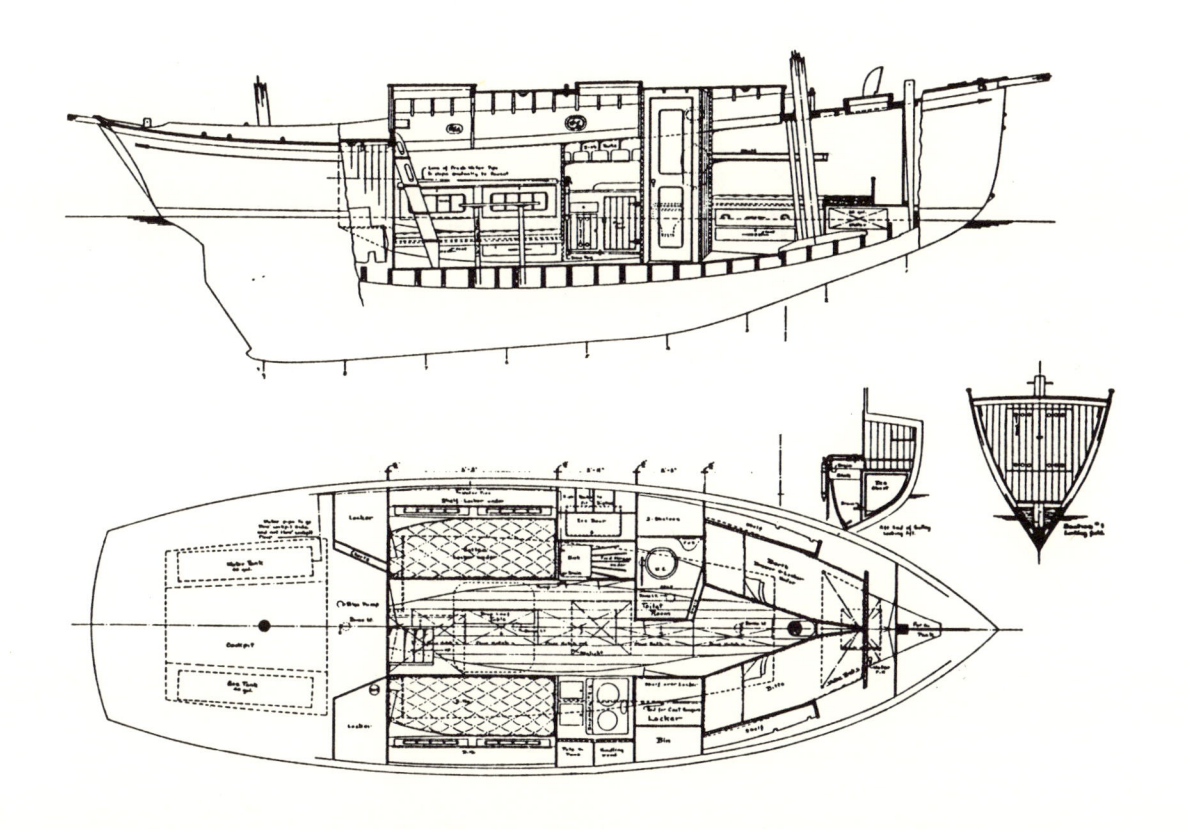

Pole Star *under sail and moving well. A Morris Rosenfeld photograph, courtesy of S. Sturgis Crocker.*

159

Design Number 159
Stonehorse Junior
Length Overall: **22 feet** 9 inches
Length on Waterline: 18 feet
Beam: 7 feet
Draft: 2 feet 6 inches
Sail Area: 159, 243 square feet
Displacement: 3,500 pounds

The sailplan for the Stonehorse Jr.

The Stonehorse Jr. was designed in 1932 for the Stonehorse Yacht Club on Cape Cod. Bill Lee built the first of the type for Palmer Putnam, and quite a few followed. Eventually, more deadwood was added to drop the ballast keel and give her more draft. There were several different rigs and deck plans drawn, but most of these involved only changes to the headsails. Eddy & Duff of Mattapoisett, Mass., started building them in fiberglass in April, 1971, and have produced well over 100, sending them all over the world.

The Eddy & Duff Stonehorse that you see today has a flush deck and may be powered by either a small inboard or an outboard motor. I think one of the things that makes this boat so attractive is the liberal use of wood trim, etc.

Left: *Stonehorse Jr. with a double headsail rig.*

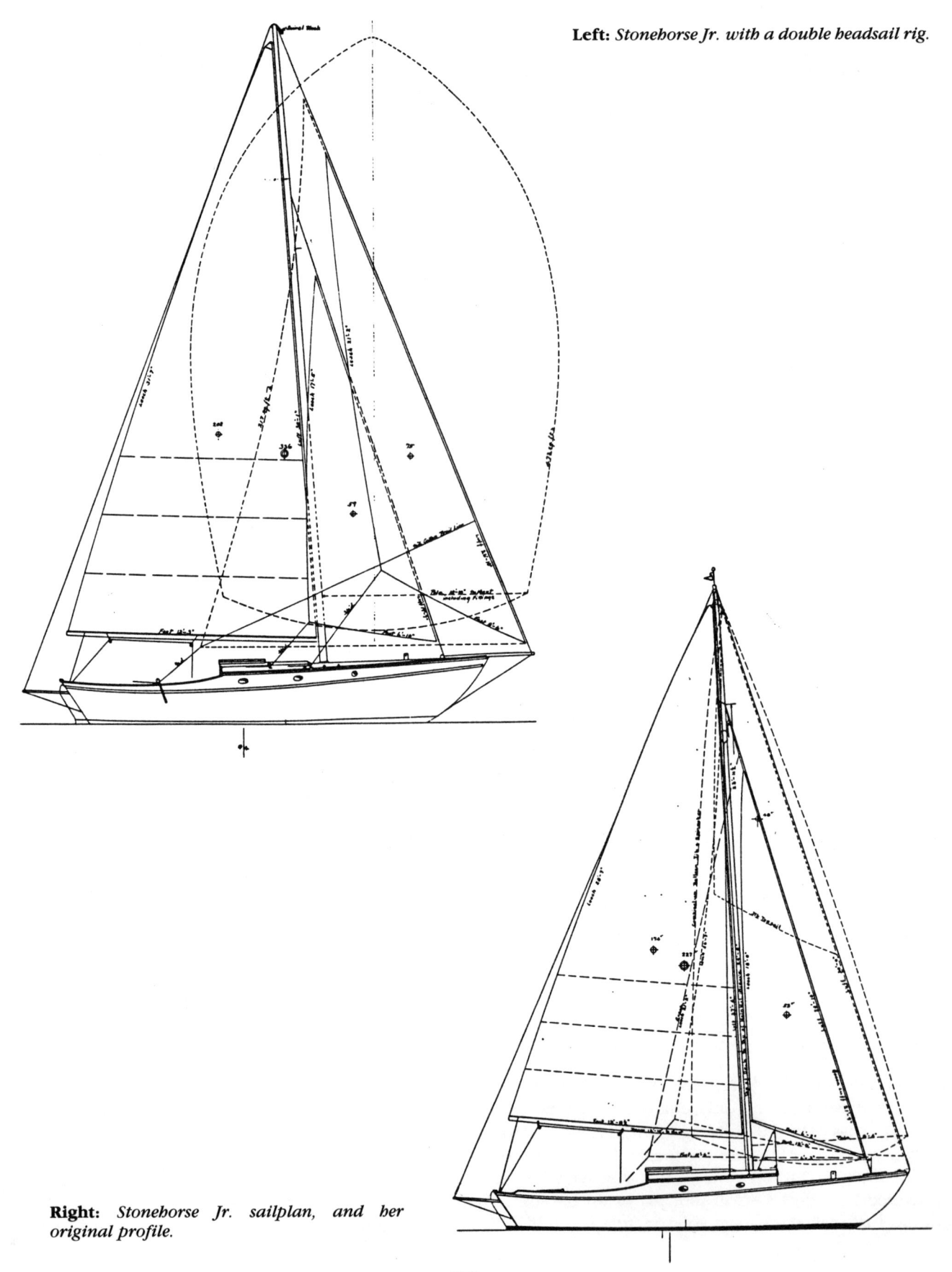

Right: *Stonehorse Jr. sailplan, and her original profile.*

Left: *Double headsails, double spreaders.*

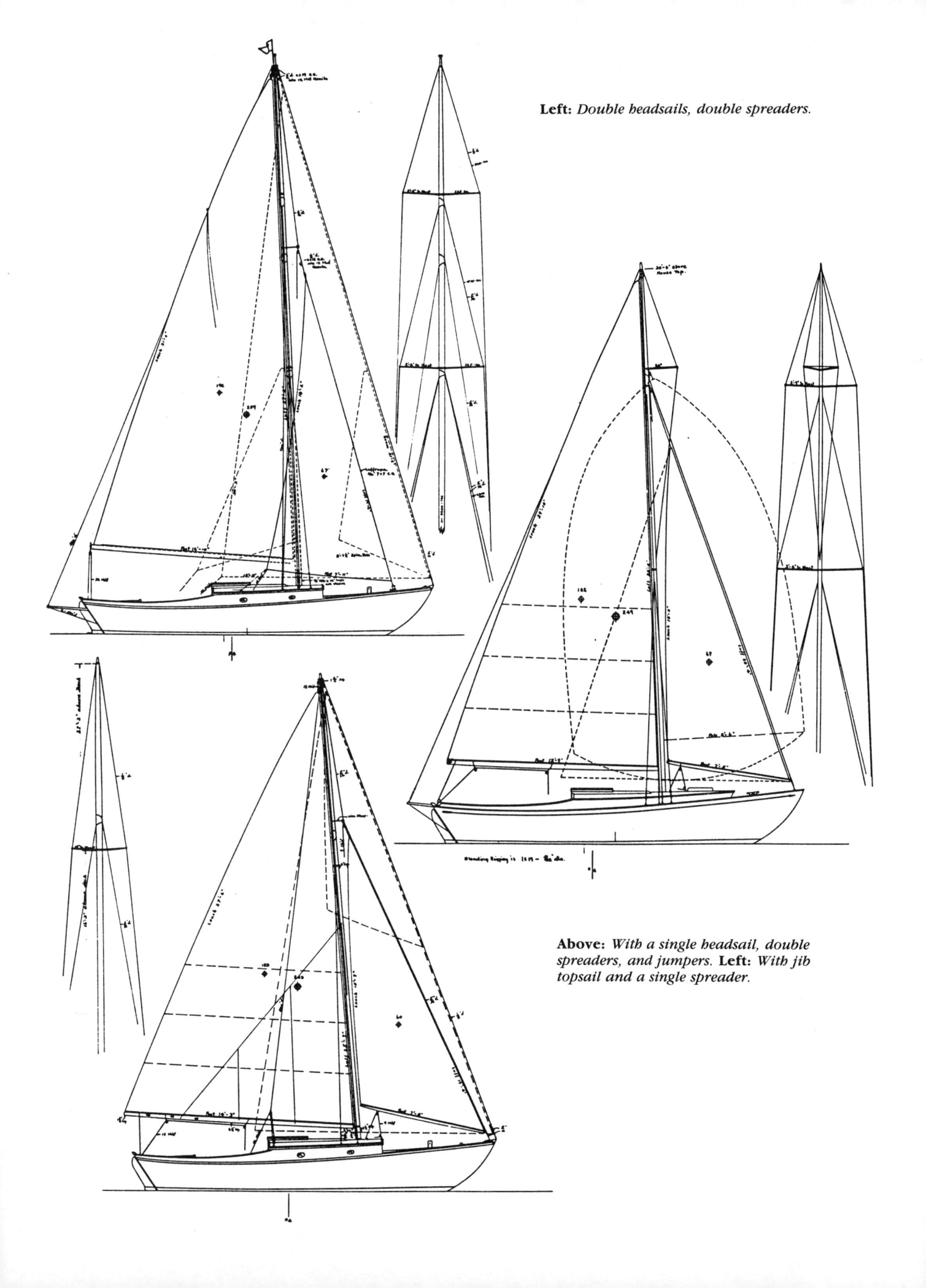

Above: *With a single headsail, double spreaders, and jumpers.* **Left:** *With jib topsail and a single spreader.*

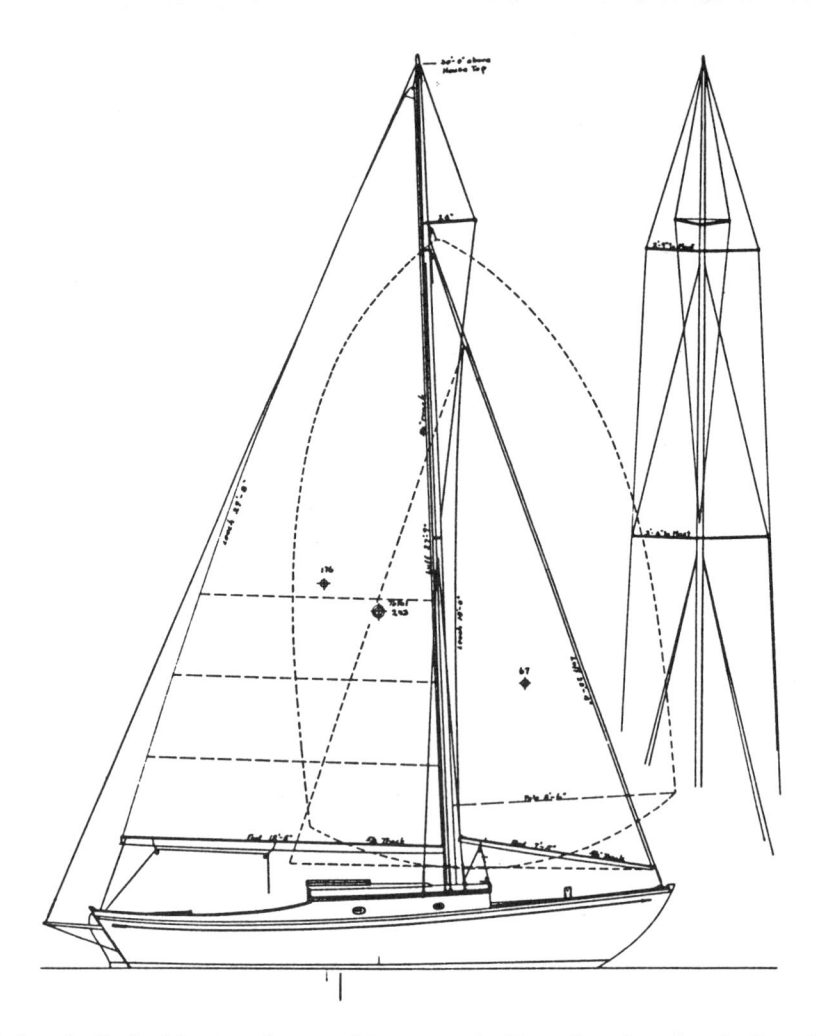

Single headsail, double spreaders, and jumpers; the lines drawings for the Stonehorse Jr.

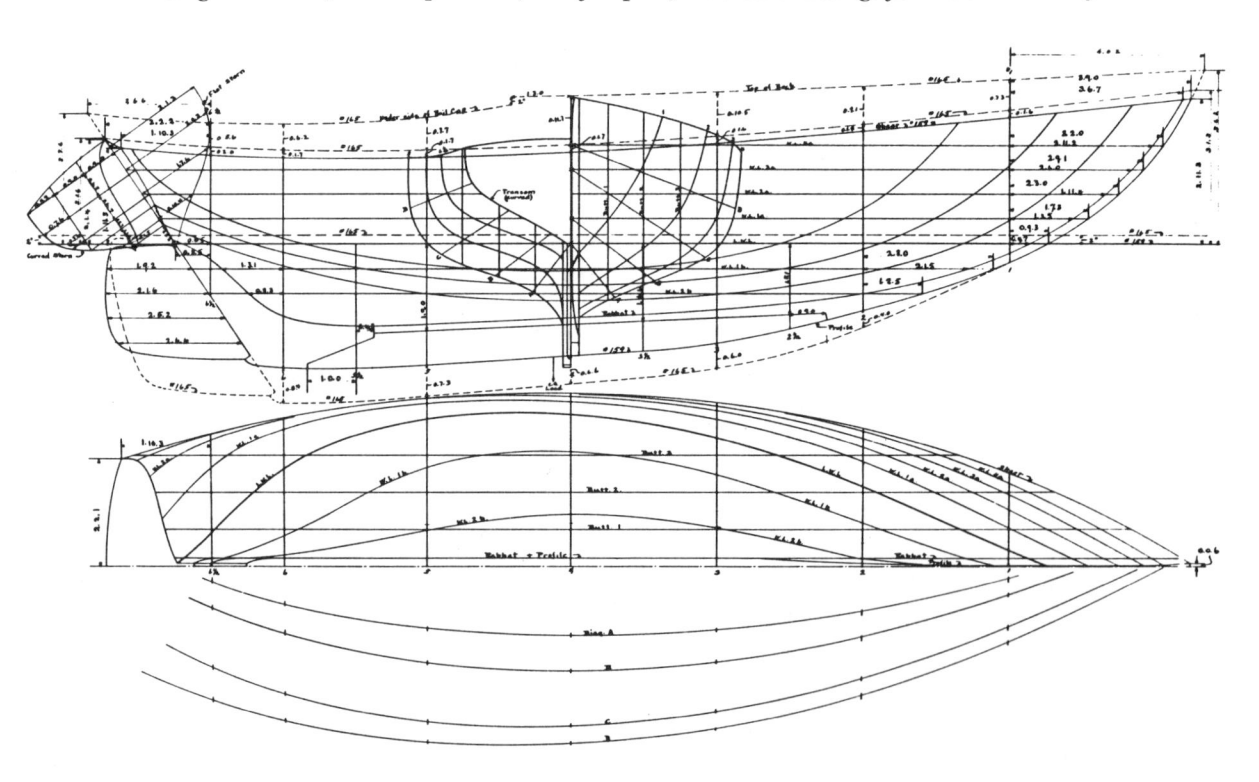

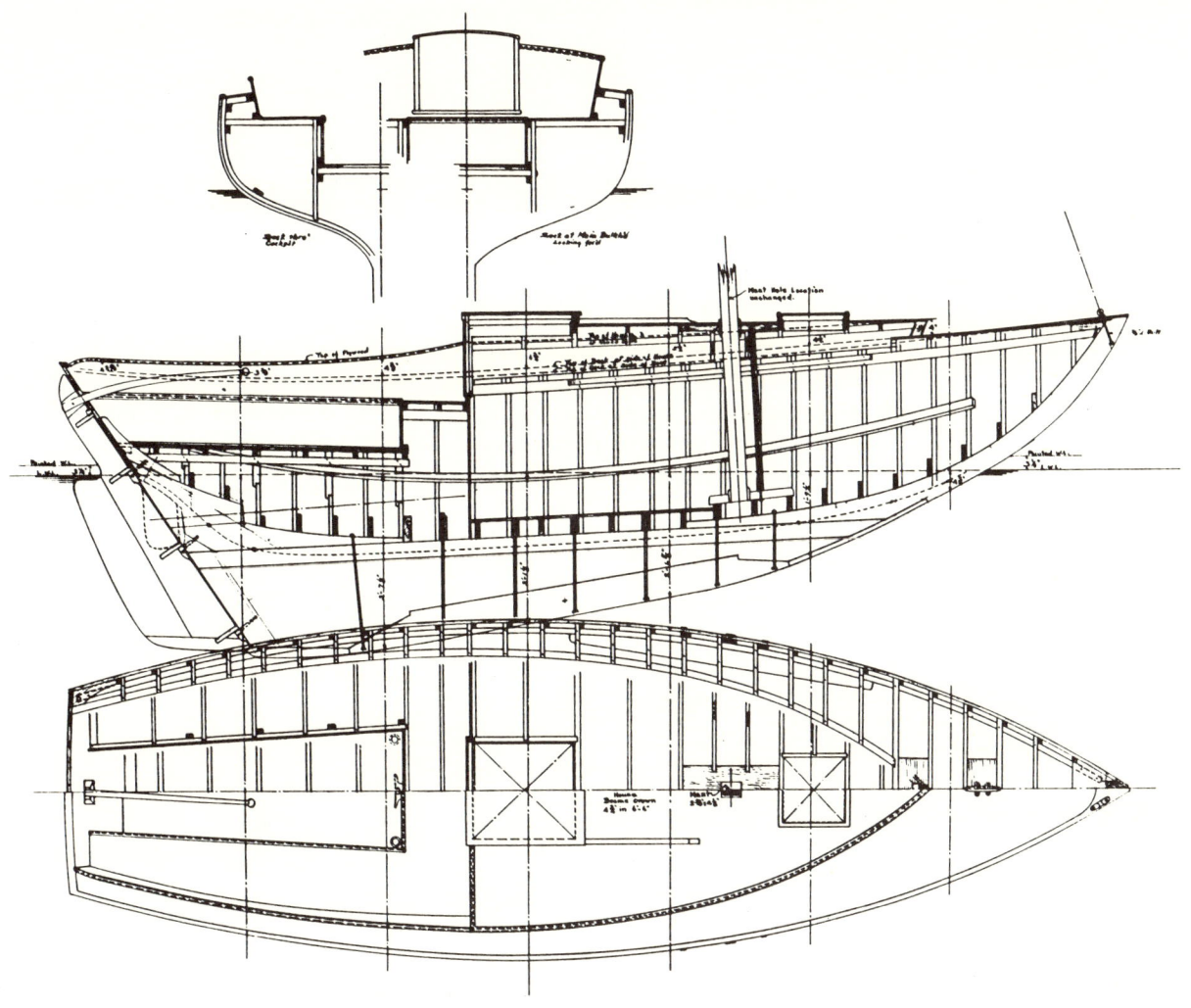

The construction drawings for number 159 and Stonehorse Jr. under sail.

135

160

Number 160: Built by George Chaisson for Tucker Neland of Brookline, Mass., in 1933, this 16-foot-by-5-foot-6-inch catboat was shipped to North Haven, Me., by the Eastern Steamship Line. She was cat rigged but certainly narrower than the usual proportions of a cat. She also had a little less than 400 pounds of lead outside.

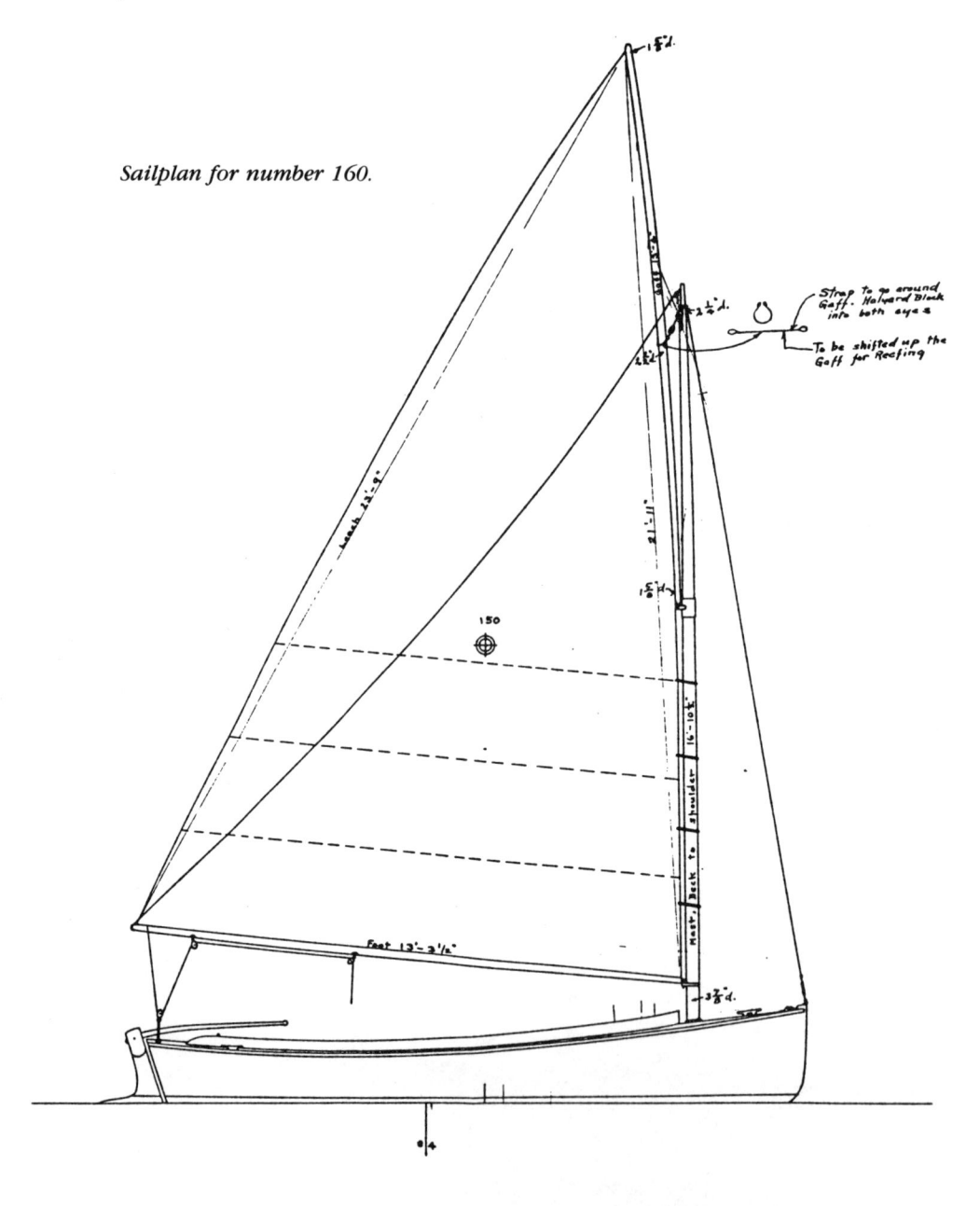

Sailplan for number 160.

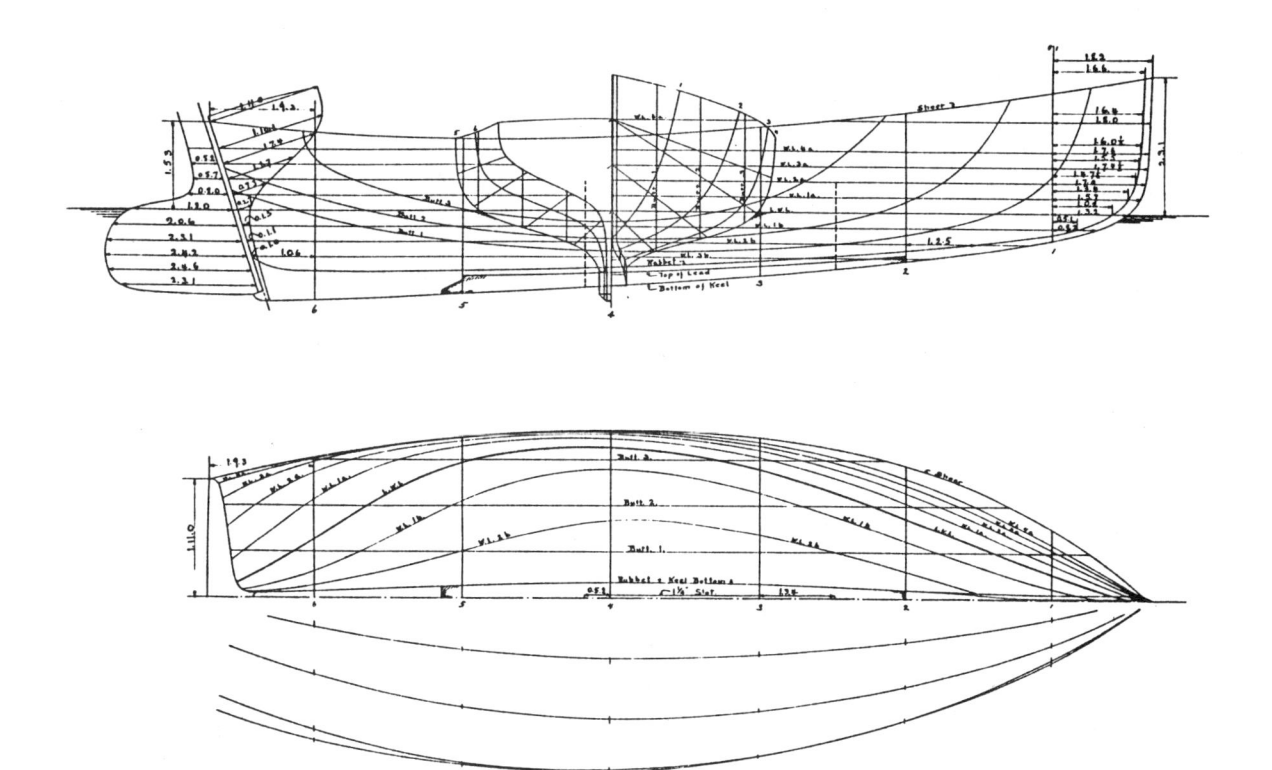

The lines for number 160 and her construction drawings.

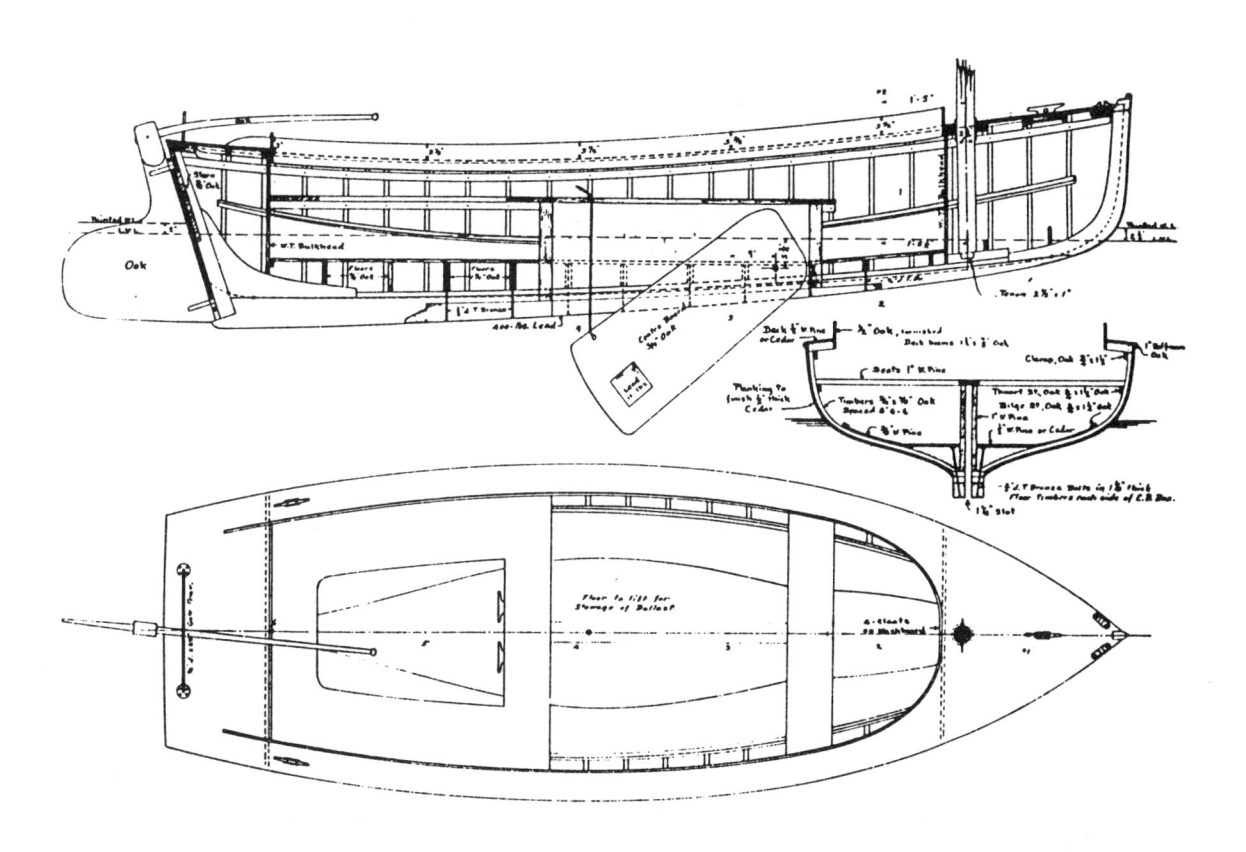

162

Design Number 162
Stonehorse Senior
Length Overall: 33 feet
Length on Waterline: 26 feet 3 inches
Beam: 10 feet 2 inches
Draft: 4 feet
Sail Area: 525 square feet
Displacement: 11,200 pounds

Dad never turned out a design without someone coming into the office and commenting that it was great, but wouldn't it be nice to have one a little bigger, smaller, deeper, or shallower. This was the case with the Stonehorse Sr. (number 162), which was 10 feet longer than her sistership and gave a lot more room and accommodations for cruising. The Seniors were designed for Lee and McMath of Harwichport, Mass., and I have records of three that were built.

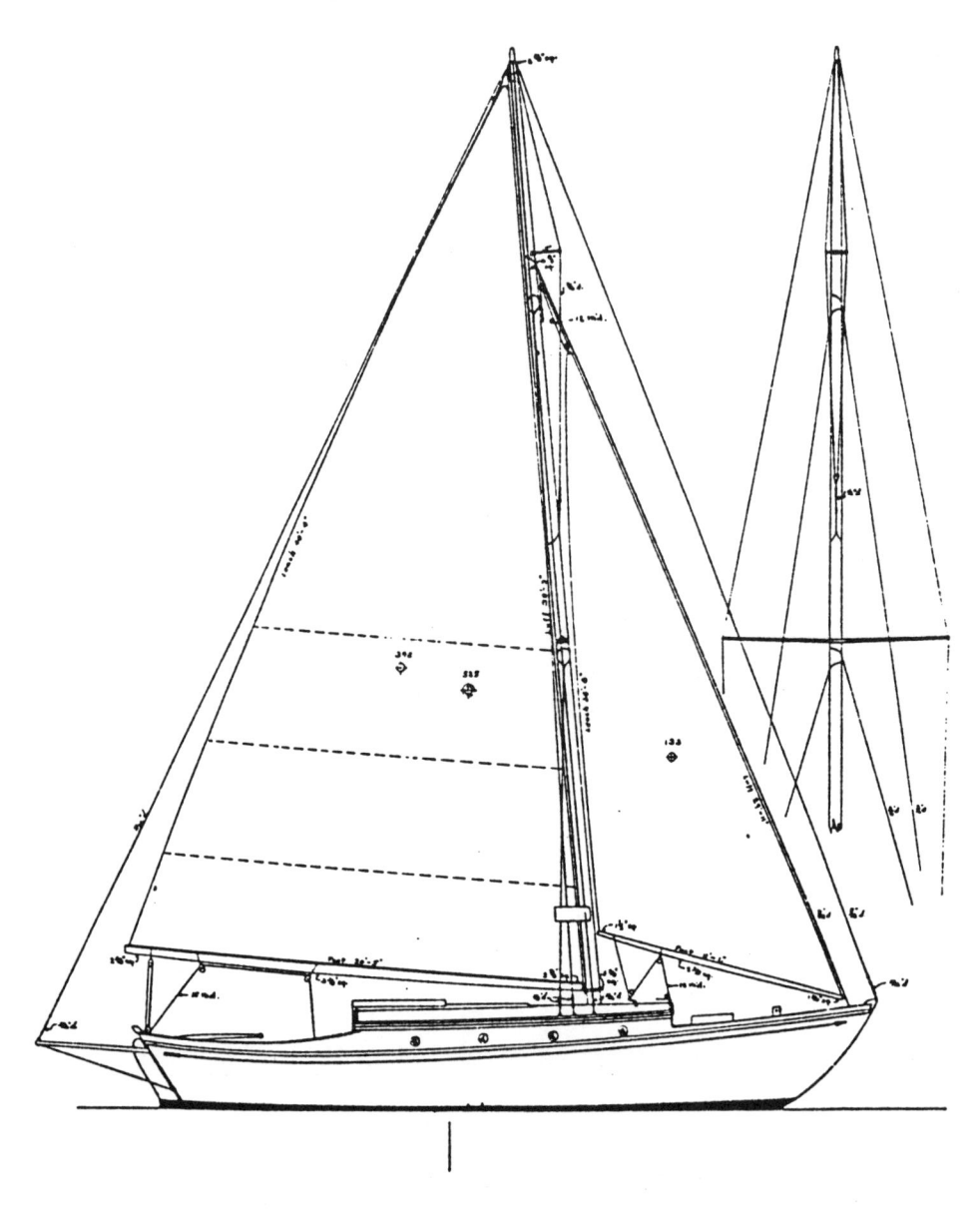

The sailplan for the Stonehorse Sr., number 162.

The lines for number 162.

Left: *The construction drawings for the Stonehorse Sr.*

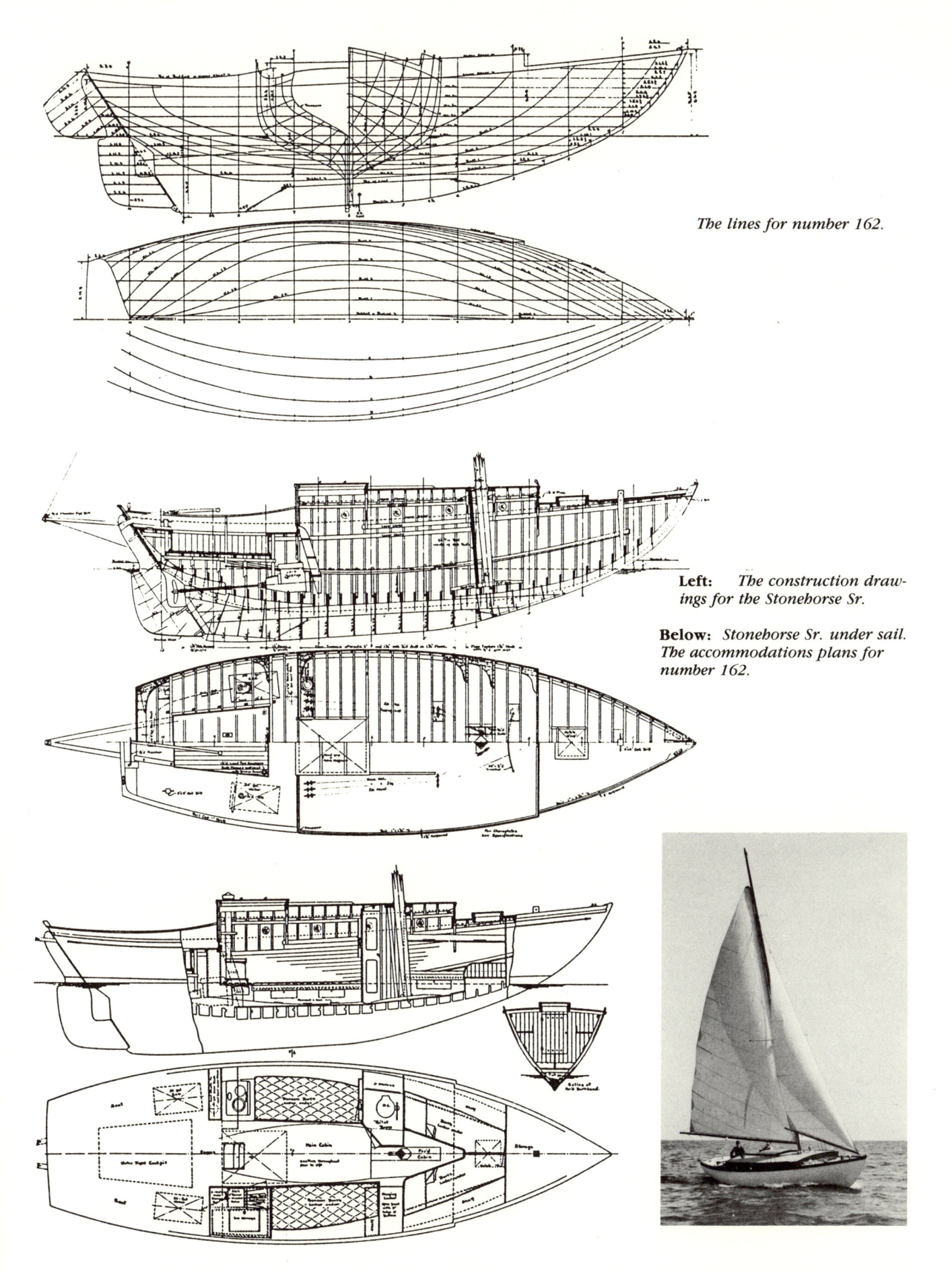

Below: *Stonehorse Sr. under sail. The accommodations plans for number 162.*

139

163 BRUNETTE

Brunette was launched in 1935 from Bill Reid's yard for Paul Whitin of Northbridge, Mass. This boat was one of the first to sport a doghouse. This was necessary because Mr. Whitin had to stay out of direct sunlight. But it must have been convenient in bad weather, too, because the boat could be handled from the doghouse as well as from the cockpit, there being an observation portlight in the overhead through which to watch the masthead pennant and mainsail.

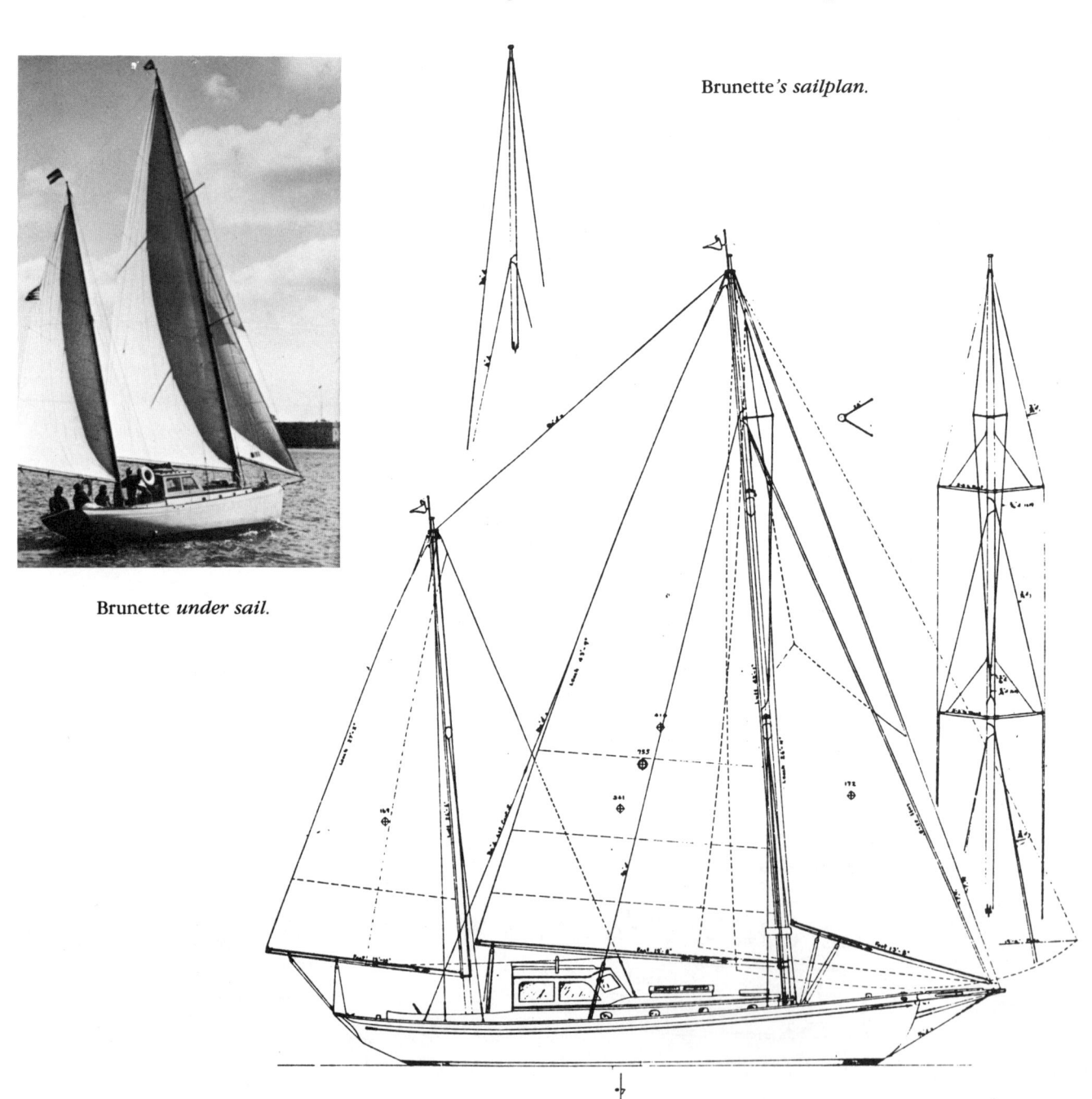

Brunette's *sailplan.*

Brunette *under sail.*

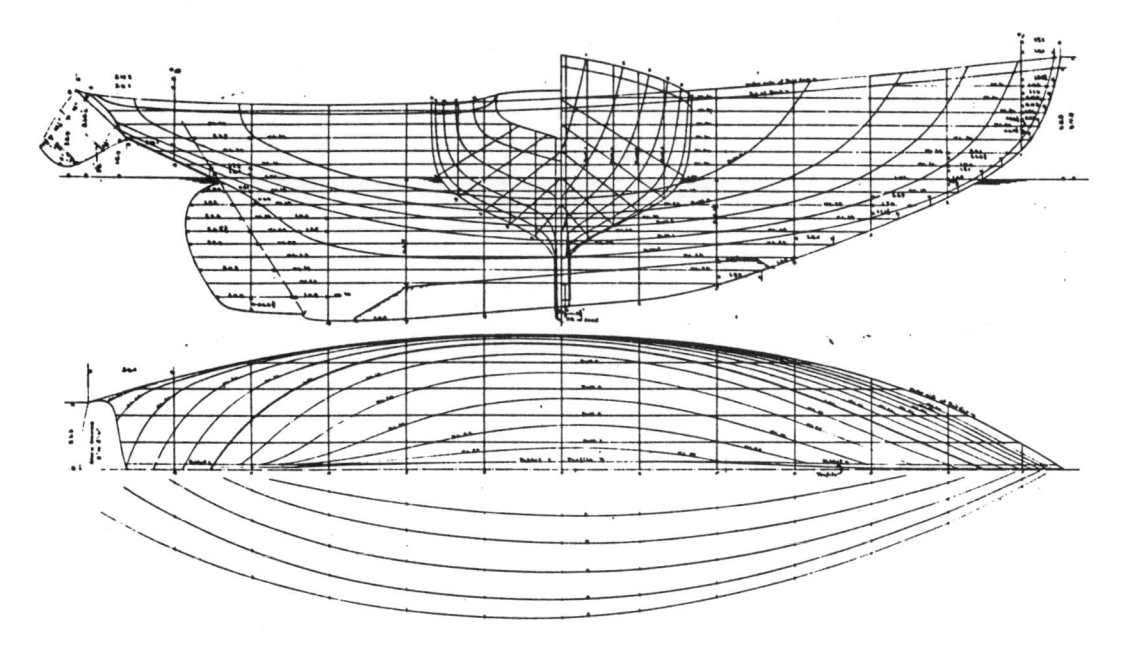

The lines for Brunette *and her construction and accommodations details.*

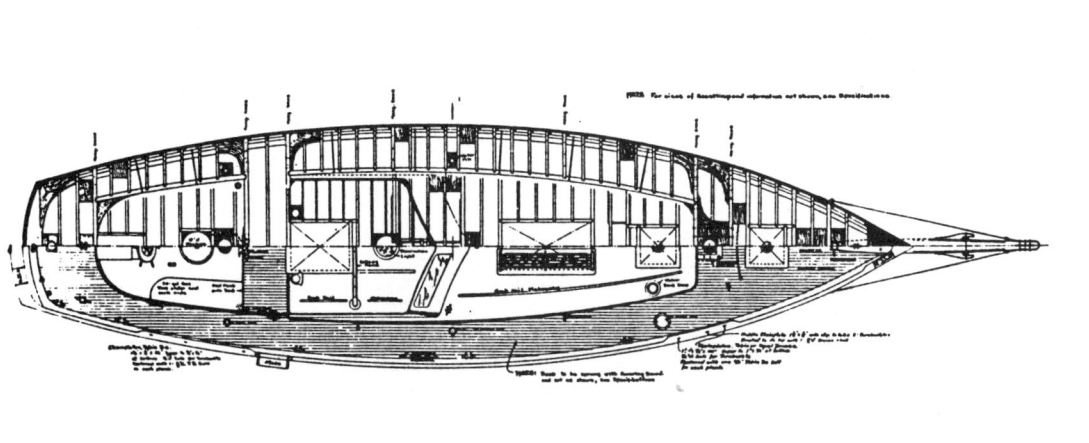

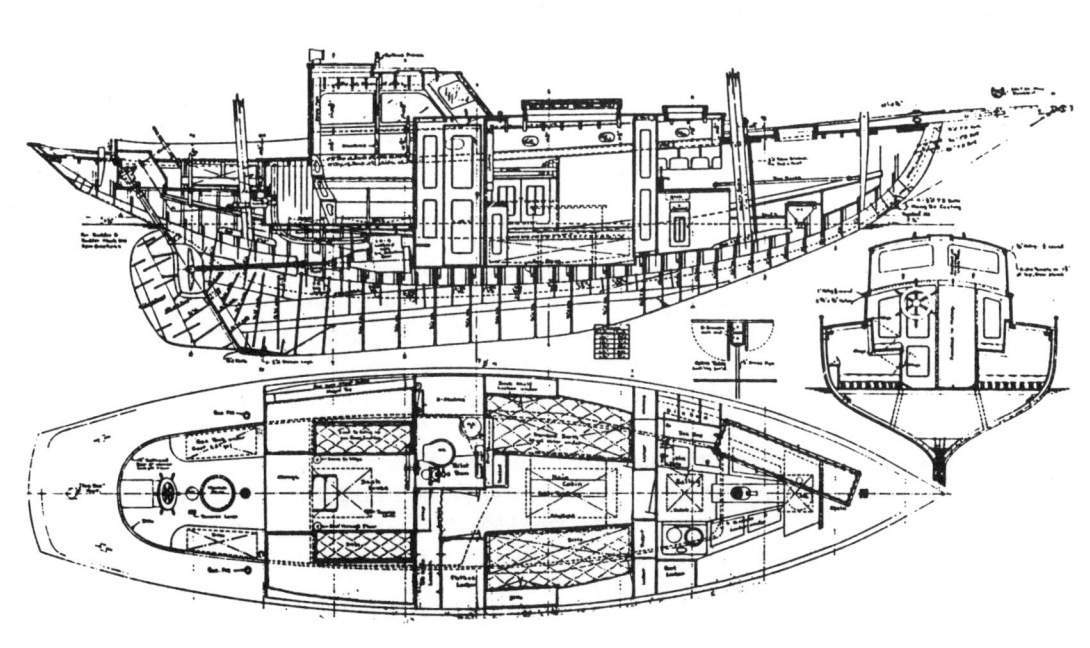

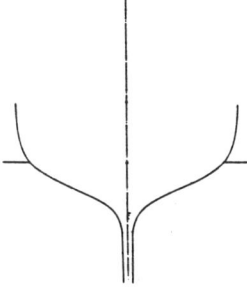

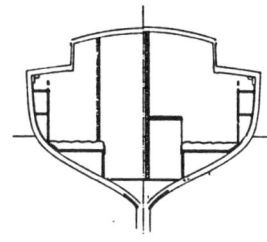

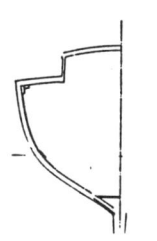

166 RANGER

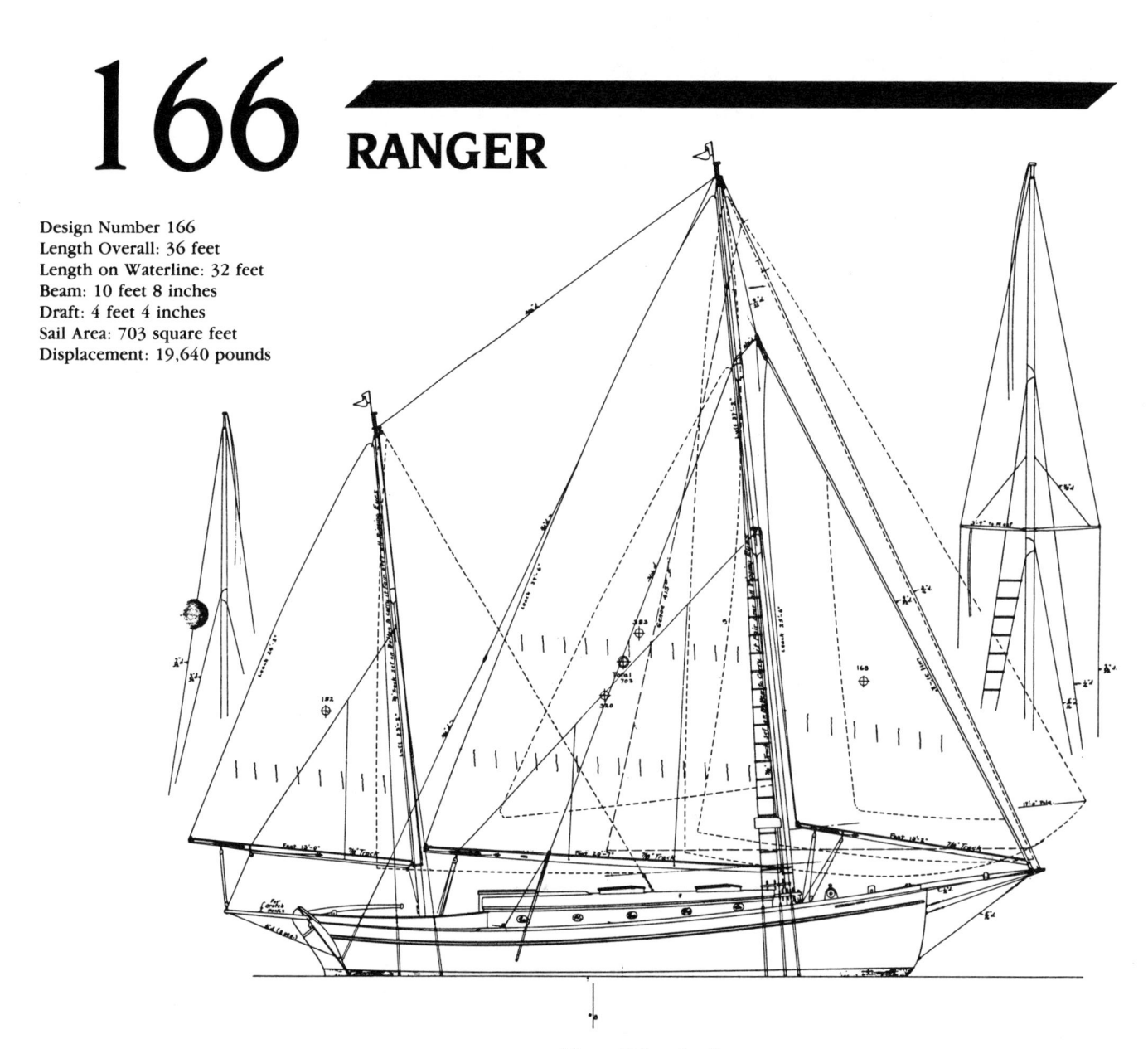

Design Number 166
Length Overall: 36 feet
Length on Waterline: 32 feet
Beam: 10 feet 8 inches
Draft: 4 feet 4 inches
Sail Area: 703 square feet
Displacement: 19,640 pounds

The sailplan for Ranger.

Ranger was designed in 1934 for H. Martyn Baker and built at Chute & Bixby's, Huntington, N.Y. Baker was a dyed-in-the-wool cruiser and had very definite ideas as to cabin arrangements. He sketched out his own cabin plan and submitted it to my father to be fitted to her lines.

The hull was similar in profile to the *Grey Gull* and was painted white up to the guard. Above this she was blue, giving the impression of bulwarks, and this was carried across the stern, which was all above the waterline and somewhat wineglass in appearance. I always thought her most attractive. The shoal draft (4 feet 4 inches) was to accommodate Florida waters, but this was changed in 1935 to give her a draft of 5 feet 1¾ inches. Auxiliary power was a Gray 4-40 gas engine.

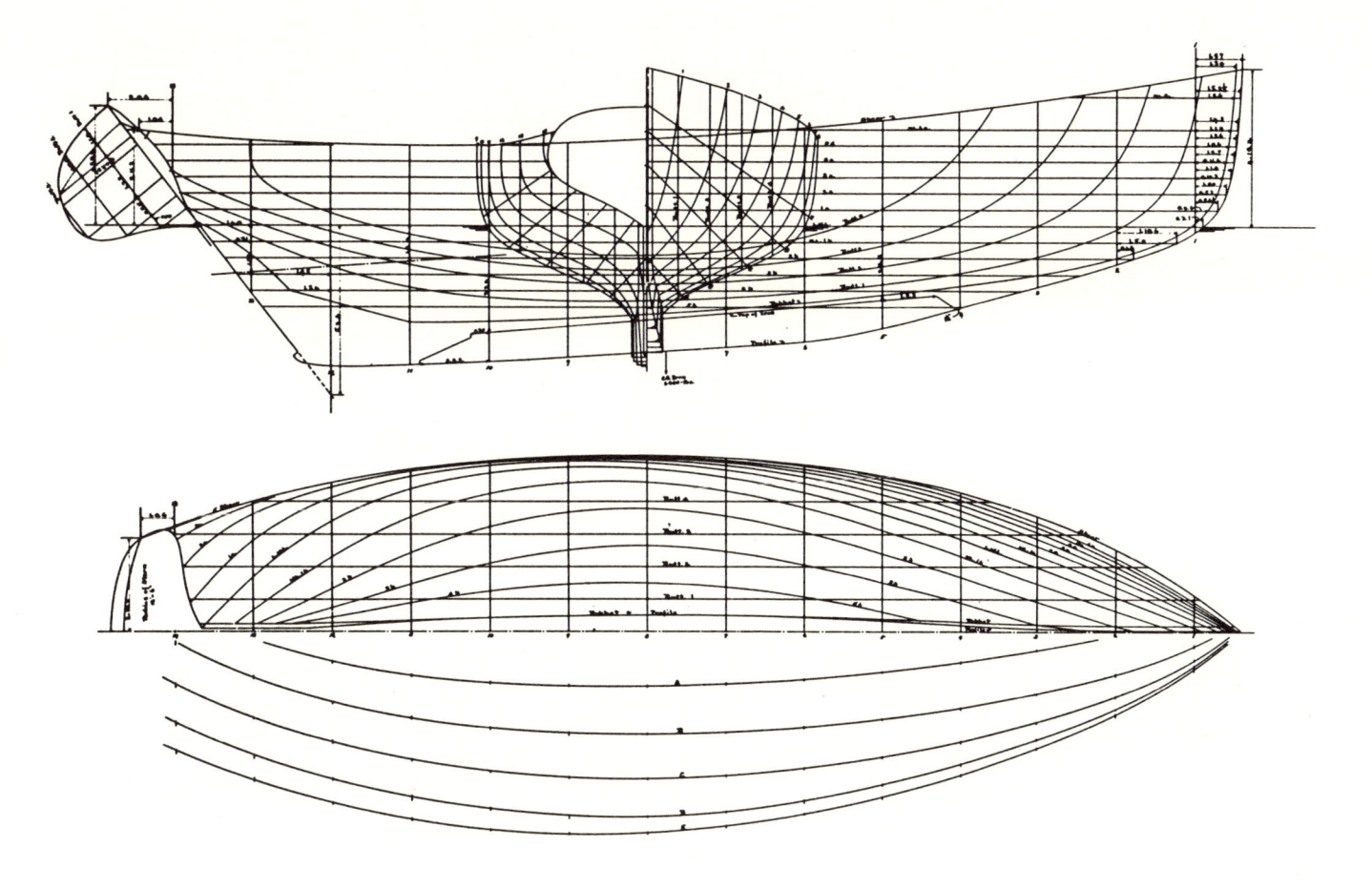

Lines and construction details for Ranger.

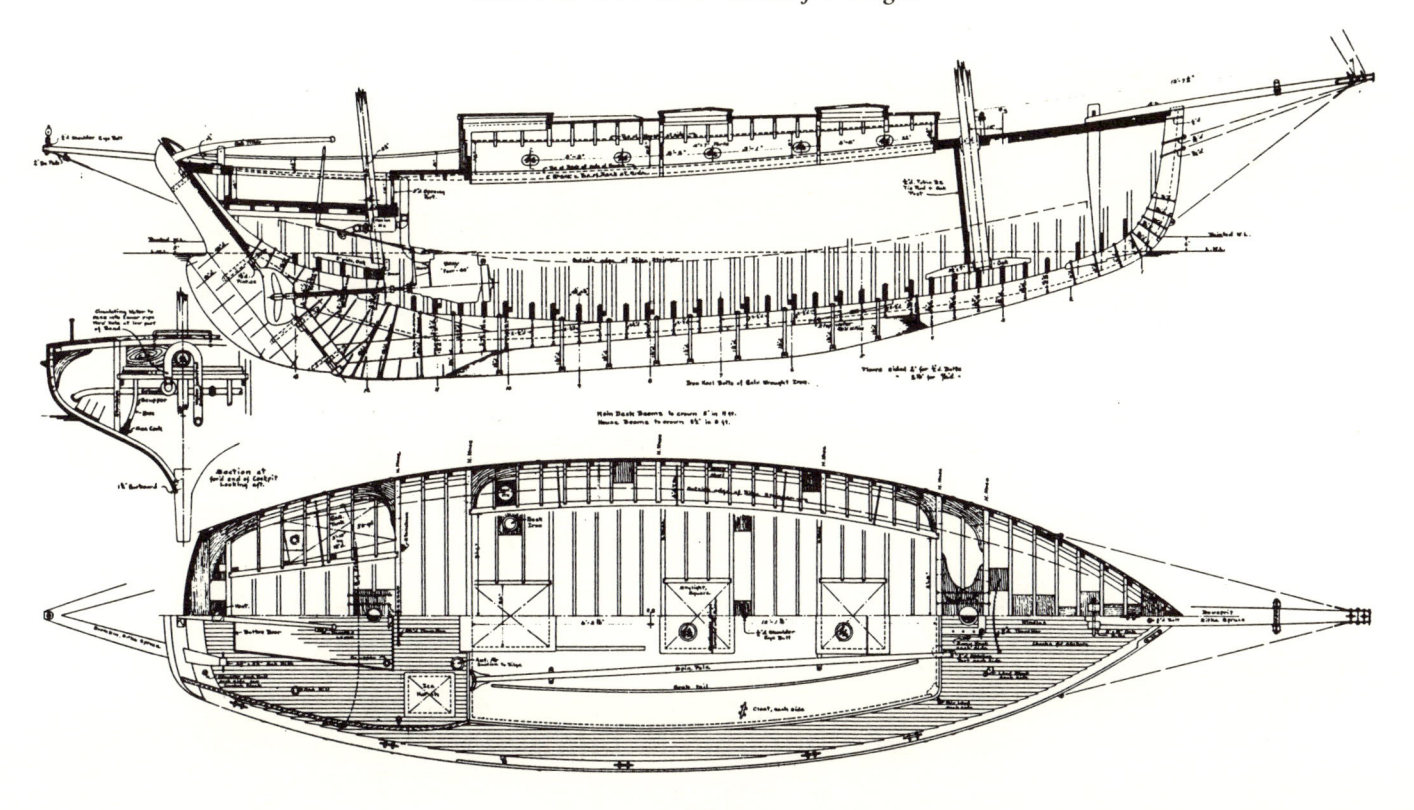

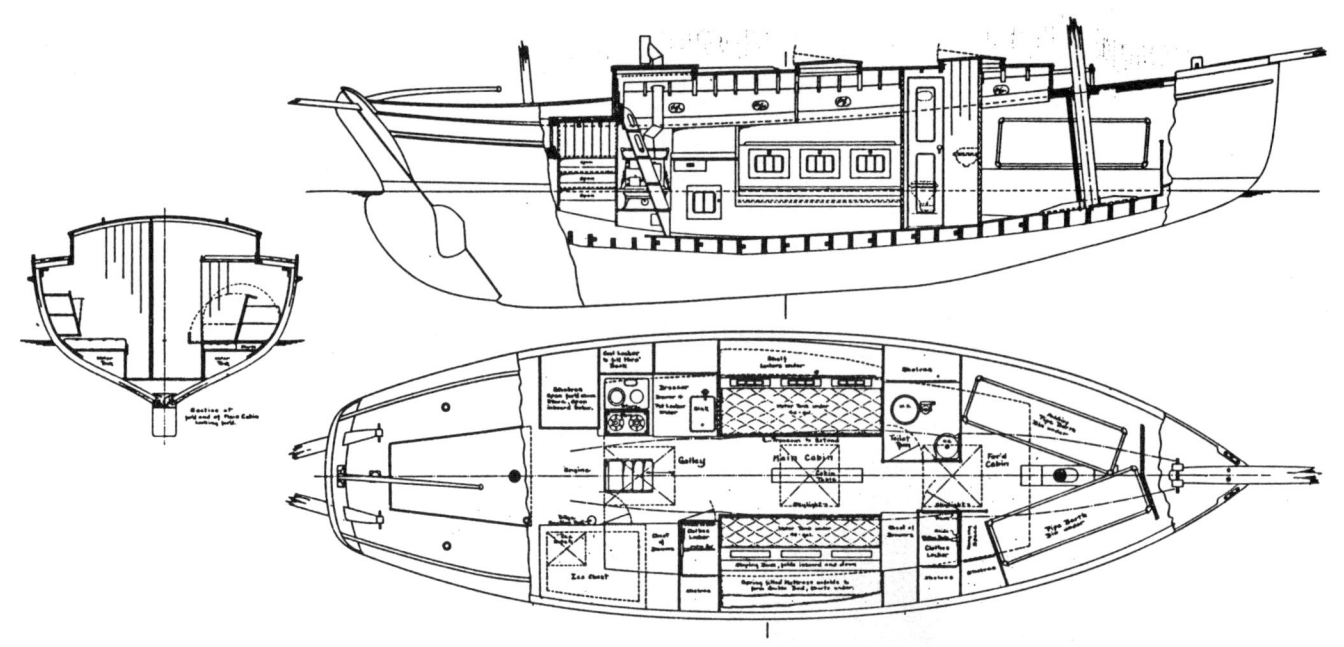

Above: *The owner-designed accommodations plans for* Ranger; **Below:** Ranger *moving along well. A Morris Rosenfeld photograph, courtesy of S. Sturgis Crocker.*

LANDS END 168

Design Number 168
Length Overall: 39 feet 3 inches
Length on Waterline: 35 feet 1 inch
Beam: 10 feet 10 inches
Draft: 6 feet
Sail Area: 868 square feet
Displacement: 24,150 pounds

The sailplan for Land's End.

Lands End was built at Britt Brothers in West Lynn, Mass., in 1935, at the same time as *Skookum III*. This is another one I worked on as a kid. I can remember when we cast the keel. The mold was set up in the shop where she was to be built, and the lead was melted outside, at least 100 feet away. When it was melted, we carried all 8,800 pounds in ladles and poured it into the mold. A stumble would have been disastrous. Lucky the Occupational Safety and Health Administration wasn't around!

Lands End was built for Lee and Henry Loomis, who cruised and raced her extensively. As a new boat, she went to Bermuda in July 1935, then sailed in the Centennial Race around Block Island and left for a month's cruise to Newfoundland the same day she finished the Block Island race. Later she was shipped to the West Coast and cruised Alaskan waters. Then she returned to the East Coast, sailing out of Manchester, and is presently in Maine.

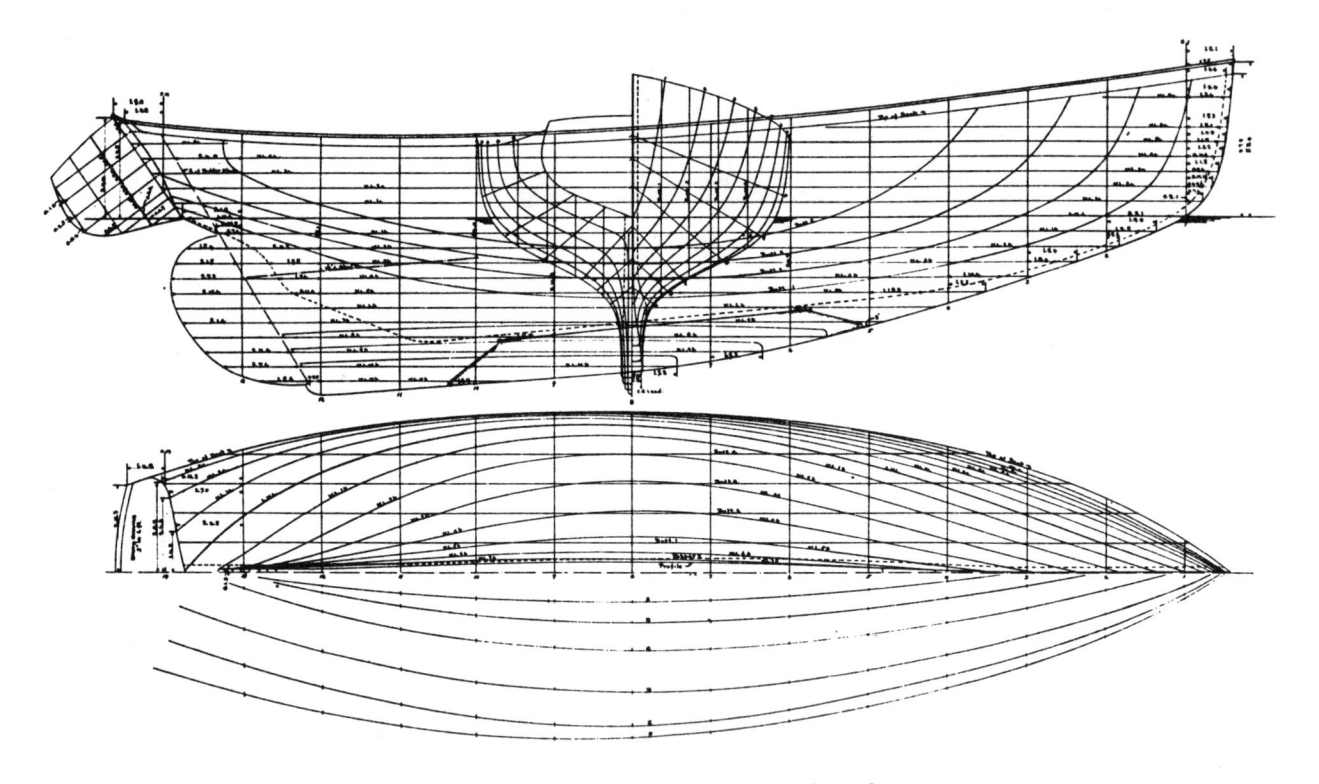

The lines for Land's End, *her construction plans.*

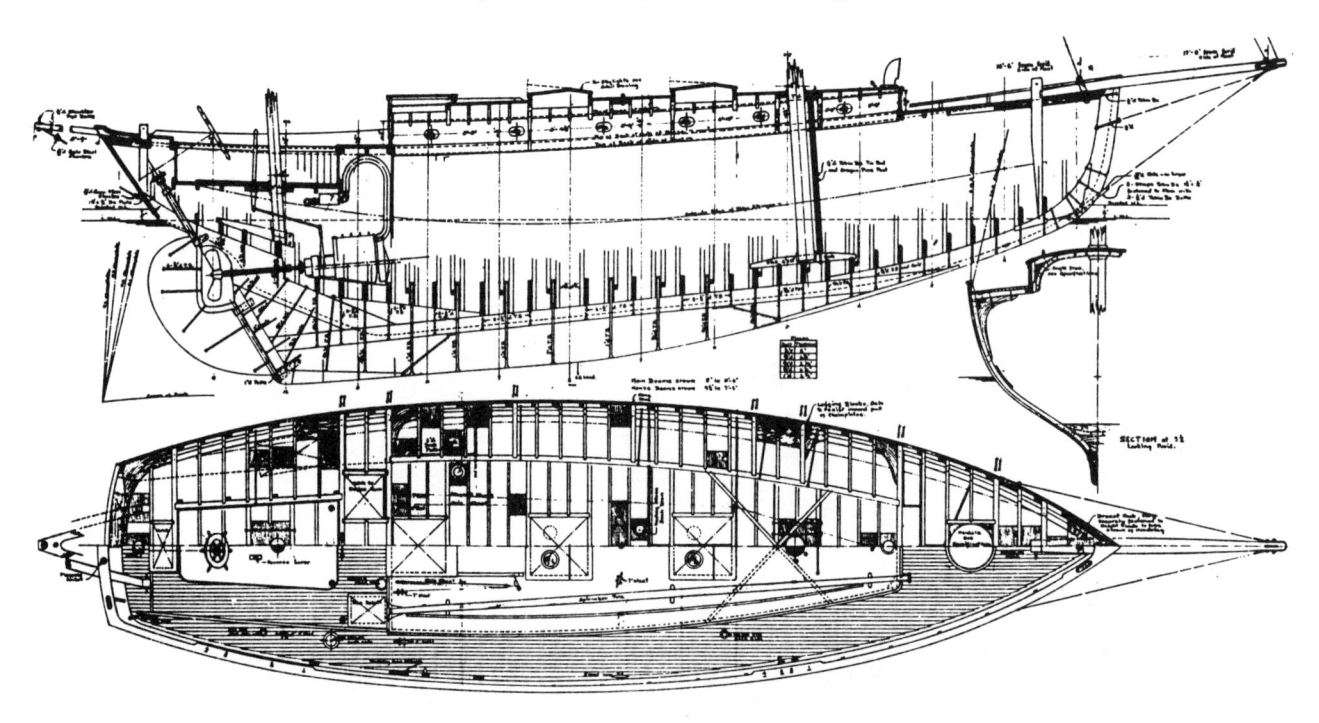

Here is an outline of *Lands End*'s life as written for me by Henry Loomis.

She was built in 1935 by Britt Brothers in West Lynn, Mass. My brother A. Lee Loomis and I owned her together. Lee had done considerable cruising and racing in *Volante,* an Alden schooner, and he worked with your father on *Lands End*'s design. Lee is 6 feet 4 inches, so the bunks were long, the galley high, and every nook and cranny used.

In the summer of 1935, Lee was skipper. He raced in several overnight races like the Whaler's Race, cruised to Bermuda, and then cruised offshore to St. John's,

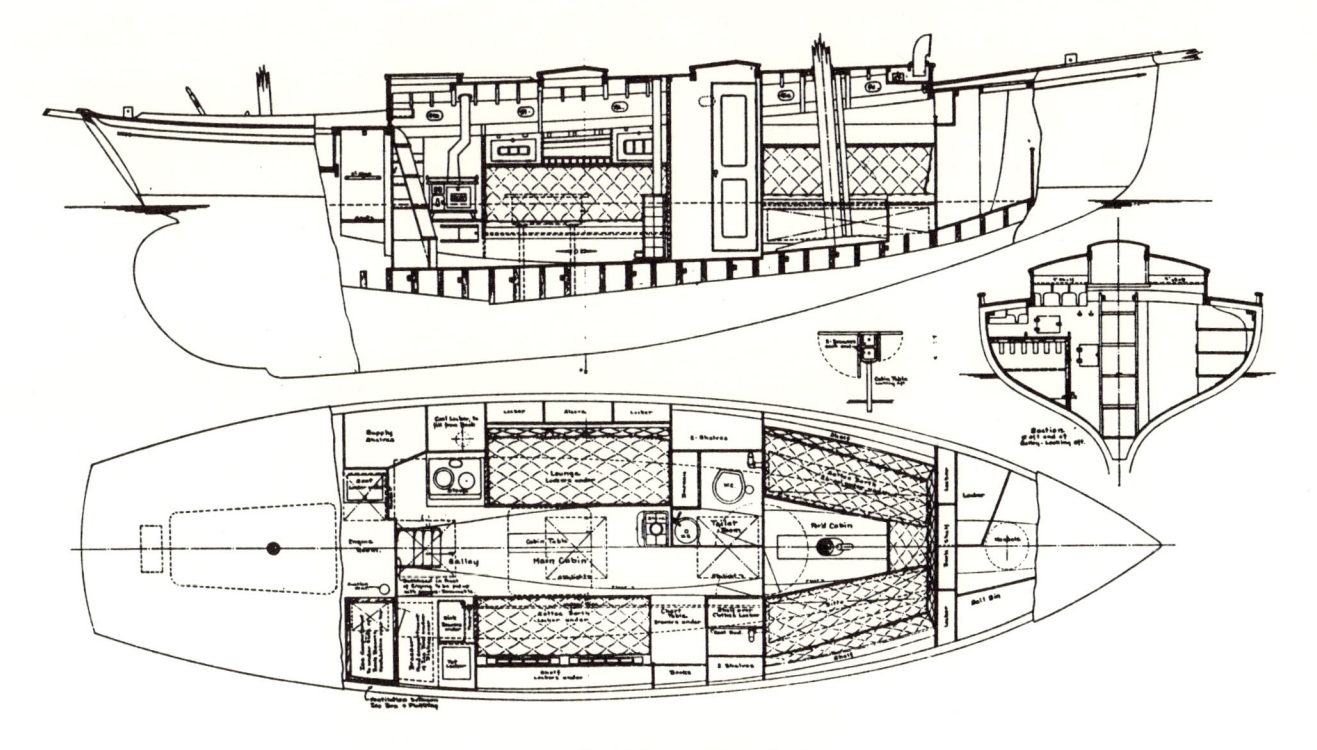

Land's End *accommodations*.

Newfoundland. The crew numbered four: two "old men," about 22 years old, and two "young men," aged 16. We were in a hurricane 200 miles south of Newfoundland, which blew out the storm trysail and double-reefed mizzen. We had to heave-to with only staysail. One wave washed over us, taking me over the side (I was lashed to the mizzen so I could get back easily) and turning her more than 90 degrees to the horizontal. The hot coals came out of the stove, hit the overhead, and set the bunks on fire, but there was plenty of water below to put the fire out. The radio broke the brass strap holding it in, gained altitude crossing the cabin, and hit the lee frame just above the head of the man off watch in the pipe berth. The dent is still visible in the beam.

In the summer of 1936, Lee skippered her in the Bermuda Race. We were the smallest boat to get there and did very well against the New York 32-foot yawls.

In the summer of 1937, I took over and cruised from Marblehead to Oyster Bay for most of the summer, usually with a crew of one or two other men.

During this period, Lands End's home port was Marblehead. She broke her moorings in the hurricanes of 1935 and 1937 and ended up on the beach both times.

In 1939 I took her to Labrador with three classmates. Our farthest journey north was to Northwest River. We went up east of Newfoundland and came back west of Newfoundland.

In 1939 we shipped her to Seattle and then sailed her to Icy Bay, Alaska — about as far north as you can go without going west. We went up on the inside passage but came back outside of Vancouver.

Lands End spent the war years at Jensen's Boat Yard in Lake Union, Seattle. I bought Lee's half from him in 1945.

In 1946, we spent a month in British Columbia and then sailed her to San Francisco. She was berthed in Berkeley, Calif., and did some day-racing in the Bay.

In 1947 she was shipped back to Boston, but was damaged being lowered from the freighter and spent the summer being repaired.

For the next 25 years, she was berthed in Manchester, Mass. I used her for daysailing and occasional cruises to Maine, Martha's Vineyard, etc. Pie Truesdale used her more than I did since I was working in Washington. She made several cruises to the Bradors. We raced in the Jeffrey's Ledge Race from 1948 to 1956.

In 1974 we sailed her to Maine, and her home port became Camden. She has been cruising the Maine coast ever since. My stepson has taken her on several cruises with his classmates, getting as far as Machias.

Land's End *under sail.* Pole Star, *number 157, is the trailing boat.*

In 1983 we moved her to Joel White's Brooklin, Me., boatyard for extensive repairs. She was showing her age.

But now she is in as good shape as ever. The only significant change is that the coal stove has been replaced with gas — much to the chagrin of all the children and grandchildren. Her home port is now Center Harbor, Me.

171

Sailplan for number 171.

Number 171: The first of these 15-foot round-bottom sailing tenders was built on our front porch. My mother was not very understanding, because you had to walk around the bow to get in the front door. I can remember my father telling my sister at lunch one Saturday what a smart pair of brothers she had. That morning I had braced a support with my foot while nailing it to the floor, and of course, the nail went through the edge of the sole of my shoe, pretty effectively anchoring me. At the same time, my brother was sanding another tender we had, but thinking the abrasive was in the block, he wasn't using any sandpaper. We kept the boat for several years, using her in Manchester and trailering her to Barnstable, Mass.

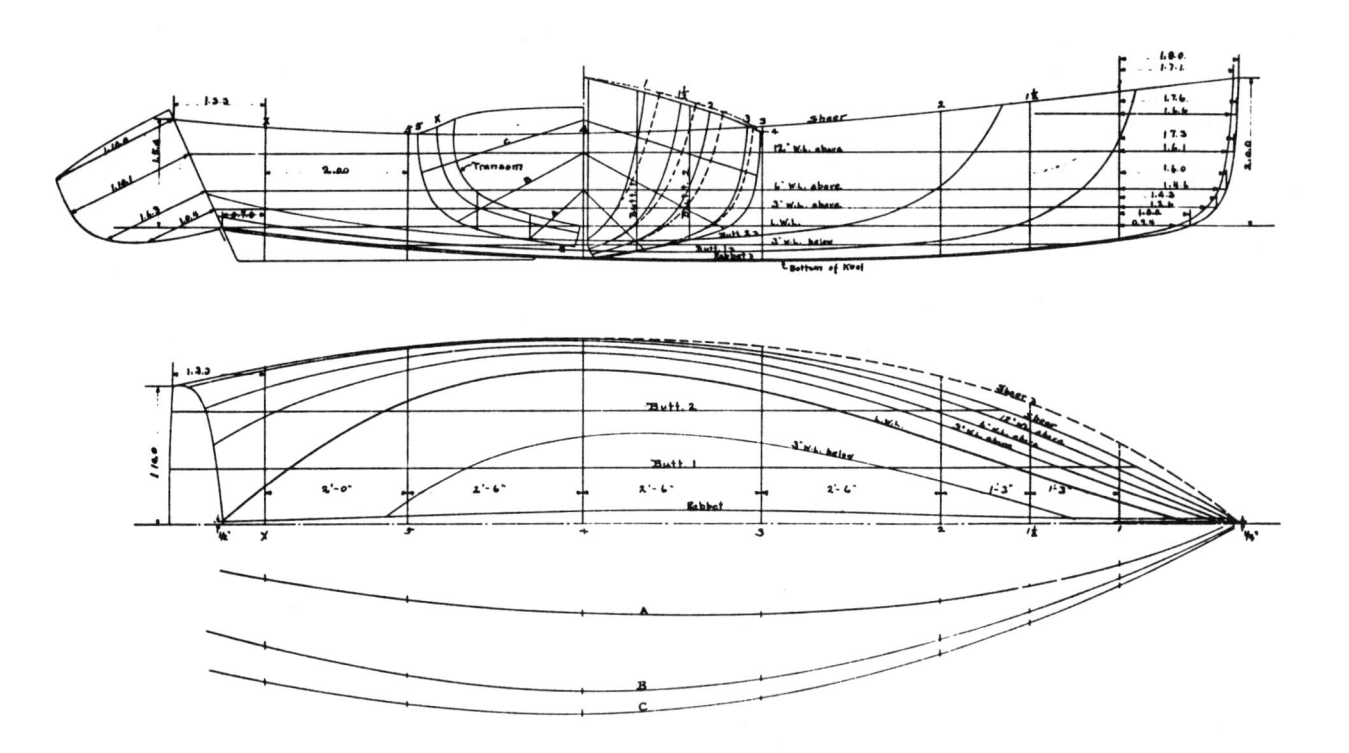

The lines for number 171 and number 171 moving along well in light wind.

175

Number 175: This 18-foot sailing dory was called the *Compass Class*. I have records of about 25 that were built, mostly by George Chaisson of Swampscott.

150

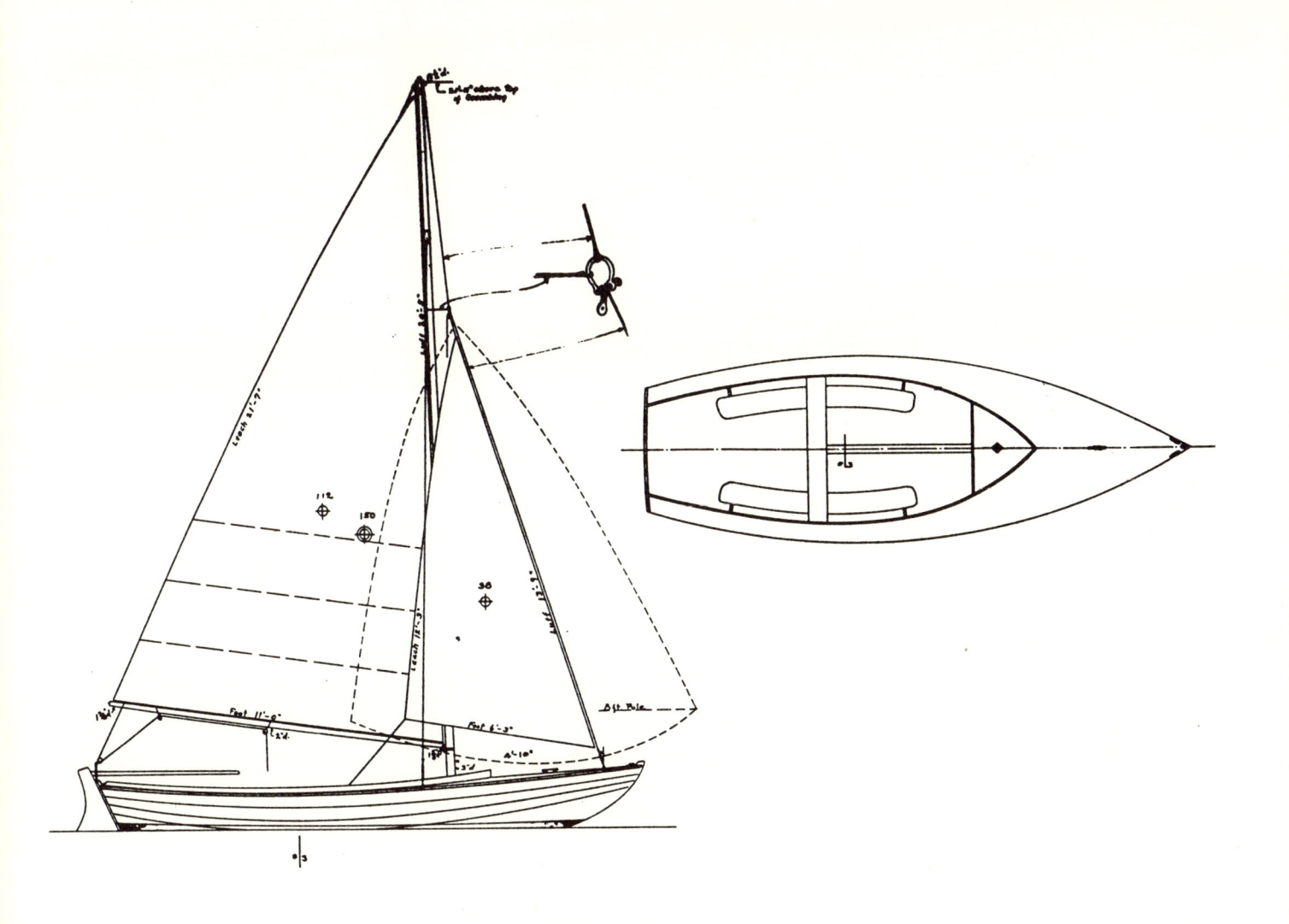

The sailplan and interior layout for number 175 and her lines drawings.

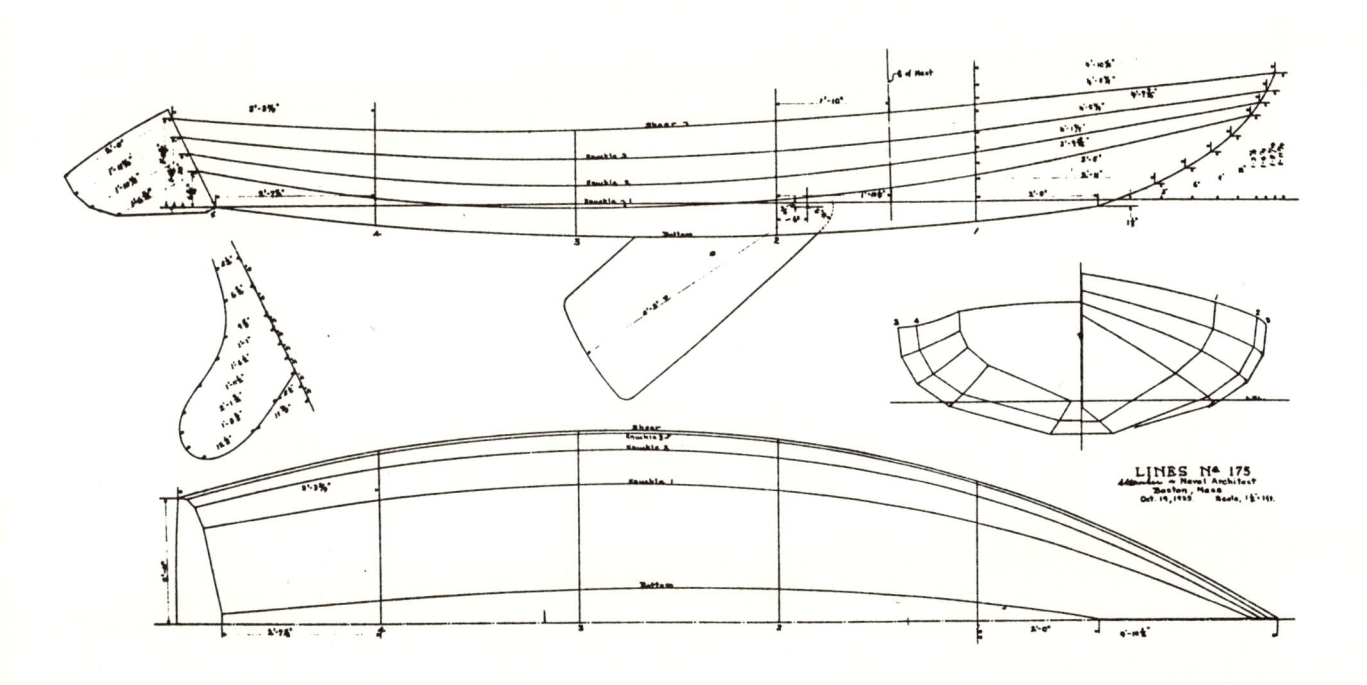

151

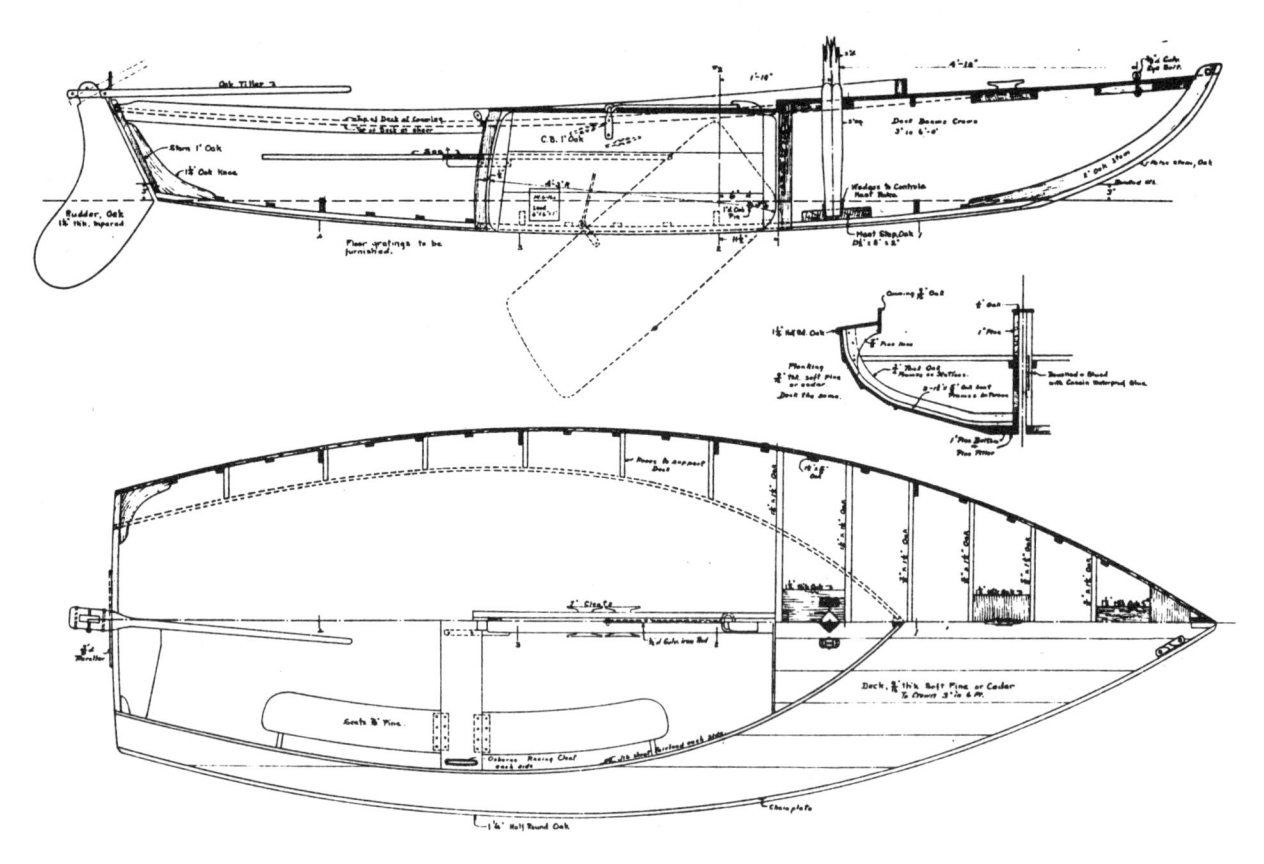

The construction details for number 175.

Compass Class *boats participating in a race off Swampscott, Mass.*

SIRIUS 176

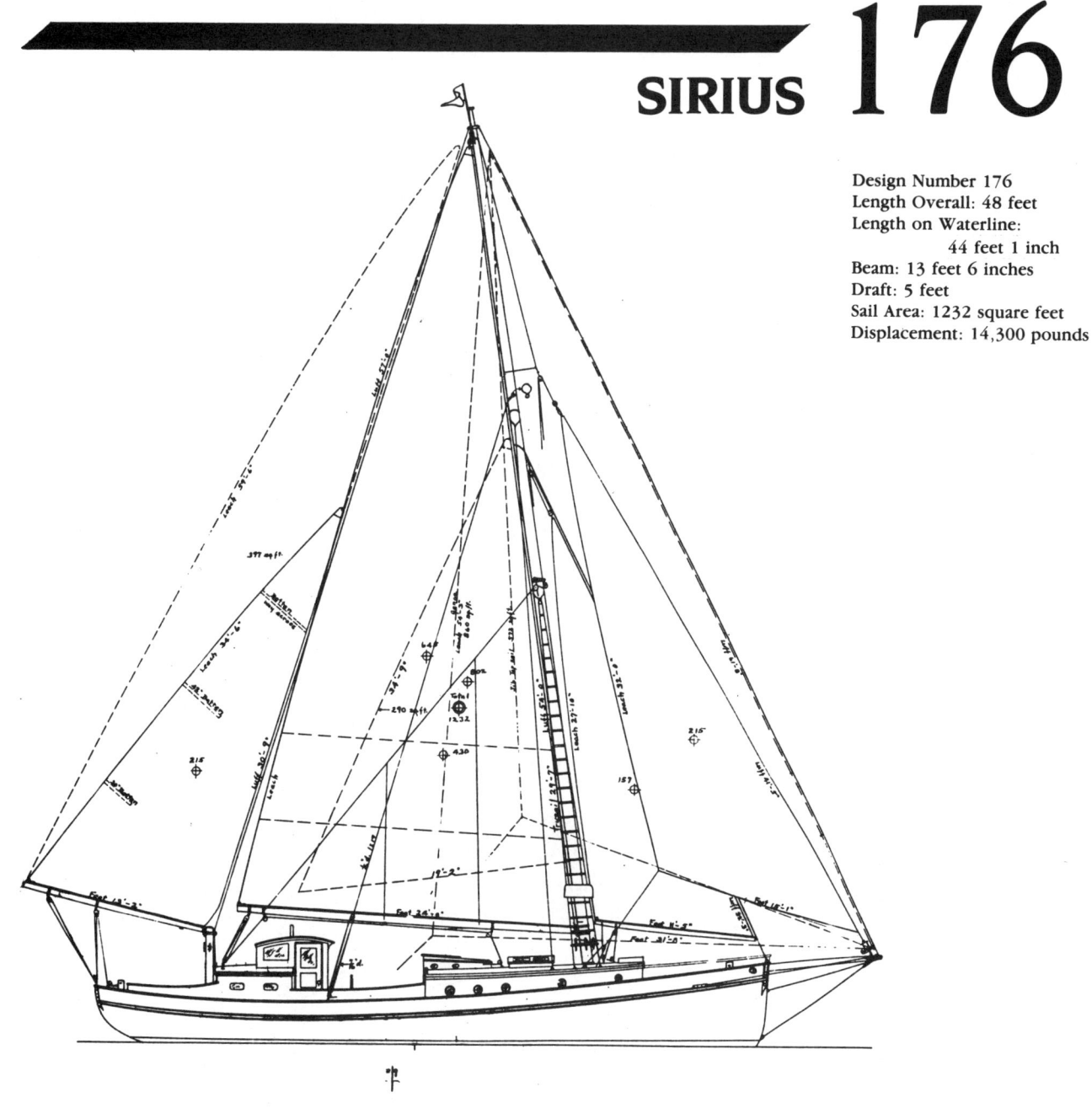

Design Number 176
Length Overall: 48 feet
Length on Waterline: 44 feet 1 inch
Beam: 13 feet 6 inches
Draft: 5 feet
Sail Area: 1232 square feet
Displacement: 14,300 pounds

The sailplan for Sirius.

    Sirius was a backstaysail ketch, sometimes called a "sketch." Originally, she had a raking mast and a backstay brought to the stub of a mizzen that supported the mizzenboom. The backstaysail was set on this stay with snap hooks. The rig was changed to the conventional ketch rig in 1939.
    Sirius was designed for H.H. Meyer, who hired a crew of shipwrights and had her built in his brother's yard in Padanaram, Mass., in 1936. She had an easily driven hull. The 130-horsepower Sterling Chevron engine drove her at a speed of eight knots when cruising and wide open at almost ten.
    In 1937 Meyer cruised her from Padanaram to Cape Smoky with a crew of

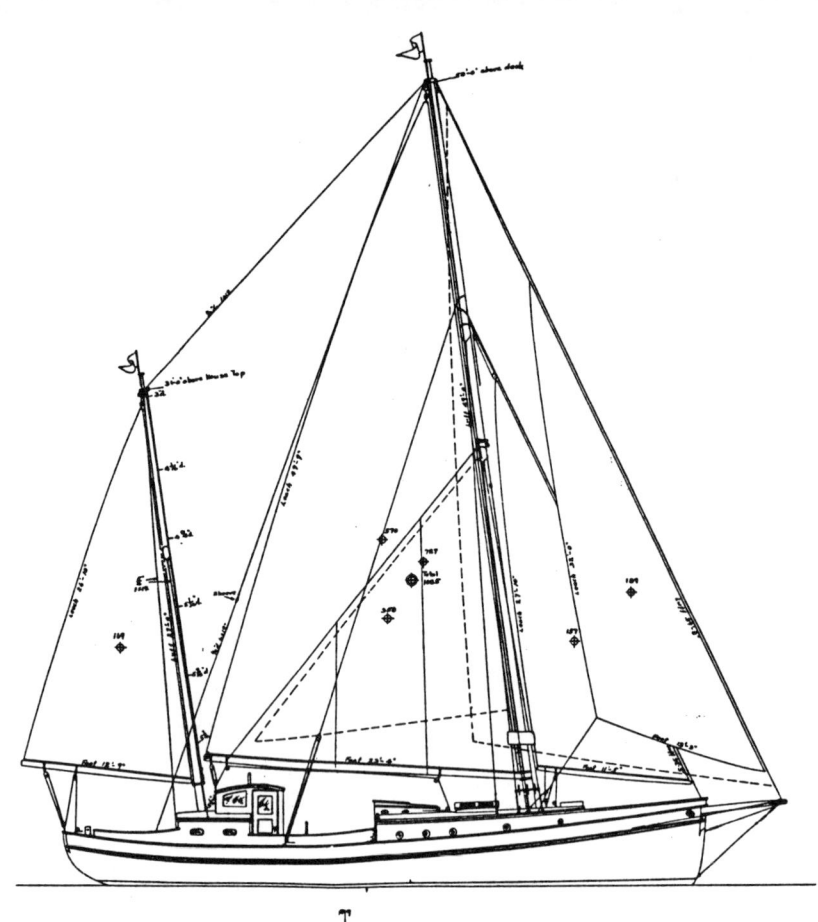

The sailplan for Sirius *as a traditional ketch, and her lines drawings.*

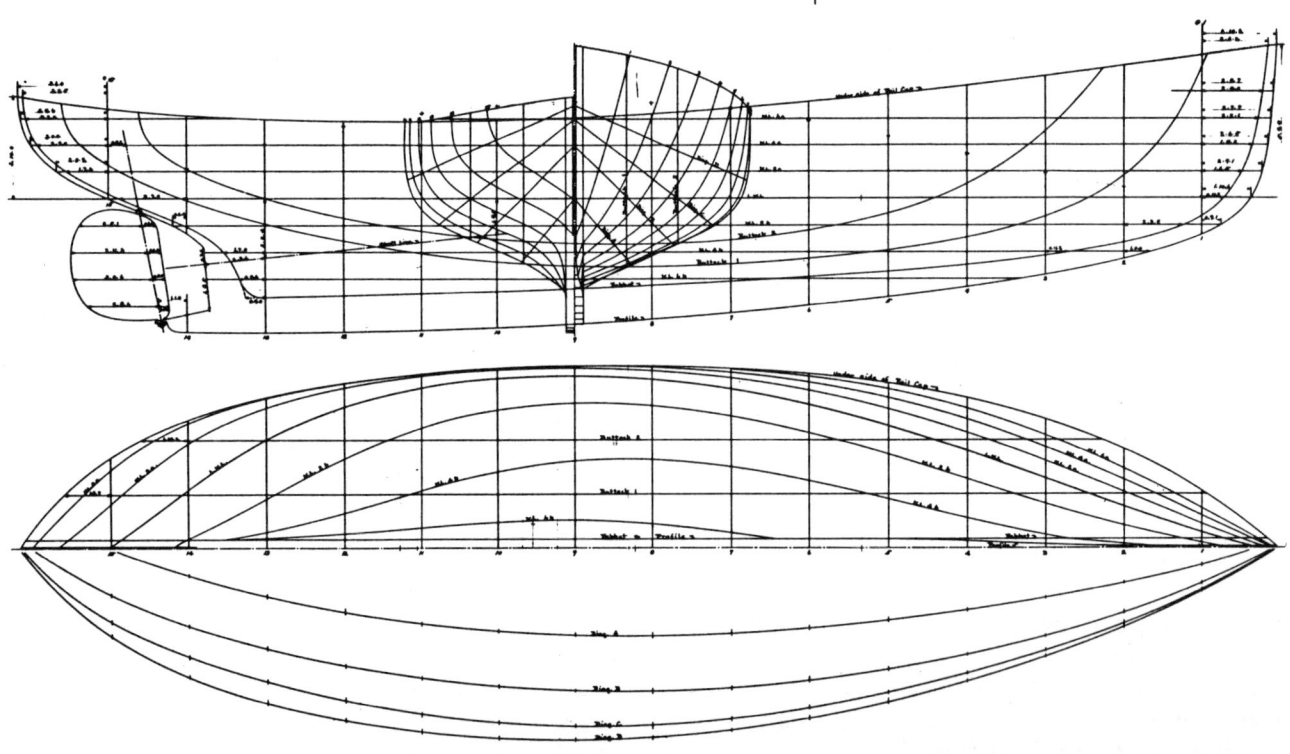

family members. This trip he described in an interesting little book, *Coasting to Smoky*. They covered 1,681 miles, visited 29 ports, and averaged 7.87 knots. Mr. Meyer also cruised her as far south as Key West. During World War II she served in the Coast Guard under command of his son. For two years she was

154

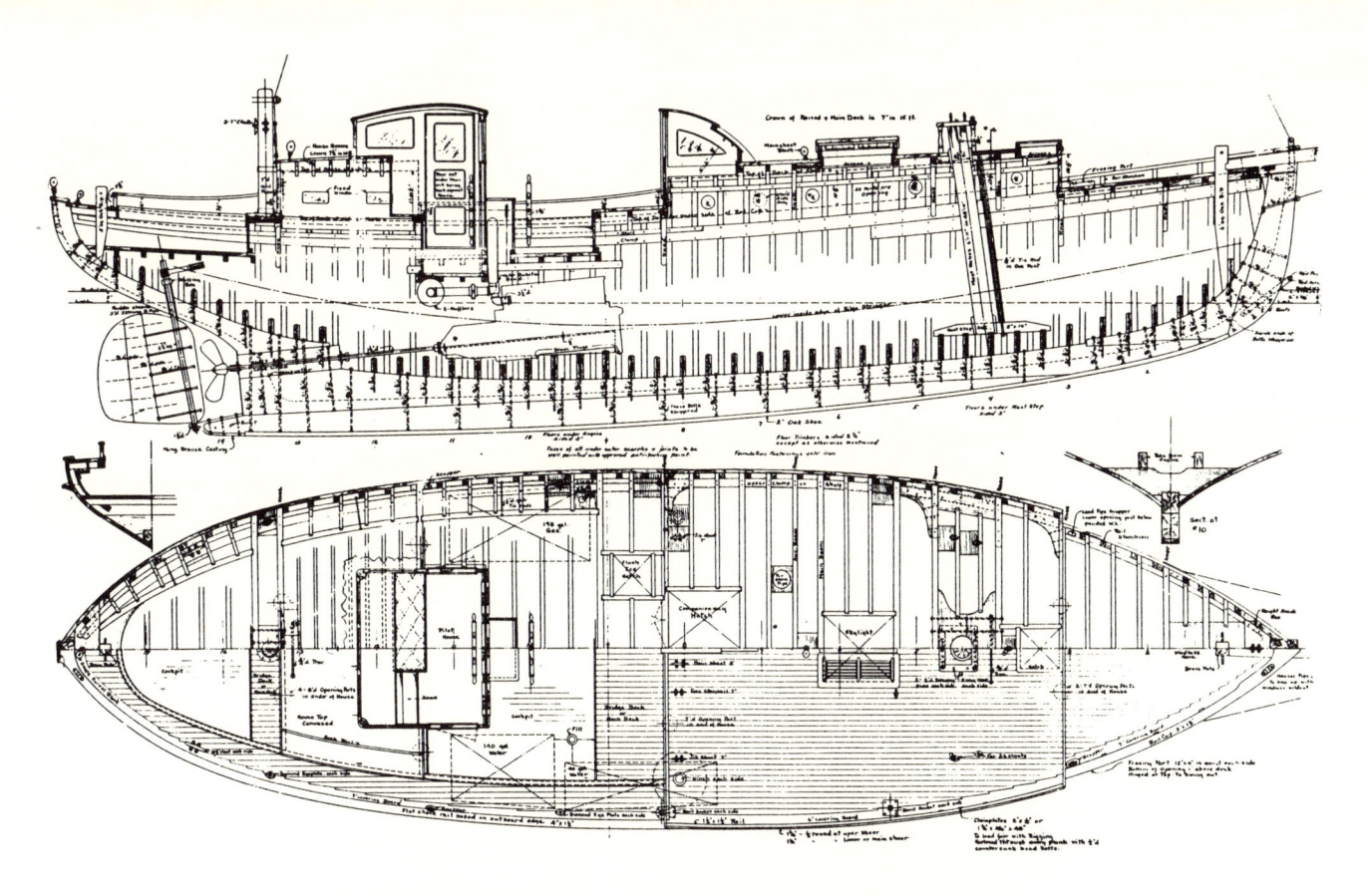

The construction drawings and accommodations plans for Sirius.

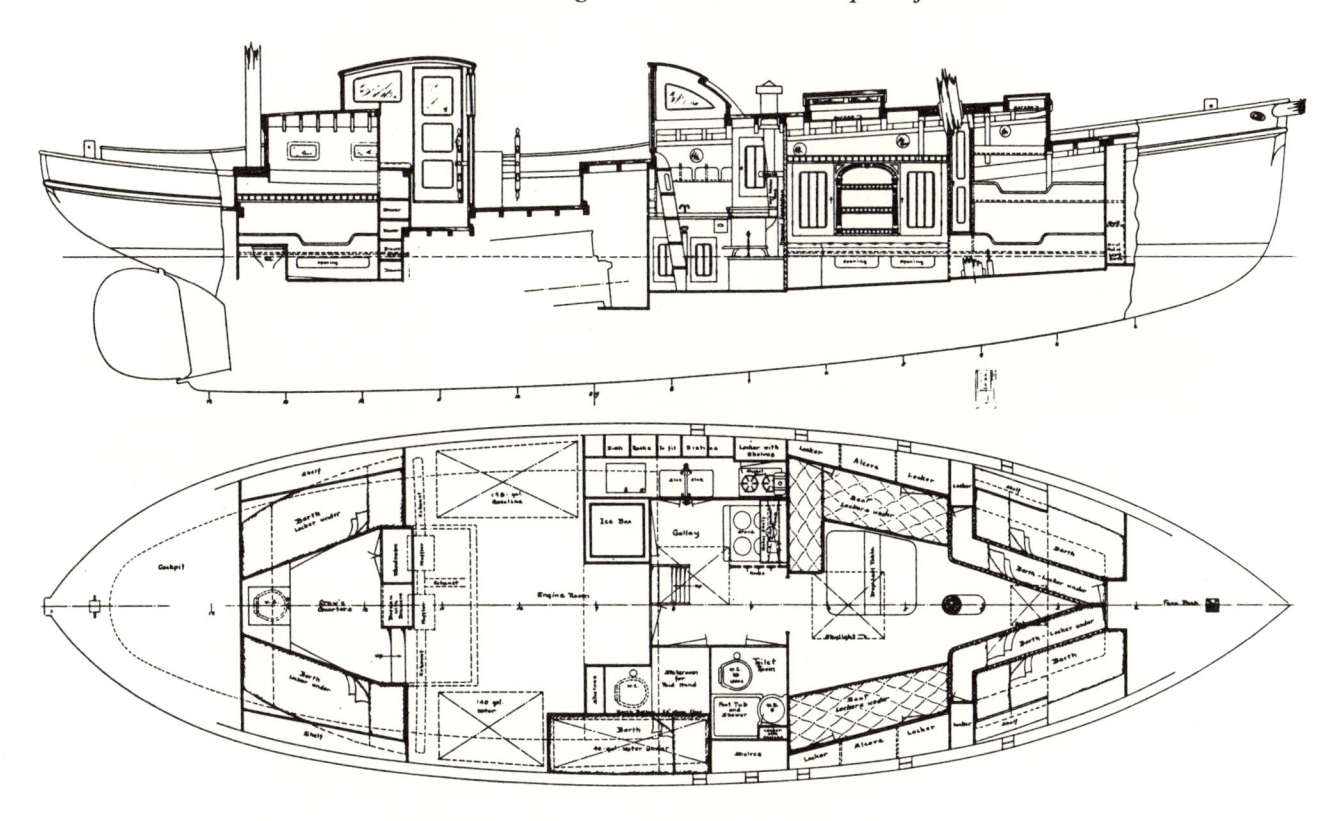

guard boat at the entrance to Narragansett Bay and was awarded three chevrons by Secretary of War James Forrestal.

In 1957 and 1958 Col. Robert F. Fulton cruised the boat from Norfolk, Va., to San Francisco, California.

Sirius *under full sail.*

BLUE PETER 178

Blue Peter was built in 1936 by Bill Reid for Robert Parsons of Providence, R.I. Her cabin interior was finished in knotty pine and trimmed with teak, and she was quite handsome. She had a loose-footed mainsail, and I can remember my father saying how critical the location of the clew was for best performance. The staysail was also loose footed. Auxiliary power was provided by a Gray 4-40 in its own compartment under the bridge deck. There is quite a story that goes along with this boat. I've included it here in the form of an excerpt from *Rudder* magazine, "The Pirating of the Blue Peter," by R. Parsons (July 1942), because it's interesting and also says, I think, something about how Dad's boats stood up to rough treatment.

Design Number 178
Length Overall:
    38 feet 10 inches
Length on Waterline: 35 feet
Beam: 10 feet 10 inches
Draft: 6 feet
Sail Area: 877 square feet
Displacement: 24,100 pounds

> The telephone rang at eight o'clock the morning of August 13 and a voice said, "The Blue Peter is not on her mooring." I raced down to the cove at East Greenwich, Rhode Island, and sure enough the boat was gone. To make certain the line had not parted, I rowed out and found the splice and buoy were intact just as though I had thrown it overboard myself.
>
> The Blue Peter is an auxiliary jib-headed cutter, thirty-nine feet overall, thirty-five feet waterline, eleven feet beam, six feet draft, designed by Sam Crocker and built by Willis Reid in 1936. She has proved to be a very satisfactory boat, being my idea of the "Perfect Ship." She has been strictly a family boat as my wife, son Sam aged nineteen and daughter Nancy, twelve, have spent every summer week-end on board and our two weeks' vacation. It was unbelievable that she had been taken and we all felt as though a member of our family had been kidnapped. We recalled with tenderness all our past good times on board and feared there would be no more. In addition we remembered that all of our most treasured belongings, our pet clothes, pipes, razors, etc., had been on the boat and now all were gone.
>
> It was very apparent that [if] she had left on or about midnight and at a speed of seven knots by nine o'clock she would be about twenty miles southeast of Block Island. She had left under ideal conditions with a strong fair northerly wind and an ebb tide. It immediately appeared to me to be the work of experts and a job well planned by someone who wished to leave the country. My first idea was to call the Quonset Naval Base as I felt their offshore patrol planes would easily pick up the boat. I pleaded with them in vain for they maintained it was a job for the Coast Guard and the Navy could do nothing for me.
>
> I called the Point Judith Coast Guard Station to report the boat missing and learned that the nearest Coast Guard Sea Plane Base is at Salem, Massachusetts. In view of this I chartered a plane from the Rhode Island airport, sending a man familiar with the Blue Peter. They went as far west as Montauk, then south of Block Island to the Vineyard and back but saw nothing of the boat.
>
> The next few days dragged on with no report of the Blue Peter and my family and I were becoming more and more despondent. I had reported the loss to the local and state police who of course were helpless as the boat was by now well out to sea. It was very difficult to convince the authorities of the seriousness of the whole affair. The insurance company wished to make sure that the boat had not sunk at her mooring, which was of course ridiculous. They stated that about a year ago a boat had been reported as stolen from the Charles River and after the authorities had spent about two weeks on the case, someone discovered she was sunk at her mooring. The Point Judith and Newport Coast Guard spent one whole day combing the shores of Narragansett Bay, believing that the boat had broken away from her mooring and drifted out of East Greenwich Cove. To do this she would have had to sail to windward under bare poles.
>
> Day after day went by with no word. The first week-end I took the family by

The sailplan for Blue Peter.

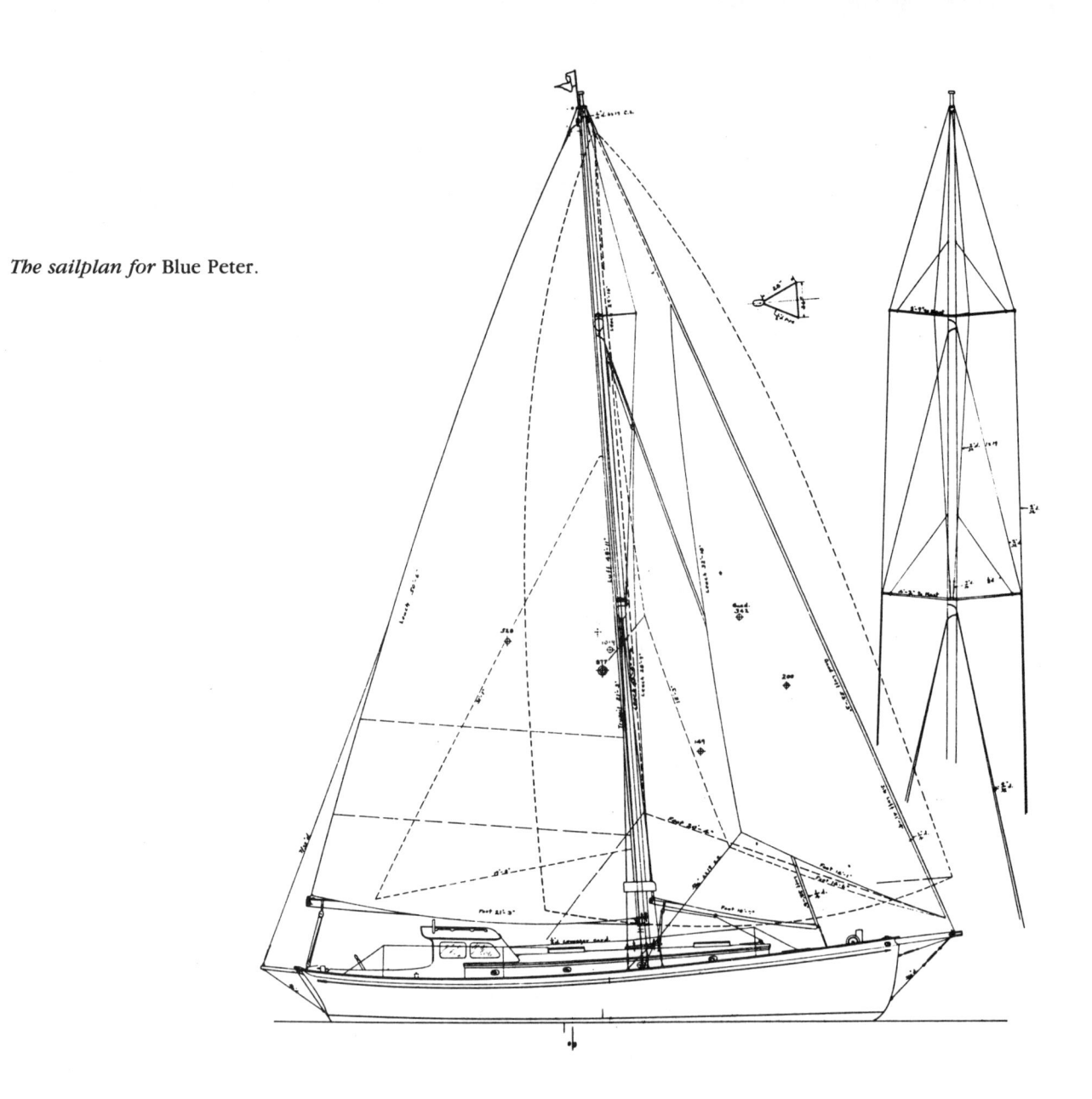

steamer to Nantucket to get away and in hopes that we might possibly run across our boat disguised somehow. We had a very interesting visit at the Coast Guard Station on the Island and were pleased that they had received the report of our missing boat and had their eyes out for her.

One week had passed and no word or clue had been received giving us any idea by whom or how the boat had been taken. We were all nearly sick with grief.

On the eighth day after the theft, while Mrs. Parsons was getting some gasoline from a neighboring filling station, the attendant tried to console her. He told her of the rumor that a couple of army deserters from one of the Bay Forts has been A.W.O.L. since the night our boat had been taken. The homes of both boys were near East Greenwich. A car belonging to one of them had been found abandoned on a back road and a skiff in the vicinity had disappeared.

There had been so many rumors that I did not pay much attention to this when I heard it, but did happen to mention it to a *Providence Journal* reporter when he called for news of the boat. This started some action. The reporter said that he would check the story and called me back in about an hour, having verified what I had told him. He felt there was no question but that these army deserters had taken the boat as a means of going South or of getting out of the country. To have some

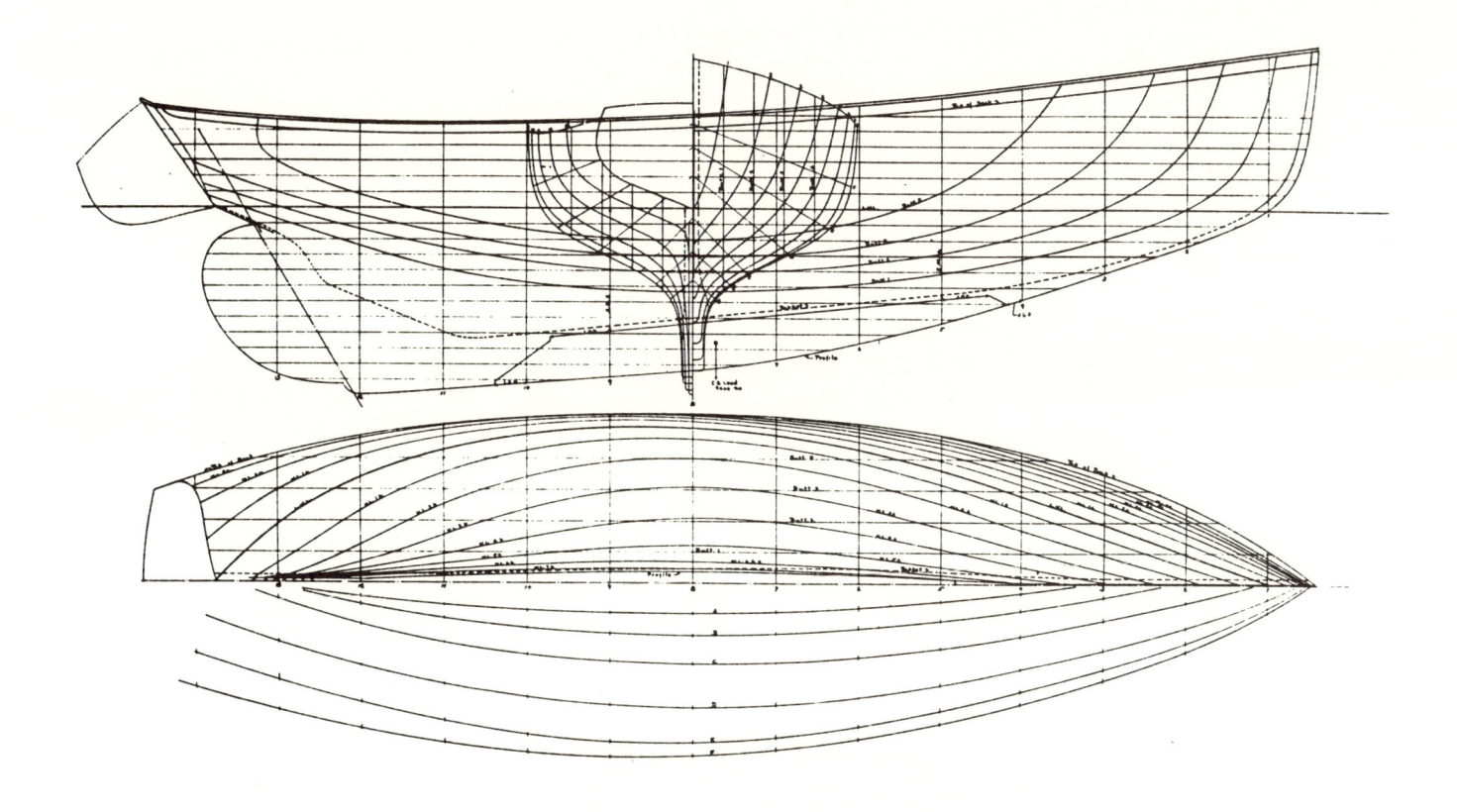

The lines and constructions drawings for Blue Peter.

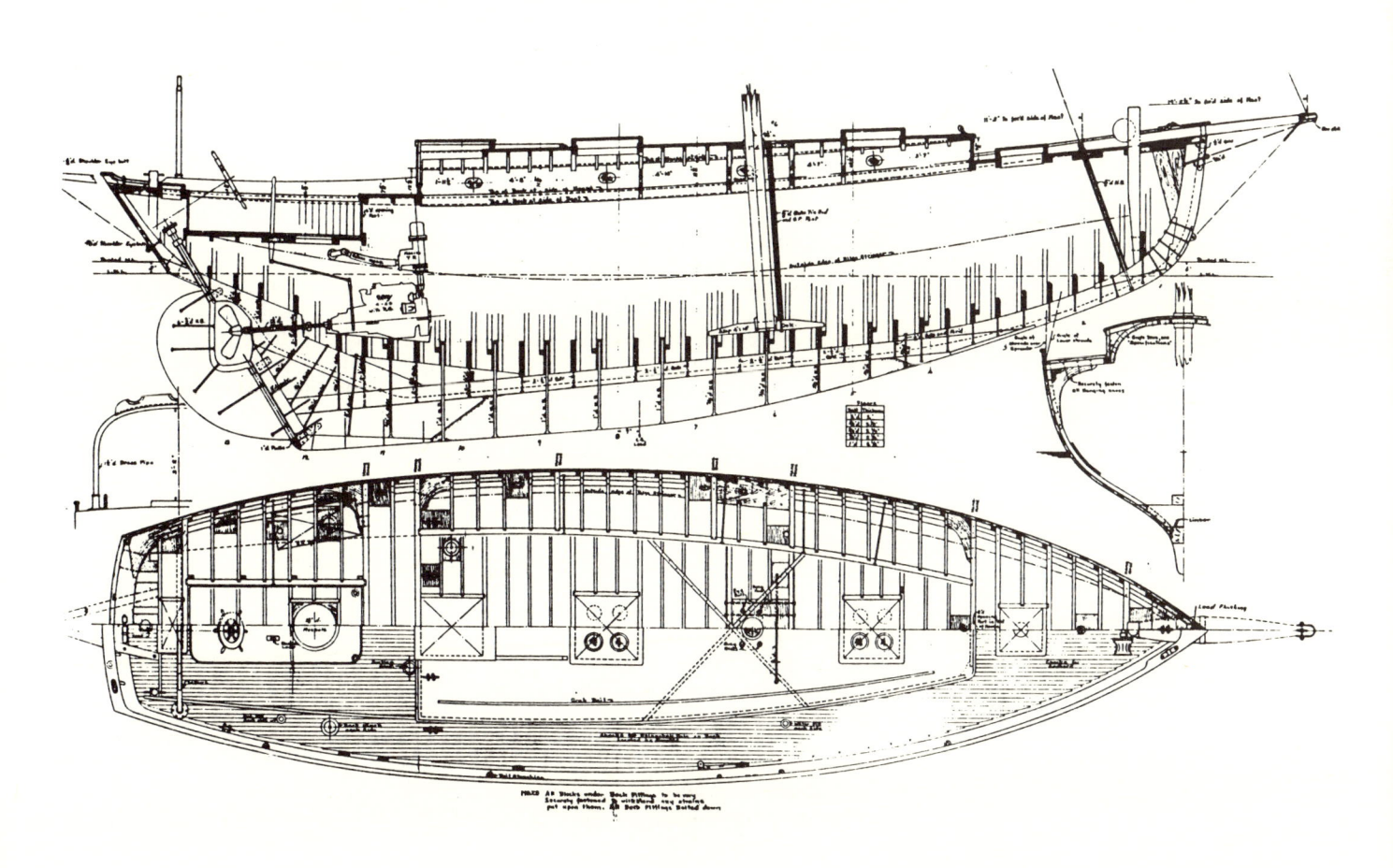

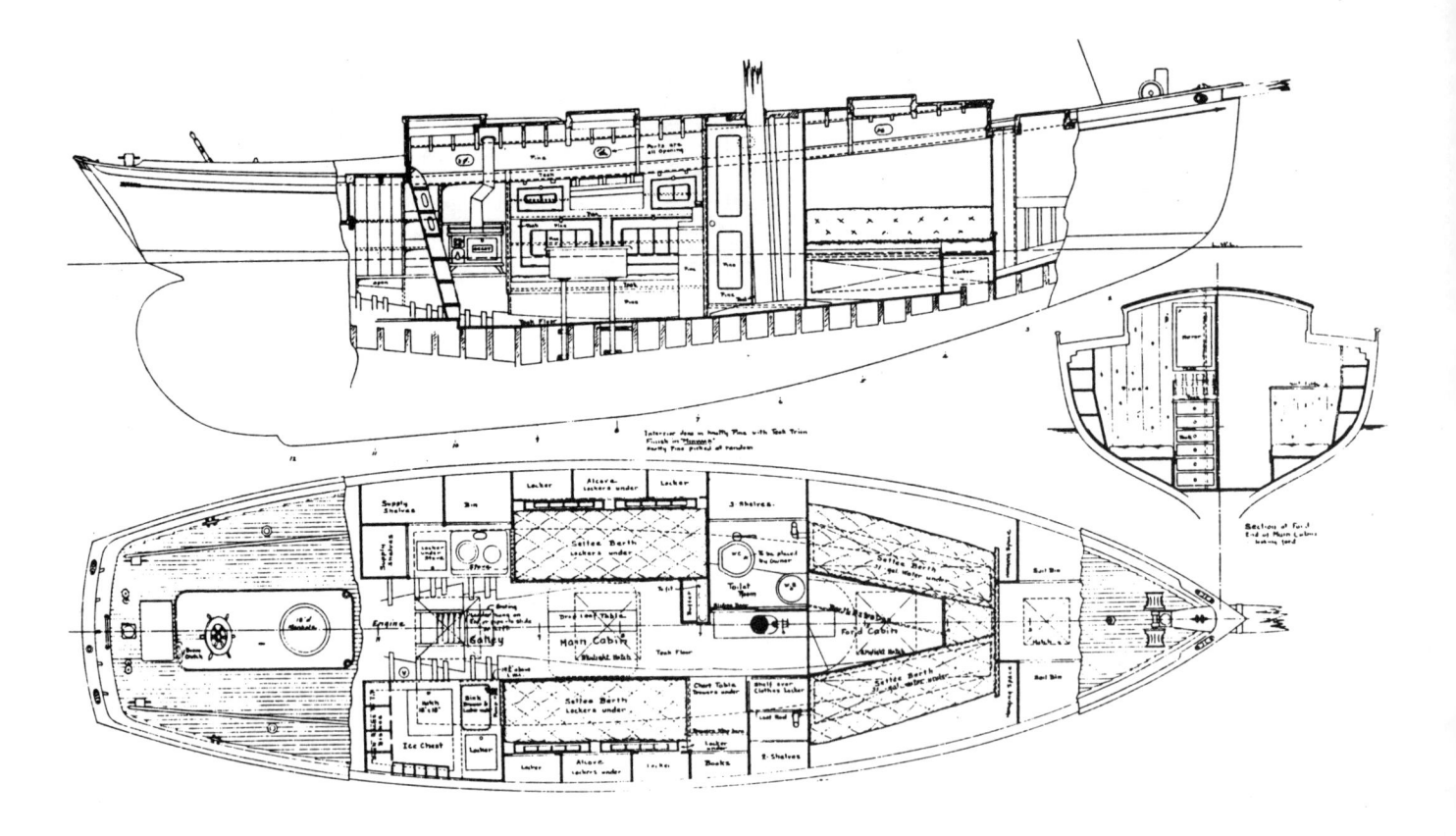

The accommodations for Blue Peter.

facts to work on gave us considerable encouragement. It seemed certain that in two weeks the boys would have to put into some port for provisions.

I had felt all along that the boat had been taken by some aliens either to get out of the country or to contact a ship offshore and then scuttle the boat. With this well-founded clue of the army deserters we began to feel that we would see our boat again even though she might be damaged.

The second week-end with no boat and no report of her brought us to Salem, Massachusetts, to check on the Coast Guard Sea Plane Base. It was most enlightening to learn how promptly they had received the original report and how it was relayed out to their planes on patrol. The stations had the report that the boat was missing at ten a.m. on the morning of August 13. I was shown the log of two planes on patrol and they both logged the message just before 10:15 of that day. The westerly limit of their flight was about in line with Block Island which accounts for their not sighting the boat. In talking with the officer in charge I learned that for some unaccountable reason the report had not gone further south than New York. Another message was immediately sent out to all the Coast Guard Stations as far south as Miami. My hopes rose as it seemed only natural the boat would have to put into some southern port, and this oversight accounted for no word having been received sooner.

Monday morning I returned to work and every time the telephone rang I expected word of the boat. About the middle of the morning I received a call from the Coast Guard in Boston stating that the Blue Peter had been boarded by one of their boats off the coast of Delaware and the person on board had given my name as owner but until I had sworn out a warrant the boat could not be seized. This certainly seemed like too much red tape that I should have to swear out a warrant for them to seize a stolen boat with a couple of army deserters aboard. So I persuaded the Warwick Police to get in touch with Boston and fix up this technicality.

Now there seemed no doubt but that we would get our boat back. However time dragged on slowly the rest of Monday and it was not until the afternoon of Tuesday, just two weeks after the boat had been stolen, that I received word the Blue Peter had been taken by a Coast Guard boat off Norfolk, Virginia. She was being towed into port and I was told to go to Norfolk and take possession. No further information regarding the condition of the boat was given, so we lived in hopes she had not been damaged.

Blue Peter *under sail. A Morris Rosenfeld photograph, courtesy of S. Sturgis Crocker.*

The next day, Wednesday, my family and I left for Norfolk and what a place to get to. We took an afternoon train out of Providence for New York and a night train from Penn. Station for Cape Charles. We left the train at 5:30 a.m. the next day, boarded a boat for Norfolk. The long but pleasant trip across the mouth of the Chesapeake over to Norfolk gave us our first sight of the Bay and an idea of its size.

We arrived at Norfolk about ten a.m. and went straight to the Federal Building where the Coast Guard have their headquarters. After a press interview and time taken to convince the authorities that I was the lawful owner of the Blue Peter, we were escorted over to the base. What a thrill to see our boat once more! She lay proudly tied up alongside of the cutter Jackson with an unknown private signal flying from her masthead. We hurried aboard to inspect her; to see what, if any, damage had been done and to lower that flag. At first appearance she seemed to be very slightly damaged outside but on going below, what a mess. Instead of seeing our own orderly familiar things we saw strange articles scattered about the cabin that gave us a most uncomfortable and weird feeling.

The Blue Peter had been picked up by the Coast Guard boat Jackson on routine patrol off Norfolk while she was apparently headed for sea. The two army deserters offered no resistance in spite of being heavily armed with a couple of pistols, rifles and shotguns. They were in the process of getting a meal when disturbed and the remains certainly gave our galley a most unhealthy look.

I left the family to collect and turn over to the Coast Guard all of the things that did not belong to us while I hunted up a boatyard or marine station where we could take the boat and prepare her for the voyage north. Norfolk is a wonderful place for vessels of 300 feet and over but there seem to be very few facilities for small boats. Nevertheless I located Forrest & Dunn's yard at the Hague, on the other side of the town, where we could tie up and go to work and get straightened out.

Upon my return to the Blue Peter I found the crew of the Jackson and my family in gales of laughter over some of the articles being brought out of the cabin. There was a quantity of clothes, tools, fishing gear and a library of about fifty books most unusually chosen, to say nothing of a large picture of a girl upside down in the frame.

After expressing our appreciation for finding our boat and presenting the "Army's" private signal to the Jackson, I started the engine and to my surprise it ran. We backed out of the slip and with waves of farewell and good luck, proceeded to Forrest & Dunn's yard where we left the boat tied up securely in a quiet inlet for the night and wended our weary way back to the hotel for supper and bed.

Fortunately the next two days, Friday and Saturday, though hot were sunny and excellent for "house cleaning" and what a job my family did. Everything was removed from the cabin and cleaned and all the inside was scrubbed with hot water and soap. To add to the confusion I had a couple of men from the yard sand and varnish the bright work. It was not long before the cabin began to have its accustomed look and the good clean smell which we had certainly missed.

We had by now taken account of stock and found that the boys had sold my Dane Direction Finder and a very nice set of end wrenches. We were minus quite an assortment of clothing, my favorite pipe, my daughter's sun glasses, a razor and numerous toilet articles. The battens in all the sails were broken and most of the pockets were torn. The fifty-pound anchor had a bad bend in the shank which I could not account for but was told it probably was caused by anchoring in a heavy seaway. The topsides were scraped and dented, and it seemed as though everywhere we looked there were signs of the boat having been abused. All her equipment was either worn or damaged; the ice box leaked, the feathering propeller vibrated, the engine was noisier, all indicating that our poor boat had had much rougher treatment than she was accustomed to.

The boys had given the press a very colorful account of their trip emphasizing how little they had known about a boat. The leader and older one had had some sailing experience in small boats but the other knew nothing about sailing. As a matter of fact the boat and her equipment were practically foolproof and as long as they kept her off the beach, no harm could come to them in the comparatively moderate going they had. The following is a copy of their log found on the boat. If the Coast Guard south of New York had been notified promptly they would have been picked up almost immediately.

Start 3:20 a.m. Aug. 13.
1 First stop Beach Haven, N.J., Aug. 14, 5:00 p.m.
2 Atlantic City, N.J., Aug. 16, 8:00 p.m.
3 Rehoboth, Del., Aug. 17, 6:30 p.m.
4 Ocean City, Maryland, Aug. 18, 11:00 p.m.
5 Chincoteague, Va., Aug. 21, 7:30 p.m.
6 Little Machipongo Inlet, Va., Aug. 22, 6:30 p.m.
7 Newport News, Va., Aug. 23, 9:00 p.m.

At four o'clock August 30 we cast off the lines from Forrest & Dunn's yard and motored out of the inlet. What a grand and glorious feeling to put on sail and shut off the engine; we were actually under sail in our Blue Peter headed for home!

About the army deserters who stole the boat. The army turned them over to the Federal authorities and they were tried for the transportation of fire arms from one state to another, receiving a sentence of two years on probation. The City of Warwick had them indicted by the Grand Jury. They appeared in court and were told by the judge if they did not make amends with the army they would be tried in his court on its last day of session. Result — the boys are back in the army where they started from.

180

This boat was designed for W.B. Lloyd. I don't have a cabin plan for it, but I do have a note that the design was turned over to Belknap & Paine for completion, so I suppose they did the cabin interior. Number 181 was the same boat stretched out to 45 feet by using a half-inch scale instead of a ¾-inch scale for the lines. This design was done for Bill Lee, who built the boat at Harwichport, Mass., and I guess he did his own cabin interior as I find no plan of it. Nor are there any photographs of either of the finished boats.

Design Number 180
Length Overall: 30 feet
Length on Waterline: 24 feet 10 inches
Beam: 7 feet 10 inches
Draft: 4 feet 6 inches
Sail Area: 346 square feet
Displacement: 8,420 pounds

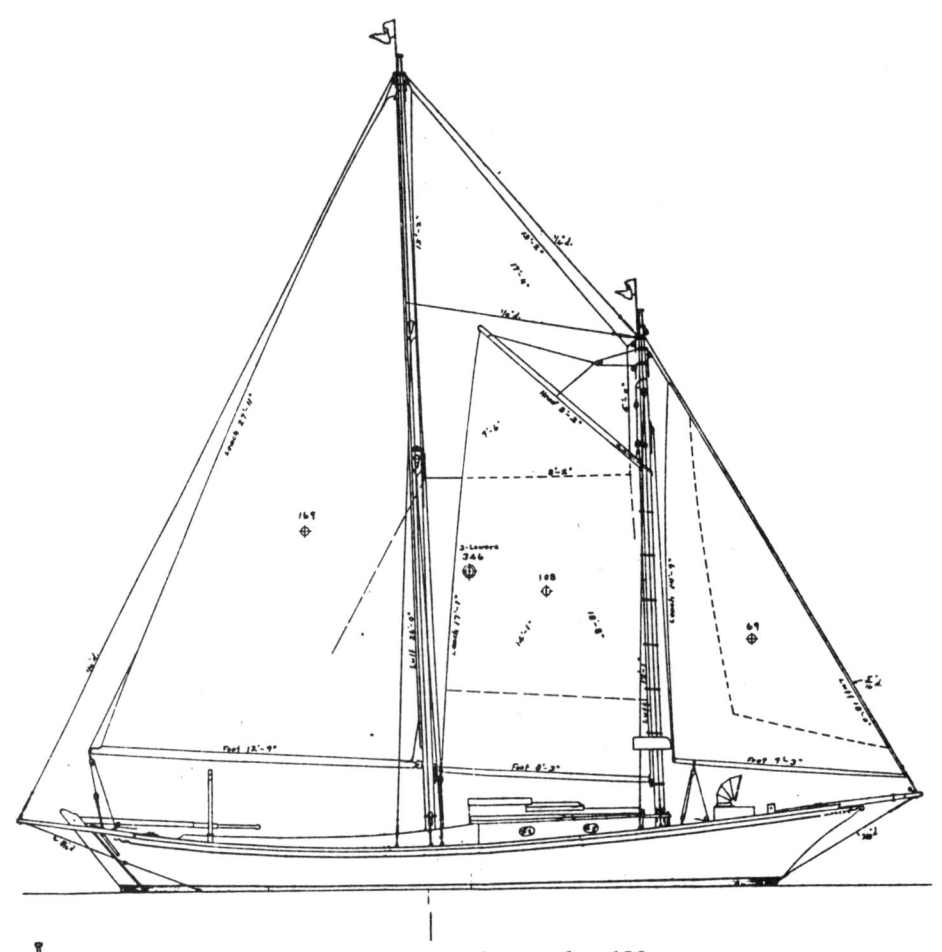

The sailplan for number 180.

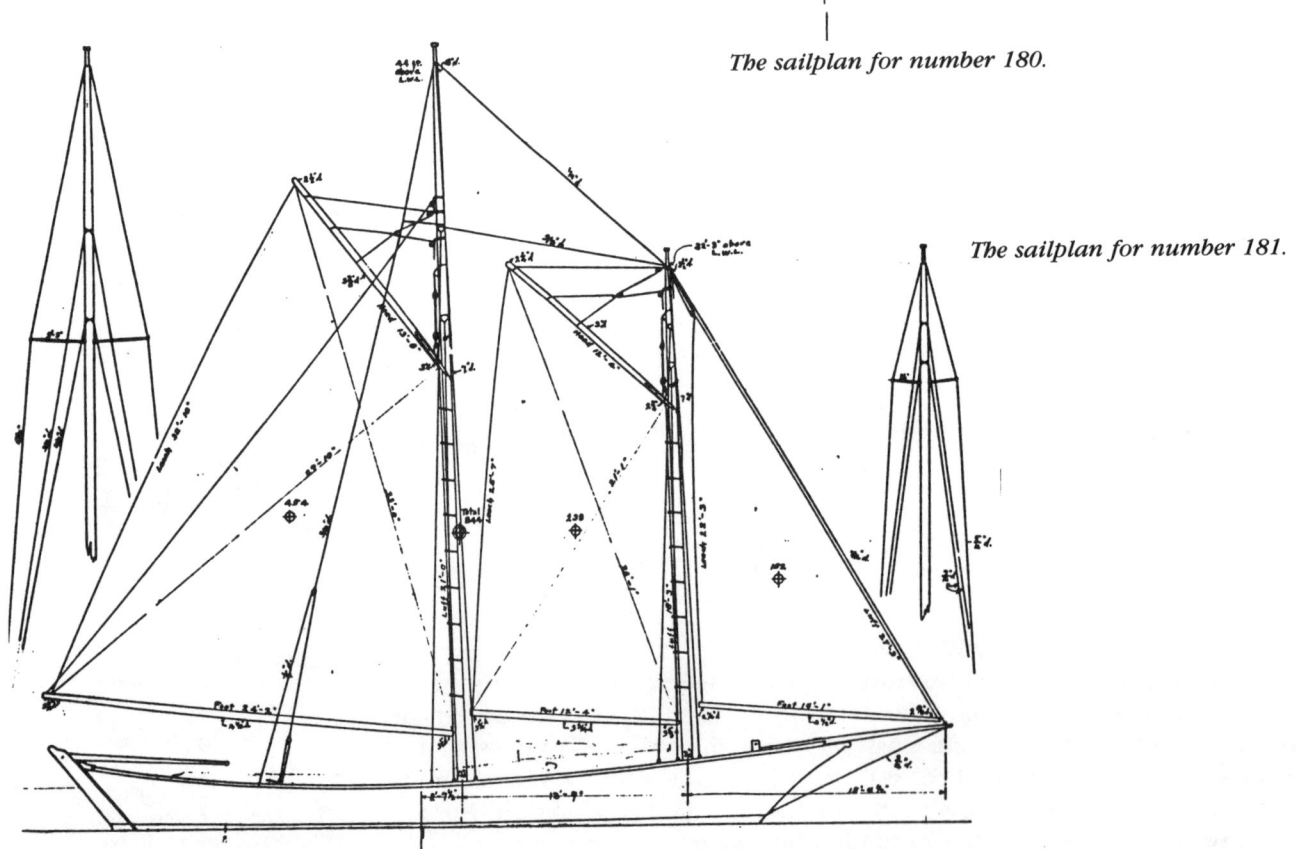

The sailplan for number 181.

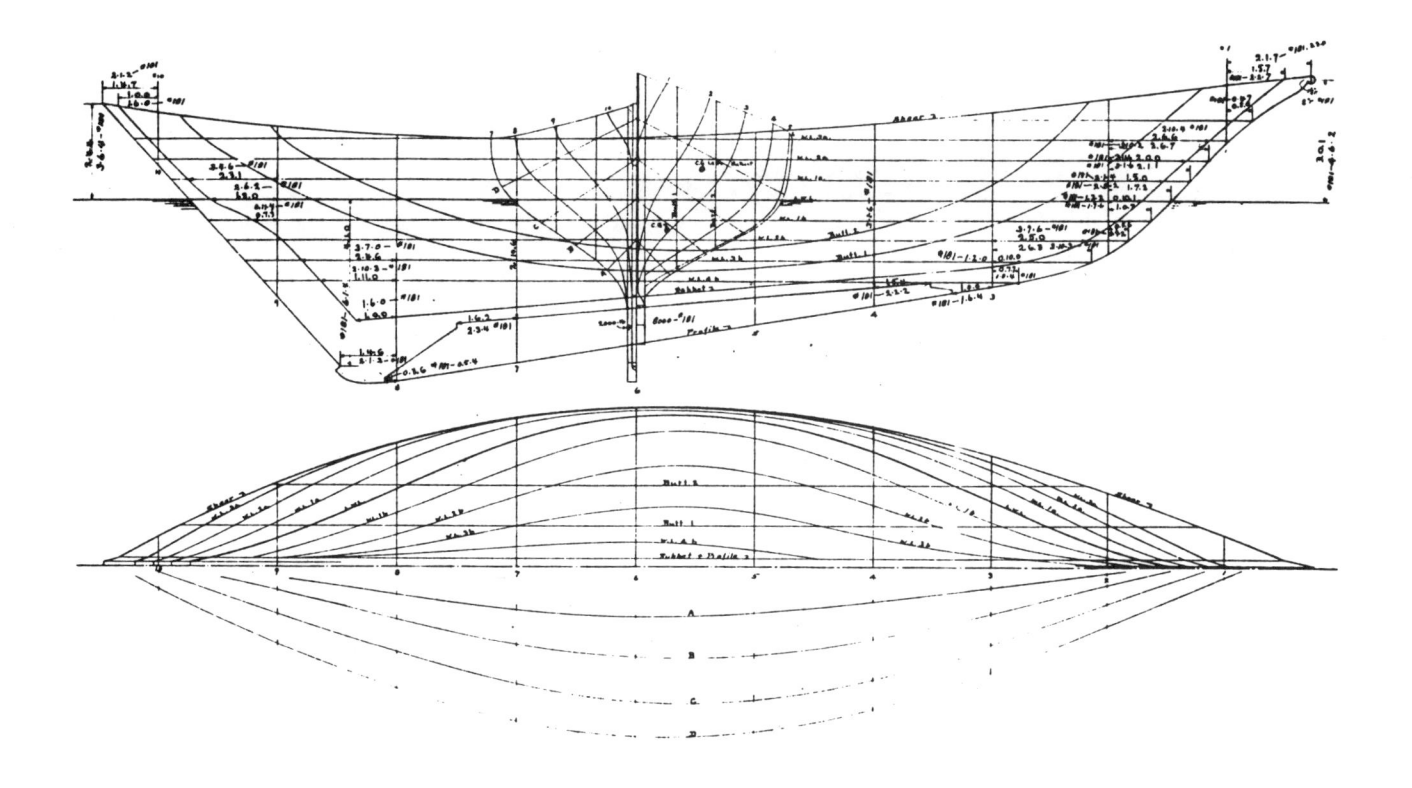

The lines for numbers 180 and 181, and the construction plans for number 180.

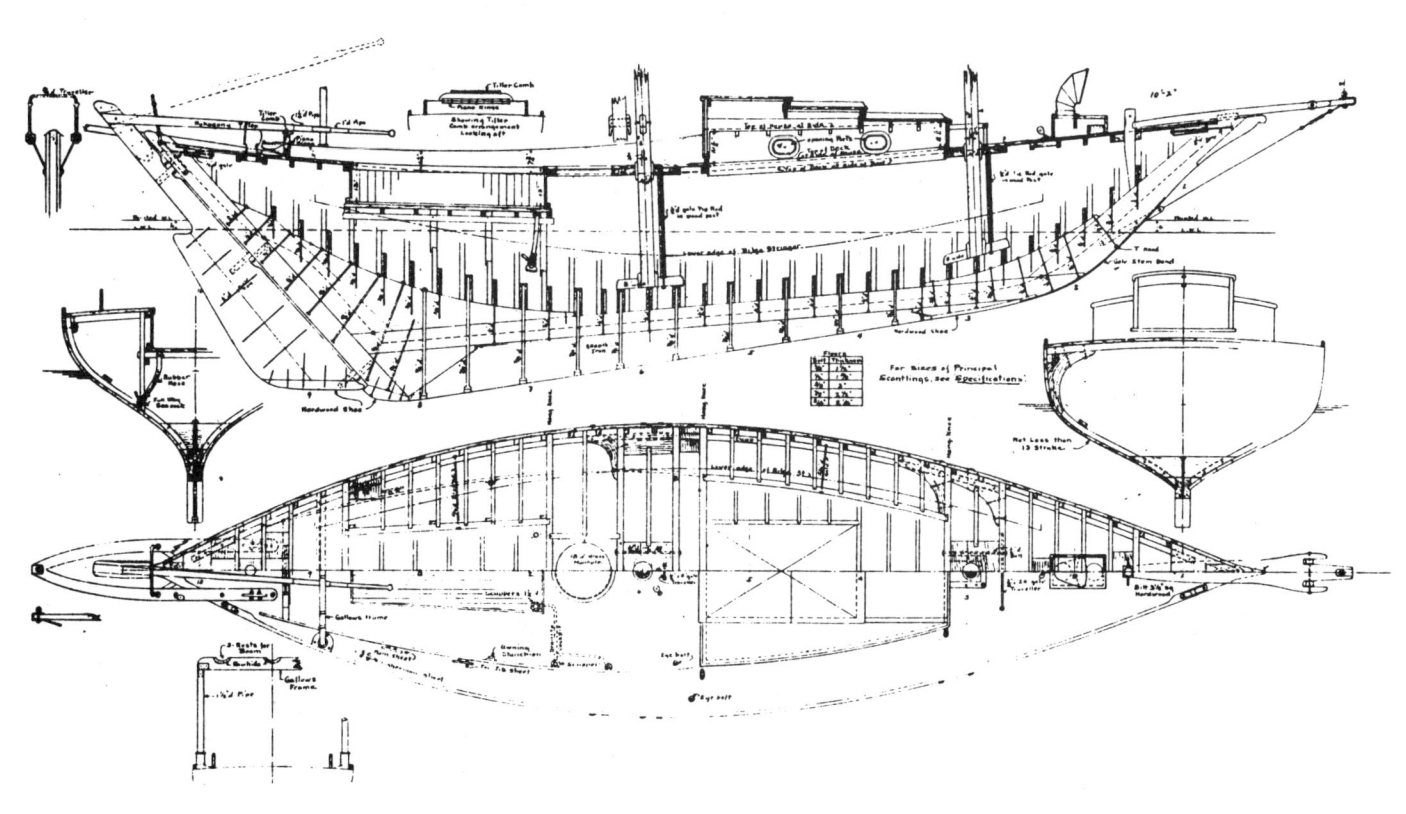

188 MILKY WAY

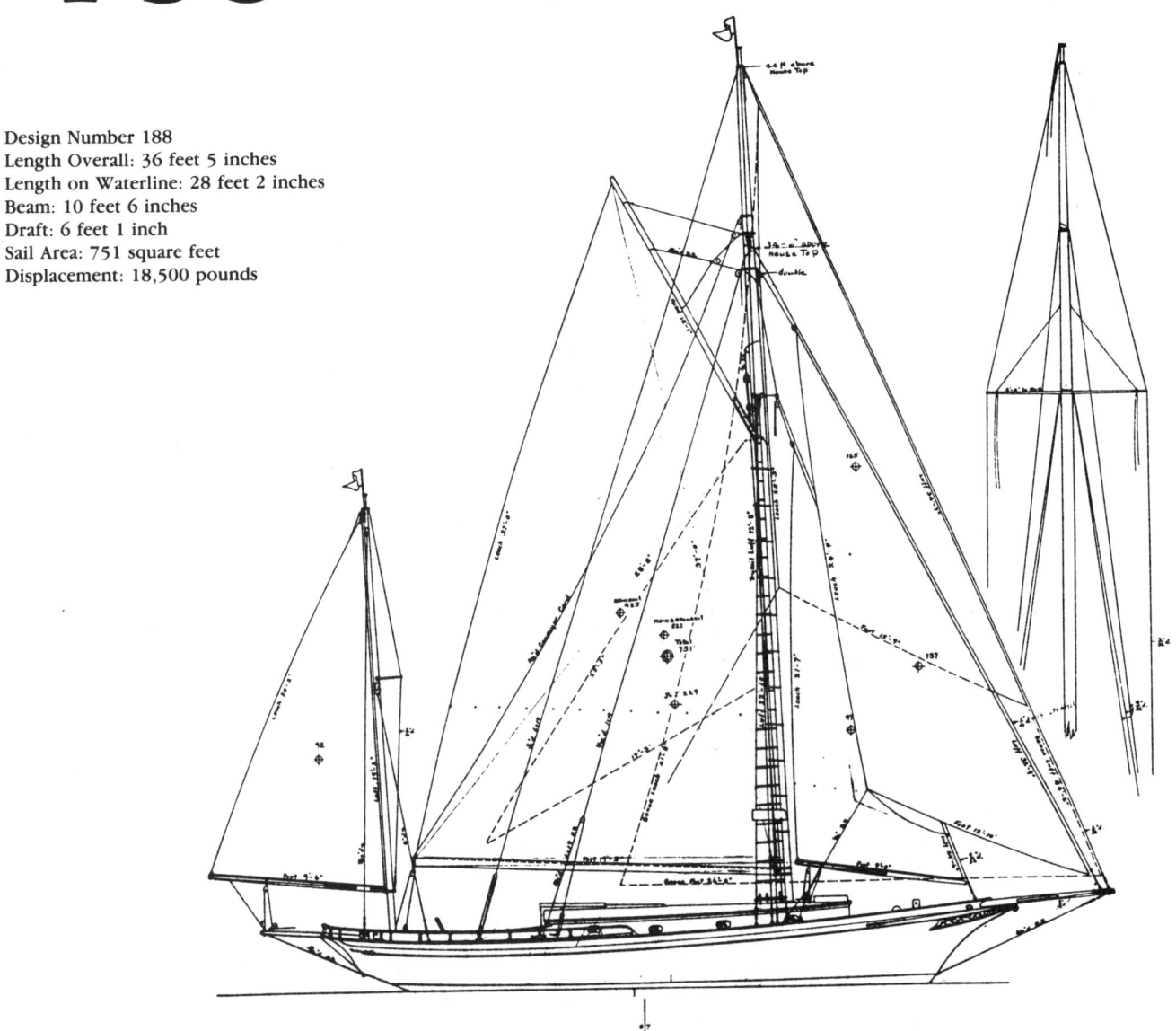

Design Number 188
Length Overall: 36 feet 5 inches
Length on Waterline: 28 feet 2 inches
Beam: 10 feet 6 inches
Draft: 6 feet 1 inch
Sail Area: 751 square feet
Displacement: 18,500 pounds

The sailplan for Milky Way.

The contract for *Milky Way* was signed in April 1937 by Simms Brothers of Dorchester, Mass. The owner is Donald Starr of Boston. She was 36 feet 5 inches by 28 feet 2 inches by 10 feet 6 inches by 6 feet 1 inch. Originally powered by a Gray gasoline 4-22 engine and gaff rigged, she was changed to marconi in 1945 and repowered with a Kermath diesel in 1950. The profile plan doesn't do her justice, because it only shows a billet head under the bowsprit. She actually had a hand-carved bust of a woman for a figurehead, followed by blue trailboards with stars. Quite an attractive boat with the teak monkey rail around the stern. In January 1985 Starr sent me the following letter:

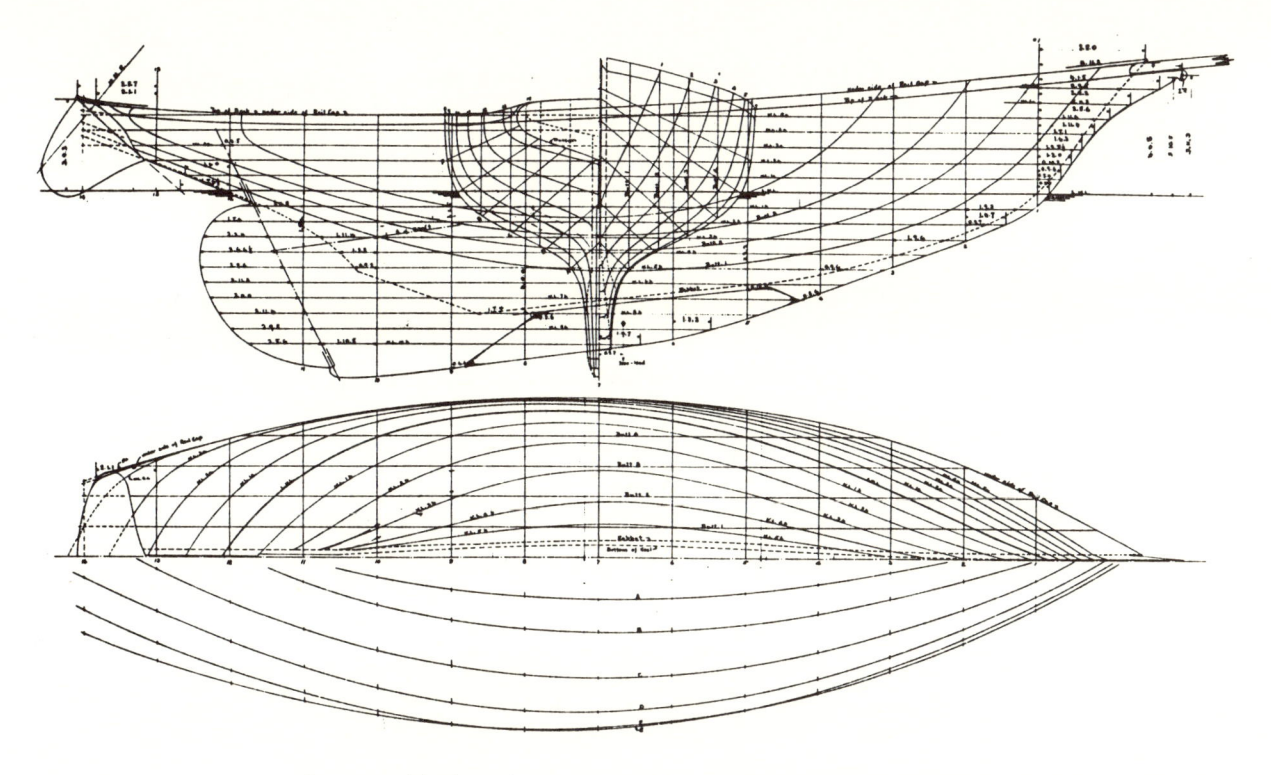

Above and below: *The lines and construction plans for* Milky Way.

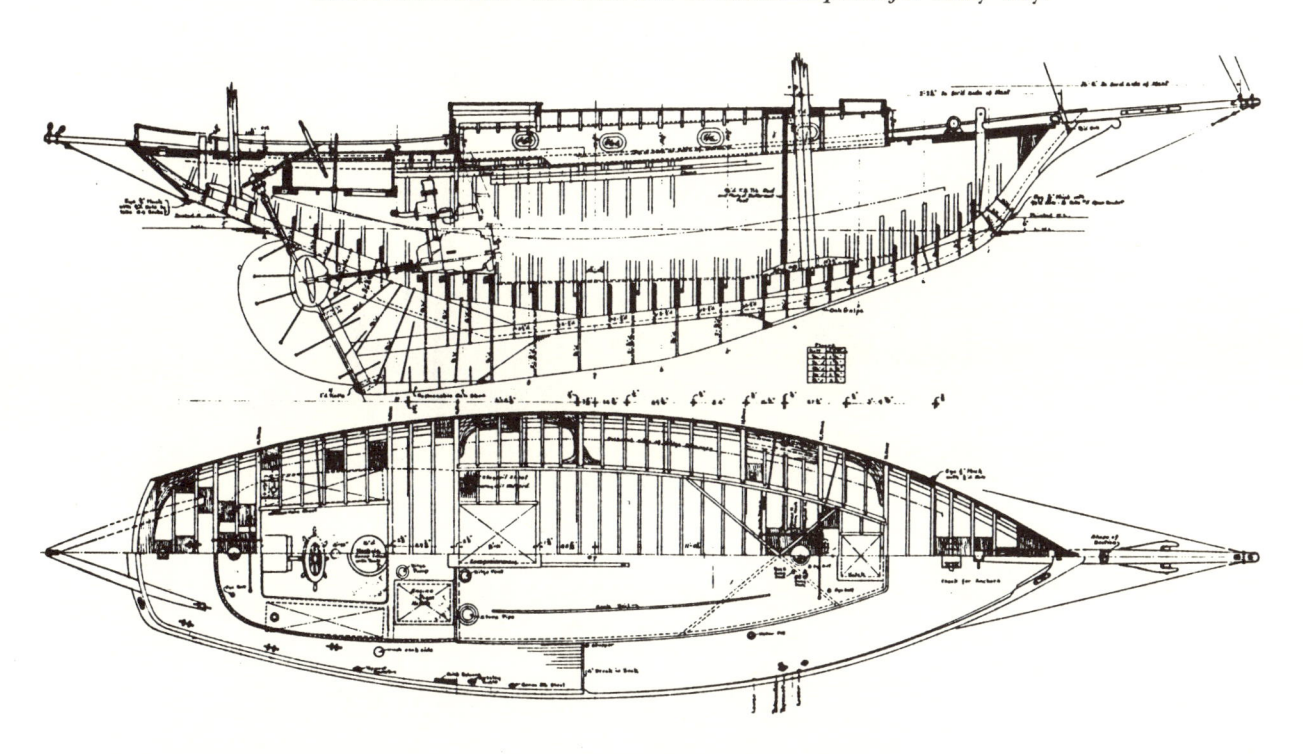

Thank you for the *Milky Way* plans; they are a fine example of the designer's art, and I was fortunate too in having the skill of the Simms Brothers artisans to translate them into the ship herself. She is referred to in John Parkinson's annals of the Cruising Club as "the lovely Crocker Yawl *Milky Way,*" and once while she was sailing among a fleet gathered at Newport to watch the start of a Bermuda Race, I heard the comment from a nearby vessel: "What a sweet little yacht!" As for her performance, the late Harold Peters, while we were tacking up the Saco River, remarked, "God, Commander, she'll do anything but eat out of your hand!"

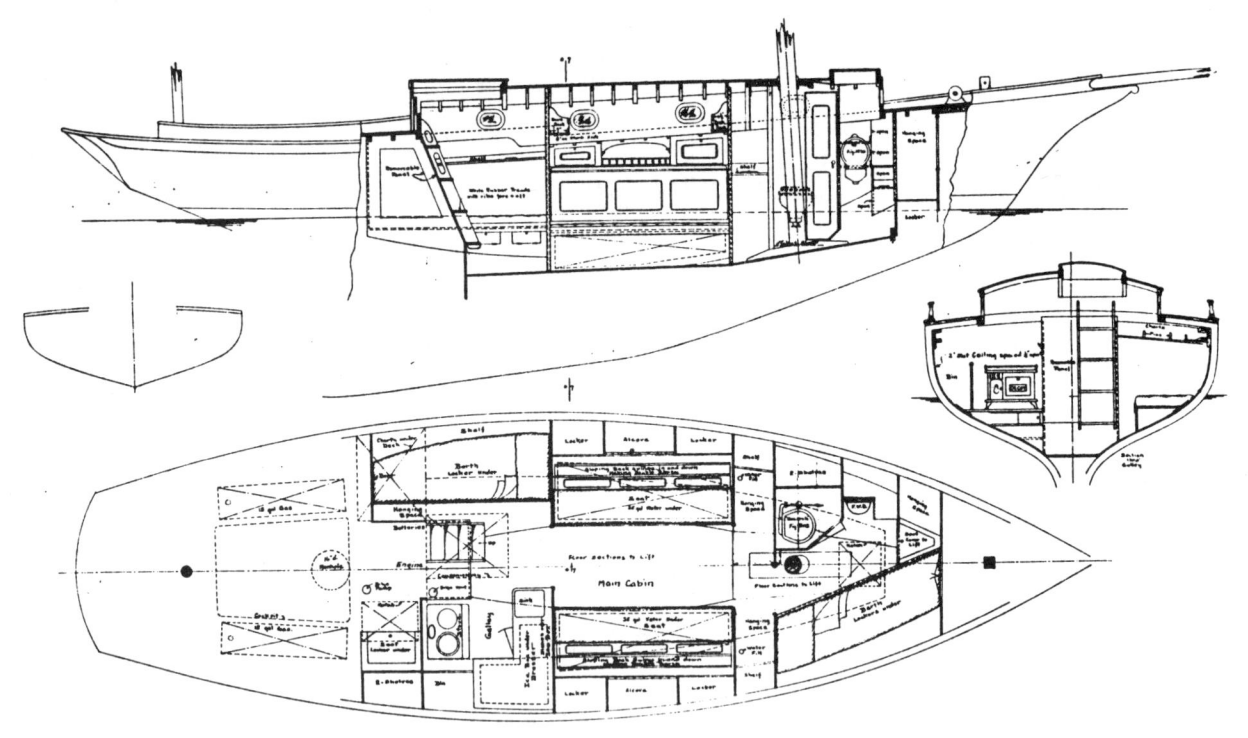

Above and right: *The accommodations for* Milky Way, *and under sail.*

BEN GUNN 190

This bugeye ketch *Ben Gunn* was designed for S.K. Dimock. She was built in 1938 by Simms Brothers of Dorchester, Mass., using the best materials: The specifications called for an African mahogany foundation, Honduras mahogany stern transom, oak frames, Honduras mahogany centerboard box, teak centerboard, cedar planking with an Oregon pine sheer strake and garboard and first two broad strakes of Honduras mahogany. Bulkheads and hull ceiling below decks were chestnut. The main deck and cockpit floor were left unfinished. Although the drawings show a billet head, she actually had a parrot with a piece of eight in his bill, which was stolen more than once. Auxiliary power was furnished by a Gray 4-22 with two-to-one reduction gear.

Design Number 190
Length Overall: 37 feet 7 inches
Length on Waterline: 32 feet 8 inches
Beam: 10 feet 6 inches
Draft: 3 feet
Sail Area: 637 square feet
Displacement: 17,400 pounds

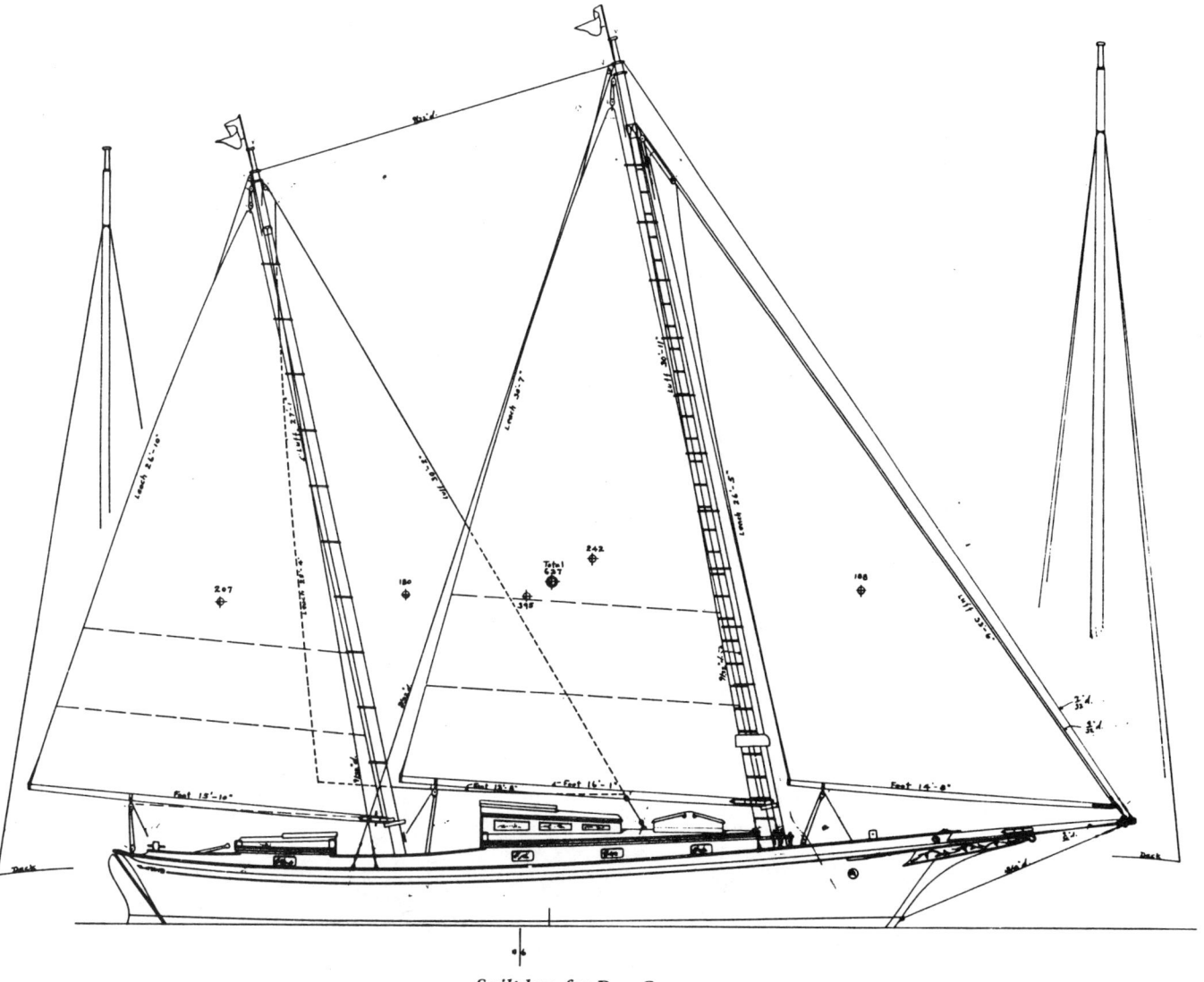

Sailplan for Ben Gunn.

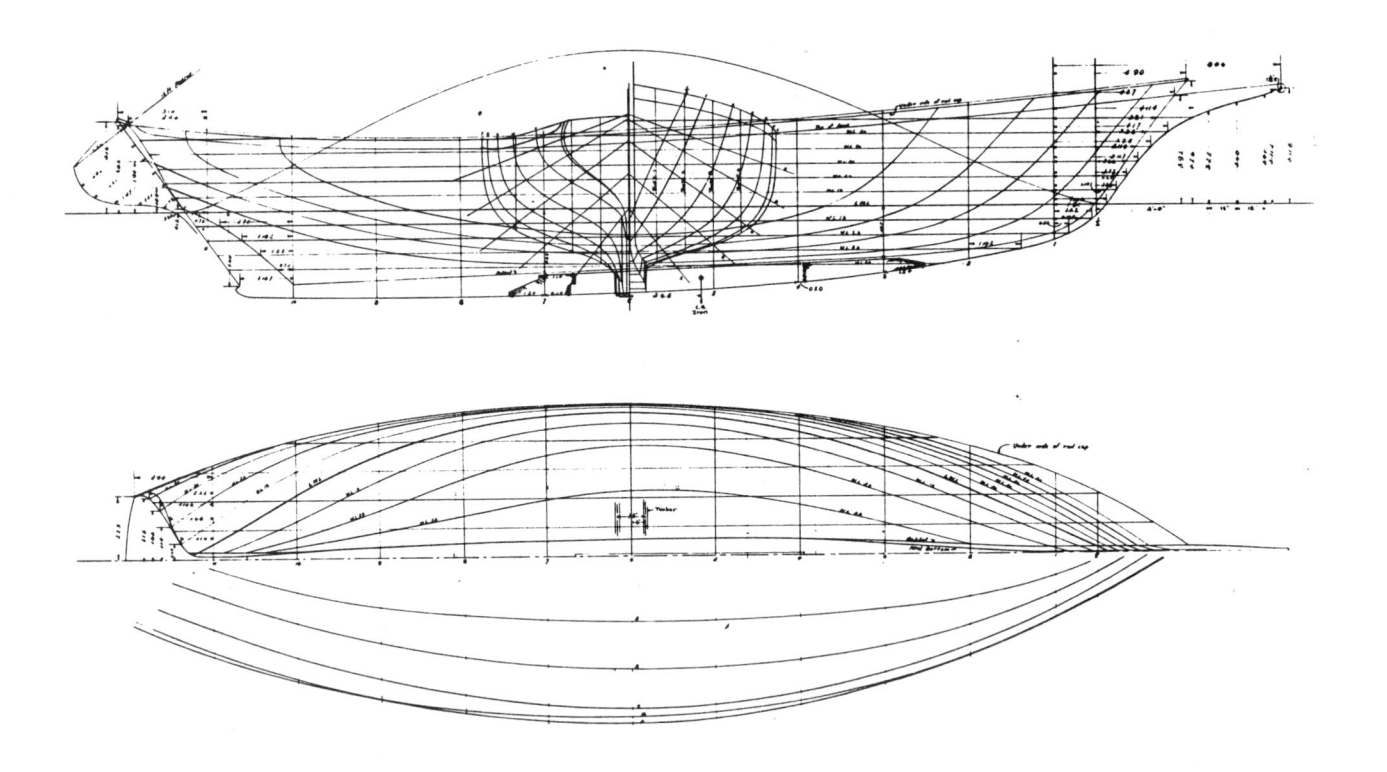

Above: *The lines for* Ben Gunn; **below,** *her construction drawings;* **top right,** *her accommodations and* **right,** *Ben Gunn moving along well in, perhaps, 15 knots of wind. Photographs courtesy of Fred Mizer Coral Gables, Florida.*

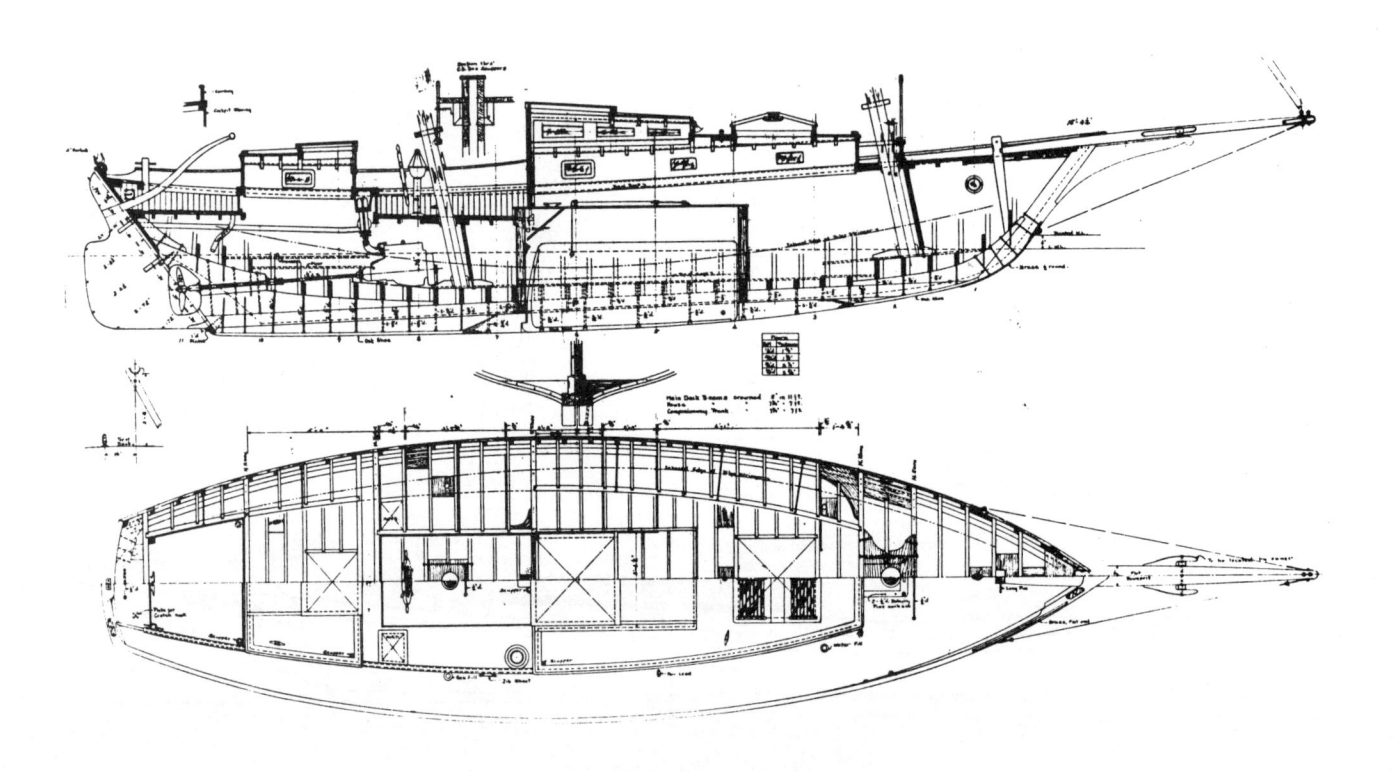

170

171

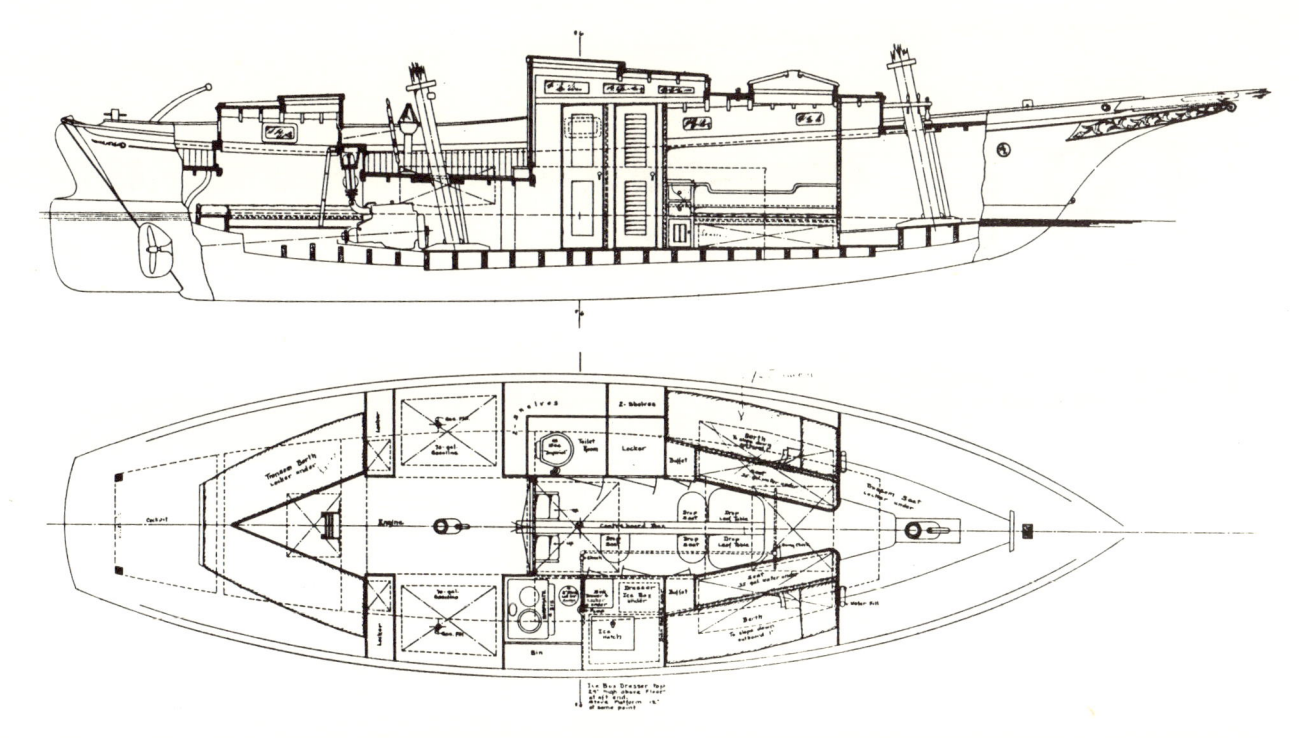

191 MERCURY

Design Number 191
Length Overall: 52 feet
Length on Waterline: 40 feet
Beam: 12 feet 6 inches
Draft: 6 feet
Sail Area: 1126 square feet
Displacement: 39,000 pounds

The sailplan for Mercury.

Mercury was launched in 1938 from the Simms Brothers yard in Dorchester, Mass. She was designed and built for J.J. Storrow, Jr., and her home port was Marblehead. She was a fine example of boatbuilding, typical of the Simms yard, with a lot of Honduras mahogany joinerwork and trim. She was also double planked with half-inch cedar covered with a ⅞-inch Honduras mahogany outer skin. Auxiliary power was furnished by a Gray 6-51 gas engine with two-to-one reduction gear. Carrying 1,200 feet of sail in an all-inboard rig, roller reefing

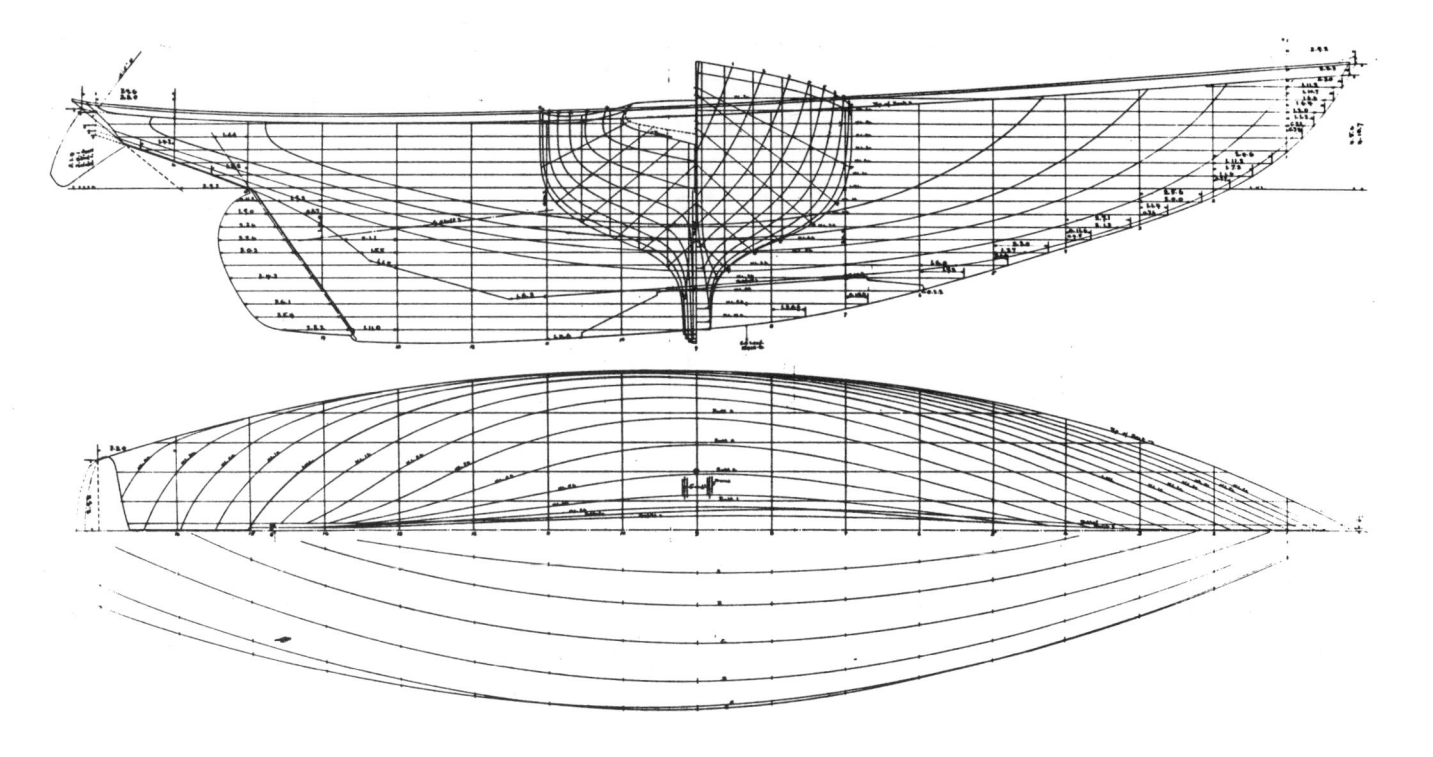

The lines drawings for number 191 and her construction plans.

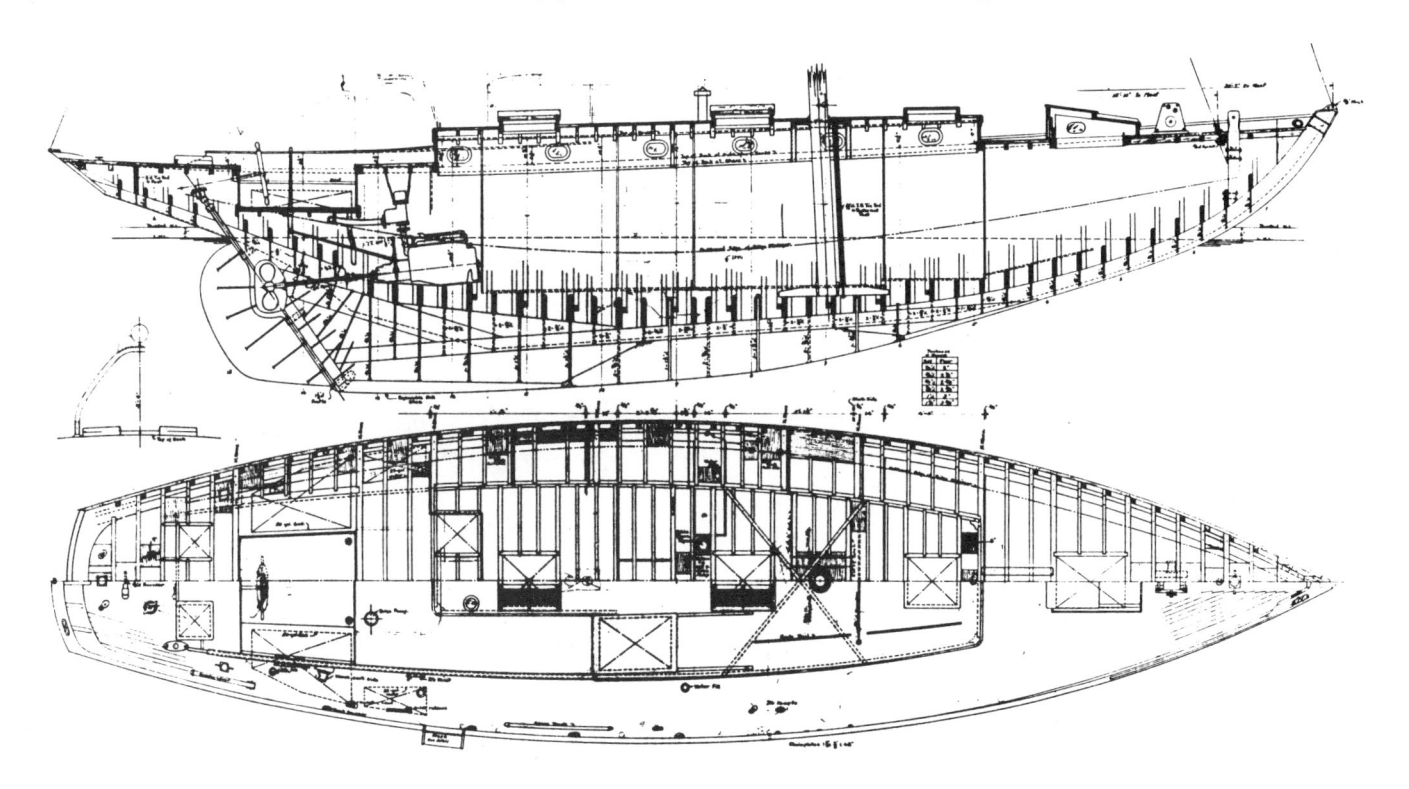

boom, and self-tending staysail, she was easily handled, even for a 52-footer. Gerry Smith of Marblehead was Storrow's captain, and he kept the boat beautifully. However, after Storrow sold her, she was caught trafficking drugs, and the last time I saw her she was sitting on the dock in Newport, waiting to be auctioned off. The people who bought her have brought her back into good condition, and she is currently in the charter business down south.

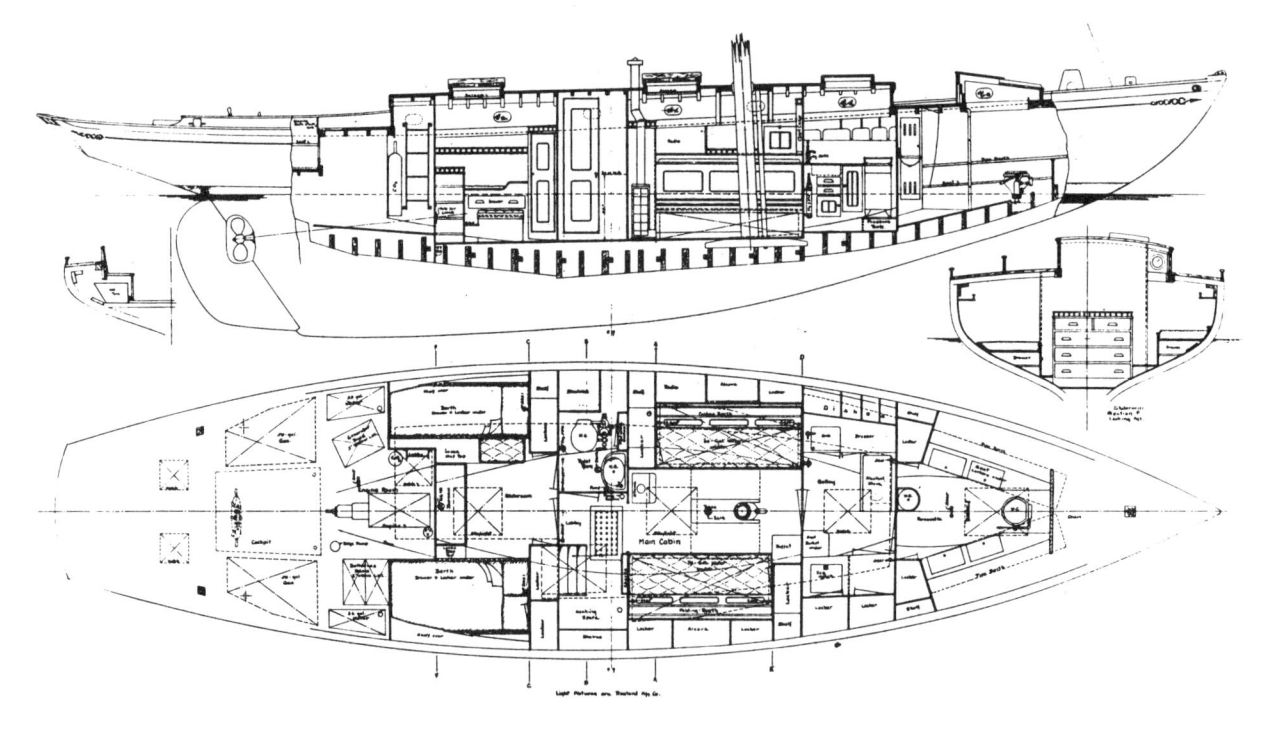

Mercury's accommodations, and under sail. A Morris Rosenfeld photograph, courtesy of S. Sturgis Crocker.

FOMALHAUT 195

Design Number 195
Length Overall: 35 feet 6 inches
Length on Waterline: 28 feet 8 inches
Beam: 10 feet 9 inches
Draft: 5 feet
Sail Area: 718 square feet
Displacement: 15,000 pounds

Fomalhaut marked the beginning of a long and pleasant association between my father and Bud McIntosh of Dover Point, N.H. Bud built *Fomalhaut* in 1939 for Edward C. Thayer of Boston. She was typical of Bud's work, being built of native pine and oak with mostly painted trim and little brightwork. With her toe rail painted dado brown to set off her sheer, plumb stem and overhanging stern, I always thought she was a most attractive boat.

The sailplan for number 195.

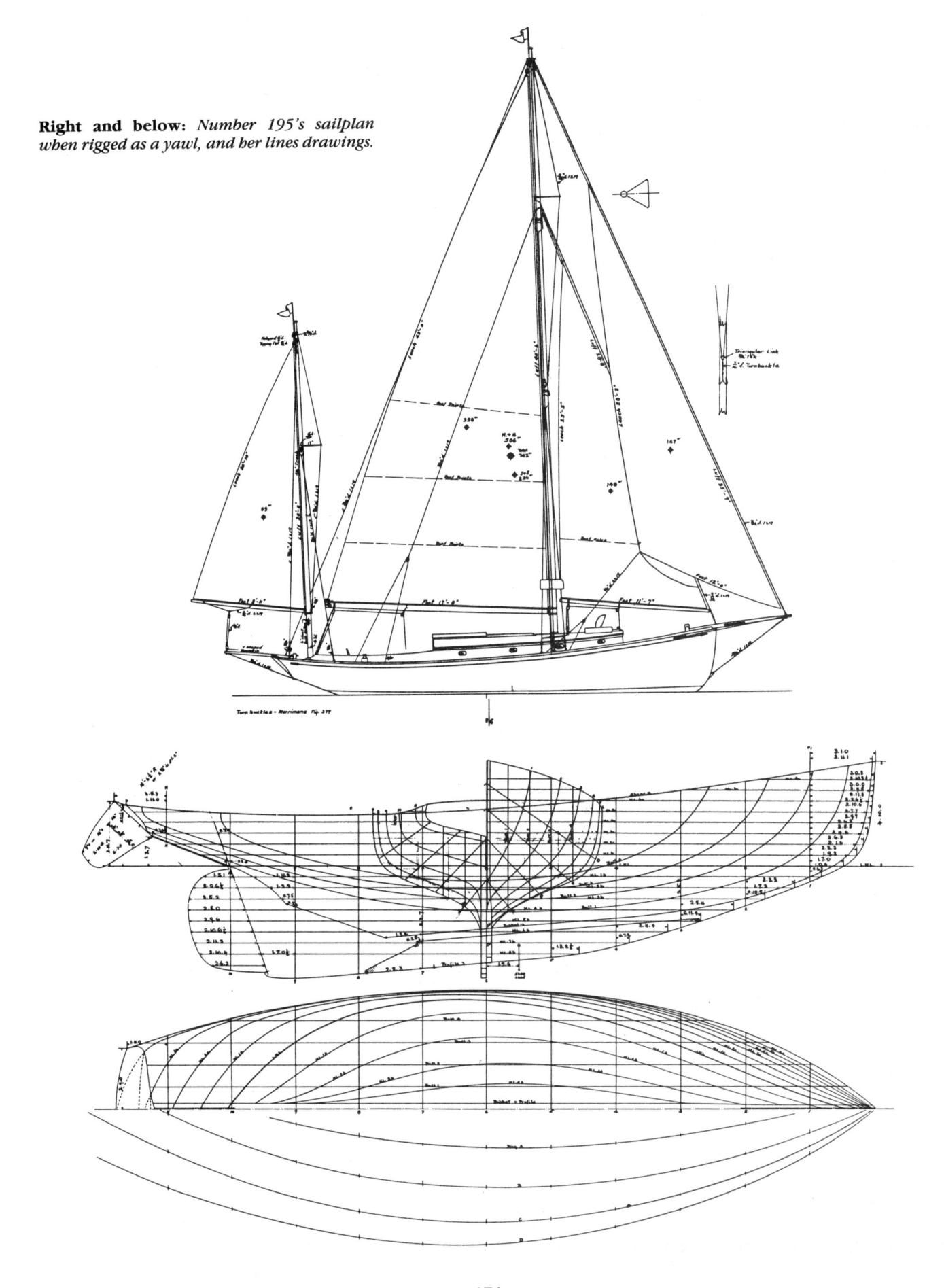

Right and below: *Number 195's sailplan when rigged as a yawl, and her lines drawings.*

176

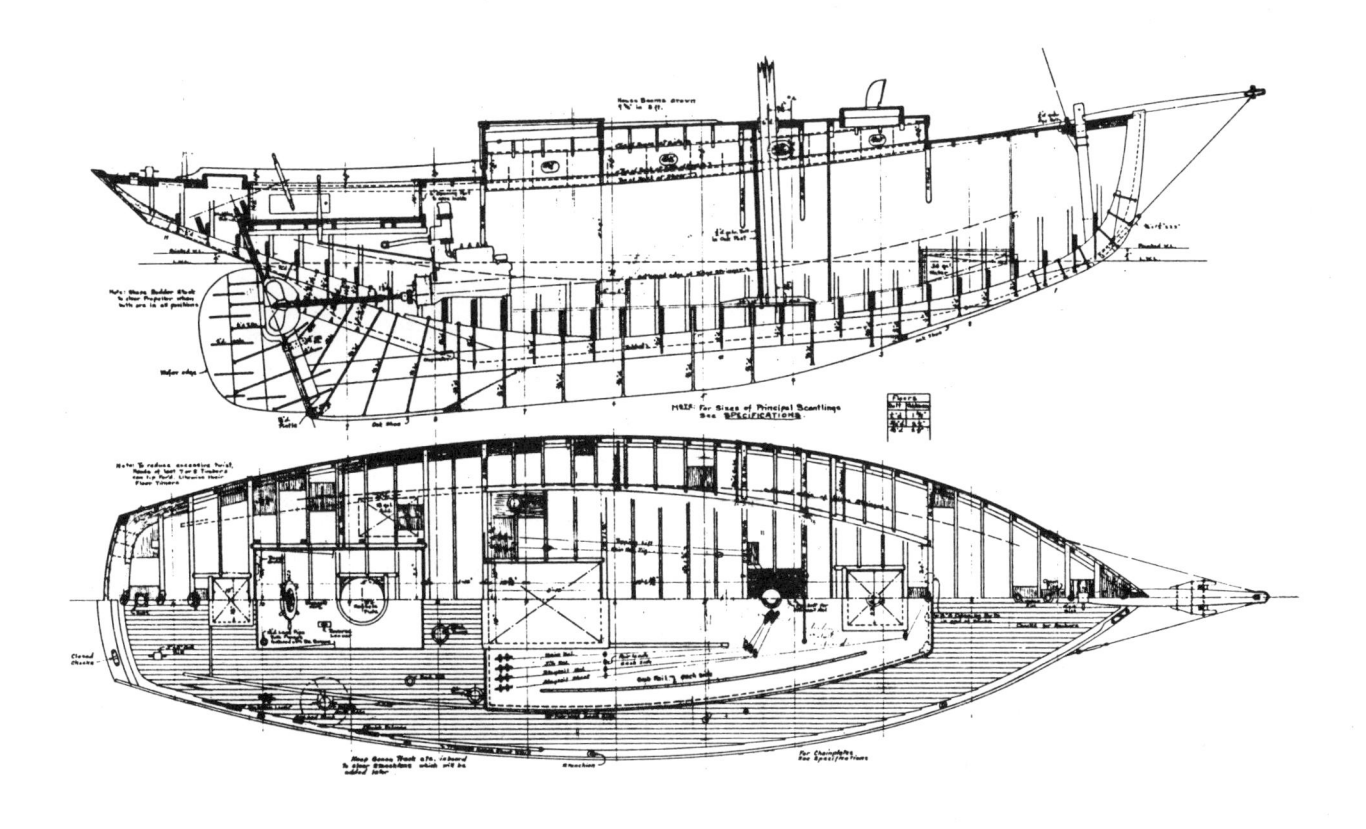

The construction details and accommodations for number 195.

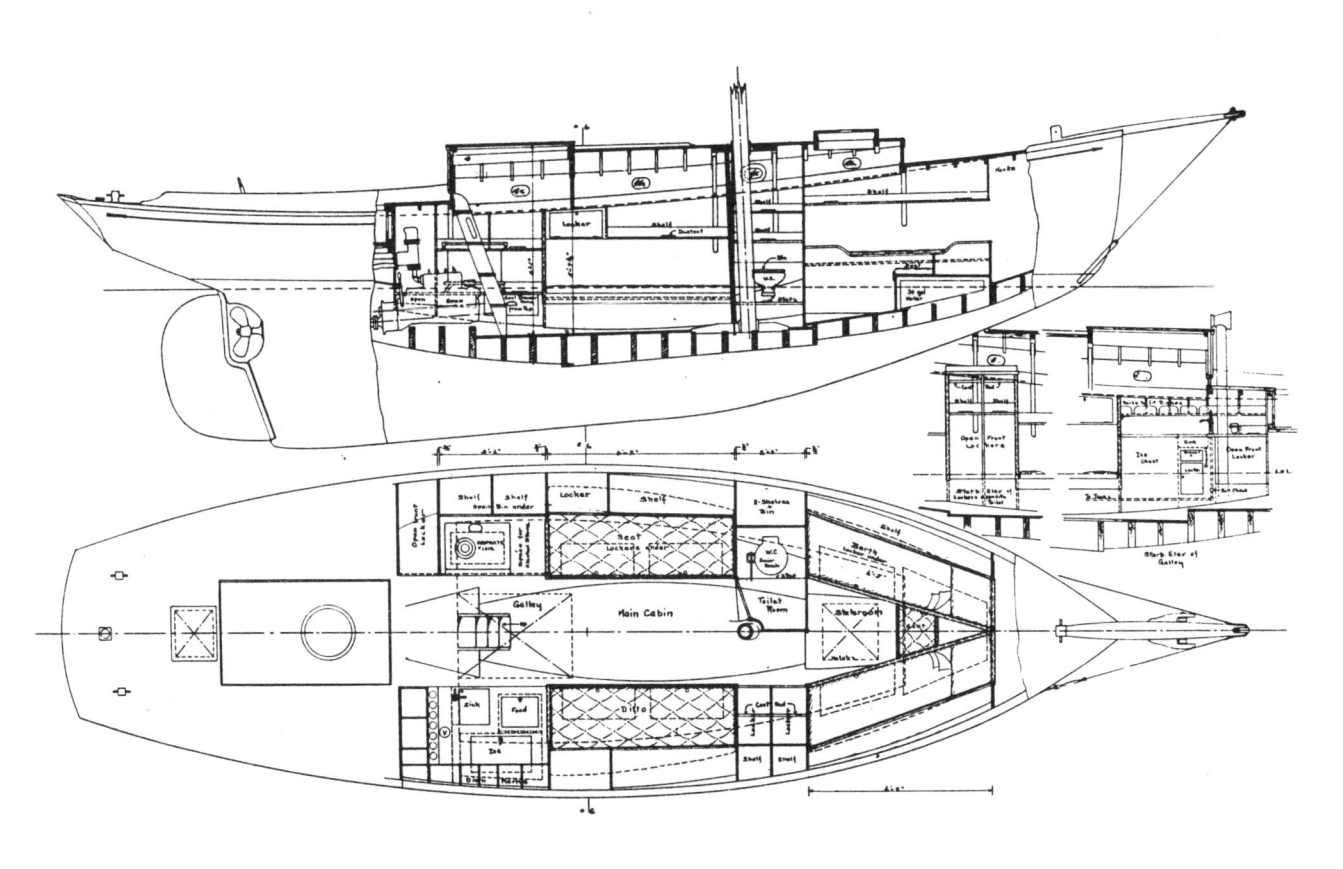

Fomalhaut *under sail off the Maine coast.*

After the war, when it became necessary to get new sails, Thayer decided to put the yawl rig on, reducing the main nearly 20 percent in area and making her easier to handle shorthanded. She was later owned by Richard Pratt; still later she went down to the Islands, where, as far as I know, she still sails.

198

Design Number 198
Length Overall: 35 feet
Length on Waterline: 28 feet
Beam: 9 feet 6 inches
Draft: 5 feet 6 inches
Sail Area: 569 square feet
Displacement: 16,620 pounds

The New Bedford 35 was designed for Carl Beetle of New Bedford, Mass., to be built as a stock boat with a base price of $6,100 in the water for the standard equipped model, or a deluxe model for $7,500. The first boat was so badly damaged in a 1938 hurricane that it was sold to the insurance company. Boat number 2 was completed in 1939, and the eleventh was completed in 1942, built to the specifications noted, with 6,300 pounds of lead outside, Philippine

The sailplan and lines for the New Bedford 35.

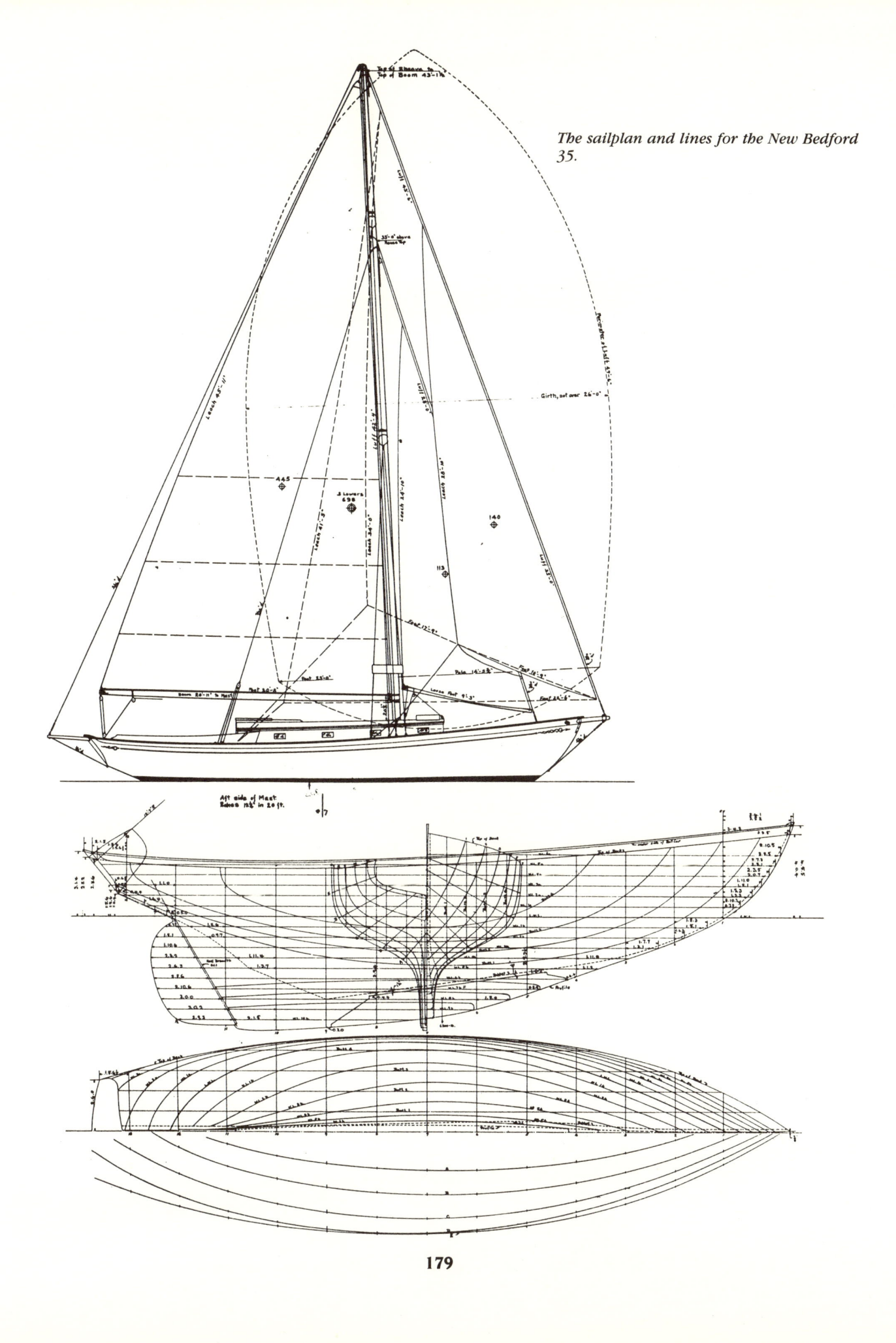

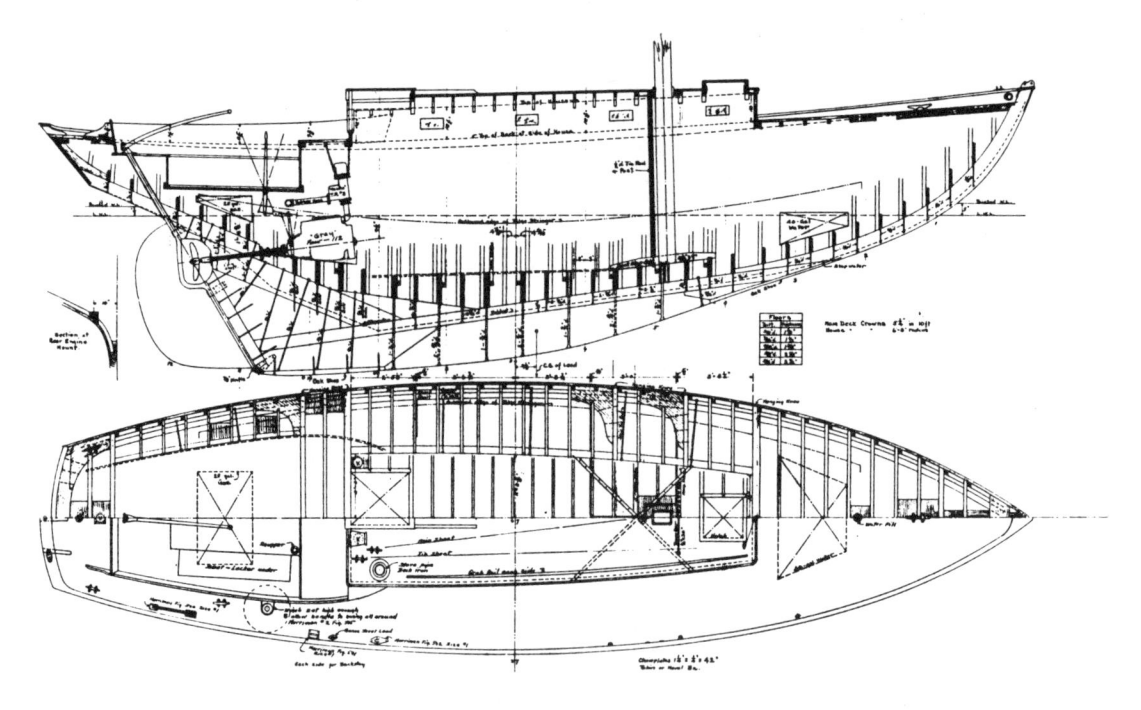

The construction plans for the 35, and under sail with problems aloft! Photograph by Norman Fortier.

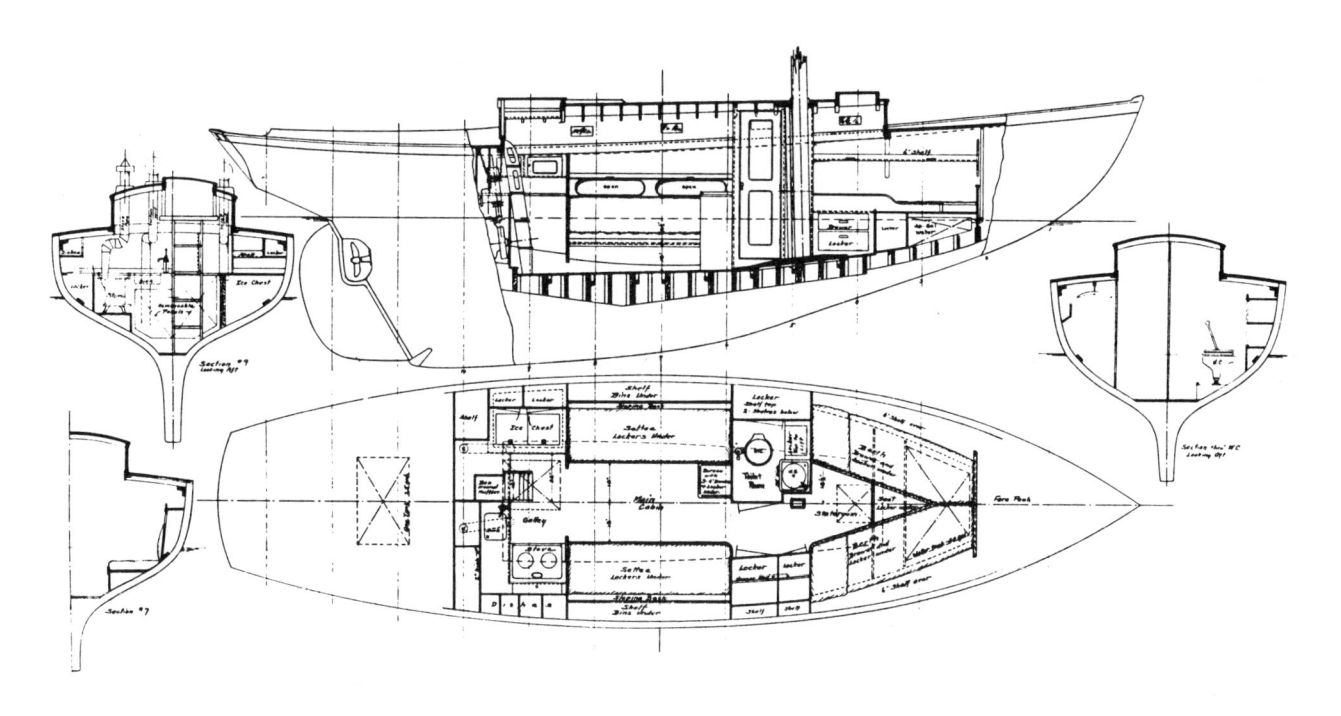

The 35's accommodations plans, and resting at sea, with a busy crew! Photograph by Norman Fortier.

mahogany planking, and bronze fastenings. Auxiliary power was a Gray 4-22 direct drive turning a feathering propeller.

The two photos show the wisdom of looking aloft once in a while. Perhaps that faulty spreader could have been detected and the boat put on the other tack until it was fixed, thereby saving the spar.

202 TYRONE

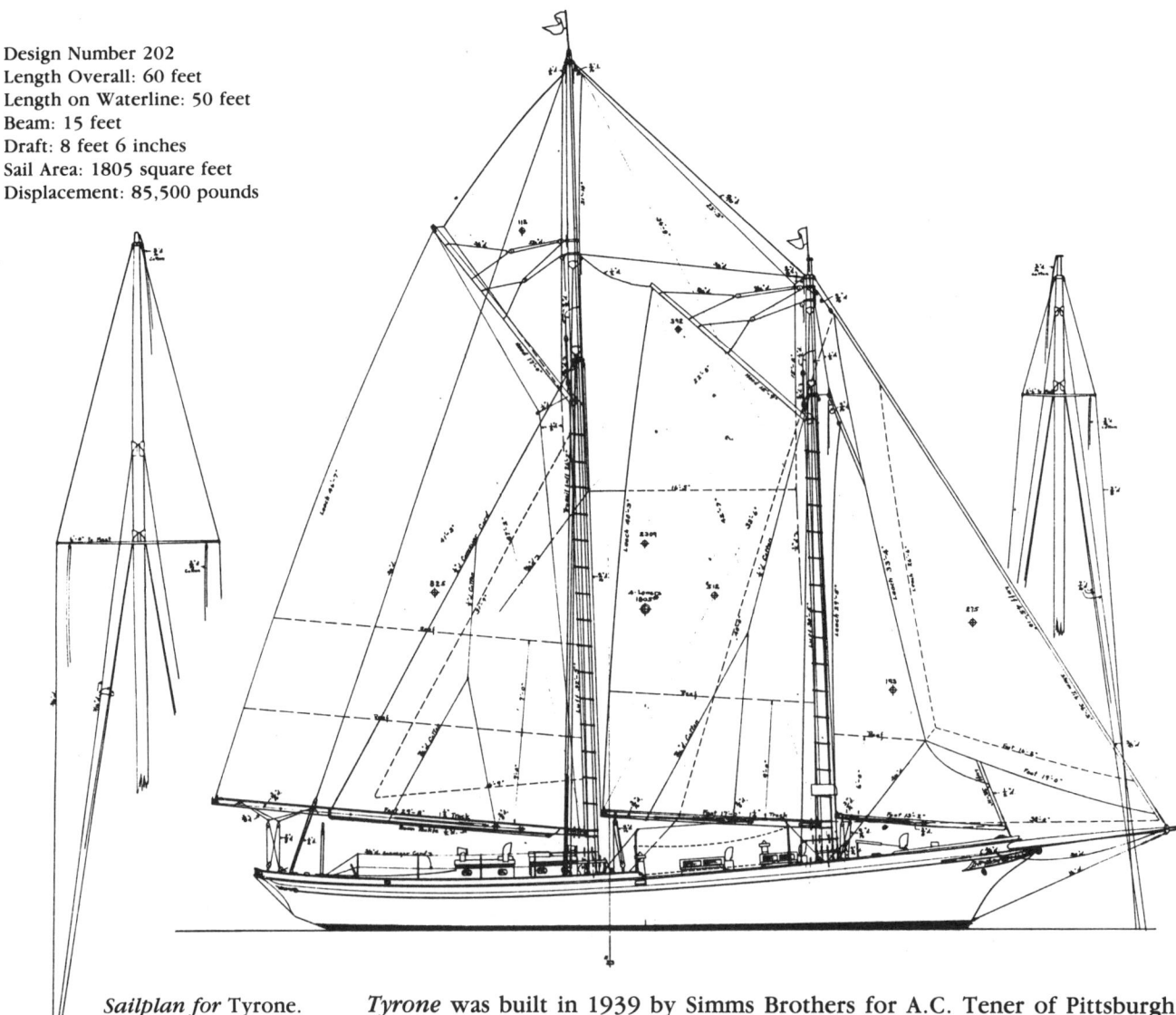

Design Number 202
Length Overall: 60 feet
Length on Waterline: 50 feet
Beam: 15 feet
Draft: 8 feet 6 inches
Sail Area: 1805 square feet
Displacement: 85,500 pounds

Sailplan for Tyrone.

Tyrone was built in 1939 by Simms Brothers for A.C. Tener of Pittsburgh, Penn. She was the subject of a lot of correspondence between Tener and my father until the plans were finished. Several different combinations of beam, draft, displacement, and freeboard were considered. The possibility of building her in steel was explored but found impractical and expensive. Tener wanted a rugged, able boat capable of weathering any kind of weather if given half a chance, and yet one that he and his captain could handle with some help from the cook. When in commission she always carried a captain and a cook.

She was heavily built, with 1⅝-inch mahogany screwed to 2½-inch double-sawn oak frames on 16-inch centers. Garboards were 2 inches thick. Power was a Lathrop Mystic 125 gas engine, and she had a 3-kilowatt, 32-volt, two-cylinder generator, to run her refrigerator and other electric powered gear.

She wintered in the water in Boothbay Harbor, Me., and went into commis-

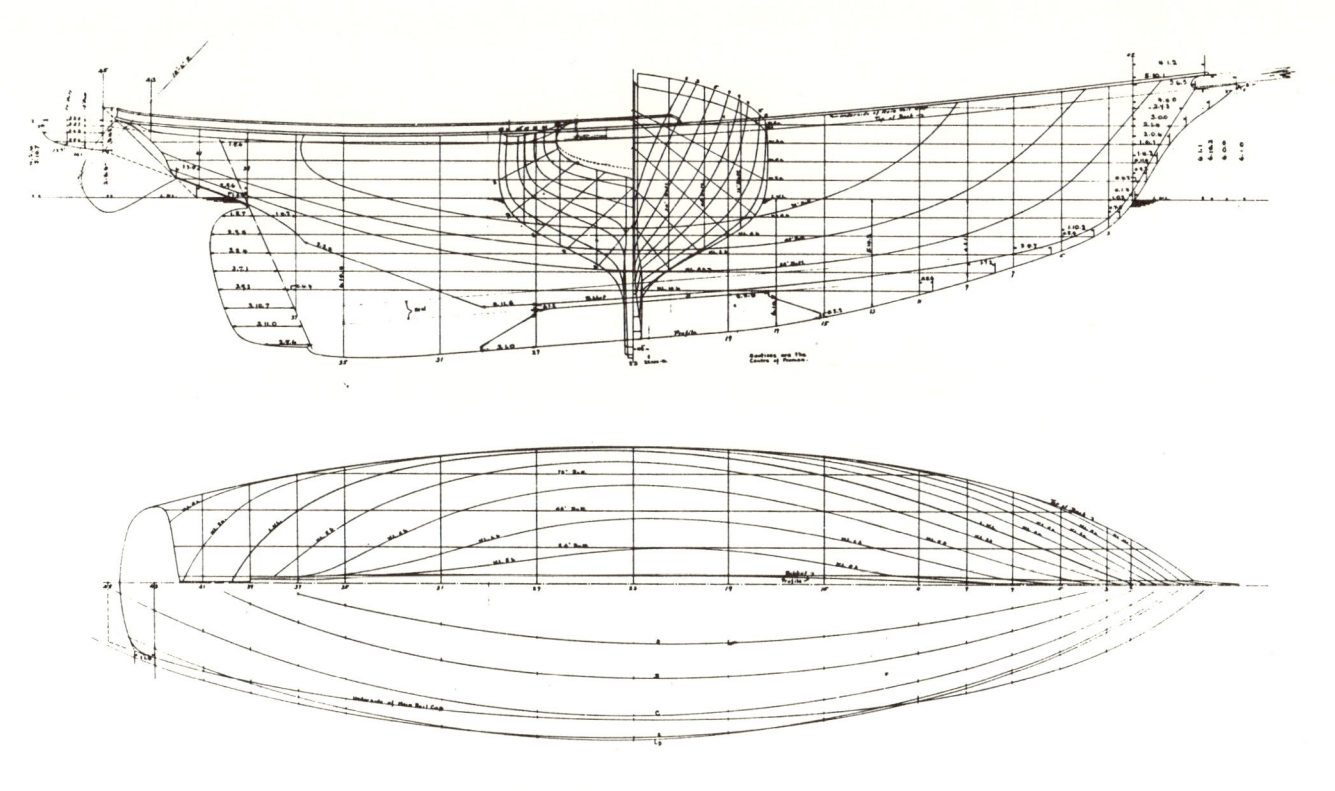

Lines for Tyrone *and her construction plans.*

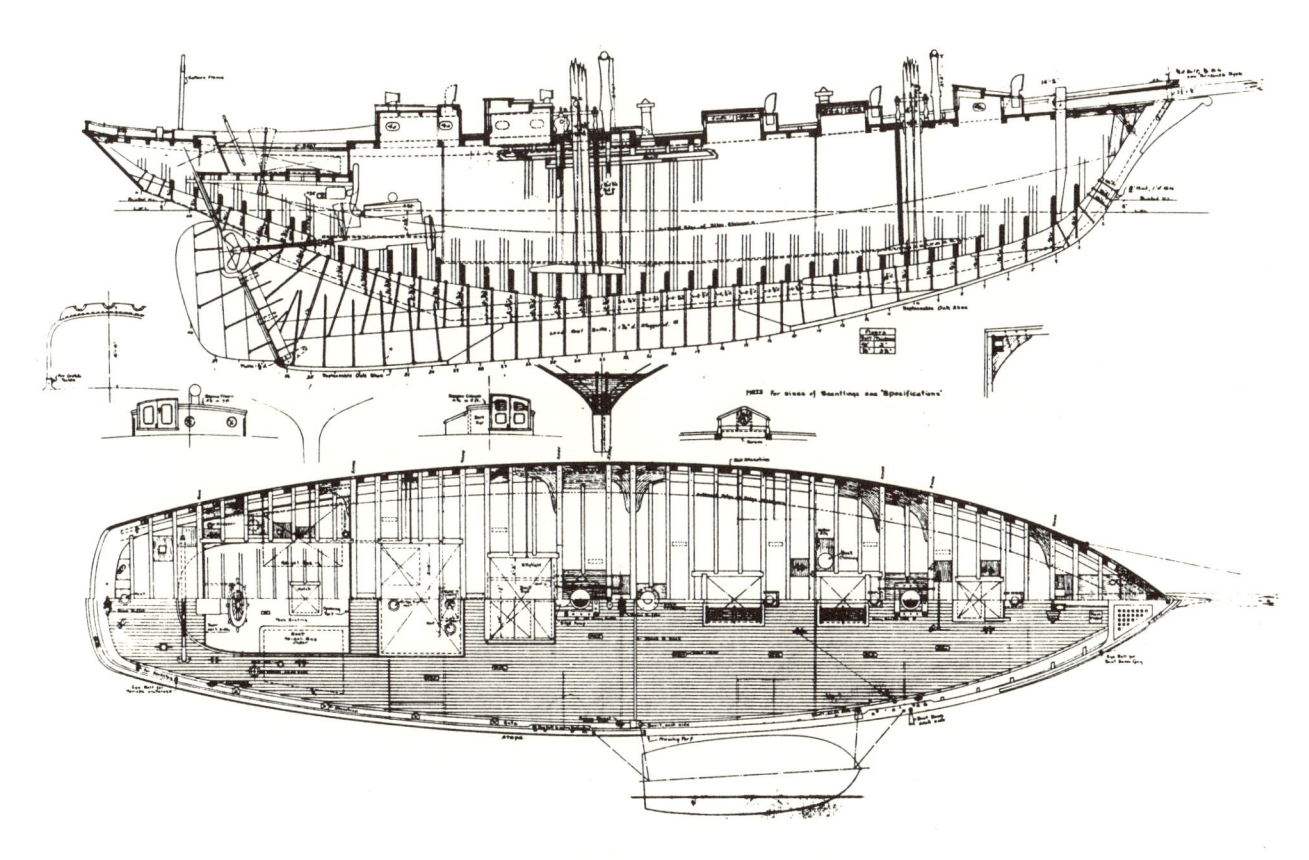

sion around April 1. In 1959 she was brought to Manchester, where we replaced some soft wood around the corners of her stern. She was too big for me to haul, so we did it all from a float while at the dock. We ended up with barrels of chain, moorings, and anything else of any weight that we could put on the foredeck to lift her stern so we could work on it. While she was with us, we all

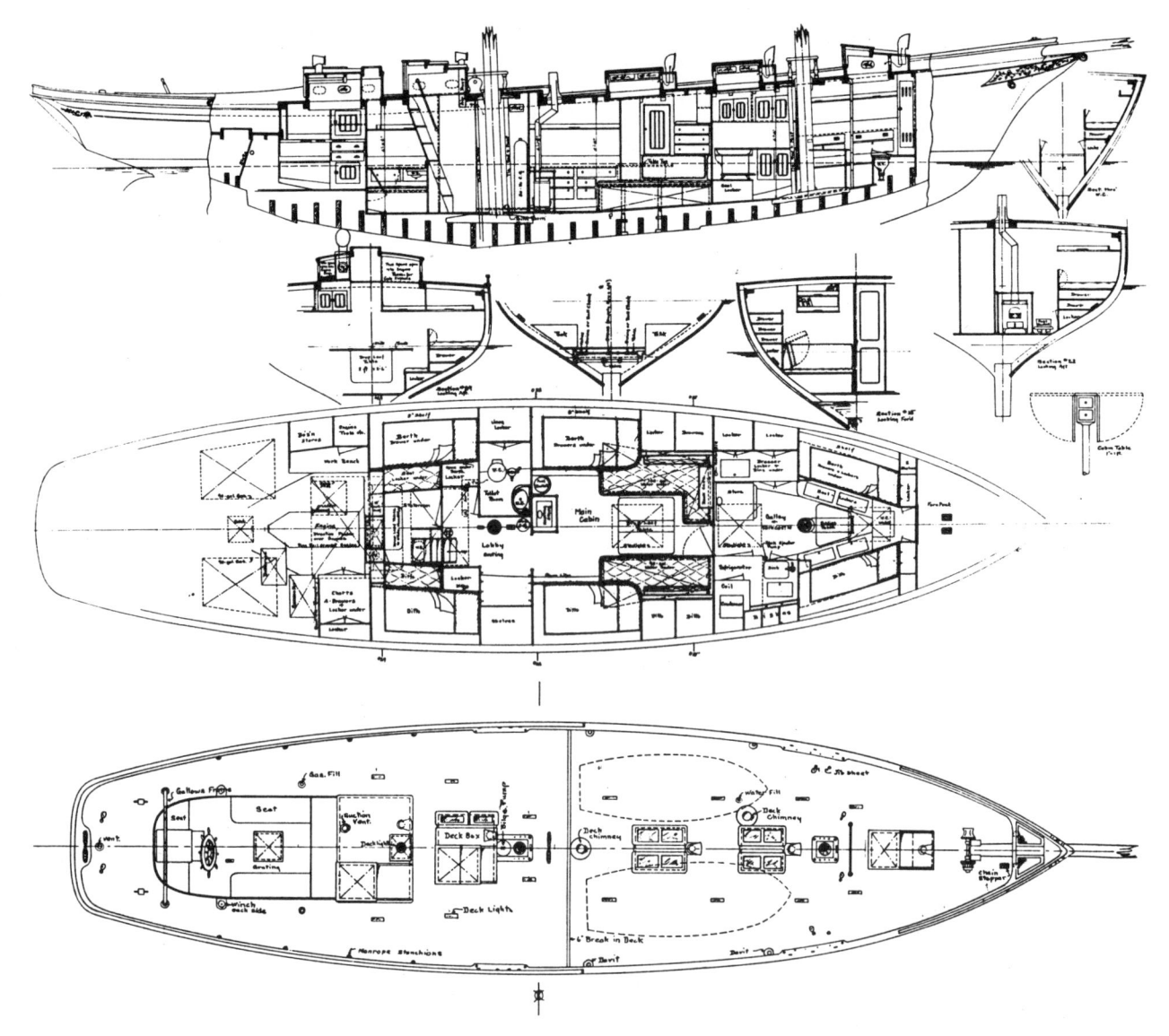

Above: Tyrone's *accommodations and deck plans.* **Right:** Tyrone *under sail.*

Tyrone *at anchor. Photograph courtesy Coast of Maine Studio.*

lived like kings and put on weight. The cook, and he was a good one, made either pies, cakes, or doughnuts every day, and on Fridays he made a fish chowder that put lobster stew to shame. He did it all on a coal-fired Shipmate that was kindled in April and never went out until the boat was laid up in the fall.

Tyrone was sold in 1966 after Tener's death to Carl Chase, and I believe she has been sold several times since. She has made several Atlantic crossings.

203 BLUE PETER

Design Number 203
Length Overall: 37 feet
Length on Waterline: 34 feet 9 inches
Beam: 11 feet 1 inch
Draft: 4 feet 1 inch
Sail Area: 540 square feet
Displacement: 21,200 pounds

Blue Peter was built in 1939 for S. Eliot Guild by Simms Brothers. She replaced the 35-foot Alden *Blue Peter,* built in 1935. For a boat of almost 11 tons designed displacement, she was well laid out for four people to cruise in comfort. The icebox was big enough for a five-gallon tank for cold drinking water, and there was a tank on the back of the Shipmate for hot water.

You might also notice that the cabin doghouse that appears in the profile drawing was not part of Dad's original thinking about this boat as it does not appear in any of the other drawings. I think its addition interrupts the lines of the boat.

Note these May 1939 comments on *Blue Peter* from *Yachting:*

> This interesting motor-sailer is from the board of S.S. Crocker, naval architect of Boston, Mass., and was designed for S. Eliot Guild, of Boston and Nahant. She is now approaching completion at the yard of Simms Brothers, in Dorchester, Mass.

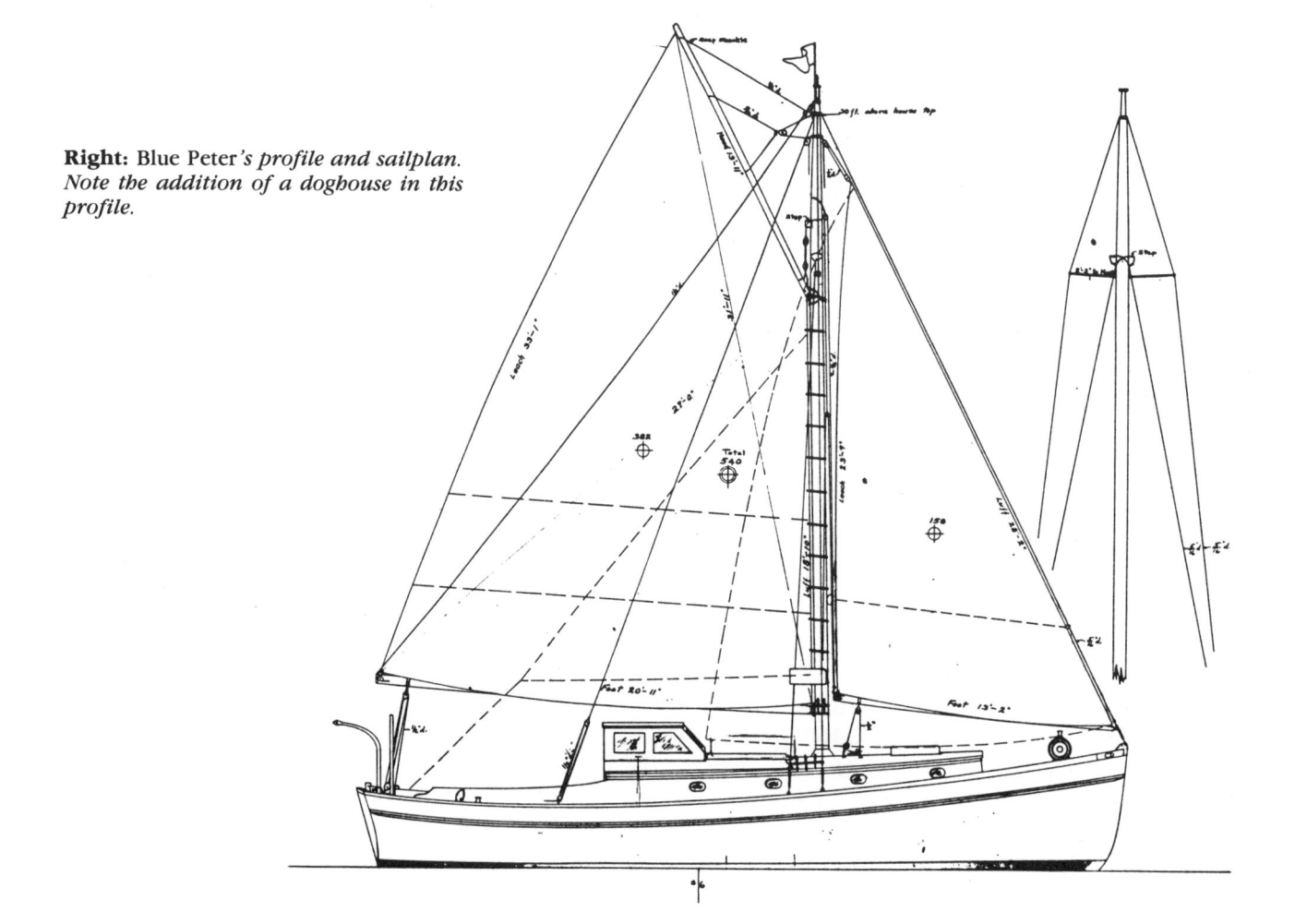

Right: Blue Peter's *profile and sailplan. Note the addition of a doghouse in this profile.*

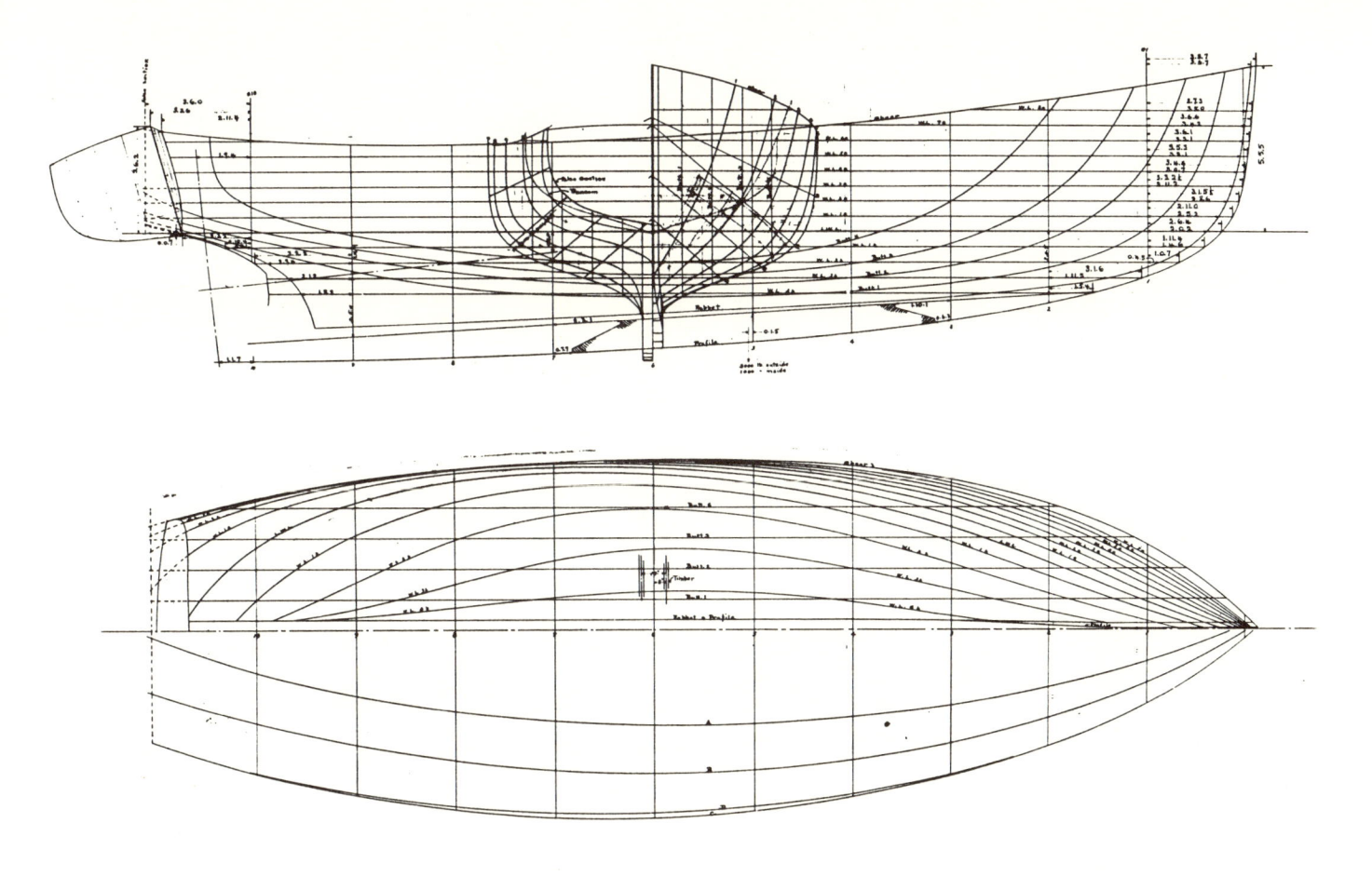

Lines for Blue Peter, *number 203.*

The principal dimensions of the new yacht are as follows: Length over all, 37'0''; length on the water line, 34'9''; beam, 11'1''; draft of water, 4'1''. She is sloop rigged, with loose-footed gaff-headed mainsail and loose-footed jib. There is also a trysail for use as a steadying sail or in a hard chance. The total area of her working canvas is 540 square feet. Of this, there are 382 square feet in the mainsail and 158 in the jib. Sails are by Manchester.

The yacht's construction is high grade. She is framed with white oak and her outside planking is of 1¼'' Oregon fir. The deck is of teak, 1¼'' in thickness. All deck joinerwork is of Honduras mahogany. She carries 3,000 pounds of iron ballast on her keel.

The power plant is a Chrysler Crown engine located on the center line under the floor of the cockpit. This 6-cylinder engine, rated 57 b.hp. at 1,600 r.p.m. to 103 b.hp. at 3,200 revolutions, is fitted with a reduction gear of 2.56:1 ratio and drives the propeller on the center line. The designed speed of *Blue Peter* is about 8½ knots, 9¾ statute miles per hour. A 90-gallon gasoline tank is located outboard on each side of the engine. A fresh water tank of 80 gallons' capacity is located under the berths in the stateroom forward.

The cabin trunk is long and low, with the mast stepped almost in the middle of it. A large hatch forward gives access to and provides ventilation for the forward quarters. The cockpit is roomy.

Below decks, the accommodation plans show a stateroom forward with a high built-in berth on each side, a seat between the berths, bureau, shelves and hanging space. Next aft is the toilet room, on the starboard side, with a large wardrobe opposite. The main cabin is provided with a wide transom on each side. Aft is the galley.

Blue Peter's equipment includes automatic steerer and ship-to-shore telephone system.

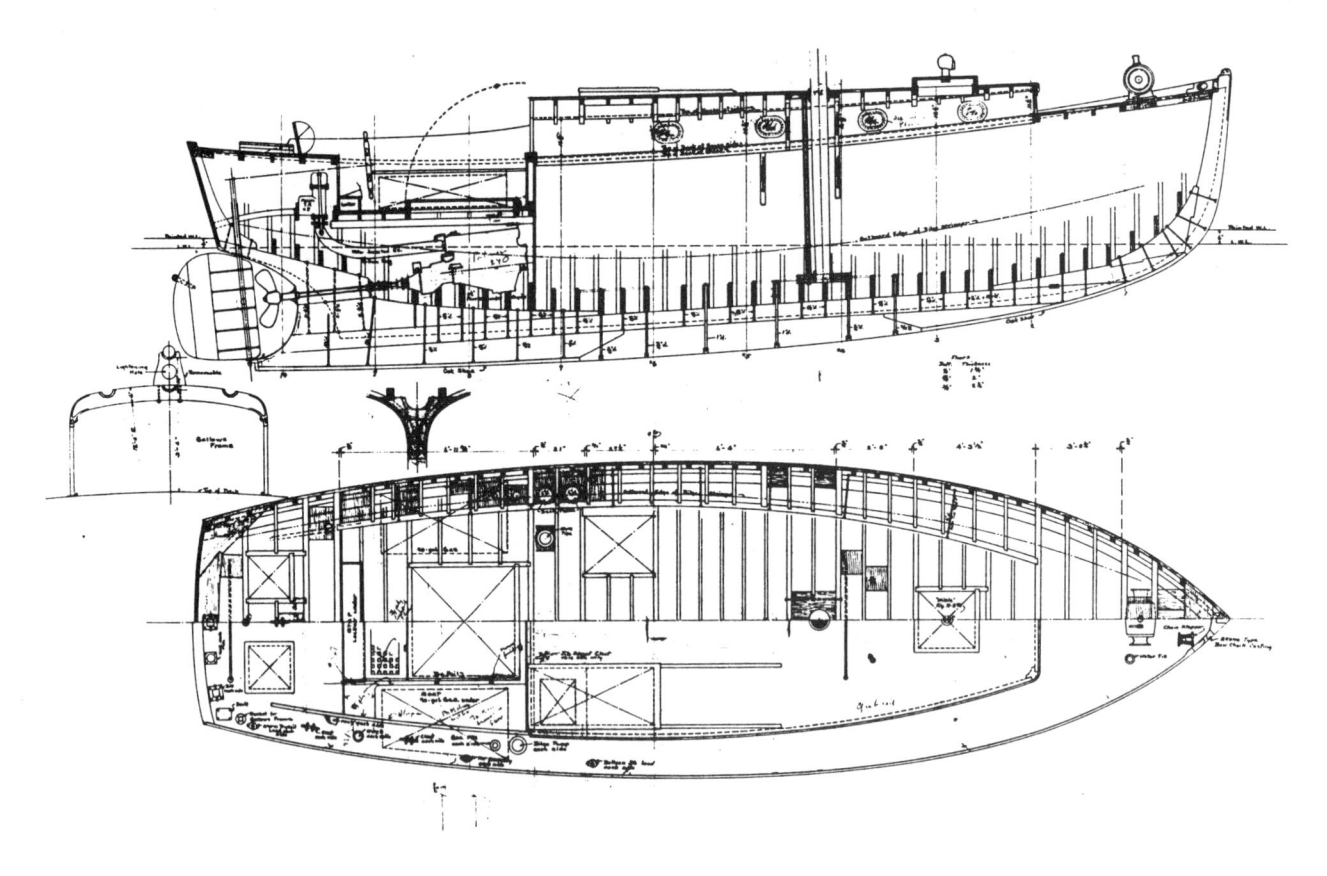

The construction drawings and accommodations plans for Blue Peter.

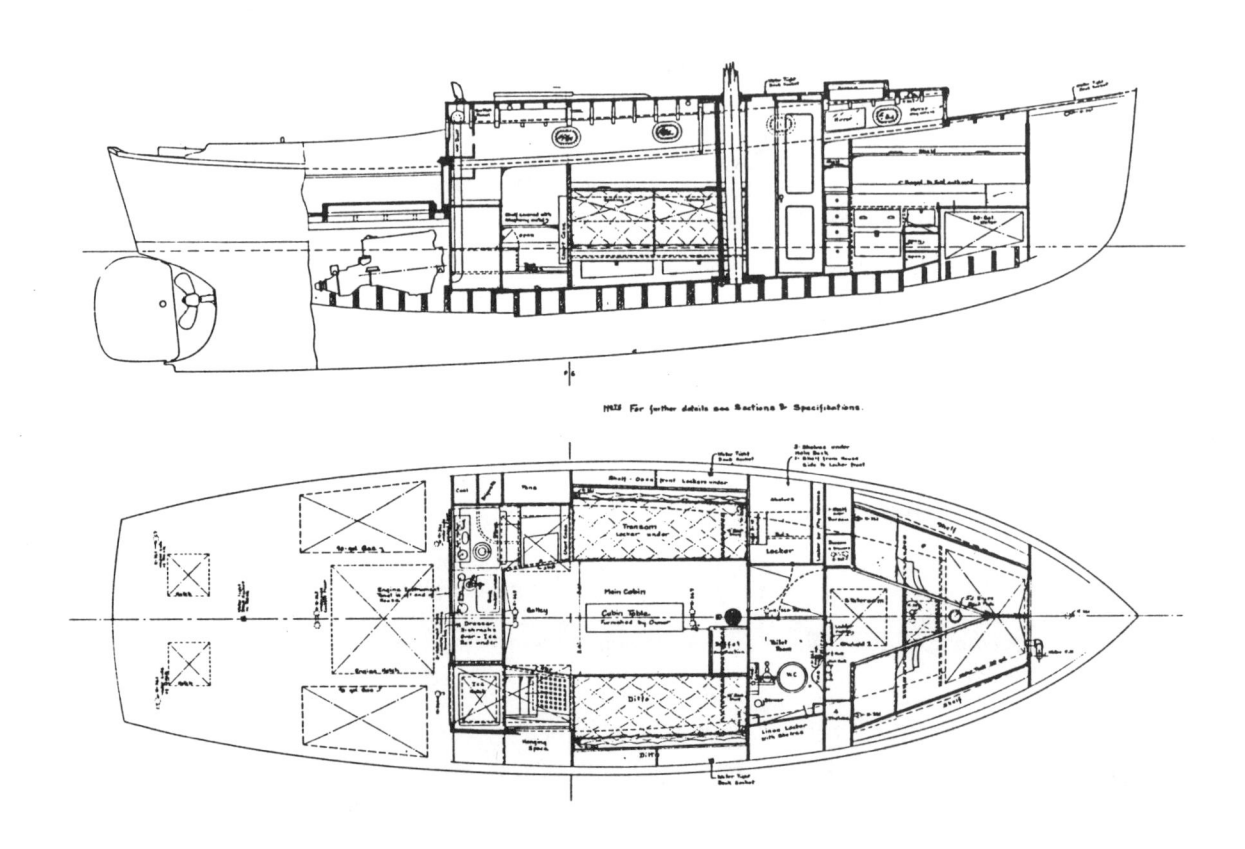

207

Number 207: I'm sure Dad took great delight in drawing up this 11-foot-9-inch scull boat for H.W. Buhler. He was probably remembering his younger days and duck hunting on the Barnstable marshes.

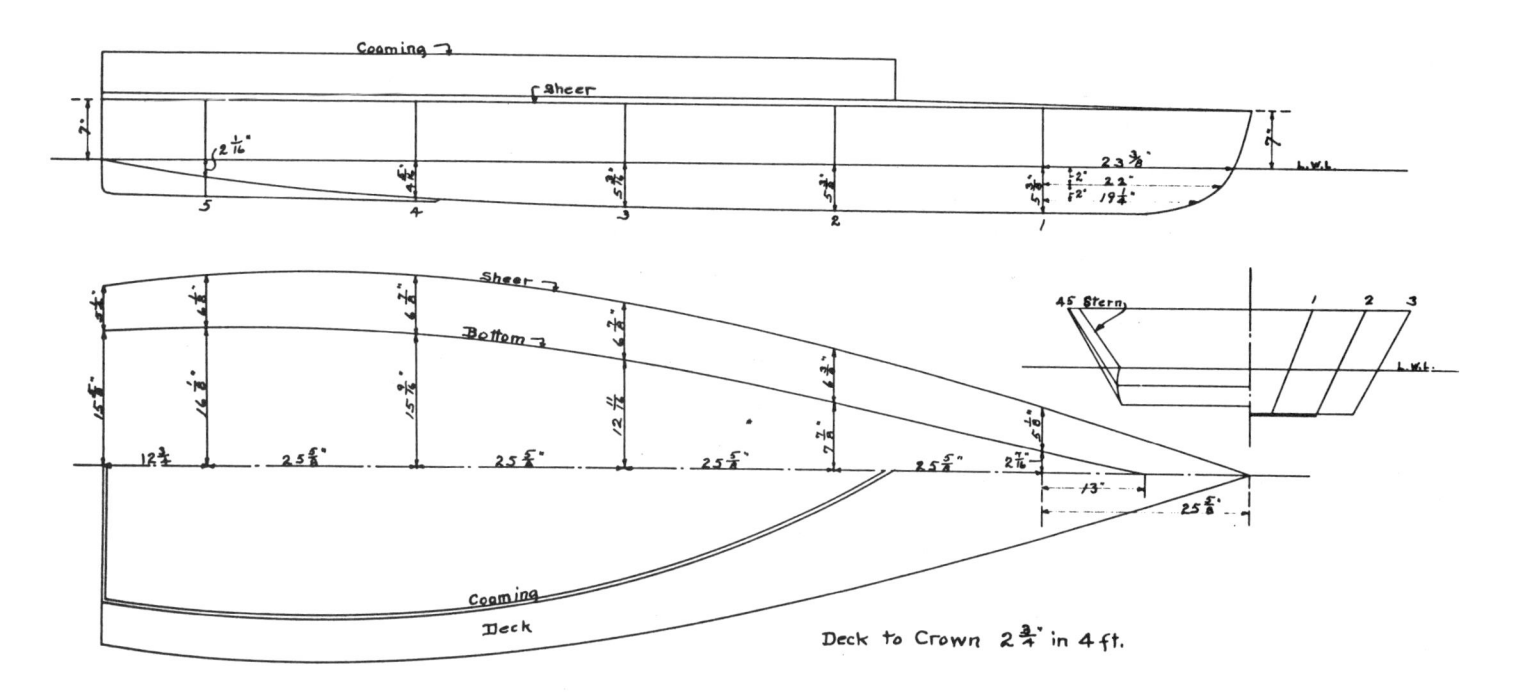

The lines for number 207.

EASTWIND 212

Eastwind was the second boat built by Bud McIntosh from my father's design. She was built for Harry Cann of Manchester, Mass., in 1940. Harry wanted a boat with a good-size cockpit for afternoon and weekend sailing out of Manchester, so the cabin was not cluttered with such things as an icebox and sink — something that is usually plugged up anyway. The occasional need for an icebox was taken care of by a portable one in the cockpit. Anyway, even without a regular icebox and sink, Harry and his wife generally were able to get away for a two-week cruise down Maine every year.

Eastwind was sold to Stuart Martin, who still owns her. She has received excellent care, and when she came into my place to have her spar lifted out for the

Design Numbers 212 and 332
Length Overall: 28 feet 1 inch
Length on Waterline: 25 feet 9 inches
Beam: 9 feet 6 inches
Draft: 4 feet 9 inches
Sail Area: 512 square feet
Displacement: 11,700 pounds

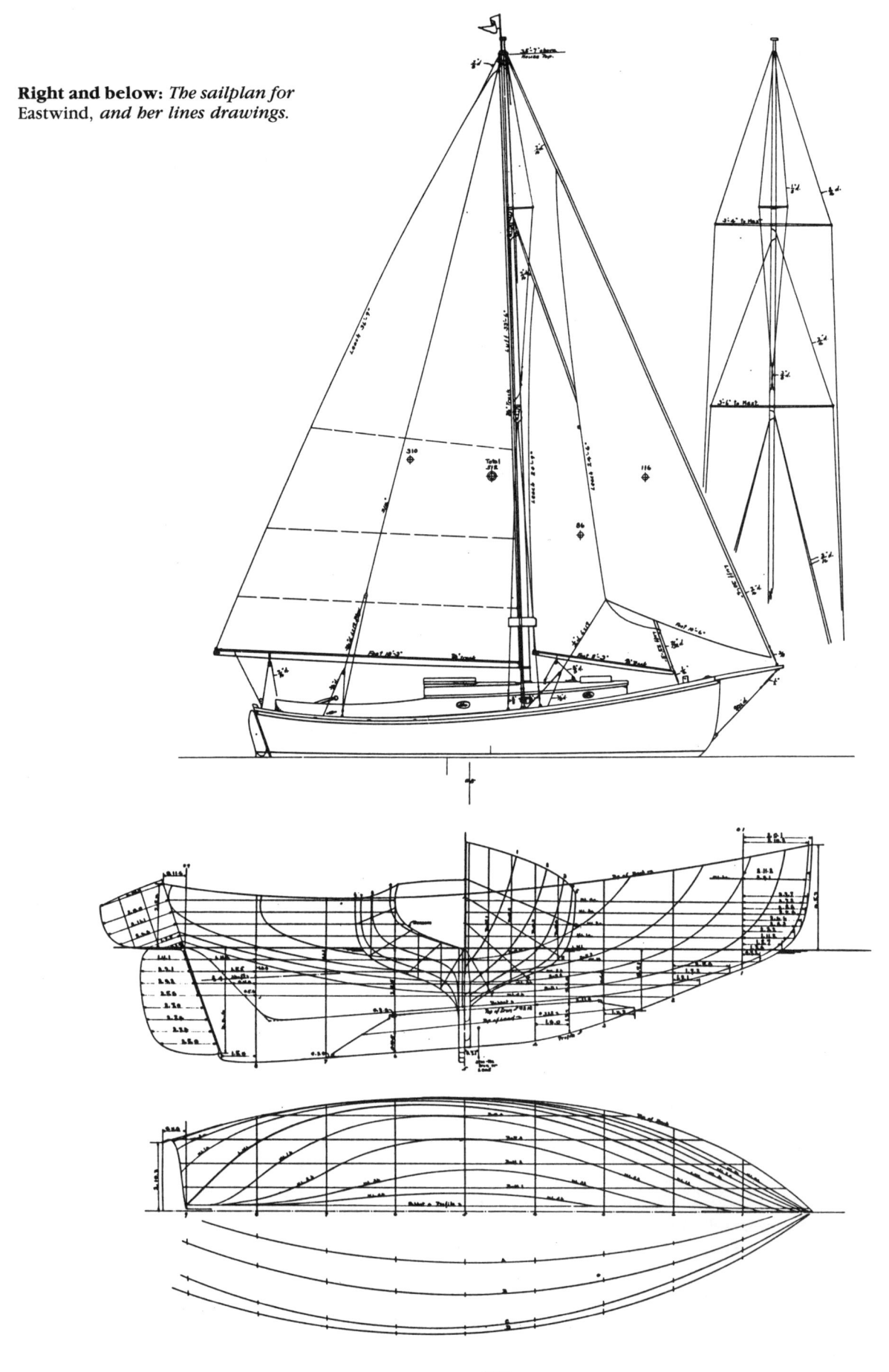

Right and below: *The sailplan for* Eastwind, *and her lines drawings.*

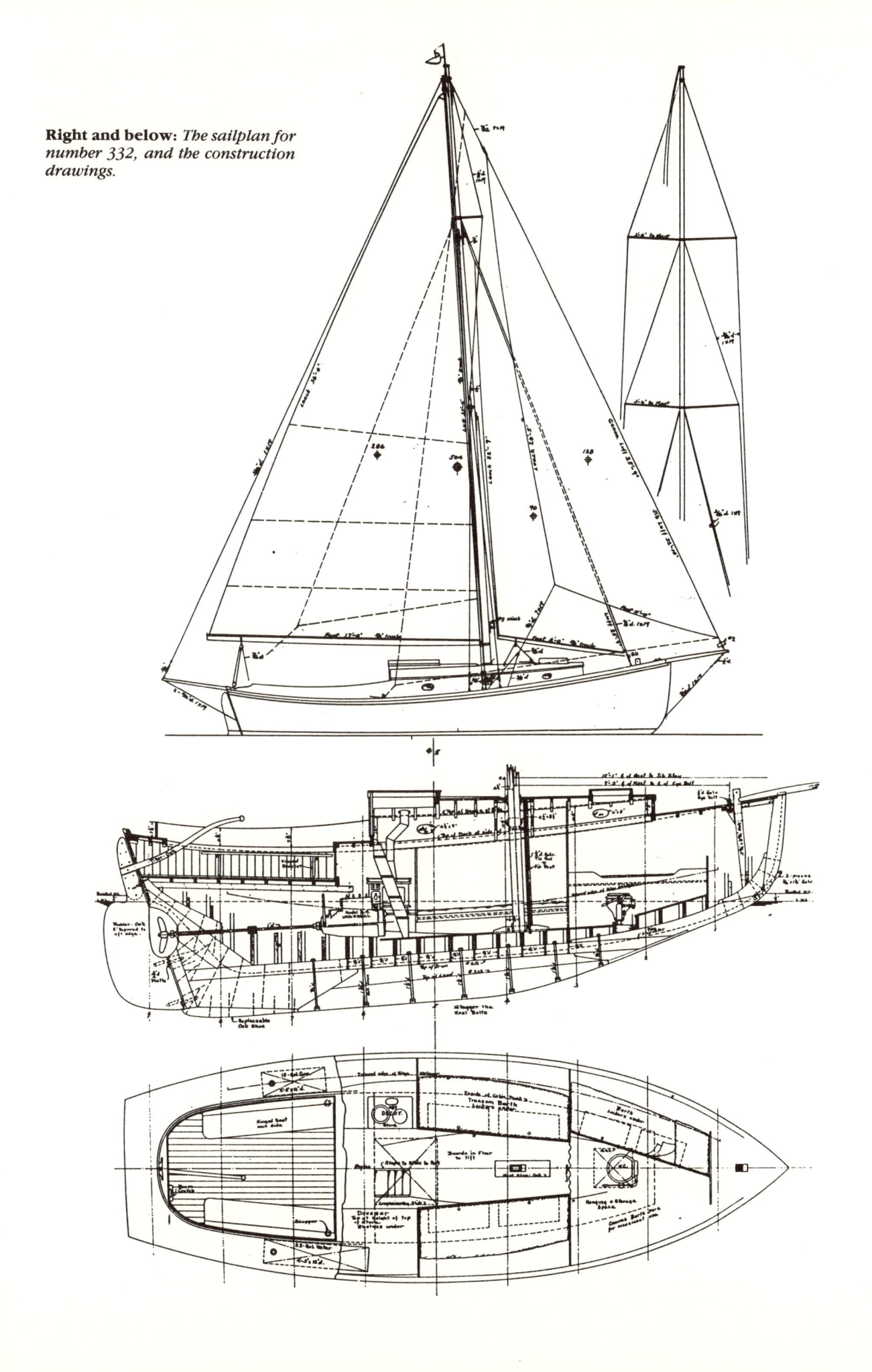

Right and below: *The sailplan for number 332, and the construction drawings.*

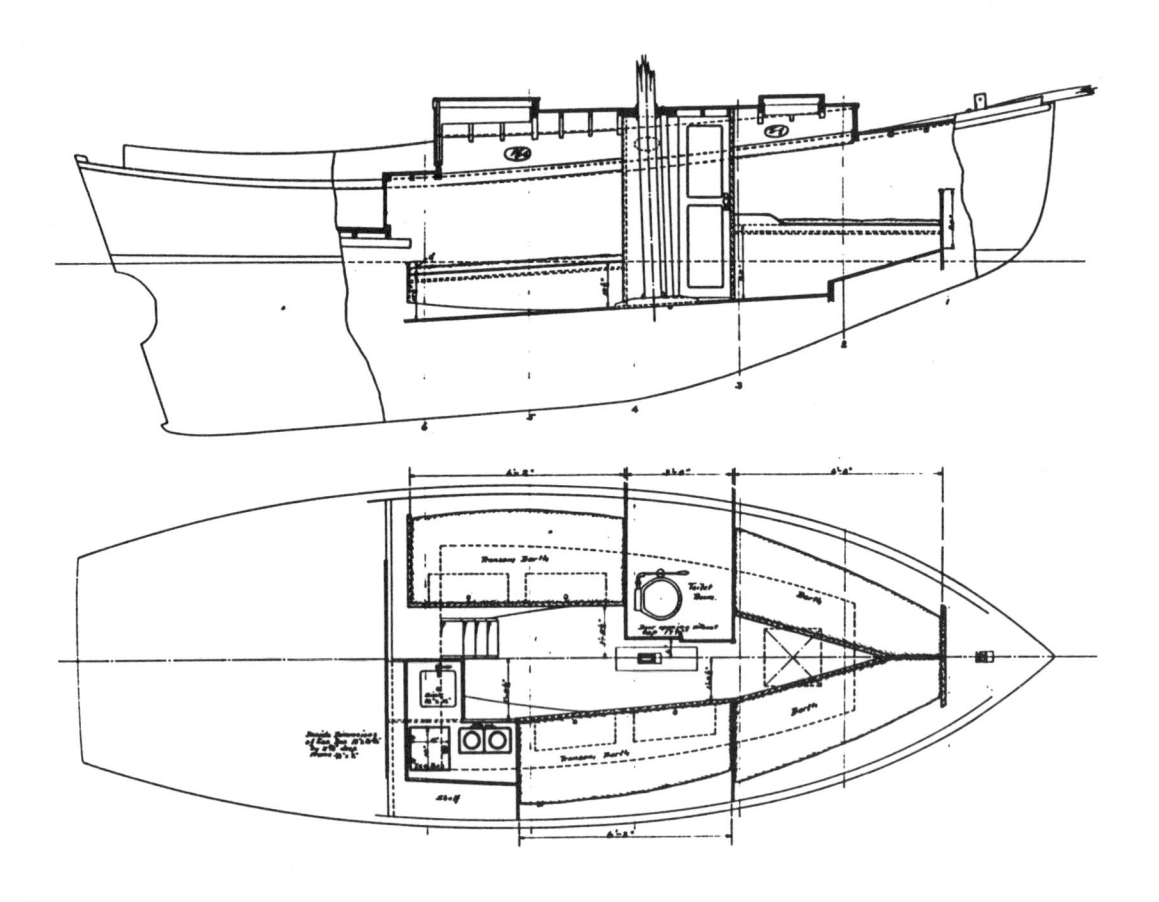

The accommodations for number 212A, and the construction plan for number 212.

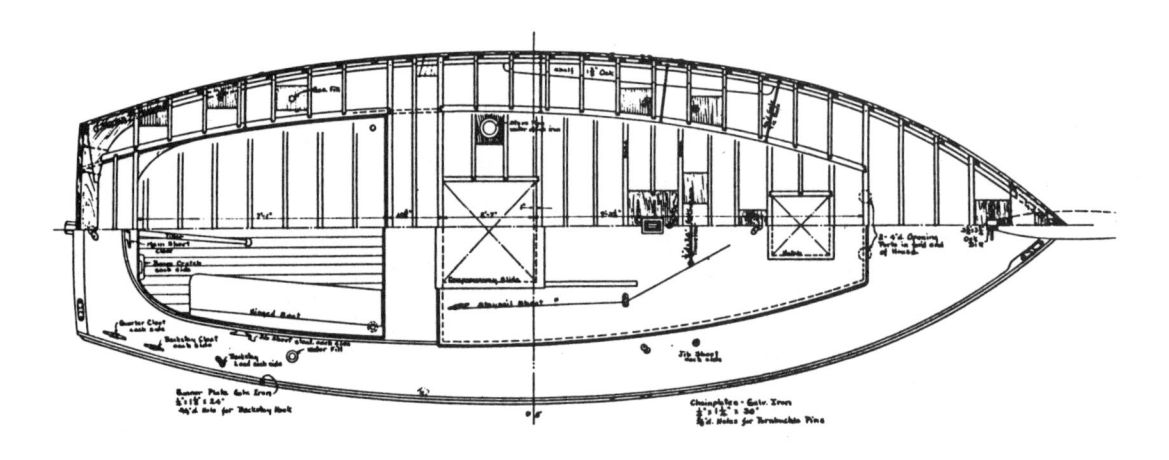

winter, her topsides were as smooth as any glass boat, even after 43 years. That speaks well of McIntosh's work. She also has the original Utility Four Universal gas engine.

At least one of these boats was built with a raised deck, which, of course, gave a lot more room below.

Cabin plan number 212A shows how the interior was arranged in the boat as built by the Greenwich Bay Shipyard and called the Greenwich Bay Cutter. The profile on number 332 shows a permanent backstay added.

192

Eastwind *under sail*.

DEVIL 216

Devil was built by Bud McIntosh for Cliff Moir of Hampton, N.H. Cliff was a guy who was bound and determined to make his living somehow or other from the ocean. I first got to know him when I worked for Bud in 1940. Cliff worked there too, and I used to pick him up in Hampton on my daily commute from Manchester to Dover Point.

Design Number 216
Length overall: 42 feet
Length on Waterline: 40 feet 6 inches
Beam: 12 feet 4 inches
Draft: 3 feet
Displacement: 15,600 pounds

193

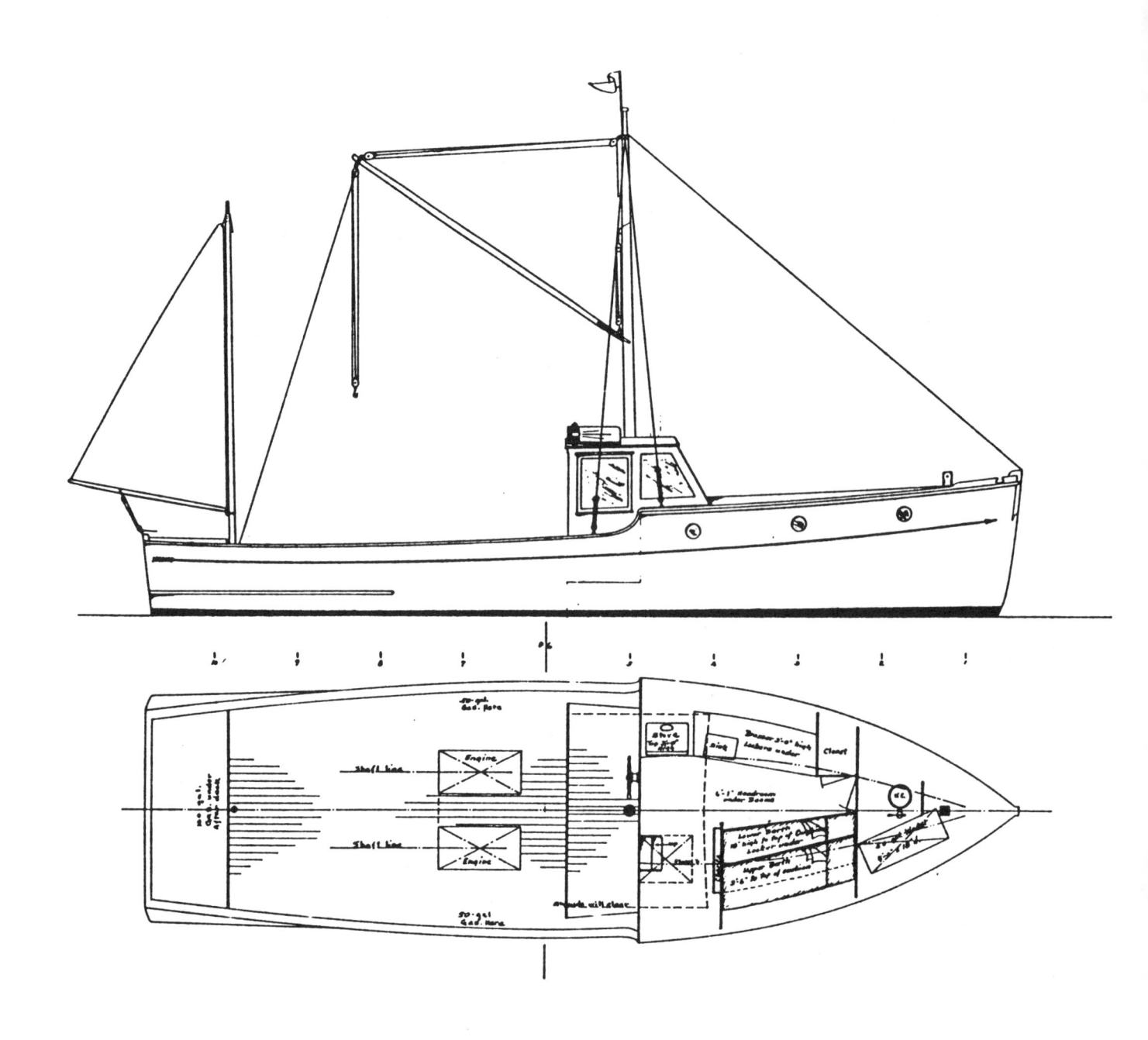

Devil's *profile and accommodations.*

    Devil was certainly an example of building on a shoestring. Bud built her after I left. He, Cliff, and Donald Whitehouse built the hull in three weeks, and as Bud says, "She showed it." The two six-cylinder Chevies cost a total of $25. Second-hand cable hooked up to a wooden quadrant and run through conduit tubing (without sheaves) steered her. To make use of some nice pine planking, she had

194

a butt block 30" side on her bottom, which had a very flat run. Backed up with floor timbers and engine beds, this didn't weaken her.

When both engines could be made to run at the same time, she went right up to 14 knots.

Cliff used her for freighting supplies to the Isles of Shoals, carrying four tons of coal in the cockpit and towing a barge loaded with six more. He also towed targets for Army and Navy target practice.

Devil *powering along.*

218

Designed in 1941 for Carl M. Beetle was the New Bedford 29. She was a smaller version of the New Bedford 35 and must have been very comfortable for two people, because there was no attempt to cram in living accommodations. I have records of only three of these boats having been built by Beetle. A four-cylinder Red Wing Meteor gas engine furnished auxiliary power.

Design Number 218
Length Overall: 29 feet
Length on Waterline: 22 feet 6 inches
Beam: 8 feet
Draft: 4 feet 7 inches
Sail Area: 386 square feet
Displacement: 10,300 pounds

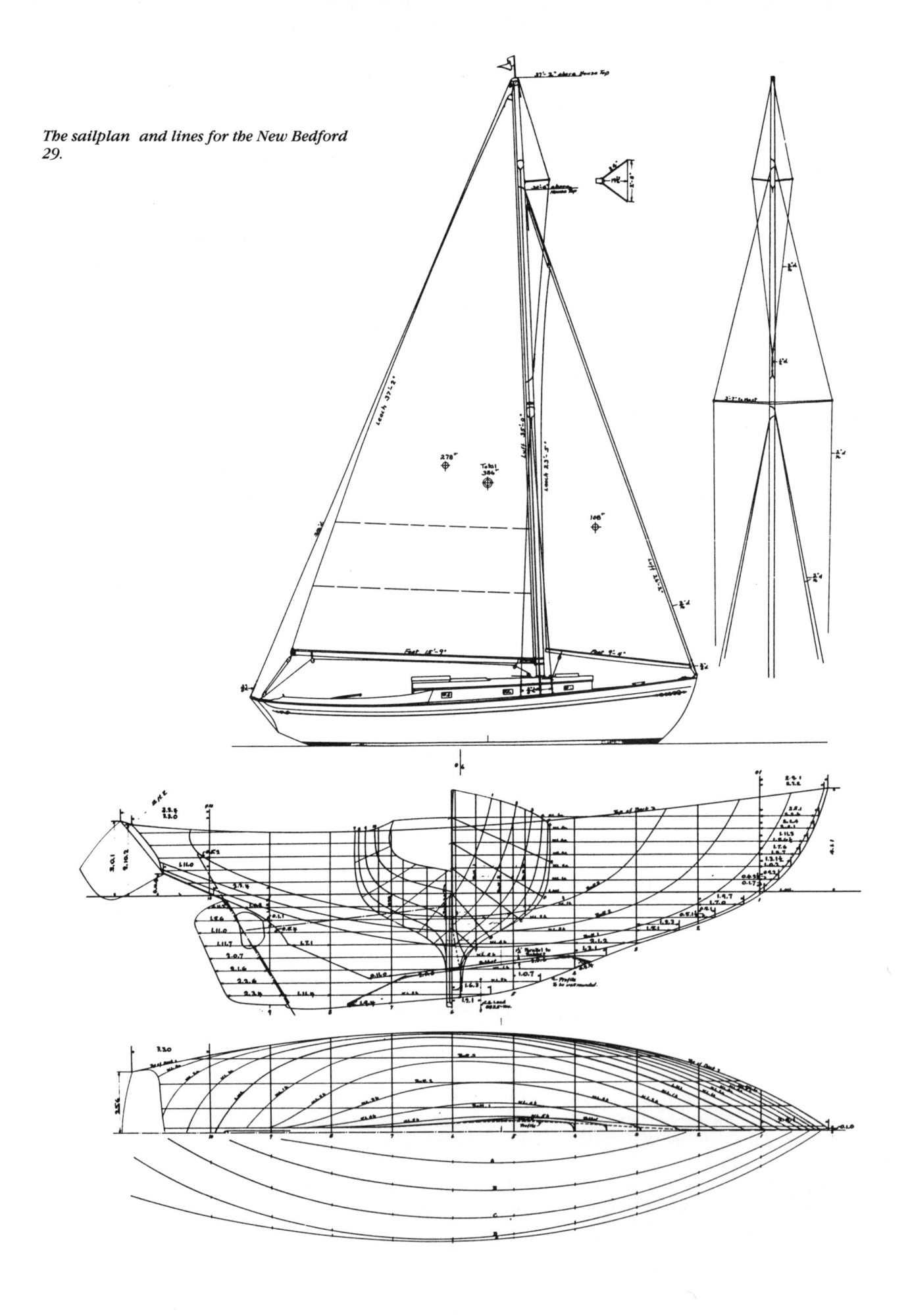

The sailplan and lines for the New Bedford 29.

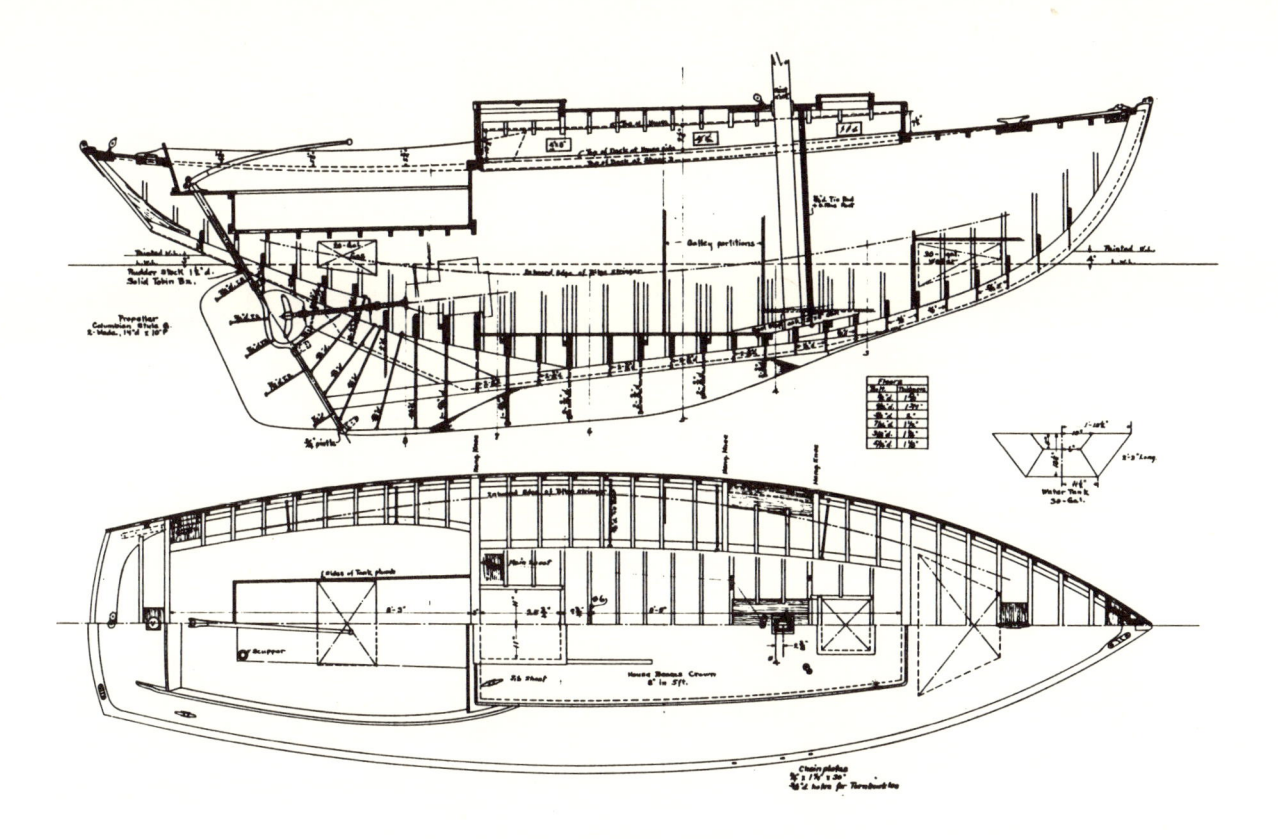

The construction plans and accommodations for the New Bedford 29.

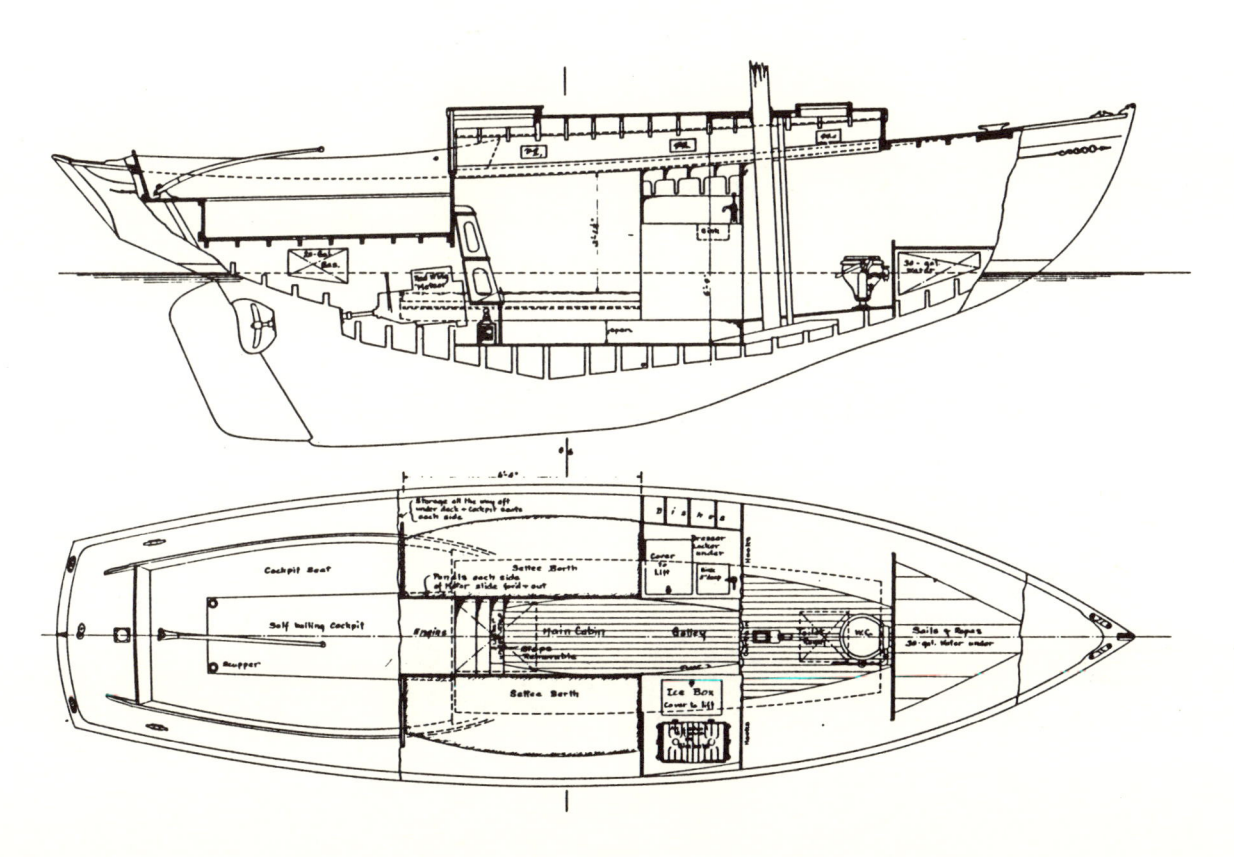

The 29 under sail.

FREE AND EASY 227

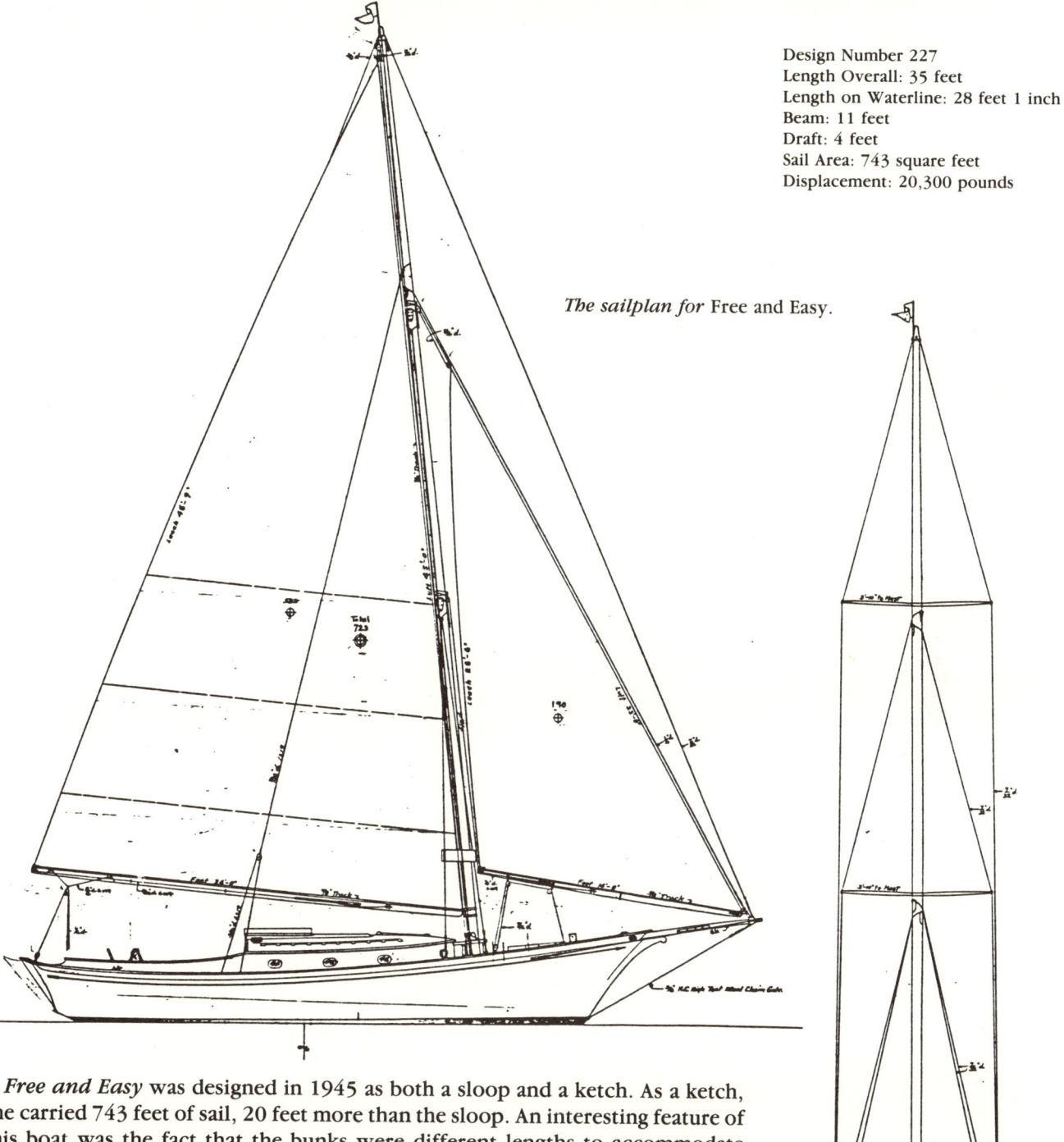

Design Number 227
Length Overall: 35 feet
Length on Waterline: 28 feet 1 inch
Beam: 11 feet
Draft: 4 feet
Sail Area: 743 square feet
Displacement: 20,300 pounds

The sailplan for Free and Easy.

Free and Easy was designed in 1945 as both a sloop and a ketch. As a ketch, she carried 743 feet of sail, 20 feet more than the sloop. An interesting feature of this boat was the fact that the bunks were different lengths to accommodate people of varying heights. Later on there was an 8,000-pound concrete keel drawn for her, increasing the draft to 4 feet 7 inches and eliminating the centerboard.

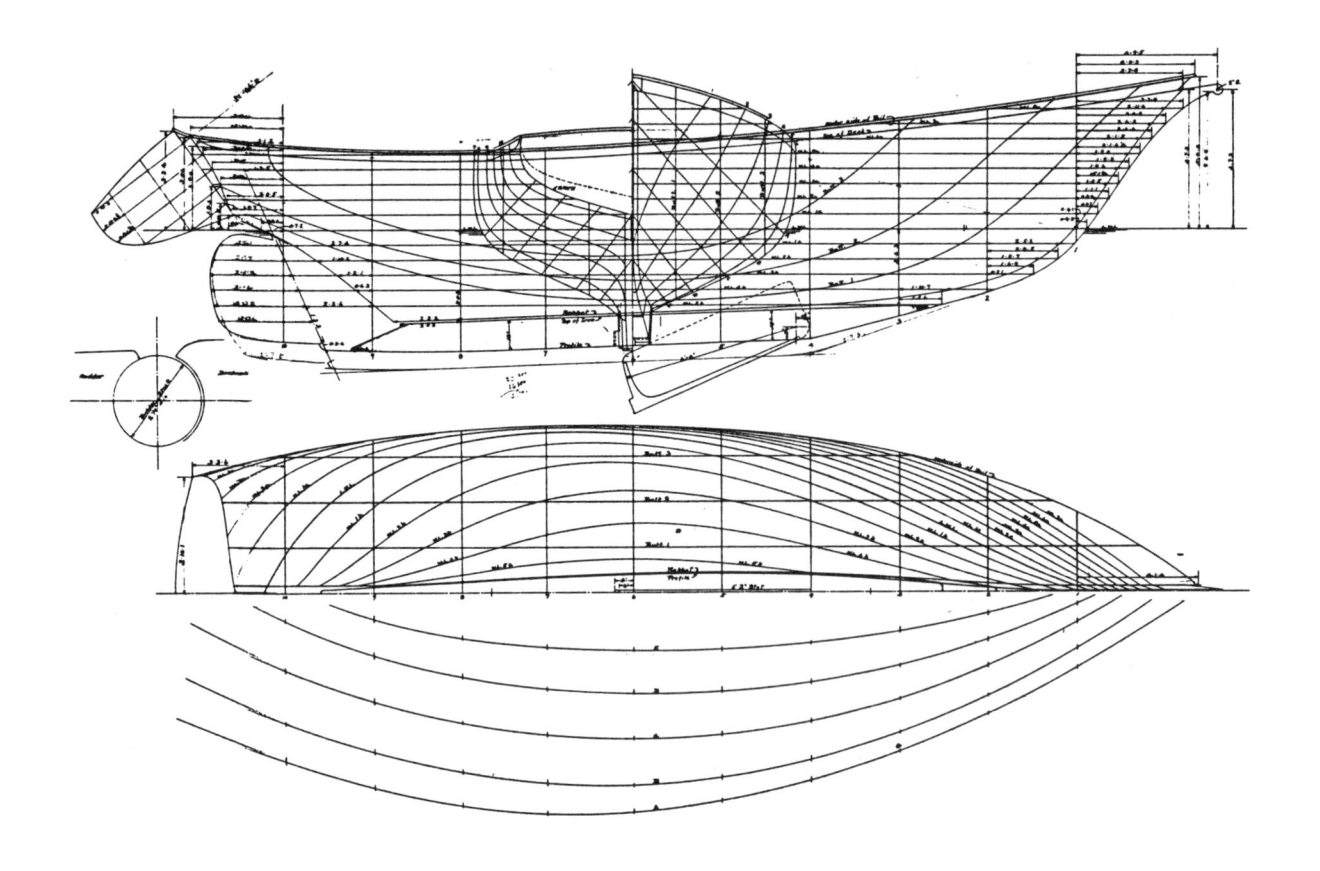

The lines and construction drawings for Free and Easy.

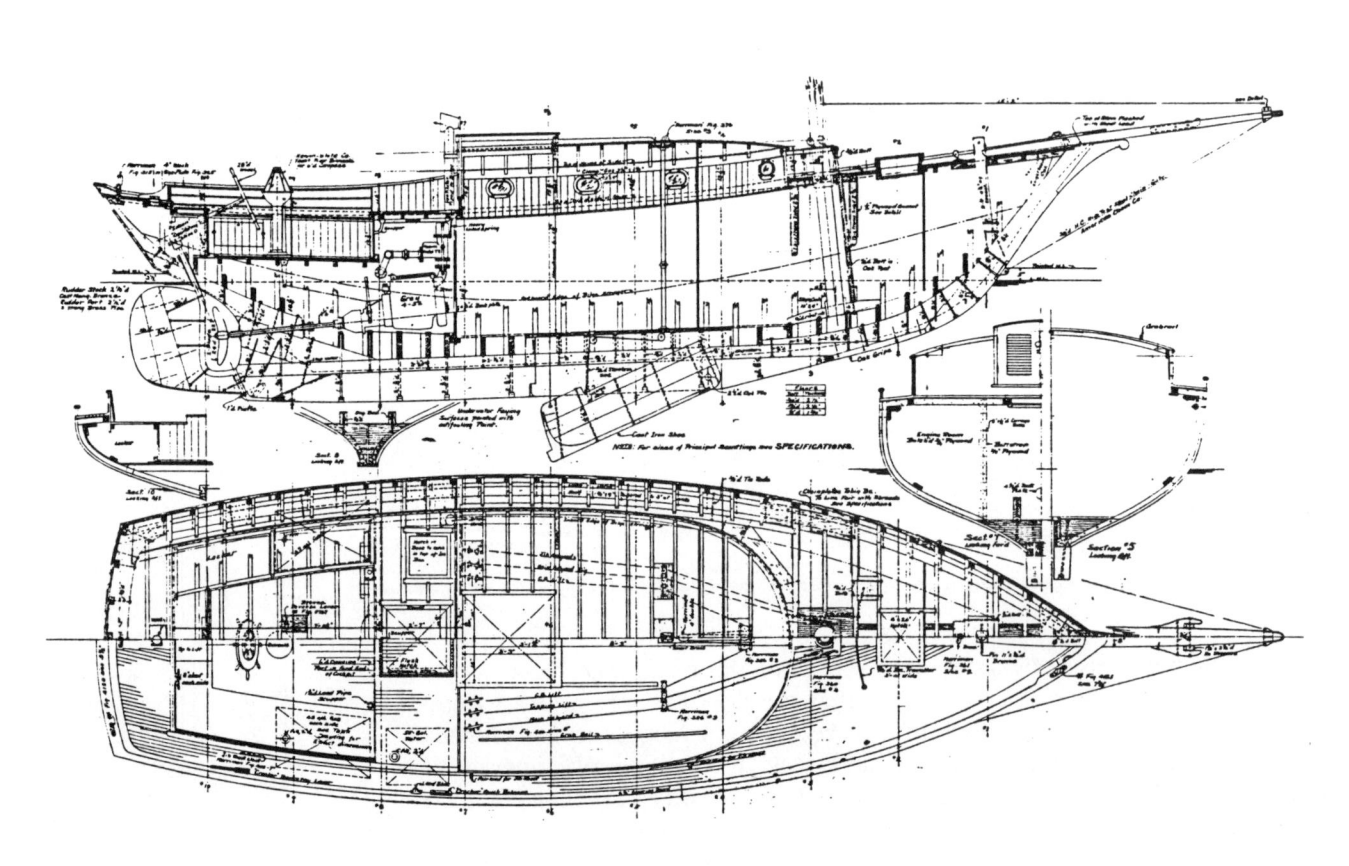

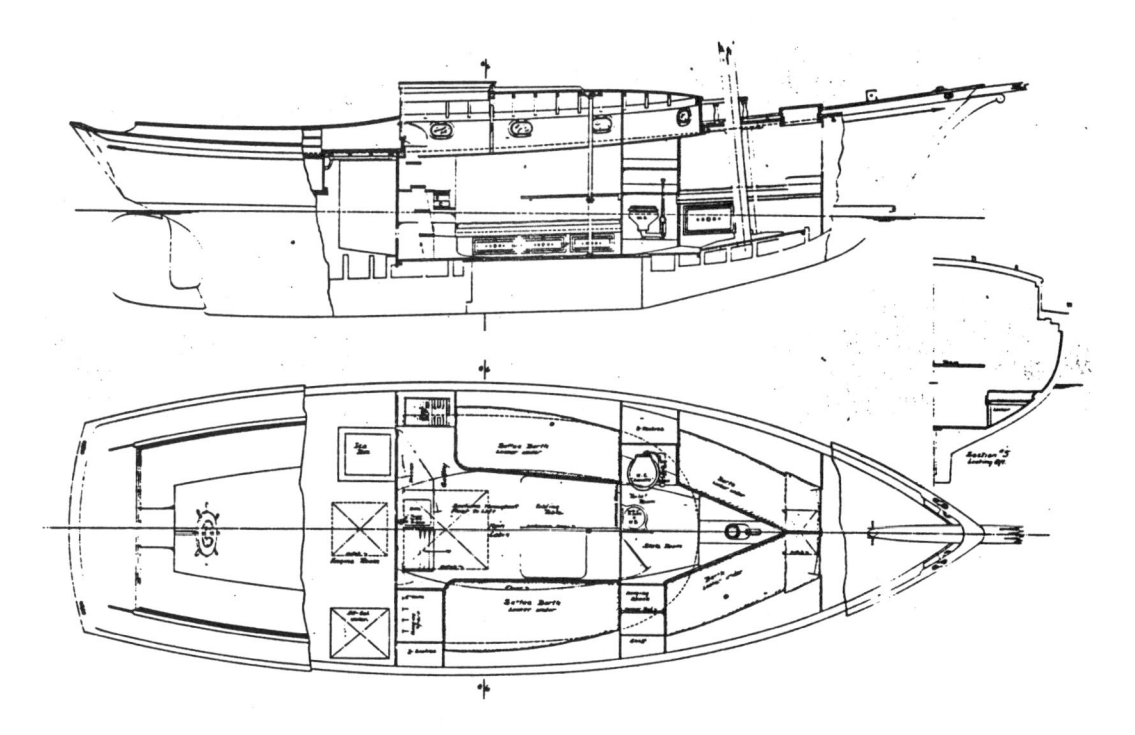

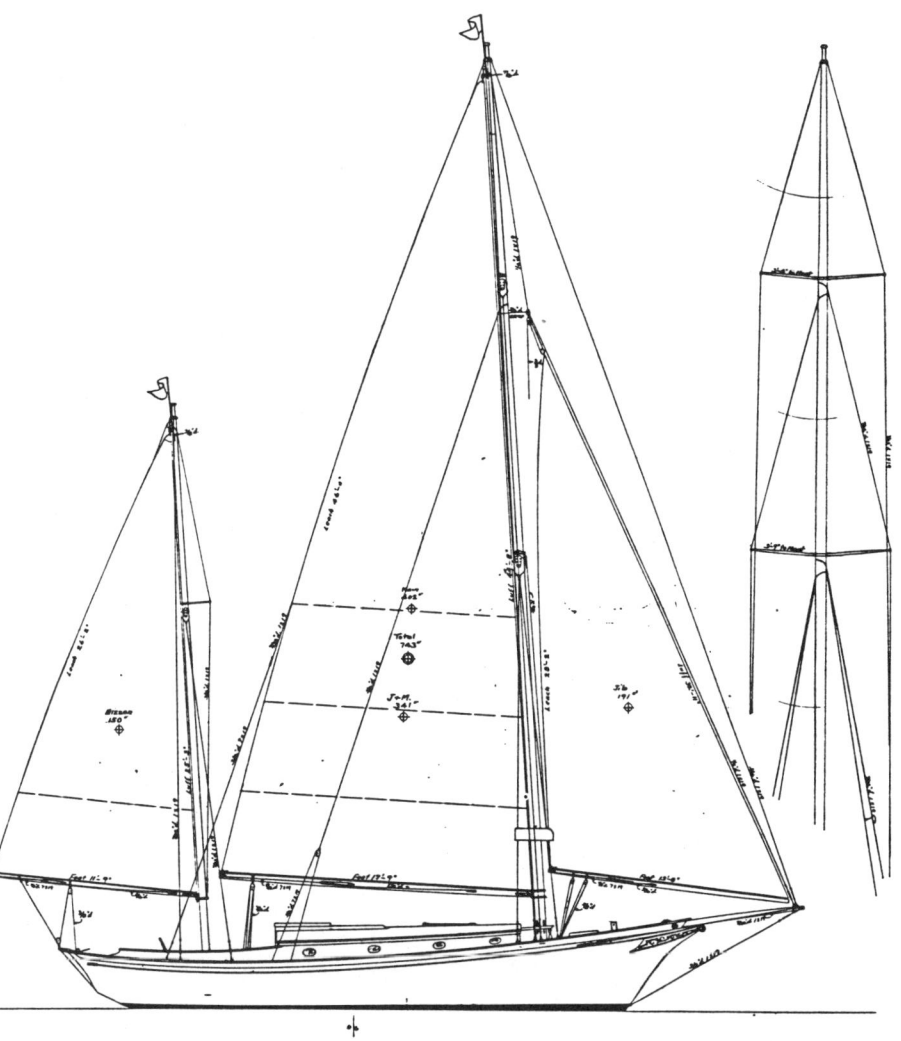

The accommodations for Free and Easy, *and her profile with a ketch rig.*

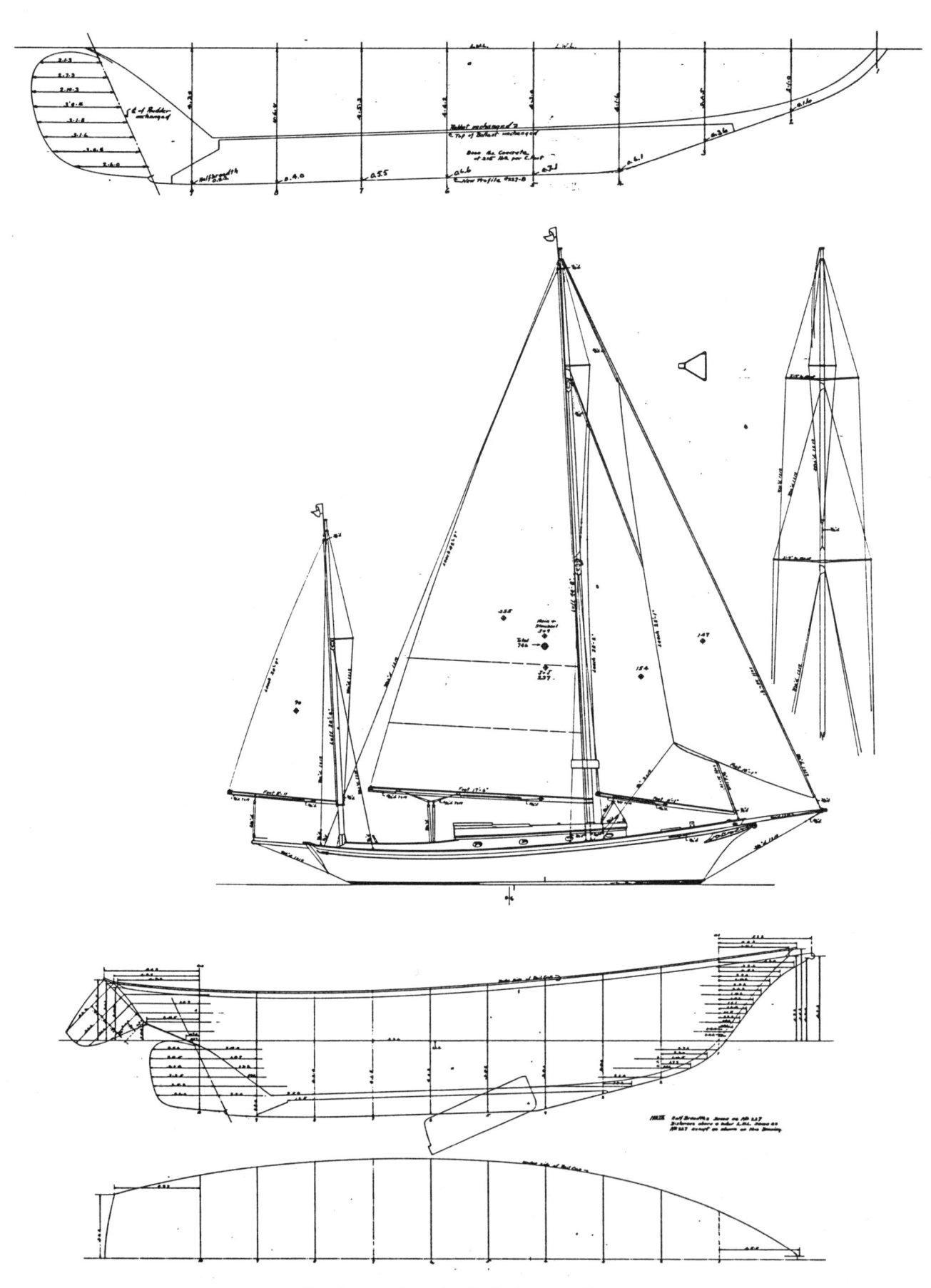

The lines and rig details for Free and Easy.

Free and Easy *with a yawl rig.*

EMILY MARSHALL 234

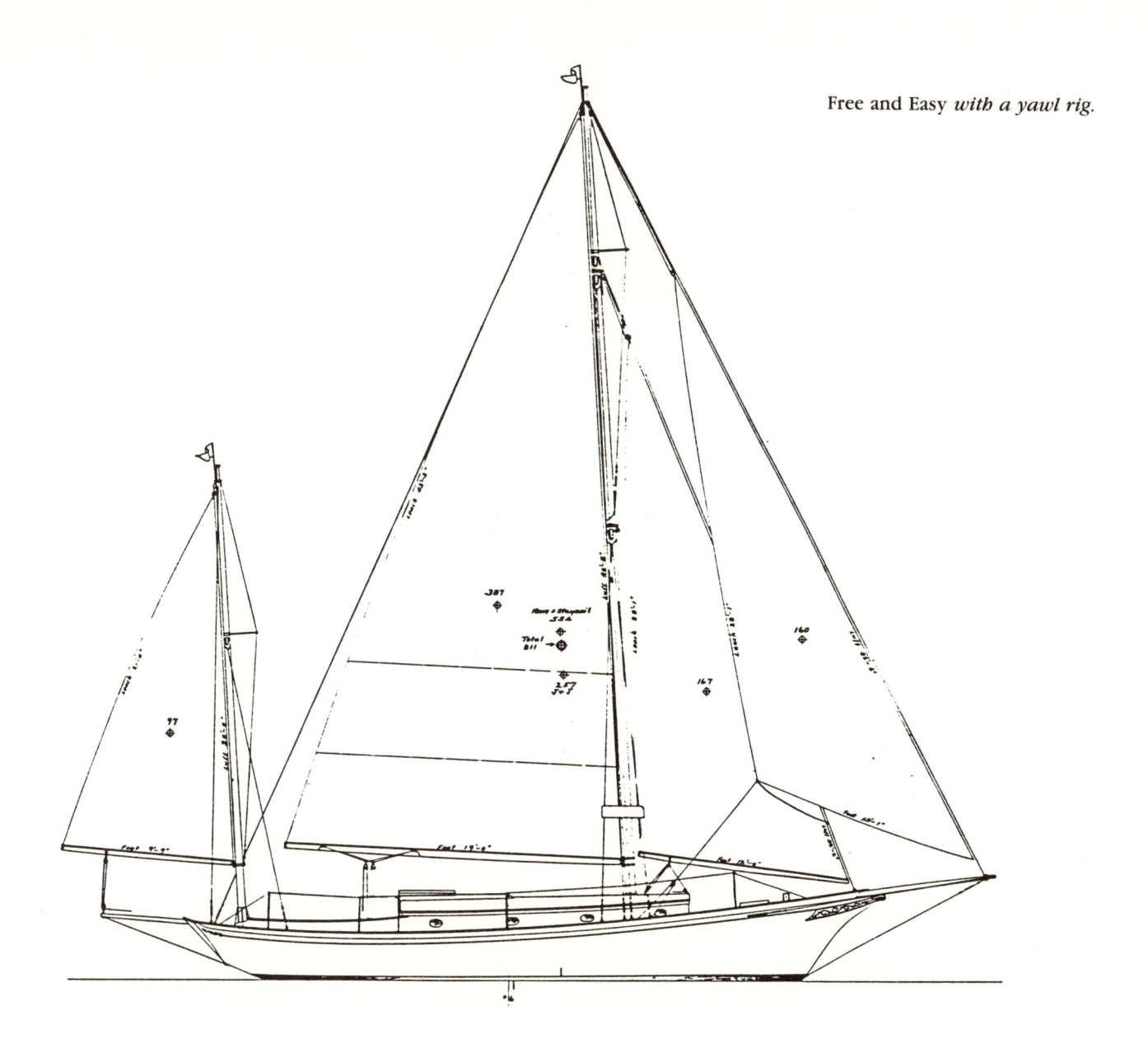

Emily Marshall was built at the George Gulliford yard in Saugus, Mass., in 1946 for then Commander, later Rear Adm. Samuel Eliot Morrison, the historian. She was built to replace a 30-footer, number 96, *Idler,* designed in 1927, which Morrison had owned. The two boats are similar in profile, but of course, *Emily* had a great deal more room below, with cruising accommodations for five. Auxiliary power was furnished by a two-cylinder, 27-horsepower Kermath diesel.

Design Number 234
Length Overall: 36 feet 6 inches
Length on Waterline: 28 feet
Beam: 10 feet 11 inches
Draft: 5 feet 6 inches
Sail Area: 763 square feet
Displacement: 18,900 pounds

203

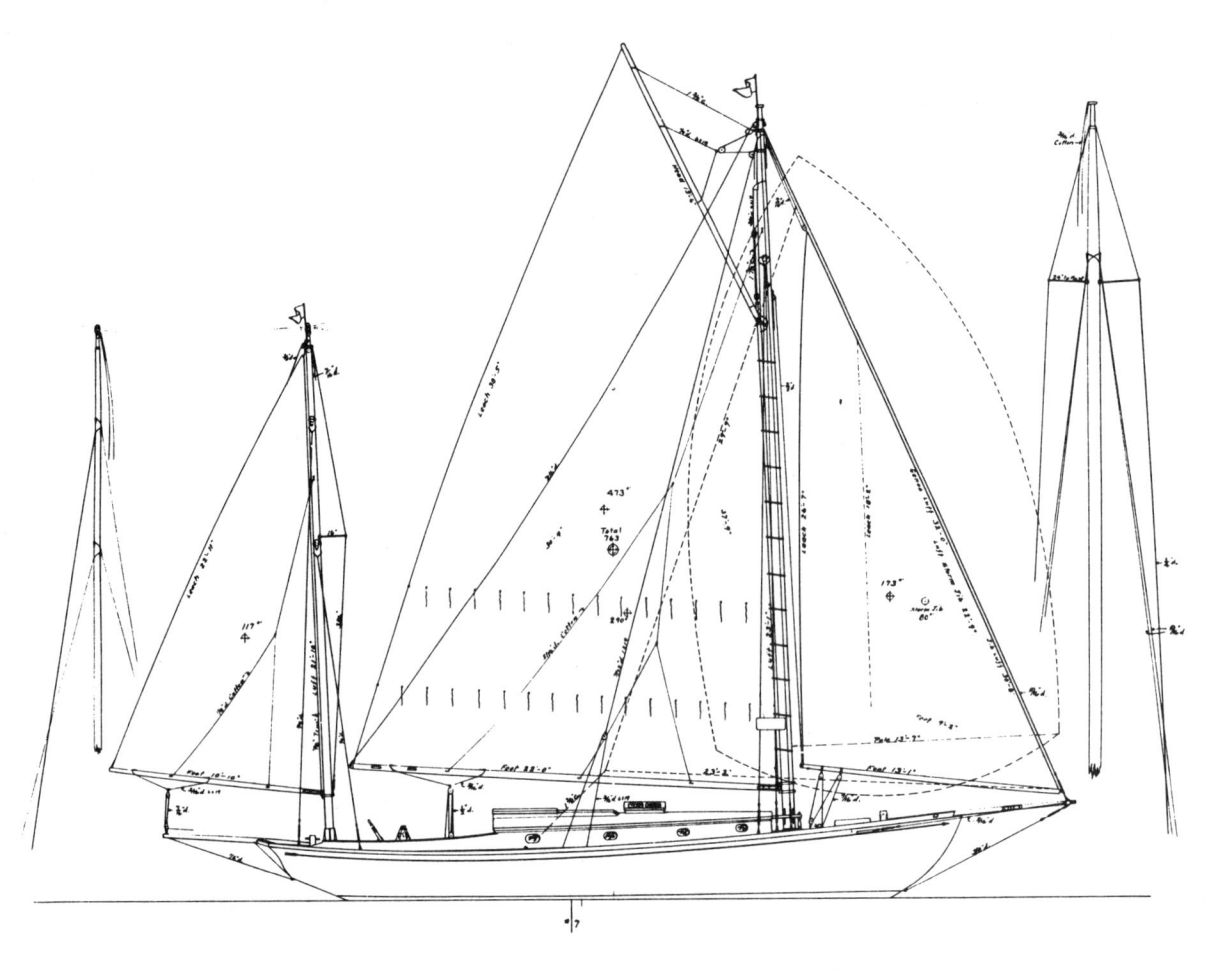

The sailplan and lines for Emily Marshall.

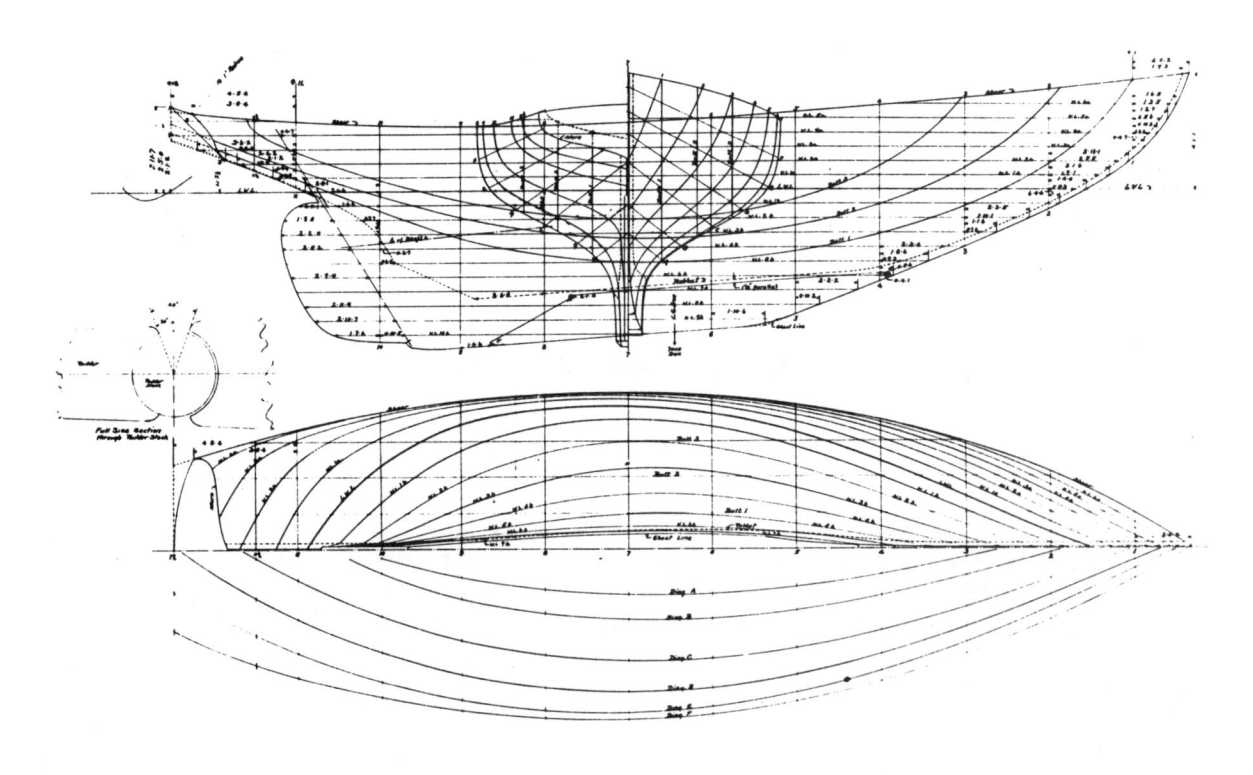

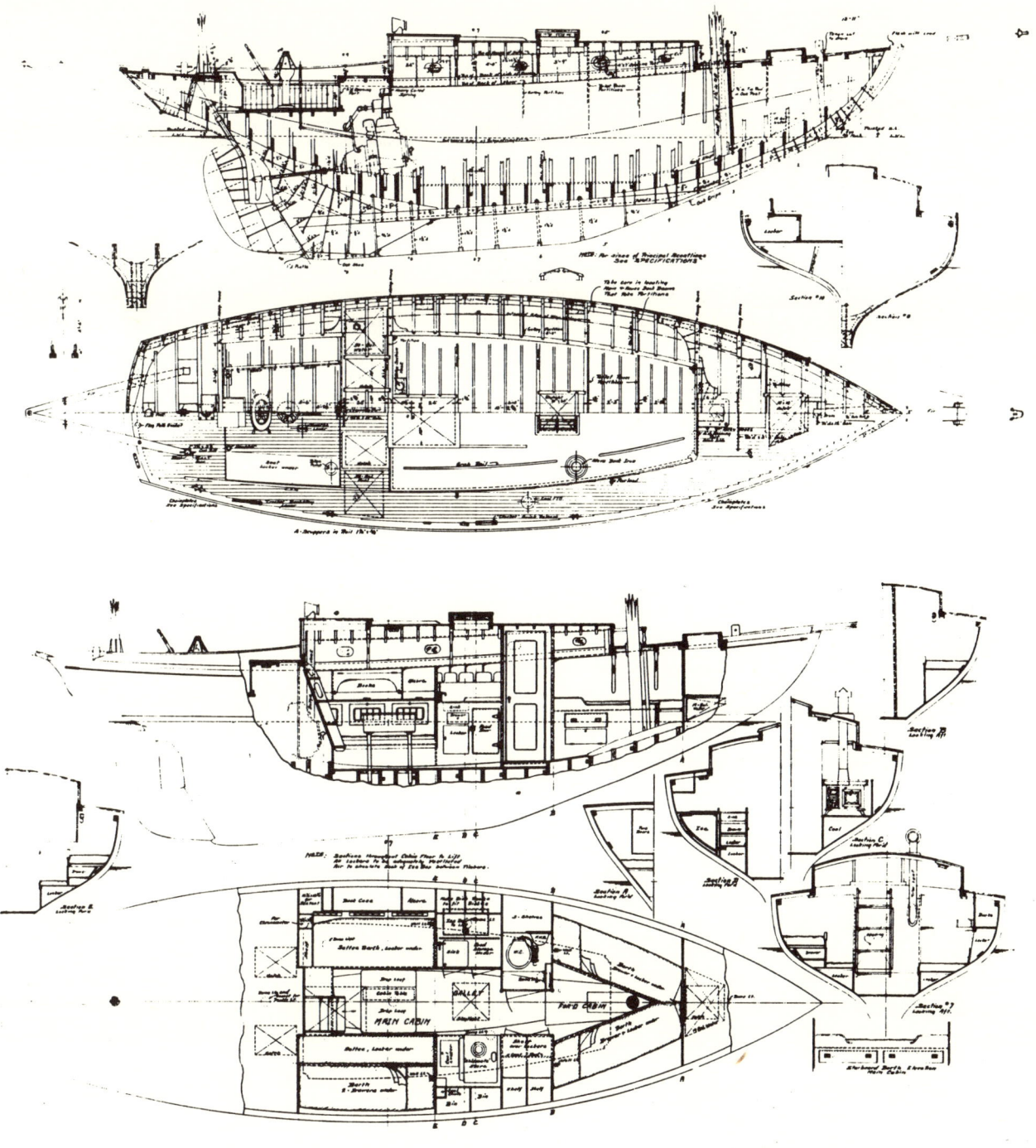

The construction and accommodations plans and Emily Marshall *under sail.*

236 DOG WATCH

Design Number 236
Length Overall: 16 feet
Length on Waterline: 15 feet 6 inches
Beam: 7 feet 6 inches
Draft: 1 foot 8 inches
Sail Area: 211 square feet

Dog Watch was started in 1945, right after World War II, by Calderwood Yacht Yard of Manchester. During construction, the yard changed hands, and I had bought the Charles While yard next door. I had done the work on *Dog Watch* up to this point, so the boat was moved to my yard for finishing. She was another boat for S.K. Dimock. As usual, when her plans came out in the magazines, inquiries came in from all over the world, and a lot of plans were sold. Auxiliary power was furnished by a single-cylinder U.S. of about six horsepower.

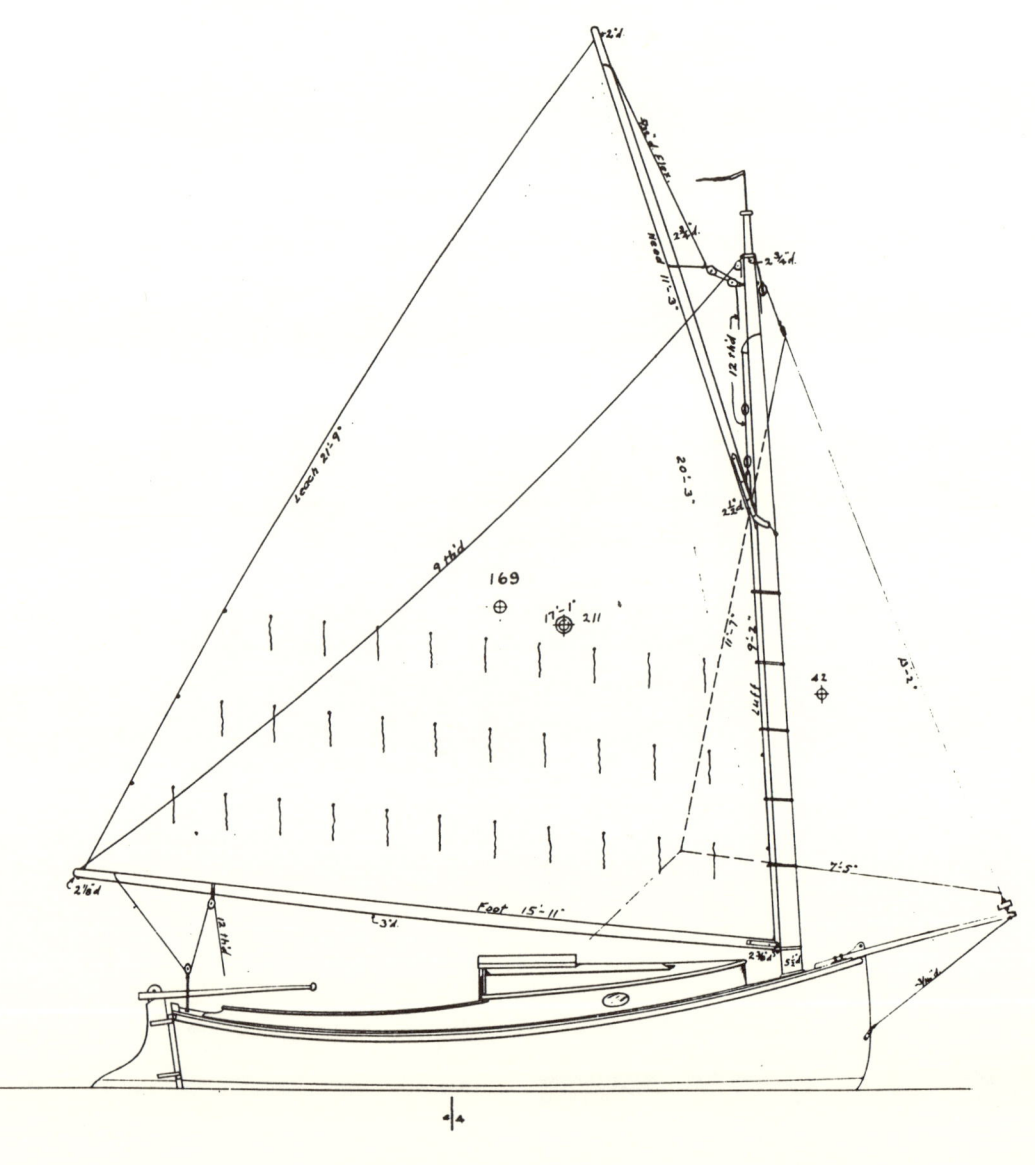

The sailplan for Dog Watch.

206

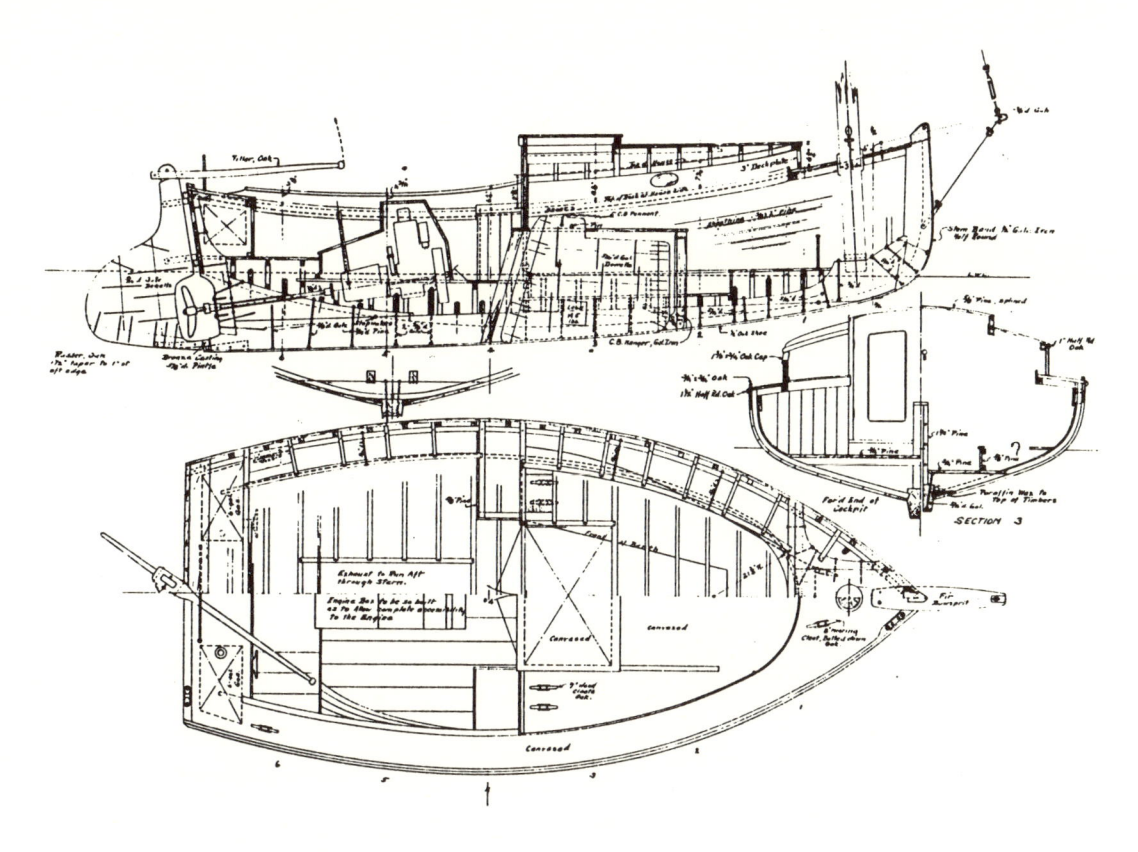

The construction plans and lines drawings for Dog Watch.

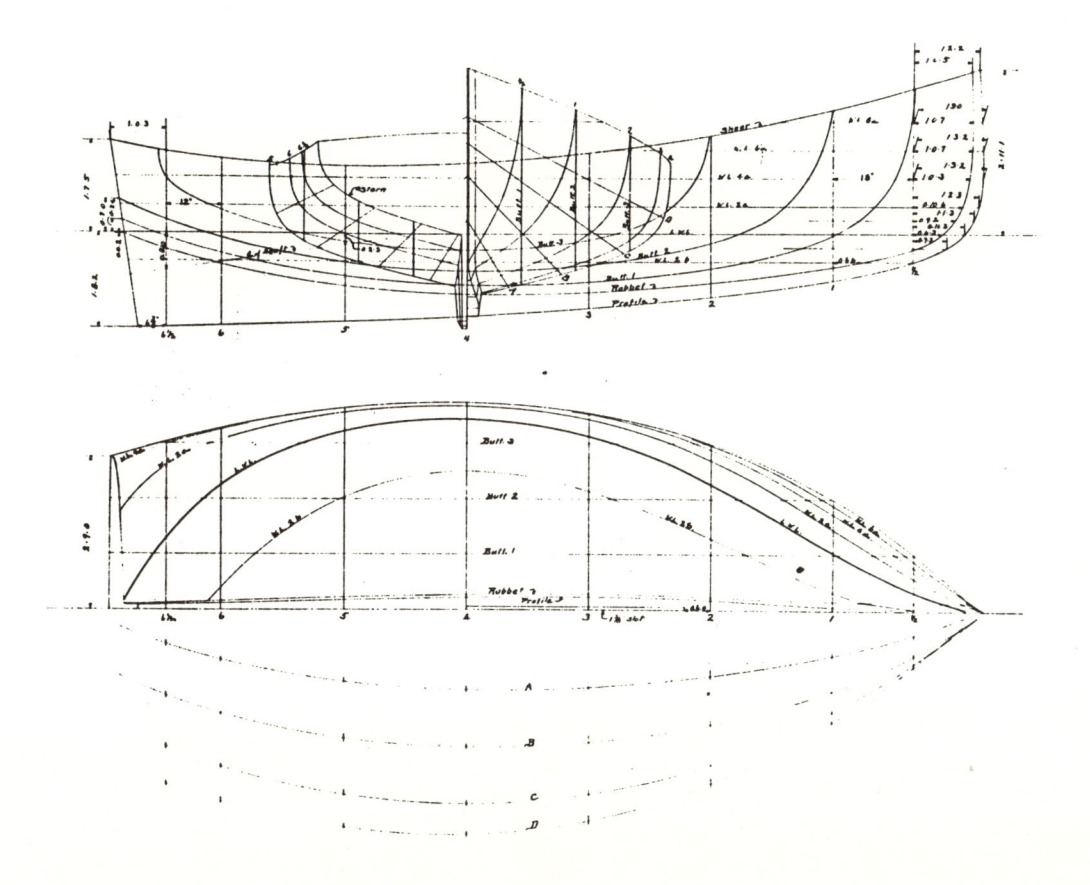

Dog Watch *under very pleasant conditions.*

238 DOLPHIN

Design Number 238
Length Overall: 52 feet
Length on Waterline: 49 feet
Beam: 14 feet
Draft: 5 feet 5 inches
Displacement: 51,800 pounds

Dolphin was built in 1947 by George Gulliford of Saugus, Mass., for three partners, Theodore D. Manning, Walter R. Kennedy, and Samuel F. Knowles. Crew's quarters were efficiently and compactly laid out forward, with the engine room just aft so there was a large working space for a boat of this size. She had the same 6-330 Gray with 3½-to-1 reduction gear as I have in *Akbar*. At 2,400 r.p.m. on the engine, she did 10 knots with a 30-inch-diameter and 25-inch-pitch wheel.

Of course, being a fisherman, *Dolphin* needed a derrick boom for lifting trawl

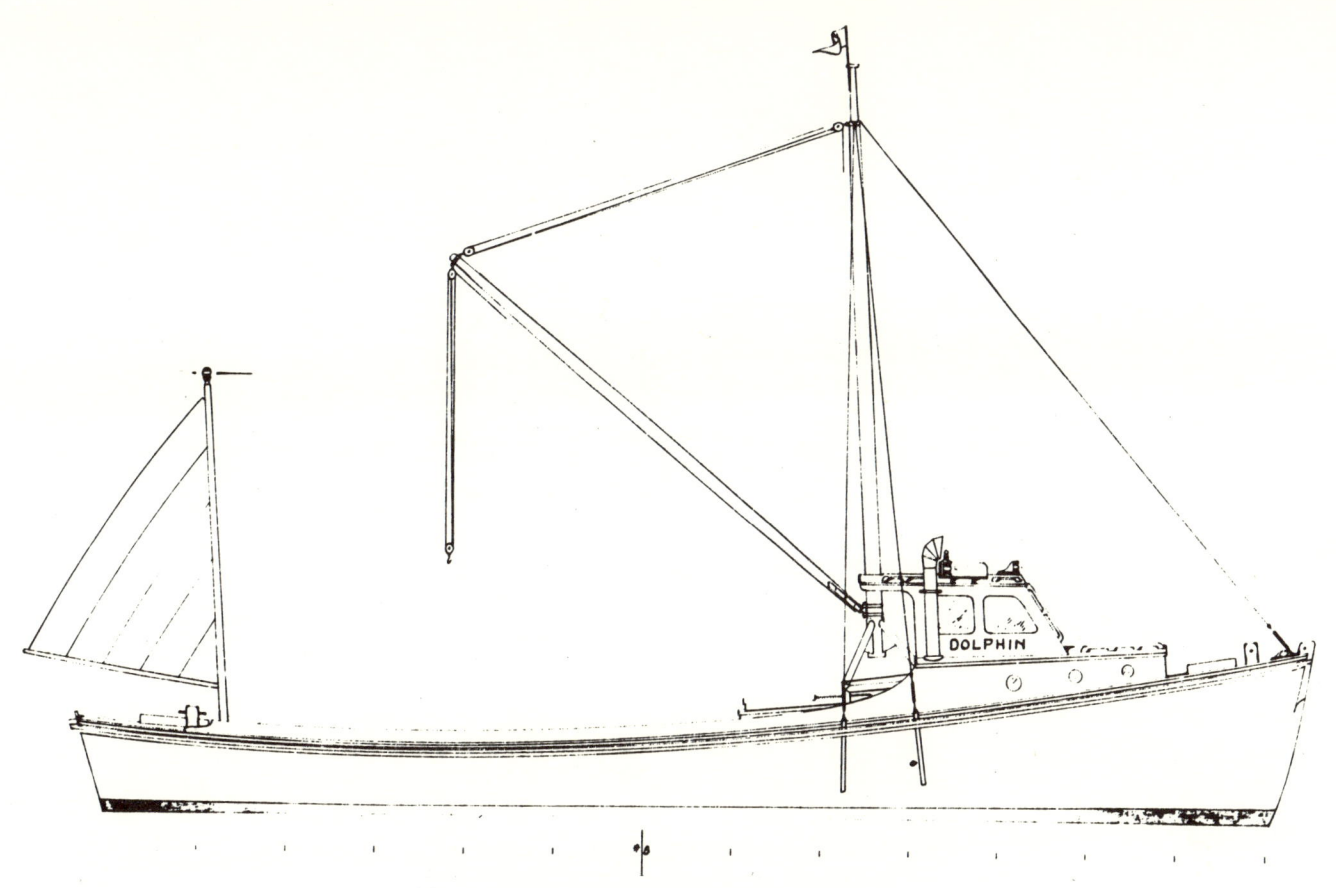

The profile for Dolphin, *and her lines drawings.*

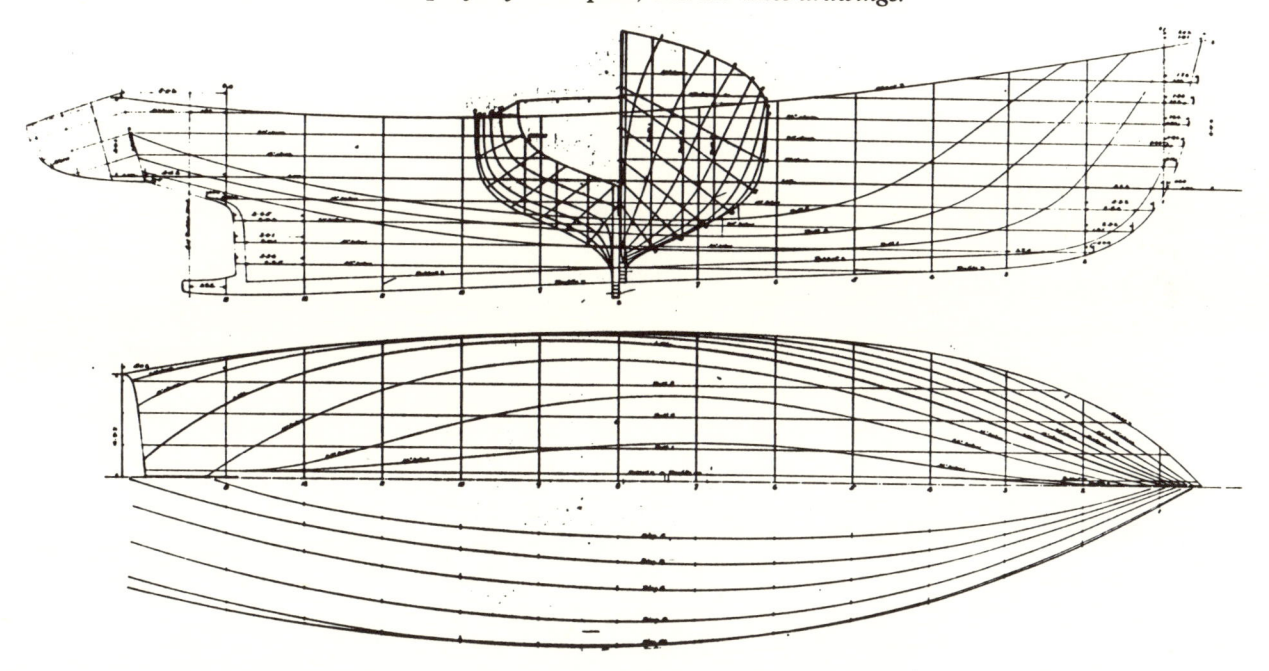

doors and nets aboard. In order not to detract from deck space, the mast was stepped over the engine house in a weldment made of 3-inch pipe. This had four stanchions to carry the end thrust down to the foundation. The whole rig was amply strong as is shown in the photo, in which she is leaving the yard with the 16-foot catboat *Dog Watch* as a deck cargo for delivery in Hartford, Conn. The *Dog Watch* has a displacement of 2,640 pounds and was lifted out of water and placed on deck with this rig.

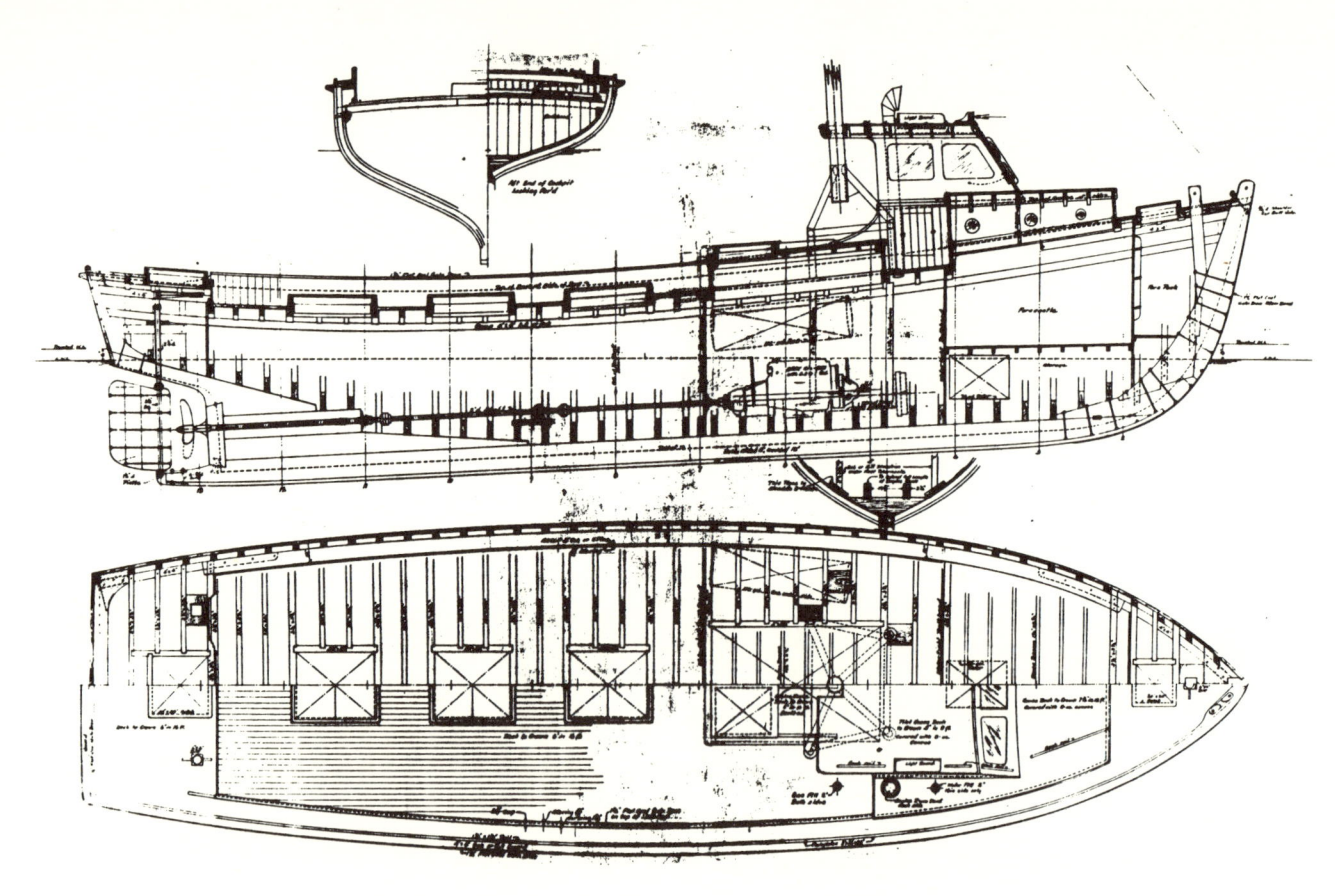

Dolphin's *construction details* and Dolphin *heading out to work*.

MASCONOMO 243

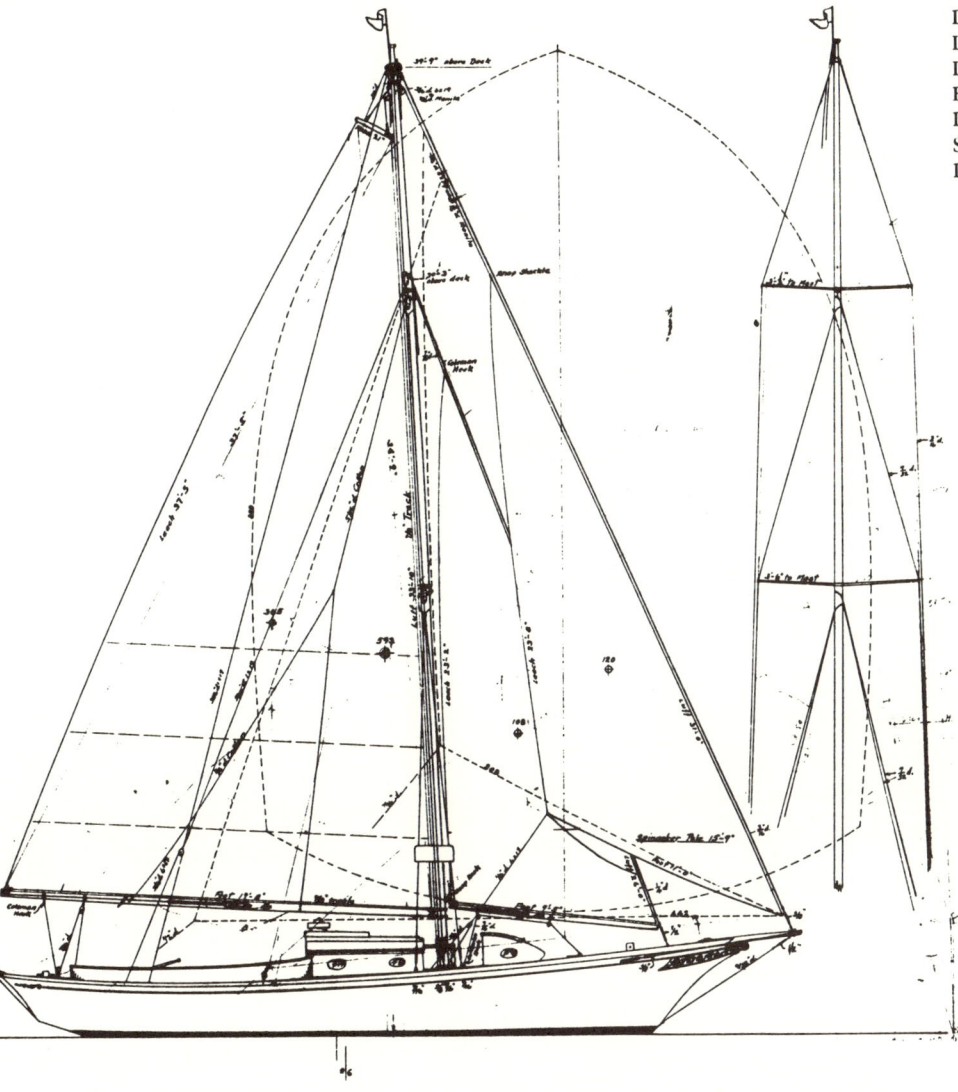

Design Number 243
Length Overall: 34 feet
Length on Waterline: 25 feet 9 inches
Beam: 9 feet 4 inches
Draft: 5 feet
Sail Area: 593 square feet
Displacement: 13,500 pounds

The sailplan for number 243.

Masconomo was Dad's own boat. I built her in 1950. She was probably not a design to satisfy most people, with so much space taken up with the cockpit, but she certainly filled the bill for us. We used her mostly for afternoon sailing and fishing, but Dad did take her on some short cruises, mostly to his home town of Barnstable on the Cape.

When we decided to build the boat, the first thing we did was mill out the native white pine decking and put it in storage to get it as dry as possible. This was 1 1/16-inch by-1 1/4-inch strips, and when it was needed it was face-nailed as well as edge nailed. It has never leaked. The deck on the cabin was glued up, and that is tight too. She has always been in the water, summer and winter, and being cedar planked, she is very smooth. The zincs on her keel have preserved her iron fastenings, but every spring it takes a coat of Rustoleum to hide the rust streaks.

The sailplan with a backstay added, and her lines drawings.

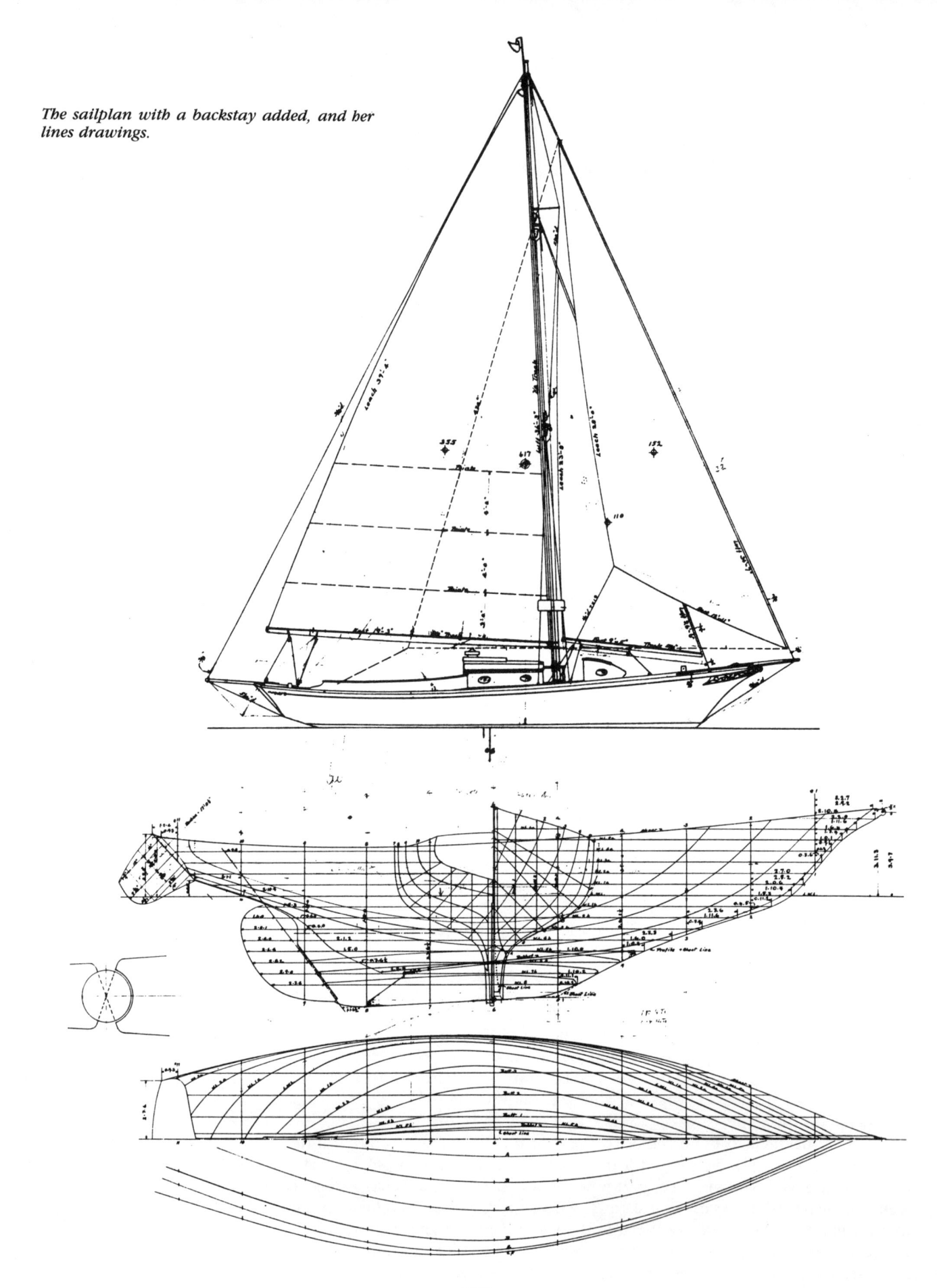

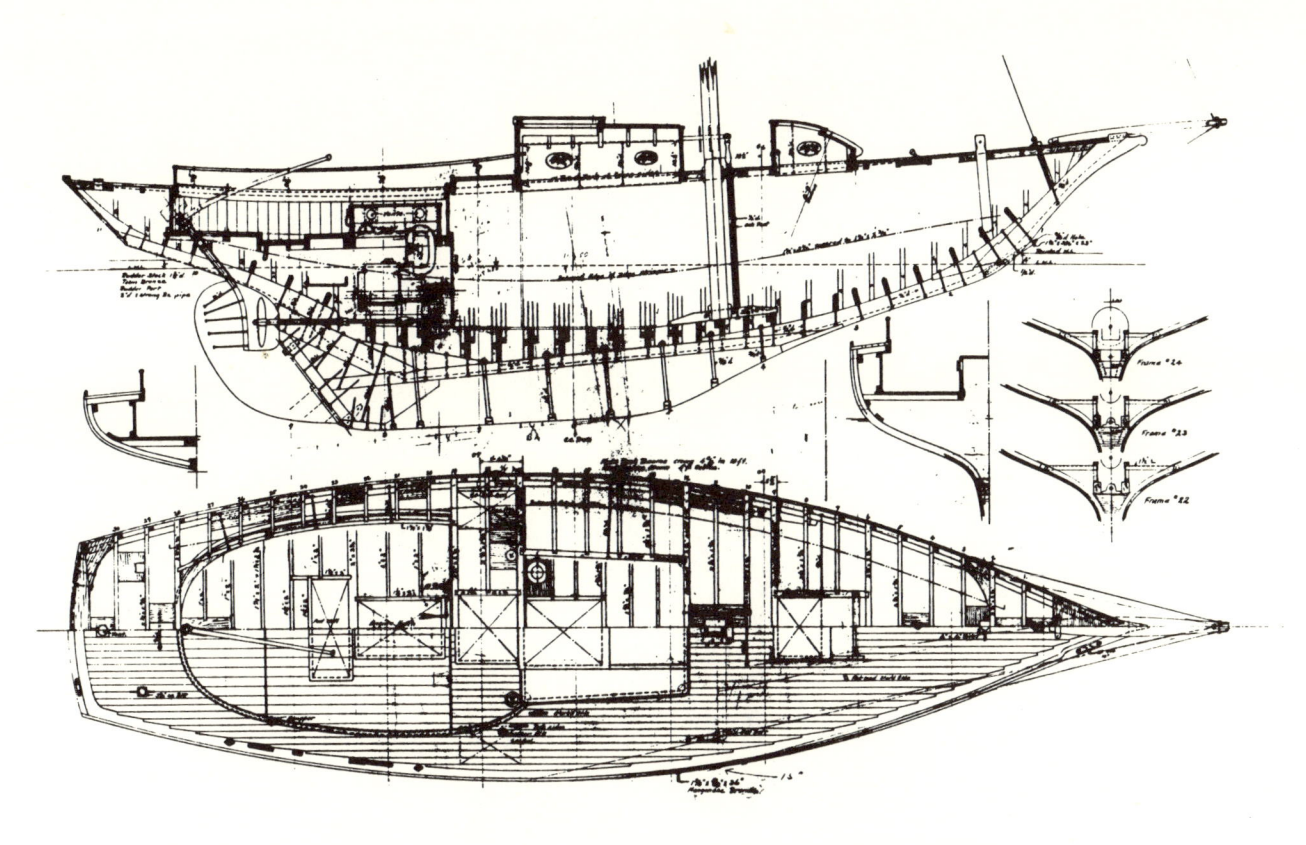

The construction plans and interior accommodations plans.

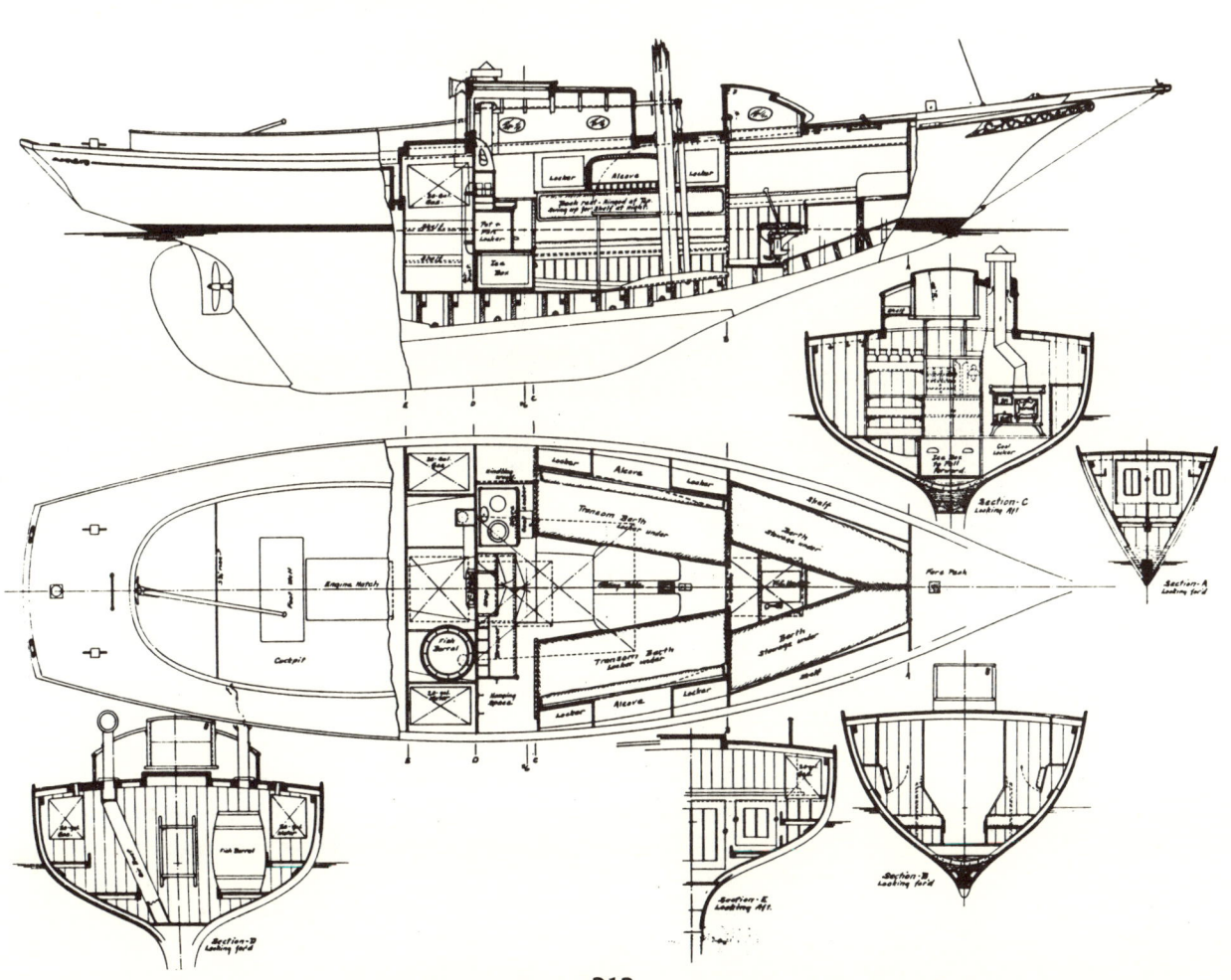

Masconomo *under sail. Photograph courtesy of Tom Sterns.*

    Originally, there was a short gaff on the main. This was an attempt to control tension on the leech, and it worked well. The four-cylinder Red Wing motor was installed backwards over the propeller shaft, and power was transmitted through V belts, thereby getting a little less than 2½-to-1 reduction.

    She was named for the Indian chief of this area when the original settlers came here and carries an Indian figurehead with headdress and feathers running back on the trailboards.

    Sold in 1966 to Tom Stearns of Amherst, N.H., she sailed and raced extensively and has taken much silverware here and in Marblehead. She was sold again in late 1984 and is now sailing Long Island Sound.

LIMULUS 245

Limulus was built in Manchester for Marine Biological Lab, Woods Hole, in 1948. She was built for taking students around Buzzards Bay and was equipped with hauling gear for dragging up ocean-floor samples for study. I found some long-length fir and was able to plank her practically without butt blocks. A Gray 6-427 gas engine with two-to-one reduction gear gave her a speed of 18½ m.p.h.

Design Number 245
Length Overall: 33 feet
Length on Waterline: 30 feet 10 inches
Beam: 10 feet
Draft: 3 feet 3 inches
Displacement: 9,500 pounds

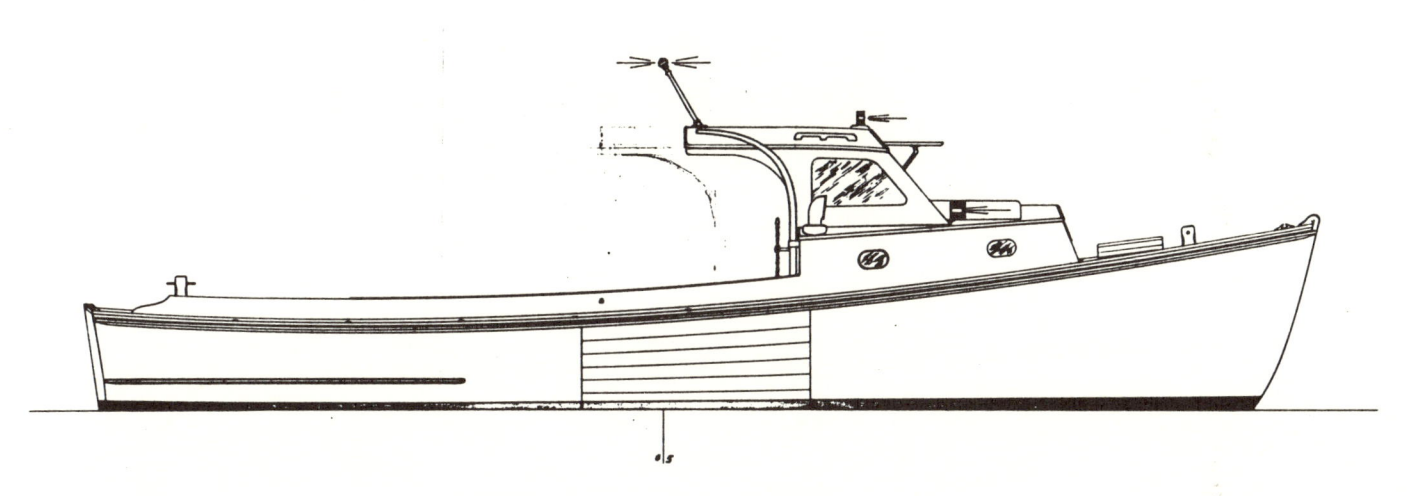

The profile for Limulus, *and her lines drawings.*

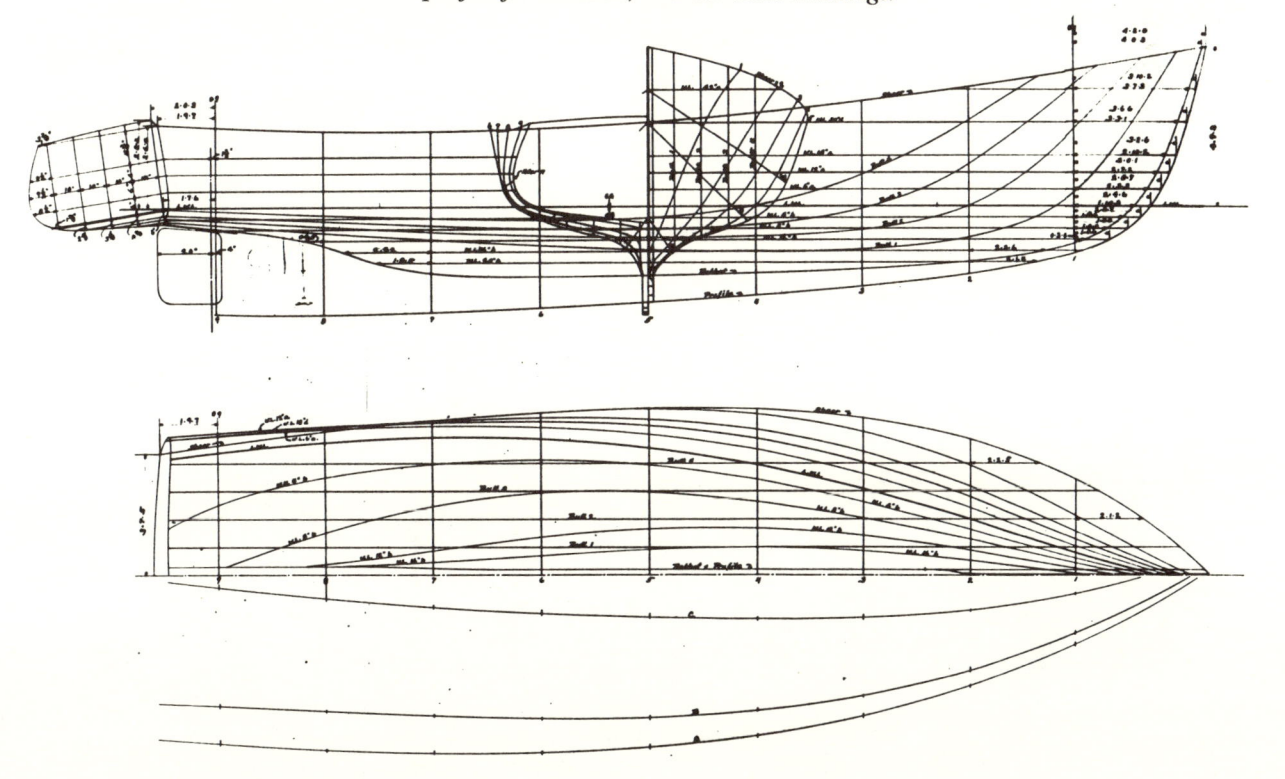

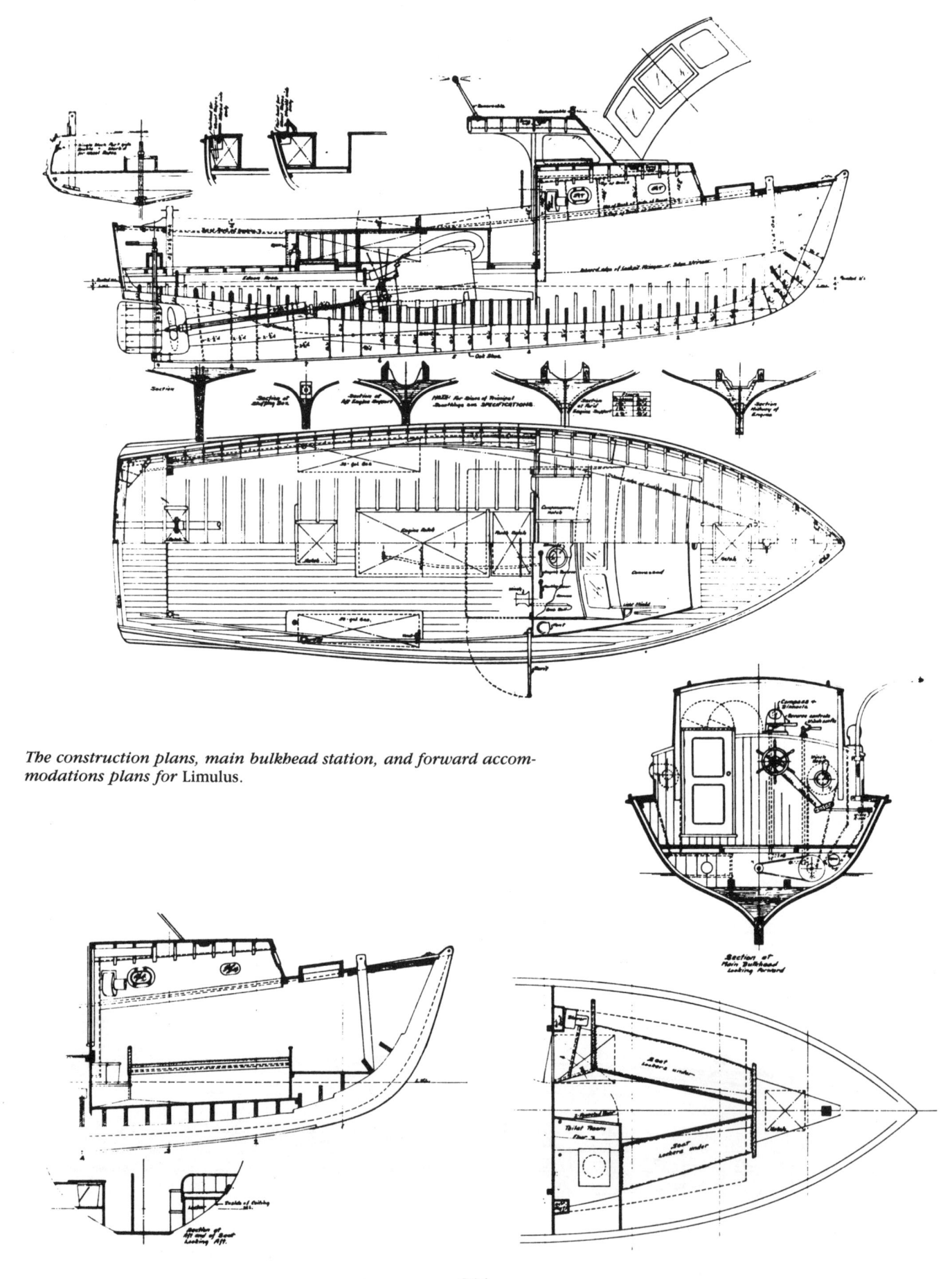

The construction plans, main bulkhead station, and forward accommodations plans for Limulus.

MARION 26 248

Design Number 248
Length Overall: 26 feet
Length on Waterline: 20 feet
Beam: 9 feet
Draft: 3 feet
Sail Area: 314 square feet
Displacement: 6,000 pounds

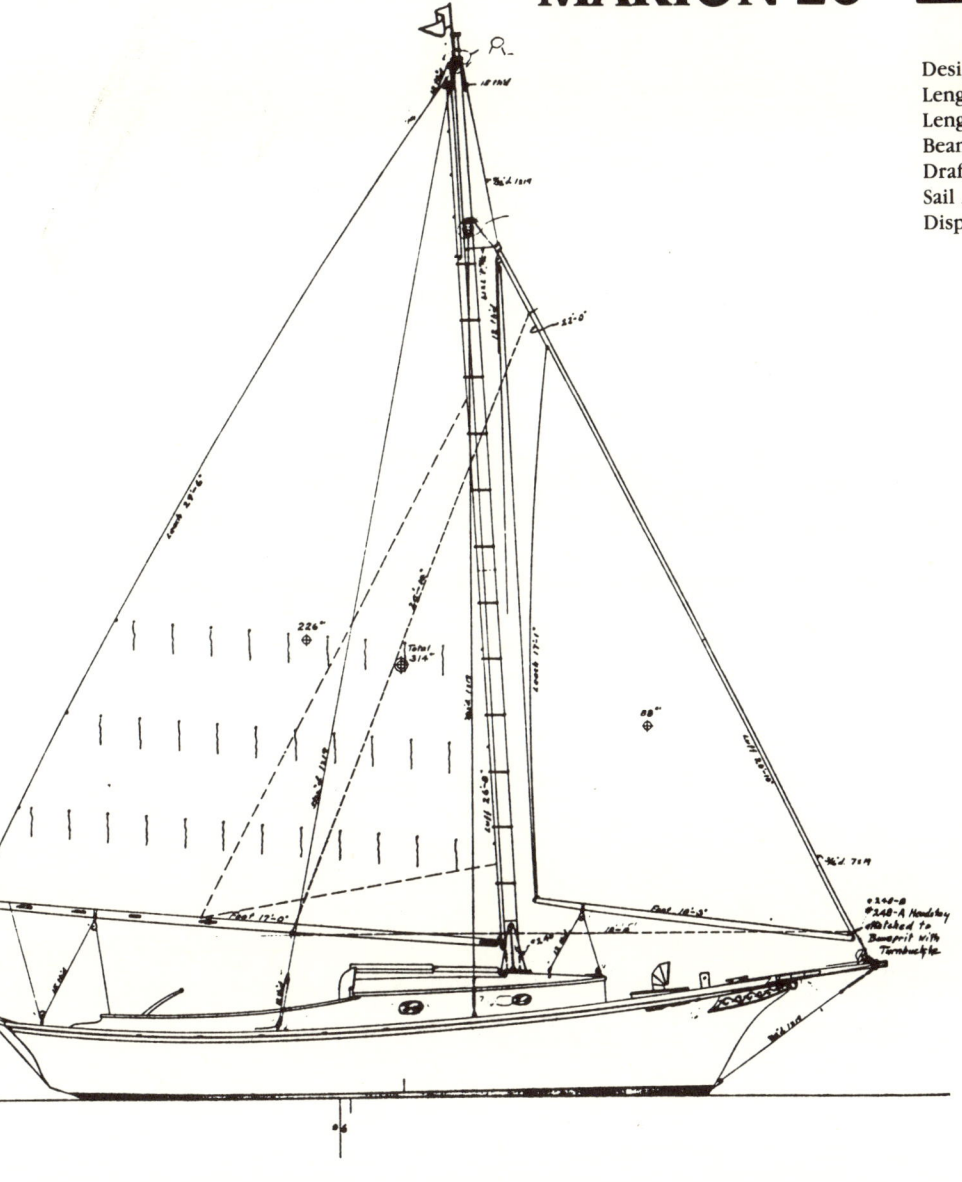

The Marion 26 came right between number 241, *Aunt Teed,* and number 252, *The Trade Winds,* which was designed for *Rudder* magazine's "How-To-Build" series. She was built in our yard in 1949 for William G. Thayer, Jr., of New York from number 241's lines. She had 800 pounds outside in a keel and deadwood, with a sliding doghouse main hatch and a little more sail in a sloop rig. Also, her mast was stepped in a tabernacle on deck so that it could be lowered for passages under nonopening bridges. Number 248A, *Wendy,* for Paul Thibodeau of Boston, had a little more sail area and 6 inches more draft. Also, her mast was stepped on the foundation. *The Trade Winds* was the same as *Wendy* with a little different arrangement below.

The sailplan for the Marion 26.

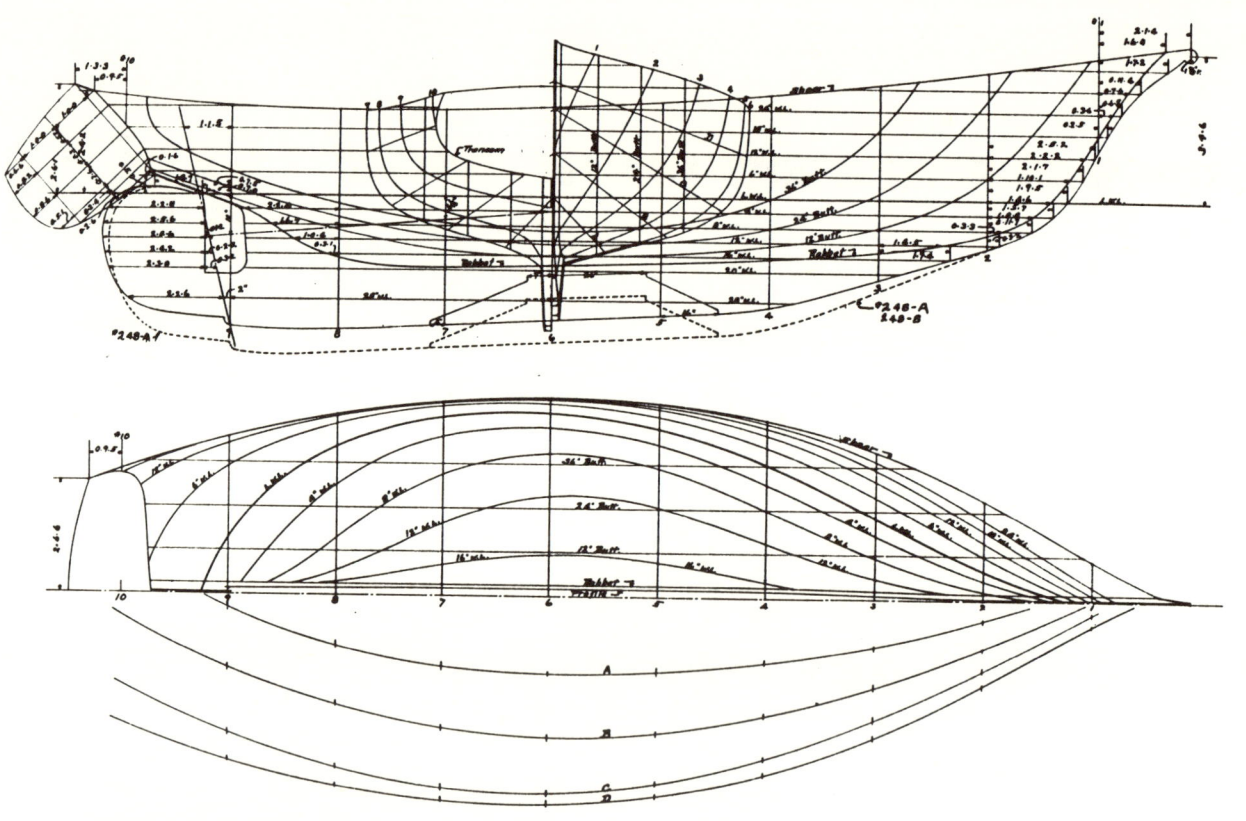

The lines and construction plan for numbers 248 and 248A. Note the added draft for 248A as indicated by the dotted line.

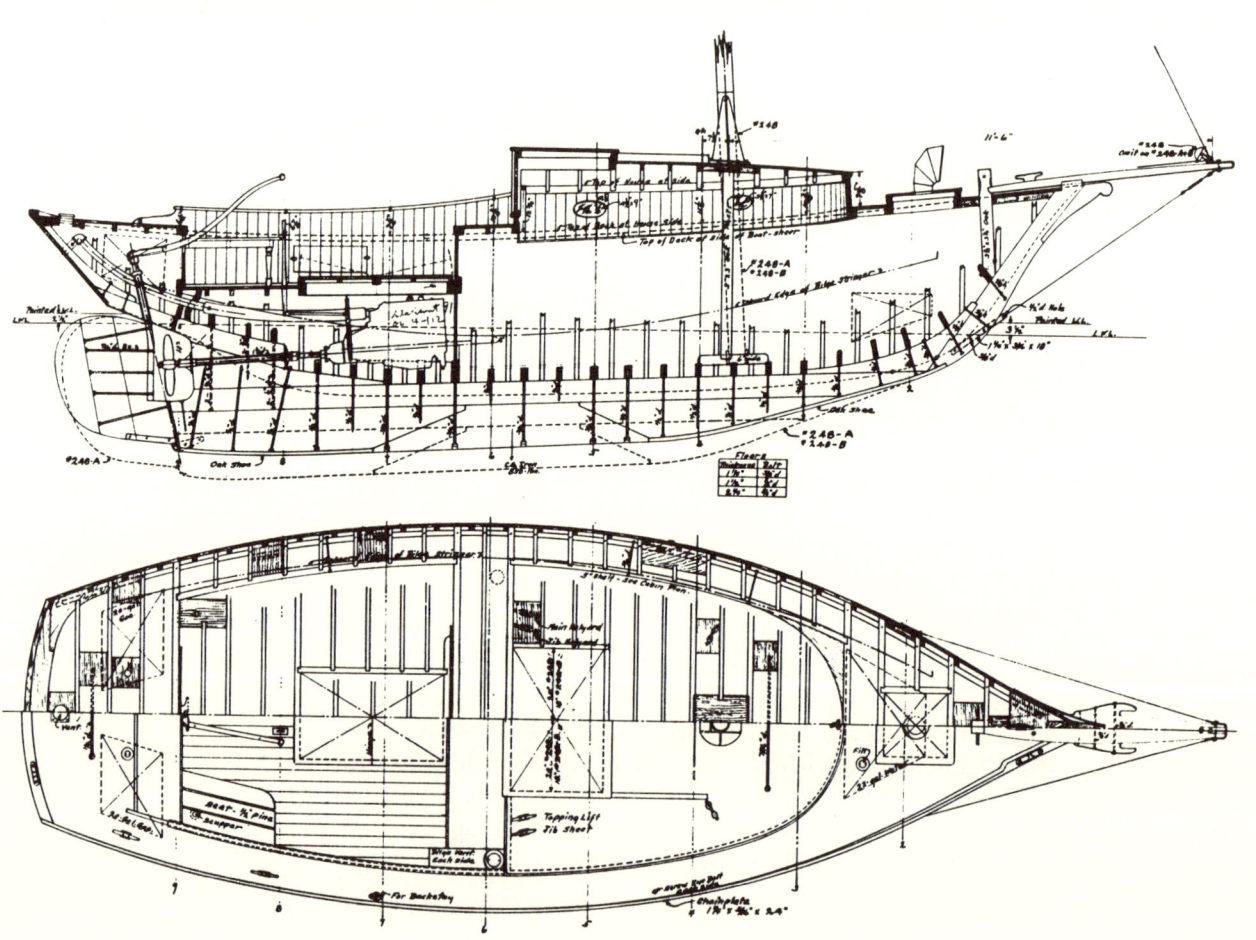

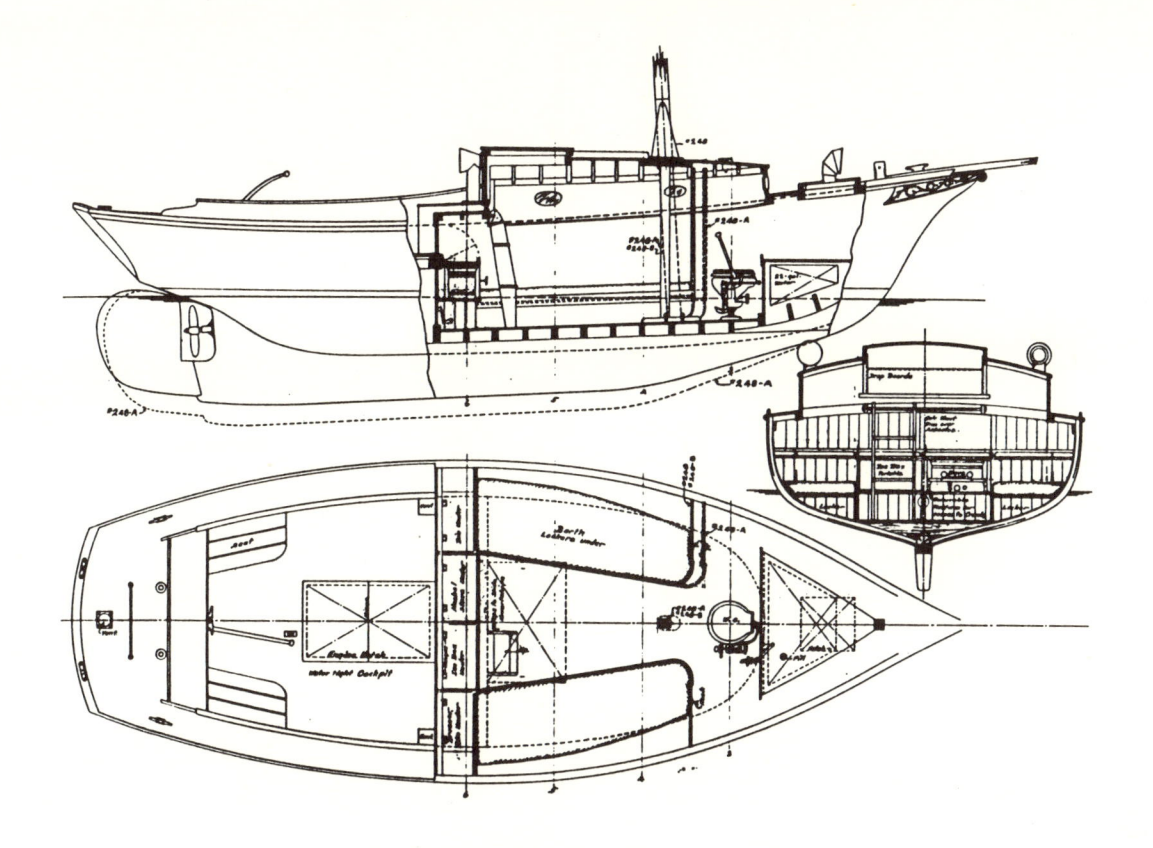

The accommodations for the Marion 26.

SPARHAWK 253

Sparhawk was built in 1940 for Talcott M. Banks, Jr., of Cambridge, Mass. This was the first of several boats that I built from these lines. I can remember my father saying that when the design was published it generated more interest than any he had published before. Coming after World War II, and with the jump over prewar prices, everything was done to keep prices down. Raised-deck construction did a lot in this direction, as well as giving a lot of room below and a nice deck to work on. Banks cruised and raced *Sparhawk* extensively and owned her for the rest of his life.

Number 256, *Old Butch,* for Francis C. Welch of Manchester, followed *Sparhawk.* She was the same boat except the raised deck was carried a little farther aft, and she had a wheel instead of a tiller. Mr. Welch took great pleasure in watching her being built and in being able to position backboards for bunks, various seacocks for easy accessibility, engine controls, etc.

Number 259, *Wendy Ann,* another boat built from these lines in 1951 for J. Stanley Churchill of Boston, was ketch rigged.

Still another was number 267, *Seafire,* built for John Lindsay of Manchester, Mass. She was planked up to the lower sheer and decked over with no cabin

Design Number 253
Length Overall: 30 feet 6 inches
Length on Waterline: 26 feet 8 inches
Beam: 9 feet 7 inches
Draft: 4 feet 10 inches
Sail Area: 595 square feet
Displacement: 12,900 pounds

Sparhawk's *sailplan and her lines drawings.*

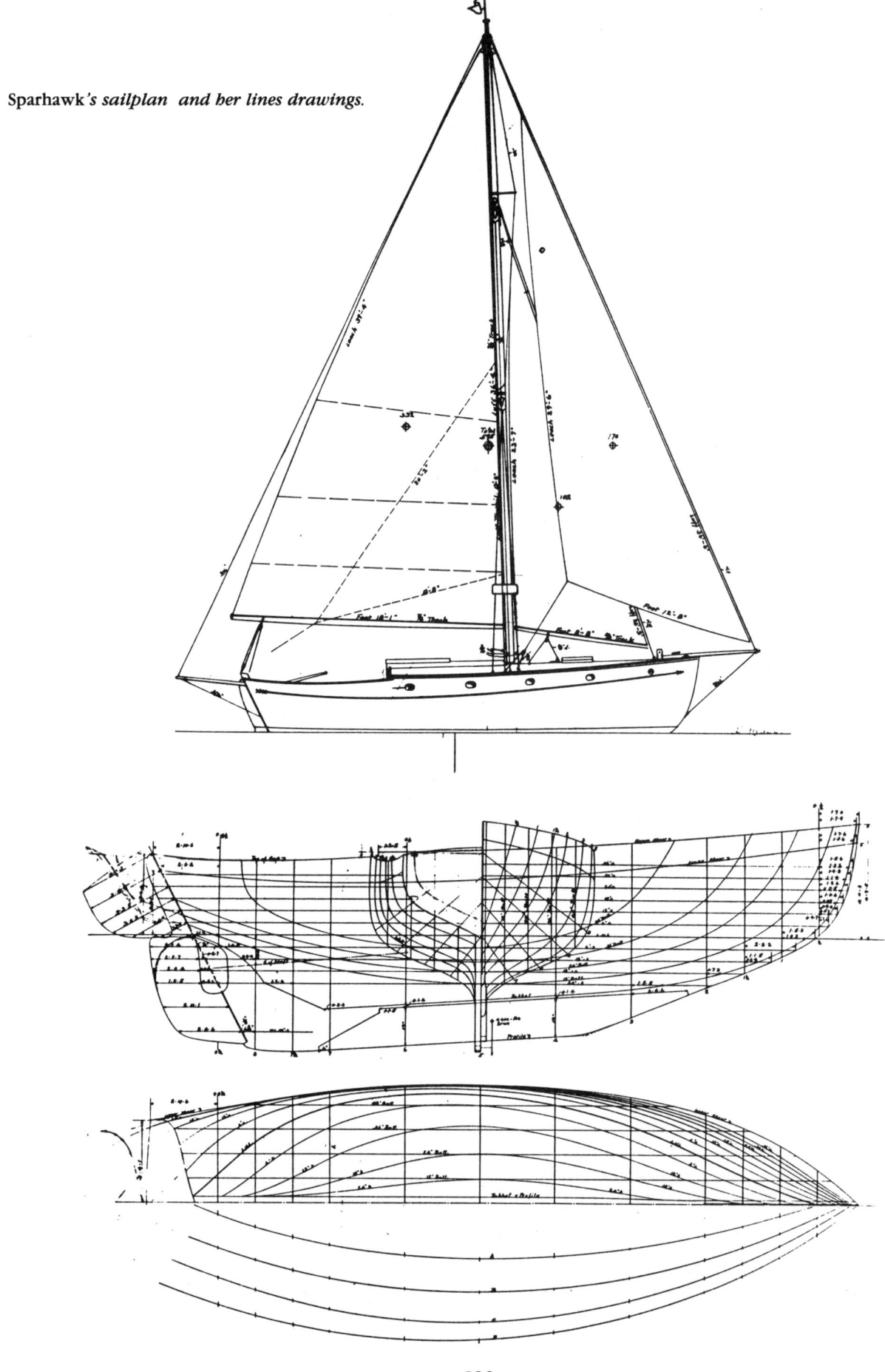

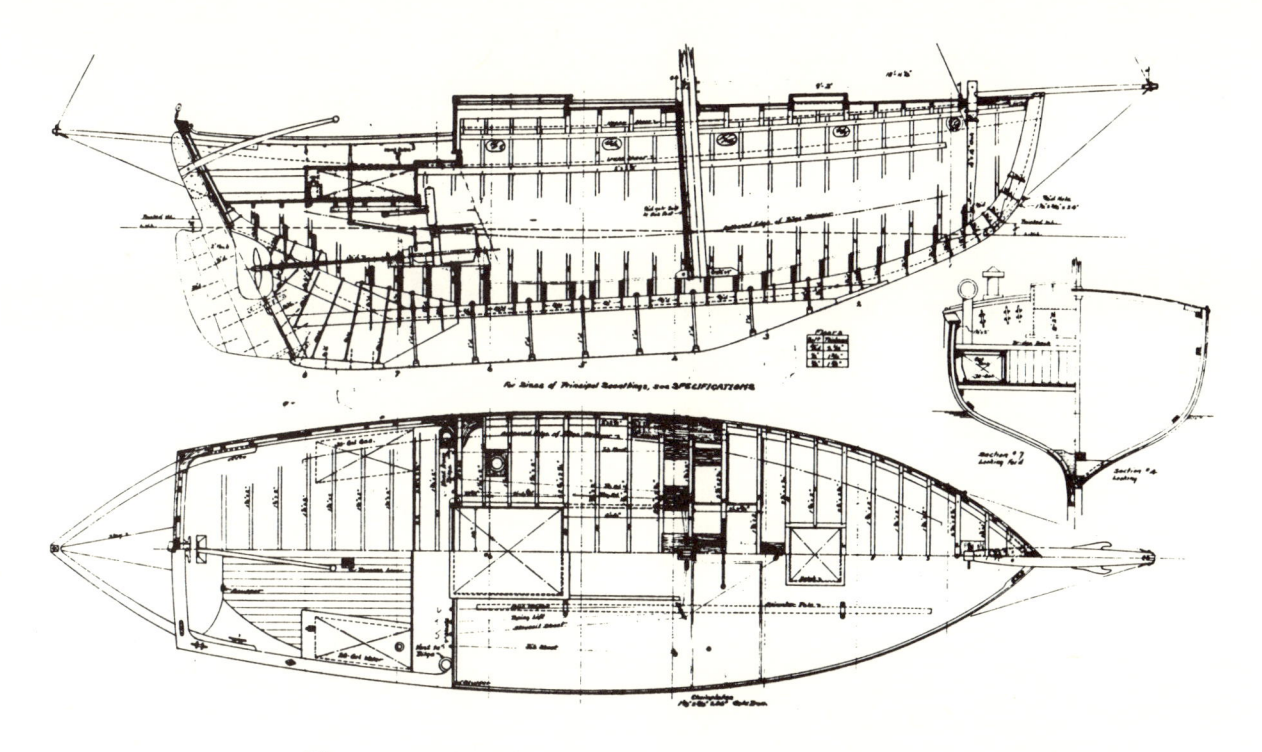

The construction plans and accommodations drawings for number 253.

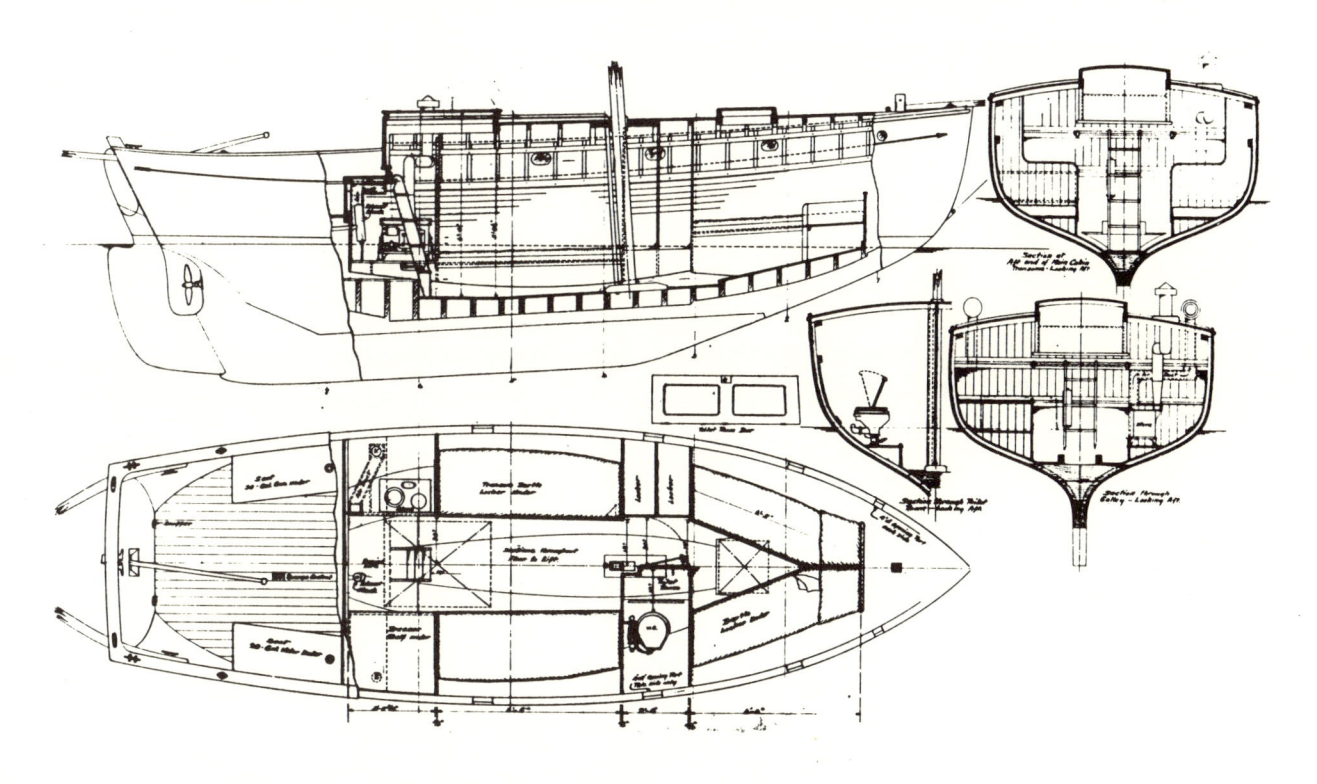

trunk. John put in his own interior. Later I put on a cabin trunk for Louis Raneri, who bought her from John. I started another of these boats but sold the foundation and other parts to Don Bugden of Beverly, Mass., who did a nice job building *Jarges Pride,* now owned by Neil MacKenna of Beverly. She had an overhanging stern, inboard rudder, and trunk cabin.

Sparhawk *under sail*.

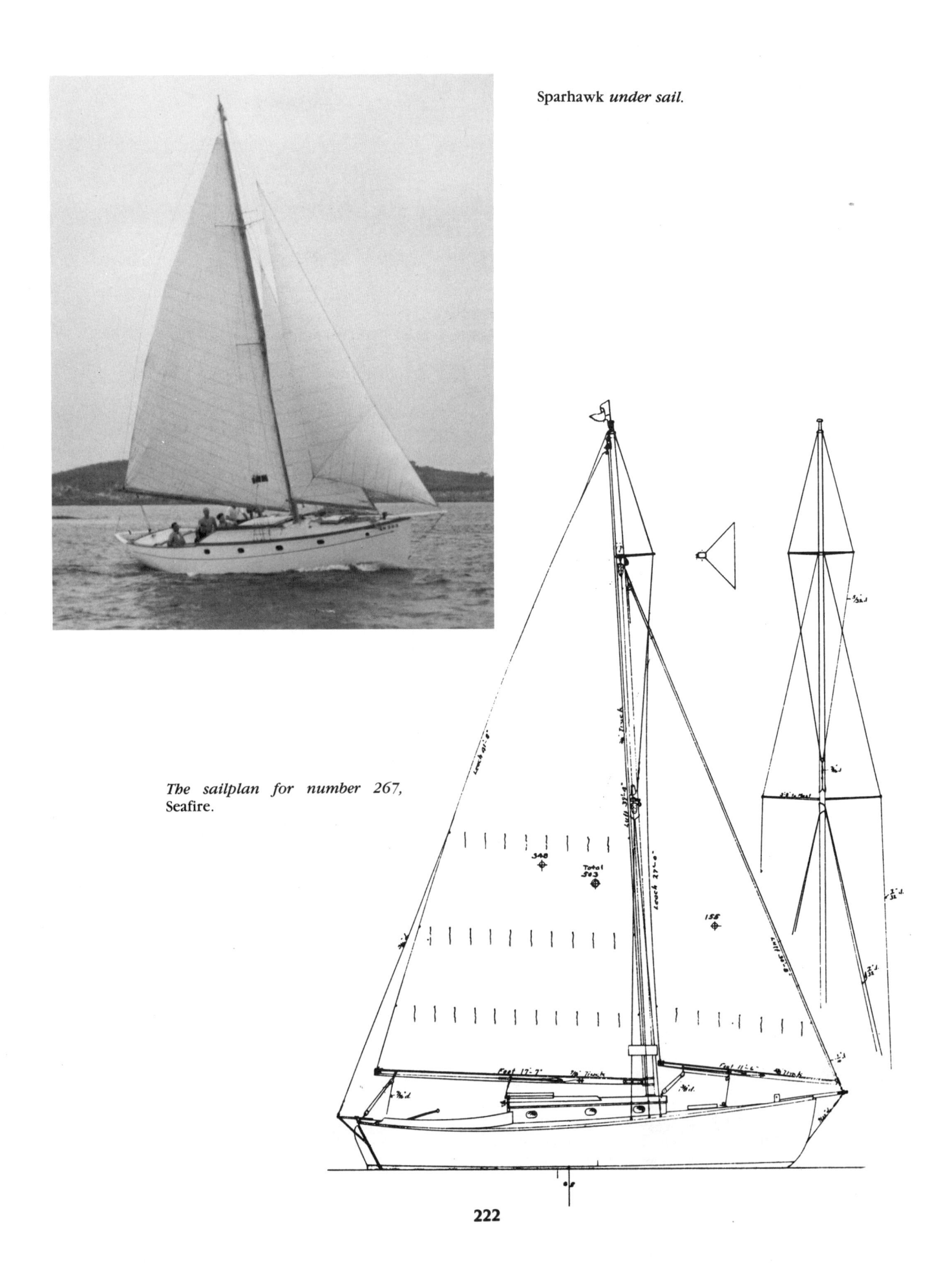

The sailplan for number 267, Seafire.

Number 256, Old Butch *under sail.*

263 AKBAR

Design Number 263
Length Overall: 30 feet
Length on Waterline: 26 feet 6 inches
Beam: 9 feet
Draft: 3 feet 9 inches
Displacement: 11,652 pounds

Akbar was designed in 1951 as a workboat for my yard. However, I was unable to complete and launch her until 1956. Rather than build molds, I used some crooked oak I had on hand to put up an oak-sawn frame on every mold station and put in three bent frames between. The bent frames consisted of two 1-inch-by-2-inch pieces, one on top of the other, to give a 2-inch-square frame. Planking was 1⅛-inch mahogany fastened with galvanized iron screws. She was covered from the rabbet to the lower guard with fiberglass for ice sheathing, and the punishment that this takes never ceases to amaze me. I keep a lot of boats at the floats in winter storage, and whenever the ice moves things around too much, we have to break them out. I have driven her through ice up to 12 inches thick by backing off and running her up onto it until her weight eventually breaks it. The power plant is a 6-330 Gray engine with 3.5-to-1 reduction gear. Originally, I had a 36-inch-diameter-by-24-inch-pitch, three-blade prop, but after breaking heavy ice it would look like a tulip. She now has a 34-inch-by-24-inch four-blade, which stands up much better, because the interval between blades doesn't admit large chunks of ice. I have probably used a couple dozen steerers out of trucks in the boats built in my yard because they are such a fine piece of machinery, and that is what *Akbar* had originally. About 10 or 12 years ago, I got a power-steering unit out of an old Plymouth and hooked it up to a cylinder at the rudderpost with a two-way valve. Now, a hard right or hard left is only a 2 inch movement of her tiller. From the forward end of the engine we run a 1¼ Jabsco bilge pump and a 1½-inch bronze-gear fire pump that can throw a stream of water 75 feet. We also put winch heads on each side of the pilot house. This, with the big sheave on the stem head, enables us to handle moorings up to 5,000 pounds. She has been a great workboat, but when it is very rough outside, you need to have your feet well spread and hang on. Her hard bilges make her pretty lively.

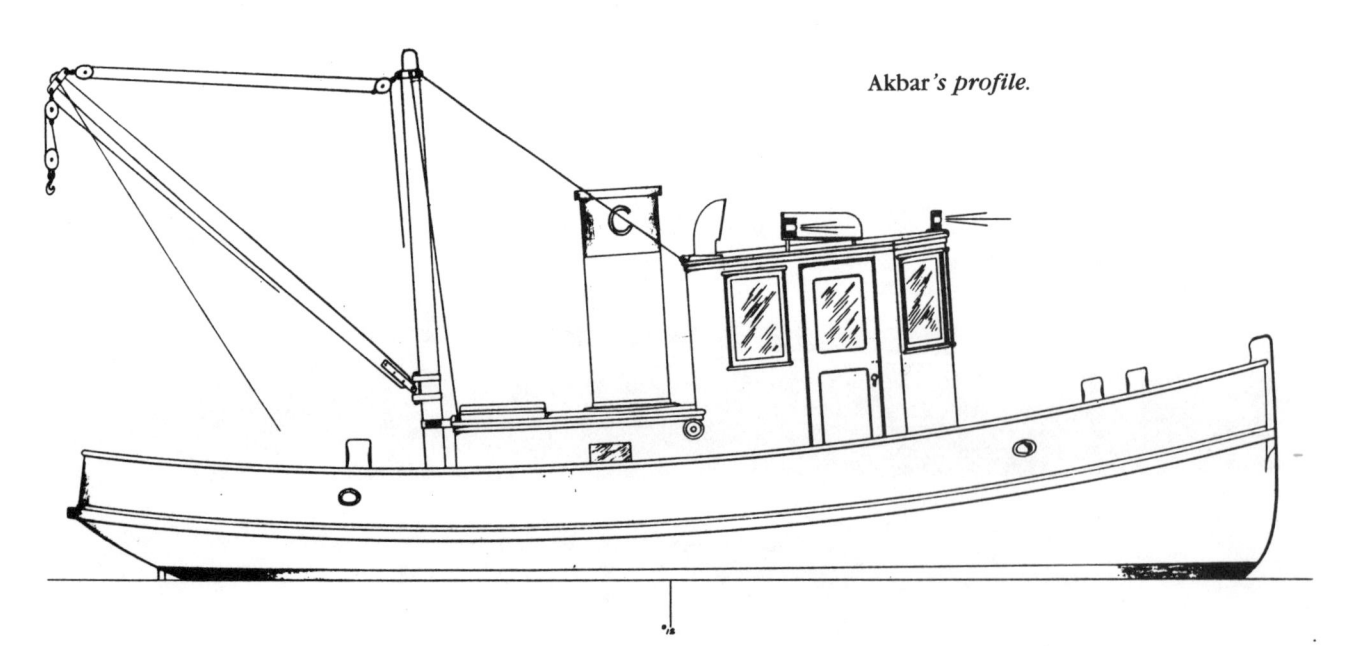

Akbar's profile.

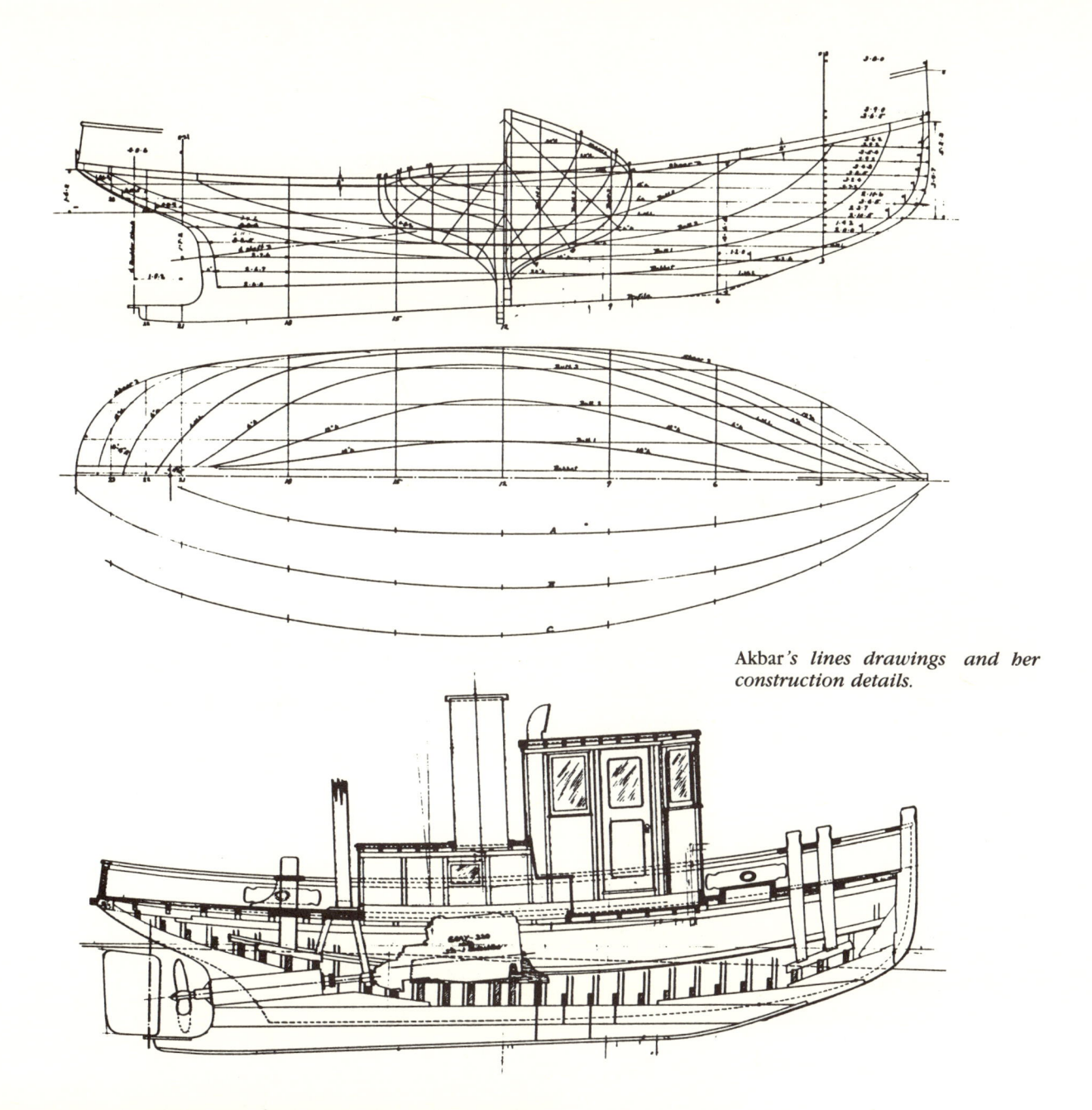

Akbar's *lines drawings and her construction details.*

Akbar *making small work of some harbor ice.*

266 CROCKER 20

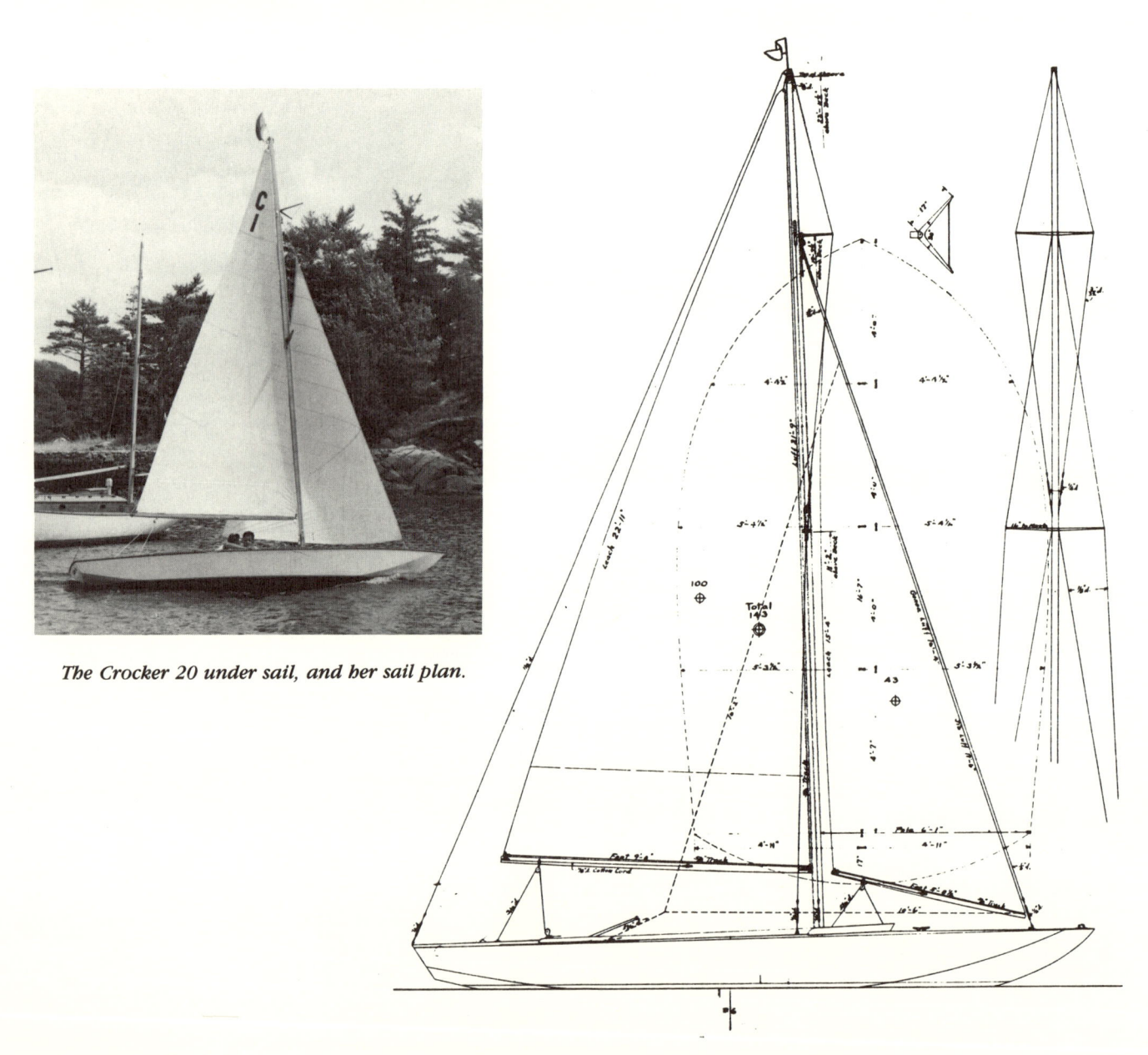

The Crocker 20 under sail, and her sail plan.

Design Number 266
Length Overall: 20 feet
Length on Waterline: 15 feet 4 inches
Beam: 5 feet 11 inches
Draft: 3 feet 7 inches
Sail Area: 143 square feet
Displacement: 1,210 pounds

In 1948 my father and several other boat owners in Manchester formed the Manchester Harbor Boat Club. Of course, boat racing followed, with everybody racing what they had. We soon saw that there was no way the boats could be handicapped, and one of the charter members, Lock Allen, proposed a one-design. As a result, Dad designed number 266, the Crocker 20. She was hard-chine construction, built of ⅜-inch marine plywood with a spruce frame and a 450-pound cast-iron keel. I built five, putting them together with Elmer's water-

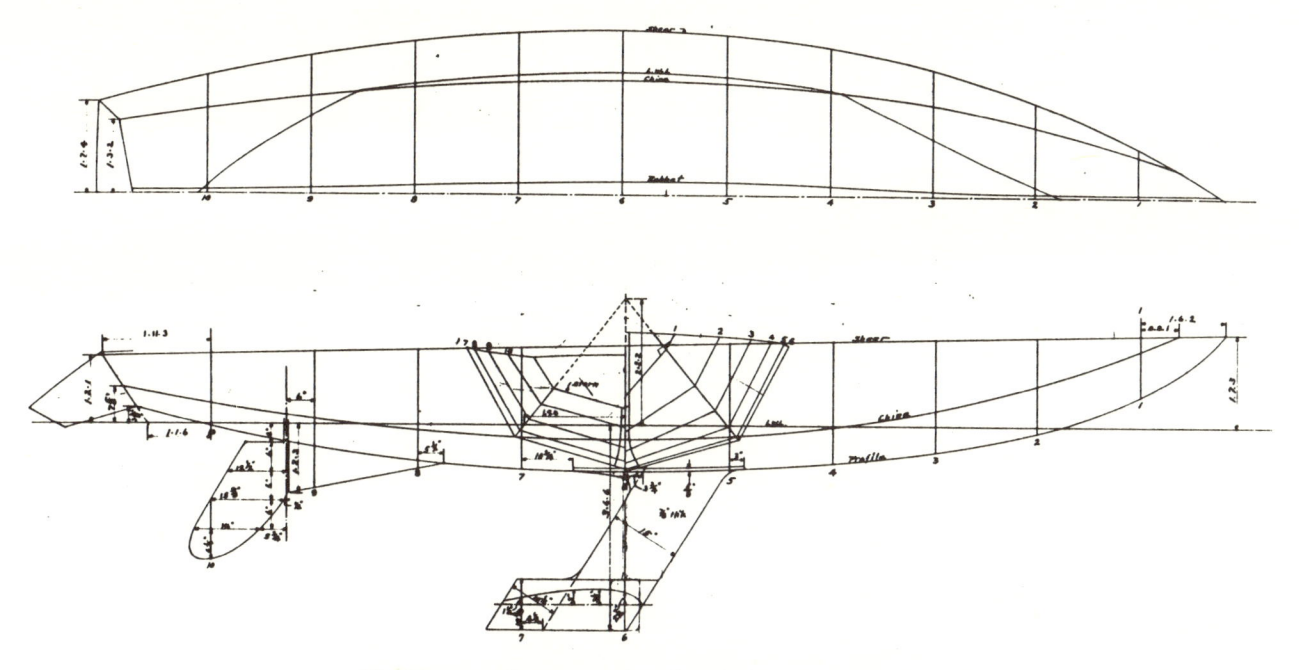

The lines, and construction details for the Crocker 20.

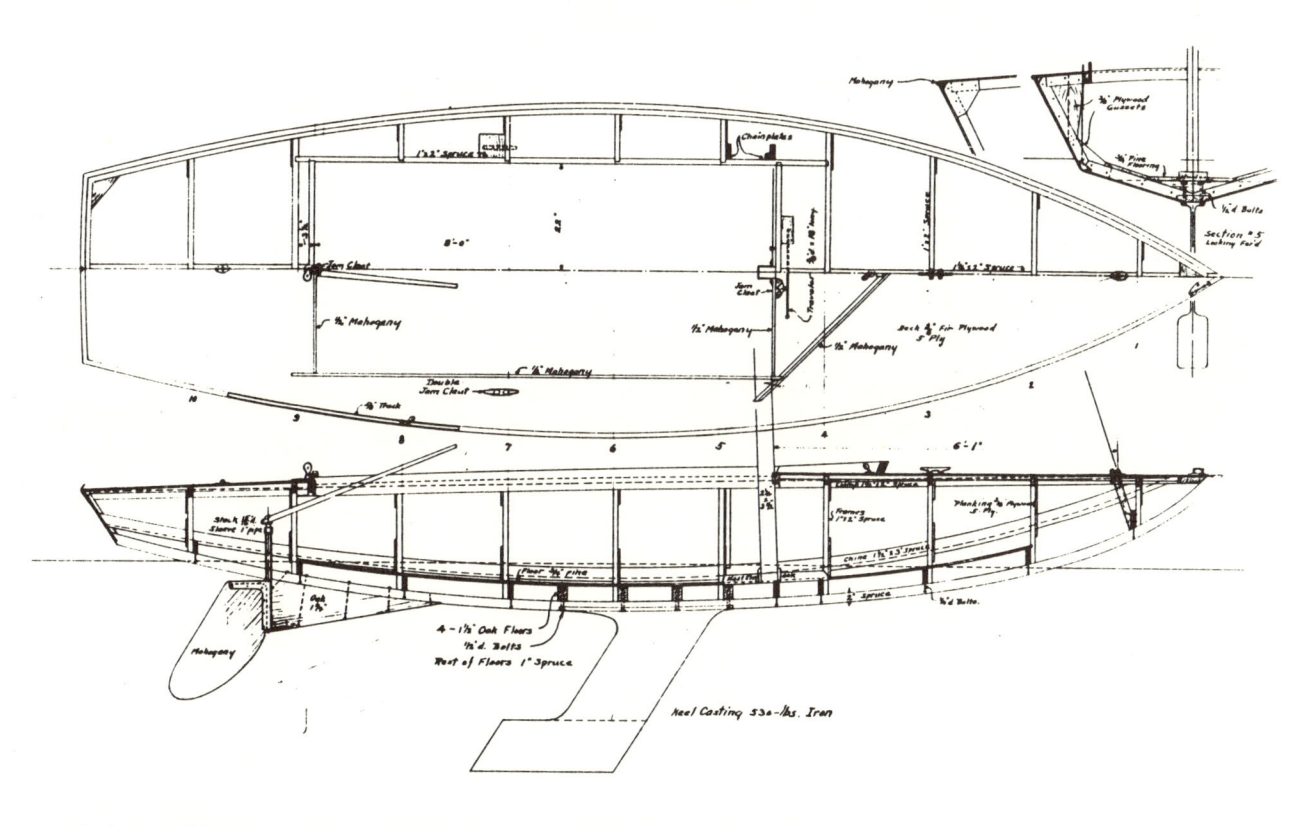

proof glue and bronze screws. The boat was unique in that the chine was dead straight, running from the stern and intersecting the sheer rather than running into the stern as is usual in chine boats. They were a joy to sail, and I think if I could have built a hundred to start it would be a going class today. People are reluctant to get into a class that is not well established. There were eight or 10 more built in Kennebunkport, Me., and plans were sold all over the world, but the class never really took hold.

268 DOLPHIN

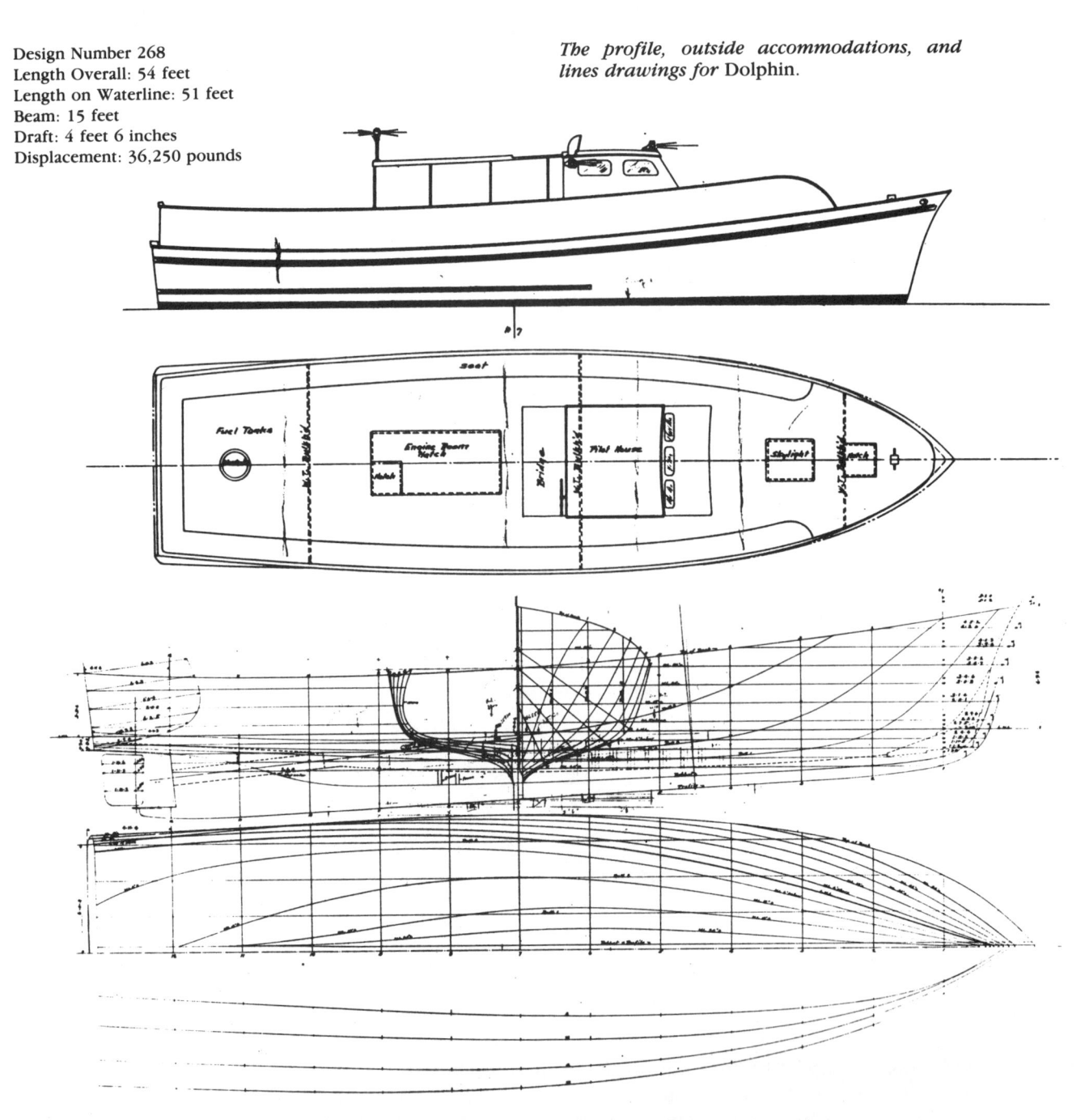

Design Number 268
Length Overall: 54 feet
Length on Waterline: 51 feet
Beam: 15 feet
Draft: 4 feet 6 inches
Displacement: 36,250 pounds

The profile, outside accommodations, and lines drawings for Dolphin.

Dolphin was a party boat designed for Capt. Albert A. Avelar, Jr., of Provincetown, Mass. She was built in 1952 by David Foster of Truro, Mass. She was designed to carry 60 people and was powered by a General Motors 671 diesel. At present she is working out of the Gateway Marina in Gloucester, Mass.

METACOMET 269

I started *Metacomet* in 1952 and finished her in 1953 for Russell Grinnell, Jr., of Gloucester, Mass. She was the biggest boat built in my yard. Russ brought a nice set of lines to my father, showing just what he wanted. My father faired up the lines, figured weights, etc., and drew the construction profile and other detailed drawings. Then Russ and I scouted the junk yards around Everett and Chelsea, where we found some beautiful hard pine planks, 2 inches by 12 inches by 20 to 24 feet, that had come out of buildings torn down to make way for the Southeast Expressway in Boston. Route 128 was being pushed through Manchester, at the time, and we walked the area to see the oak and pine that was to be cut to make way for it. I remember one oak that had been deflected so that it made a 90-degree bend. Fortunately, it was sound and about 24 inches in diameter. Russ put his hand on it and said, "I want it for a stem knee." It was a truckload in itself, but we landed it in the yard and it turned out a beautiful knee.

We bent in 1½-inch-by-3-inch oak for a frame and then put another 1½ inches by 3 inches on top of it to end up with a 3-inch-by-3-inch bent frame. The hard pine planking finished 1¾ inches and was bolted on with 5/16-inch galvan-

Design Number 269
Length Overall: 62 feet
Length on Waerline: 55 feet
Beam: 14 feet 6 inches
Draft: 7 feet 3 inches
Sail Area: 1147 square feet
Displacement: 87,000 pounds

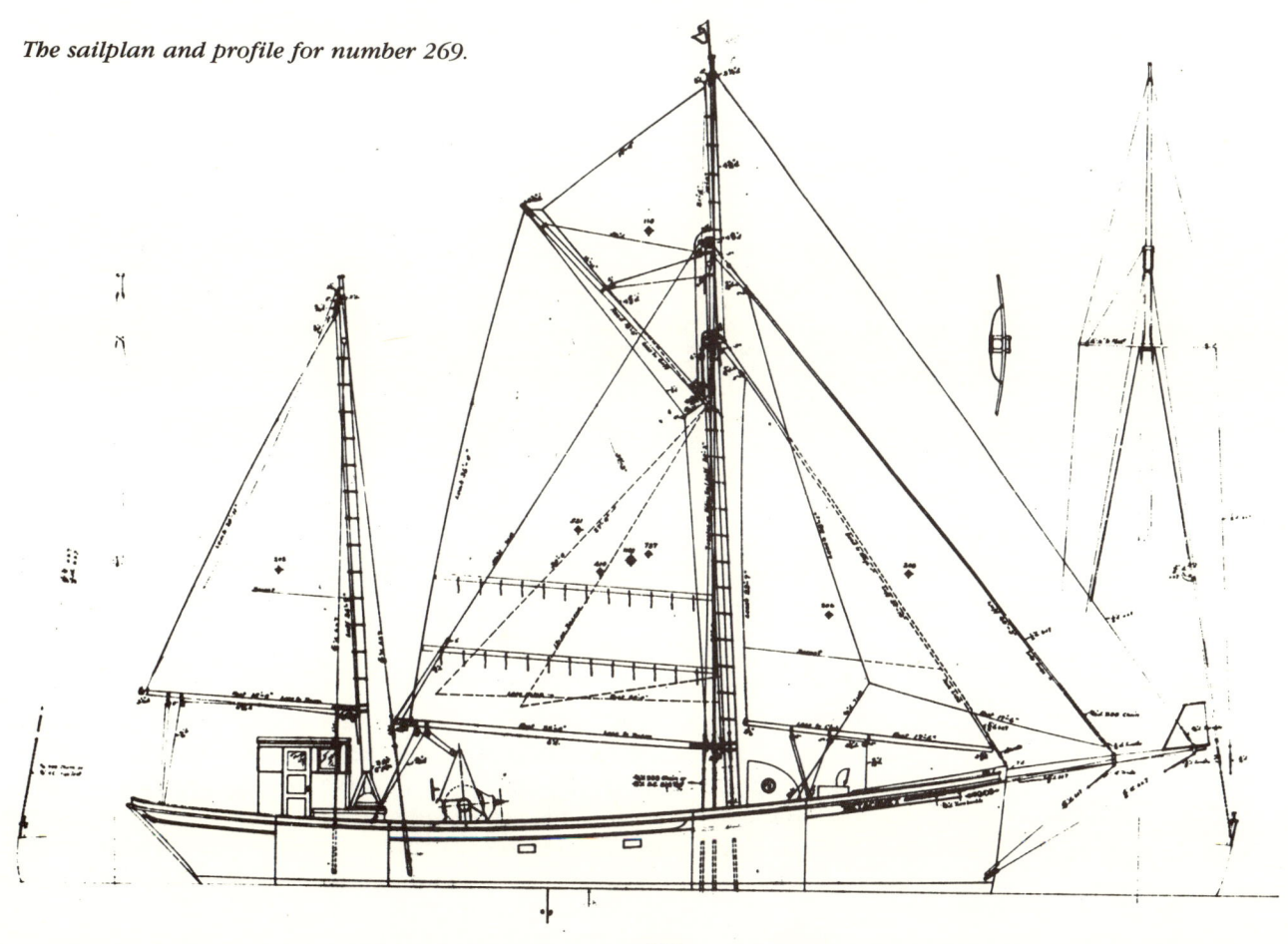

The sailplan and profile for number 269.

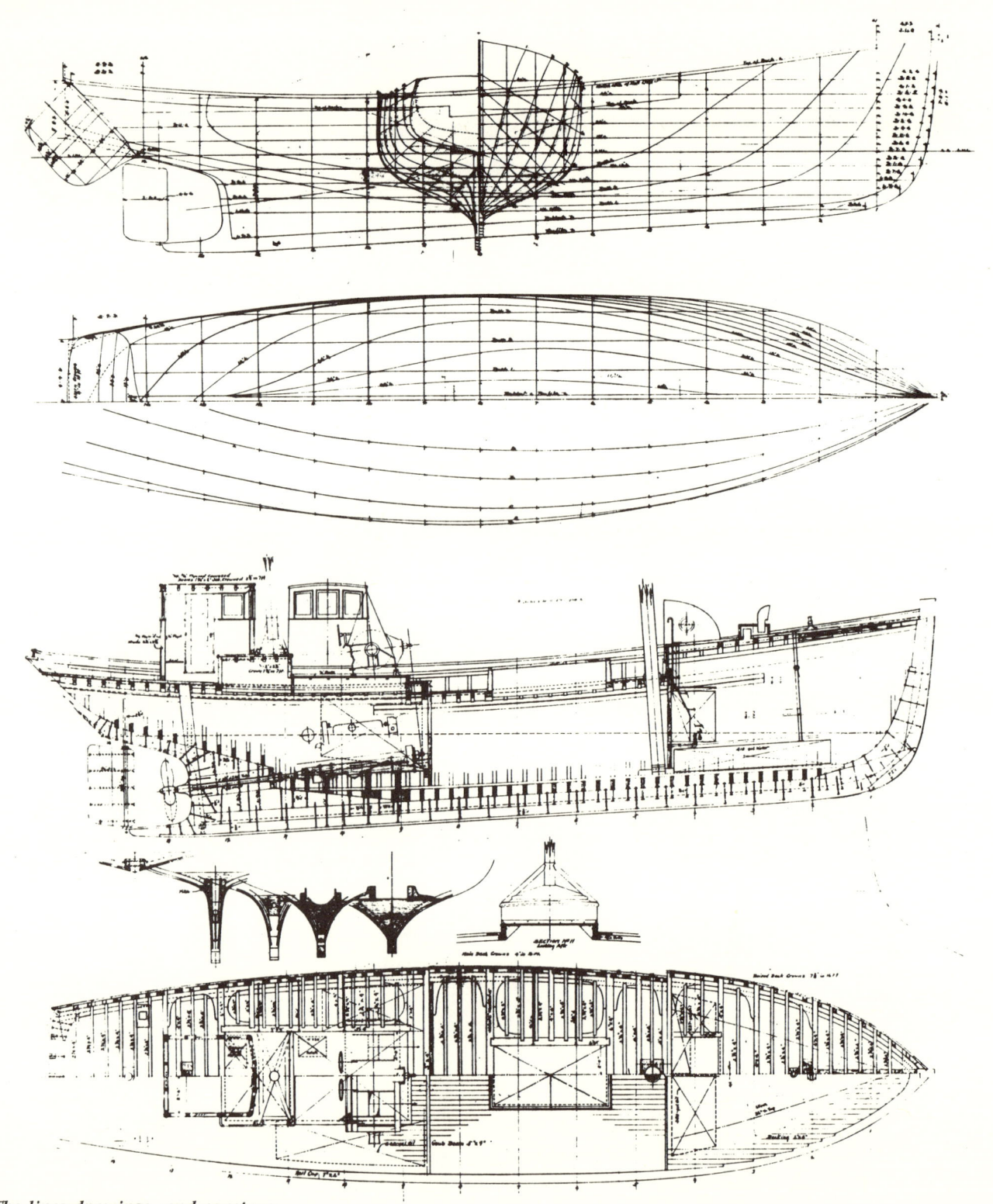

The lines drawings, and construction details for Metacomet.

ized carriage bolts, making the whole structure very strong. For a steering gear, it was back to the junk yard, where we took the rear end from a 1½-ton Ford truck. We placed it on end with one axle connected to the rudder stock and a sprocket on the drive shaft to be connected to the steering wheel with a roller chain. She steered easily, without the one thing both Russ and I couldn't abide, backlash and slack from cables. We couldn't think of a use for the other axle

The frames in Metacomet *looking aft, and under power off Gloucester.*

sticking up, so it was cut off and the opening in the housing capped. Her spars were hewn from pine trees cut in Manchester. Russ had a complete suit of sails made, but I don't think they were ever bent on. She's still fishing out of Gloucester, but I note she has steel spars. A six-cylinder 200 model General Motors diesel with 3¾-to-1 reduction and a 48-inch propeller gave 10 knots at 1,600 r.p.m.

270 AUNT EMMA

Design Number 270
Length Overall: 37 feet 2 inches
Length on Waterline: 26 feet 8 inches
Beam: 9 feet 7 inches
Draft: 5 feet 4 inches
Sail Area: 549 square feet
Displacement: 15,000 pounds

I built *Aunt Emma* in 1953 for Dr. Donald Brown of Beverly, Mass. She was auxiliary-powered by a four-cylinder Arnolt Sea-Mite, which was installed backwards above the propeller shaft and connected to the shaft by V belts. This gave it the reduction necessary to swing a fairly large prop. The contract was signed in 1952 for delivery in 1953. Don left for a month's trip to Europe in May 1953, right after the iron keel casting was delivered. I can still see the expression on his face when he got back and drove down Ashland Avenue, only to see the keel in the same position it had been in a month earlier. I had been so busy trying to finish up *Metacomet,* I hadn't been able to touch Don's boat.

We did get him sailing before layup time that fall but without much cabin interior. Don wrote:

> Due to the late launching, the 1953 season was restricted to a few shakedown daysails. The following year, we cruised down east with Harrison and Elizabeth Cann, they in their *East Wind*. On the return trip, following a brisk squall, Harry suggested that we head for South Freeport. He knew the way, and we should follow him. Well, Harry inadvertently cut a buoy, and we both went hard aground on a going tide. Some fishermen came and took my wife Eileen and our three children, ages 4, 6, and 8, to one of their homes for the night. We floated off about 2 a.m. On our return to Manchester, I told Sam Crocker to put the boat on the market. I will always remember the kindly twinkle in his eyes as he counseled me to "wait a spell and see if things didn't look better." Needless to say, we still own *Aunt Emma*.

The lines drawings for Aunt Emma.

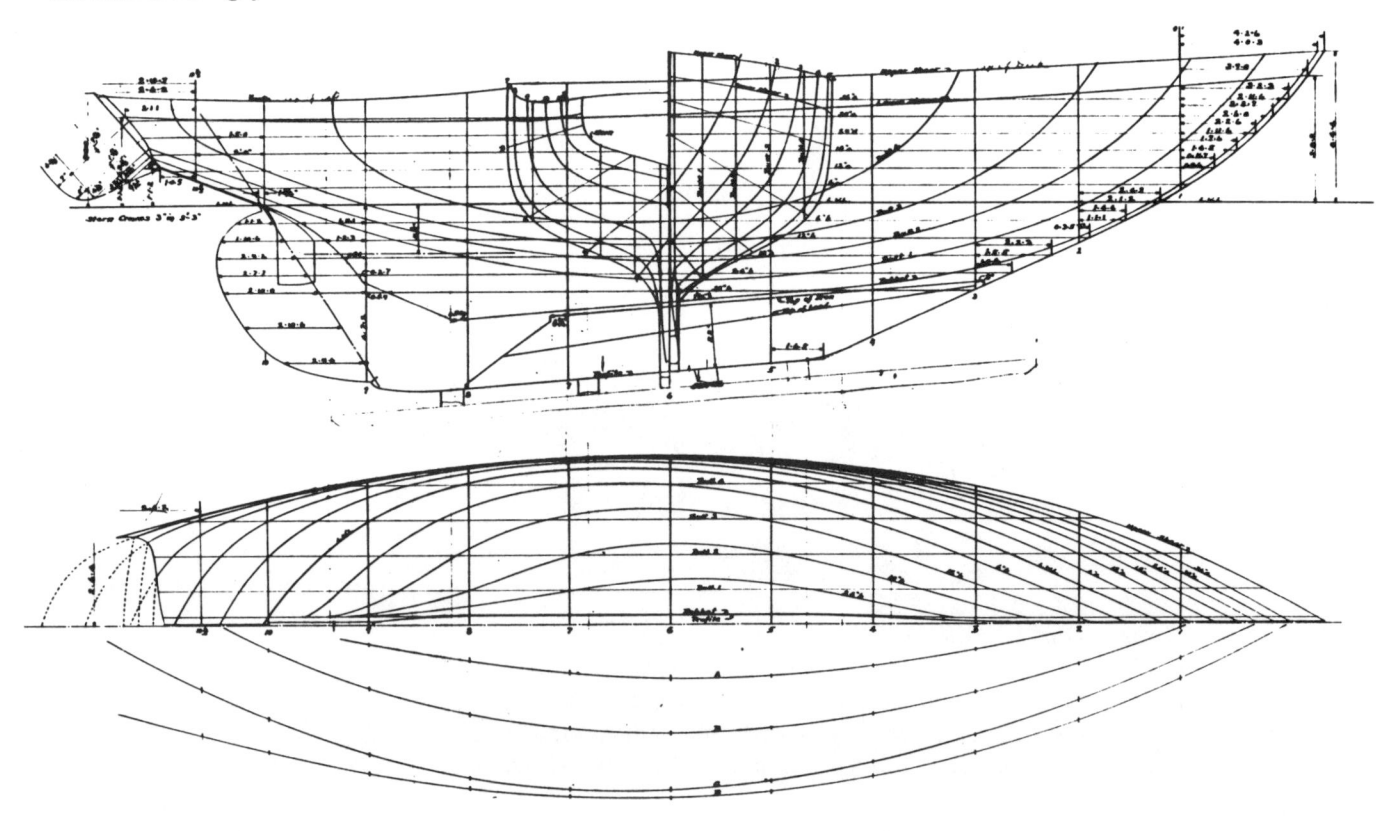

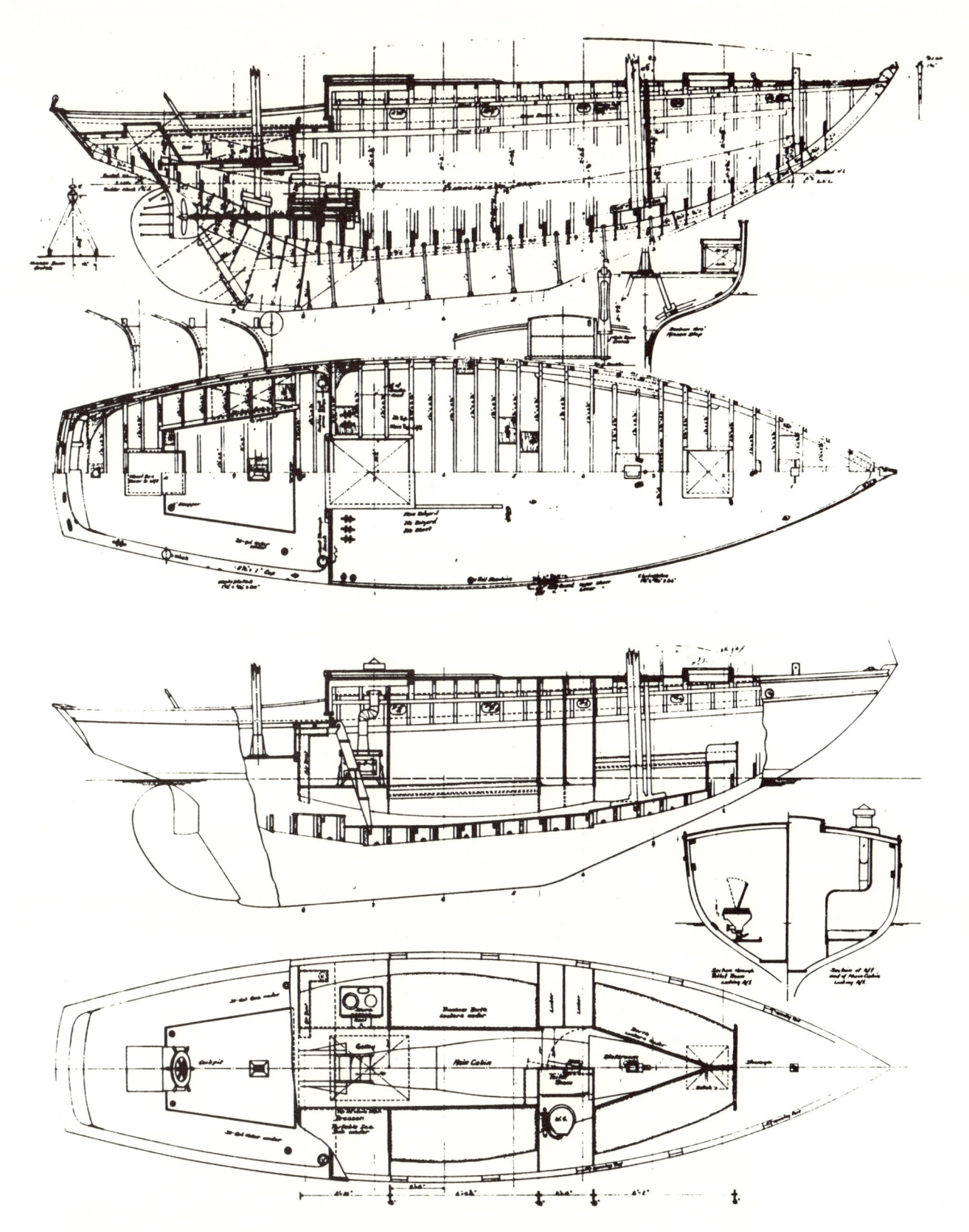

We moved to New Jersey, and every summer the family cruised back at least to Manchester and sometimes down east as far as Bucks Harbor. *Aunt Emma*'s standing rigging has been replaced with stainless, a new Universal Atomic Four was installed in 1966, and she is on her third suit of sails. In 1980, she was refastened, and in a manner of speaking, so was I. She was done by a ship's carpenter, and I was done by a cardiac surgeon. She is ready to go cruising, but I am not too sure about myself.

The construction drawings and accommodations plans for Aunt Emma.

We have retired to Manchester, and my crew is all grown up with families of their own, but my wife and I can handle the *Aunt Emma* in any reasonable sort of weather. She is an easy boat to sail, and her large cockpit is sheer luxury for the type of sailing we do. The somewhat unorthodox engine mounting has never given a minute's trouble. The five V belts have been replaced once in 32 years. There has been hardly a day when we are sailing that someone does not hail us to ask if she is a Crocker boat or to comment on her graceful lines. Although she won't sail as close to the wind as a sloop or cutter, once she's underway, she can hold her own with

Aunt Emma *under sail*.

almost anyone. She is an old and well-loved member of the family. We have been together in many harbors and at many boat yards. It is nice to be back in Manchester.

Seneca (number 258) was the same boat but with more rake to stem and stern, and was 38 feet on deck. She was built for George R. Poor of Marblehead in 1954. Both these boats had galvanized rigging with poured zinc sockets, one of the best systems of rigging there ever was. However, after the war, we never got as good galvanized wire as before, and it didn't stand up. I can remember George looking over his rigging in my loft before commissioning in 1963. It was quite rusty, but he decided to get another year out of it. Then he sold the boat, and the new owner took her to the Chesapeake. They got into a northeast gale; they estimated winds of 80 knots and heard over the radio of planes grounded at LaGuardia Airport and winds of 70 m.p.h. I've included a letter from the owner, G.L. Cochran, and an article he did for *Yachting* (February 1964) on the incident.

Dear Sam:
I'm not sure I can answer your question on why the *Seneca*'s spars were still in her after we rolled, but I'll try. As far as I can tell, she rolled from port to starboard until she was completely upside down, at which time she rolled back in the same direction. She did not go all the way over in a complete circle. The three of us in the cockpit were underwater. John Klopp and my wife were below and were thrown to the starboard side, then to the ceiling, then back to starboard, then to the bunk. I don't know why we didn't lose the spars or spreaders. I have since been up both masts, and found no evidence of any part being cracked or harmed in any way. I hope you build and design all of your boats as well as you did the *Seneca*.

Sincerely, G.L. Cochran

The thing is, none of us had ever actually been in a sailboat that was upside down before. Our experience of a lifetime began with the purchase of a 38-foot Crocker-designed and built, flush-deck ketch. We bought her in Marblehead, Mass., in January, and started planning for the cruise offshore to our home port, Middle River on the Chesapeake Bay.

Food lists were prepared, gear was bought, borrowed, or made, and the crew chosen. The gear included extra life-jackets, liferings, night light, safety harnesses for all hands, a gimbal stove for rough weather, sextant, taffrail log, RDF, charts and Dramamine pills.

Our crew, which would be hard to beat, included my wife, Jean, who had shared my long-time dream of an offshore cruise. Nils Olssen, first mate, lives aboard his own boat, *Phyllis II,* a 45-foot flush-deck ketch. He is a Past Commander of the Coast Guard Auxiliary and one of the best seamen I know. John Klopp, our navigator, lives aboard the *Sinbad,* a 30-foot Tahiti ketch which he built himself, and plans extensive ocean cruising on her. Leight Johnson has been (and still is) recommended as a good hand. He has crewed in many Bay races and has his own day sailer.

Sunday, April 9, we sailed from Marblehead to Onset, where we lay over a day to wait out a gale. The next day's trip down Buzzards Bay was roughly like rounding Cape Horn in winter (Dramamine saved the day), and most of us were feeling quite salty by the time we reached Cuttyhunk, where we optimistically put in for supplies and gas. Having seen this attractive island harbor during the summer, and being accustomed to the longer sailing season on the Chesapeake, we expected to pull in to the gas pier and top our tanks. But Cuttyhunk's few year-round residents were astonished to see a yacht in early April. Oh well, our 30-gallon tank was nearly full (we told ourselves) and ice was no problem in temperatures close to freezing. *Seneca* was snug in the land-locked harbor overnight, and the charcoal fireplace made the cabin cozy and pleasant. An early start for Block Island was decided upon.

"Wednesday fair, with southwesterly winds, shifting to north-easterly, 20-30 knots, Wednesday night and Thursday, with some rain likely." So went the forecast by the Boston marine operator on Wednesday, April 12, promising an easy run to Delaware Bay. After sailing all day under clear skies, we heard the forecast con-

Aunt Emma's sailplan.

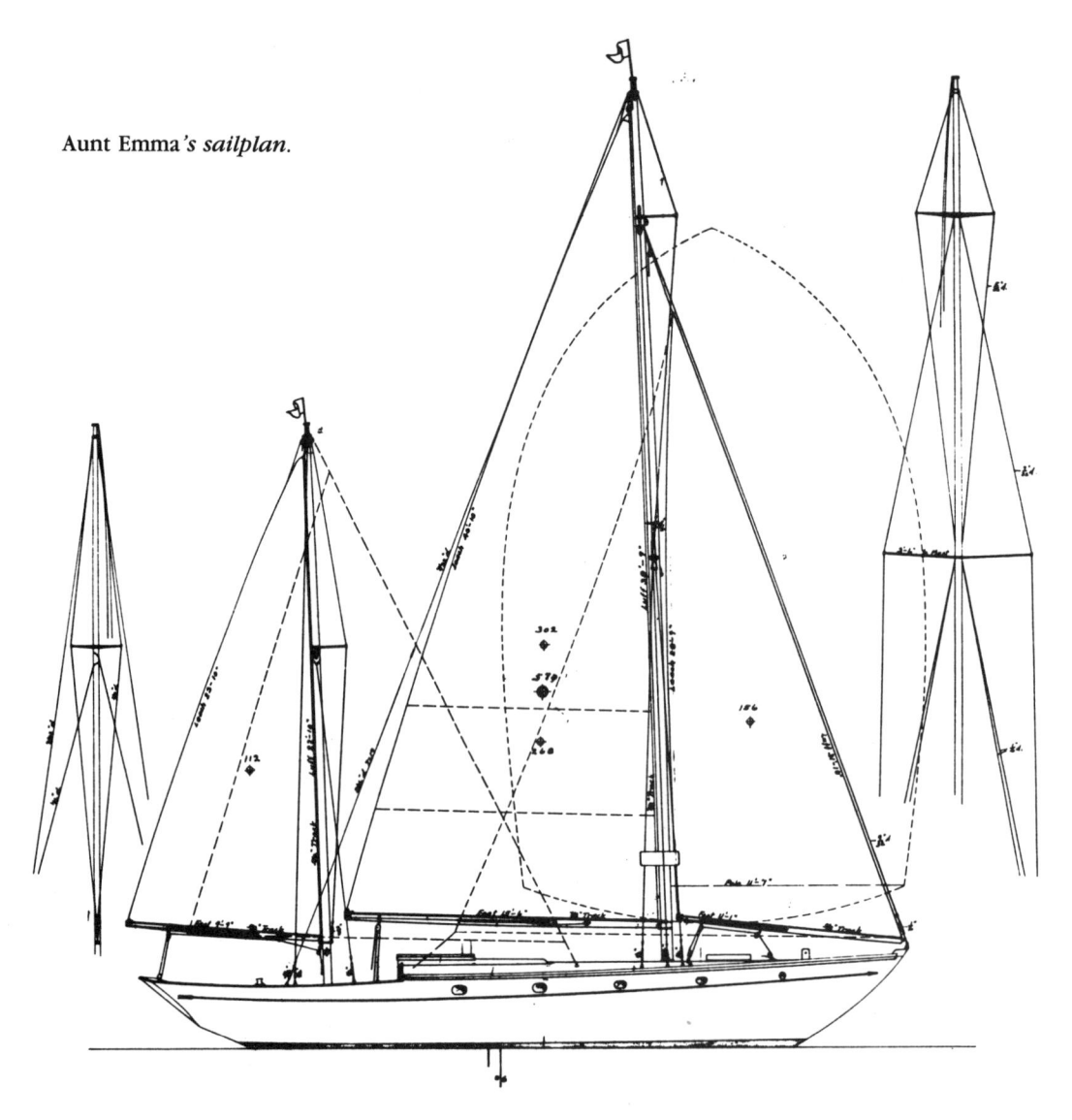

firmed on the evening broadcast, and headed confidently offshore, passing Block Island at dusk.

John Klopp, Jean and I had the evening watch while Ole and Leight did the last loafing they were to do for several days. Soon the rain came, foul weather gear was put on, and Jean was sent below. "No point in you getting wet," I told her. Little did she know this was the last time she would be on deck for a day and a half.

During this watch the wind built up rapidly. The mainsail was dropped and furled securely. The wind continued to increase and soon, with the mizzen also furled, we were scudding along under jib alone. When Ole and Leight took over at midnight the wind, already from the northeast, had risen to near-gale force, driving us before it through luminous, hissing seas. It was too late to change course or beat back to Montauk Point and the dubious safety of Long Island Sound. We began to wonder about the weather predictions we had heard. John and I attempted to get a fix with the RDF but were unable to do so as it was impossible to hold a steady course in these tremendous seas.

Concerned about how much sea room we had, I decided to drop the jib and rig a drogue to slow us down. The sail had jibed several times and had a small three-cornered tear. After a few hectic moments on the foredeck, the jib was lashed down and we improvised a sea anchor off the stern. A heavy canvas sea bag was filled with canned goods and spare parts and dragged at the end of our new nylon anchor line. This made the boat's motion easier, and we continued until daylight, which brought only a sobering view of the huge seas. A cheery-voiced New York disc jockey was not reassuring with his announcement that Hudson River ferries and the George Washington Bridge were closed by the storm with planes at LaGuardia

Seneca under sail.

grounded by 70 m.p.h. winds. At sea, we estimated the wind at 80 knots. We knew now that Ole had been serious in his remark, "Out where we're going we'll need steel cables for tell-tales!"

Still scudding under bare poles, we knew *Seneca* was rapidly approaching the Jersey Coast, and that the seas which towered above our 50-foot mast would steepen and break, swamping us long before we could see land. The anxious crew improvised more drogues, using sailbags filled with more canned goods, tools, spare parts, even our galley stove — anything to slow us down! Even then, under bare poles, we seemed to be making about eight knots. Finally, in desperation, we started our engine, hauled in the drogues and headed into the wind, hoping to work southerly to gain more sea room.

We spent the next hour dodging the big waves, and climbing over the ones that weren't breaking. At the wheel I felt like a rabbit ducking through the bushes. Every chance I got, I headed south, angling away from the coast. Our exhausted crew began to feel more optimistic about our chances of making it.

The wind finally eased off and we decided to set a storm trysail and conserve our dwindling gas. We did this, eased the throttle, found that we had control with the sail, and shut off the engine. Ole took the wheel while Leight and I rested in the cockpit (all of us, while on deck, hooked on with safety lines). Jean and John were down below, trying to fix our position.

We had been under sail for about ten minutes when Leight let out a yell. Suddenly a huge sea broke over *Seneca,* rolling her completely upside down and sending me flying over the mizzen boom and overboard. My foot was caught in the upper rigging. I managed to yank it free and was attempting to release my safety line, as I believed no 38-foot boat could survive in such a sea. But in a moment *Seneca* had righted herself, rolling back the same way she had gone over, and had pulled me to the surface by the lifeline. The cockpit, which is extremely large, was filled from rail to rail. Her freeboard, normally about three feet, was down to less than a foot. I grabbed the rail, pulled myself on board and found both Ole and Leight still on deck.

A quick check below showed Jean and John scrambling anxiously out from under a mountain of drawers, bunk mattresses, dishes, cans, radios, etc. The cabin was a shambles with water up to the bunks but no one seemed to be seriously injured. Two hatches in the cockpit had broken loose and the water was pouring into the bilges.

We quickly organized a bucket brigade, fearing at any moment that the next sea would finish us. Looking back, I believe we may hold a world's record for the amount of water bailed out in about ten minutes! During this time Ole had stayed at the wheel and was having great difficulty in steering. At first, we feared that the rudder had been fouled by gear washed overboard but a quick check showed it to be clear. We finally found that Ole, clinging to the wheel when *Seneca* broached, had bent the one-inch shaft so far out of line that it wouldn't turn. Three of us, pushing with all our remaining strength, were able to straighten it enough so that, by loosening a bearing we could steer.

Another fast survey showed that our moment of bottom-up sailing had cost us, among other things, our main anchor and davit, the two hatch covers (a serious loss in breaking seas), our taffrail log and a smashed sextant. The masts and standing rigging were still intact! The trysail sheet had parted, which accounts for *Seneca*'s being able to right herself so quickly.

Below decks was a most disheartening sight. Water and debris, clear across the ceiling, was already inky black from the dissolving charcoal brickets in the bin. All drawers on the port side had slid out and dumped their contents into the bilge. We had gone over far enough for the dipstick to fall from the engine and a sliding shield between the fireplace and bunk had slid up off its vertical track. The crew had cuts and bruises from stem to stern but no major injuries!

While the rest of us were getting shipshape on deck, John had been working feverishly on the engine. He replaced the batteries, which had fallen out of their deep boxes, dried the distributor and all electrical parts. Miraculously the engine started, and we were under way once more.

Now new difficulties arose. The wind had died down while we were making *Seneca* seaworthy, shifted to the northwest, creating the most mixed-up sea I ever hope to sail in. That night it piped up to 35-40 knots, with the familiar glowing, curling waves, and we spent a second consecutive night running before a storm under bare poles, this time away from the coast. Sleep was out of the question, with tricks on watch shortened to less than an hour. By this time we were all completely exhausted but in much better spirits as we were being blown offshore and had plenty of sea room.

Friday morning the wind moderated, the sun shone briefly and after a few minor repairs we were under full sail again. John attempted to take sights, and concluded that the sextant had been damaged in the knockdown. Though the RDF was working properly, he was unable to get strong enough signals so far offshore. We had to be content with sailing southwest and knowing we would make a landfall eventually. The tired crew, having subsisted on snatches of coffee and stew since Wednesday was treated to a real meal of bacon and eggs. Yes, the three dozen eggs in cardboard cartons were unbroken!

A Navy blimp circled us that morning and came around again for another look. The wet gear and blankets strung up on deck and the bearded crew must have been a sight! Finally convinced that we were not refugees from behind the Iron Curtain, they flew away. It was nice to know someone knew where we were. The good sailing weather Friday and Saturday would have been enjoyable had there been enough dry clothes and bunks to go around.

We homed in on Five Fathom Lightship Saturday and by nightfall entered Delaware Bay. The run up to the C&D Canal was routine, if you discount a couple of near-misses by freighters that seemed bent on running us down in the early morning fog (outside the channel), and forgetting the final stretch with rising winds and steepening seas at our backs, breaking aboard.

Sunday morning's gale warnings (What else?) sounded familiar, but we heard them from the shelter of the canal, while we reflected on such things as the absence of any loose inside ballast that might have dropped through the deck, the second wave that didn't hit us while we were crippled, and the boat that had survived hurricane winds and a knockdown without a rigging or a structural failure.

We all felt extremely lucky, and appreciated being alive. Credit for our having made it is given to the Crockers, Jr. and Sr., who designed and built *Seneca* to take more than I ever thought possible, and to my crew who wouldn't quit.

LAST CALL 273

Design Number 273
Length Overall: 26 feet
Length on Waterline: 21 feet 3 inches
Beam: 8 feet 6 inches
Draft: 4 feet 3 inches
Sail Area: 365 square feet
Displacement: 8,450 pounds

Last Call. number 273, was built in my yard for C. Gardner Akin, Jr., of New Bedford, Mass., in 1955. Akin was an associate of my father's who had his first Amantha.

I built two of these — *Last Call* and *Mehitabel*, for Clark Dixon of North Chelmsford, Mass. *Wendy Ann,* number 286, built in 1956 for J. Stanley Churchill of Cohasset, is the same boat but with overhanging ends, inboard rudder, and trunk cabin.

The sailplan for Last Call.

The lines for number 273.

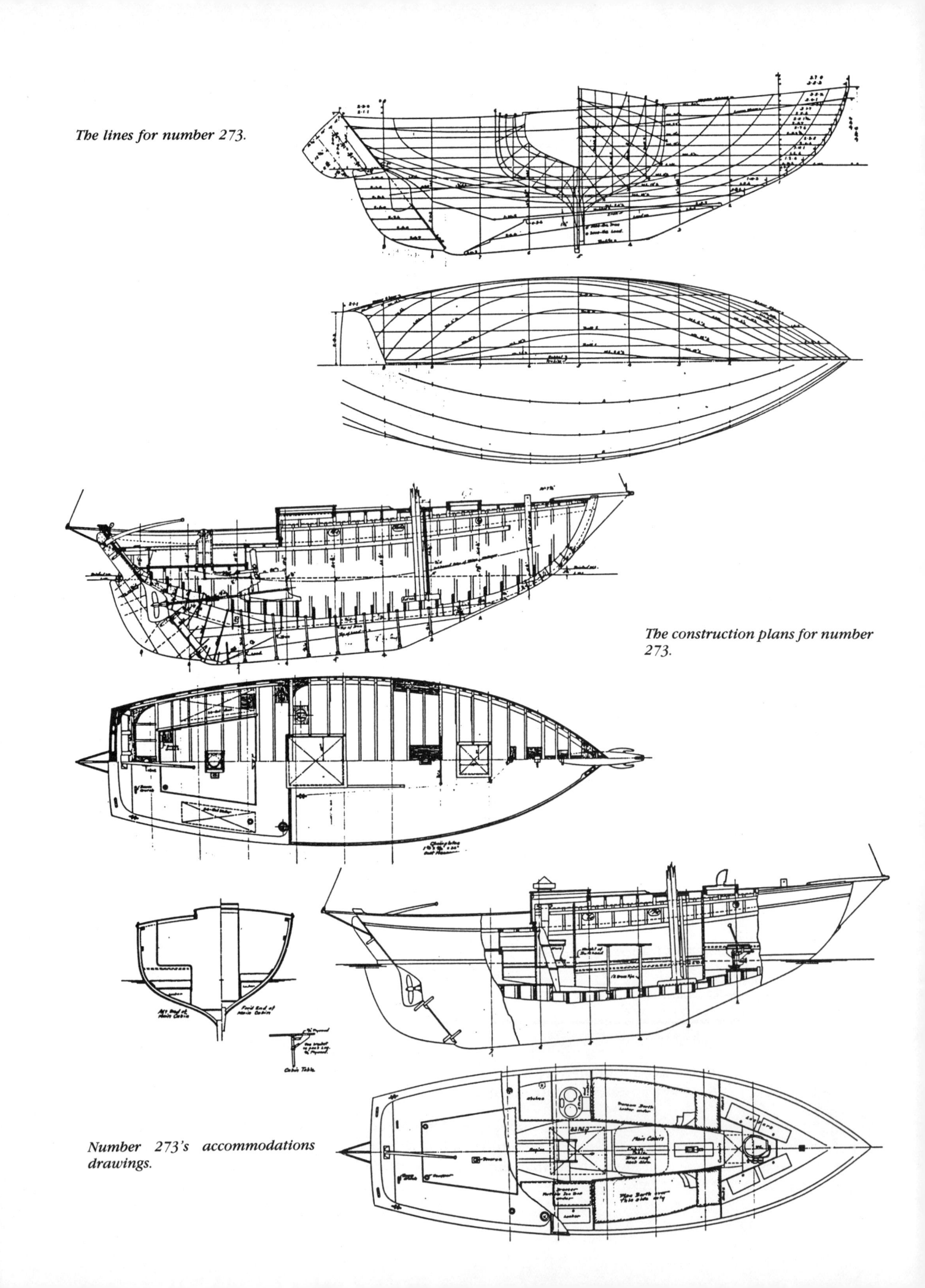

The construction plans for number 273.

Number 273's accommodations drawings.

Last Call *moving along well. Photograph courtesy of Norman Fortier.*

The sailplan and accommodations for number 286, Wendy Ann.

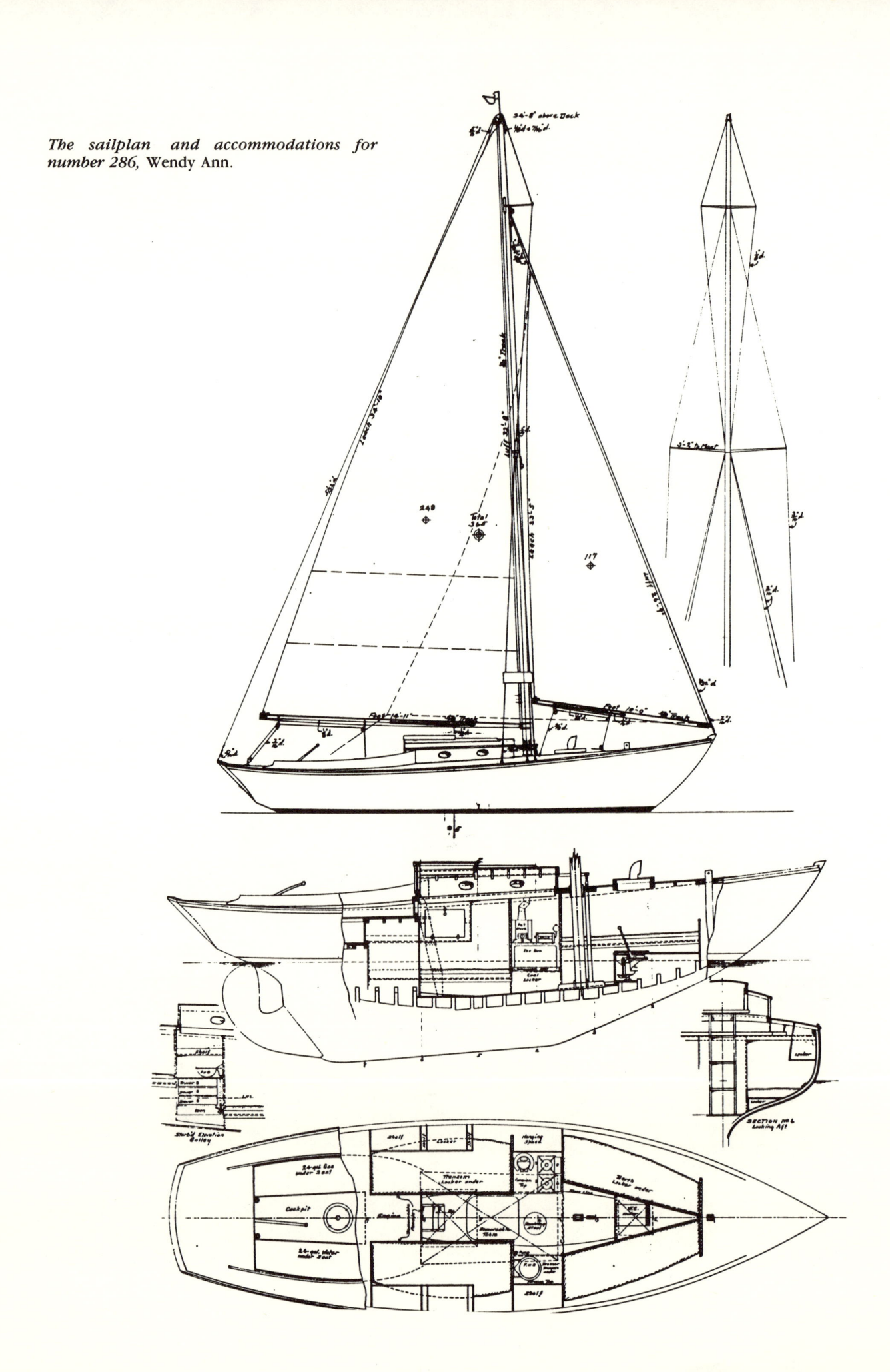

CALISTA III 277A

Calista II was built by Elmer Collemer of Camden, Me., in 1956 for A.J. deGozzaldi of Saxonville, Mass. He used her in New England waters and took her to the Bahamas, winters. On one of her trips back to this yard one spring early in the 1960s, she disappeared with all hands. I don't know that any trace of her was ever found.

Design Number 277A
Length Overall: 39 feet 6 inches
Length on Waterline: 32 feet
Beam: 11 feet 7 inches
Draft: 4 feet 6 inches
Sail Area: 797 square feet
Displacement: 16,400 pounds

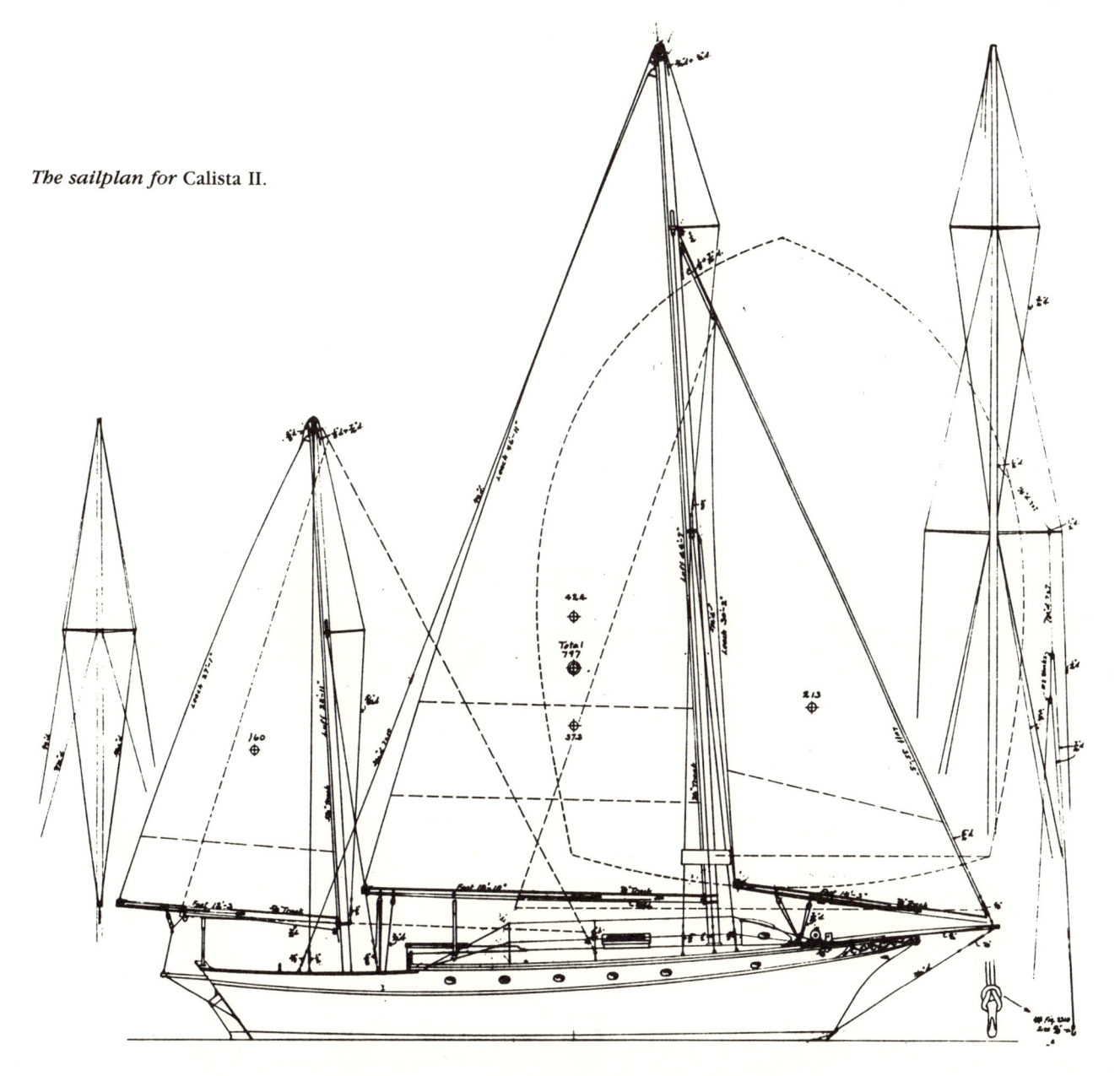

The sailplan for Calista II.

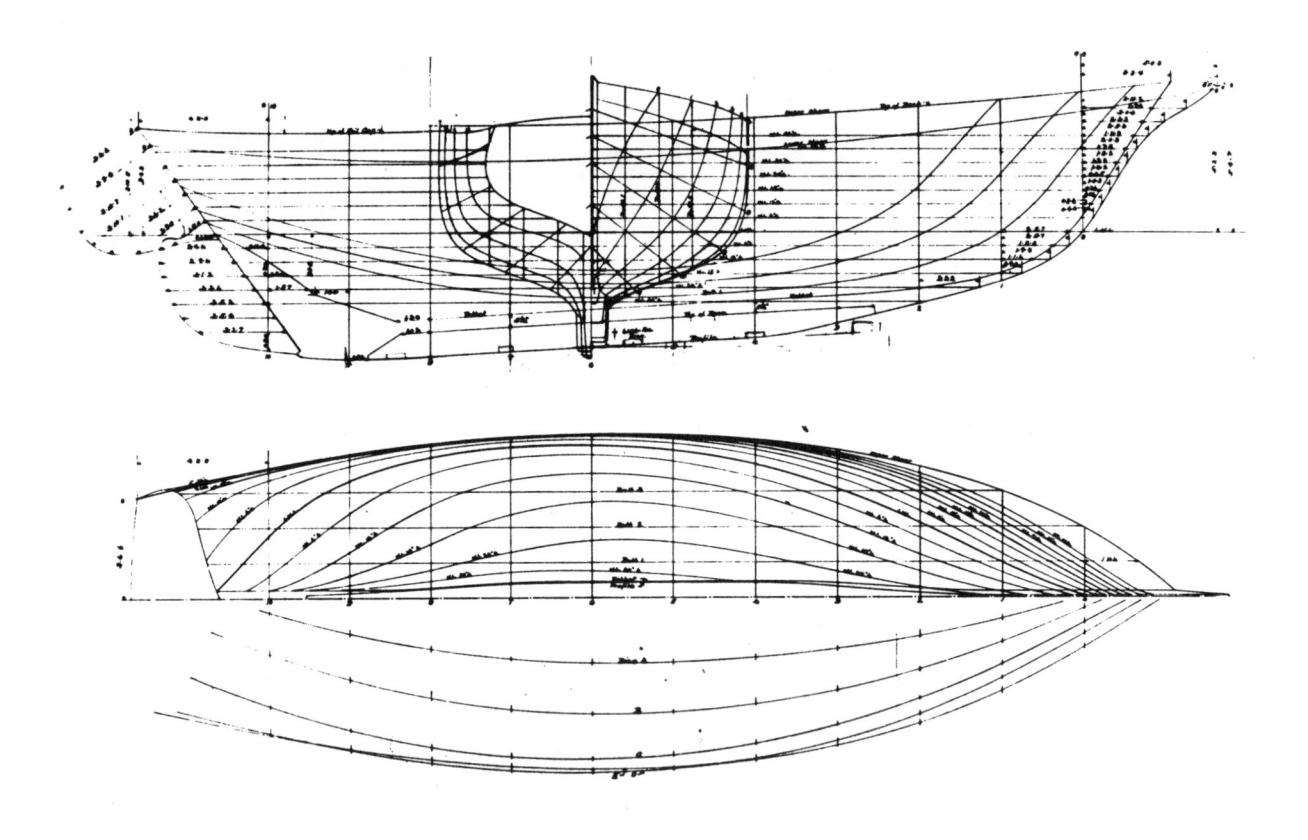

The lines drawings and construction details for Calista II.

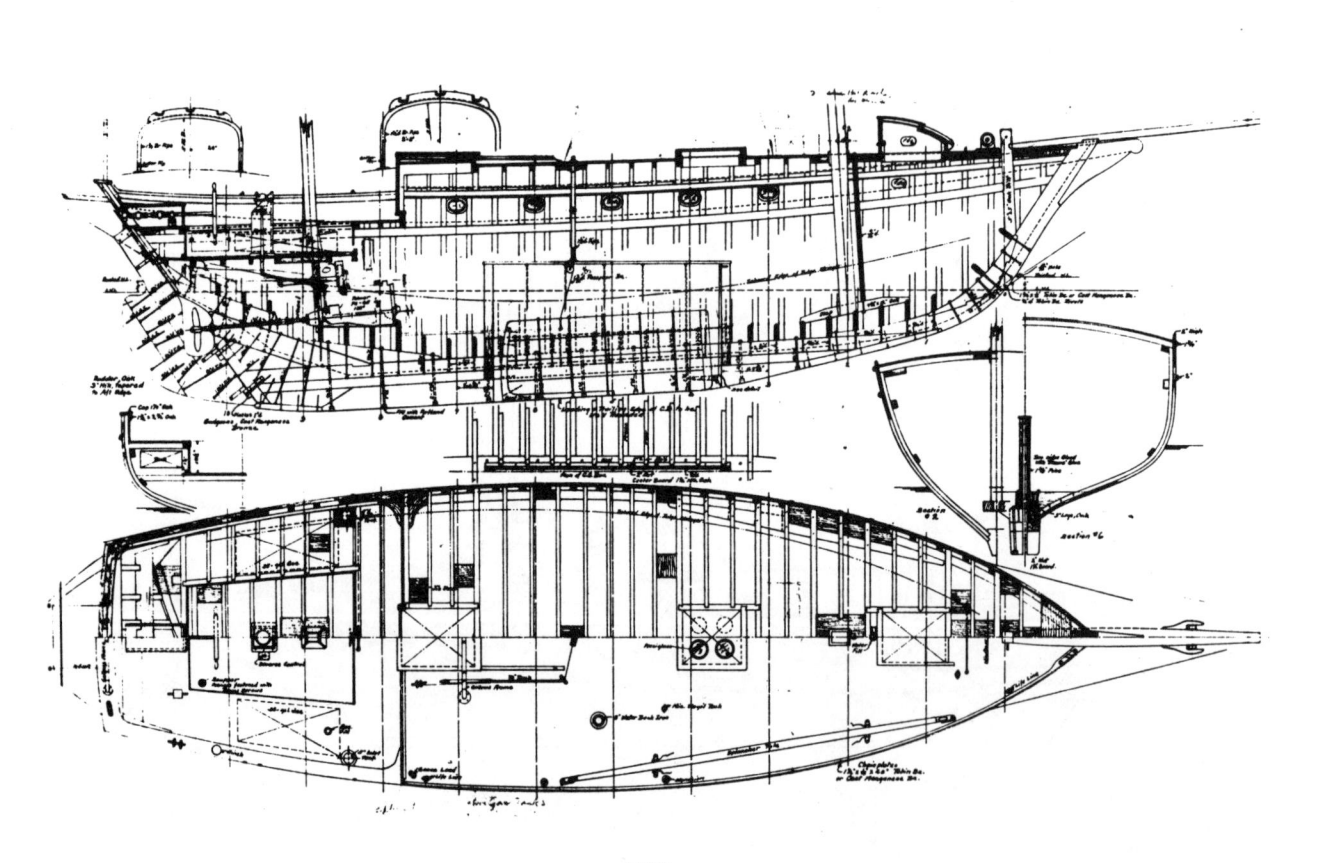

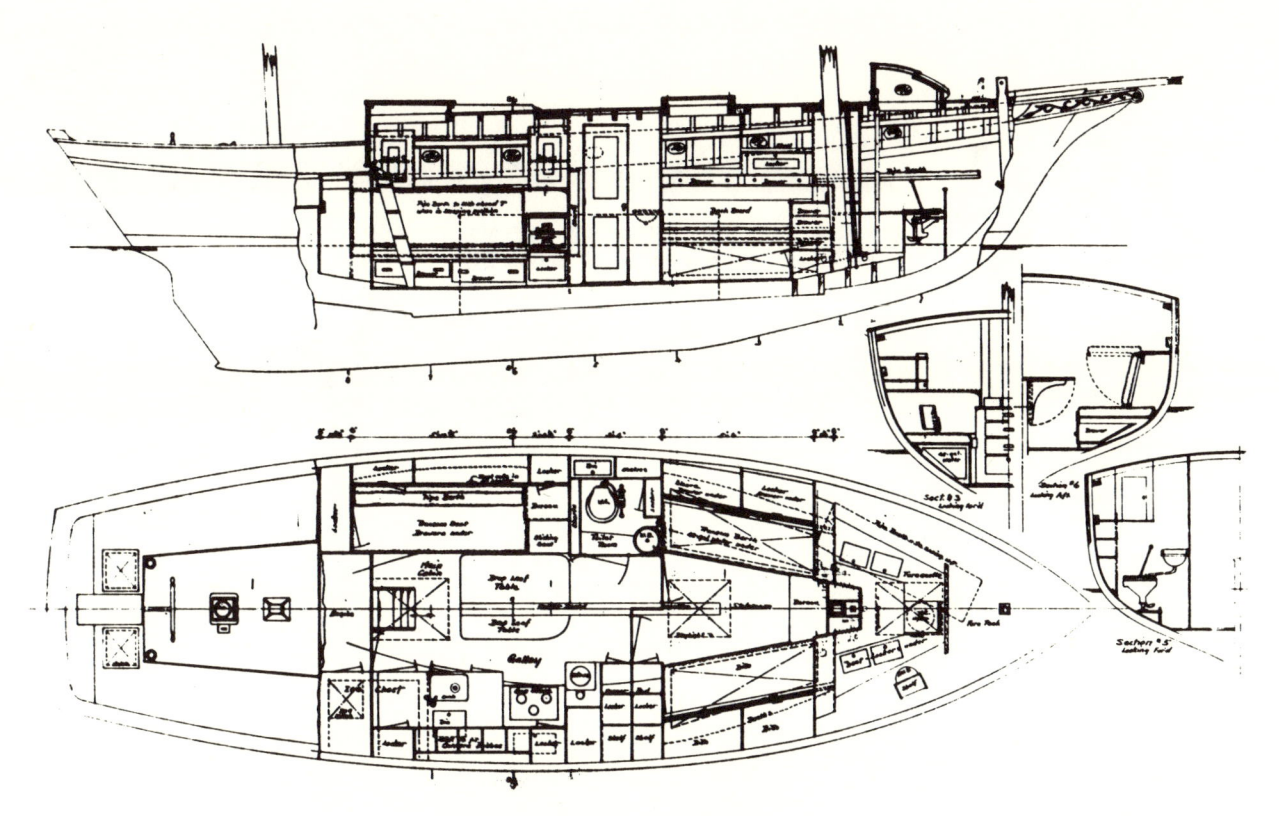

The accommodations for Calista II.

Calista II, *under sail.*

280 SALLEE ROVER

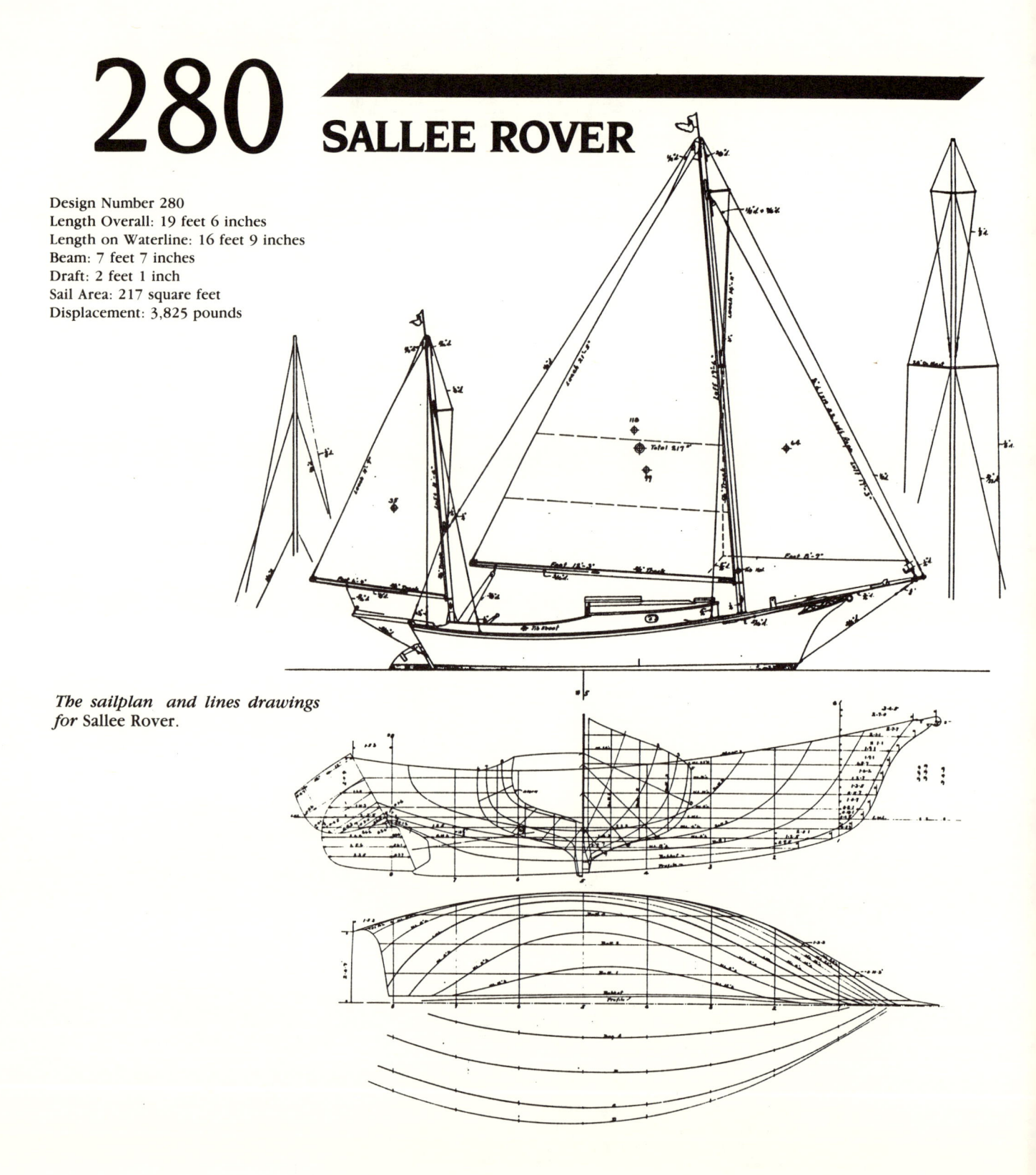

Design Number 280
Length Overall: 19 feet 6 inches
Length on Waterline: 16 feet 9 inches
Beam: 7 feet 7 inches
Draft: 2 feet 1 inch
Sail Area: 217 square feet
Displacement: 3,825 pounds

The sailplan and lines drawings for Sallee Rover.

Sallee Rover was built in Manchester for S.J. Dimock. She was heavily built, because Dimock didn't want any outside ballast, and rather than use a lot of inside ballast, we put the weights into the hull to pull her down to her designed

Number 280's sailplan under a sloop rig.

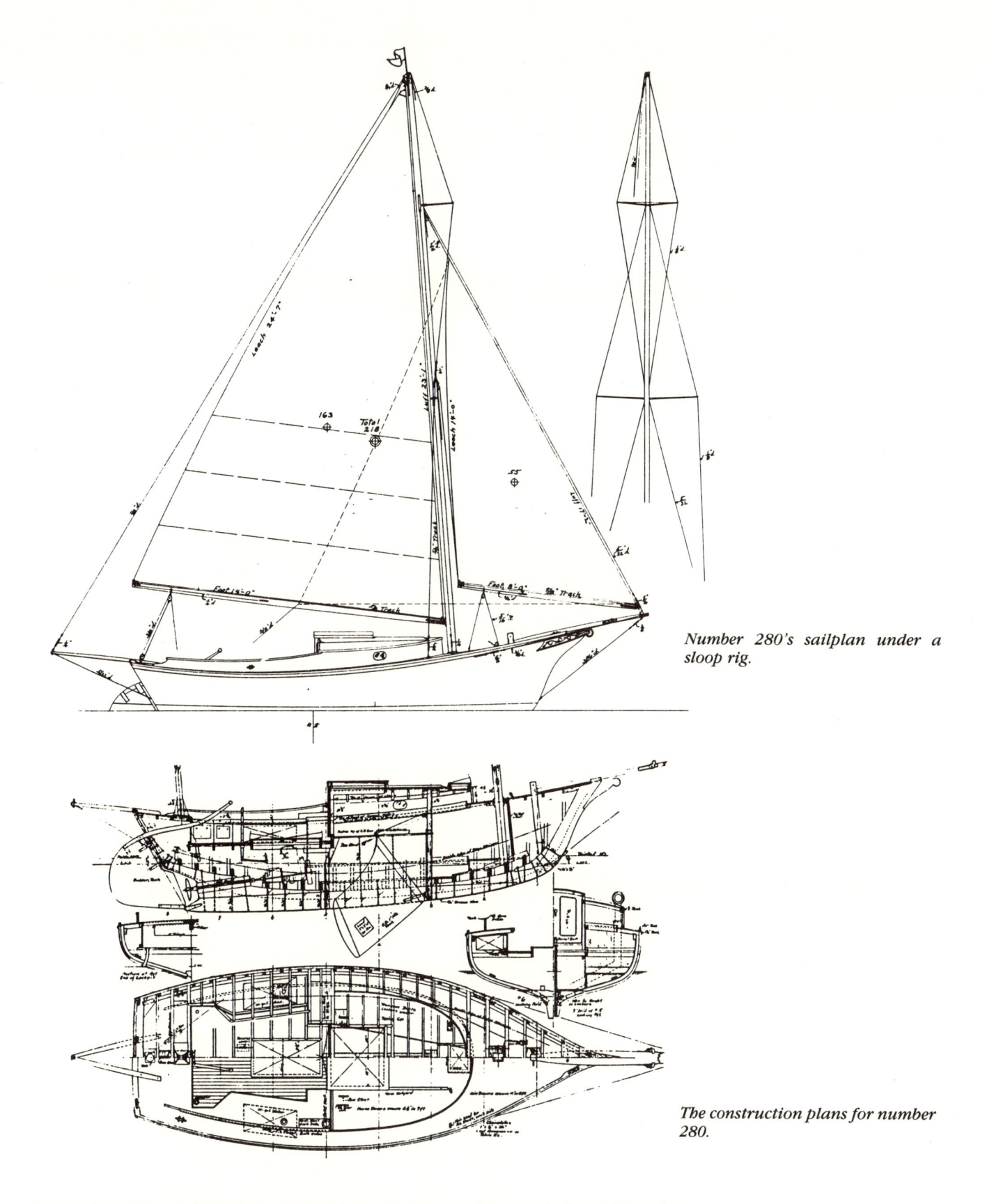

The construction plans for number 280.

lines. She only carried 300 pounds of lead inside. A single-cylinder Palmer six-horsepower furnished auxiliary power. Number 300, *Quahog,* was the same boat, built by Myron Cowden in Amesbury, Mass., for Roger Merrill, Jr., in 1950.

Sallee Rover.

283

Design Number 283
Length Overall: 19 feet 5 inches
Length on Waterline:
18 feet ½ inch
Beam: 6 feet 8 inches
Draft: 1 foot 5 inches
Displacement: 2,100 pounds

This handy little outboard cruiser was built for Paul Whitin in 1955 by Morrison Boat Shop of Berwick, Me. Power was provided by a Mercury 18-horsepower. She was of strip construction, using ¾-inch-by-¾-inch pine strips glued and edge fastened. Paul was very pleased with the boat's performance in bad weather. He went from this to the big 30-foot Long Shore with two outboards, then to a sailboat. He also had us build another from design number 283 (the plans for which he still has) and cruised and trailered her all up and down the coast from Maine to Maryland.

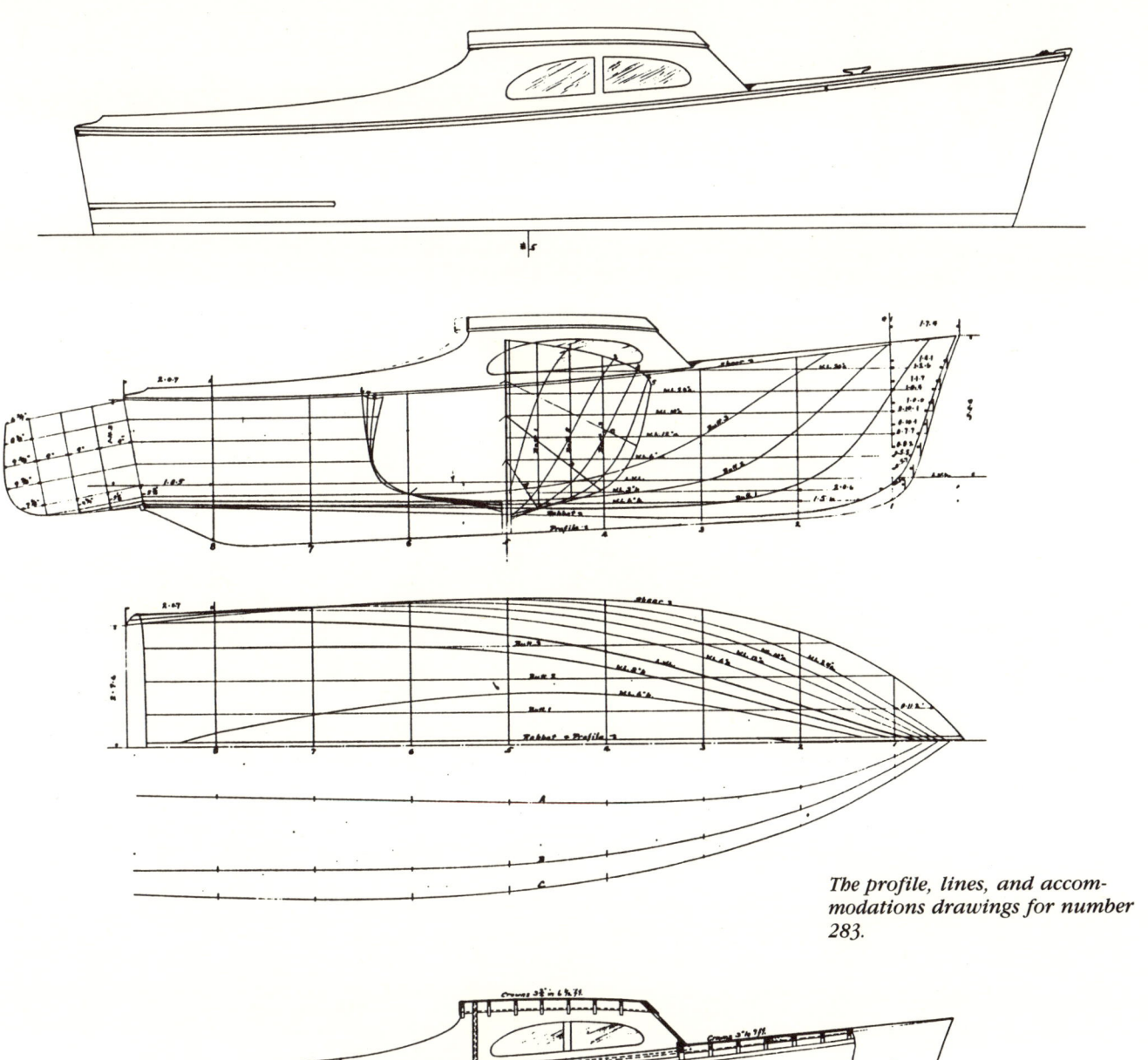

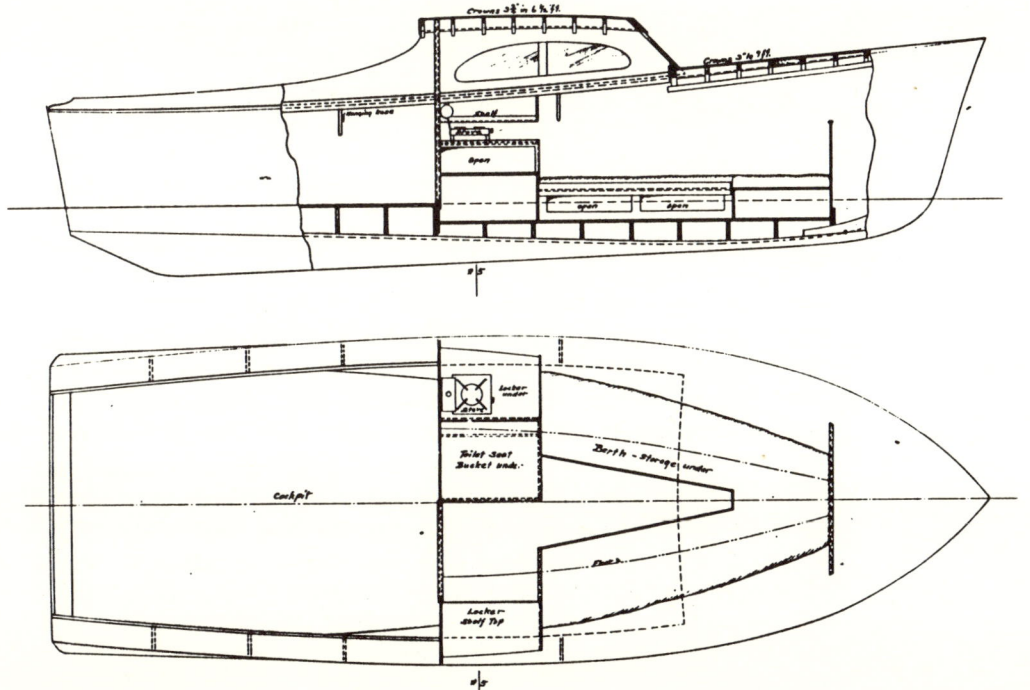

The profile, lines, and accommodations drawings for number 283.

284 CHIEF GRAMATAN

Design Number 284
Length Overall: 27 feet 3 inches
Length on Waterline: 22 feet 8 inches
Beam: 11 feet
Draft: 3 feet
Sail Area: 400 square feet
Displacement: 8,740 pounds

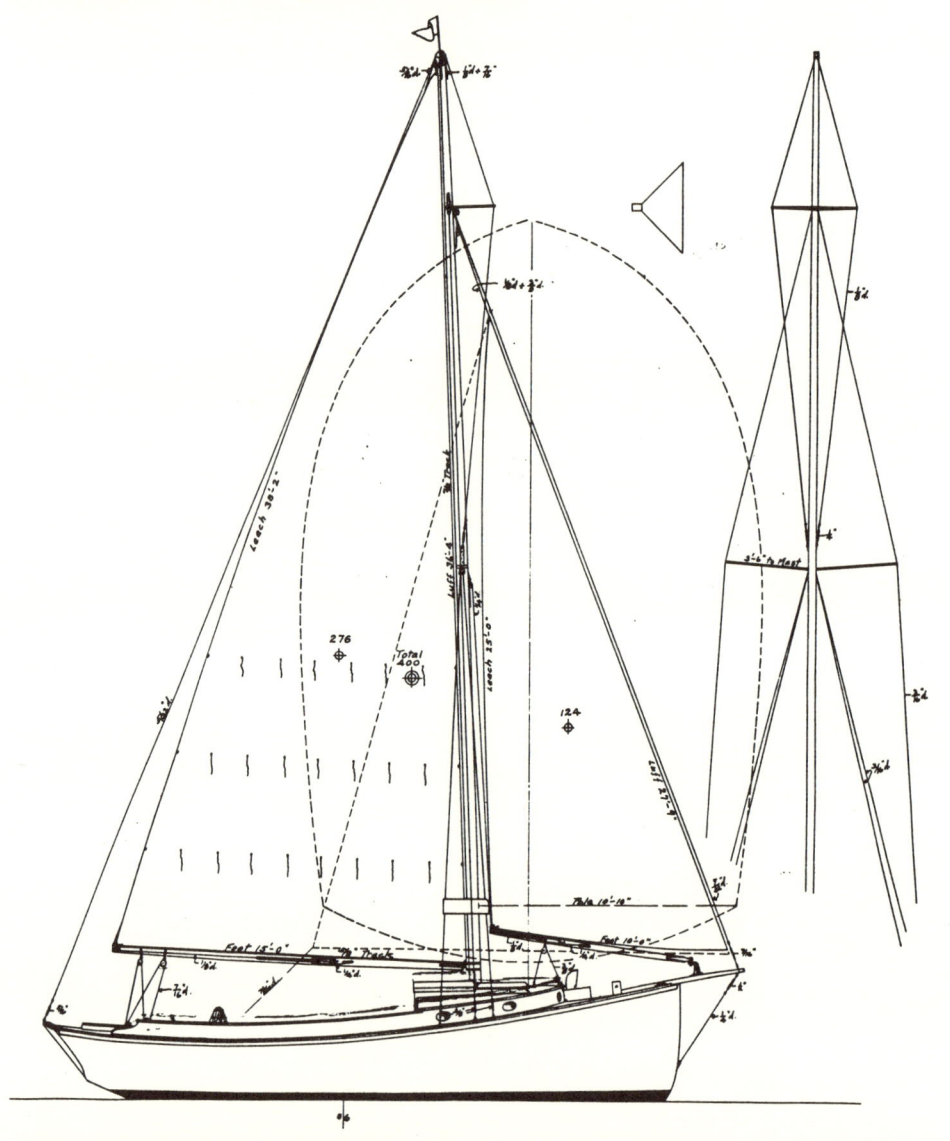

The sailplan for Chief Gramatan.

  Chief Gramatan was designed in 1954 for Jackson Chambers. Cecil Bigelow of Monument Beach in Plymouth, Mass., was the builder, but Hurricane Carol wiped his yard out before the boat was completed. The boat was hardly scratched, even though one of the buildings came down on top of her. She was taken over to the Chester Crosby yard in Osterville and completed for a 1955 launching. A Lathrop LH4 with reduction gear furnished auxiliary power.
  With a cockpit 11 feet long and 8½ feet wide, *Chief Gramatan* can sail an army. Her cabin, while little over 6 feet in length, can accommodate a couple for limited cruising. The *Chief* is distinguished by excellent detailing and choice of materials. The decks, coamings, stavings, hatches, rails, centerboard trunk, rudder, and interior are all upland teak — 1,200 board feet in all. Her topsides are white cedar; her bottom select cypress; and her framing white oak. No plywood

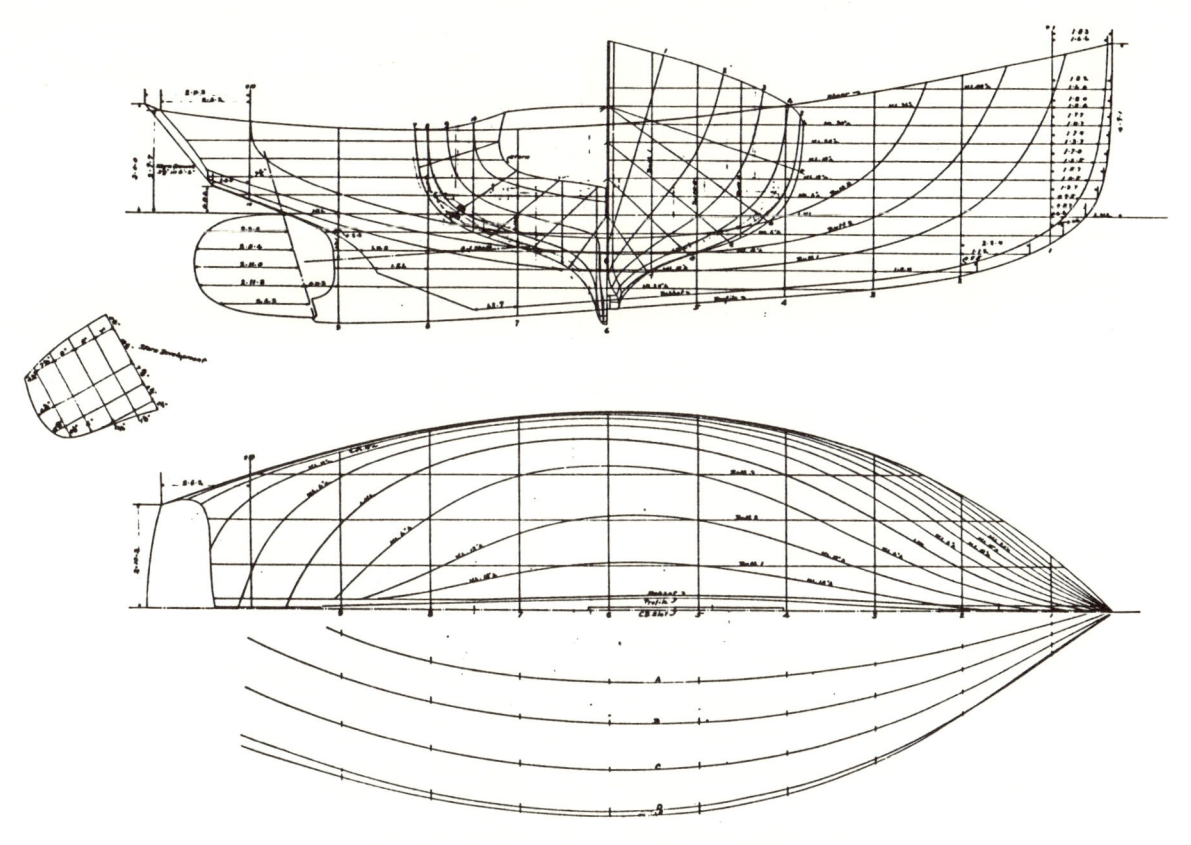

The lines and construction plans for Chief Gramatan.

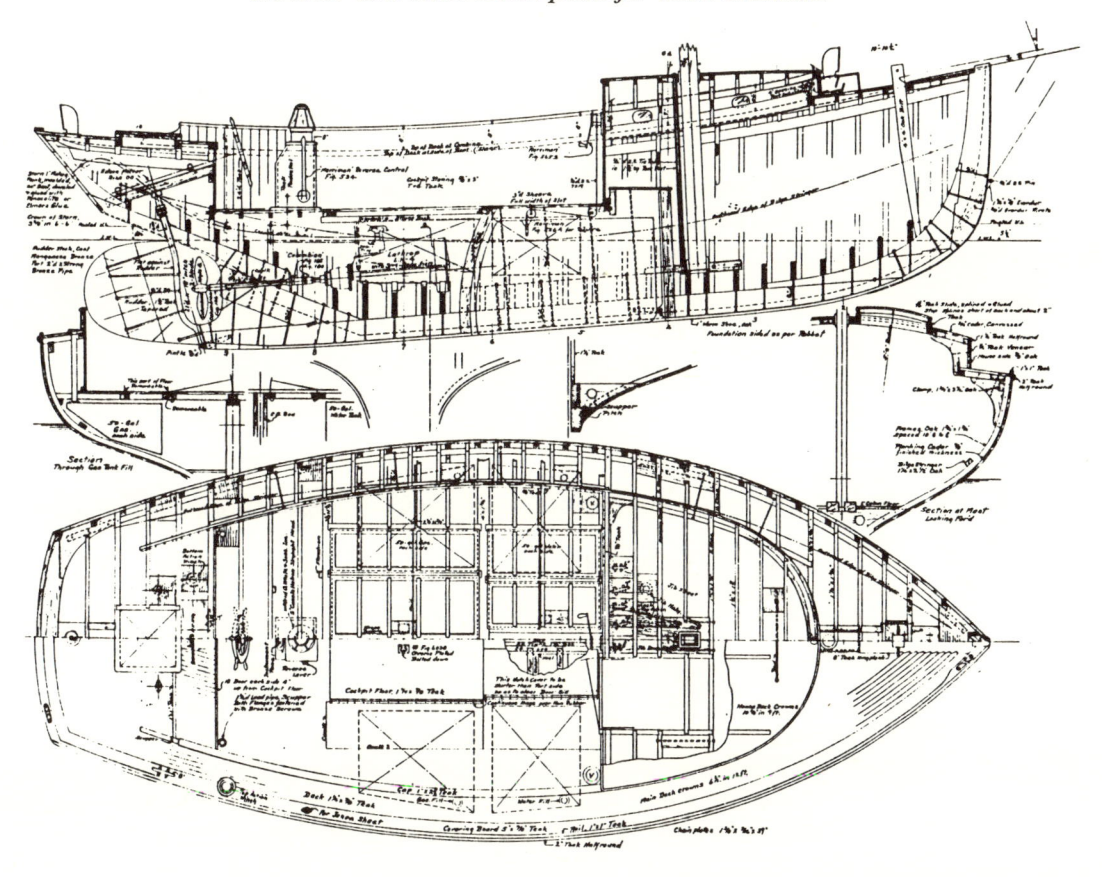

251

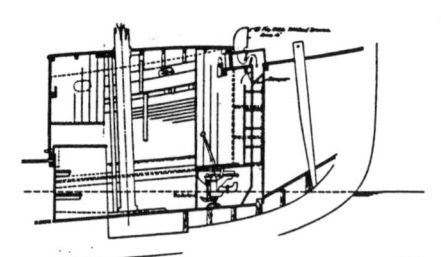

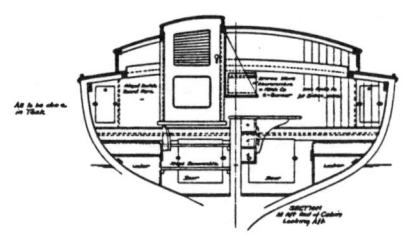

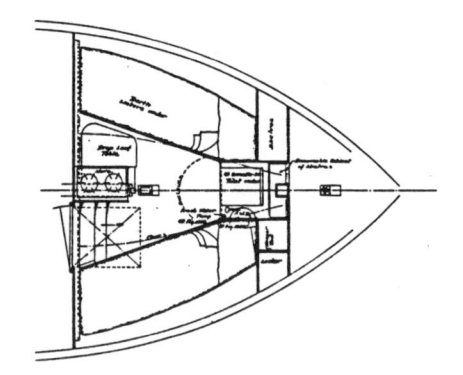

The forward accommodations plans for number 284.

was used in her. She carries 100 gallons each of fuel and water in monel tanks and is fastened with monel screws and bolts.

The many pages of correspondence between Dad and the original owner give fascinating insight into the evolution of the design. She started out as a marconi cat, 22 feet by 11 feet, with a vertical stern and boomkin. Because the owner wanted to do away with the boomkin at no penalty in sail area, and because the designer wanted to ease the lines, she gained a counter stern and afterdeck and grew to 27 feet. To cope with the choppy waters of Vineyard Sound, my father gave her a very hollow entrance with ample reserve buoyancy.

Three of the most famous catboat builders assisted in her creation. Manuel Schwartz molded her, laid her keel, and left. Cecil Bigelow laid a new keel, altered the molds, and built her up to the deck, only to lose his shed and business to Hurricane Carol. Chester A. Crosby finished the deck, accommodations, wiring, and engine installation and commissioned her.

My father was pleased with the *Chief* when he wrote on April 4, 1954:

> On last Thursday afternoon, I went down to Crosby's together with Ike Manchester and we tried out *Chief Gramatan*. Everybody we had aboard seemed enthused with her performance. I could hardly get the wheel away from Chester Crosby. It was blowing real hard and as a matter of fact if Ike Manchester had not been there, I would have questioned whether or not to have taken her out.

The present owners, Lee Eiseman and Mary Runkel, have cruised in her from Shelter Island and Martha's Vineyard to Frenchman's Bay and enjoyed daysailing from my father's boatyard for several summers. They think she's the loveliest day boat afloat.

291 DOROTHY

Design Number 291
Length Overall: 36 feet 10 inches
Length on Waterline: 28 feet 2 inches
Beam: 10 feet 8 inches
Draft: 2 feet 11 inches
Sail Area: 635 square feet
Displacement: 14,100 pounds

The presto-type schooner *Dorothy* was designed in 1961. She was built for Robert Duncan by Reid's Shipyard in Boothbay, Me. Some of the ballast was outside in the form of a 3,000-pound cast-iron shoe. This made more room for inside ballast, but most importantly, it gave solid protection to the bottom of the boat and centerboard slot. Auxiliary power was furnished by a four-cylinder Palmer I H 60 with a two-to-one reduction gear.

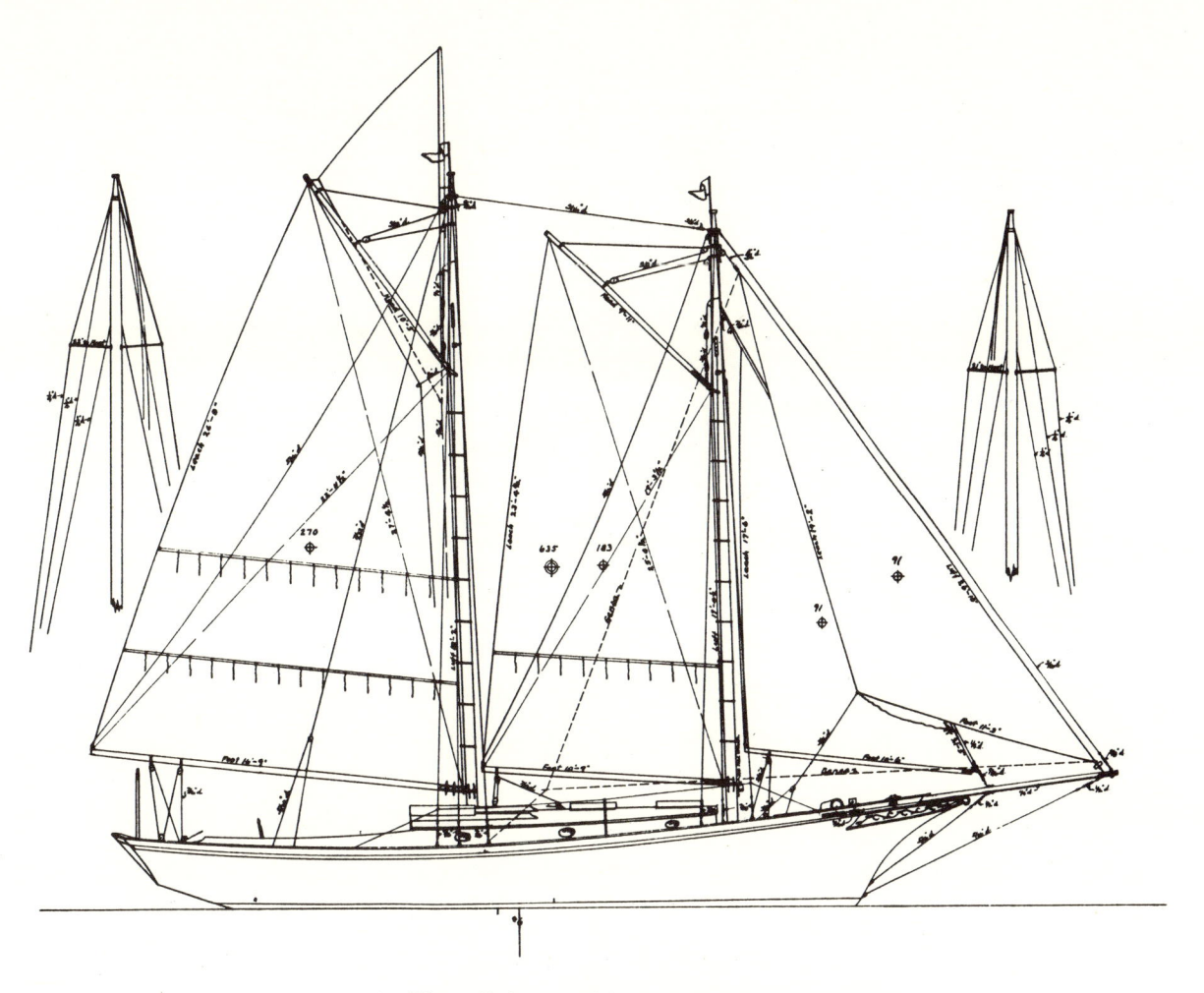

The sailplan and lines drawings for Dorothy.

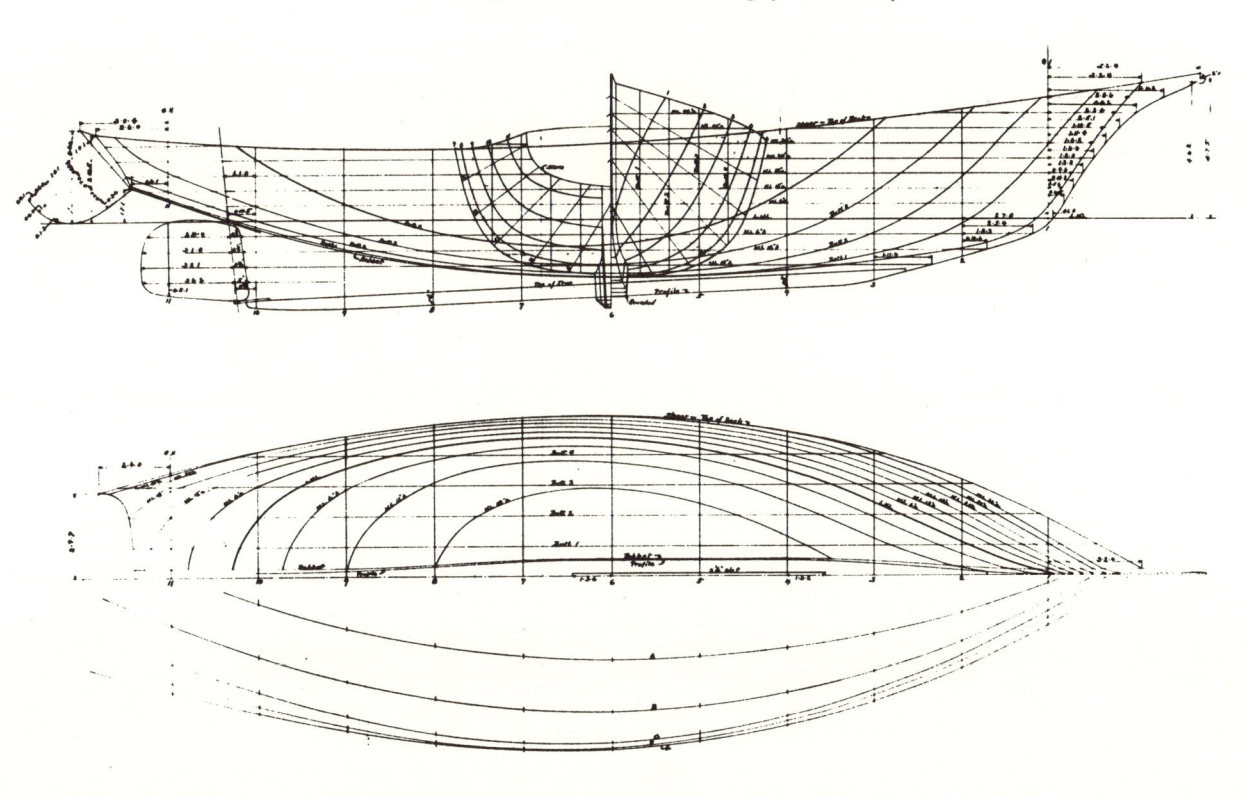

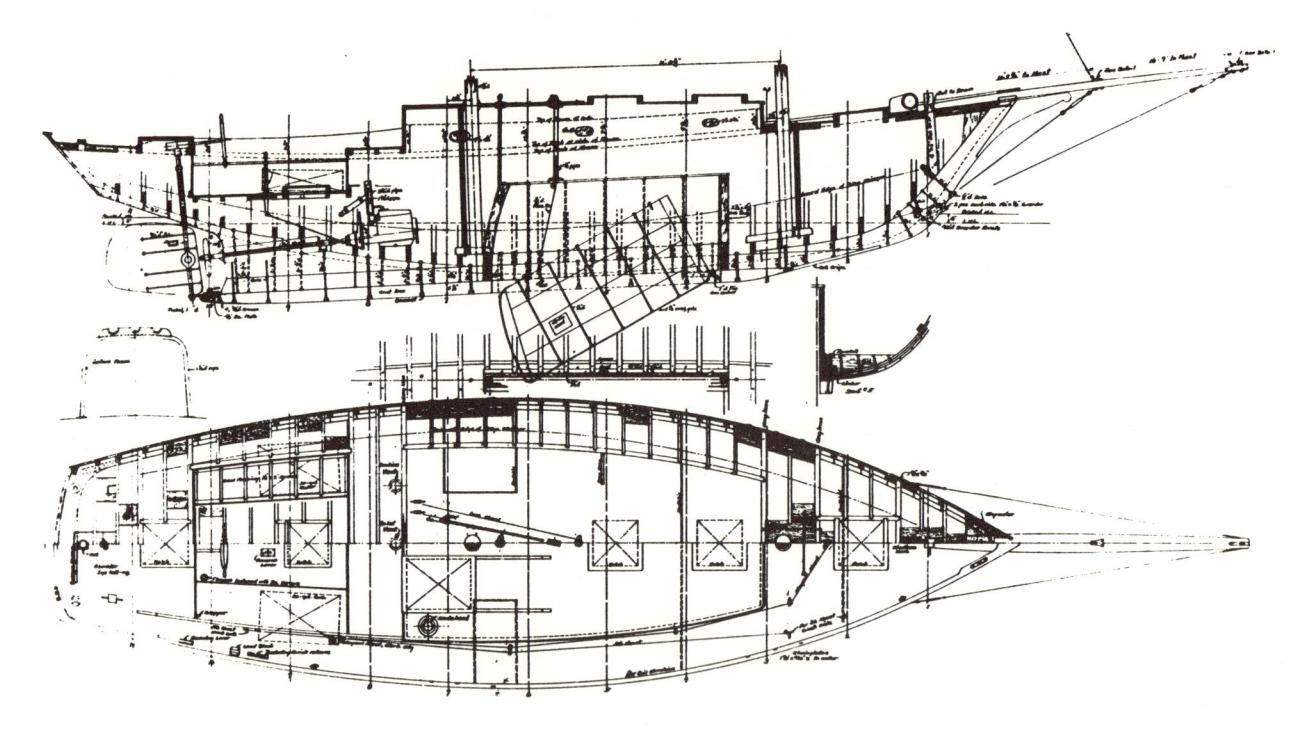

The construction plans and Dorothy *under sail.*

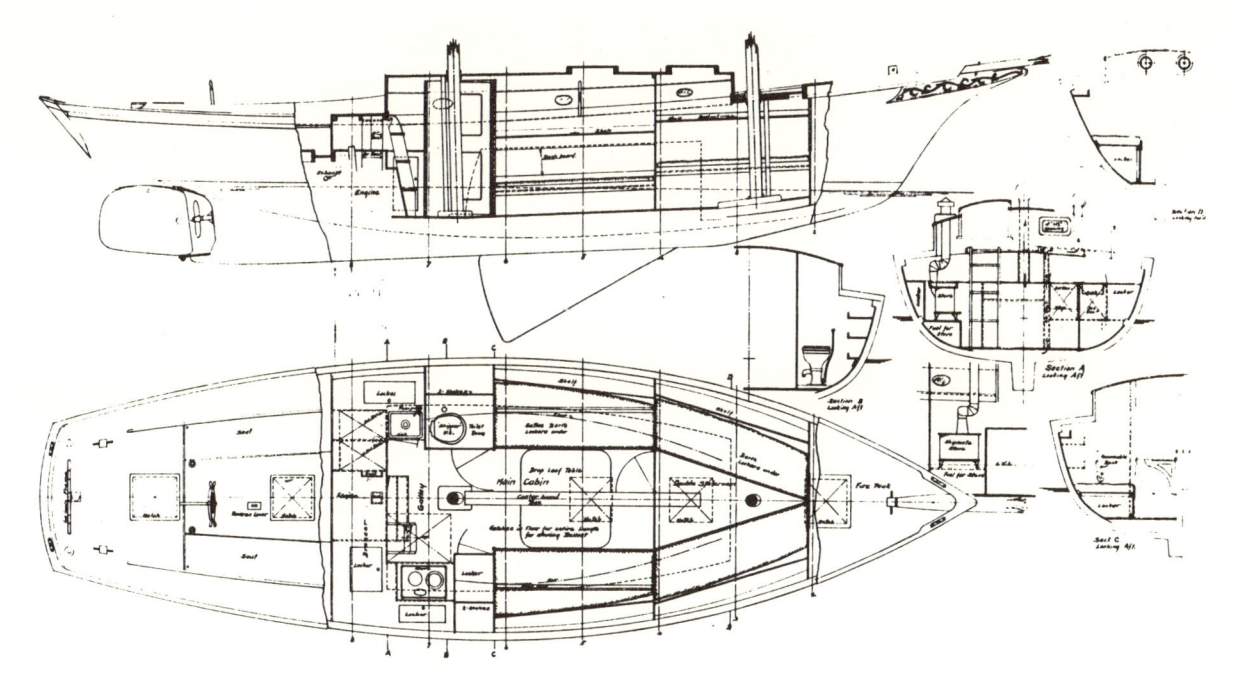

Dorothy's accommodations plans.

STROMBOLI 292

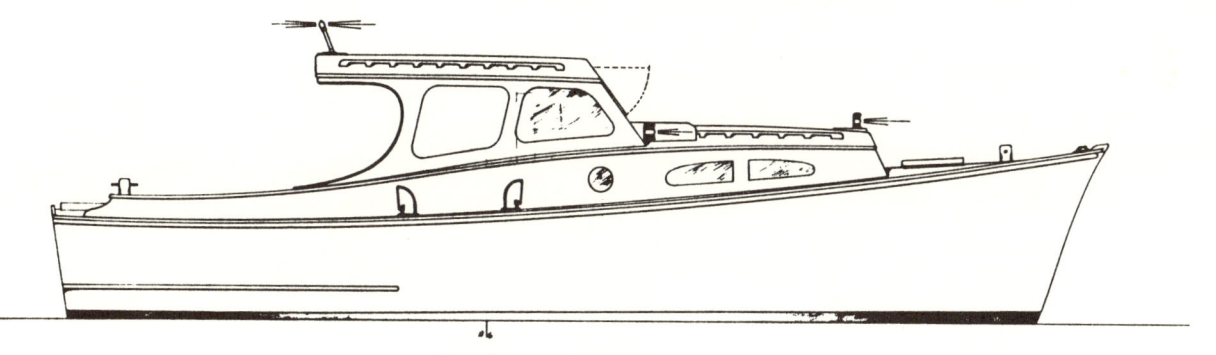

Number 292's profile.

There were at least three boats built around here from these lines. One was *Stromboli,* built for Joseph Bonsignor of Wakefield, Mass., by William Smith of Amesbury, Mass., in 1956. The other two were built in Kennebunkport, Me., by Reid & Prendergast. Abbot Prendergast's boat, the *Lively Lady,* was the same as *Stromboli* but with a little more power. The *Long Shore* was built for Paul Whitin. She was glued strip construction using 1¼-inch cedar strips and had twin 70-horsepower Mercury outboards for power. She cruised at 22 m.p.h. with a top speed of 28 m.p.h., almost 10 m.p.h. faster than *Lively Lady* with inboard power. The acceleration of this boat was unbelievable.

Design Number 292
Length Overall: 30 feet
Length on Waterline: 27 feet 5 inches
Beam: 10 feet 6 inches
Draft: 2 feet 8 inches
Displacement: 7,800 pounds

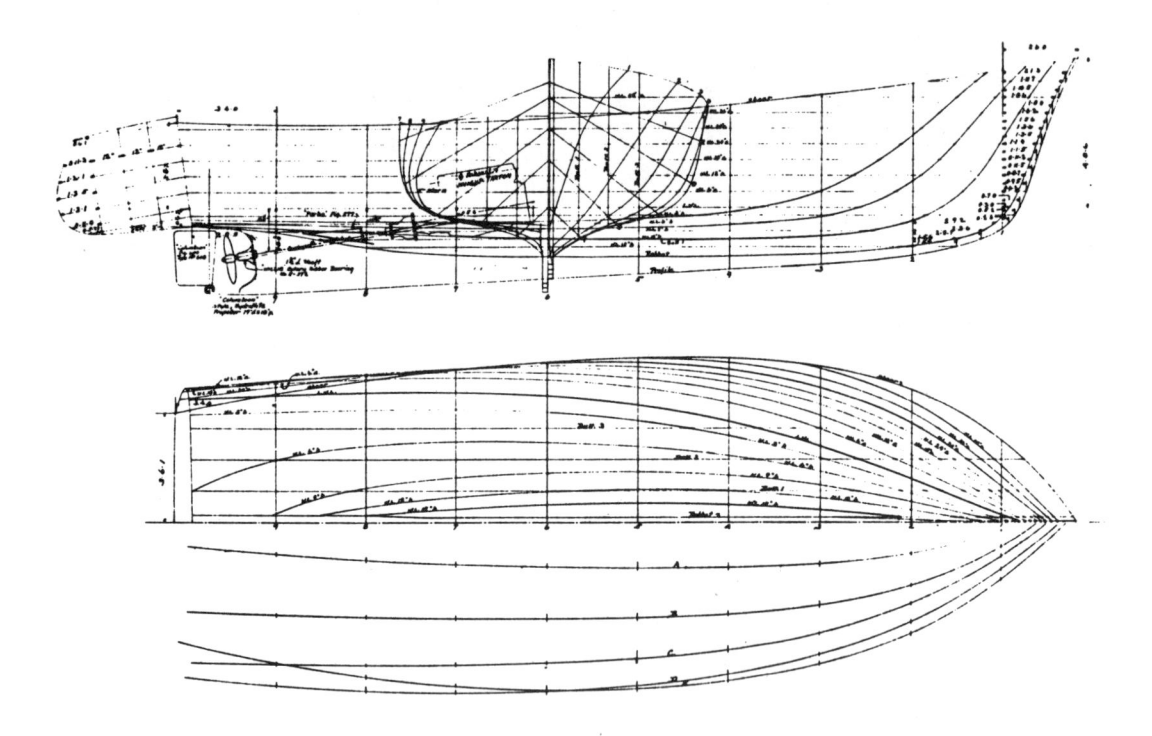

The lines, construction plans, and accommodations drawings for number 292.

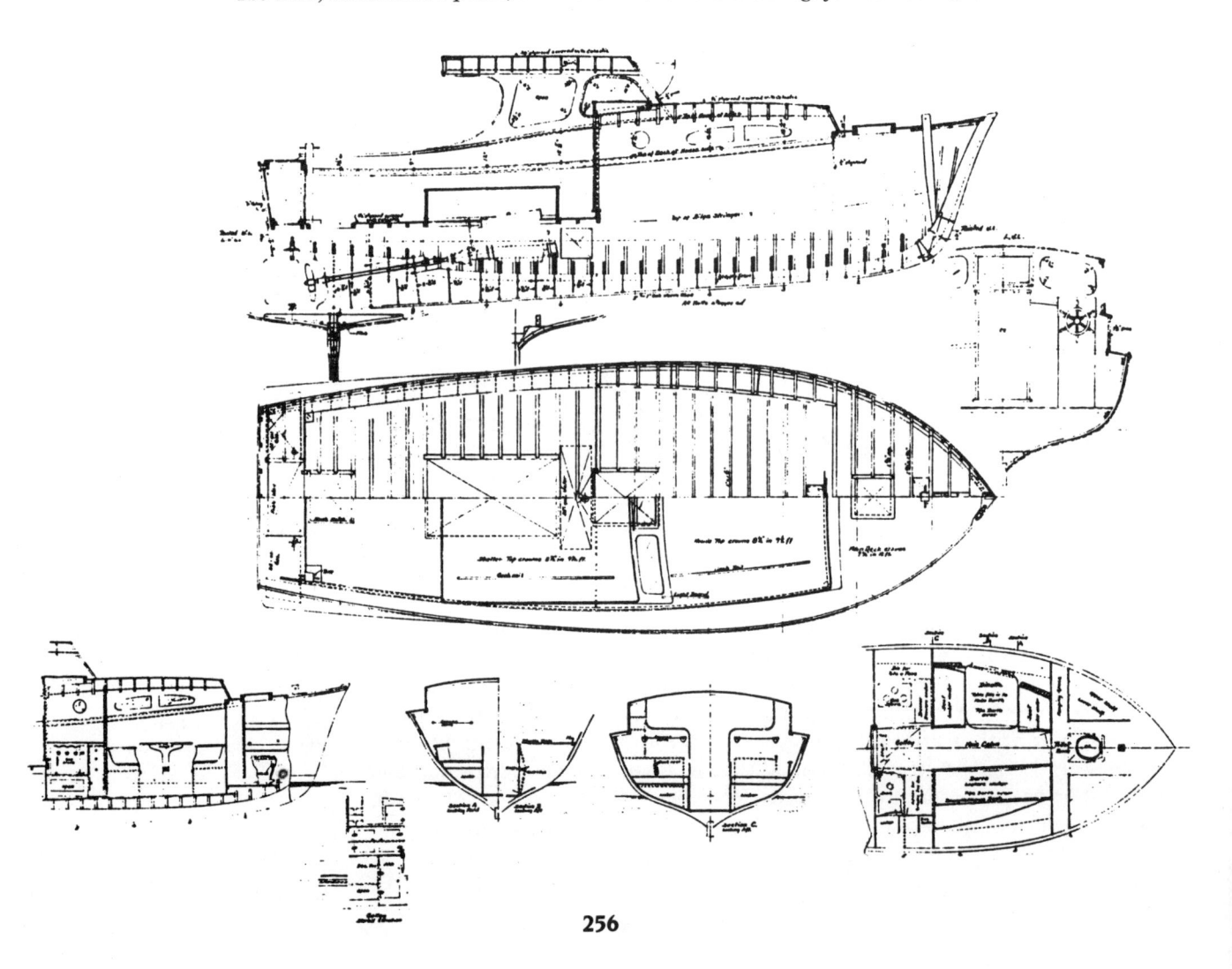

TORINO 297

Design Number 297
Length Overall: 33 feet
Length on Waterline: 26 feet 7 inches
Beam: 10 feet 10 inches
Draft: 4 feet
Sail Area: 615 square feet
Displacement: 15,300 pounds

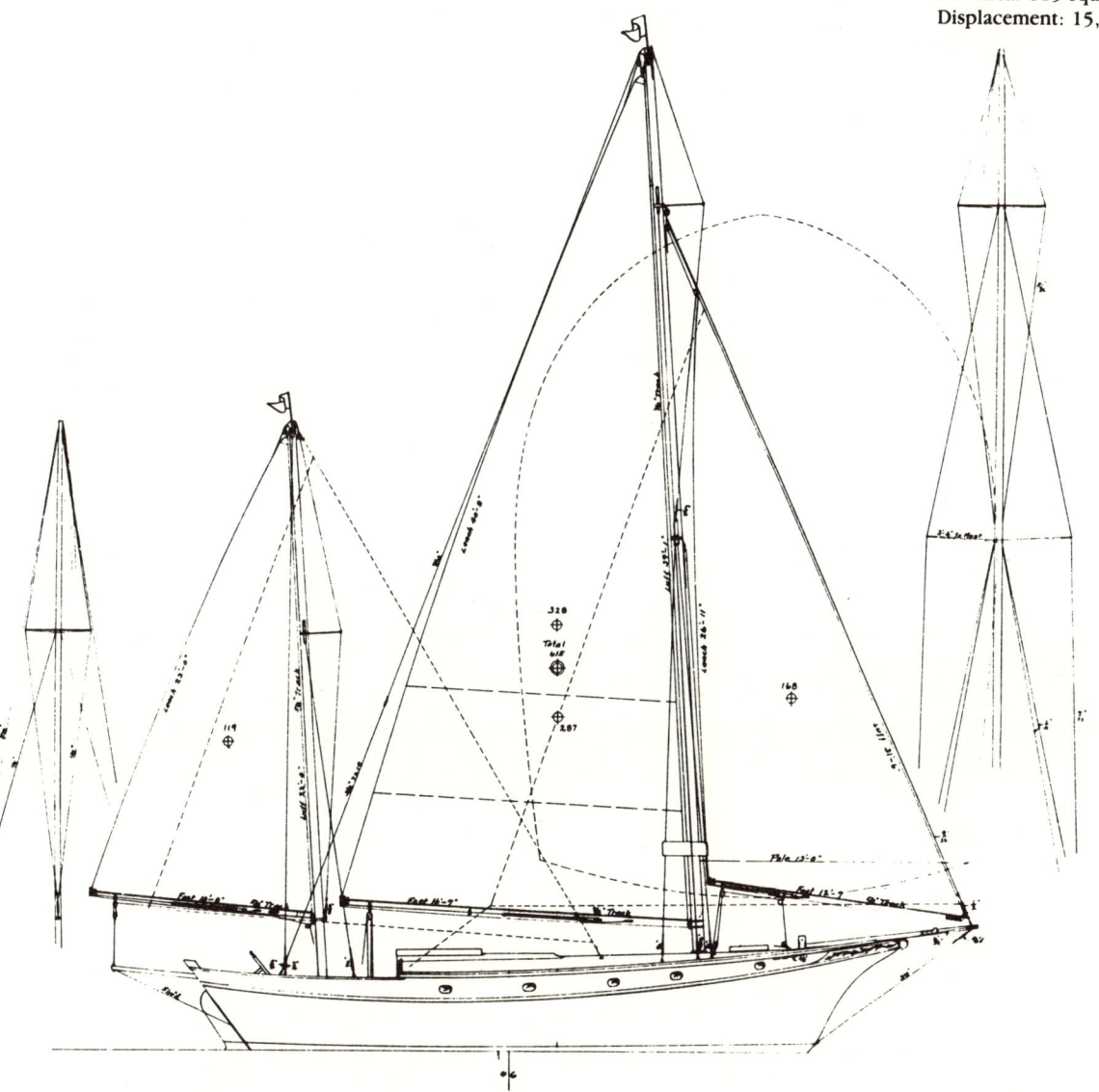

I built *Torino* for George Lee in 1956. Being of raised-deck construction, she has a lot of room below with a lot of locker space. Refrigeration was gained by building in portable iceboxes. With all three working sails on booms, she is easily handled. A Universal Utility Four with 2¼-to-1 reduction gear furnished auxiliary power. Number 317 shows her as a sloop.

The sail plan for Torino.

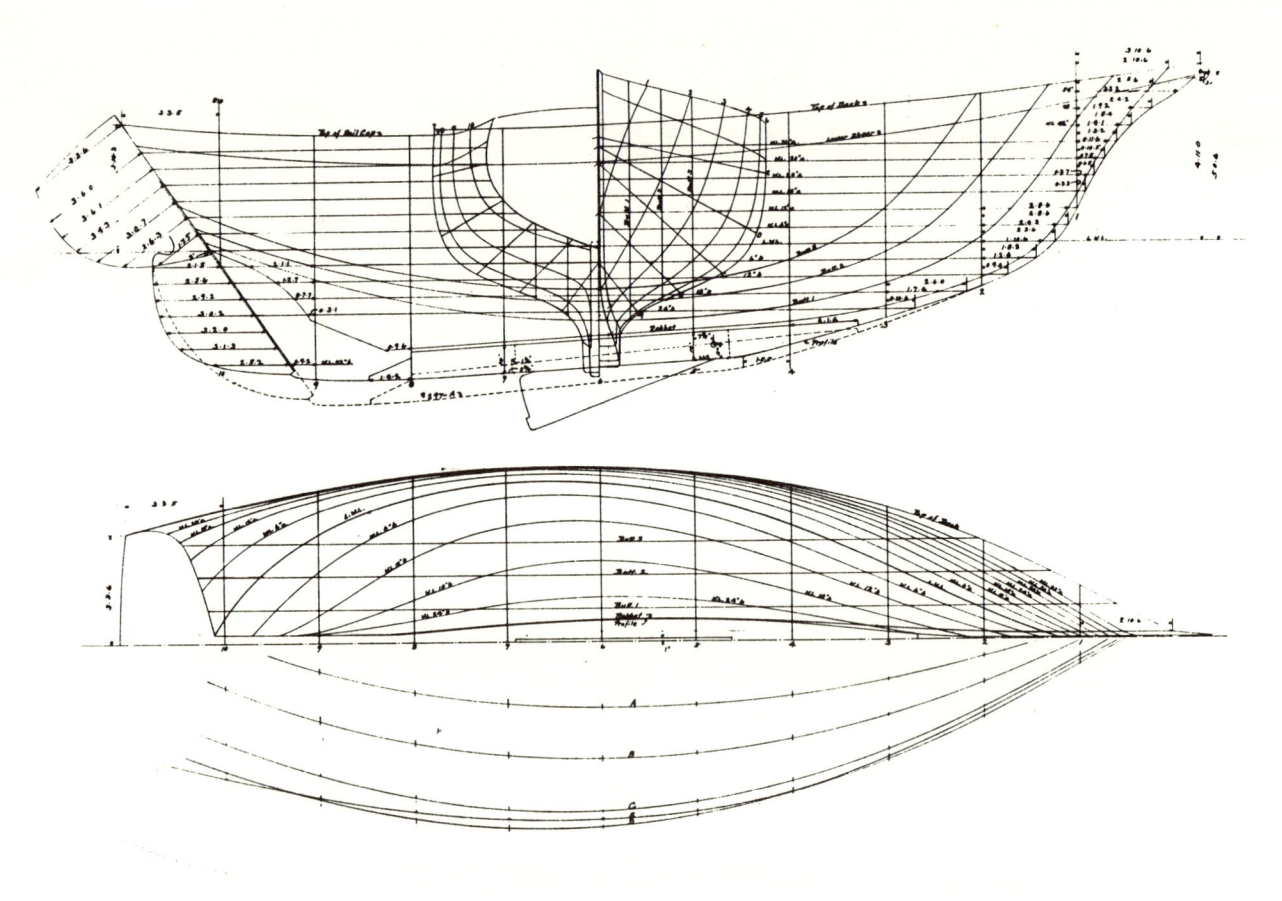

The lines drawings and construction plans for Torino.

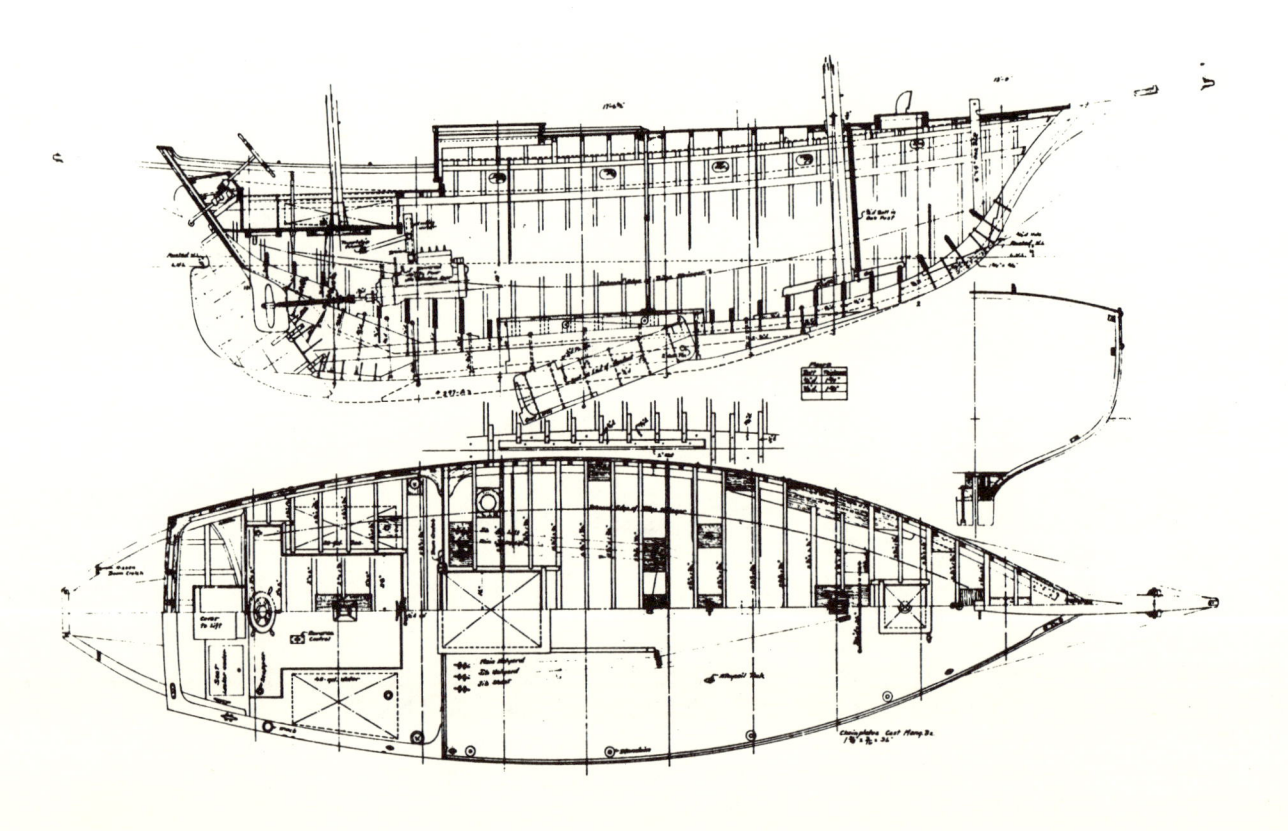

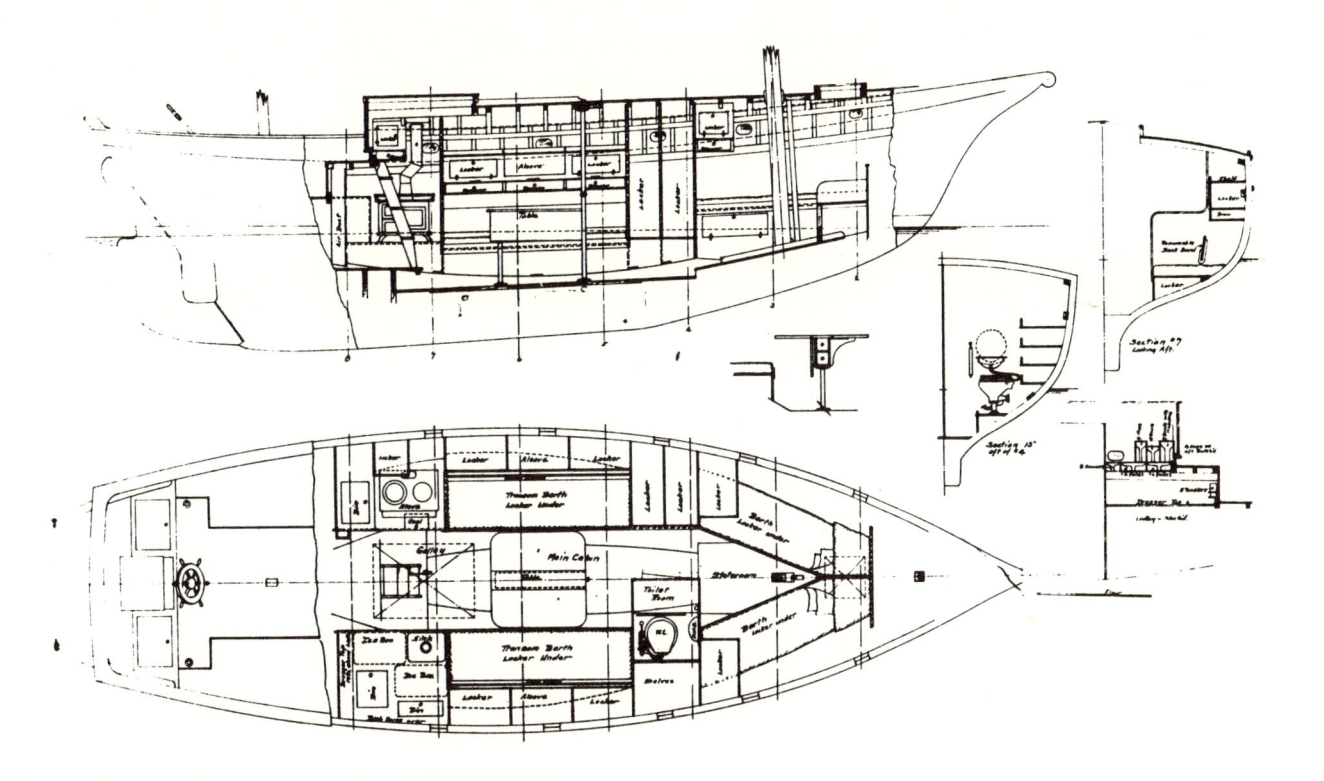

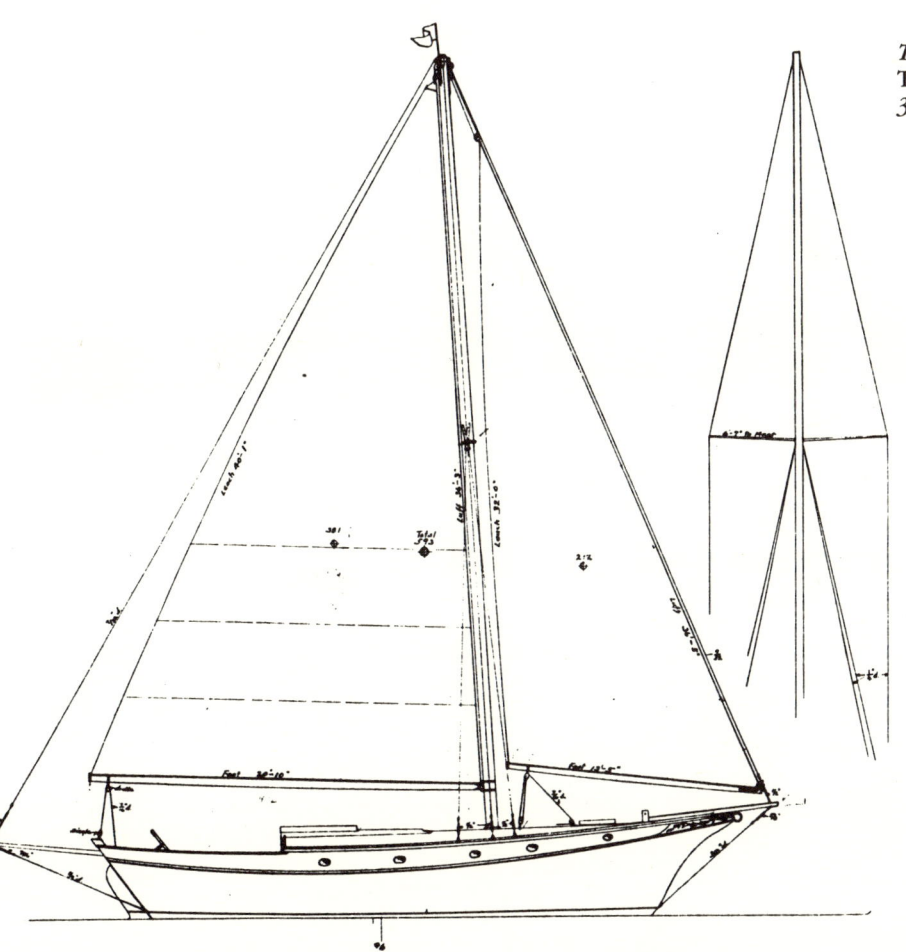

The accommodations drawings for Torino, *and the sailplan for number 317.*

259

Torino *under sail*.

GOLDEN EAGLE 301

Golden Eagle was built by Grandville Davis for Edward Earle in 1956. Built of cedar and oak with mahogany trim and Sitka spruce spars, she had, her owner reported, good sailing and handling qualities. With a 4BDMR-182 Buda Diesel swinging a two-blade, 22-inch-by-16-inch prop through a two-to-one reduction gear, she did 8.5 knots at 1,300 r.p.m. and 6.6 knots at 950 r.p.m.

Design Number 301
Length Overall: 40 feet 7 inches
Length on Waterline: 32 feet 9 inches
Beam : 11 feet 10 inches
Draft: 4 feet
Sail Area: 808 square feet
Displacement: 24,640 pounds

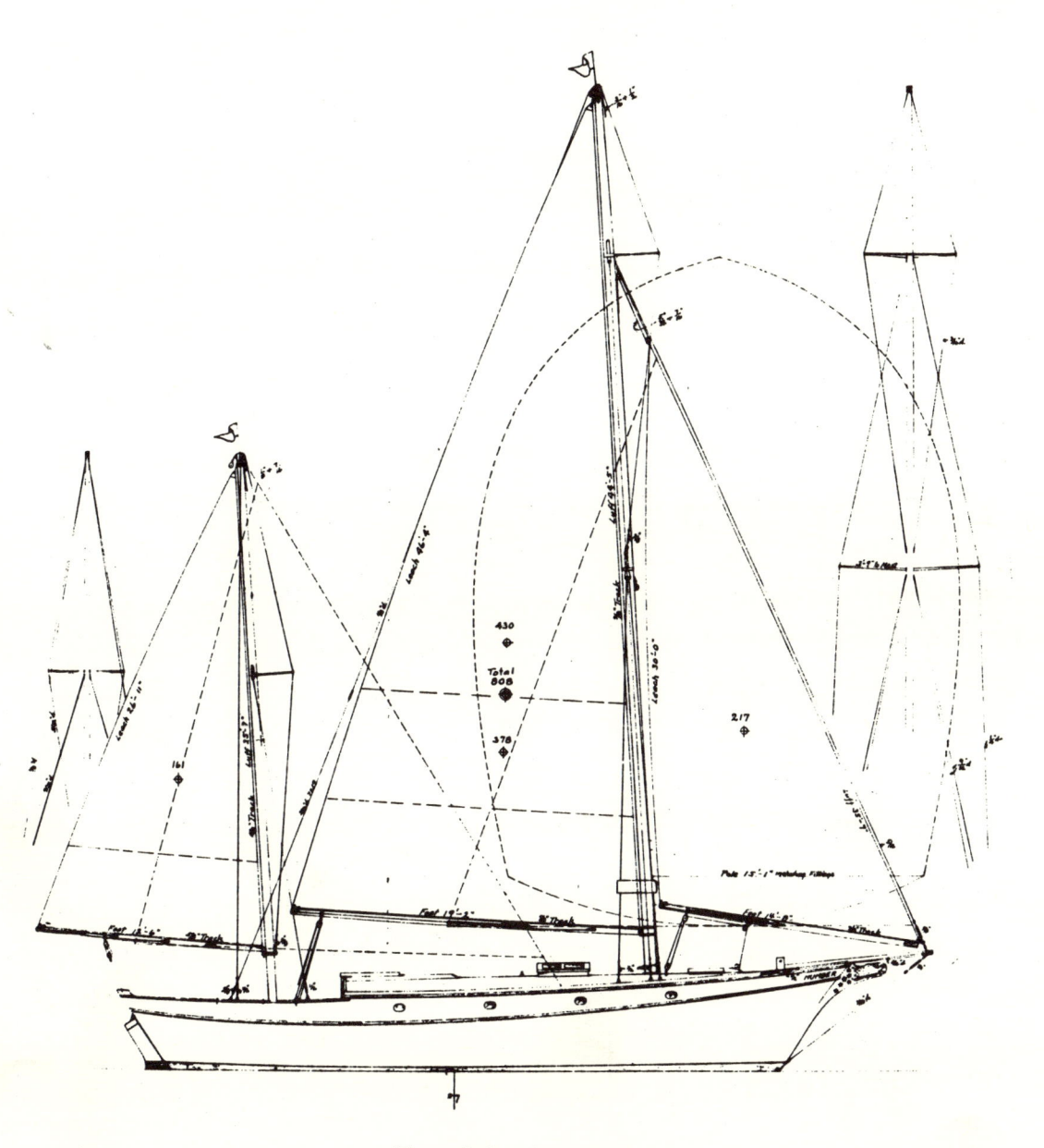

The sailplan for Golden Eagle.

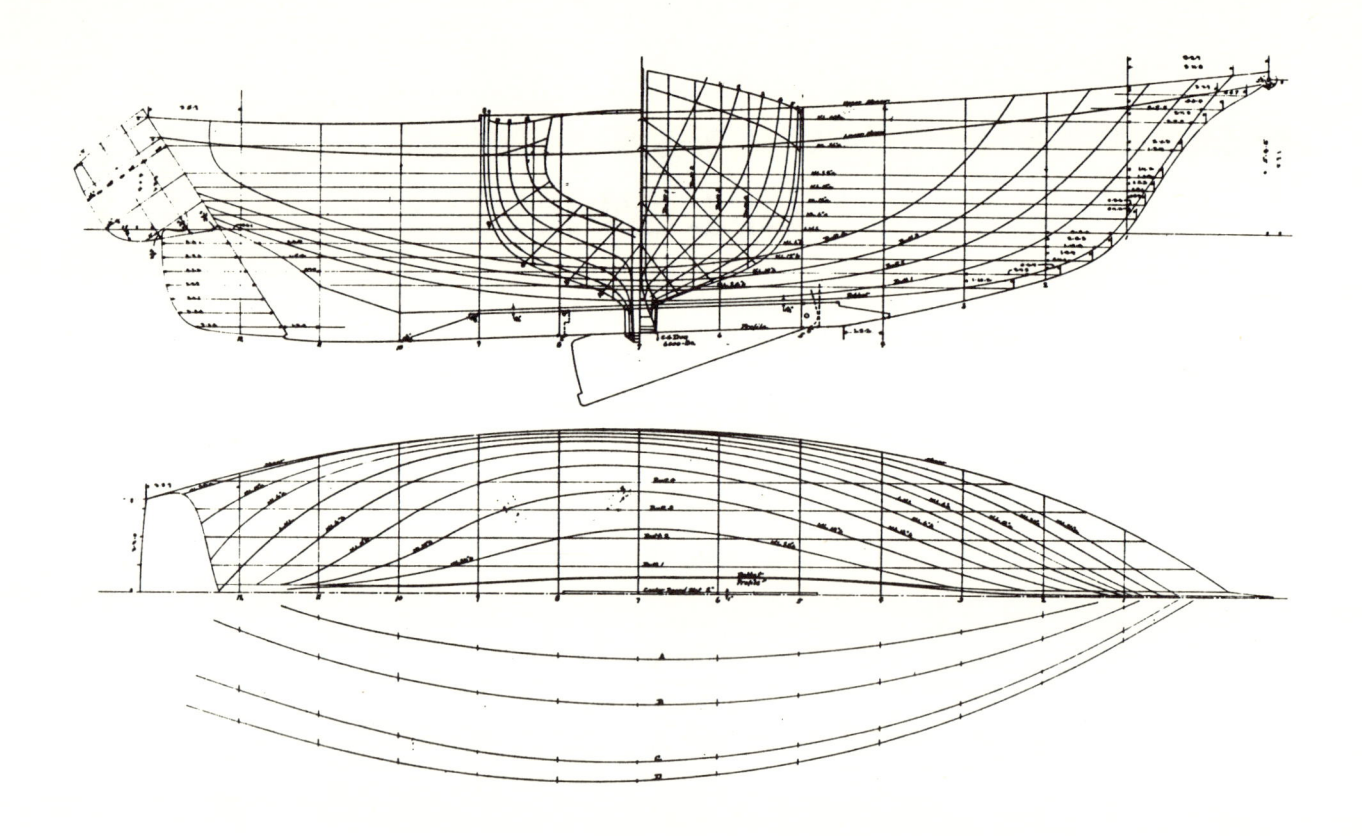

The lines drawings and construction drawings for Golden Eagle.

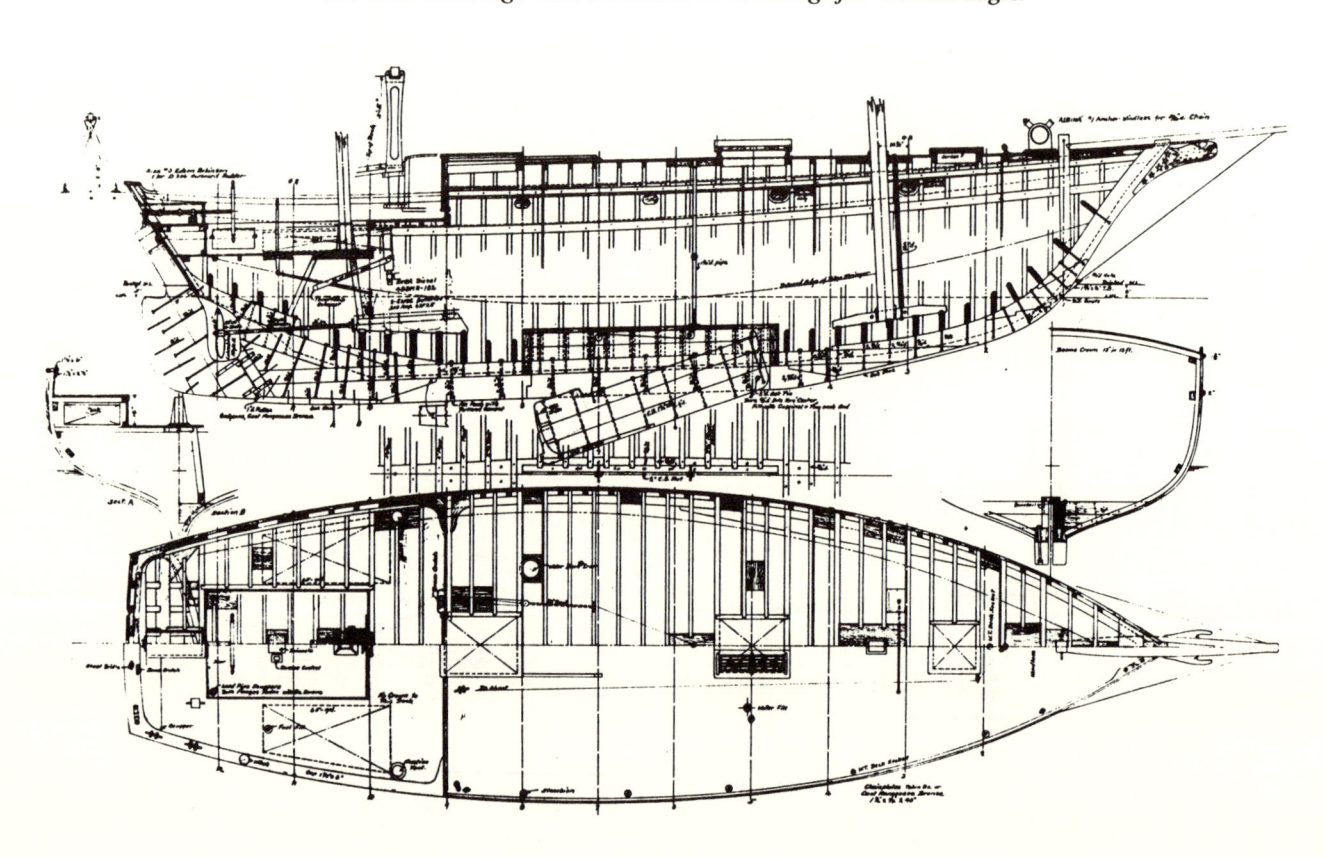

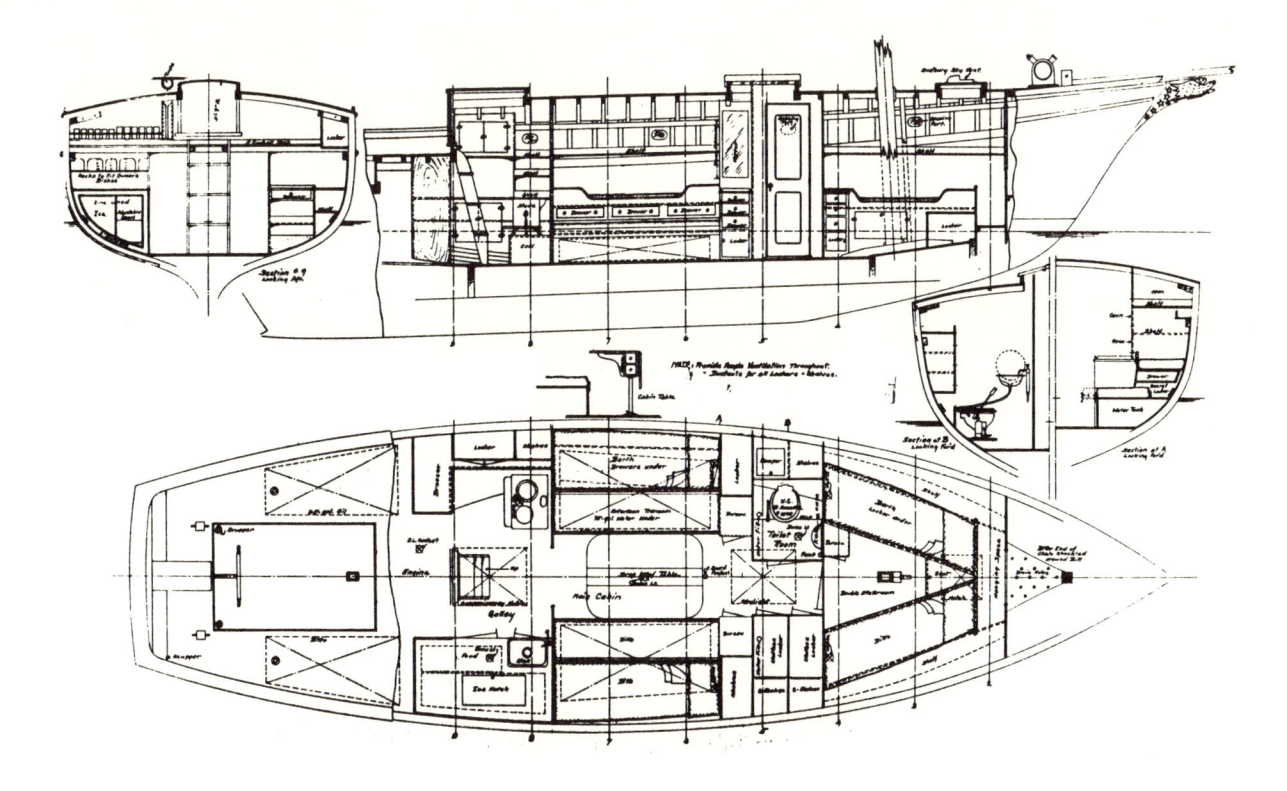

The accommodations plans for Golden Eagle.

MACAW 302

Macaw was a presto-type ketch built in Manchester for Lawrence Holloway in 1956. My father was dubious about the seaworthiness of this type of hull, but the more he worked with the lines, the more enthusiastic he became and found it had ample sail-carrying ability. Holloway proved it when he took her south in October. Incidentally, that good looking suit of sails (see the photograph on page 266) was made by Holloway in his New York apartment.

In a letter to my father, Holloway stated:

Design Number 302
Length Overall: 36 feet
Length on Waterline: 28 feet 6 inches
Beam: 10 feet 8 inches
Draft: 2 feet 6 inches
Sail Area: 593 square feet
Displacement: 14,100 pounds

We left in a flat calm at first light October 24, 1956. About 10 a.m., the wind started from the NE, and by noon it was blowing 20-25 knots. We spent the afternoon long and short tacking for Plum Gut under the four lowers. As we approached the Gut, the mizzen was taken in for better steering. We passed through the Gut just before dark and were glad to find it quite smooth. Close-reaching for Montauk Point, we cleared it about 8 p.m. The wind had been slowly increasing. About midnight, we took in the main and jib, and continued under forestaysail alone, wind NE 40 knots. On Thursday, we set the storm trysail in addition to the staysail. The additional drive threw spray on occasion, but no solid water came aboard. Once in a while a following sea would slap aboard and almost completely fill the cockpit. For a while the boat was quite sluggish, but with the scuppers and some bailing, we soon

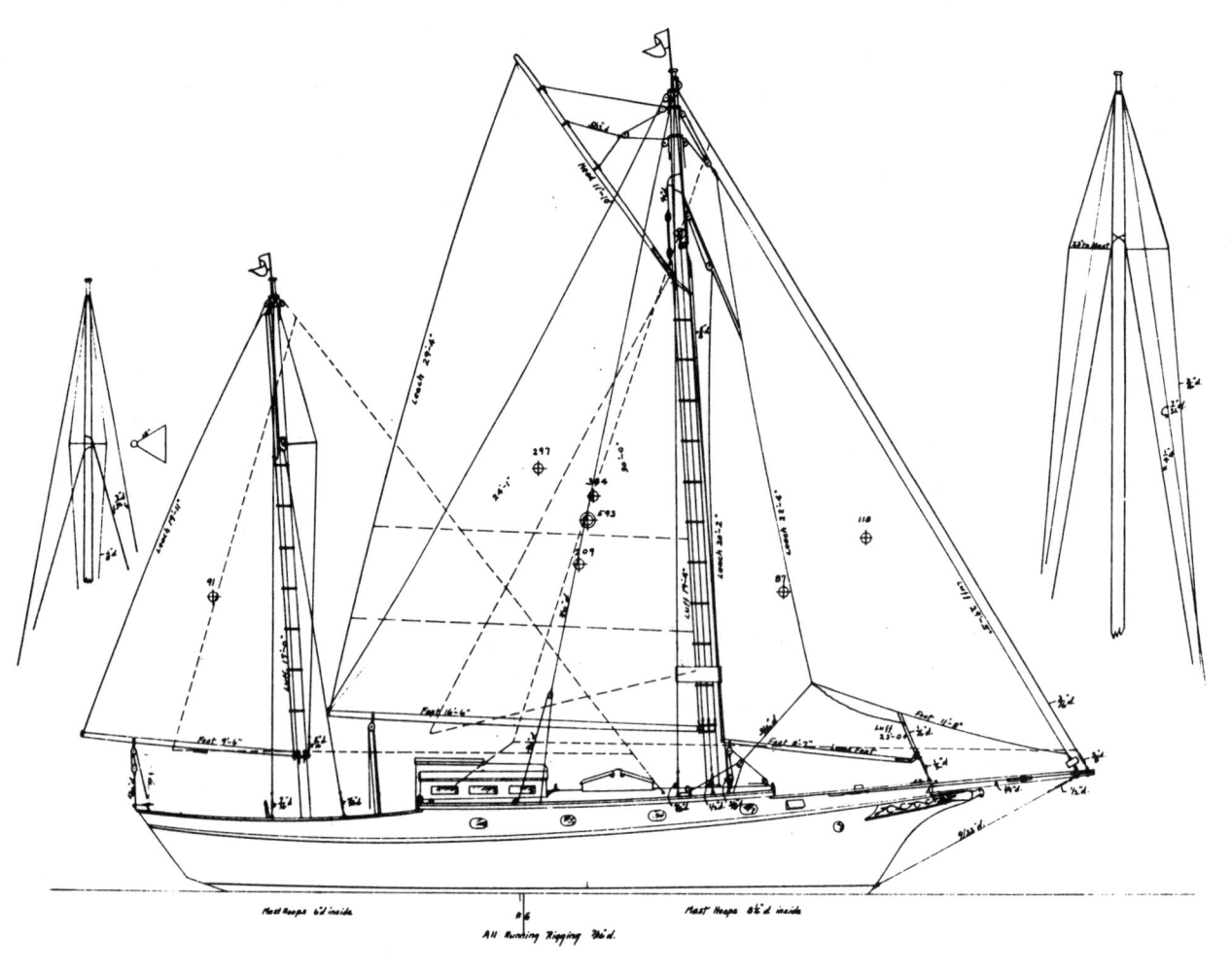

The sailplan and lines drawings for Macaw.

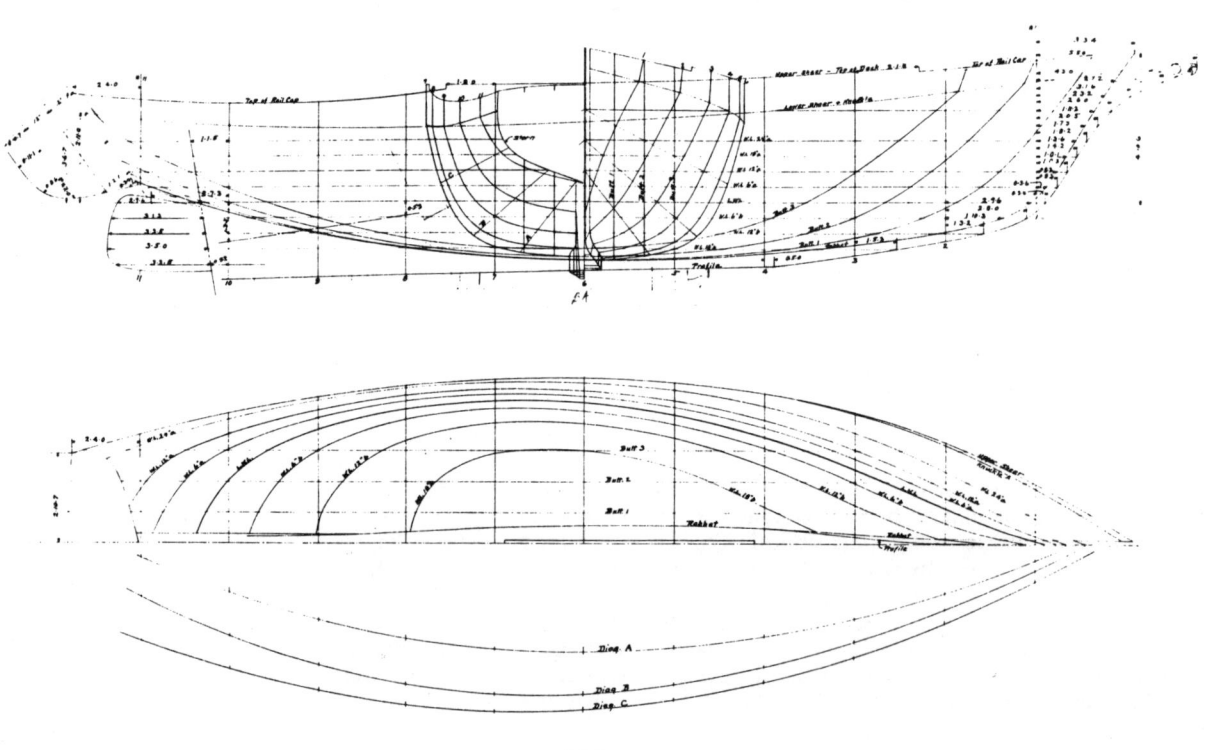

The construction drawings for Macaw.

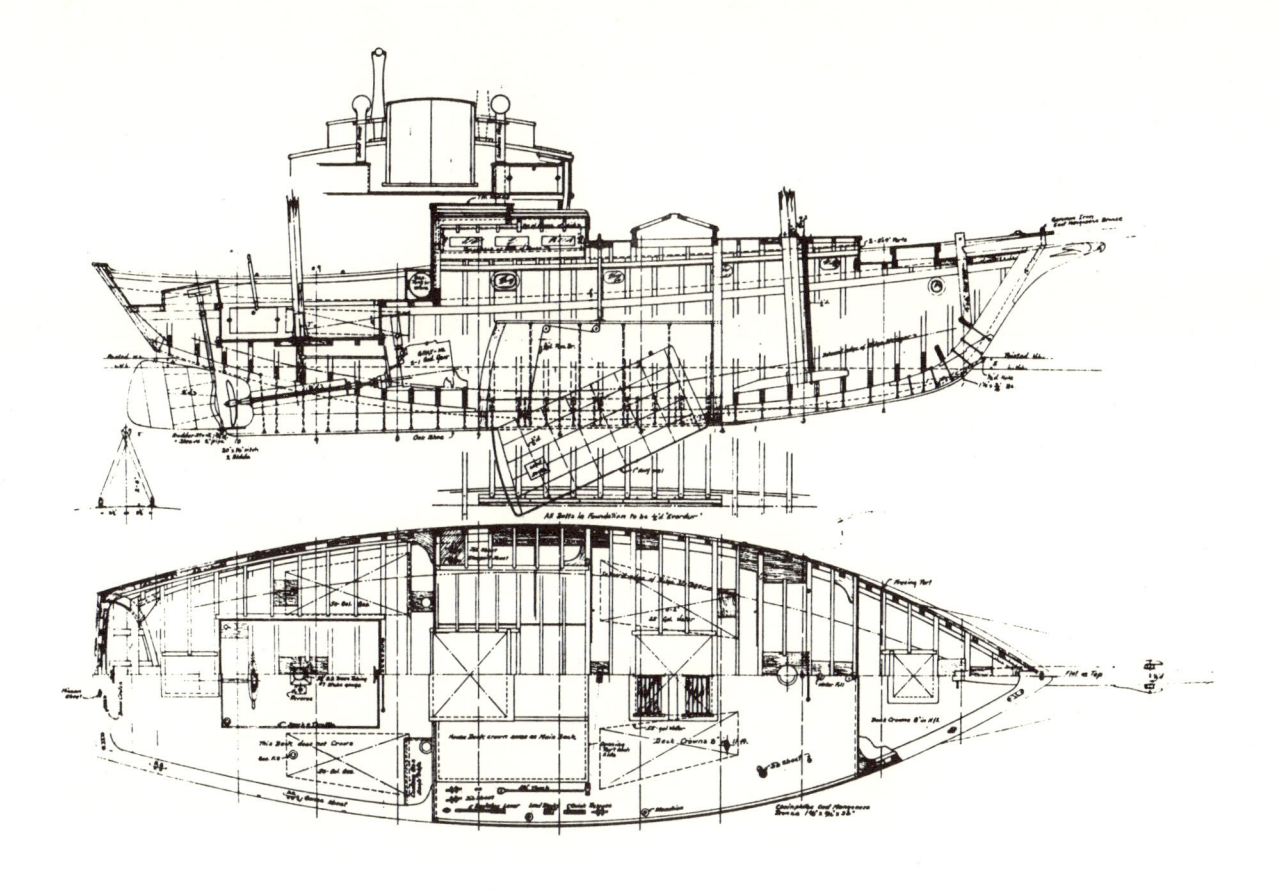

emptied the cockpit. We were now plagued with heavy rain. The wind had shifted to E x S and had increased to about 50 knots. The seas were getting quite high — 20-25 feet.

We carried on 'til Saturday evening. We had now decided that this was no ordinary nor-easter. (We later found that Hurricane Greta had reached her northernmost travel.) We were about 180 nautical miles ESE of Norfolk, which seemed the only reasonable coastal port to try to enter. We altered course but soon found it a dangerous one to steer. We then lay-to on the starboard tack. With the storm trysail quite flat and the helm full up and centerboard up, she lay quietly, quartering the seas [on the bow] and making between one-half and one knot leeway toward Norfolk.

We lay-to for 36 hours, and were quite comfortable during this time — only a little spray came aboard. I estimate (and have confirmed the probability with a meteorologist) that the sustained velocity of the wind was 60 knots with higher gusts.

Monday morning we were able to get underway. At about 10 p.m., we sighted Cape Henry and found that we would have to keep hard on the wind if we were to fetch the point. It was still blowing 40 knots, and the sea was very sloppy. We flattened the storm trysail, put the forestaysail on her, and drove to windward. She went to windward amazingly well and ran six nautical miles between two buoys in one hour. Total sail area — less than 200 square feet.

Finally, after slopping through a foul tide around Cape Henry, we slipped into Hampton Roads and quiet water about 2 a.m. Tuesday morning.

We motored the rest of the way inside. We found she would cruise seven knots at 1,700 r.p.m. and six knots at 1,500 r.p.m. We completed the passage without further incident, except that I found that the vent in on the starboard fuel tank was partially obstructed and that the filler pipe leaked near the deck. I still haven't had a chance to check into this.

In conclusion, I feel that your design leaves very little to be desired. That she is well constructed is certainly attested to by the fact that at no time during this passage were there any indications of any undue stress or strain.

265

Macaw under sail.

Another well-known boat from this design is *Varuna,* built by Phil Fessenden in Ipswich, Mass., and owned by Jack Picard. Still another was the *I.B.G.,* home built by the owner, Porter Blanchard in California. She was strip built and marconi rigged. Blanchard was a well-known silversmith and operated a business that originated in Milford, N.H., in 1788. When he saw plans of *Macaw* published, he decided to build her, and he paid my father for the plans in handmade silver trinkets, such as a sugar bowl and creamer, mint-julip goblets, etc. They were quite pretty.

304 GULL

Design Number 304
Length Overall: 30 feet 6 inches
Length on Waterline: 24 feet 7 inches
Beam: 9 feet 3 inches
Draft: 4 feet 10 inches
Sail Area: 462 square feet
Displacement: 11,400 pounds

Gull was the first of these 30-footers. She was built by me for Dave Livingston in 1956. The design became very popular, and I built two more. Plans were sold all over the world. It's no wonder when you look at the cabin plan and note the accommodations in a 30-foot hull. However, with all six bunks spoken for, I think locker space would be at a premium. Raised-deck construction gives a lot of space both above and below decks, and a dinghy can be carried across the boomkin. In 1972-1973 *Gull* made the trip down the Intracoastal Waterway, through the Bahamas, Abacos, Exumas, and back, handling all sea conditions nicely.

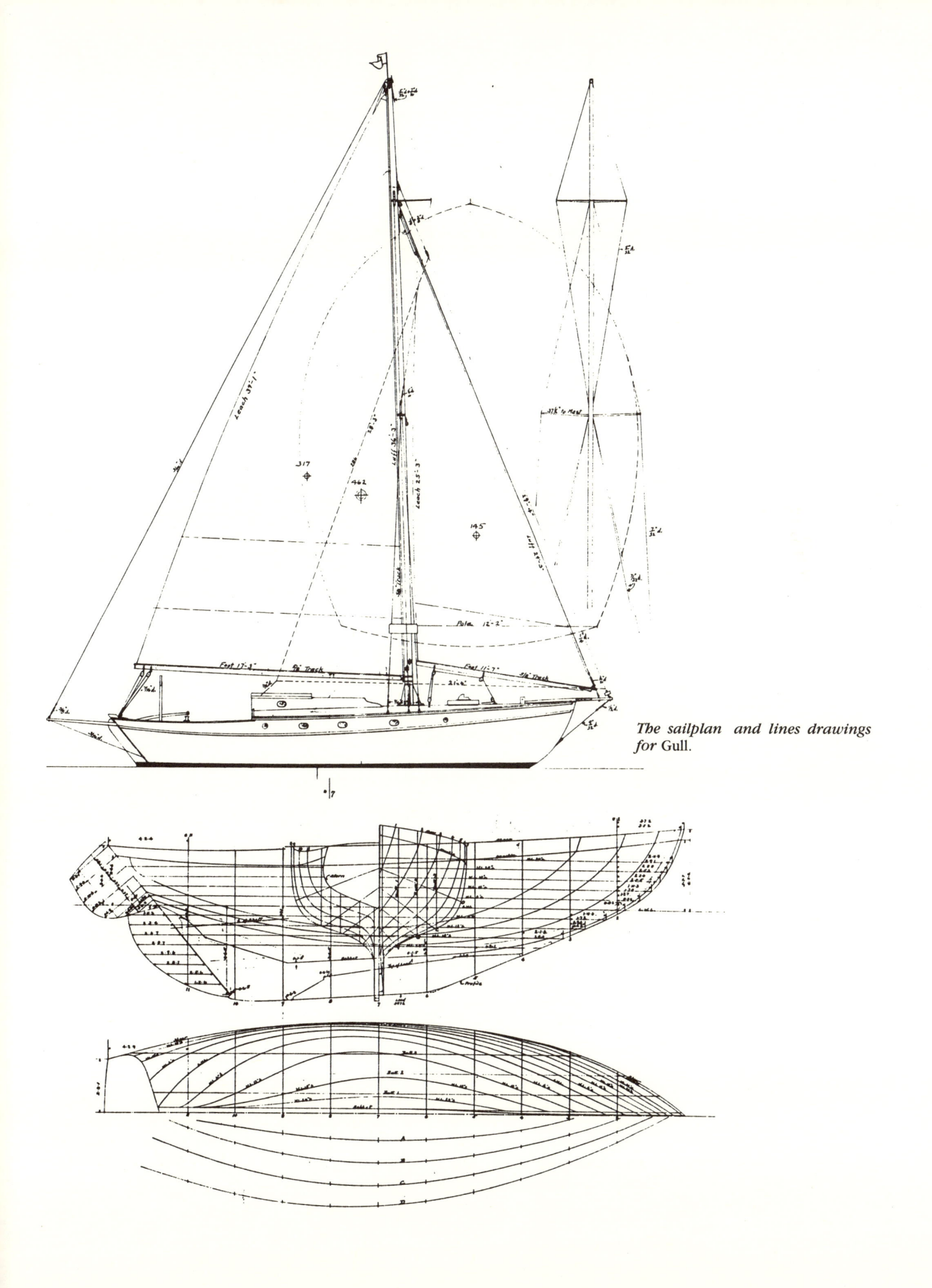

The sailplan and lines drawings for Gull.

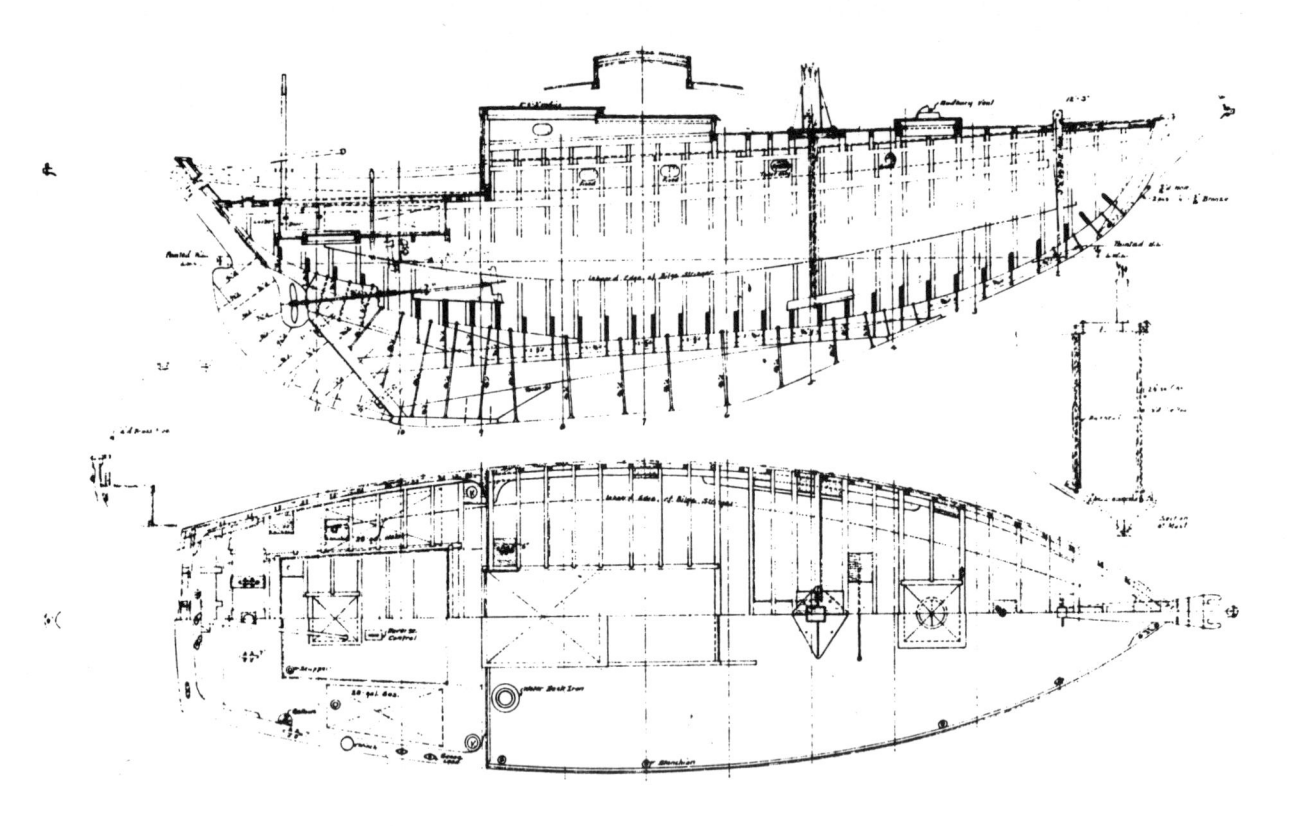

The construction and accommodations drawings for Gull.

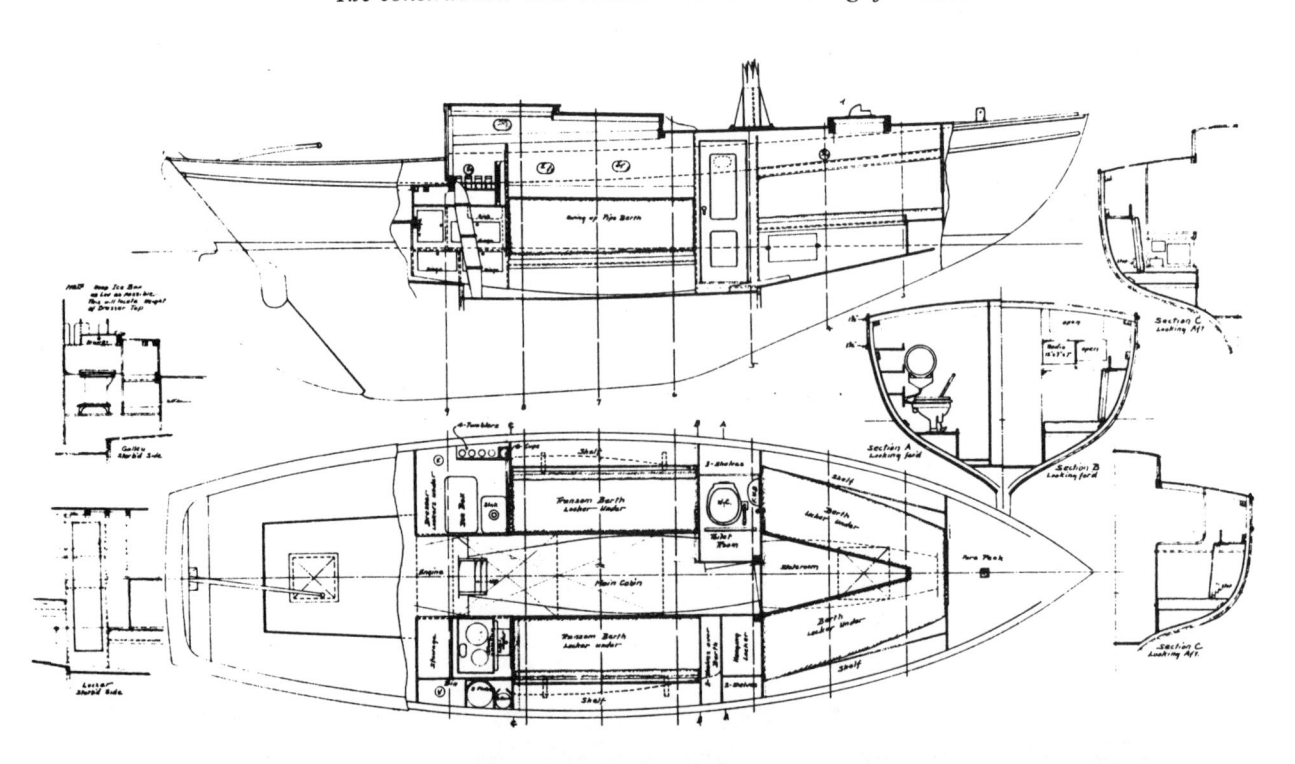

I built number 334, *Sunset,* in 1963 for Mary Ann and Al Higgins on these lines but with the house carried a little farther aft to get more room below. Wanting a little more room in the head, they wondered how much a bulkhead would have to be moved to be noticeable. My father's reply was: "To move that bulkhead an inch would be like adding an inch to the end of your nose." They lived aboard her and cruised her from New York to Canada.

Gull sailing well.

305

This 22-foot keel cat sloop, built in 1957 by Bud McIntosh for John Lindsay, was called *Sea Fire*. When she was all planked up, she was covered with fiberglass in an effort to cut down on year-to-year maintenance. She had 1,700 pounds of lead outside. She is a smart and comfortable sailer. Another design, number 312, was the same boat with a ketch rig.

Design Number 305
Length Overall: 22 feet 2 inches
Length on Waterline: 20 feet 2 inches
Beam: 9 feet 7 inches
Draft: 3 feet 6 inches
Sail Area: 425 square feet
Displacement: 6,200 pounds

The sailplan and lines drawings for Sea Fire.

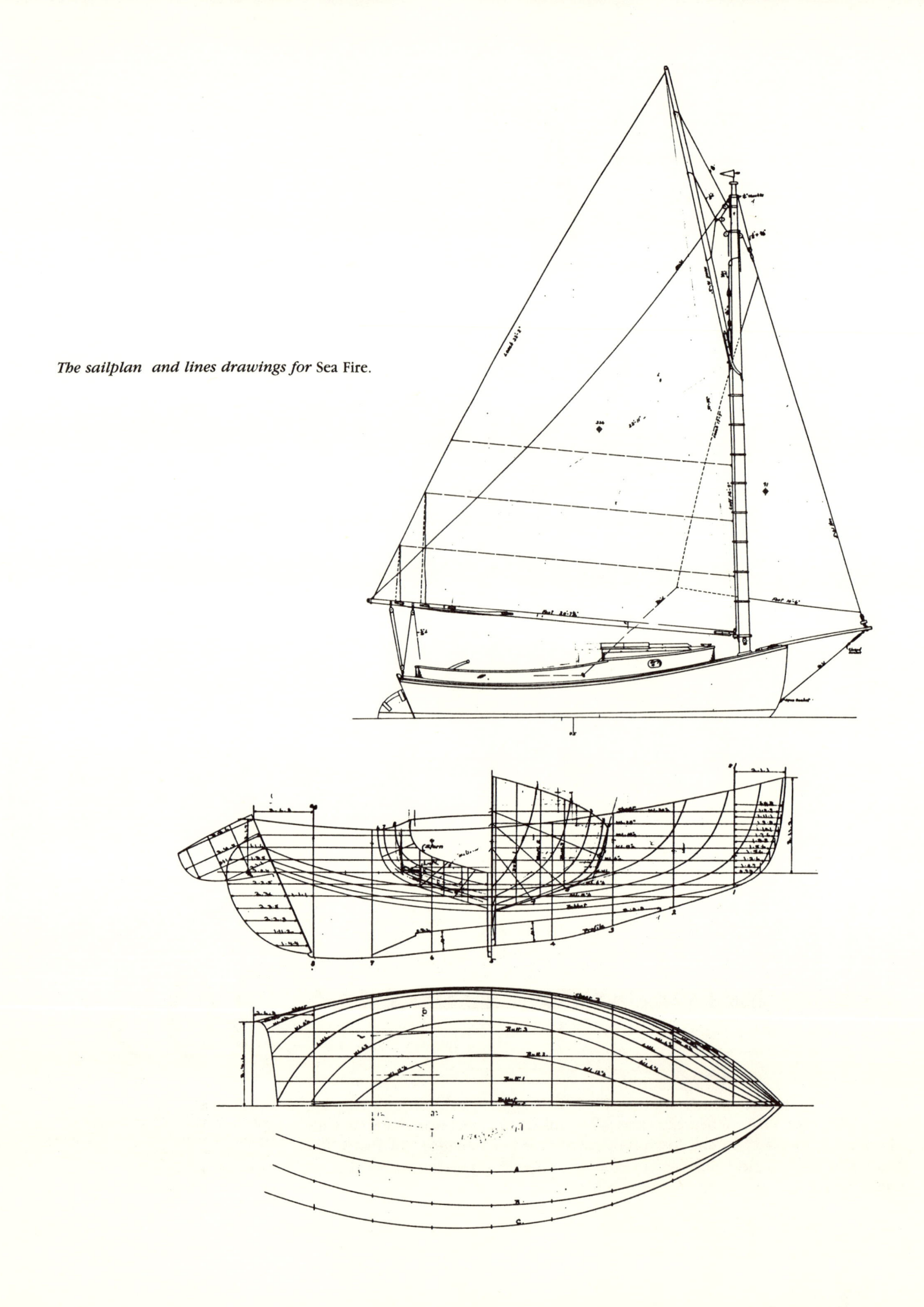

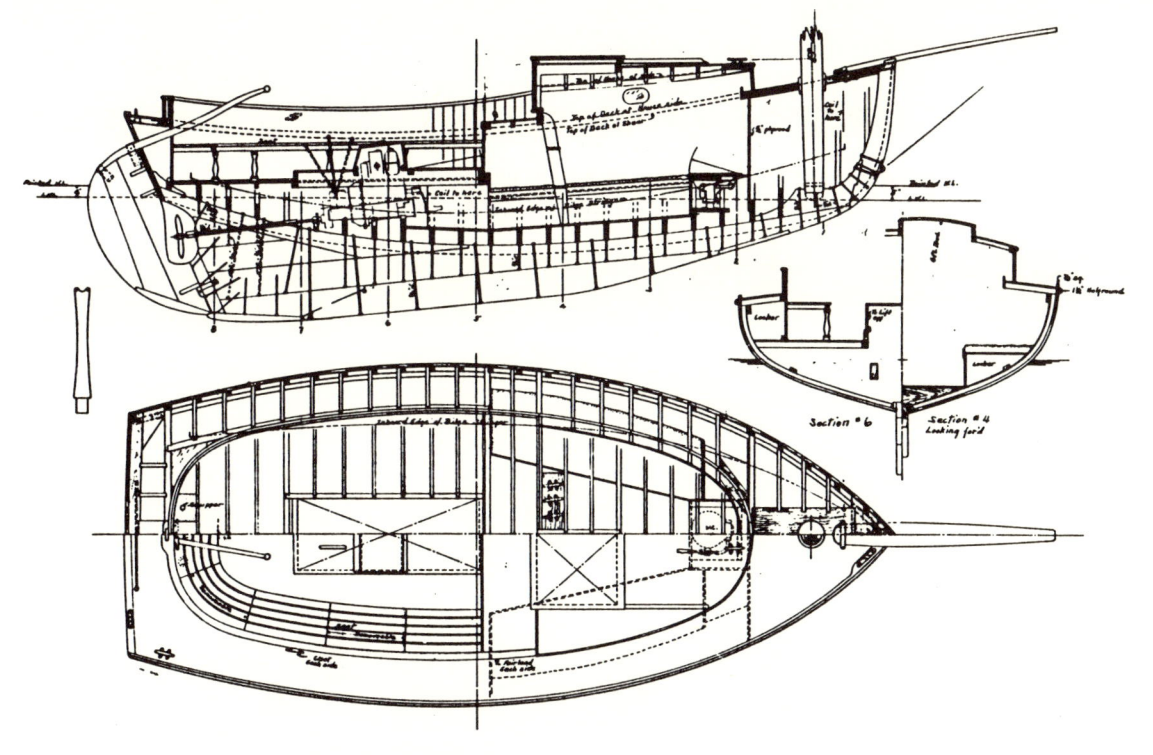

The construction drawings and Sea Fire under sail.

310 COUSIN ELIZABETH

Design Number 310
Length Overall: 42 feet 9 inches
Length on Waterline: 36 feet 6 inches
Beam: 12 feet 2 inches
Draft: 6 feet
Sail Area: 880 square feet
Displacement: 32,850 pounds

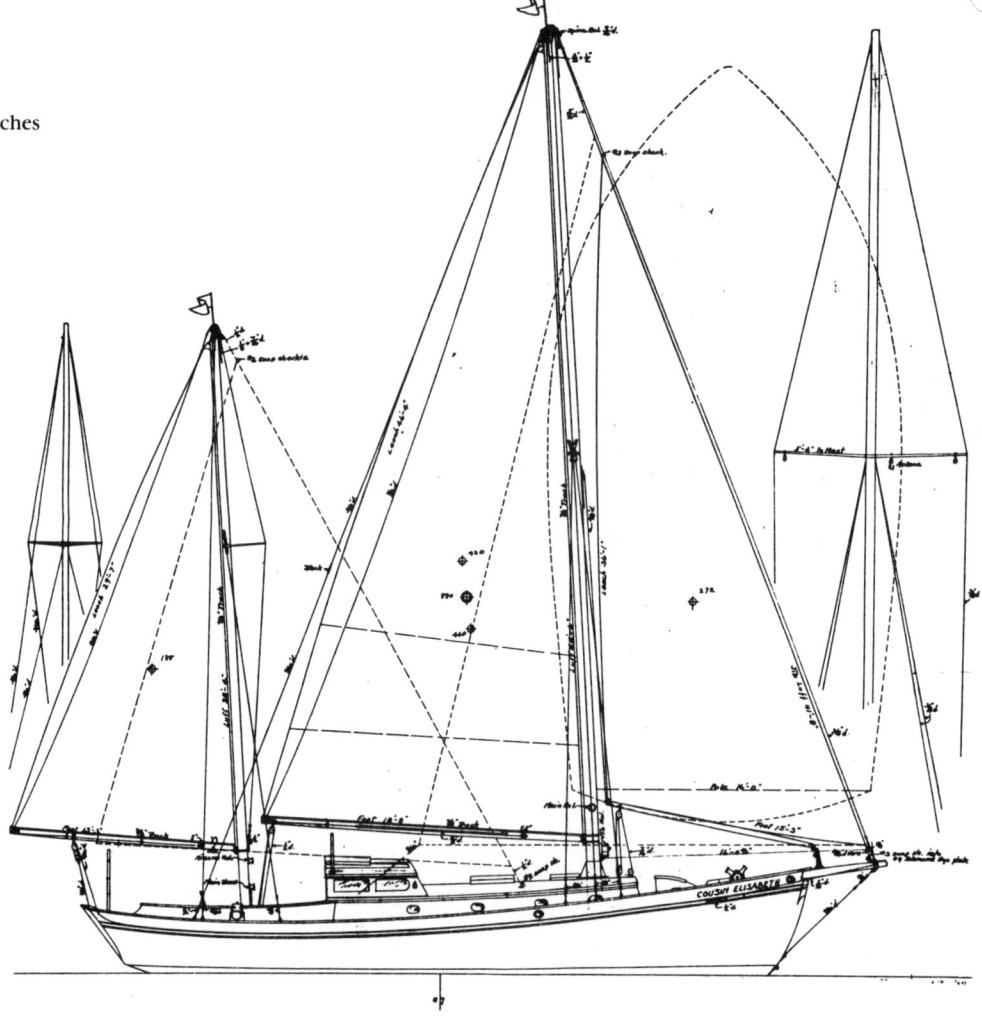

The sailplan for Cousin Elizabeth.

Cousin Elizabeth, launched in 1958, was built in Manchester for Sandy Moffat.

My father and Sandy were old friends; in fact, Sandy was Dad's first client when he opened his office on Washington Street in 1924.

Sandy once said:

> When I had *Cousin Elizabeth* designed, I had certain definite ideas in mind and went to your father because I felt he would be sympathetic with my thinking.
>
> The following were the criteria we took into consideration: (1) she must be a comfortable cruising auxiliary with adequate berths for my family, (2) she must have a sheltered cockpit, (3) she must have six-foot-six headroom, (4) she must have a three-cylinder General Motors diesel, with which I had had highly successful experience.
>
> My experience as skipper of a sub chaser in World War II made me all too familiar with what the Atlantic can offer in the way of weather. I wanted my new boat to be able to handle anything I might be likely to encounter. *Cousin Elizabeth* met this criterion very successfully.

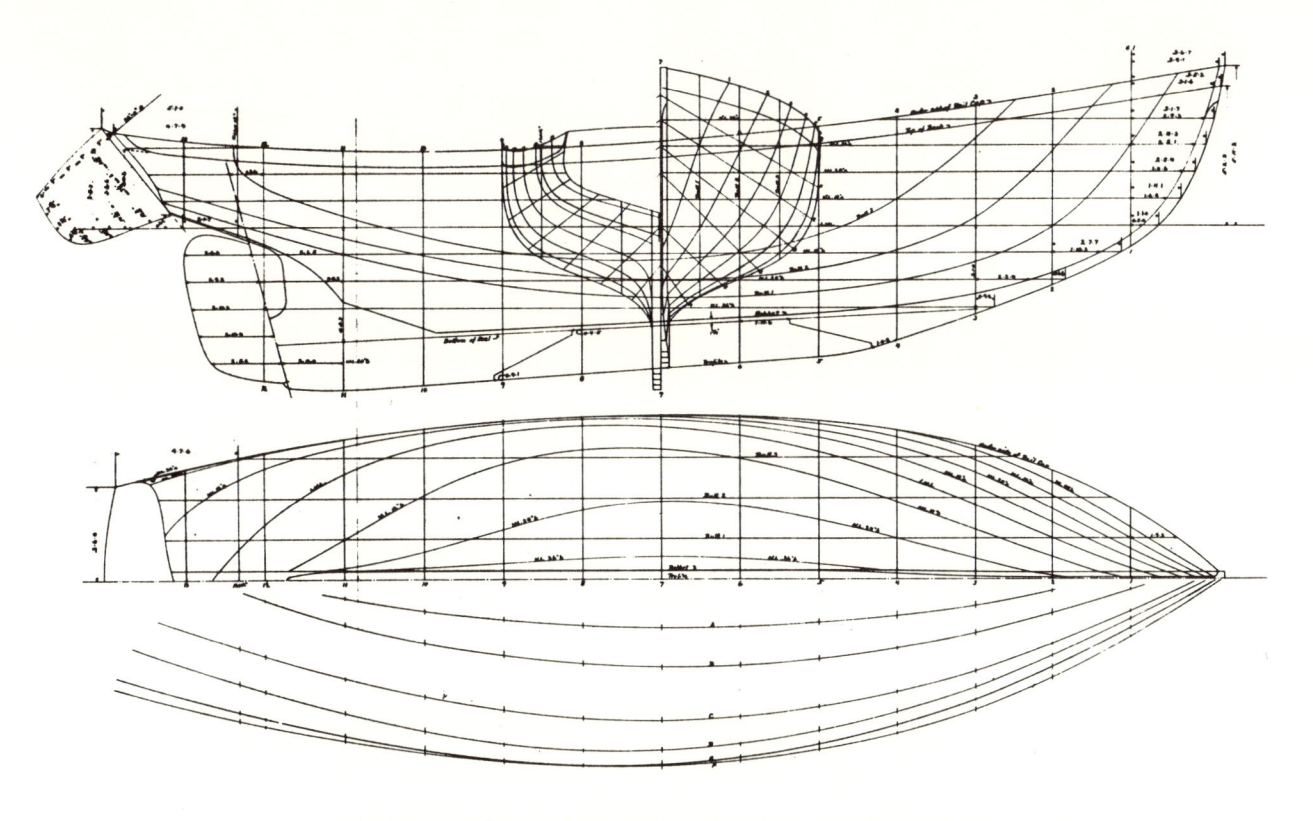

The lines and construction drawings for Cousin Elizabeth.

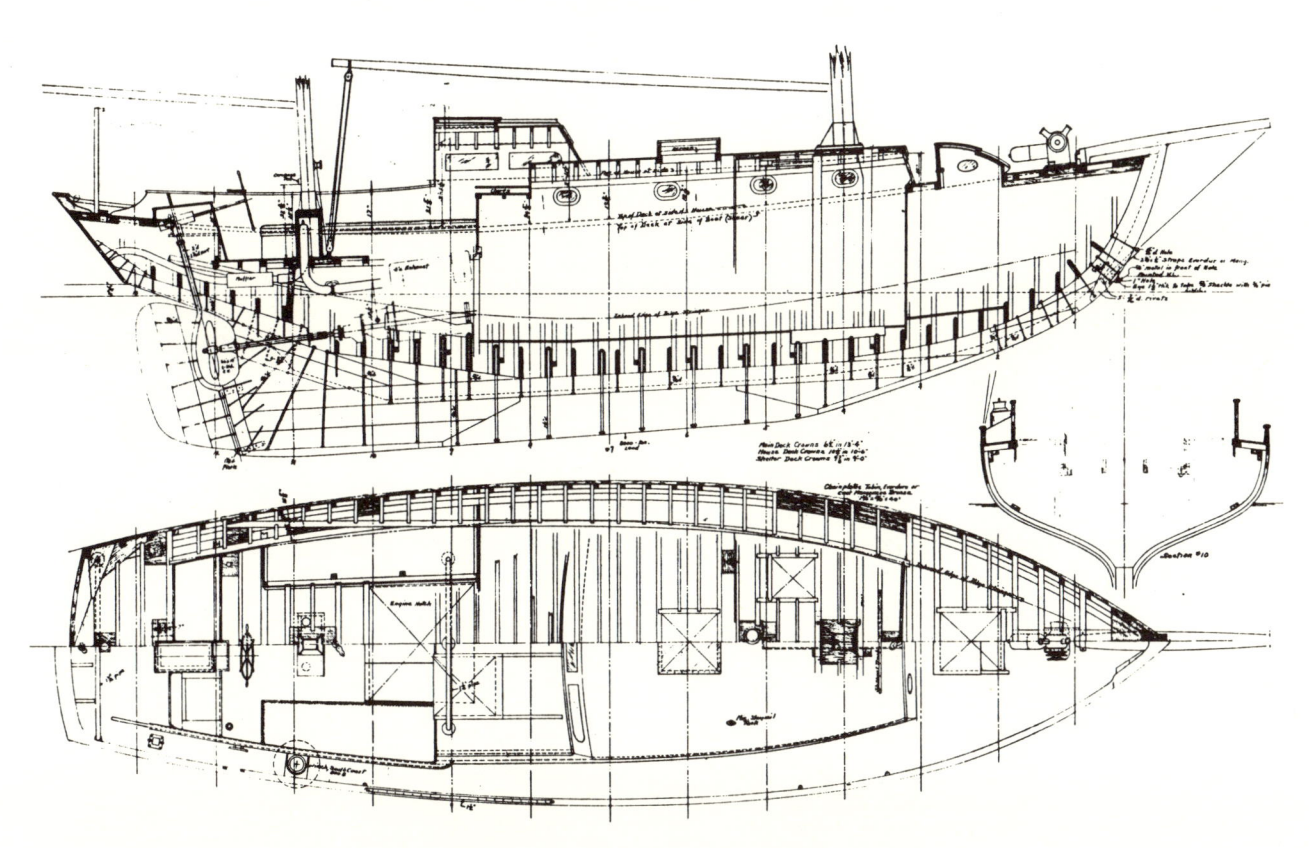

The same considerations applied to *Mahdee*. After all, if you want a proper ship, you first pick your architect.

273

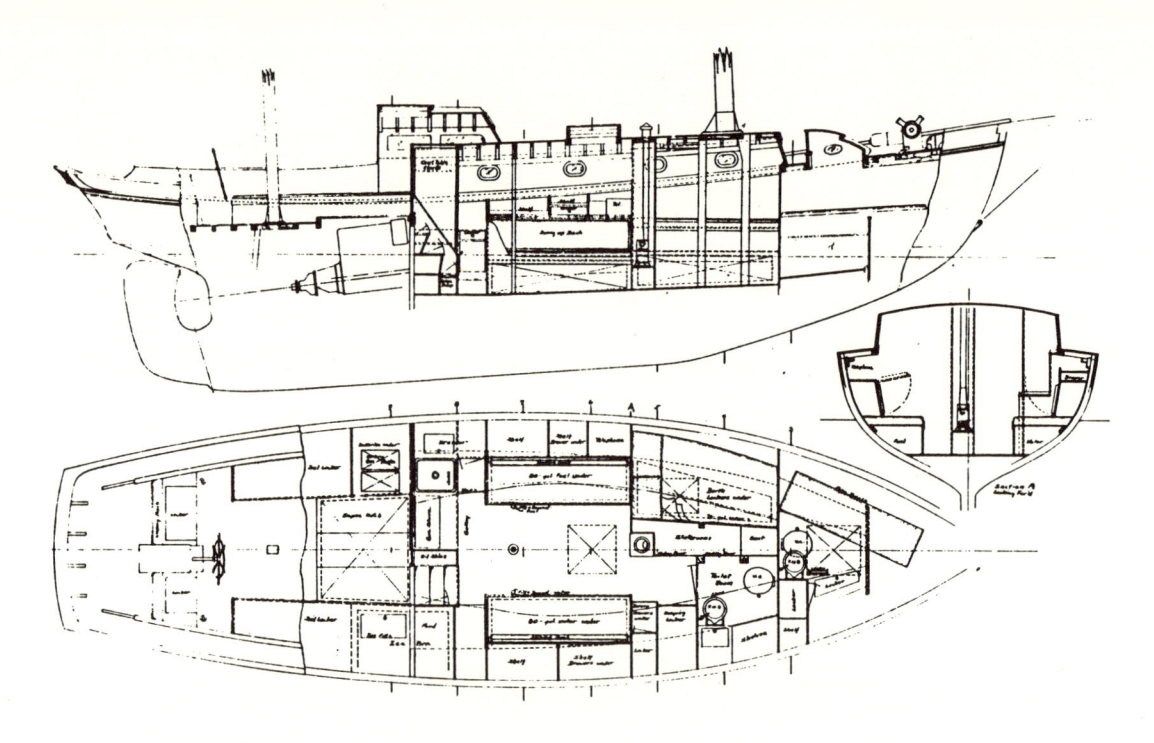

Cousin Elizabeth's *accommodations drawings and under sail in light air*.

JINGO 311

Jingo was launched in 1959 for A.P. Loring. She is a centerboard ketch and presto hull. Spars are on tabernacles so they can be lowered for passage under nonopening bridges. A note from Gus describes the boat better than I can:

> In the fall of 1957, I approached your father and asked him if he would design a boat for me. The ground rules were that if she grounded out, she would have a list of not more than 15 degrees so that I could at least sleep on the bunks without rolling out. During the winter of 1957-1958, I dropped by his office on Washington Street once a week to watch the plans develop. It was one of the most enjoyable exercises I have ever been through. He immediately came up with the idea of a presto hull. I had not thought of a centerboard boat, and I liked it. I told him early on that I preferred to have a ketch, and I certainly wanted a gaff rig. This, he thought, made all sorts of sense and, I think, was instrumental on his settling on the presto lines. I

Design Number 311
Length Overall: 35 feet 10 inches
Length on Waterline: 31 feet 5 inches
Beam: 10 feet 9 inches
Draft: 3 feet
Sail Area: 619 square feet
Displacement: 17,900 pounds

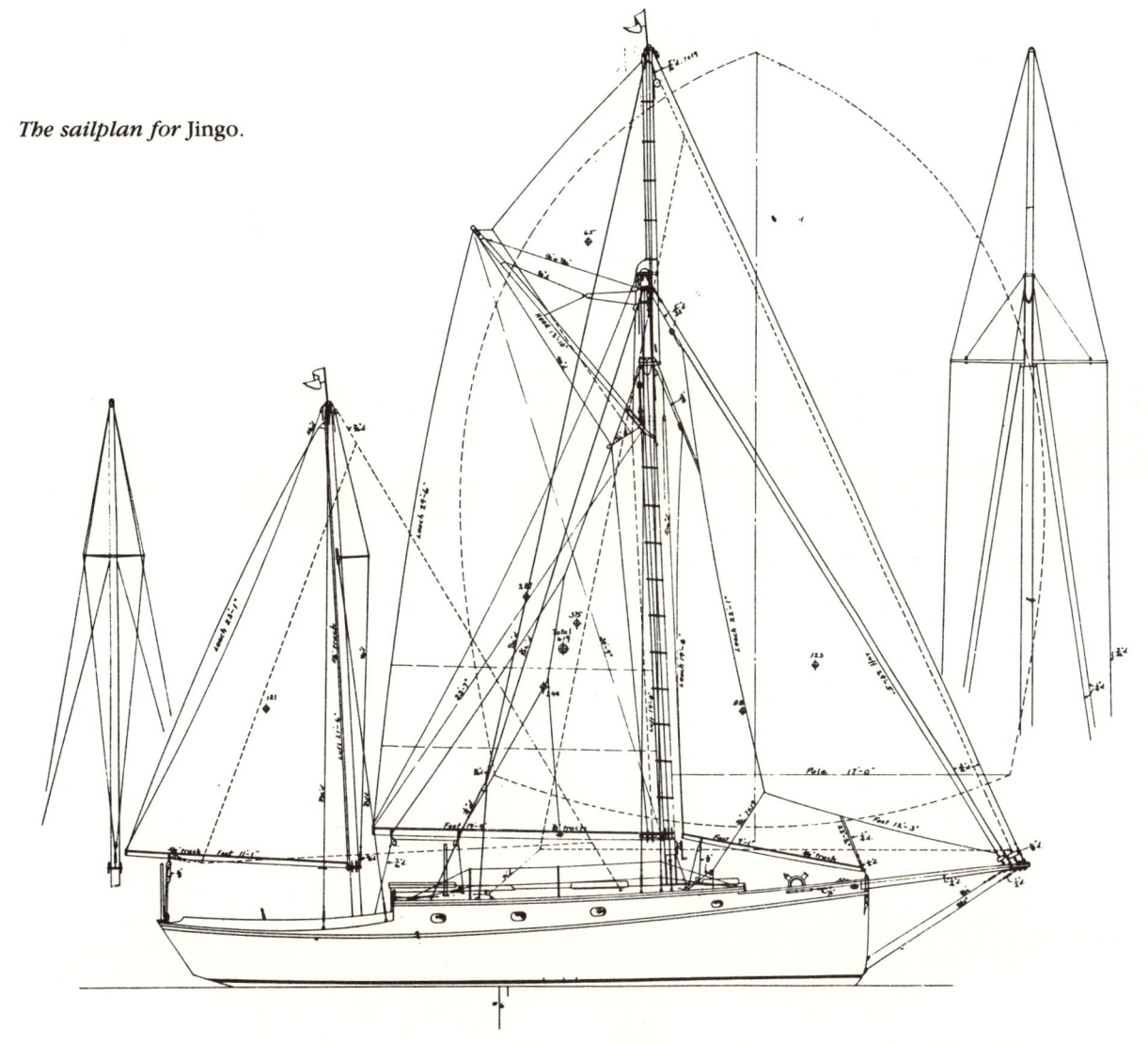

The sailplan for Jingo.

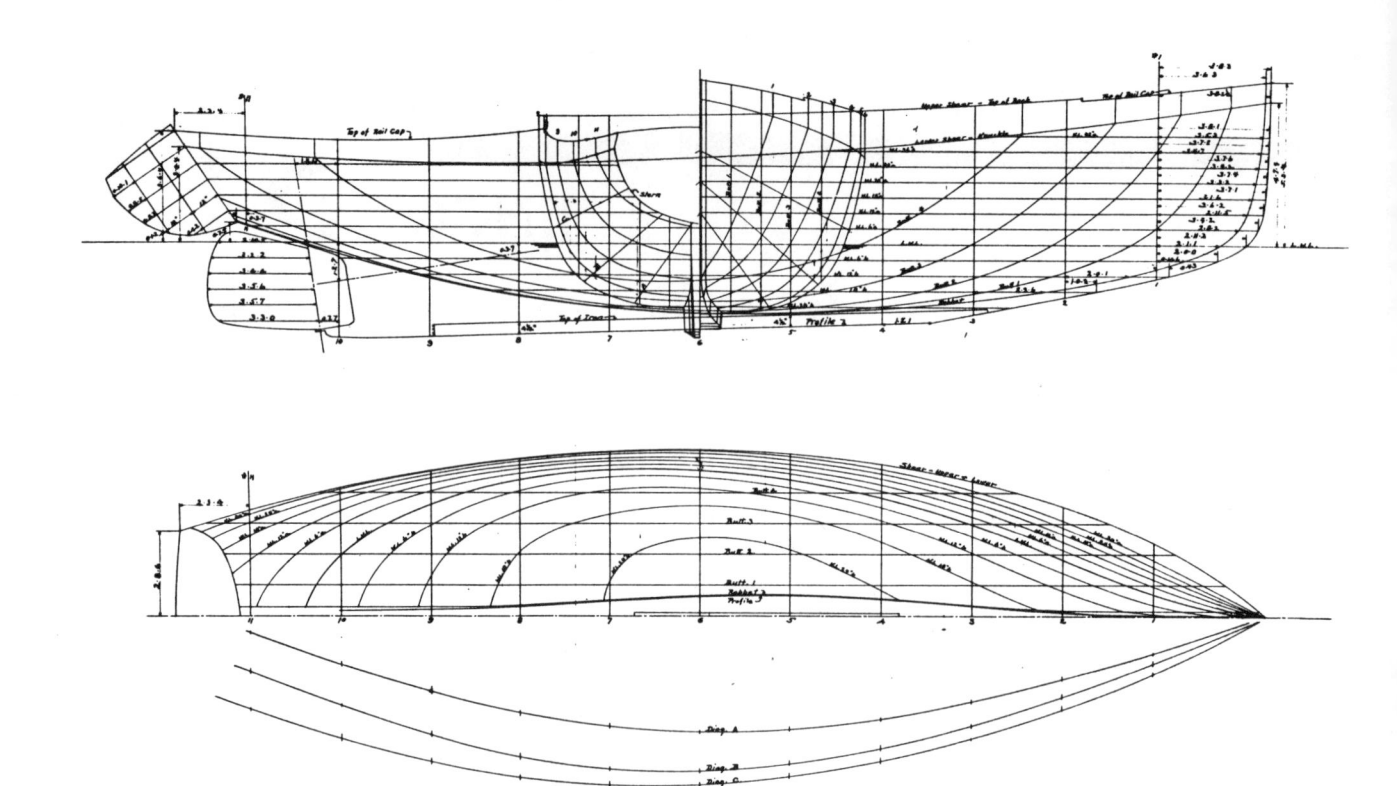

The lines and construction drawings for Jingo.

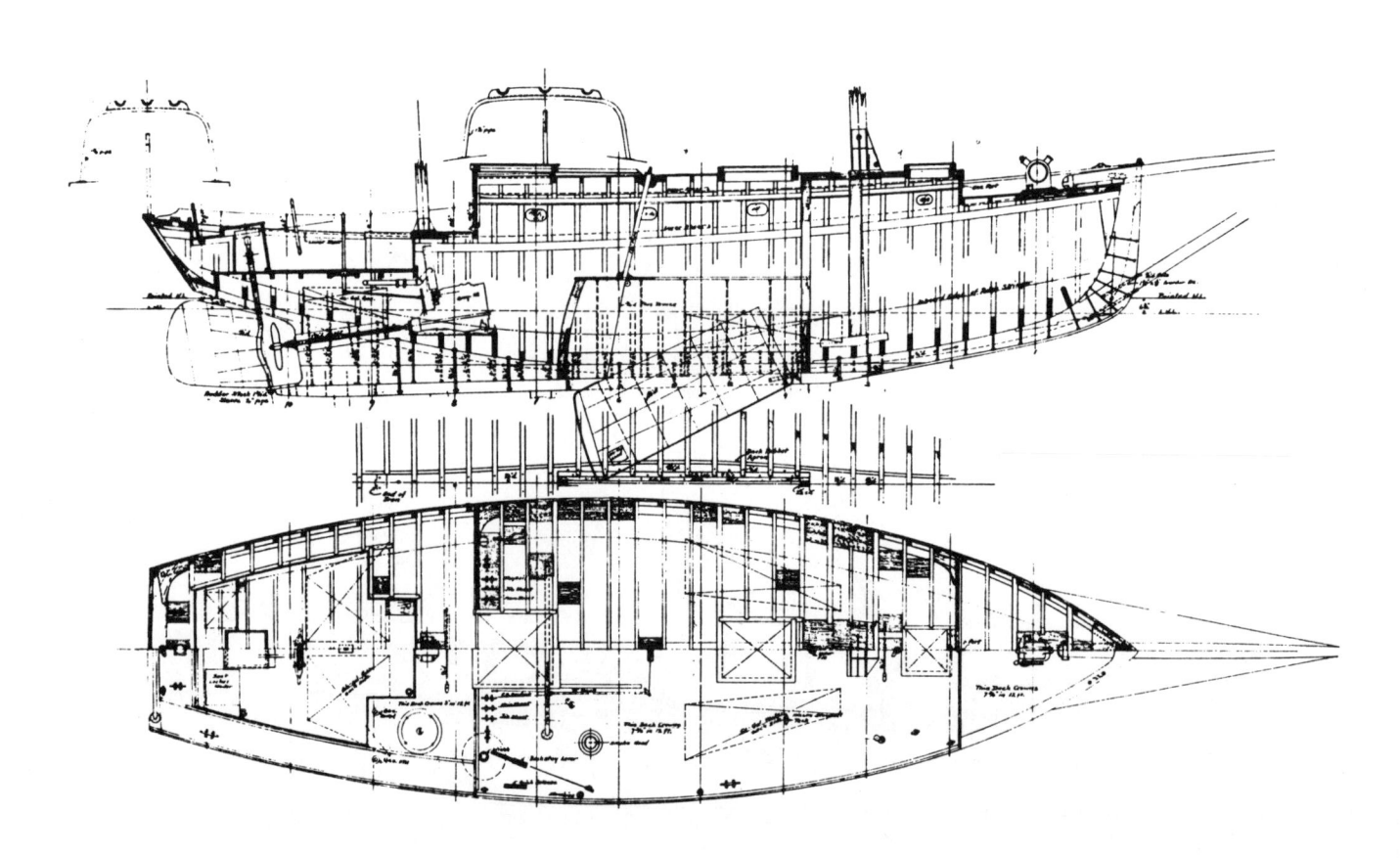

Jingo's *accommodations drawings.*

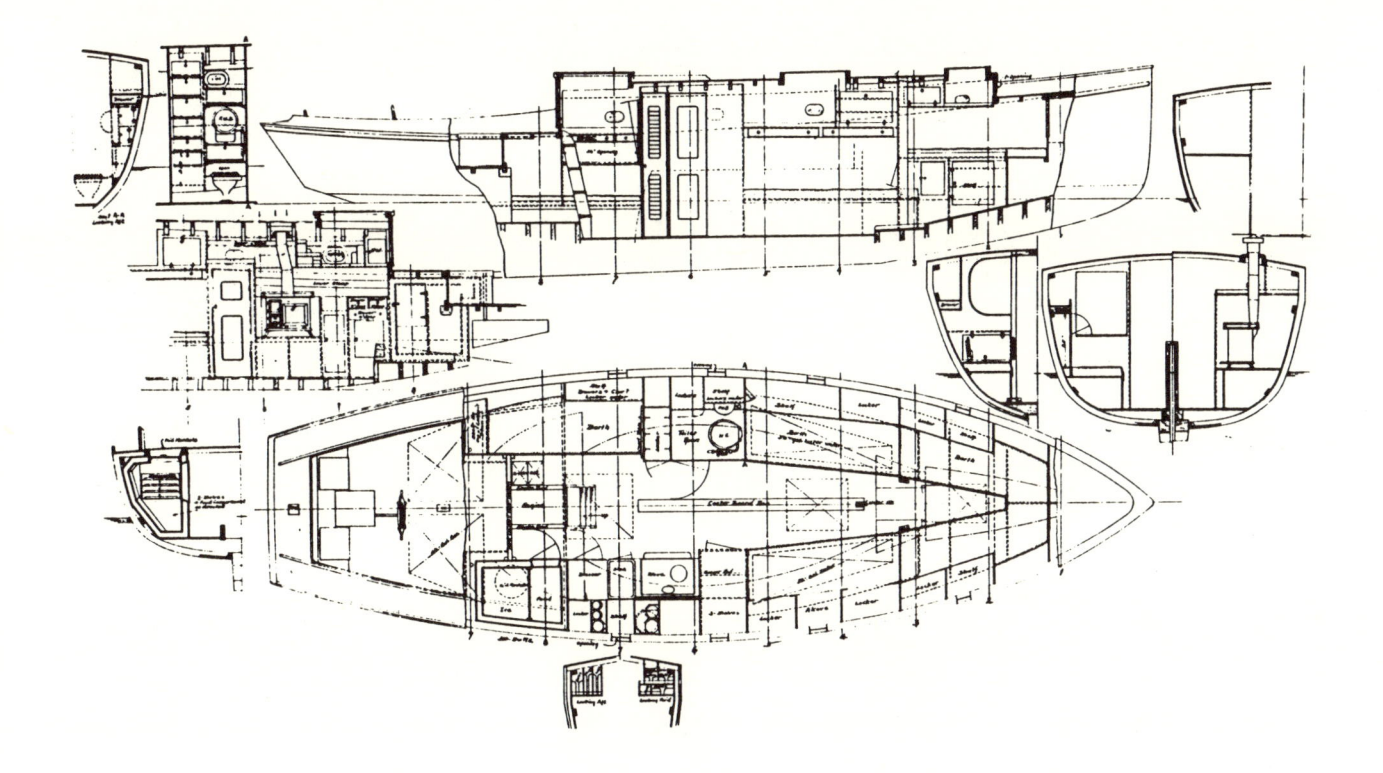

also said I wished to have a plumb stern. There were several trial sketches, but we soon settled on the basic lines that ultimately developed into the *Jingo*.

I then had the fun of laying out the cabin. This continued up to the [bitter] end, and I think I got exactly what I wanted. One of the ground rules in the cockpit was that I would be able to have a deck chair, and he liked this idea, and hence the removable seats. I had originally wanted the cabin completely open but changed my mind after the boat was three-quarters built and you very adroitly closed the opening between the two forward bunks and the main cabin. The position of the stove, chopping block, etc., was fundamentally mine. He, however, put in wonderful refinements that I would not have thought of, and they have been absolutely invaluable. We got together to make sure that every conceivable space could be used for storage, and as a result, I think I have more storage space on the *Jingo* than on any comparable boat her size.

Originally, no topmast was envisioned. I thought I would dress the boat up a lot, so I suggested it. He thought it was a wonderful idea, and the result was the large roller furling genoa, which he said would be "just like turning on the motor," and so it has proven in light weather. Without it, the *Jingo* would have been sluggish; with it, she is great, particularly off the wind.

I was fortunate in having him move to Manchester the year you built her, and I think going over the boat with him once or twice a week added a dimension that I shall never forget, and I feel that a lot of his personality went into the boat because he was there to see exactly how things developed and could make what changes were necessary.

She has proven to be exactly what I wanted. She is not the greatest yacht going to windward, but I did not expect she would be. She is wonderful a little off the wind and can keep up with anybody else. The only time I have raced her was in a Patton Bowl race 15 years ago. In that race, I surprised some of the fancier, more modern boats by keeping even with them and only ran into trouble when the wind shifted and I had to beat. I was then out of luck.

Having a centerboard was a revelation to me. I would never again want to have a cruising boat that drew more than three feet. It opens up a wealth of harbors that are closed to the normal modern yacht. The ability to ground out has served me well, particularly on the two trips I have taken to the upper regions of the Bay of Fundy. The rugged keel has enabled me to sit comfortably leaning against docks.

Jingo under sail.

The ratlines have been another source of pleasure in that they have enabled not only me, but my children, particularly my daughter, to learn to climb up and down the mast, and we love it.

All in all, I think that I could not have asked for a more comfortable boat or one that better filled my needs. It is great.

GREEN HERON 313

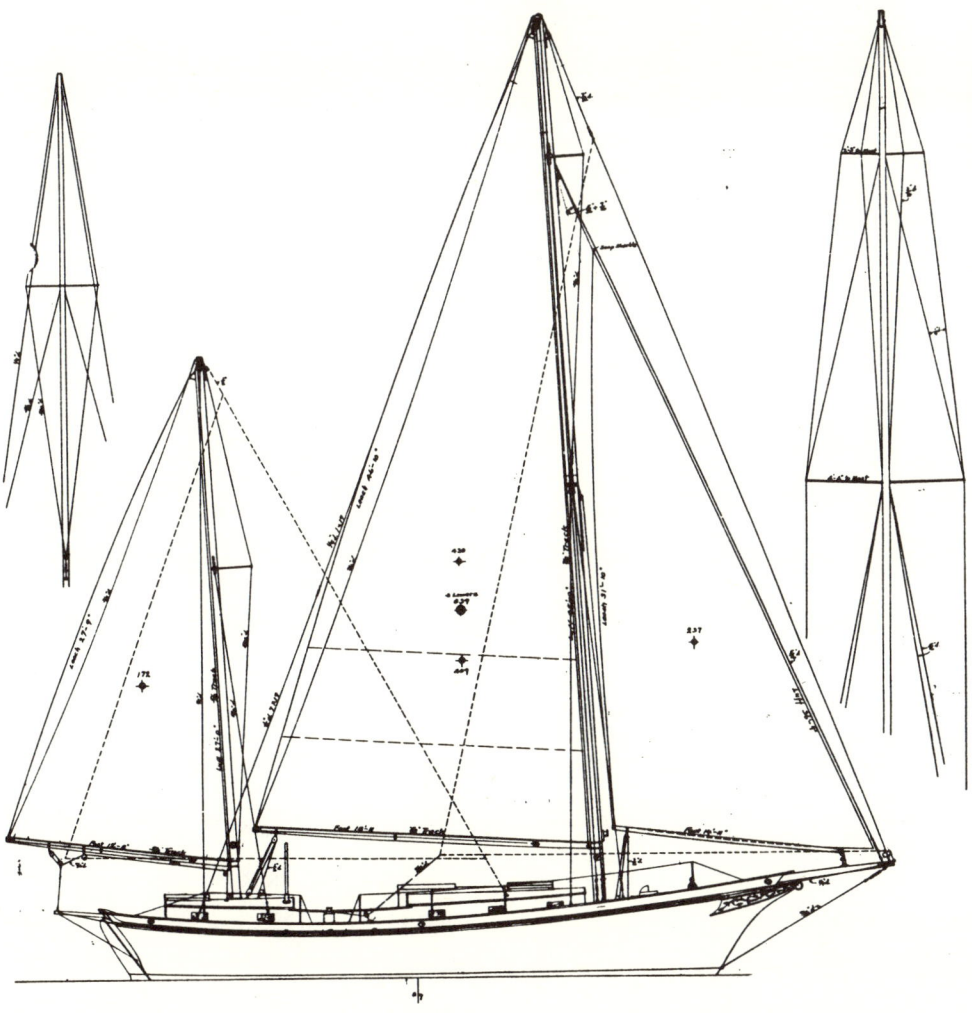

Design Number 313
Length Overall: 39 feet 6 inches
Length on Waterline: 32 feet 4 inches
Beam: 11 feet 9 inches
Draft: 5 feet
Sail Area: 839 square feet
Displacement: 25,750 pounds

Green Heron was built in 1959 by Bob Reid in Kennebunkport, Me. Now Sunset, owned by M.A. and G.A. Higgins of Castine, Me., she was the first of this design, built for Norton V. Ritchey. The double-cabin arrangement drew nothing but favorable comment, and the boat has proven to be an excellent sea boat, handling rough weather between Connecticut and Annapolis very well. In a letter in October 1959 Ritchey stated:

The sailplan for Green Heron.

> At the close of our first short season, I wanted you to know how pleased we are with the performance of Green Heron. She is now laid up in Annapolis in wet storage at Arnold Gay's Yacht Yard.
> She handles very easily whether we have a full crew or with Ruth and myself. She is extremely comfortable for cruising a party of four or even for five or six. The privacy of the after cabin with its own head and lavatory is a great luxury.
> I was very pleased with her windward ability as I was a bit skeptical of the 5-foot draft which I had specified. She has a fine turn of speed on every point of sailing, and it doesn't take much wind to move her.

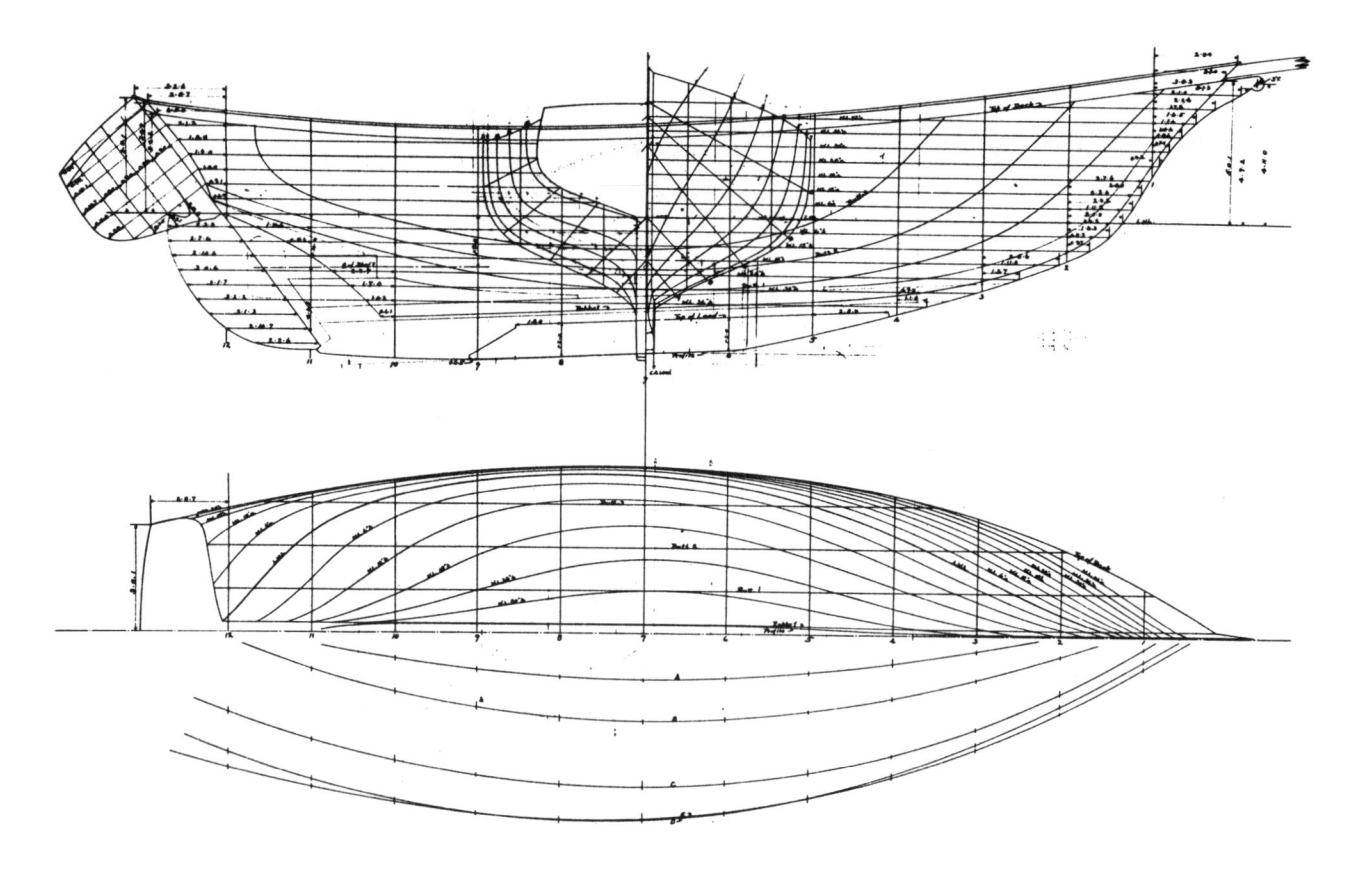

The lines drawings and construction plans for Green Heron.

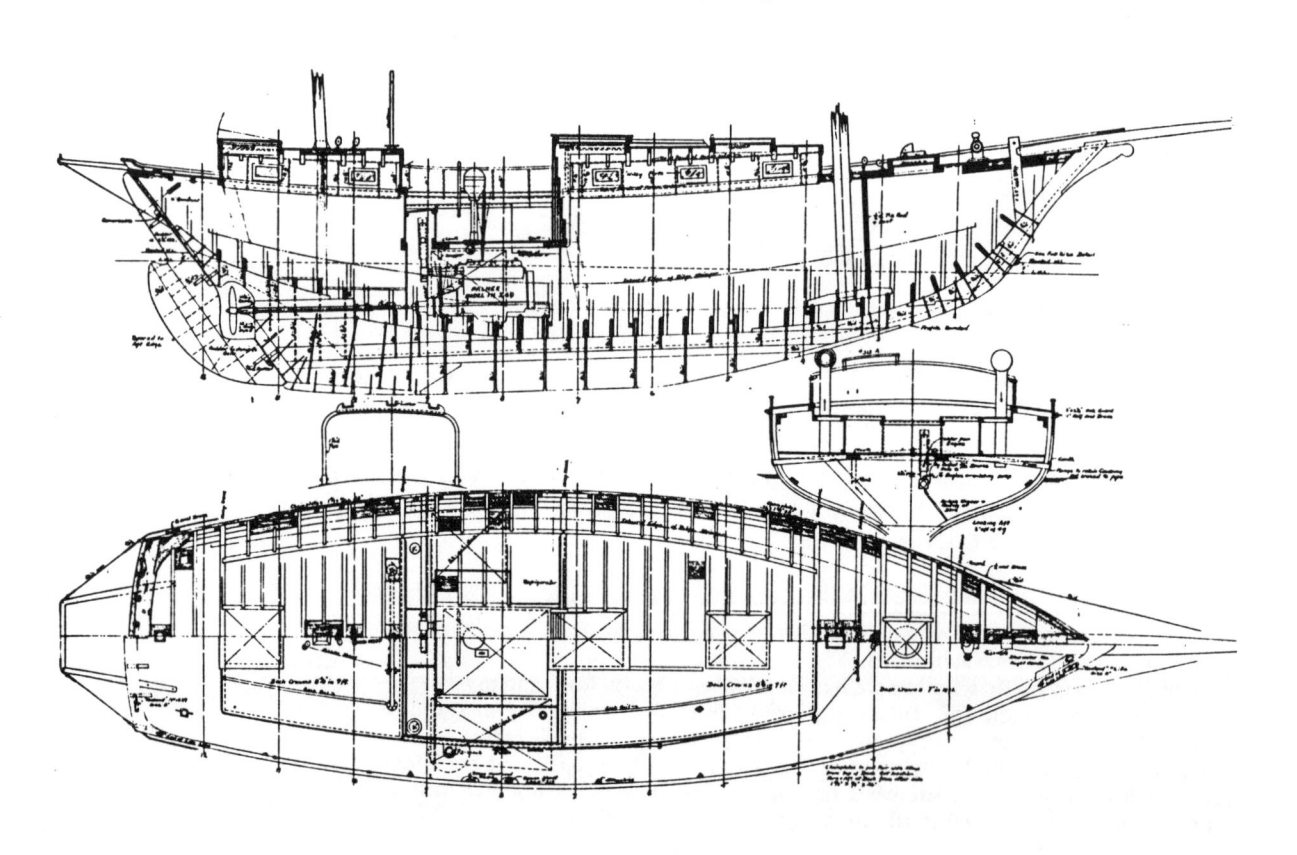

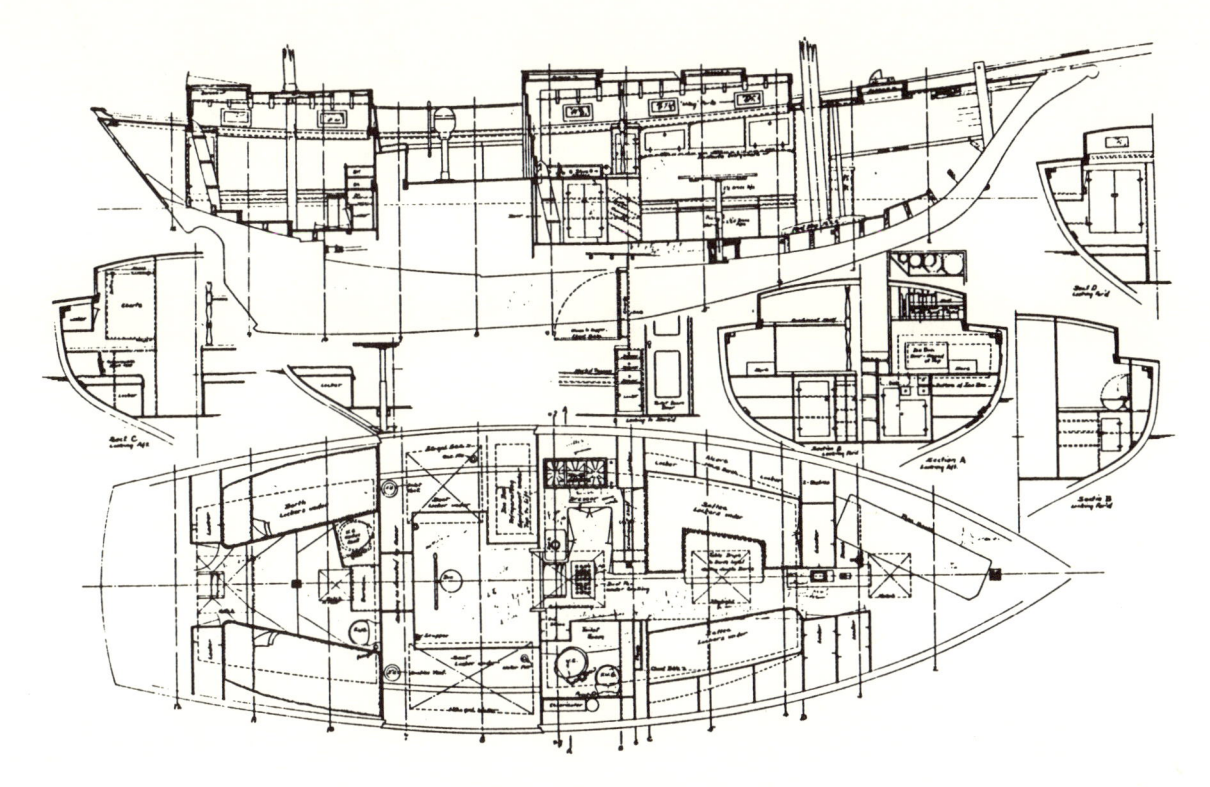

The accommodations drawings.

FIVE PLY 325

One of the admirers of the Crocker 20 was Paul Whitin of Kennebunkport, Me., who also had had several of Dad's boats. He got Sam to sketch the 20 into a 40-foot yawl. I liked the looks of it and started fooling around with the sketch, not as a yawl but as a 40-foot sloop. Thus, with my father doing most of the work, *Five Ply* was born, with her light displacement, probably 20 years ahead of her time. Originally, she was a doubled-up 20, with a three-quarter rig and as such, we cleaned up in the 1966 Patton Bowl. However, on a spinnaker reach into Gloucester from the A buoy, she carried such a weather helm, and my shoulders were so lame, that I moved the rudder 4 feet aft. On that run into Gloucester, we twisted a piece of extra heavy 1¼-inch bronze pipe that connected the rudder to the tiller about five to 10 degrees. I discovered this the next morning when I had to hold the tiller way off to starboard to go straight ahead. No wonder my shoulders ached! With the rudder moved back and a wheel in place of the tiller, she balanced beautifully. With the ability to hold the short headstay of the three-quarter rig straight, it was amazing how the boat would point and still keep going. However, I got sick and tired of being first to the weather mark, only to see the masthead boats climb over our stern on the downwind legs, so I shortened the mast, ran the headstay to the top, and pushed the point of attachment out to the stemhead.

Another thing that improved performance, especially in light air, were the

Design Number 325
Length Overall: 39 feet 7 inches
Length on Waterline: 28 feet
Beam: 11 feet 7 inches
Draft: 6 feet 7 inches
Sail Area: 577 square feet
Displacement: 9,000 pounds

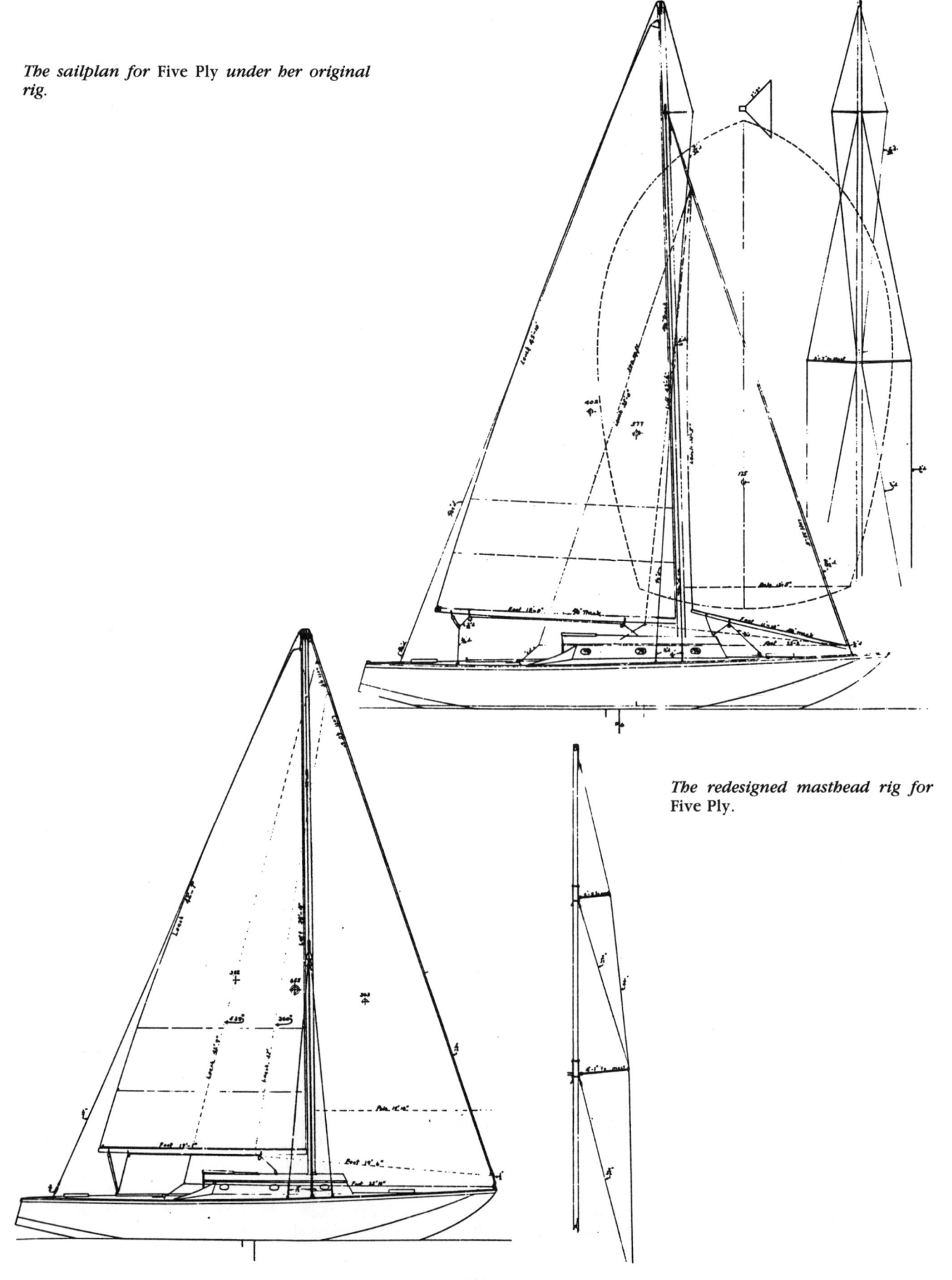

The sailplan for Five Ply *under her original rig.*

The redesigned masthead rig for Five Ply.

282

The construction details for Five Ply.

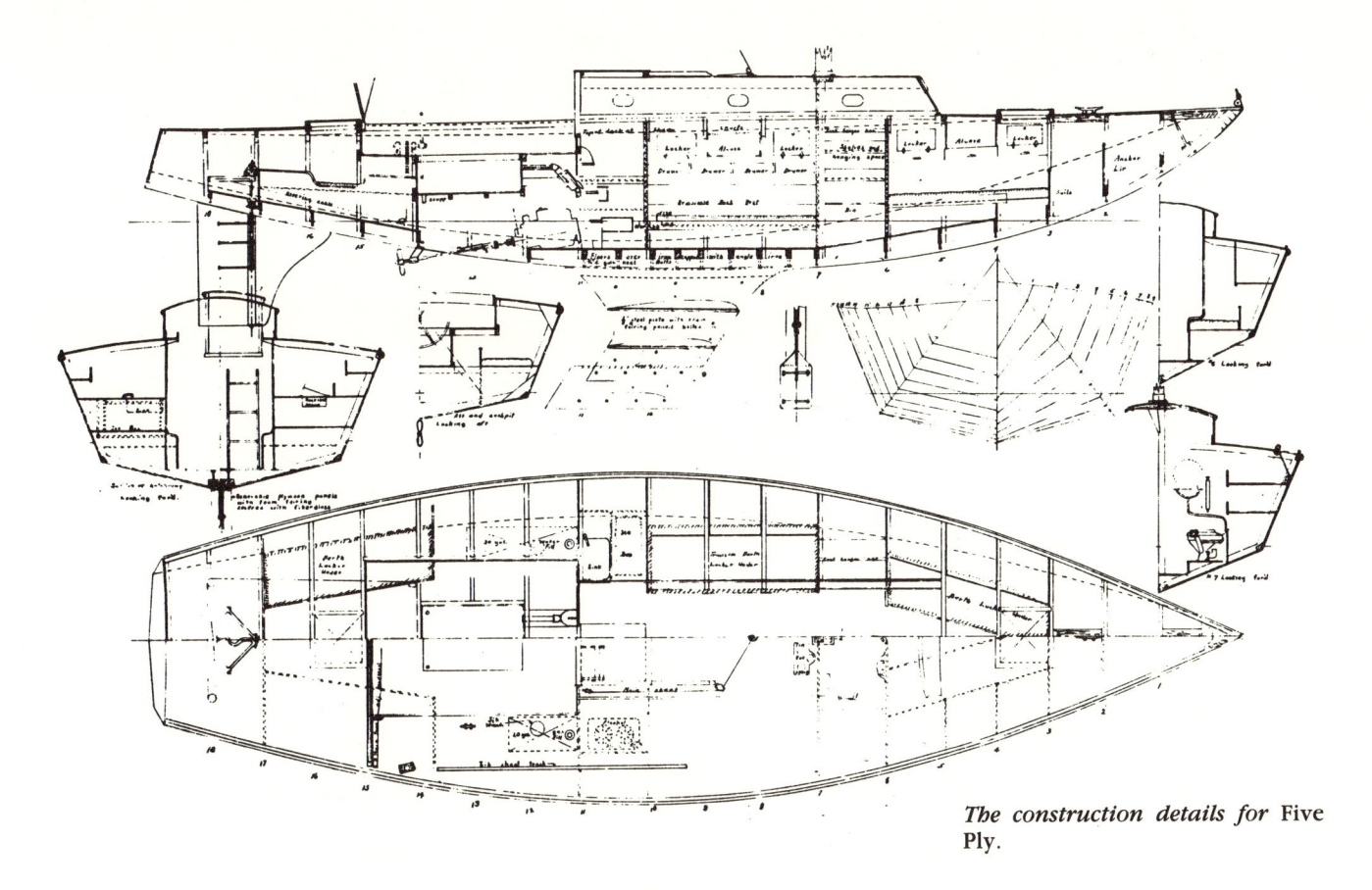

pads I bolted on the sides of the steel keel plate. I knew this would work, but I hated to cover that ⅝-inch-thick piece of steel. I made up some plywood panels with the streamlining on them and bolted them through and through. Now I can take them off for periodical maintenance of the plate. She is planked with ¾-inch plain exterior plywood with ⅝-inch harborite on deck. All framing is native spruce out of the local lumber yard as is the plywood. She is all screwed and glued together with special attention paid to plywood edges. The original design figured out to about 9,000-pound displacement, but this was increased to just under 13,000 pounds, and now I guess she weighs 14,000 with all that I have added to her. She certainly has filled the bill for something quick, cheap, and easy to build. Yet she is a good performer. People sometimes ask if she pounds. The answer is a definite yes, and yet she seems to do her best when it is blowing pretty fresh.

All the sections are straight lines from sheer to chine and chine to keel, so I didn't bother with a table of offsets but just picked these points off the floor from the full-size lay-down. Sections are generally 24 inches apart, but I spread them a little in the way of the main cabin to give transom berths a little over 6 feet. These sections were made up out of spruce, 2 inches by 3 inches, complete with deckbeam. All joints were secured with a half-inch plywood gusset glued and nailed unless they carried a bulkhead, in which case, of course, the bulkhead was used to hold the frame. The keel, fabricated out of steel, is bolted through floor timbers capped with galvanized angle iron. The bunk fronts come down on the outer ends of these, which pretty well distributes the strain of the keel in the event of a knockdown. The mast is stepped on deck with a post at the corner of the toilet room to transmit its thrust down to the keel. First launched in 1964, she is still going strong, and we've had a lot of fun in her.

Five Ply *sailing well off Manchester, Mass. The author is second from the left in this photograph.*

327

SCAUP

Design Numbers 327 and 330
Length Overall: 37 feet 6 inches
Length on Waterline: 34 feet 4 inches
Beam: 11 feet 9 inches
Draft: 4 feet 7 inches
Sail Area: 605 square feet
Displacement: 22,250 pounds

Scaup (now *Illusion*) and *Whampoa* are practically sisterships built from the same lines, the only difference being that *Whampoa* is a little longer on deck because the stem and stern have more rake. *Whampoa* also has a little more outside ballast and a little more sail. I built the decked-over hull and spars of *Scaup* for Fred Johnson. He had her trucked to his home in Andover, Mass., where he put the interior in. Fred is a fine craftsman and did a nice job on the interior.

Fred said he wanted something a little faster than his Alden ketch and a comfortable cruising boat for alongshore sailing, mostly down east. With no intention of going to sea, and after a lot of figuring, he went ahead with the big cockpit. The fact that the Palmer 6-240 would push her along at 7½ knots should allow her to high-tail it to safety if caught in bad weather. Under sail she continues to surprise people. Fred sold the boat to Alvin Doane, who now owns her. Al took her to Florida in 1977. Summers, he lives aboard. The 1983 Jeffrey's Ledge Race was made for her, with a reach on each of three legs. We came in second, even though dragging a 20-inch blade prop. *Whampoa* was built for Bill Endicott, She was laid out below, though, the same as *Scaup*. Endicott sold her to Robert Jacobs, who shortened the mainboom and put a mizzen on her. He sold her to Donald Bugden, who restored the original rig. Both boats are kept at my floats, summer and winter. *Whampoa* also has been cruised to Florida. The two boats cruise together in the summer and attract a lot of attention when rafted up together.

284

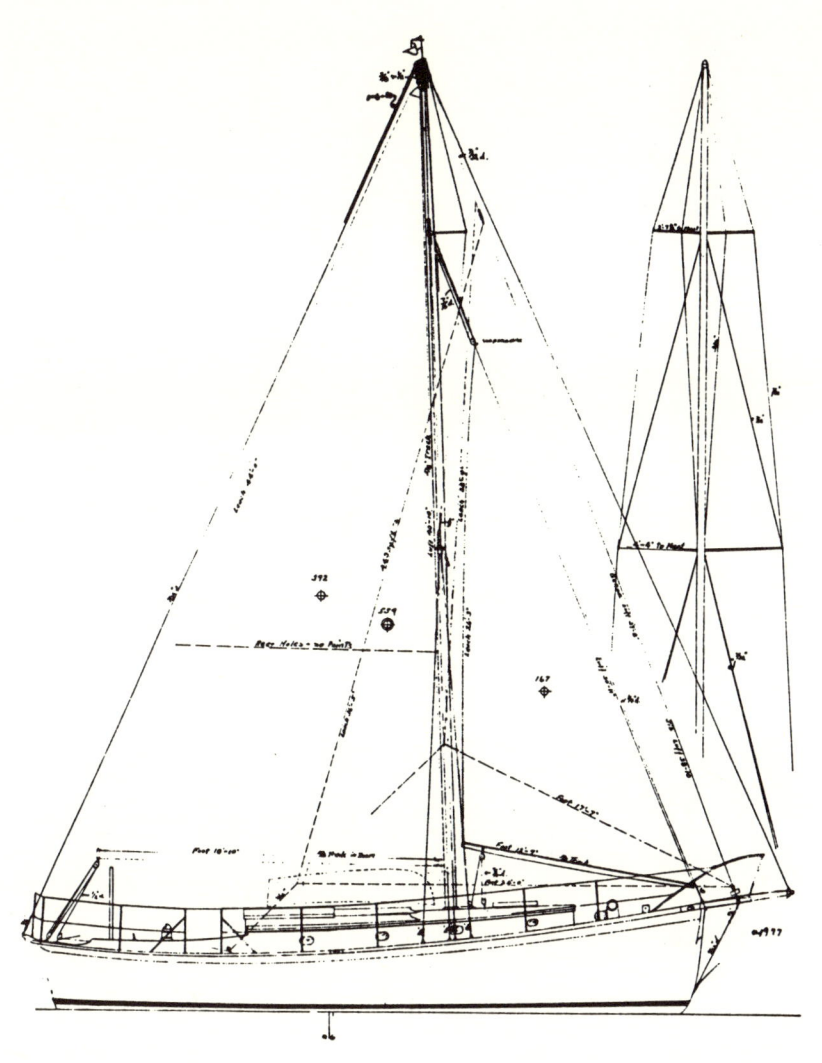

The sailplan and construction plans for Scaup, number 327.

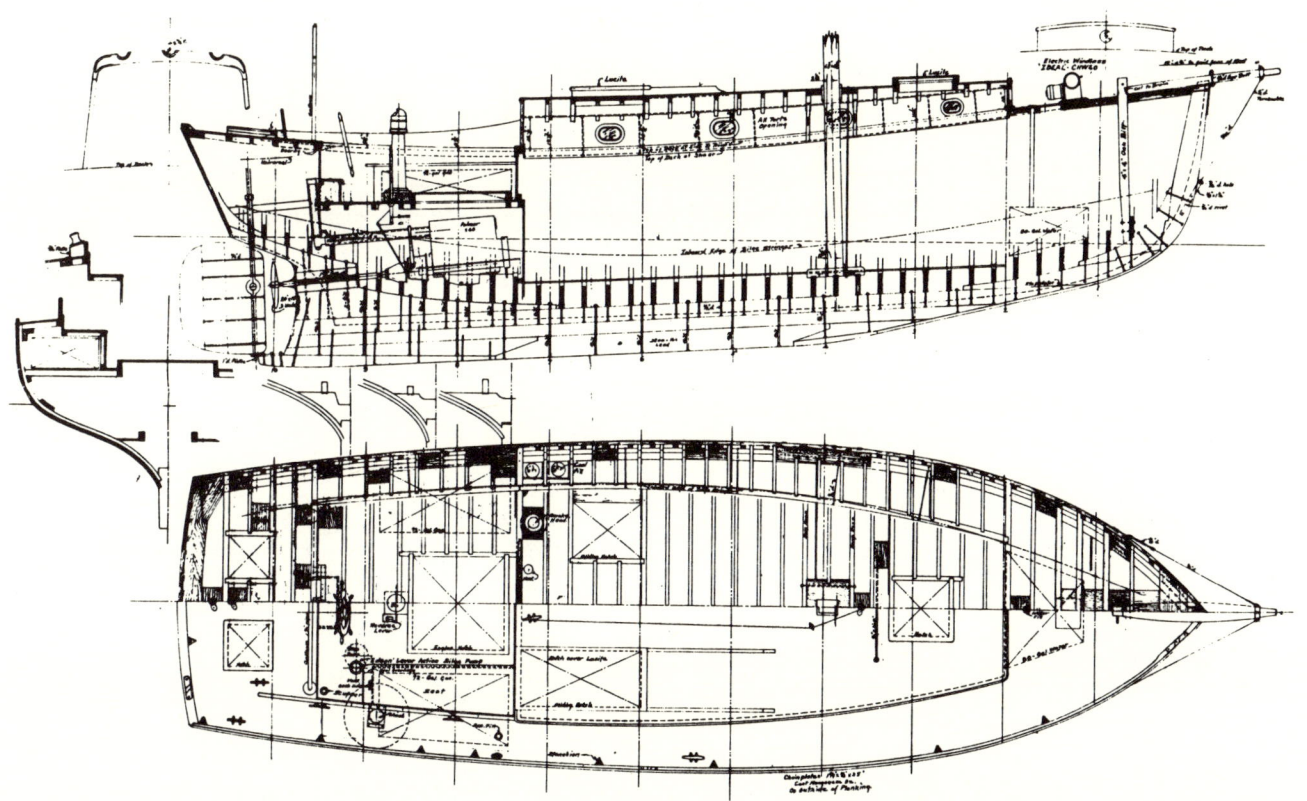

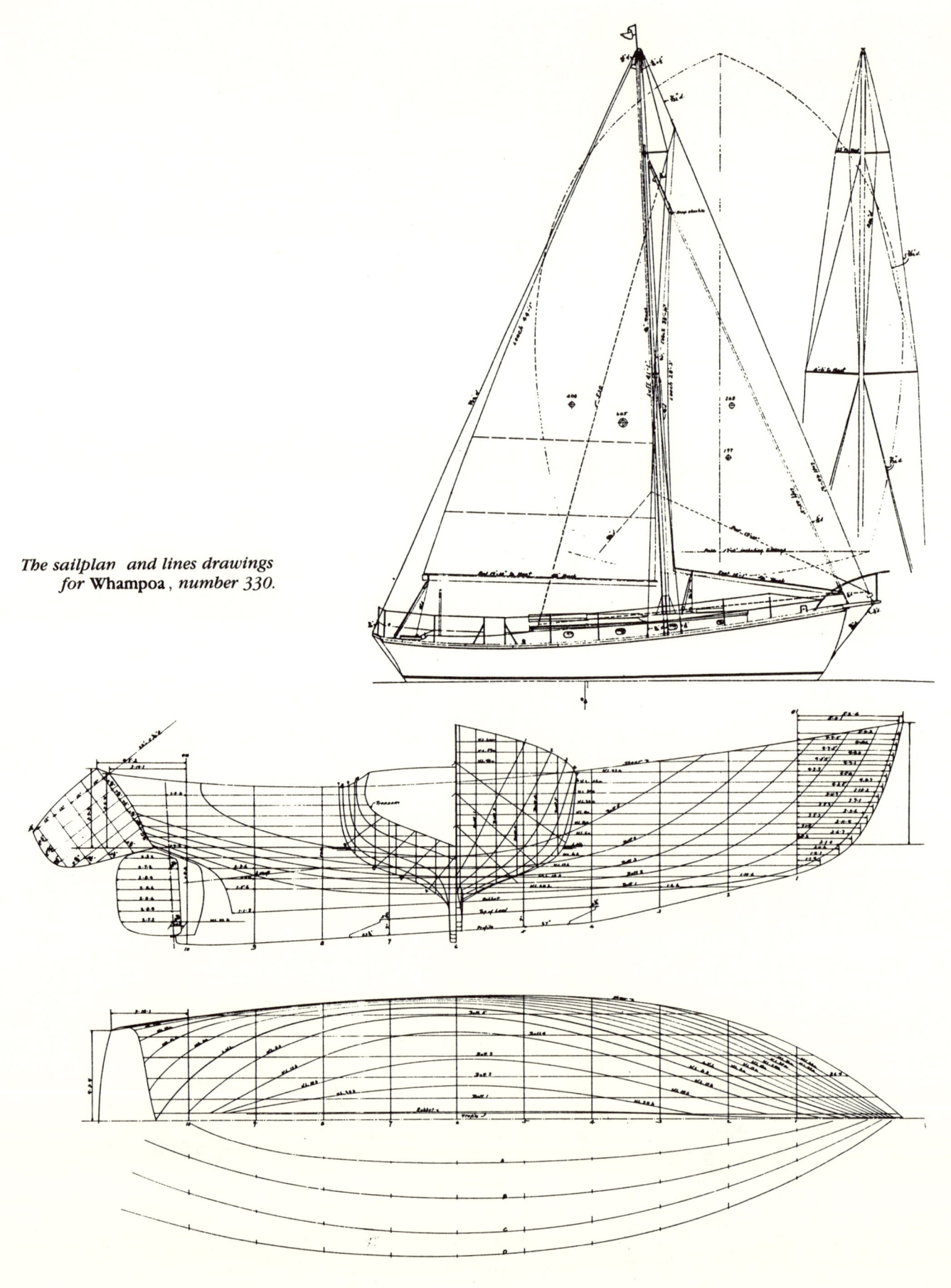

The sailplan and lines drawings for **Whampoa**, *number 330.*

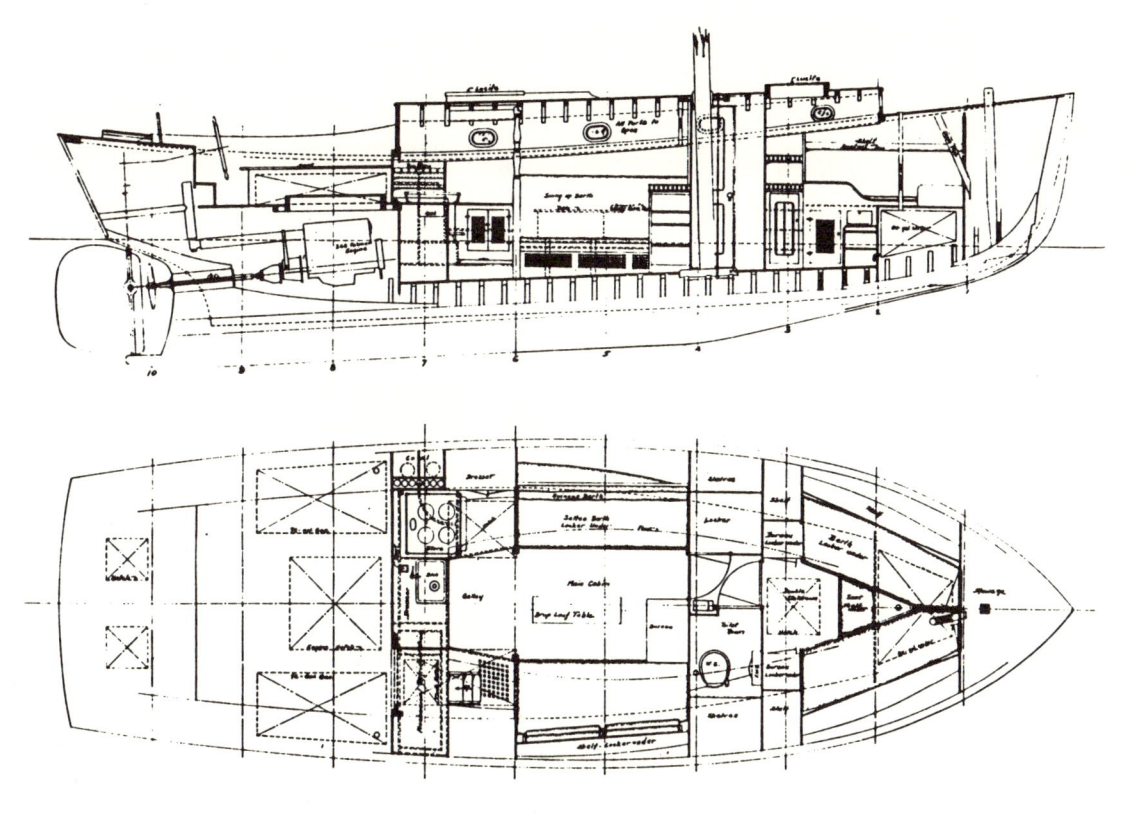

Whampoa's *accommodations*, Scaup (Illusion) *and* Whampoa *under sail. Photograph courtesy of Tom Sterns.*

337 DIONE

Design Number 337
Length Overall: 27 feet 6 inches
Length on Waterline: 25 feet
Beam: 10 feet 6 inches
Draft: 4 feet 6 inches
Sail Area: 428 square feet
Displacement: 13,800 pounds

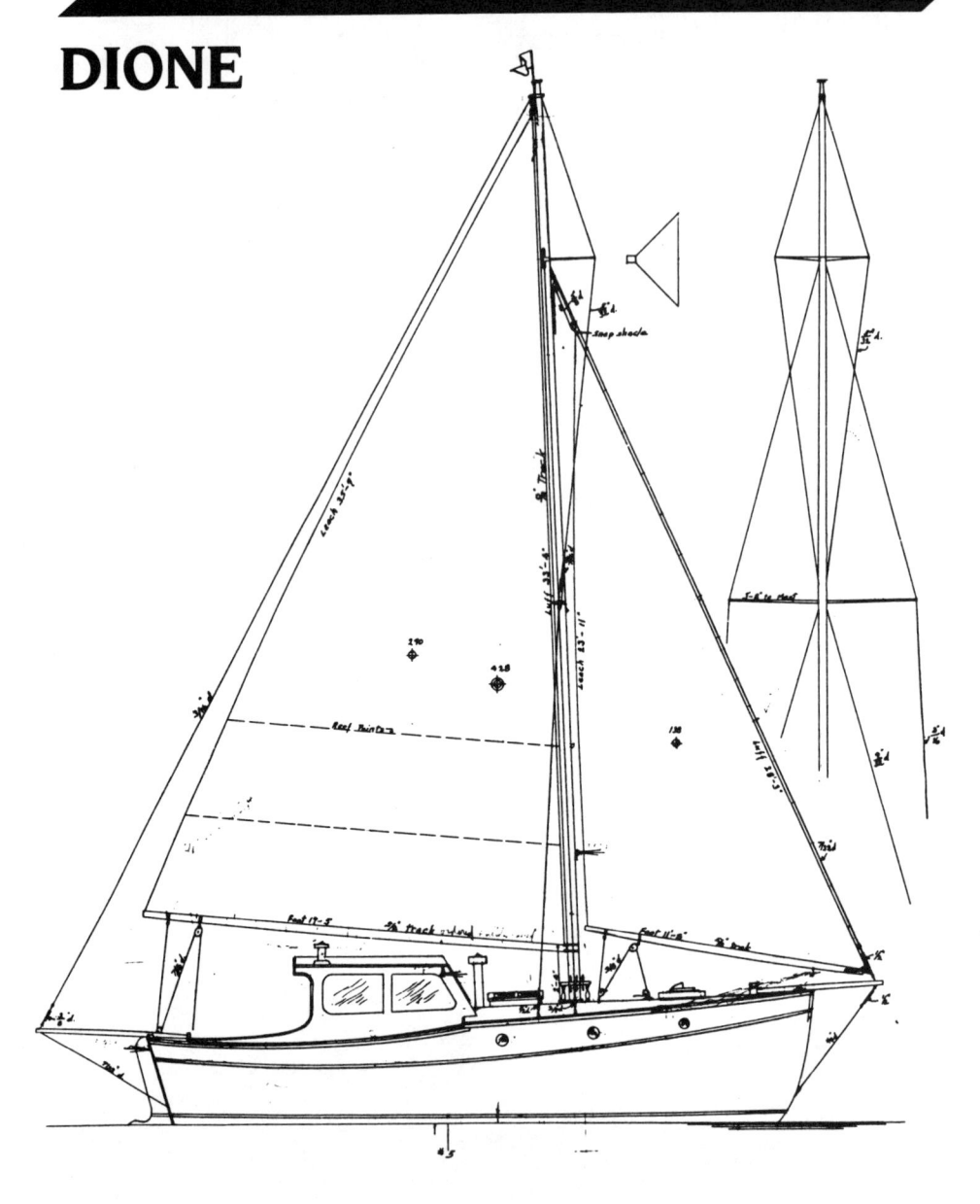

The sailplan for Dione.

Dione was another boat for Adm. Samuel E. Morrison. He previously had owned number 234, *Emily Marshall.* The admiral liked rough but sturdy construction and found his own builder to build this boat in Canada. She certainly was rough and probably sturdy. However, the builder didn't refer to the plans or specs too often, and the boat was pretty much a disaster. It's too bad, because she certainly was well laid out with an awful lot of accommodations for a 28-footer. I made up the rigging and when she was launched drove to Campobello with my father to make up the lower ends. When we first saw her, we could hardly believe she was the boat to have been built from these plans. Naturally, in order to get all the accommodations the owner wanted in 28 feet, she had to be somewhat chunky. The design accomplished this and still pro-

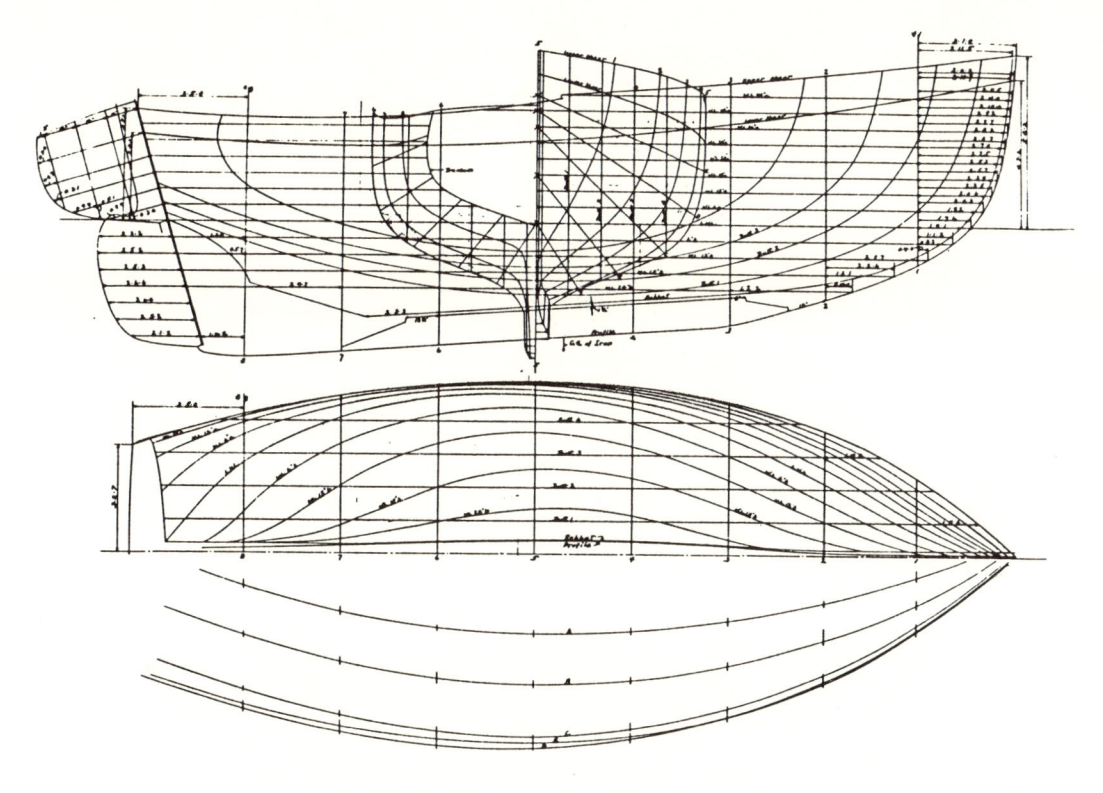

The lines and construction drawings for Dione.

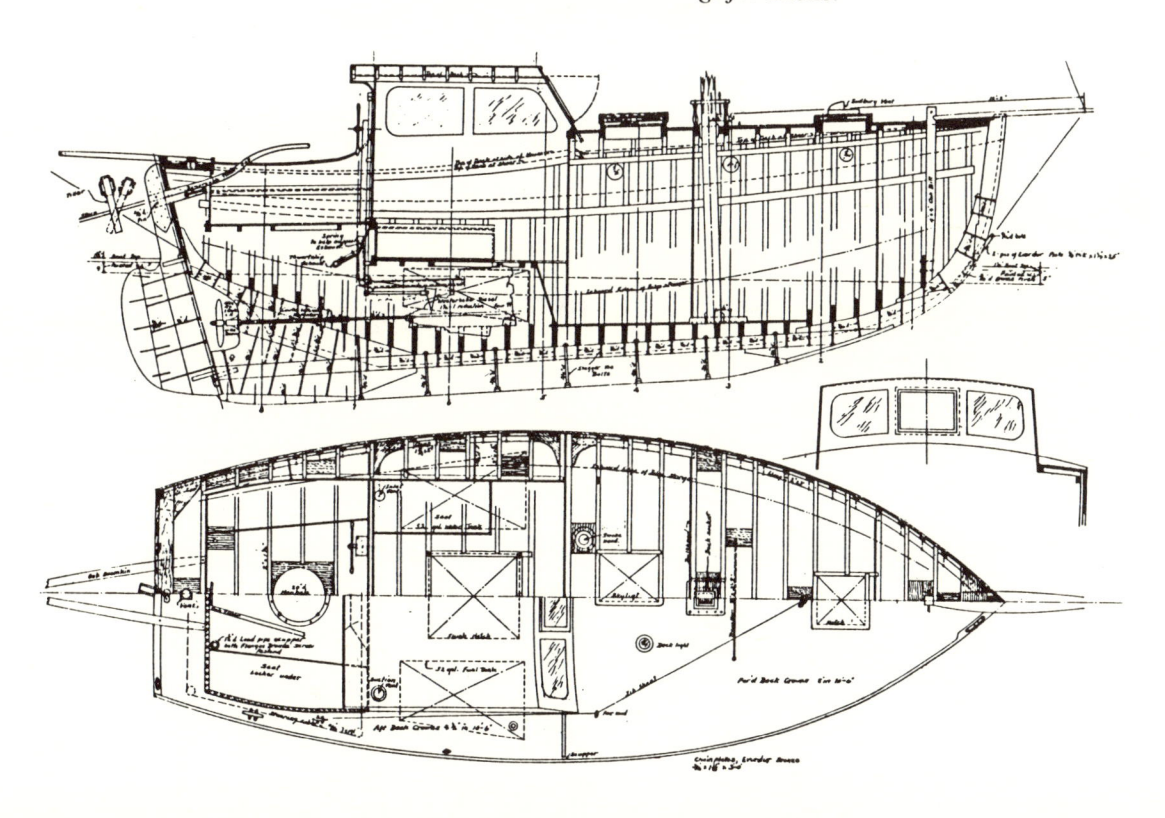

duced a good looking profile. The builder must have lost the offsets in places, because the whole raised deck was higher than it should have been. I don't think the admiral ever used her.

289

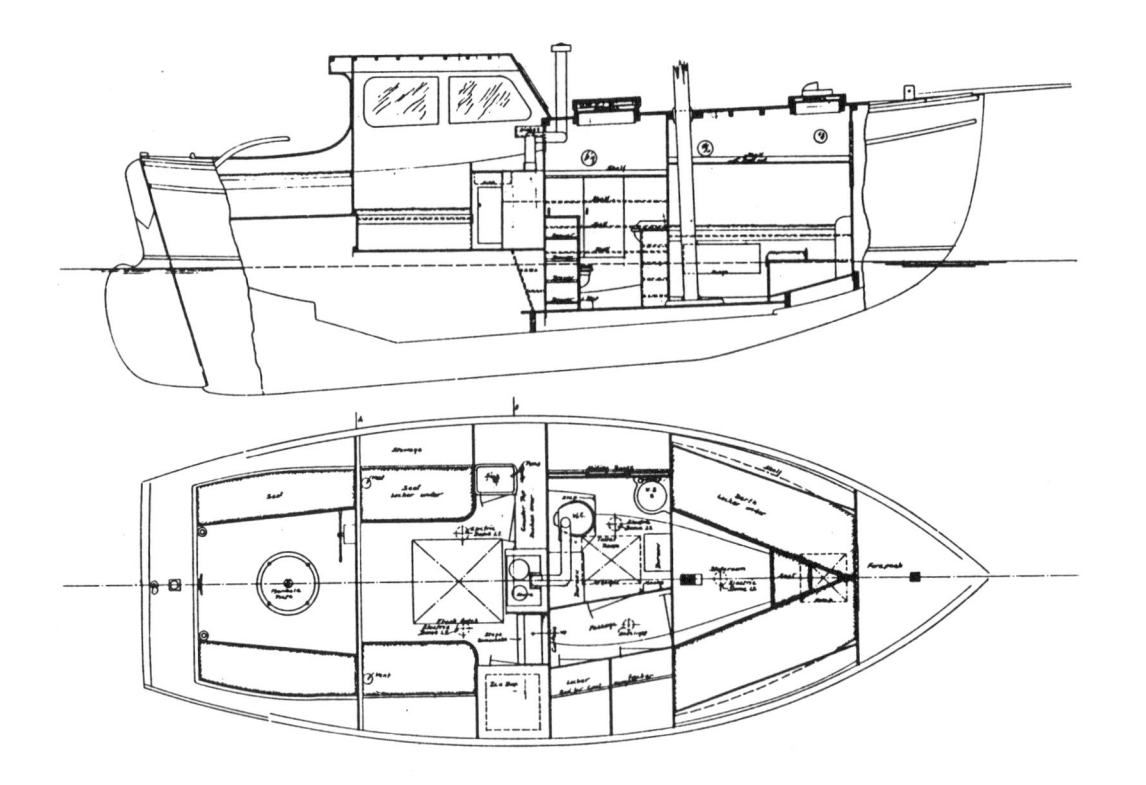

The accommodations for Dione.

338

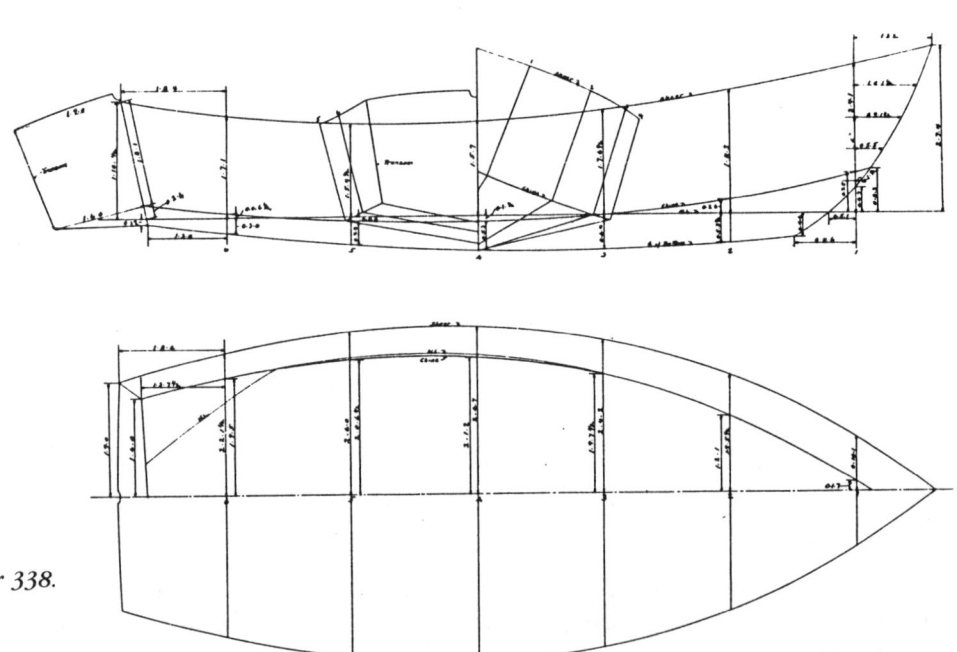

The lines drawings for number 338.

The sailplan for number 338.

The construction drawings for number 338.

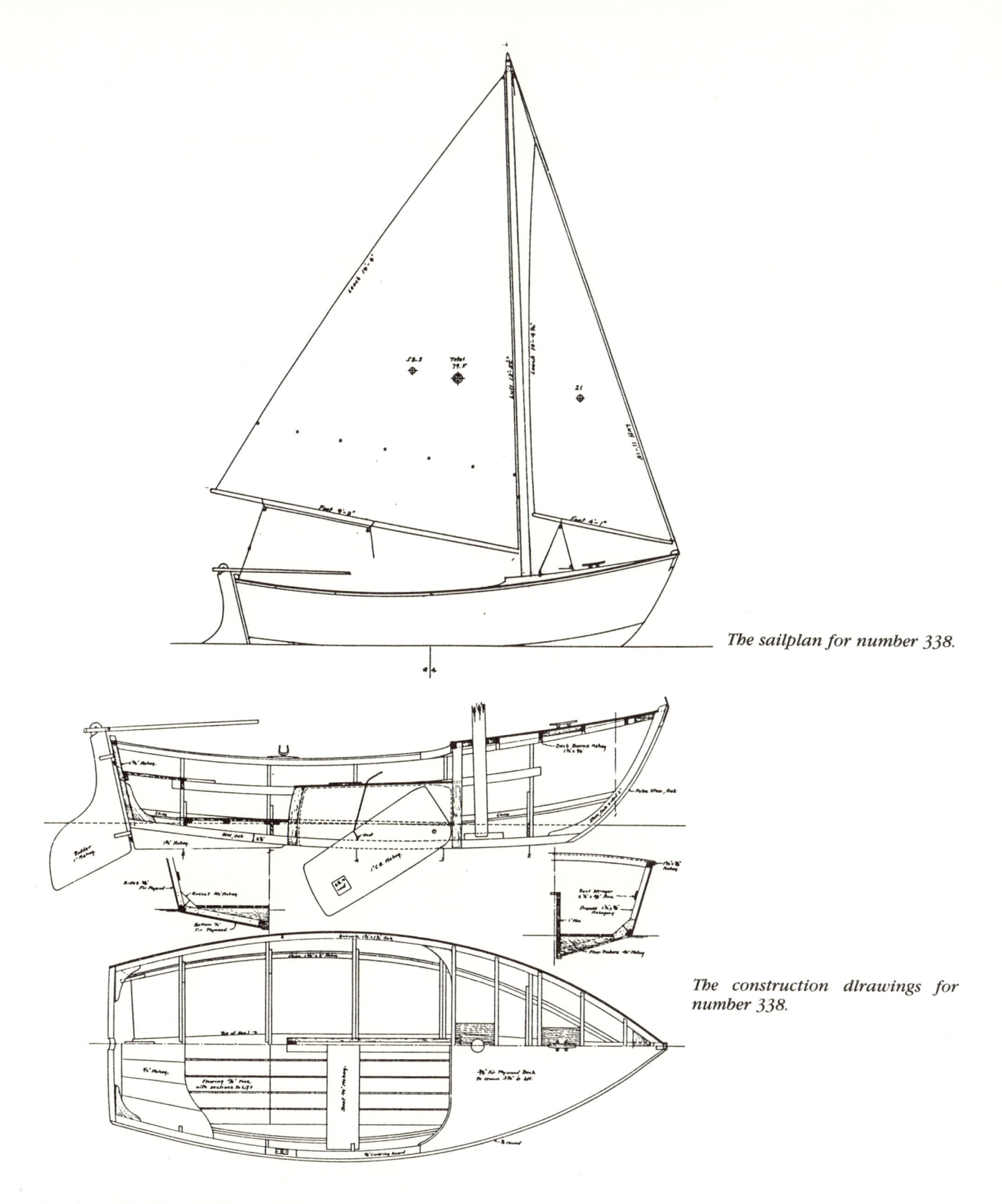

Number 338: This 13-foot V bottom was for S.K. Dimock. With her V-bottom, chine construction boarded in with plywood, she should be very easy for the amateur to build. While almost every design for Dimock had some kind of sailplan, they were usually moderate, and most people would probably want more sail on this one.

344 MARY HARDING

Design Number 344
Length Overall: 46 feet
Length on Waterline: 40 feet
Beam: 13 feet 6 inches
Draft: 5 feet 7 inches
Sail Area: 961 square feet
Displacement: 38,500 pounds

The sailplan for Mary Harding.

Mary Harding was my father's last design. He worked on the plans right up until a week before he died. She was designed for Donald K. Evans and his son-in-law Rogers M. Doering. I built the hull and spars and put in the main bulkheads, tanks, and engine. We built the decked-over hull with main bulkheads, deckhouse, cockpit, etc. The owner put in his own interior and did a nice job. He brought enough of it up from New York for us to install so that she could be cruised away soon after launching. We also built the spars and rigged her.

She had the usual oak foundation, steam-bent frames, mahogany plank, and locust stern. She had 12,500-pound lead outside and 1,000-pound inside for trimming. Frames were 2 inches by 2½ inches on 12-inch centers, with about 10 auxiliary frames in the way of the outside ballast extending from bilge stringer to bilge stringer in one piece. Fastenings were all bronze, using Phillips screws for the planking. These screws work out well and speed a job up because they automatically center the bit of an electric screwdriver so that the bung hole is not chewed up by an off-center screwdriver bit. The main deck was ¾-inch

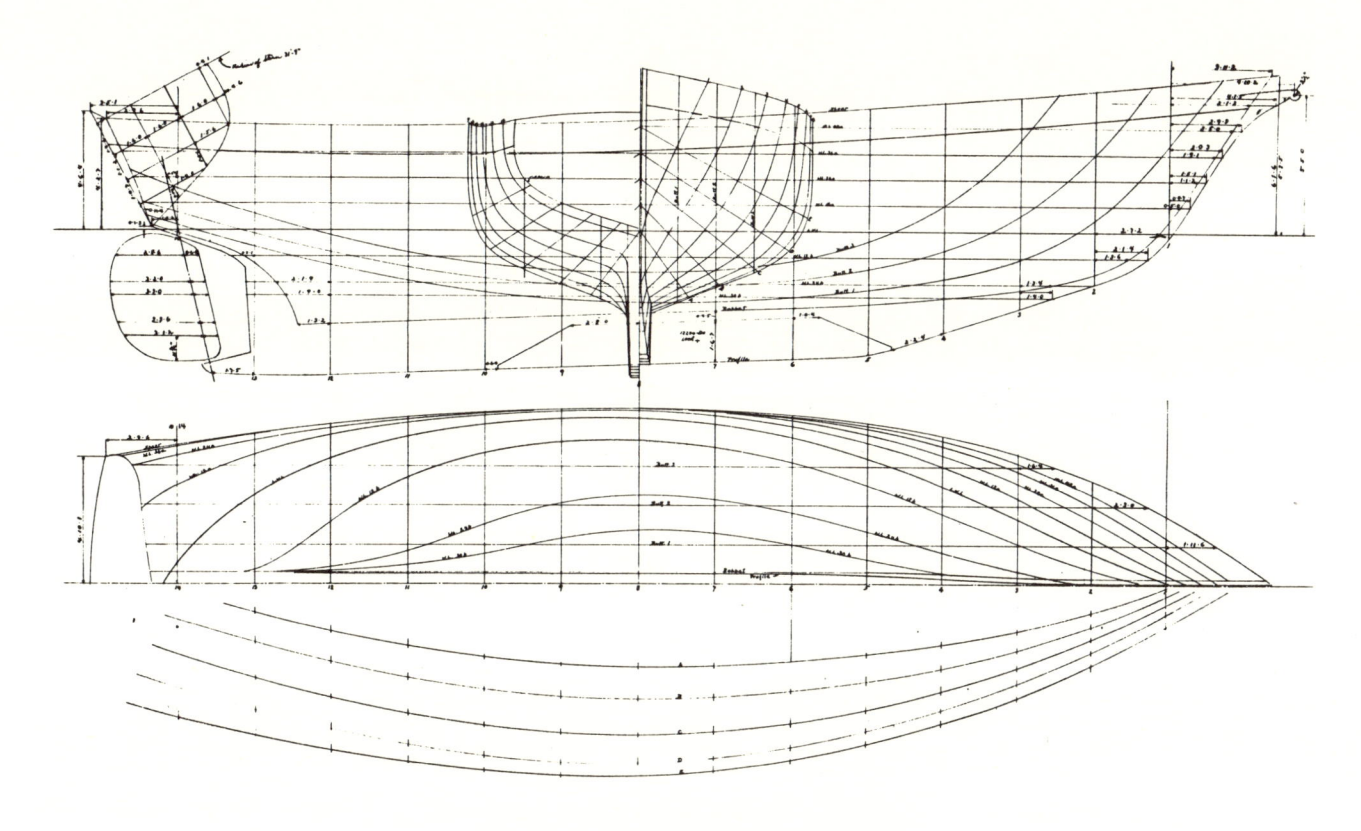

The lines drawings for Mary Harding.

plywood covered with celastic, the butts in the plywood being made between beams with a ¾-inch plywood butt-strap fitted from beam to beam for the length of the joint. The top of the shelter was treated in the same manner, using half-inch plywood. Bulkheads were also of plywood ⅝ inch thick and were fitted out to the skin of the boat and well fastened for strength members. The main and mizzen were box-section Sitka spruce, and the small spars were solid. Both spars folded down on deck on bronze hinge arrangements cast to patterns of the owner's design and maufacture. Other spar hardware was custom made in Manchester, either cast or cut from sheet bronze. The engine was a IHD301 diesel with 2.5-to-1 reduction gear turning a 26-inch-diameter-by-16-inch prop.

Here's what Evans had to say about her in 1978:

> Our object with the *Mary Harding* was a boat that could be handled easily by two people, that would be very comfortable for four; which would sleep eight if necessary. That we have, except that we didn't allow quite enough hanging lockers for all eight people.
>
> We were afraid that the boat might not be fun to sail. It is true that four points off the wind she just won't move. But five points off, and she really travels. We have averaged 8.5 knots from Cuttyhunk to Newport. The boat never takes a drop of solid water on board. She will balance with every combination of sail we have tried. She is a joy to work on, with her huge flush deck and dropped bow section. Most particularly, I like being able to sit at the wheel and see easily over the doghouse.

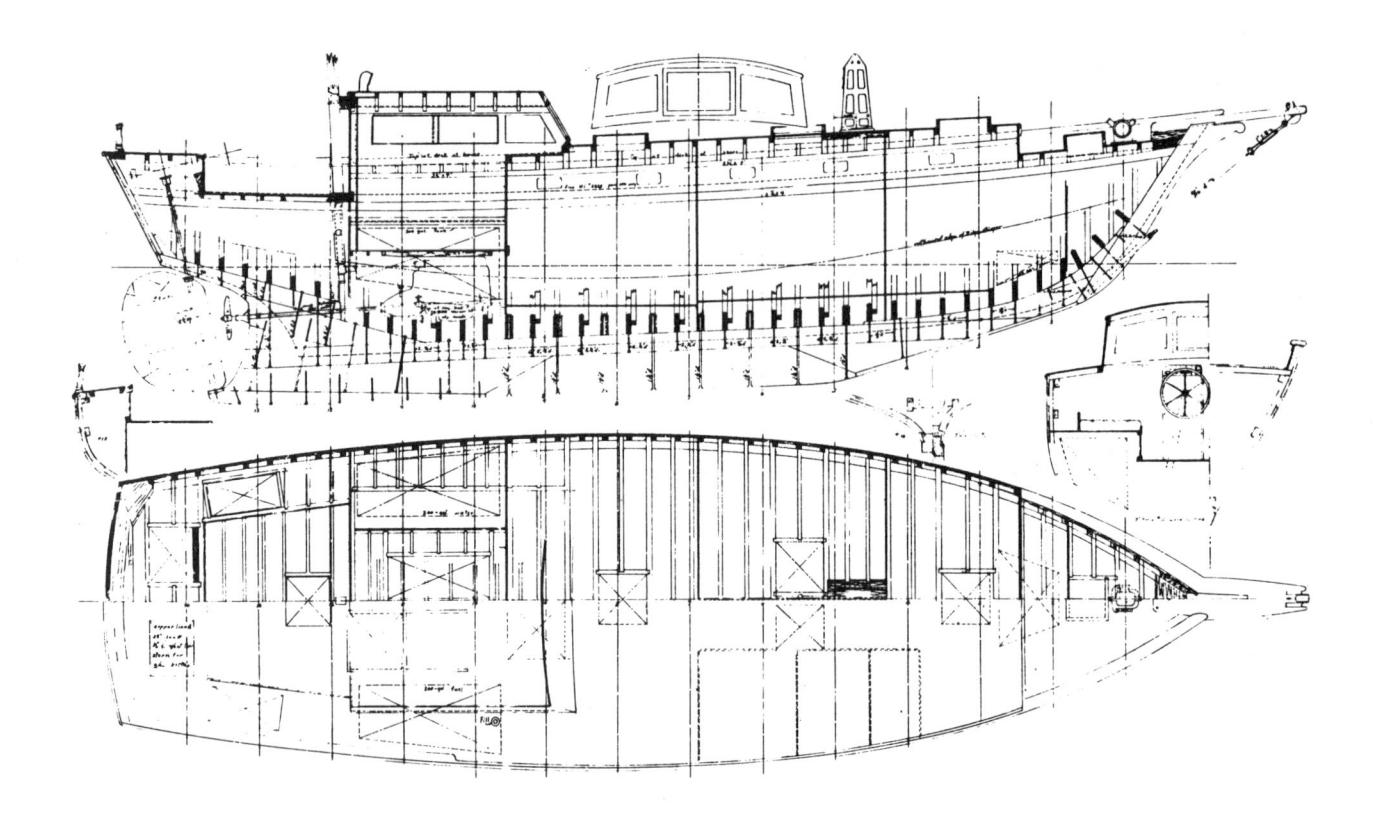

The construction plans and accommodations for Mary Harding.

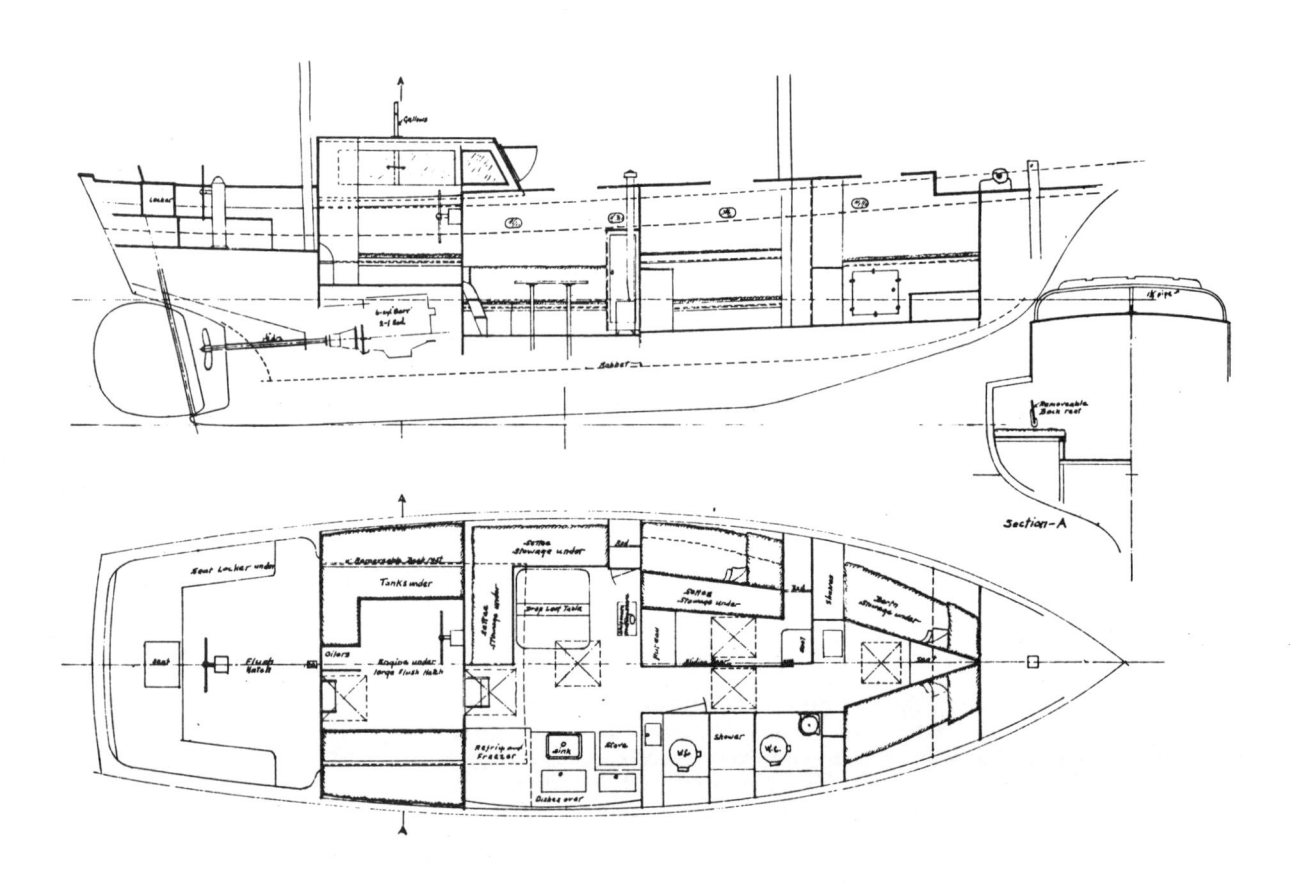

Mary Harding *under sail. A Morris Rosenfeld photograph, courtesy of S. Sturgis Crocker.*